W9-DFZ-523

Introducing Public Administration

Eighth Edition

JAY M. **SHAFRITZ**

*Professor Emeritus, Graduate School of Public and
International Affairs, University of Pittsburgh*

E. W. **RUSSELL**

School of Public Health, La Trobe University

CHRISTOPHER P. **BORICK**

Department of Political Science, Muhlenberg College

PEARSON
Prentice
Hall

Pearson Education International

Boston   Columbus   Indianapolis   New York   San Francisco   Upper Saddle River
Amsterdam   Cape Town   Dubai   London   Madrid   Milan   Munich   Paris   Montreal   Toronto
Delhi   Mexico City   São Paulo   Sydney   Hong Kong   Seoul   Singapore   Taipei   Tokyo

If you purchased this book within the United States or Canada you should be aware that it has been imported without the approval of the Publisher or the Author.

Assistant Editor: Stephanie Chaisson
Executive Marketing Manager: Wendy Gordon
Media Supplements Editor: Lisa Dotson
Production Manager: Denise Phillip
Project Coordination and Electronic Page Makeup:
S4Carlisle Publishing Services

Cover Designer: Bernadette Travis

Senior Manufacturing Buyer: Dennis J. Para
Photo Researcher: Melody English
Printer and Binder: R. R. Donnelley/Crawfordville

Photo Credits: Page 4: © Landov; **Page 37:** © Landov; **Page 101:** © REUTERS/Win McNamee; **Page 114:** © The Granger Collection, NYC — All rights reserved.; **Page 156:** © Time & Life Pictures/Getty Images; **Page 168:** © Portrait of Niccolo Machiavelli (1469–1527), Santi di Tito (1536–1603) / Palazzo Vecchio (Palazzo della Signoria) Florence, Italy / The Bridgeman Art Library International; **Page 179:** © AP Photo/White House Photo; **Page 207:** © AF archive/Alamy; **Page 222:** © Bettmann/ CORBIS; **Page 287:** © Francis G. Mayer/CORBIS; **Page 373:** © CORBIS; **Page 442:** © JIM YOUNG/Reuters/Corbis; **Page 492:** © AF archive/Alamy; **Page 517:** © The Granger Collection, NYC — All rights reserved.; **Page 362L:** © GL Archive/Alamy.; **Page 362R:** © Splash/Newscom

Copyright © 2013, 2011, 2009, 2005 by Pearson Education, Inc.

All rights reserved. Manufactured in the United States of America. This publication is protected by Copyright, and permission should be obtained from the publisher prior to any prohibited reproduction, storage in a retrieval system, or transmission in any form or by any means, electronic, mechanical, photocopying, recording, or likewise. To obtain permission(s) to use material from this work, please submit a written request to Pearson Education, Inc., Permissions Department, One Lake Street, Upper Saddle River, New Jersey 07458, or you may fax your request to 201-236-3290.

1 2 3 4 5 6 7 8 9 10

ISBN-13: 978-0-205-92246-8
ISBN-10:   0-205-92246-5

BRIEF CONTENTS

DETAILED CONTENTS

CHAPTER 5 Honor, Ethics, and Accountability 166

CHAPTER 6 The Evolution of Management and Organization Theory 205

PREFACE

This is the eighth edition of a text first published in 1997. There's only one audience for a book of this nature—students and teachers of public administration. The fact that we have been given this eighth opportunity to summarize the field for this readership means that a significant percentage of all instructors of college and university courses in public administration has approved of our past efforts. These instructors vote approval by adopting this text for their students. We consider their approval a great honor—and an even greater responsibility. Thus our goal is to maintain this text at a standard that is worthy of them and us.

In the original preface to this book we explained that we sought to create a text that would bridge two worlds, a text that would be informal enough to be accessible to undergraduates, yet comprehensive enough for beginning graduate students. We're pleased to now be able to report that we have succeeded—at least to the extent that the publisher, after scrupulously studying the adoption statistics, has asked us to prepare this new edition.

As we've said since the first edition of this text, public administration is an exciting and fascinating field of study, full of the stuff of fiction, only true. We try to capture this sense of drama and excitement by beginning each chapter with a good story—what we call a keynote—that highlights a major aspect of the subject. These accounts deal with a rich variety of topics, including the attack on the World Trade Center in New York, how Moses better led the Israelites with the aid of a management consultant, the famous mutiny on the *Bounty*, and that Thomas Becket was murdered because he disagreed with administrative policies of England's King Henry II. All of these keynotes have significant public policy and public management implications that are developed further in their respective chapters. We trust they'll lead to many stimulating class discussions. To facilitate this we have included "For Discussion" questions at the end of each keynote.

The material in each chapter is then presented in an order that shouldn't surprise anyone familiar with public administration. We've made every effort to keep the tone lively so that students, as well as their professors, might take some pleasure in reviewing the material. When a word appears in red in the text, it's defined at the side of its page. The key concepts at the end of each chapter supplement, rather than duplicate, these red-lettered definitions. Readers also will find a list of recommended books and a list of related Web sites at the end of each chapter. These have been included as guides to further information on chapter topics for any interested reader—student or instructor.

Every effort has been made to keep the material as current as possible. Thus there is extensive coverage of the movement to reinvent government, privatization, and contracting out. Because American public administration is increasingly influenced by technological innovations, we pay increased attention to advancements in communications and information management that are reshaping the field.

NEW TO THIS EDITION

- This text has been physically redesigned and is now presented to you in color. Many of the photographs are offered as they were meant to be viewed. The headings have been color coded and all of the tables, charts, and boxed materials have been given pastel tints.

- All statistical information, tables, and bibliographies have been updated as appropriate. All recommended Web sites have been annotated for the first time.
- New initiatives of the Barack Obama administration—especially those concerned with economic, financial management, and budgetary policy—have been incorporated where appropriate.
- Numerous chapters examine the effects of the 2008 economic meltdown on areas of public administration such as regulation of financial markets, cut-back management, and social equity.
- Three case studies and/or keynotes have been added to this edition, with two others significantly revised:

  Chapter 4: Keynote: The Intergovernmental Problem of Marijuana

  Chapter 5: A Case Study: Parallel Bloody Hands—Comparing the Administrative Ethics of Secretaries of Defense Robert McNamara and Donald Rumsfeld

  Chapter 10: Keynote: The Hedgehog, the Fox, Henry V, or the "Hidden- Hand" Golfer

  Chapter 11: A Case Study: The Spectacular Rise and Modest Decline of Public Employee Unions

  Chapter 12: Keynote: A Tale of How Two States and Their Governors Weathered the Fiscal Storms of 2011

- This edition also contains several new and substantially revised sections:

  Chapter 3 contains new sections on (1) the separation of powers and (2) pressure for privatization and nonprofit management alternatives.

  Chapter 4 contains a new section on welfare reform.

  Other new sections examine the use of social networks by federal, state, and local governments (Chapter 8), the importance of optimism for political leaders and public administrators (Chapter 10), mentoring as management development (Chapter 11), public administration and social equity (Chapter 12), and the influence of F. A. Hayek (Chapter 13).

- More than two dozen new boxes and tables exploring subjects such as the debt ceiling, writing in public administration, and the work of ratings agencies.

A NOTE ON NOTES

There are no traditional footnotes in this book. Generally, if a work or author is referred to in a chapter, the corresponding full citation will be found in that chapter's bibliography. The major exceptions are works or statements so famous and existing in so many formats—such as excerpts from the Bible and Shakespeare's plays—that further bibliographic information was deemed unnecessary. Most long quotations are kept in boxes, separate from the main body and rhythm of the text. This informal format was used very successfully through five editions of the Shafritz et al. text *Personnel Management in Government* (New York: Marcel Dekker, 1978–2001). Sometimes it was too awkward to incorporate a reference to a citation in the body of the text. These "fugitive" quotations have their sources identified in an appendix.

GIVE YOUR STUDENTS CHOICES

In addition to the traditional printed text, *Introducing Public Administration,* Eighth Edition is available in the following format to give you and your students more choices— and more ways to save.

The **CourseSmart eText** offers the same content as the printed text in a convenient online format—with highlighting, online search, and printing capabilities. Visit **www.coursesmart.com** to learn more.

MySearchLab® WITH PEARSON eTEXT

MySearchLab is an interactive website that features an eText, access to the EBSCO ContentSelect database and multimedia, and step-by-step tutorials which offer complete overviews of the entire writing and research process. MySearchLab is designed to amplify a traditional course in numerous ways or to administer a course online. Additionally, MySearchLab offers course specific tools to enrich learning and help students succeed.

- **eText:** Identical in content and design to the printed text, the Pearson eText provides access to the book wherever and whenever it is needed. Students can take notes and highlight, just like a traditional book. The Pearson eText also is available on the iPad for all registered users of MySearchLab.
- **Flashcards:** Review important terms and concepts from each chapter online. Students can search by chapters or within a glossary and also access drills to help them prepare for quizzes and exams. Flashcards can be printed or exported to your mobile device
- **Chapter-specific Content:** Each chapter contains Learning Objectives, Quizzes, Media and Flashcards. These can be used to enhance comprehension, help students review key terms, prepare for tests, and retain what they've learned. To order this book with MySearchLab access at no extra charge use ISBN: 0205910009

Learn more at www.mysearchlab.com

INSTRUCTOR RESOURCES

A comprehensive Instructor's Manual and Test Bank, as well as a PowerPoint Presentation prepared by Breena Coates, Chairman & Professor of Global Strategy, Department of Management, College of Business & Public Administration, California State University, San Bernardino will accompany this new edition of *Introducing Public Administration*. These resources are available for download at www.pearsonhighered.com/irc (access code required).

ACKNOWLEDGMENTS

No book is born without debts. We wish to express our thanks to the following faculty reviewers—Peter Cruise of Mary Baldwin College; Craig Curtis of Bradley University; Jane Hansberry of University of Colorado, Denver; Jared J. Llorens of the University of Georgia; Theo Edwin Maloy of West Texas A&M University; Richard T. Middleton of the University of Missouri, St. Louis; Dale Nesbary of Oakland University—who helped to prepare this current edition. We're also happy to acknowledge the helpful suggestions of David H. Rosenbloom of American University; Albert C. Hyde of the Brookings Institution; Elizabeth Hecker of Boise State University; Carol Edlund of California State University–Hayward; Richard Wandling of Eastern Illinois University; Barbara Yarnold of Florida International University; John Sacco of George Mason University; Gashaw W. Lake of Kentucky State University; Michael L. Vasu of North Carolina State University; Christopher A. Simon of the University of Nevada Las Vegas; Curtis R. Berry of Shippensburg University; Ari Halachmi of Tennessee State University; William H. Stewart of the University of Alabama;

Daniel Martin of the University of Baltimore; Kenneth L. Nichols of the University of Maine; Gary S. Marshall of the University of Nebraska at Omaha; Gordon P. Whittaker of the University of North Carolina; Jean Wahl Harris of the University of Scranton; Sharon Ridgeway of the University of Southwest Louisiana; David H. Davis of the University of Toledo; J. Steven Ott of the University of Utah; Frank Bryan of the University of Vermont; Richard Crockett of Western Illinois University; Robert E. Colvin of Christopher Newport University; William N. Thompson of the University of Nevada, Las Vegas; Arthur Sementelli of Stephen F. Austin State University; Dwight S. Cropp of George Washington University; Christine J. Brehan of Bentley College; John Carhart of Texas A&M University at Galveston; R. Steven Daniels of California State University at Bakersfield; Jeremy L. Eccles of Marygrove College; Anne M. Gurnack of the University of Wisconsin, Parkside; Jeffrey Kraus of Wagner College; Michael E. Meagher of the University of Missouri; Fred A. Meyer, Jr. of Ball State University; Norman H. Runge of Wilmington College; Samuel T. Shelton of Troy State University; Robert Stock of San Diego State University; Pamela Stricker of California State University, San Marcos; and R. Lawson Veasey of Jacksonville State University.

Some colleagues have been especially helpful. We're particularly grateful for the many helpful suggestions of Breena Coates of United States Army War College; Jeffery K. Guiler and Michele Cole of Robert Morris University; Paul A. Danczyk, David Young Miller, and Sarah Pennock of the University of Pittsburgh; and Gerald Caiden of the University of Southern California, who had an entire class of graduate students write very useful critiques of the text that he then sent on to us. We would also like to thank Sarah Niebler, Jill Batdorf, Steven Fischer, Elisa Zaehringer, and Katherine Sharga of Lehigh University, and Micahel Wiener of Muhlenberg College for their tremendous assistance in gathering research for the book.

This book started many years ago as a collaboration by two friends at opposite ends of the world: Melbourne, Australia, and Pittsburgh, Pennsylvania. The collaboration grew by one when a younger colleague from Allentown, Pennsylvania, joined with us during the writing of the fifth edition. While separated by generations and many miles, we're kindred academic spirits. Despite the fact that we were bred in differing administrative cultures, we were in accord on what we wanted to say. And we're very grateful that what we have had to say has found a wide audience. We're hopeful that this text will continue to find sufficient acceptance that subsequent editions will be warranted. Thus, suggestions for improvements and enhancements will always be welcome.

JAY M. SHAFRITZ
PROFESSOR EMERITUS
UNIVERSITY OF PITTSBURGH
shafritz@yahoo.com

E. W. RUSSELL
LA TROBE UNIVERSITY
ewrussell@hotmail.com

CHRISTOPHER P. BORICK
MUHLENBERG COLLEGE
cborick@muhlenberg.edu

KEY EVENTS IN PUBLIC ADMINISTRATION

1776
- Declaration of Independence is signed.
- Adam Smith in *The Wealth of Nations* advocates "the ability to pay" principle of taxation.

1781
- Articles of Confederation adopted.

1787
- Northwest Ordinance provides for future states to enter the union and for federal aid to local public schools.
- Constitutional Convention convenes in Philadelphia.

1789
- U.S. Constitution adopted.
- Congress establishes the first federal administrative agencies (the Departments of State, War, Treasury, and the Office of the Attorney General).
- The Federal Judiciary Act creates the Supreme Court.
- New York City becomes the first capital of the United States.

1790
- First census sets U.S. population at 4 million.
- U.S. capital moved from New York to Philadelphia.

1791
- Bill of Rights (the first 10 amendments) added to the Constitution.
- Congress passes the first internal revenue law; a tax on alcohol.

1800
- U.S. capital moved from Philadelphia to Washington, D.C.

1803
- The Supreme Court first asserts the right of judicial review in *Marbury v. Madison*.

1819
- The Supreme Court in *McCulloch v. Maryland* establishes the doctrine of implied constitutional powers and the immunity of the federal government from state taxation.

1829
- Andrew Jackson becomes president.

1832
- Senator William L. Marcy gives title to the spoils system when he asserts in a Senate debate that politicians "see nothing wrong in the rule, that to the victor belongs the spoils of the enemy."

1836
- Alexis de Tocqueville publishes *Democracy in America,* his classic study of American political institutions and political culture.

1840
- President Martin Van Buren establishes the 10-hour day for most federal employees.

1844
- The New York City Police Department is established.

1849
- The U.S. Department of the Interior created.

1851
- Massachusetts enacts the first law permitting towns to use tax revenues to support free libraries.

1861
- Abraham Lincoln becomes president; the Civil War begins.

1862
- The Morill Land Grant Act endows state colleges of agriculture and industry.

1863
- President Lincoln issues the Emancipation Proclamation.

1865
- New York City establishes the first fire department with full-time paid firefighters.
- Civil War ends; Reconstruction begins.
- The Thirteenth Amendment abolishes slavery.

1868
- President Andrew Johnson is impeached by the House, but tried and acquitted by the Senate.
- Congress mandates an eight-hour workday for federally employed laborers and mechanics.

1881
- President James Garfield is assassinated by deranged office seeker.

1883
- The Pendleton Act creates the U.S. Civil Service Commission.

1886
- Henry R. Towne's paper "The Engineer as an Economist" encourages the scientific management movement.
- American Federation of Labor formed.

1887
- Congress creates the Interstate Commerce Commission, the first federal regulatory commission.
- Woodrow Wilson's "The Study of Administration" is published in *Political Science Quarterly.*

1901
- Galveston, Texas, is the first city to install the commission form of government.
- Oregon becomes the first state to adopt the initiative and referendum.

1903
- The American Political Science Association founded.
- U.S. Department of Commerce and Labor is established.
- The Boston police are the first to use an automobile, a Stanley Steamer, for regular patrol.

1904
- Lincoln Steffen's muckraking *Shame of the Cities* finds Philadelphia to be "corrupt and contented" and arouses sentiment for municipal reform.

1905
- New York City starts the first police motorcycle patrol.

1906
- Bureau of Municipal Research founded in New York City to further the management movement in government.
- Pure Food and Drug Act passed.

1908
- Staunton, Virginia, appoints the first city manager.

1910
- Ohio is the first state to empower its governor to prepare an executive budget for legislature review.

1911
- Frederick W. Taylor publishes *The Principles of Scientific Management.*

1912
- Taft Commission calls for a national executive budget.
- Position classification first adopted at the municipal level in the city of Chicago.
- Sumter, South Carolina, is first to install a council-manager form of city government.
- Congress approves an eight-hour day for all federal employees

1913
- Hugo Munsterberg's *Psychology and Industrial Efficiency* calls for the application of psychology to industry.
- Woodrow Wilson becomes president.
- The Sixteenth Amendment to the Constitution creates the first permanent federal income tax.
- The Federal Reserve Act creates a central bank responsible for monetary policy.
- The U.S. Department of Commerce and Labor is divided into two separate departments

1914
- The City Manager's Association is formed.
- The University of Michigan creates the first master's program in municipal administration.
- Dayton, Ohio, is the first major city to have a city manager.
- World War I begins.

1918
- World War I ends.

1919
- The failure of the Boston police strike sets back municipal unionization and makes Calvin Coolidge, the governor of Massachusetts, a national hero.

1920
- The Retirement Act creates the first federal civil service pension system.
- The Nineteenth Amendment gives women the right to vote.

1921
- The Budget and Accounting Act establishes (1) the Bureau of the Budget in the Department of the Treasury and (2) the General Accounting Office as an agency of the Congress.

1922
- Max Weber's structural definition of bureaucracy is published posthumously.

1923
- The Classification Act brings position classification to Washington-based federal employees and establishes the principle of equal pay for equal work.

1924
- Hawthorne studies begin at the Hawthorne Works of the Western Electric Company in Chicago; they will last until 1932 and lead to new thinking about the relationship of work environment to productivity.

1926
- Leonard D. White's *Introduction to the Study of Public Administration* is the first text in public administration.
- Mary Parker Follett, in calling for "power with" as opposed to "power over," anticipates the movement toward more participatory management styles.

1929
- The University of Southern California establishes the first independent professional school of public administration.
- Stock market crashes; Great Depression begins.

1930
- Durham County, South Carolina, is first to install county-manager form of county government.

1933
- President Franklin D. Roosevelt's New Deal begins.
- Francis Perkins, the first woman in a president's cabinet, is appointed Secretary of Labor.
- The Tennessee Valley Authority (TVA) is established by Congress as an independent public corporation.

1935
- The National Labor Relations (Wagner) Act establishes the right of private sector employees to organize and bargain collectively.
- Social Security program created.

1936
- J. Donald Kingsley and William E. Mosher's *Public Personnel Administration* becomes the first text in this field.
- John Maynard Keynes publishes his *General Theory of Employment, Interest, and Money,* which calls for using a government's fiscal and monetary policies to positively influence a capitalistic economy.
- E. Pendleton Herring in *Public Administration and the Public Interest* asserts that bureaucrats, by default, must often be the arbiters of the public interest.

1937
- The Brownlow Committee's report says that the "President needs help" and calls for the reorganization of the executive branch.
- Luther Gulick calls attention to the various functional elements of the work of an executive with his mnemonic device POSDCORB.

1938
- The Fair Labor Standards Act provides for minimum wages, overtime pay, and limits on child labor.
- Chester I. Barnard's *The Functions of the Executive* foreshadows the postwar revolution in thinking about organizational behavior.

1939
- American Society for Public Administration is founded.
- The Reorganization Act enables the creation of the Executive Office of the President and the transfer of the Bureau of the Budget from the Treasury to the White House.
- The Hatch Act is passed to inhibit political activities by federal employees.
- The federal government first requires the states to have merit systems for employees in programs aided by federal funds.

1940
- *Public Administration Review* is first published.

1941
- James Burnham's *The Managerial Revolution* asserts that as the control of large organizations passes from the hands of the owners into the hands of professional administrators, the society's new governing class will be the possessors not of wealth, but of technical expertise.
- Japanese attack on Pearl Harbor brings the United States into World War II.

1943
- Abraham Maslow's "needs hierarchy" first appears in *Psychological Review*.
- Withholding for federal income tax begins as a temporary wartime measure.

1944
- J. Donald Kingsley's *Representative Bureaucracy* develops the concept that all social groups have a right to participate in their governing institutions in proportion to their numbers in the population.

1945
- With the dropping of the atomic bomb and the end of World War II, the suddenly public Manhattan Project marks the federal government's first major involvement with science in a policymaking role.
- Paul Appleby leads the postwar attack on the politics/administration dichotomy by insisting in *Big Democracy* that apolitical governmental processes went against the grain of the American experience.

1946
- The Employment Act creates the Council of Economic Advisors and asserts that it is the policy of the federal government to maintain full employment.
- The Administrative Procedure Act standardized many federal government administrative practices across agencies.
- Herbert A. Simon's "The Proverbs of Administration" attacks the principles approach to management for being inconsistent and often inapplicable.

1947
- President Harry S. Truman announces his namesake doctrine.

1949
- The First Hoover Commission recommends increased managerial capacity in the Executive Office of the President.
- The National Security Act creates the Department of Defense.

1951
- David Truman's *The Governmental Process* calls for viewing interest groups as the real determinant of, and focal point of study on, public policy.
- Kurt Lewin proposes a general model of organizational change consisting of three phases, "unfreezing, change, refreezing" in his *Field Theory in Social Science*.

1954
- Peter Drucker's book, *The Practice of Management*, popularizes the concept of management by objectives.
- The Supreme Court, in *Brown v. Board of Education*, holds that racially separate educational facilities are inherently unequal and therefore violate the equal protection clause of the Fourteenth Amendment.
- Senator Joseph McCarthy (and in effect McCarthyism) is censured by the U.S. Senate.
- Lakewood, California, pioneers the service contract, whereby a small jurisdiction buys government services from a neighboring large jurisdiction.

1955
- The Second Hoover Commission recommends the curtailment and abolition of federal government activities that are competitive with private enterprise.
- The Department of Health, Education and Welfare (HEW) is created.
- AFL-CIO is formed by the merger of the American Federation of Labor and the Congress of Industrial Organization.

1957
- C. Northcote Parkinson discovers his law that "work expands so as to fill the time available for its completion."
- Chris Argyris asserts in *Personality and Organization* that there is an inherent conflict between the personality of a mature adult and the needs of modern organizations.
- Douglas M. McGregor's article, "The Human Side of Enterprise," distills the contending traditional (authoritarian) and humanistic managerial philosophies into Theory X and Theory Y.

1958
- NASA is created.

1959
- New York City is the first major city to allow collective bargaining with its employees.
- Wisconsin is the first state to enact a comprehensive law governing public sector labor relations.
- The Advisory Commission on Intergovernmental Relations is established.
- Charles A. Lindblom's "The Science of 'Muddling Through'" rejects the rational model of decision making in favor of incrementalism.
- Herzberg, Mausner, and Snyderman's *The Motivation to Work* puts forth the motivation-hygiene theory.

1960
- Richard Neustadt's *Presidential Power* asserts that the president's (or any executive's) essential power is that of persuasion.

1961
- President Dwight D. Eisenhower in his farewell address warns of "the military-industrial complex."
- President John F. Kennedy's Executive Order 10925 requires that "affirmative action" be used in employment.
- The Peace Corps is established.
- Alan B. Shepard becomes the first American astronaut to fly in space.
- The Rand Corporation helps the Department of Defense install PPBS.

1962
- President John F. Kennedy issues Executive Order 10988, which encourages the unionization of federal workers.

1963
- During the "March on Washington," Martin Luther King Jr. delivers his "I Have a Dream" speech.
- President John F. Kennedy is assassinated; Vice President Lyndon B. Johnson becomes president.

1964
- The Civil Rights Act prohibits discrimination in private sector employment and public accommodation.
- Aaron Wildavsky publishes *The Politics of the Budgetary Process,* which becomes the classic analysis of the tactics public managers use to get budgets passed.
- The Economic Opportunity Act becomes the anchor of President Lyndon B. Johnson's "war on poverty" and other Great Society programs.

1965
- PPBS made mandatory for all federal agencies.
- The Department of Housing and Urban Development is established.
- Medicare is created through amendments to the Social Security Act.

1966
- The Freedom of Information Act allows greater access to federal agency files.
- Morton Grodzins in *The American System* asserts that the federal system is more like a marble cake than a layer cake.

1967
- The Age Discrimination in Employment Act is passed.
- The National Academy of Public Administration is organized; its first members will be all of the living past presidents of the American Society for Public Administration.
- Edward A. Suchman's *Evaluation Research* asserts that evaluation is a generic field of study.
- Terry Sanford in *Storm over the States* develops the concept of "picket-fence federalism," which holds that bureaucratic specialists at the various governmental levels exercise considerable power over the nature of intergovernmental programs.

1968
- "Younger" public administration scholars meeting at Syracuse University's Minnowbrook Conference site call for a "new public administration" that would emphasize social equity.
- Martin Luther King Jr. is assassinated.
- Robert F. Kennedy is assassinated.
- Richard M. Nixon is elected president.

1969
- Laurence J. Peter promulgates his principle that "in a hierarchy every employee tends to rise to his level of incompetence."
- Theodore Lowi's *The End of Liberalism* attacks interest group pluralism for paralyzing the policymaking process.
- Neil Armstrong, an American astronaut, becomes the first man to walk on the moon.

1970
- The Bureau of the Budget is given more responsibility for managerial oversight and renamed the Office of Management and Budget.
- The Postal Reorganization Act creates the U.S. Postal Service as a public corporation within the executive branch.
- Hawaii becomes the first state to give state and local government employees the right to strike.
- Environmental Protection Agency established.

1971
- The Supreme Court attacks restrictive credentialism in *Griggs v. Duke Power Company.*
- PPBS is formally abandoned in the federal government by the Nixon administration.

1972
- The Equal Employment Opportunity Act amends Title VII of the Civil Rights Act to include prohibitions on discrimination by public sector employers.
- The Watergate scandal erupts when men associated with the Committee to Reelect the President are caught breaking into the campaign headquarters of the Democratic opposition, located in the Watergate hotel-office-apartment complex.
- The Equal Rights Amendment is passed by Congress; it never becomes law because too few states will ratify it.
- Revenue sharing is introduced with the passage of the State and Local Fiscal Assistance Act (it will expire in 1986).

1973
- Vice President Spiro Agnew resigns after pleading "no contest" to a charge of tax evasion; Gerald R. Ford becomes vice president.
- Pressman and Wildavsky publish *Implementation* and create a new subfield of public administration and policy analysis.

1974
- The Congressional Budget and Impoundment Control Act revises the congressional budget process and creates the Congressional Budget Office.
- The Supreme Court in *United States v. Nixon* denies President Nixon's claim of absolute executive privilege; Nixon is forced to resign in the face of certain impeachment because of Watergate.
- Gerald R. Ford becomes president and grants former president Nixon a full pardon for all possible crimes.
- An amendment to the Social Security Act provides for automatic cost-of-living adjustments in Social Security payments.

1976
- Colorado is the first state to enact "sunset laws" as a method of program review and evaluation.

1977
- Zero-based budgeting is required of all federal agencies by the new Carter administration.
- The Presidential Management Intern Program is established as a special means of bringing public administration masters' graduates into the federal bureaucracy.
- The Government in the Sunshine Act requires all multi-headed federal agencies to have their business sessions open to the public.
- The Department of Energy is created.

1978
- The Civil Service Reform Act abolishes the U.S. Civil Service Commission and replaces it with (1) the Office of Personnel Management, (2) the Merit Systems Protection Board, and (3) the Federal Labor Relations Authority.
- The Ethics in Government Act seeks to deal with possible conflicts of interest by former federal employees by imposing postemployment restrictions on their activities.
- Proposition 13, requiring reductions in local property taxes, is voted into law in California.
- The Pregnancy Discrimination Act is passed.

1979
- The Department of Health, Education, and Welfare is divided into (1) the Department of Education and (2) the Department of Health and Human Services.

1980
- The EEOC issues legally binding guidelines holding that sexual harassment is sex discrimination prohibited by Title VII of the Civil Rights Act and that employers have a responsibility to provide a place of work that is free of sexual harassment or intimidation.

1981
- President Carter's zero-based budgeting requirements are rescinded by President Ronald Reagan.
- David Stockman, director of the Office of Management and Budget, tells the *Atlantic Monthly* that "none of us really understands what's going on with all these numbers."
- Professional Air Traffic Controllers (PATCO) strike; President Reagan responds by firing 11,500 of them for striking in violation of federal law.

1982
- The Grace Commission, the President's Private Sector Survey on Cost Control, finds widespread inefficiencies in the federal government.

1983
- The birthday of Martin Luther King Jr. is made a national holiday.

1985
- The Gramm-Rudman-Hollings Act is signed into law; it seeks to balance the federal budget by mandating across-the-board cuts over a period of years.

1986
- The Supreme Court in *Meritor Savings Bank v. Vinson* finds that sexual harassment is prohibited by the Civil Rights Act of 1964.
- The space shuttle *Challenger* explodes on take-off.
- The national debt passes $2 trillion.
- The Iran-Contra Scandal begins to unfold.

1988
- George Bush is elected president.
- The United States and Canada reach a free trade agreement.

1989
- The Financial Institutions, Reform, Recovery, and Enforcement Act is passed to help clean up the $500 billion savings and loan scandal.
- The National Commission on the Public Service, the Volcker Commission, calls for a revitalization of the public service.

1990
- The Budget Enforcement Act amended the Gramm-Rudman-Hollings Act to require that new spending be balanced by new taxes or spending reductions.
- The national debt passes $3 trillion.
- The Chief Financial Officers Act requires federal agencies to create a chief financial officer position to oversee agency finances.

1992
- Bill Clinton is elected president.

1993
- National debt passes $4 trillion.
- Osborne and Gaebler publish *Reinventing Government*.
- The Government Performance Results Act requires agencies to justify their budget requests on the basis of the results or outcomes to be achieved.
- The North American Free Trade Agreement is ratified.

1995
- Republicans take control of both houses of Congress.

1996
- Congress gives the president the line-item veto.
- The national debt passes $5 trillion.
- Welfare Reform Act passes.

1998
- The Supreme Court vetoes the presidential line-item veto.
- President Clinton is impeached by U.S. House of Representatives.

1999
- President Clinton is tried and acquitted by U.S. Senate.

2000	• George W. Bush is elected president.	2008	• Barack Obama elected president.
2001	• The War on Terror begins.	2009	• The national debt passes $12 trillion.
2003	• The war in Iraq begins.	2010	• Republicans win control of the House of Representatives.
	• Department of Homeland Security created.		
2004	• George W. Bush is reelected.	2011	• Standard and Poor's downgrades the credit rating of the United States.
2005	• The national debt passes $8 trillion.		
2006	• Democrats win control of both houses of Congress.	2012	• The national debt passes $15 trillion.

Defining Public Administration

CHAPTER OUTLINE

KEYNOTE: Go Tell the Spartans

At 8:48 on the morning of September 11, 2001, Adam Mayblum, 35, an investment firm employee, was in his office on the 87th floor of the north tower of the World Trade Center in New York. Suddenly, it seemed like a huge bomb exploded on the floors above—the building shook as if in an earthquake, lighting fixtures fell down, the ceiling collapsed in several areas, and paper flew everywhere. The halls quickly filled with smoke, but the phones were still working. Mayblum immediately called home and left a message for his wife that a bomb had gone off and he was on his way out. Next he took off his undershirt, tore it into three pieces, and gave two of the pieces to coworkers. They soaked the fabric in water and tied the torn T-shirt pieces around their faces as improvised air filters. Then the trio started down a smoke-filled staircase.

As Mayblum walked down the crowded and smoky stairs, he called his parents on his cell phone. Soon after, his sister-in-law called him. Everybody with a cell phone was making calls to or taking calls from friends and relatives. On the 53rd floor they found a "heavyset man" just sitting on the stairwell. Mayblum and his friends offered to carry him, but he preferred to wait for professional help. As they approached the 44th floor, they first started seeing firefighters and police officers on their way up. Mayblum stopped several of them and told them about the man on the 53rd floor and also about a friend who was missing on the 87th.

The next day, in a 2,000-word e-mail that was written for friends but ultimately distributed to thousands, Mayblum told of his narrow escape. He wrote that he "felt terrible" about telling the rescuers to go further up the stairs. "They headed up to find those people and met death instead. . . . I realize that they were going up anyway. But it hurts to know that I may have made them move quicker to find my friend."

Mayblum is only one of thousands who fled down the stairs to safety from the inferno of the World Trade Center towers as firefighters and other rescue workers raced up the stairs into deadly danger. The essence of the firefighters' bravery can be summed up by an old observation: Firefighters don't run from burning buildings; they run into them. Peggy Noonan, a speechwriter for Presidents Reagan and Bush (the elder), wrote, "You think to yourself: Do we pay them enough? You realize: We couldn't possibly pay them enough. And in any case, a career like that is not about money." But if it is "not about money," what *is* it about? The answer is that it is about duty.

For almost 2,500 years "Go tell the Spartans" has been the most famous classical reference to a duty done unto death. When it became shockingly evident that more than 300 firefighters died that day, those who knew ancient history might well have thought of another group of 300 heroes who died in the line of duty. In 480 B.C.E., soldiers from the Greek city of Sparta fought a delaying action against invaders from Persia (now Iran). Taking up a defensive position in the mountain pass of Thermopylae, they fought off massive waves of assaulting Persians for three days. The Spartans knowingly sacrificed themselves—fought until they were all killed—so that their fellow Greeks would have the time to organize and eventually defeat the enemy.

The similarities between the New York City firefighters and the Spartans of ancient Greece go far beyond the number 300. And that number is not accurate in either case. The 343 firefighters who died were in the company of 136 other rescue workers (New York City police, Port Authority police, private security guards, etc.) who also died. The Spartans had auxiliaries (somebody had to cook) and small combat units from other cities, including about 1,000 Thespians (not actors, but soldiers from Thespiae). Nevertheless, the number 300 resonates because it was the Spartans who fought to the death while others retreated. And it was the firefighters who personified the rescue effort.

Societies have always expected their soldiers to die in large numbers if necessary—but not their firefighters, who are pacifistic warriors seeking only to fight fires and save lives. In the past, firefighters only occasionally died in the line of duty. Until 2001 about 100 died in the United States each year. Previously, in the worst fire disaster in New York City, 12 firefighters died. To have 343 die in a single day was, until September 11, unthinkable.

Both the firefighters and the Spartans sacrificed themselves according to the ethics of their crafts. And though their actions were separated by two-and-a-half millennia, they were both fighting the same enemy: a despotism from the East that then sought to suppress the budding democracy of ancient Greece and now seeks to wipe out the flourishing democracies of the Western world.

After the Greeks won their war, Simonides (556–468 B.C.E.), a famous poet of the time, was commissioned to write an appropriate inscription for a memorial plaque to be placed at Thermopylae to honor the Spartan heroes. Some Greeks were shocked when he turned in only two lines. But these two lines have become the most meaningful and best-known epitaph in the history of Western civilization:

> Go tell the Spartans, thou who passest by,
> That here obedient to their laws we lie.

There would eventually be a fitting memorial to all those who died on that infamous 11th of September. But the firefighters, police officers, and other doomed rescuers already had one memorial. They all share the epitaph of the Spartans because they died bravely in the line of duty, "obedient to their laws."

Although the approximately 3,000 dead from the attacks were in New York, western Pennsylvania, and at the Pentagon in northern Virginia, it was the whole nation that cried with their families. This was not just another office building complex. Towering over Wall Street, these office buildings represented the capitalistic might of the United States. The barbarous attack wounded the entire country because it was an act of war against all of us. In the days following the blast the news media put forth much banal talk about America's "loss of innocence" along with the increasing statistics, the body count, on the loss of the innocents.

That no one would be found alive in the rubble after the first day was impossible to know at the time. Soon out-of-state rescue teams arrived to help. These teams, deployed by the Federal Emergency Management Agency, included search dogs. They are trained to bark if they detect a live person and whine when they locate a body. The dogs spent most of their time whining. While less dramatic, it is often just as dangerous to recover a body at a disaster site as it is to rescue a survivor.

TABLE 1.1

Annual Police and Firefighter Deaths in the Line of Duty

Year	Police	Firefighters
1996	133	95
1997	163	94
1998	156	91
1999	134	112
2000	151	102
2001	230	446
2002	147	102
2003	146	111
2004	153	110
2005	145	106
2006	157	106
2007	181	118
2008	138	118
2009	117	90
2010	162	87

Source: Federal Emergency Management Agency/National Fire Data Center/National Law Enforcement Officers Memorial Fund.

The heroic efforts of the rescuers received massive publicity. The stories many of the survivors told of the bravery and daring of the rescue teams were heartrending. But one point was largely missed in all the news reports. All these highly trained search and rescue professionals were public employees. They, and the administrative apparatus that sustains their organizations, are part of the government. They are representative of the bureaucrats whom so many people—even some who were then lauding them as heroes—had often described as overpaid and inefficient.

These everyday heroes got so much attention after September 11 because they were doing wholesale what they did retail on a daily basis. It is a common, if not everyday, occurrence in America for firefighters to rescue people from burning buildings. But this was the first time that they rescued thousands and died themselves in the hundreds.

Why is this photo of Air Force One flying between New York and New Jersey like an invasion from Mars? Because both caused widespread panic. The "invasion" came in 1938, as a radio drama of the H. G. Wells novel *War of the Worlds*. Because it was broadcast as a simulated newscast, listeners thought it was real. It caused a memorable Halloween night of disorder. Similarly, when on April 27, 2009, a 747 jumbo jet was seen flying low over the Statue of Liberty followed by a fighter jet, people on the ground reasonably assumed that another 9/11 terrorist attack was only minutes away. Panic ensued. Office buildings emptied. Antacids were taken. But no attack was under way. It was just that Louis Caldera, the civilian head of the White House Military Office, thought that this would be a great day to get some publicity photos of the presidential airplane. So he sent Air Force One to fly a mere 1,000 feet over the Statue of Liberty with a fighter along to take pictures. It never occurred to him to notify all local authorities or to allay public fears by alerting the media. But this Harvard-trained lawyer did justify the more than $300,000 cost of the photo shoot by asserting it was a training mission. The people who panicked were furious. The mayor of New York was furious. President Obama was furious. And this bureaucrat of such poor judgment was certainly furious with himself when he lost his job over this. This incident proves two things: (1) that there is some sense of accountability in the Obama White House and (2) that New Yorkers are still very sensitive about low-flying jetliners over Manhattan. And rightly so!

Citizens the world over complain about their governments. But once disaster strikes—whether caused by nature or terrorists—they expect instant service. When there is an earthquake in California, when the Mississippi River floods, or when an Atlantic hurricane wreaks havoc in Florida, volunteers come running. But usually only those with special training can save someone from the raging torrent that was once a gentle stream or the cage of twisted metal that was once a car. And the lasting help that disaster victims need—from social services to low-interest loans for rebuilding—is generally available only from government. Suddenly these "bureaucrats" are angels of mercy. When danger lurks, they become our modern versions of medieval knights in shining armor. Call 911 in most U.S. cities and within minutes you'll have a career public servant at your door ready to risk his or her life for you and yours.

Yet, when our modern heroes do not live up to the high expectations that we place on them, the public disappointment is obvious. During the darkest hours of Hurricane Katrina in 2005, a number of New Orleans police officers failed to uphold their solemn oath to defend and protect the citizens of their city, causing outrage throughout the nation. How could so many men and women who pledged to serve the public interest fail in the time of greatest need? For the many New Orleans police officers who stayed on the job, the disappointment in their colleagues must have been overwhelming. To be sure, the men and women of the NOPD who deserted their posts were no Spartans.

There were certainly heroes in New York and in New Orleans. And there are heroes in your city, too, but most of them are invisible to you. The modern public service allows vast scope for heroism. Throughout history, classic heroes used their special skills for the public good, usually by performing feats of military prowess and physical bravery. And some societies recognized other kinds of heroes, too. For example, Michelangelo, who became one of the greatest heroes of Renaissance Italy, was known only for his prowess with a chisel and a paintbrush.

Today's police officer and firefighter heroes are joined by great numbers of quiet unsung heroes: public works department engineers who provide safe drinking water, highway department drivers who work all night clearing snow in a blizzard, and public health officials who keep diseases from becoming epidemics. These virtually invisible heroes often hold our lives in their hands no less than their uniformed coworkers. More than that, they make modern life—civilization as we know it—possible.

Then there are those public employees who do not deal with life-and-death issues. Their concerns are instead with quality of life. They are, for example, the teachers who inspire students to excel, the social workers who find a loving home for a suddenly orphaned child, the economic development officers who bring hundreds of new jobs into a community, and the public managers who reinvent programs so that costs can be cut and taxes lowered. While not called on to be physically brave, their efforts are often heroic. The public service has a wide variety of heroes. Some are just more visible than others.

For Discussion: *Are the first responders (police, firefighters, etc.) where you live more prepared now for a terrorist attack than they were before September 11, 2001? Has the election of President Barack Obama to the presidency changed your attitude toward public servants and public service careers?*

THE DEFINITIONS OF PUBLIC ADMINISTRATION

It is easy to define public administration if you are content with being simplistic: it is government in action—the management of public affairs or the implementation of public policies. Such a facile definition, while accurate, is not adequate for such an important task. Consider the scene in Edmond Rostand's play *Cyrano de Bergerac* in which somebody insults the hero's big nose to provoke him into fighting a duel. But the challenger's insult of "rather large" is so commonplace that Cyrano then lectures him on "the great many things" he might have said if he'd had "some tinge of letters, or of wit." Defining public administration poses a similar challenge—even without the ensuing swordplay.

The authors of this book believe that nothing is more important to an introduction to public administration than the most expansive definition possible. How else can we explore its richness and subtlety and savor its historical significance, universal application, and present development? How else can we gain an appreciation for the later technical chapters? Nevertheless, the discussion that follows is inherently incomplete. Public administration is so vast that there is no way to encompass it all with only one definition. So we have written 18 of them and clustered them into four categories: political, legal, managerial, and occupational. This quartet of definitions essentially expands on the trio—managerial, political, and legal—established by **David H. Rosenbloom**. But even with such an array of definitions, the authors are in the uncomfortable position of Cyrano's challenger. We would have said more if we'd only had the wit!

Political Definitions of Public Administration

Public administration cannot exist outside of its political context. It is this context that makes it public—that makes it different from private or business administration. Consequently, our first definitions of public administration focus on its political nature.

Public Administration Is What Government Does

It is a White House chef preparing the menu of a state dinner for a visiting **chief of state**, a Department of Agriculture inspector examining beef at a slaughterhouse, and a Food and Drug Administration scientist determining the number of rodent hairs that food processors can safely and legally leave in chocolate, popcorn, and peanut butter. It is a firefighter rescuing a child from a disintegrating building, a meter reader attaching a ticket to your automobile for overlong parking, and a state prison official injecting deadly fluids into the veins of a condemned criminal. It is an astronomer exploring the furthest reaches of outer space, a CIA agent decoding captured messages from suspected terrorists, and a sewer crawler seeking to discover what has clogged up a municipal drainpipe. It is giving **food stamps** to the poor, mortgage interest deductions to homeowners, and hot meals to evacuees of a Gulf Coast hurricane.

Throughout the world, government employees do things that affect the daily lives of their fellow citizens. These things range from the heroic (as we saw in New York City) to the mundane. Usually these efforts are beneficial, but sometimes they are not. Most of the time, in most countries, public administrators tend to the public's

---

David H. Rosenbloom (1943–) ■

The leading authority on the constitutional aspects of public employment. His paradigm of public administration as the intersection of management, politics, and law has become a standard way to analyze and teach the subject.

Chief of state ■

The ceremonial head of a government, such as a king, queen, or president. This is in contrast to the chief executive of a government, such as a prime minister, chancellor, or president. The American presidency combines in one office—one person— the roles of chief of state and chief executive.

Food stamps ■

A welfare program designed to improve the nutrition of the poor. Administered by the Department of Agriculture and state and local welfare organizations, the program provides coupons (stamps) that can be used to pay for food at many grocery stores.

business; for example, they build bridges and highways, collect garbage, put out fires, plow snow, spray for mosquitoes, and provide essential social services for the less fortunate. But in other lands public employees may torture the innocent and murder children. When **Amnesty International** publishes its annual report on the states that brutalize and violate the civil rights of its citizens, who do you think does all this brutalizing and violating? It is none other than the local public administrators! Of course, such nefarious activities are usually organized within some innocuous-sounding program having to do with "population control" or "internal security." Thus, modern public relations try to put a friendly face on ancient atrocities.

As a profession, public administration has developed values and ethical standards. But as an activity, it has no values. It merely reflects the cultural norms, beliefs, and power realities of its society. It is simply government doing whatever government does—in whatever political and cultural context it happens to exist. In 1955, **Dwight Waldo** was the first to insist that analysts "see administration in terms of its environment" because "it enables us to understand differences in administration between different societies which would be inexplicable if we were limited to viewing administration analytically in terms of the universals of administration itself." So, essentially similar administrative acts can be performed differently in different cultures. Thus, a routine customs inspection in one state parallels the solicitation of a bribe by a corrupt customs official in another. The same act that is performed honestly in one state (because of a culture that supports honesty) may be performed corruptly in another (where the culture supports corruption by government officials).

Public administration is the totality of the working-day activities of all the world's bureaucrats—whether those activities are performed legally or illegally, competently or incompetently, decently or despicably! British scientist J. B. S. Haldane wrote that "the universe is not only queerer than we suppose, but queerer than we *can* suppose." Things are much the same with public administration. It is not only far vaster in scope than most people suppose, but it is so extensive and pervasive in modern life that not even the most imaginative of us can imagine it all.

Public Administration Is Both Direct and Indirect   It is direct when government employees provide services to the public as varied as mortgage insurance, mail delivery, and electricity. It is indirect when government pays private contractors to provide goods or services to citizens. For example, **NASA** operated the space shuttle, but the shuttle itself was built by private corporations. Similarly, security officers protecting American construction workers in Iraq's oil fields are not part of the U.S. armed forces but employees of private firms contracted by the defense department. Does the fact that these workers are employed by private companies put them outside the realm of public administration? Not at all. Remember that a government agency must hire, evaluate, and hold all employees and contractors accountable for the quality of their performance—whether they are building rockets or guarding oil rigs.

Governments have used private contractors since ancient times. For example, the executioner who once operated and maintained the guillotine in France was an independent contractor who earned a fee per head chopped off (literally severance pay). The current trend toward greater **privatization** of government functions, which began most notably in the 1980s during the Reagan administration in the United States and the Thatcher administration in the United Kingdom, is

Amnesty International ■
A worldwide organization that seeks to gain the release of political and religious prisoners by publicizing their plights and by lobbying governments. It has been especially effective in exposing cases of government-sanctioned torture. In 1972 the organization was awarded the Nobel Peace Prize.

Dwight Waldo (1913–2000) ■
The preeminent historian of the academic field of public administration.

NASA (National Aeronautics and Space Administration) ■
The federal agency created by the National Aeronautics and Space Act of 1958 to conduct research on problems of flight and to explore outer space.

Privatization ■
The process of returning to the private sector property (such as public lands) or functions (such as trash collection, fire protection) previously owned or performed by government.

BOX 1.1 | How the Inherent Criminality of Some Public Administrators Is Hidden by Political Language

It was the British political essayist George Orwell (1903–1950) who most famously observed that the speeches and writings of politicians are often the "defense of the indefensible," because the language used is too euphemistic and excessively vague. Innocent villagers are murdered and their homes burned in an effort at "pacification." Citizens are imprisoned without trial or sent to slave labor camps in a process called "elimination of unreliable elements." According to Orwell, such euphemistic phraseology is needed so that people can avoid thinking of the ugly reality of murder and torture. Consequently, the language of politicians and their administrators "is designed to make lies sound truthful and murder respectable."

Orwell's "Politics and the English Language," in *Shooting an Elephant and Other Essays* (New York: Harcourt Brace, 1946) has had a rhetorical influence that remains alive and well. For example, a week after the September 11, 2001, attack, President Bush told a joint session of the Congress, "Whether we bring our enemies to justice or bring justice to our enemies, justice will be done." In the classic Orwellian tradition he was using a relatively innocuous word to mean something far harsher. Only those not familiar with the innate subtleties of the English language did not understand that his "justice" meant death to the terrorists. Note that his administration continued to pay homage to Orwell when it renamed torture "enhanced interrogation techniques." ▲

now worldwide. This trend has been reinforced by the growth of the nonprofit sector, which receives much of its funding from government contracts—especially for social services and research. Much of the budgets of private nonprofit organizations providing human services now comes from the government. According to former New York Governor Mario Cuomo, government funds account for two out of every three dollars spent by Catholic Charities USA, a national network of some 1,400 social service organizations. By comparison, Lutheran Social Ministries obtains 54 percent of its funding from government sources, and the Salvation Army obtains 15 percent from such sources. Thus we may conclude that privatization has not necessarily reduced the total amount of public administration in the world; it has simply forced it to take different forms.

The increasingly expansive nature of public administration, branching out into the private and nonprofit sectors, has given new meaning to the word *governance*. What was once a synonym for the process of government has evolved to refer to interorganizational efforts to cope with cross-boundary problems by using networks of people and organizations. Thus public administration has gone from being merely indirect to being extremely convoluted as well.

Public Administration Is a Phase in the Public Policymaking Cycle   Public policymaking never ends. Government perpetually suffers from a problem similar to that faced by Shakespeare's Hamlet, the indecisive prince of Denmark, who struggled with whether "to be or not to be." Governments are in a constant flurry over whether to do or not to do. And whatever they do or do not do is public policy. All such decisions (including decisions not to make a decision) are made by those who control political power and implemented by the administrative officers of the bureaucracy. Thus public policy and public administration are two sides of the same coin. One decides, the other does. They cannot be separate because one side cannot exist without the other. But because policymaking is a continuous process, it cannot end with **implementation**. Whenever government does something, critics will suggest ways to do it better. This feedback can be informal—from citizen complaints to journalistic investigations—or it can take the form of an agency or legislative program evaluation. In any case, new decisions must be made even if the decision is to avoid making a decision.

Public Administration Is Implementing the Public Interest   Public interest is the universal label in which political actors wrap the policies and programs that they advocate. Would any **lobby**, public manager, legislator, or chief executive ever propose a program that was not "in the public interest"? Hardly! Because the public interest is generally taken to mean a commonly accepted good, the phrase is used both to further policies that are indeed for the common good and to obscure policies that may not be so commonly accepted as good. A considerable body of literature has developed about this phrase, because it represents an important philosophic point that, if successfully defined, could provide considerable guidance for politicians and public administrators alike. **Walter Lippmann** wrote that "the public interest may be presumed to be what men would choose if they saw clearly, thought rationally, acted disinterestedly and benevolently." Clear eyes and rational minds are common enough. Finding leaders who are disinterested and benevolent is the hard part.

In the early twentieth century, **E. Pendleton Herring** examined the problems posed by the dramatic increase in the scope of the administrative discretion of government. He accepted that laws passed by legislatures are necessarily the products of legislative compromise; thus they are often so vague that they need further definition. The bureaucrat, by default, then has the task of giving defining detail to the general principles embodied in a statute by issuing supplemental rules and regulations. "Upon the shoulders of the bureaucrat has been placed in large part the burden of reconciling group differences and making effective and workable the economic and social compromises arrived at through the legislative process." In effect, it becomes the job of the anonymous administrator to define the public interest.

Herring's discussion of the public interest and the critical roles played by bureaucrats and interest groups in public policy formulation correctly anticipated many of the critical issues still being grappled with in schools of public policy and administration today. Herring is a significant voice in what political science calls group theory, a school of thought that views government as representing various group interests and negotiating policy outcomes among them. According to Herring, the most basic task of a bureaucrat has been to establish working relationships with the various special interests so that their concerns can be more efficiently brokered.

The role that Herring would have public administrators play is that of **Edmund Burke's** trustee, a representative who exercises personal judgment and doesn't just follow the exact orders of a legislature or the perceived opinion of a constituency. In his classic 1774 "Speech to the Electors of Bristol," Burke

Implementation ■
Putting a government program into effect; the total process of translating a legal mandate into appropriate program directives and structures that provide services or create goods.

Lobby ■
Any individual, group, or organization that seeks to influence legislation or administrative action.

Walter Lippmann (1889–1974) ■
A journalist who went beyond being the preeminent political pundit of his time to being a political philosopher who wrote pioneering analyses of public opinion and foreign policy.

E. Pendleton Herring (1903–2004) ■
One of the most influential of the pre–World War II scholars of public administration. His *Group Representation Before Congress* (1929) was one of the pioneering works in the study of pressure groups. His *Public Administration and the Public Interest* (1936) remains a major analysis of the relations between government agencies and their constituencies.

BOX 1.2 | Edmund Burke Versus the Tea Party

Edmund Burke, the British parliamentarian, was in England when he heard of the original Tea Party in 1773 Boston. In a 1774 speech in the House of Commons, "On American Taxation," he supported the Boston tea dumpers and urged the repeal of the tax on tea. His policy was simple. "Leave America . . . to tax herself." Despite his feelings about American efforts to reduce taxes on tea, he, if alive today, would be vexed by the current Tea Party movement which seeks to contradict his famous statement on the role of a legislative representative.

Burke's classic 1774 "Speech to the Electors of Bristol" specifically rejects the notion that an elected representative be bound by pre-election

"instructions" from his constituents. Tea Party activists often demand that the candidates they support pledge never to raise taxes of any kind and never allow laws to tolerate abortion under any conditions, even in cases of rape and incest. The clear implication is that representatives would be punished at the next election if they stray in the least from their mandates.

Burke's "speech" is a famous reproach to Tea Party rigidity and a call for representatives to exercise judgement. Thus Burke, the best-known British supporter of the original Tea Party, would likley question many of the actions of its current reincarnation. ◣

Edmund Burke (1729–1797) ■
The British political philosopher and member of parliament who is often referred to as the father of conservative thought.

Tragedy of the commons ■
A story illustrative of the principle that maximization of private gain will not result in the maximization of social benefit. When herdsmen sought to maximize individual gain by adding cattle to the common, it caused overgrazing, with the result that the common could no longer be used for grazing at all. The concepts involved with the tragedy of the commons apply to societal problems.

told the voters, "Your representative owes you, not his industry only, but his judgment; and he betrays, instead of serving you, if he sacrifices it to your opinion." Few would argue with the desirability of using good judgment in the furtherance of the public interest. However, some would argue that the interest-group broker role that Herring espouses for high-level public administrators is inherently undemocratic.

Public Administration Is Doing Collectively That Which Cannot Be So Well Done Individually   This is Abraham Lincoln's understanding of the "legitimate object of government . . . to do for a community of people, whatever they need to have done, but cannot do, at all, or cannot, so well do, for themselves—in their separate, and individual capacities." Thus, public administration is the mature manifestation of the community spirit. What started as voluntary service (such as fire protection or care for the poor) became institutionalized as people indicated a preference (via elections) to pay taxes so that once-voluntary activities could become government functions. Similarly, collective action is the remedy for the "tragedy of the commons," where individuals acting in their self-interest destroy public resources such as land and water. In this context public administration is central to the process of regulating individual behavior in the interest of the common good.

Twenty-first-century communications have brought about a "revolution of rising expectations" whereby the people of traditionally poor countries realize just how poor they are relative to industrialized states. Similarly, the citizens of these rich states benefit from programs that they increasingly resent paying for. Senator Ernest Hollings of South Carolina often told the story of the veteran who returned from Korea and went to college on the **GI Bill**, bought a house with a Federal Housing Administration loan, started a business with a Small Business

Administration loan, got electricity from Tennessee Valley Authority, and, later, got clean water from an Environmental Protection Agency project. His parents, who were receiving Social Security, retired to a farm, got their electricity from the Rural Electrification Administration, and had their soil tested by the U.S. Department of Agriculture. When his father became ill, the family was saved from financial ruin by Medicare, and his father's life was saved with a drug developed through the National Institutes of Health. His kids participated in the school lunch program, learned physics from teachers trained in a National Science Foundation program, and went on to college with guaranteed student loans. He drove to work on the interstate and moored his boat in a channel dredged by the Army Corps of Engineers. When his home was flooded, he took **Amtrak** to Washington, D.C., to apply for disaster relief, and while there, he spent some time in the Smithsonian Institution museums. One day he got mad, so he sent his congressman an angry letter. "Get the government off my back!" he wrote. "I'm tired of paying taxes for all those programs created for ungrateful people!"

But we all want—and indeed expect—government employees to literally pull our backs out of the rubble when disaster strikes, as it did in New York City. Volunteers could do the easy tasks, such as driving the walking wounded to local hospitals, but only the highly trained public service professionals could do the real rescue work. Their organizations—the police and fire departments—were created, in Lincoln's words, to be available to do what the citizens "cannot do, at all, or cannot, so well do, for themselves."

Legal Definitions of Public Administration

Because public administration is what a state does, it is both created and bound by an instrument of the law. Indeed, in many communities, such as those of continental Europe, it is an academic subject that has never escaped from the faculties of law. While public administration in the United States is not a "legal" subject, its foundations are always legal.

Public Administration Is Law in Action   Public administration is inherently the execution of a **public law**. Every application of a general law is necessarily an act of administration. Administration cannot exist without this legal foundation. In the United States, the Constitution of 1787 as amended is the law of the land. All legislation must conform to it or at the very least not violate it in a manner obvious to the U.S. Supreme Court. The law that creates an agency or program is known as its enabling legislation—the law that legally "enables" a program to exist. In theory, no government administrator can do anything if it is not provided for in the legislation or in the rules and regulations that the legislation allows the agency to promulgate. And how much government money can the president of the United States spend on his own without the approval of the Congress? Not a penny! Everything the president does, if it involves spending public money, must have a basis in legislation. This is often difficult for people in less democratic regimes to understand. Tip O'Neill, the former **Speaker** of the U.S. House of Representatives, wrote in a memoir, "I must have met Deng Xiaoping of China a half-dozen times, and every time he would ask, 'The president has to go to you for his money?'"

GI Bill ■
The American Servicemen's Readjustment Act of 1944. It provided low-interest, no-down-payment home mortgages and education benefits that allowed a whole generation of working-class veterans to go to college and advance into the middle class.

Amtrak ■
The National Railroad Passenger Corp., the federally subsidized corporation created in 1970 to operate intercity rail passenger service.

Public law ■
A legislative act that deals with the citizenry as a whole; a statute that applies to all. This is in contrast to a private law that affects only one person or group.

Speaker ■
The presiding officer of a legislature such as a House of Representatives or a House of Commons, elected by its members. Thomas P. "Tip" O'Neill was speaker from 1977 to 1987.

O'Neill always answered this question the same way: "Yes, and the president had better not forget it." And the same is true of governors and mayors who must go to their respective legislative bodies for appropriations.

While many books have been written about the implementation of this or that government program, there is ultimately only one thing that government is in essence capable of implementing: the law. Of course, the law is often in turmoil. The legislative basis of programs, or specific agency rules and regulations, is constantly being challenged in court by those who oppose as well as those who support the program involved. The opposition wants the enabling legislation declared unconstitutional and the program destroyed, while supporters often want the program administered even more generously. From the **New Deal** to the first years of the Barack Obama administration, a pattern has emerged with controversial legislation. After its passage, opponents challenge its legality in court, hoping that the judicial branch will overturn it. In effect, there is a new final phase to the legislative process: a **judicial review** that confirms that the new law is constitutional.

While public administration is the law in action, the law of how, when, and where these actions can be taken is called administrative law. In the American context, administrative law does not deal with the substantive content of agency policies and practices. Instead, it focuses on the procedures that agencies use in exercising their authority. For example, Congress requires federal agencies such as the Environmental Protection Agency (EPA) to notify the public when the agency is creating a new rule that affects citizens. If the agency doesn't follow the specific guidelines on how and when to notify the public, its new rules can be declared illegitimate by the courts. In effect, administrative law is the totality of constitutional provisions, legislative statutes, court decisions, and executive directives that regulate the activities of government agencies.

Public Administration Is Regulation   It is government telling citizens and businesses what they may and may not do. Regulation is one of the oldest functions of government. The Code of Hammurabi in ancient Babylonia provided that "the mason who builds a house which falls down and kills the inmate shall be put to death." While not exactly a modern building code, this nevertheless proved an effective means of regulating the soundness of housing.

Our lives are constantly governed, or interfered with, by regulation. We are not officially born until we have a birth certificate—regulation. We must attend school up to a certain age—regulation. We cannot engage in many occupations without a license from the state—regulation. Finally, we cannot be declared legally dead without a death certificate—regulation. And it doesn't even end there. We can be buried only in government-approved cemeteries, and our estate taxes must be paid—regulation. As you will see in Chapter 9, regulation can also be used as a tool to reach the strategic goals of government. From preservation of natural resources to controlling obesity levels within the population, public administrators turn to regulation to help them achieve an array of desired outcomes.

Public Administration Is the King's Largesse   "The king's largesse" is whatever goods, services, or honors the ruling authority decides to bestow. This was the earliest meaning of public administration. Since everything was owned by the crown,

New Deal ■
The domestic programs and policies of the administration of Franklin D. Roosevelt, who was president from 1933 to 1945.

Judicial review ■
Any court's power to review executive actions, legislative acts, or decisions of lower courts (or quasi-judicial entities, such as arbitration panels) to either confirm or overturn them.

whatever was granted to the nobles and peasants was a gift. In the modern world, this version of public administration can be seen in traditional monarchies and dictatorships, where hospitals, schools, parks, and such are touted as something given by the autocrat to a grateful people. The last vestige of this kingly largesse in **representative government** can be seen on the plaques often attached to public buildings and bridges indicating that the edifice was built during the tenure of Mayor Smith or Governor Jones. Of course, whenever representative governments grow corrupt, largesse as an operating mode of public administration reasserts itself. Then citizens may only get public services such as police protection and welfare benefits if they are deserving in the eyes of the rulers.

The traditional big-city **political machine** lasted only as long as there was largesse to distribute. For example, in Cambridge, Massachusetts, during the Great Depression, Democratic party **ward heelers** were authorized to distribute up to 50 "snow buttons" each time there was a major snowstorm. Each button entitled the holder to a day's work shoveling snow for the city. This was a highly prized benefit sought by unemployed men in each ward. While certainly at the low end of the patronage food chain, this largesse bought the ward heeler loyalty that translated into votes for the party. Snow buttons are a relic of the past. So are political machines, because welfare benefits as a matter of right, as an entitlement, have made them superfluous. Thus the comprehensive public services of the welfare state have driven out the informal welfare system of the machines. Without largesse, the political machines could not hold the loyalty of their audience.

Public Administration Is Theft   There are those who believe that a government should do little more than provide police and military protection; other than that, it should not interfere—either for good or ill—in the lives of its citizens. A major intellectual force advocating such **libertarianism** was Ayn Rand, the **objectivist** philosopher who attacked welfare state notions of selflessness and sacrifice for a common good in novels such as *The Fountainhead* (1943) and *Atlas Shrugged* (1957). In *Capitalism: The Unknown Ideal* (1966), she wrote, "The only proper function of the government of a free country is to act as an agency which protects the individual's rights, i.e., which protects the individual from physical violence." Such **reactionary** attitudes are an extreme form of **conservatism**.

Rand, because of her philosophy of positive selfishness and government minimalism, has become an icon of the Tea Party Movement; they have conveniently forgotten that she was a proselytizing atheist and unapologetic abortion rights advocate.

Conservatives are continuously fearful of public policies involving redistribution, such as social welfare policies and programs whose goal is to shift wealth or benefits from one segment of the population to another. The welfare state is founded on this notion of redistribution. The basic mechanism for redistribution is taxation. However, the laws themselves can sometimes redistribute benefits. For example, **tax loopholes** benefit one group of taxpayers at the expense of others; and civil rights legislation, through equal employment opportunity mandates, gives economic benefits to one segment of the population at the theoretical expense of another. Redistribution is one leg of political scientist Theodore J. Lowi's three-part classification of all domestic public policies into distribution,

Representative government ■
A governing system in which a legislature freely chosen by the people exercises substantial power on their behalf.

Political machine ■
Historically, an informal organization that controlled the formal processes of a government through corruption, patronage, intimidation, and service to its constituents.

Ward heeler ■
A local political functionary.

Libertarianism ■
A political doctrine holding that a government should do little more than provide protection; other than that, it should not interfere—for either good or ill—in the lives of its citizens.

Objectivist ■
One who believes that reason and logic are the only means to knowledge, that self-interest determines ethics, and that capitalism should prevail in society.

Reactionary ■
A person who supports outmoded ideas of the past; a derogatory reference to political malcontents who yearn for a previous status quo.

Conservatism ■
Adherence to a political disposition that prefers the status quo and accepts change only in moderation.

Tax loophole ■
An inconsistency in the tax laws, intentional or unintentional, that allows the avoidance of some taxes.

Pierre-Joseph Proudhon (1809–1865) ■
The French journalist who is considered the intellectual father of anarchism.

regulation, or redistribution. Obviously, redistribution is more popular with some classes of society than with others. Playwright George Bernard Shaw put this succinctly: "A government which robs Peter to pay Paul can always depend on the support of Paul."

And just who is the government's chief robber in this Robin Hood game? None other than your local public administrator! This is why so many citizens with their assets at risk consider thieving the underlying occupation of the public administrator. It is a long-standing legal maxim that government regulation that goes too far amounts to a taking. This conservative attitude is strikingly similar to the famous invective issued in 1851 by anarchist **Pierre-Joseph Proudhon** against all governments: "To be governed is to be watched over, inspected, spied on, directed, legislated at, regulated, docketed, indoctrinated, preached at, controlled, assessed, weighed, censored, ordered about, by men who have neither the right nor the knowledge nor the virtue."

Proudhon was wrong about at least one thing. Public administrators *do* have the right under law to do what they do. A controversial example of the power of public administrators to "take" from the public was provided in a 2005 U.S. Supreme court ruling. The decision in *Kelo v. New London* allows government authorities to take private property from individuals for private sector economic projects in the same way that government can take one's land to build a new road. Thus, a local redevelopment agency seeking to bring in a new Walmart can make you sell your property even if you wish to maintain ownership.

While many government actions could be construed as theft by portions of the populace, there is a line separating metaphorical and actual thievery. Just as the fictional British secret agent James Bond had a "license to kill," government employees in some countries consider their jobs a license to steal—usually by soliciting bribes. This is extremely common in developing countries where bureaucrats are not paid reasonable wages and have almost no choice but to engage in petty corruption. Often an informal system of fees evolves that tells the citizen, for example, how much is expected to "fix" a parking ticket or to speed up a building permit.

Managerial Definitions of Public Administration

Alexander Hamilton (1755–1804) ■
George Washington's aide during the Revolutionary War. A supporter of a strong national government, coauthored the *Federalist Papers* to help get the Constitution ratified. When Washington became president, he made Hamilton secretary of the treasury.

Public administration is so much a branch of management that many graduate schools of management (or business or administration) are divided into public and private—and now increasingly nonprofit—programs. Its legal basis allows public administration to exist, but without its management aspect, not much of the public's business would get done.

Public Administration Is the Executive Function in Government   In democratic states, whether they are republics or constitutional monarchies, it is government agencies putting into practice legislative acts that represent the will of the people. According to **Alexander Hamilton**, writing in *The Federalist*, No. 72, "The administration of government . . . in its most usual, and perhaps most precise signification . . . is limited to executive details, and falls peculiarly within the province of the executive department." In dictatorial regimes similar agencies do

BOX 1.3 | The Legal "Crimes" of Government

President Richard M. Nixon often took the position and literally said that: "When the President does it, that means that it's not illegal." This attitude got him into a lot of trouble during the Watergate scandal (see Chapter 5) especially after the U.S. Supreme Court disagreed in the 1974 decision of *United States v. Nixon* that forced his resignation.

Still, Nixon had a point. Many things done by governments would clearly be illegal if undertaken by individuals. If someone takes your money by threatening to kidnap you and hold you prisoner if you don't pay up, that is clearly a crime. Yet, the government does, in essence, the same thing when it threatens to put you in jail if you don't pay your income taxes.

There is an almost infinite number of laws and regulations that allow the government to do things to you that would otherwise be criminal. Consider child molestation. Ever since a passenger on an airliner futilely sought to ignite a bomb hidden in his underwear, your federal government has been authorizing the gloved hands of designated public administrators to feel the intimate parts of children while searching for explosive materials. Thus child molestation becomes an instance of homeland security administration when those molesting hands belong to an agent of the Transportation Safety Administration. To be fair to these agents, we should also note that they "molest" the adults as well. The "groin checks" or "love pats" at airport security gates are a daily example of just how intrusive public administrations can be. ◣

the bidding of the people who hold power. But the process is far more interactive and dynamic than any separation of powers diagram would suggest. While the executive, legislative, and judicial branches are separate and distinct in the United States, all sides struggle to influence the others. A president, governor, or mayor is constantly recommending new programs to the Congress, state legislature, or city council. Modern government executives at all levels do not meekly sit back and merely "execute" the will of the legislature. They actively compete to influence that will and to fight for the enactment of programs they are anxious to implement. Because this can lead to dramatic and highly publicized confrontations, the impression is often given that this is what executives do: fight for new legislation, fight for the annual budget, and fight for or against various interest groups. The reality is far less dramatic and more mundane. Most of what an executive does is to manage existing programs, to run the bureaucracy. This work is virtually invisible to the public except when something goes wrong and the media circus begins.

Public Administration Is a Management Specialty   Management refers both to the people responsible for running an organization, and to the running process itself—the use of numerous resources (such as employees and machines) to accomplish an organizational goal. Top managers make the big decisions and are responsible for the overall success of the organization. In government the top managers are always the political leaders of society, whether they gain power by election, appointment, or assassination. When a new president comes into office in the United States, he or she may appoint persons into approximately 3,000 jobs as the top managers who will be responsible for implementing policy. These appointees, while functioning as top managers with significant management responsibilities, are seldom professional managers and seldom think of themselves as management experts. They tend to be simply old friends, political-party loyalists, campaign contributors, and representatives of interest groups.

Consequently, the public administrators of a jurisdiction (the actual management specialists) are to be found in the vast area of middle management—the group responsible for the execution and interpretation of top-management policies and for the day-to-day operation of the various organizational units. These individuals often have advanced degrees in general fields such as public administration or business administration or technical fields such as public health or social work. These are the people who have made the management of government programs their life's work. They typically have supervisory or first-level managers—those responsible for the final implementation of policies by rank-and-file employees—reporting to them. These middle managers, despite their disparity in functions and technical backgrounds, largely constitute the management specialty of public administration. They spend their working lives fighting as officers in the administrative wars started by their political leaders.

Public Administration Is Mickey Mouse This otherwise innocent cartoon rodent has lent his name as a pejorative term for many aspects of governmental administration. When Walt Disney's famous mouse made it big in the 1930s, he appeared in a variety of cartoon shorts that showed him building something (such as a house or a boat) that would later fall apart, or generally going to a great deal of trouble for little result. So Mickey gradually gave his name to anything requiring considerable effort for slight results, including many of the Mickey Mouse requirements of bureaucracy. The term is also applied to policies or regulations felt to be needless, inane, silly, or mildly offensive. For example, President Ronald Reagan used the term to good effect when he complained in 1982 that "the United States government's program for arriving at a budget is about the most irresponsible Mickey Mouse arrangement that any government body has ever practiced."

Mickey Mouse is often used to mean *red tape*, the symbol of excessive formality and attention to routine. This has its origins in the red ribbon with which clerks bound official documents in the nineteenth century. The ribbon has disappeared, but the practices it represents linger on. Herbert Kaufman of the Brookings Institution found that the term "is applied to a bewildering variety of organizational practices and features." Organizations create and retain such seemingly rigid "practices and features" because they promote efficiency and equity on the whole—even though this may not be true in many individual cases. After all, according to Kaufman, "one person's 'red tape' may be another's treasured procedural safeguard."

Public Administration Is Art, Not Science—or Vice Versa Some people have a gift for administration. We have all met such natural administrators. They are not only perpetually organized but have a knack for getting people to work together harmoniously. The administrative art comprises judgment, panache, and common sense. But the artist is useless without tools—without the technical skills (the science) that allow for the digestion and transference of information. Nothing is more pointless than to argue whether the practice of public administration is more art or science. It is inherently both. Of course, the more science you have, the better artist you'll be. But "book learnin'" won't make you an artist if you don't possess an element of the gift in the first place.

At the beginning of the American Civil War, Henry Wager Halleck was perhaps the most knowledgeable northerner on the art and science of war. His textbook *Elements of Military Art and Science* (1846) and translations of foreign military texts were used at West Point, where he taught. He was nicknamed "Old Brains," and much was expected when he was given a field command. But while he knew all the science, he just didn't have the art to be a leader in actual battle. Although he ended up as the **chief of staff** of the U.S. Army, he is on nobody's list of great generals. By contrast, Ulysses S. Grant, the winning general of the Civil War, dismissed books on tactics as "nothing more than common sense." He wrote in his *Memoirs* (1885) that he didn't believe his officers "ever discovered that I had never studied the tactics that I used."

So are you more likely to be an "Old Brains" Halleck—all science and no art, good at **staff** work but incapable of command—or a Grant—all art and no science, the archetypal line officer? Just because you have a master's degree or even a doctorate in public administration or a related field doesn't mean that you can function as a high-level administrator. Being highly educated does not always equate with being professionally able. If your goal is to make it as a city manager or agency administrator, you may wish to avoid staff jobs. Get out there and run something! Gradually prove with progressively more responsible jobs that you are an artist—that you can cope with and thrive among the usual administrative chaos.

It is the same in all professions. You prepare yourself by doing smaller versions of the big thing you really want to do. Organizational theorist Antony Jay wrote of the advice traditionally given to aspiring actors: If you want to be a leading actor, you must only play leading parts—"much better to play Hamlet in Denver than **Laertes** on Broadway." You thus learn "to lead a big organization by leading smaller ones." But lead you must! When selection committees are seeking a manager for a major agency, those with only staff experience are not as likely to make the short list of finalists. Appointing authorities may not have heard of the historical Halleck, but they have all seen a Halleck—and don't want to see one in the administrative structure of their group.

Chief of staff ■
An army's highest-ranking officer.

Staff ■
Specialists who assist line managers in carrying out their duties. Generally, staff units do not have the power of decision, command, or control of operations. Rather, they make recommendations (which may or may not be adopted) to executives and line managers.

Laertes ■
A supporting role in Shakespeare's *Hamlet*; Laertes and Hamlet have the big sword fight in the final act.

Occupational Definitions of Public Administration

One of the joys of public service occupations is the frequent opportunity to participate in analyses and evaluations of public programs. However, not all public sector workers seek to engage in the public debate over policies, laws, and management practices. But all of them are interested in their jobs. So let's look at public administration—as an occupation.

Public Administration Is an Occupational Category It is whatever the public employees of the world do. It ranges from brain surgery to street sweeping. Most of the people in this broad occupational category do not even think of themselves as public administrators. They identify with their specific professions (physician, engineer, or teacher) and trades (carpenter, electrician, or plumber). While it is true that they may not be administrators in the sense of being managers, they are nevertheless, whether they realize it or not, ministering (in the sense of providing services) to the public. In 2010 the United States had just under 18 million civilians working for its local, state, and federal governments. And only the smallest portion of them would define their work as public administration. They simply see themselves as police officers, social workers, or forest rangers, but they are also, unavoidably, public administrators.

In 1995 Richard Klausner became the director of the federal government's National Cancer Institute. He then defiantly told the *New York Times,* "I am not an administrator." He asserted that he was "a scientist and a physician." But the *Times* was not fooled by Dr. Klausner. Its lengthy profile of him was headlined "New Administrator Is 'Not an Administrator.'" Administrators, even if they, like Dr. Klausner, are in denial, are still administrators.

Public Administration Is an Essay Contest   People in bureaucratic careers tend to rise or fall on how well they can write. In a game of shuffling paper, the person whose memorandum ends up on top wins. It is a legendary truism in the U.S. State Department that nobody who's good writes his or her own memos. If you are considered talented enough, you will be asked to write your boss's memos. Then, because you're too busy writing the boss's memos, you find a younger talent to write yours. When your boss gets that big promotion, you go along for the ride with your own promotion. And, of course, you bring along the person who's been writing for you. Remember that Thomas Jefferson was offered the job of writing the Declaration of Independence because of his reputation as a fine stylist. And his eventual elevation to president came because he made the most of this writing opportunity. When General Douglas MacArthur was head of the U.S. Army in the 1930s, a young captain (later a major) wrote the general's reports and speeches. Coworkers knew that Dwight D. Eisenhower was an officer who was going places, because he could write.

Oral presentation skills are also essential, but because more people can speak than write effectively, writing is more decisive in determining whose ideas get advanced. All organizations place great value on the person who can write succinctly in times of stress. That is the person who will be turned to when an important opportunity comes up. This is why public administration is an essay contest: because your writing reputation creates your administrative persona of winner or loser. According to a U.S. Department of State report, the Foreign Service "has prized drafting ability above almost all other skills. We emphasize this skill in recruitment and reward it generously in our promotion system. The prize jobs in the service are the reporting jobs." Donald P. Warwick, in his analysis of the State Department's bureaucracy, found that "following the classic model of the gentleman generalist, the Foreign Service exalts graceful prose and the well-turned phrase." Other agencies with fewer "gentlemen" are equally anxious to reward "graceful prose."

If you examine the personal histories of the best-known and most influential members of the George W. Bush administration—Vice President Richard (Dick) Cheney, Secretary of State Condoleezza Rice, and Secretary of Defense Robert Gates—you will find that when they were lowly bureaucrats they each jumpstarted their careers because of their ability to write. And while President Bush was not known by most as one to whom "graceful prose" comes naturally, the man that replaced him has been widely hailed for his ability to put words together.

Writing Your Way to the Presidency:
BOX 1.4 | John F. Kennedy Compared to Barack H. Obama

In the early 1950s a young senator from Massachusetts, John F. Kennedy, knew he wanted to run for president but also knew that he had no substantial record of accomplishment upon which to run. So he and his father, Joseph P. Kennedy, one of the richest men in the country, arranged for him to win the prestigious Pulitzer Prize for biography. That'd show them!

First they found a talented staffer (Theodore Sorensen) to ghost write most of the book, *Profiles in Courage* (1955), a collection of essays on eight senators who behaved courageously at the risk of their political careers. In *Counselor,* a memoir he wrote more than half a century later, Sorensen admitted that he wrote "first drafts" of all of the chapters in *Profiles in Courage.* Second, the Kennedys arranged for—paid for—massive purchases of the book to make it an acknowledged best-seller. Then the elder Kennedy used his considerable influence on the Pulitzer Prize committee to effectively buy his son the prize. Result: instant gravitas for an otherwise insignificant junior senator.

With his now award-winning bestseller in hand Kennedy could be considered a serious candidate for vice president at the 1956 Democratic National Convention. While he lost his bid for the nomination and his party lost the subsequent presidential election, the concomitant favorable publicity about this handsome prize-winning war hero senator laid the foundation for his successful presidential campaign four years later in 1960.

Not every president has had a reputation as a fine writer, whether real or "store bought." But nowadays all presidential candidates make the effort to publish a book or two. And unlike in Kennedy's time, they

don't even make the pretense that they wrote it themselves. Indeed, today it is fashionable to list the person who wrote the book for you as your coauthor. Of course, none of these books has won the Pulitzer Prize since Kennedy did. But no candidate since Kennedy has had a father as rich as his was.

In contrast, Senator Barack Obama had an even more modest legislative record than Senator John F. Kennedy. Nevertheless, he took a page from Kennedy's book and wrote himself some gravitas. But unlike Kennedy he had to do it all the work himself. That's the problem with starting out poor in life; you lack a readily available ghost writer. Nevertheless, Obama soon had millions from his book sales. Poor no more.

With two bestselling books (one a memoir and the other a romp for policy wonks), he was suddenly a serious contender for the Democratic nomination for president. Obama could not only write books, he could write speeches, too. And deliver them in a compelling fashion. That is a winning combination. That attracts campaign donations and volunteers. One who volunteered was Theodore Sorensen, the same man who 60 years earlier "helped" Kennedy write *Profiles in Courage* and because of that was able to help him write his inaugural address ("Ask not what your country can do for you. . ."). Now Kennedy's ghost was ghosting for Obama. How sweet! Not only had the Kennedy torch been passed but so had the ghost. Sorensen, the old ghost, was the young lawyer from Nebraska who through his own writing, under his own name or not, won more wealth and esteem than he had ever dreamed of as a boy. He saw a kindred soul in Obama—a fellow contestant in the essay contest of life. And a winner, too. ▲

In fact, while Barack Obama's oratory skills often draw high levels of public recognition, it is important to note that he is often the writer of the script that he is following. His skill with words made him the editor of the *Harvard Law Review.* All his big professional and political breaks derive from that accomplishment—including his bestselling books and subsequent public offices.

Public Administration Is Idealism in Action   Many people enter public service careers because they are idealists; they believe in and seek to advance noble principles. "Noble" is the key word here because traditionally the nobility had public service obligations. They were the warrior class, so it was their obligation to heroically protect the weak and less fortunate, to accept the notion of **noblesse oblige**. Gradually, their duties expanded from military affairs to the whole realm of public affairs. High-level government service, which was once the prerogative of the well-born, the financially well off, and the well connected, is now also open to those who were born with talent but without money or connections.

Noblesse oblige ■
A French term meaning "nobility obliges"; the notion that the nobles (or those of the upper class) have a special obligation to serve society.

Idealism draws people into public administration because it provides them with worthwhile—and exciting—things to do with their lives. Nowhere else can someone without private wealth achieve such vast power so quickly. Even the children of the very wealthy—such as the Kennedys and Rockefellers—tend to enter public service for the same reasons other people do: because it's fun, it offers ego gratification, and, most importantly, because it satisfies their dual desires to do good works and exercise power. When someone asked the multimillionaire presidential candidate John F. Kennedy why he wanted to be president, he candidly replied, "Because that is where the power is."

The idealism associated with public administration goes far beyond the individual. The goal is the mystical one of building "a city upon a hill," an ideal political community thoroughly fit for others to observe as an example. This phrase comes from John Winthrop, governor of the Massachusetts Bay Colony. In 1630 he wrote, "For we must consider that we shall be as a city upon a hill. The eyes of all people are upon us." This is a famous statement in Massachusetts history, and both Presidents Kennedy and Reagan favored using it in speeches. It also illustrates how the nondenominational religious elements of public administration allow participants to gain satisfaction by becoming involved with a cause greater than themselves. During the 2008 presidential campaign, Barack Obama updated the "city upon a hill" idealism when he stated that "hope is what led me here today—with a father from Kenya, a mother from Kansas; and a story that could only happen in the United States of America. Hope is the bedrock of this nation; the belief that our destiny will not be written for us, but by us; by all those men and women who are not content to settle for the world as it is: who have the courage to remake the world as it should be."

Rugged individualists ■
Those who staunchly believe that citizens should take care of their own economic needs and not be dependent on government for the necessities of life. Rugged individualists also tend to oppose paternalistic government welfare programs out of concern that the poor will have their character undermined. This philosophy was most associated with Presidents Hoover and Reagan.

It is strange how these idealists in government who only want to do good for their fellow citizens are considered not much better than thieves and social parasites by others—usually not by those who need government help but by those **rugged individualists** who don't. Many who seek careers in public service believe that government is a legitimate vehicle for solving social problems—and they want to be driving that vehicle when the problem gets solved. What's the good of doing good if you can't have fun doing it? This attitude is similar to that of the sixteenth-century Spanish conquistador Bernal Díaz del Castillo, whom Samuel Eliot Morison quotes as saying, "We came here [to the Americas] to serve God and also to get rich." Today's public administration idealists know that getting rich in terms of money is unlikely; the riches they seek are those of the joys of experience, the sense of personal satisfaction, and the building of "a city upon a hill."

Public Administration Is an Academic Field It is the study of the art and science of management applied to the public sector. But it traditionally goes far beyond the concerns of management and incorporates as its subject matter all of the political, social, cultural, and legal environments that affect the running of public institutions. As a field of study, it is inherently cross-disciplinary because it encompasses so much of political science, sociology, business administration, psychology, law, anthropology, medicine, forestry, and so on. Indeed, it can be argued that because public administration borrows so much from other fields, what is left as its core is hardly worthy of being considered a legitimate academic field at all. Yet, there is a center about which the parts of public administration have coalesced (see Figure 1.1).

While **Woodrow Wilson** and many others of the **progressive movement** called for a "science of administration," new intellectual fields evolve amorphously. It is difficult to trace the exact moment of their conception. What is certain is that the first real American public administration text is *Introduction to the Study of Public Administration* by **Leonard White**, published in 1926.

While Woodrow Wilson provided the rationale for public administration to be an academic discipline and professional management specialty, it remained for White to most clearly articulate its preliminary objectives. In his pioneering text, he noted four critical assumptions that formed the basis for the study of public administration:

1. Administration is a unitary process that can be studied uniformly, at the federal, state, and local levels.
2. The basis for study is management, not law.

Woodrow Wilson (1856–1924) ■
Before Wilson became president of the United States (1913–1921), he was a professor of history and political science who rose to be president of Princeton University (1902–1910) and governor of New Jersey (1911–1913).

Progressive movement ■
While the term has its origins in religious concepts that argued for the infinite improvability of the human condition, by the end of the nineteenth century it had come to refer to a political and cultural movement that focused on reforming industrialized societies to provide for greater democratic participation, and the application of science and specialized knowledge to the improvement of life.

Leonard White (1891–1958) ■
The University of Chicago professor who wrote the first public administration text in 1926. He is the author of the standard administrative histories of the U.S. government in the nineteenth century.

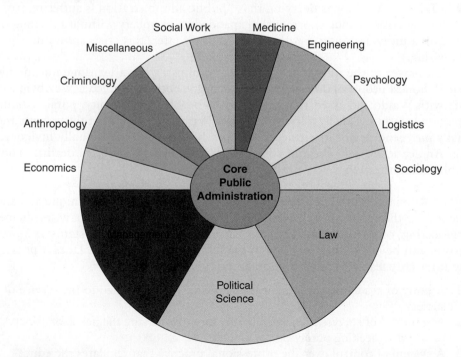

FIGURE 1.1
The interdisciplinary nature of public administration

3. Administration is still art, but the ideal of transformation to science is both feasible and worthwhile.
4. Administration "has become, and will continue to be the heart of the problem of modern government."

White's text was remarkable both for its influence over four decades (the fourth and last edition was published in 1955) and for its restraint in not taking a prescriptive cookbook approach to public administration. He recognized that public administration was above all a field of study that had to stay close to reality—the reality of its largely untrained practitioner base that still professed great belief in the art of administration.

As an independent academic field, public administration has always been controversial. First, it was the stepchild of political science. And in many colleges, the field is still represented by a few courses within the political science curriculum. Later, schools of business or management began to offer it as one of a variety of administrative specialties. In recent decades, independent departments and graduate schools of public administration have been created. But as the field of public administration matured, its constituent elements began to intellectually fly away. The public policy analyst increasingly identified with the mathematical rigor of political science methodologists. Public finance has been claimed by the economists. The core management elements have drifted toward the field of public management. Increasingly, the field seems to be less a discipline than a holding company for disparate intellectual components. This is hardly new. In 1975 Dwight Waldo was decrying that "public administration is suffering from an identity crisis, having enormously expanded its periphery without retaining or creating a unifying center." A third of a century later, this crisis shows no signs of abating.

In answer to the question, "Is public administration a legitimate academic field?" honest people of differing views will argue both pro and con. We obviously side with Waldo and assert that, whatever its problems with unity, public administration is most decidedly a legitimate field. We also contend that the growth and frisky independence of its elements are both healthy and intellectually invigorating. An academic field without controversy must necessarily be in decline. Thus public administration is very healthy indeed.

Public Administration Is a Profession   It is the application of its unique arts and sciences to the problems of society. But is it a profession, such as law, medicine, engineering, or architecture? The case for public administration's status as a profession can be made by applying to it the test of professionalism. Does it possess the three core features common to traditional professions?

1. A body of academic and practical knowledge that is applied to the service of society
2. A standard of success theoretically measured by serving the needs of society rather than seeking purely personal gain
3. A system of control over the professional practice that regulates the education of new members and maintains both a code of ethics and appropriate sanctions

Public administration amply meets all three of these criteria even though, unlike law or medicine, it cannot control entry to practice through licenses and examinations. However, public administration acts such as these long-established professions by drawing on different fields of specialization to solve problems and prepare new practitioners. While public administration is not a pure social science, as some would have it, it is fully equal to these more traditional fields of study. Perhaps it supersedes many in one respect. Society's original professionals were clergy because they professed the word of God. Such people were said to have a "calling." Why? Because God was said to have called them. Public administration, with its idealistic notions of building "a city upon a hill," is closer to this original religious conception of professionalism than many other professions today.

THE EVOLUTION OF PUBLIC ADMINISTRATION

There was nothing preordained about the preceding discussion of definitions. It is a product of the life experiences of the authors. It could have been written in a radically different framework and accomplished essentially the same task. Similarly, public administration itself did not have to evolve the way it did. As with any evolutionary process, there was a seemingly infinite number of possible outcomes. Biologist Stephen Jay Gould in his book about the Burgess Shale, a fossil-rich limestone quarry in the Canadian Rockies, shows how animal evolution had any number of starts and stops. According to Gould, no "handicapper, given Burgess evidence as known today, would have granted very favorable odds" that the vertebrate creatures from which humans evolved would have survived. The most disturbing thing about this kind of natural selection, according to Gould, is the random nature of it—that so much of evolutionary history takes on the character of a lottery.

So it has been with public administration. The administrative institutions that we presently have could so easily have been radically different. How humans learned to approach the practice and definition of public administration could so easily have taken a surprising turn. For example, if the Greeks had insisted that administration was household management on a grand scale, they might have developed it as a female occupation. And it might have been copied that way by the Romans, who adopted so much else of Greek science and culture. If the classical world developed the notion that men were fit only for war and physical toil, women might have evolved a beneficent administrative matriarchy. And there is a third possibility: rule by eunuchs. (No joke!)

For more than 2,000 years and into the twentieth century, eunuchs—males with their external sex organs amputated—were the public administrators of choice. Why? Because their missing parts meant that they could be trusted—first with the rulers' wives and concubines, and then with other administrative chores. Eunuchs proved to be particularly effective and loyal administrators. As slaves usually long removed from any family, they knew that the only way to thrive was to do well by the only people who could enrich and protect them. The eunuchs formed a kind of civil service system. Entrance was typically limited to captured slave boys from the edge of the empire, who were castrated by the thousands. While a large percentage died from the crude surgery, the survivors were put into service as court eunuchs. There they could work their way up to the highest level of administrative responsibility. Eunuchs grew to be the servant class most trusted by the rulers of ancient Syria, Persia, China, and Rome. In an era rife with nepotism (hiring of relatives), they were immune from such influences. While Christian Byzantium made extensive use of eunuchs in government posts, Western Christendom did not.

The last of the traditional bureaucrat-eunuchs were still to be seen in imperial China and the Ottoman Empire only a century ago. Thus for most of recorded history administration by eunuchs was a "normal" means by which states managed their affairs. The advantages they offered—absolute loyalty and apathy—are not to be sneered at. Fortunately today there are ways to instill high standards of ethics in government officials without sending castration technicians to visit the bureaucrats of Washington, **Whitehall**, and the **Kremlin**.

The Core Content

But even if public administration had evolved along radically different lines, it would have had to come out about where it is concerning its core content. While there is no agreement on all the details, there is broad general agreement about the subject matter. Thus all public administration introductory texts have chapters similar to those that follow, except for the method of presentation. But there is almost universal agreement that organization theory, bureaucratic behavior, personnel management, public finance and budgeting, policy analysis, program evaluation, and administrative ethics, among other topics, are essential to a basic understanding of the field. This essential information is all here.

It is an underlying premise of this book that public administration cannot be properly understood without an appreciation of its political dynamics. All of the actors in the public administration world must accept their political fate—they cannot pretend either to themselves or to the public that they operate as a public sector counterpart to industrial management. And the political nature of public administration must be faced maturely. Just as the first step in arresting alcoholism is to have the alcoholic admit that he or she is an alcoholic and will always be an alcoholic even after he or she stops drinking, the first step toward putting public administration operations on a more realistic footing is for public managers to admit that public sector administration is an inherently political process.

Public administration is increasingly a cross-governmental field. Yet too many of the comprehensive texts available for introductory courses in the United States are decidedly parochial in that they focus on the national government. This is an incongruous situation when you consider that a relatively small percentage of American public administrators work for the federal government. While the United States has one federal government, it has more than 80,000 units of state, county, metropolitan, and local governments led by administrators as esteemed as governors and as unnoticed as the executive director of a mosquito abatement district. In all, state and local governments employed just under 15 million Americans in 2009, compared to only 2.8 million individuals working for the federal government in civilian positions (see Table 1.2). Most public administration students in the United States will go into state and local government or are foreign nationals who expect to return home with readily applicable skills. Still others will work in nonprofit organizations. The end of the Cold War in 1989 has only encouraged

Whitehall ■
That area of London between Trafalgar and Parliament Squares in which government buildings have historically (since the time of Henry VIII) been concentrated. Thus it has come to refer to the most senior members of the British civil service.

Kremlin ■
The Moscow citadel where the main offices of the Russian government are located.

TABLE 1.2

Government Employment in 2009

Level of Government	Number of Employees	Total Monthly Payroll*
Federal Government	2,823,777	$15.1 billion
State Government	3,836,544	$19.4 billion
Local Government	11,114,889	$50.7 billion

Source: U.S. Bureau of the Census Annual Survey of Government Employment, 2009: http://www.census.gov/govs/apes/

*Monthly payroll figures calculated from payrolls in March 2009 for the federal, state, and local governments.

an ever-increasing worldwide market for Western-oriented public administration. Thus to a large extent this text takes a unified approach—appropriate for U.S. students at all levels (federal, state, and local) but generic enough to be truly useful to students of other countries and cultures.

Most of the content of introductory public administration texts can be universally applicable. There exists a unified whole (public administration in general) that is greater than the sum of its parts (public administration in each jurisdiction). The core concept of the unified approach to introducing public administration is to write the material in such a manner that it can be readily applied to the differing political systems within the American federal system and throughout the rest of the world. Indeed, no public administration textbook can be comprehensive today if it is not cross-governmental in the most expansive sense. National administration figures from the president on down hardly ever make a major speech without some reference to government policies and practices in Asia, Europe, and elsewhere. This is just the latest evidence of how imperative it is that American students of public administration develop a greater international perspective.

This will not be a "how-to" book written for people who want to be public administration experts in ten easy lessons. It will be a "what is it?" book written for people who seek or are engaged in managerial careers in the public sector and are in need of a basic introduction to, or a review of, public sector administrative practices. The "nuts and bolts" of administrative processes vary considerably from jurisdiction to jurisdiction. Because of differing laws and customs, it would be futile to present the "one right way" for any given procedure. Instead, the procedural chapters (on personnel, budgeting, strategic management, etc.) concentrate on the historical evolution, essential theory, and future trends of their subjects. With this information, diligent readers will have the kind of conceptual foundation that will allow them to rapidly digest and master the procedural nuts and bolts that differ with every jurisdiction.

It's an Adventure!

The U.S. Navy once used this recruiting slogan: "It's not just a job, it's an adventure." So is it with public administration. A public service career is often the most exciting thing individuals can do with their lives. Walter Lippmann often observed that "the joys of private life" are much overrated. "For the truth is that public life, once a man [or woman] has been infected with its excitement and importance, is something that few ever get over." Whether one comes to a capital to expand government or to contract it, it is a worthy personal quest, a great personal adventure—and equally worthy and adventurous if you serve in a national capital, a state capital, a city hall, or a neighborhood association. Public service, like adventures, comes in all sizes.

Many of you would not be holding this book if you were not engaged in or contemplating a public service career. Consider what follows not so much as a guidebook—the field is too vast to be encompassed in one or even one hundred books—but as a reconnaissance. Herein is the lay of the land that you will encounter in a public administration adventure. Learn how to tinker with the machinery of government, discover the ancient secrets of modern strategic management, review the arcane rules of public personnel administration, buy into the politics of the budgetary process, and finally examine how ethical it all is. Public administration not only has a cast of millions, but it is a show that has been playing for more than 5,000 years. The goal of the authors has been to make your journey in the sometimes wild and woolly public sector more successful by giving necessary historical perspectives on this strange world and by alerting you to the dangers and opportunities that lie ahead. You, as the adventurer, must make the most of them. Enjoy the trip!

A CASE STUDY: | How a President Undeservedly Received Credit for Founding a Discipline

In 1885 Woodrow Wilson, having not yet completed his doctoral program at Johns Hopkins University, began his teaching career at the newly founded Bryn Mawr College for Women. While reportedly a lecturer of genius, he resented having to teach women. As he told an associate, such an activity "relaxes one's mental muscle." In 1887 he summed up his life by saying, "Thirty-one years old and nothing done!" In retrospect, Wilson seems to have been like many other ambitious academics seemingly stuck in a post that did not do justice to talent. And he chose as the way out the now traditional road to high academic fame, fortune, and position: He wrote and published and was saved!

American public administration as a field of study traditionally traces its origin to an 1887 *Political Science Quarterly* article by this frustrated young academic. In "The Study of Administration," Wilson attempted nothing less than to refocus the newly emerging field of political science. Rather than be concerned with the "lasting maxims of political wisdom," he argued that political science should concentrate on the more generally neglected details of how governments are administered. This was necessary because "it is getting harder to *run* a constitution than to frame one."

Wilson wanted the study of public administration to focus not only on the problems of personnel management, as many other reformers of the time had advocated, but also on organization and management in general. The reform movement of the time had an agenda that did not go beyond the abolition of the spoils system and the installation of a merit system. Wilson regarded civil service reform "as but a prelude to a fuller administrative reform." He sought to push the concerns of public administration into investigations of the "organization and methods of our government offices" with a view toward determining "first, what government can properly and successfully do, and secondly, how it can do these proper things with the utmost possible efficiency and at the least possible cost either of money or energy." He was concerned with overall organizational efficiency and economy—that is, productivity in its most simplistic formulation. What could be more current—then or now?

In his essay, Wilson also proclaimed the existence of a major distinction between politics and administration. This was a common and necessary political tactic of the reform movement because arguments that public appointments should be based on fitness and merit, rather than partisanship, necessarily had to assert that "politics" was out of place in public service. As Wilson said, "Although politics sets the tasks for administration, it should not be suffered to manipulate its offices." In reinforcing what became known as the "politics–administration dichotomy," Wilson was really referring to "partisan" politics. While this subtlety was lost on many, Wilson's main themes—that public administration should be premised on a science of management and separate from traditional politics—fell on fertile intellectual ground. The ideas of this then obscure professor eventually became the dogma of academic public administration.

And what happened to the young Bryn Mawr professor who plaintively wrote in 1888, "I have for a long time been hungry for a class of *men*"? Shortly thereafter, he took up an appointment at Wesleyan University in Connecticut. From there he went to Princeton, made good, and became president of that university. In later life he found a job in Washington.

But if Wilson had not found that job in Washington, had not become president, his now seminal article would have continued to enjoy the obscurity its verbosity warrants. The article's significant influence came only after World War II—more than half a century after it was published. Administrative historian Paul van Riper found that none of the early public administration scholars, Wilson's contemporaries, cited the article in their otherwise heavily referenced works. "In reality, any connection between Wilson's essay and the later development of the discipline is pure fantasy! An examination of major political and social science works of the period between 1890 and World War I shows no citation whatever of the essay." So how did it get rediscovered and become required reading for generations of students? According to a historical analysis by Daniel W. Martin, "The simple answer . . . is the glowing reprint of Wilson's article in the December 1941 *Political Science Quarterly*. It was a masterwork of public relations, complete with a photostatic copy of Wilson's tentative letter of submission." Thereafter, Wilson's essay, cited only modestly in the interwar period, grew to its current influence.

For Discussion: *Do you think that public administration can, or should, ever be totally separate from politics? Can the current Obama administration be considered "Wilsonian" in its similar concern with efficiency and economy?* ▲

SUMMARY

Public administration can be defined from political, legal, managerial, and occupational perspectives. However defined, its vast scope encompasses whatever governments do. Public administration cannot exist outside of its political context. It is this context that makes it public—that makes it different from private or business administration. Public administration is what a state does. It is created by and bound by the law and is an instrument of the law. It is inherently the execution of public laws. Every application of a general law is necessarily an act of administration. Its legal basis allows public administration to exist, but without its management aspect, not much of the public's business would get done.

Public administration as an academic field is the study of the art and science of management applied to the public sector. But it traditionally goes far beyond the concerns of management and incorporates as its subject matter all of the political, social, cultural, and legal environments that affect the running of public institutions. It is inherently cross-disciplinary, encompassing so much of other fields—from political science and sociology to business administration and law. American public administration as a field of study is traditionally traced to Woodrow Wilson's 1887 article "The Study of Administration." The discipline of public administration, after developing as part of political science, emerged as an independent field in the second half of the twentieth century.

As a profession, public administration offers significant opportunities for idealism in the pursuit of public service—and even heroism, as we saw on September 11. Concerns about an increasingly effective or more expansive public service ebb and flow with the changing political philosophies of differing administrations. But the provision of public services—whether by career public servants or by contracted private sector employees—remains the very essence of public administration.

REVIEW QUESTIONS

1. How would you define public administration in one phrase, one paragraph, or an essay?
2. Is public administration among the oldest or newest areas of study, or both?
3. Is public administration an amalgam of various areas of study or a field unto itself?
4. Is public administration a profession or just an occupation?
5. How does a public administration career offer the potential of a great adventure?

KEY CONCEPTS

Administration The management and direction of the affairs of governments and institutions; a collective term for all policymaking officials of a government; the execution and implementation of public policy.

Executive branch The part of a government responsible for applying or administering the law. Thus a president, governor, or mayor and the supporting bureaucracies are the executive branches of their respective jurisdictions.

Management   A word that refers to both the people responsible for running an organization and the running process itself; the use of numerous resources (such as employees and machines) to accomplish an organizational goal.

Professional   A member of an occupation requiring specialized knowledge that can be gained only after intensive preparation. Professional occupations tend to possess three features: a body of academic and practical knowledge that is applied to the service of society, a standard of success theoretically measured by serving the needs of society rather than seeking purely personal gain, and a system of control over the professional practice.

Public administration   Whatever governments do for good or ill. It is public administration's political context that makes it public—that distinguishes it from private or business administration.

Public interest   The universal label in which political actors wrap the policies and programs that they advocate.

Public policy   Decision making by government. Governments are constantly concerned about what they should or should not do. And whatever they do or do not do is public policy.

Red tape   The ribbon that was once used to bind government documents; the term now stands as the symbol of excessive official formality and overattention to prescribed routines.

Regulation   The totality of government controls on the social and economic activities of its citizens; the rulemaking process of those administrative agencies charged with the official interpretation of laws.

MySearchLab® EXERCISES

Apply what you learned in this chapter on MySearchLab (*www.mysearchlab.com*).

BIBLIOGRAPHY

Cuomo, Mario. (1995). *Reason to Believe*. New York: Simon and Schuster.

Edelman, Murray. (1964). *The Symbolic Uses of Politics*. Urbana: University of Illinois Press.

Friedman, Thomas L. (1998). "Desperado Democracies," *New York Times* (July 14).

Galbraith, John Kenneth. (1956). *American Capitalism*. Boston: Houghton Mifflin.

Gould, Stephen Jay. (1989). *Wonderful Life: The Burgess Shale and the Nature of History*. New York: Norton.

Haldane, J. B. S. (1928). *Possible Worlds and Other Essays*. New York: Harper.

Halleck, Henry W. (1863). *Elements of Military Art and Science*, 3rd ed. New York: Appleton.

Herring, E. Pendleton. (1936). *Public Administration and the Public Interest*. New York: McGraw-Hill.

Irving, Clive, ed. (1995). *In Their Name: Dedicated to the Brave and the Innocent— Oklahoma City, April 1995*. New York: Random House.

Jay, Antony. (1967). *Management and Machiavelli*. New York: Holt, Rinehart and Winston.

Kaufman, Herbert. (1977). *Red Tape: Its Origins, Uses, and Abuses*. Washington: Brookings Institution.

Kirschbaum, Erik. (2003). "Iran Asks: Why Are Earthquakes So Deadly?" Reuters (December 30).

Kugler, Sara. (2001). "One WTC Survivor's E-Mail Touches Hundreds Worldwide," Associated Press (December 25).

Lippmann, Walter. (1955). *The Public Philosophy*. Boston: Little, Brown.

Lowi, Theodore J. (1969). *The End of Liberalism*. New York: Norton.

Martin, Daniel W. (1988). "The Fading Legacy of Woodrow Wilson," *Public Administration Review* 48 (March–April).

Morison, Samuel Eliot. (1974). *The European Discovery of America: The Southern Voyages*. New York: Oxford University Press.

Noonan, Peggy. (2001). "Courage under Fire," *Wall Street Journal* (October 5).

O'Neill, Tip. (1994). *All Politics Is Local and Other Rules of the Game*. New York: Times Books.

Rosenbloom, David H. (1990). *Public Administration*, 2nd ed. New York: Random House.

Rossiter, Clinton, and James Lare, eds. (1963). *The Essential Lippmann: A Political Philosophy for Liberal Democracy*. New York: Random House.

Shaw, George Bernard. (1944). *Everybody's Political What's What?* New York: Dodd, Mead.

Tocqueville, Alexis de. (1835; translation 1899). *Democracy in America*. New York: Appleton.

U.S. Department of State. (1970). *Diplomacy for the 70s*. Washington: U.S. Department of State.

Van Riper, Paul. (1983). "The American Administrative State: Wilson and the Founders—An Unorthodox View." *Public Administration Review* 43 (November–December).

Waldo, Dwight. (1955). *The Study of Administration*. New York: Random House.

———. (1975). "Education for Public Administration in the Seventies." In *American Public Administration: Past, Present, Future*, ed. Frederick C. Mosher. Tuscaloosa: University of Alabama Press.

Warwick, Donald P. (1975). *A Theory of Public Bureaucracy: Politics, Personality, and Organization in the State Department*. Cambridge, MA: Harvard University Press.

Wilson, Woodrow. (1887). "The Study of Administration," *Political Science Quarterly* 2 (June); reprinted 50 (December 1941).

Winthrop, Robert C. (1971). *Life and Letters of John Winthrop*. New York: Da Capo Press.

Woodward, Bob. (2002). *Bush at War*. New York: Simon and Schuster.

RECOMMENDED BOOKS

Fry, Brian, Jos C. N. Raadschelders. (2008). *Mastering Public Administration: From Max Weber to Dwight Waldo*, 2nd ed. Washington DC: CQ Press. A comprehensive review of the lives and scholarship of the leading theorists in the field of public administration.

Kettl, Donald F. (2002). *The Transformation of Governance: Public Administration for Twenty-First Century America*. Baltimore: Johns Hopkins University Press. An explanation of how governance—the set of processes and institutions, formal and informal, through which social action occurs—is transforming the nature of public administration.

Shafritz, Jay M., editor in chief. (1998). *International Encyclopedia of Public Policy and Administration*. Boulder, CO: Westview Press. Nine hundred articles defining and analyzing every aspect of public administration; the first place to go to look up a concept, practice, theory, or issue in the field.

Shafritz, Jay M. (2004). *The Dictionary of Public Policy and Administration*. Boulder, CO: Westview Press. A detailed collection of terms and definitions within the areas of public administration and policy.

Waldo, Dwight. (1984). *The Administrative State: A Study of the Political Theory of American Public Administration*, 2nd ed. New York: Holmes and Meier. The classic work on the philosophy of public administration (originally published in 1948) wherein the prevailing "gospel of efficiency" is rejected and administrative value neutrality is denied.

RELATED WEB SITES

www.apsanet.org
American Political Science Association (APSA)
This is a reference site for scholarly information about the field of political science. Members of the organization have access to scholarly journals and articles through the site. It also contains information about conferences and gatherings organized by APSA to promote political science and research in the field.

www.aspanet.org
American Society for Public Administration
The American Society for Public Administration, which has been representing the public service arena since 1939, presents an array of information on the field of public administration at this site. Among the most useful features of this site are links to career opportunities for those interested in working in the public service field.

www.appam.org
Association for Public Policy Analysis and Management
This organization offers a multidisciplinary annual conference that attracts the highest-quality research on a wide variety of important current and emerging policy and management issues, and its Web site is structured to encourage substantive interaction among participants. The site also has information on recent articles in the organization's peer-reviewed journal and updates on opportunities in the field of public management.

www.csg.org
Council on Licensure, Enforcement, and Regulation
CSG is a region-based forum that fosters the exchange of insights and ideas to help state officials shape public policy. Its site provides information and research about states' biggest ticket issues as well as ways to contact experts with knowledge in these fields. Useful location for finding information pertaining to state laws, policies, and interactions, and information about how states are interacting with one another.

www.naspaa.org
National Association of Schools of Public Affairs and Administration (NASPAA)
The NASPAA serves as a national and international resource for the promotion of excellence in education and training for public service. Its institutional membership includes more than 260 U.S. and non-U.S. university programs in public affairs, public policy, public administration, and public management. Its site offers information for grad students looking to enter these fields, as well as teachers looking to better their teaching in these fields.

The Political and Cultural Environment of Public Policy and Its Administration

KEYNOTE: Who Decides Whether the United States Should Wage War?

A decision to go to war is arguably the most important public policy decision made by a state. The U.S. Constitution (Article I, Section 8) unambiguously gives Congress the authority "to declare war." However, the president, as commander in chief, has implied powers to commit the military forces to action. Article III, Section 2, of the Constitution says that "the president shall be commander in chief of the army and the navy of the United States and of the militia of the several states when called into the actual service of the United States." The last president to exercise his authority as commander in chief to literally command troops in the field was James Madison during the War of 1812. At Bladensburg, Maryland, the American forces, under the direct command of the president, met the British and were soundly defeated. The British then marched on Washington, D.C., to burn the White House, the Capitol, and most other public buildings. No subsequent president has sought to personally lead men in battle while in office.

But many subsequent presidents have sent U.S. forces to fight in foreign lands without waiting for or even asking Congress to exercise its constitutional responsibility "to declare war." Formal declarations of war seem to be rapidly becoming quaint relics of diplomatic history. Declarations of war first came about when states felt it necessary to separate their military actions from the activities of bandits, pirates, and privateers (a pirate ship authorized by a government to prey on its foes). Therefore, before the beginning of hostilities, a formal statement of intention—a declaration—to make war on another state was promulgated. In 1907 this practice was formalized by the Hague Convention Relative to the Opening of Hostilities. This established an international obligation on the part of the signatories to announce that a legal state of hostilities existed with another state by making a formal declaration to this effect. And formal meant *formal*. For example, here is the declaration that started World War I:

> The Royal Serbian Government not having answered in a satisfactory manner the note of July 23, 1914, presented by the Austro-Hungarian Minister at Belgrade, the Imperial and Royal Government are themselves compelled to see to the safeguarding of their right and interests, and, with this object, to have recourse to force of arms. Austria-Hungary consequently considers herself henceforward in state of war with Serbia.

These are the courtly words that initiated the greatest mass slaughter the world had seen to date. When British Prime Minister Winston Churchill had to justify why the declaration of war against Japan on December 8, 1941, was made in similar diplomatic language, he responded, "When you have to kill a man, it costs nothing to be polite."

World War II was the last war the U.S. Congress actually declared. The Congress was called into an emergency joint session by President Franklin D. Roosevelt the day after the Japanese attack on Pearl Harbor (December 8, 1941). The president said:

> Yesterday, December 7, 1941—a date which will live in infamy—the United States of America was suddenly and deliberately attacked by naval and air forces of the empire of Japan. . . .
> I ask that the Congress declare that since the unprovoked and dastardly attack by Japan on Sunday, December 7, 1941, a state of war has existed between the United States and the Japanese Empire.

Pearl Harbor, the American Pacific fleet headquarters in Hawaii, had about 5,000 casualties, half of them deaths. The attack incensed the American public not just because it was a surprise, which is to be expected in war, but because it was a sneak attack when there was no state of war. Indeed, Japanese emissaries were in Washington at the same time purportedly negotiating in good faith to resolve United States–Japan differences. The Japanese had intended to notify the Americans that a state of war existed one half hour before the attack. But because of decoding difficulties, the war message was not delivered until after the attack was well under way. This time difference was the difference between an honorable surprise attack and a dishonorable sneak attack. So how did Pearl Harbor cause the United States to fight Nazi Germany as well? Because Germany's 1937 treaty of alliance with Japan was a defensive one, its pact did not require Germany to declare war on the United States after the Japanese attack on Pearl Harbor. (It would have been required if the United States had attacked Japan.) Because Japan was clearly the aggressor, Hitler's declaration of war against the United States was both gratuitous and, as it turned out, stupid.

While World War II was the last time formal declarations of war were widely used, things started to get constitutionally messy with the Korean War. This war, between communist North Korea and non-communist South Korea, began on June 25, 1950, when the North invaded the South. The American intervention was a symbolic signal to the Soviets that the United States was determined to halt the spread of communism. With the encouragement of the United States, the United Nations Security Council (with the Soviet Union temporarily absent) asked member nations to aid the South in resisting the invasion. Thus the war, called a "police action," was fought under the flag of the United Nations by U.S. forces with small contingents from more than a dozen other nations.

The Vietnam War of 1956 to 1975 was between the non-communist Republic of Vietnam (South Vietnam) and the communist Democratic Republic of Vietnam (North Vietnam), which resulted in the victory of the North over the South and the unification of the two countries into the communist Socialist Republic of Vietnam on July 2, 1976. The United States first offered financial support to South Vietnam during the Eisenhower administration. Military assistance began with the John F. Kennedy administration in 1961. By 1963, the United States had 16,000 military "advisors" in South Vietnam. In 1964, the Gulf of Tonkin Resolution allowed the administration of Lyndon B. Johnson to expand U.S. involvement in spite of the fact that Johnson had promised, notably in a campaign speech in Akron, Ohio, on

TABLE 2.1

Wars: Declared and Undeclared

Declared Wars	Undeclared Wars
War of 1812	Korean War 1950–1953
Mexican War, 1846	Vietnam War 1962–1974
Spanish-American War, 1898	Grenada Invasion 1983
World War I, 1917	Panama Intervention 1989
World War II, 1941	Persian Gulf War 1990–1991
	War on Terrorism 2001–
	Iraq War 2003–

October 21, 1964: "We are not about to send American boys nine or ten thousand miles away from home to do what Asian boys ought to be doing for themselves."

With the Gulf of Tonkin Resolution, the U.S. Congress sanctioned the Johnson administration's use of great numbers of American forces in an expansion of the Vietnam War. It was based on a presumed attack on U.S. ships in the Gulf of Tonkin by North Vietnamese naval units. The Johnson administration would treat this as the moral and legal equivalent of a declaration of war. Later, those who opposed the war would denounce it as a fraud because there was no solid evidence that there ever was an attack on American ships in the Tonkin Gulf. Indeed, Barbara W. Tuchman in *The March of Folly* (1984) would write, "With evidence accumulating of confusion by radar and sonar technicians in the second clash, [President] Johnson said privately, 'Well, those dumb, stupid sailors were just shooting at flying fish.' So much for *casus belli*." But there was little initial opposition. The House of Representatives passed it unanimously. In the Senate there were only two dissenting votes. Senator Jacob K. Javits, who voted for the resolution, would later write in *Who Makes War* (1973), "In voting unlimited presidential power most members of Congress thought they were providing for retaliation for an attack on our forces and preventing a large-scale war in Asia, rather than authorizing its inception."

By 1968, the United States had more than one-half million men engaged in the most unpopular foreign war in American history. As a direct result, the Democrats lost control of the White House to Republican Richard M. Nixon. The Nixon administration's policy of "Vietnamization" called for the South Vietnamese to gradually take over all the fighting from the Americans. The Americans continued to pull out, and the South held off the North for a while. As the American forces dwindled, the North got more aggressive and successful. Finally, the North's January 1975 offensive led to the South's unconditional surrender by April. More than 58,000 Americans died in the Vietnam War; another 150,000 were wounded.

Because of the unhappy experience of the Vietnam War, Congress passed the War Powers Resolution of 1973, the law that seeks to clarify the respective roles of the president and Congress in cases involving the use of military forces without a declaration of war. The president "in every possible instance" shall consult with Congress before introducing troops and shall report to Congress within 48 hours. The use of the armed forces is to be terminated within 60 days (with a possible 30-day extension by the president) unless Congress acts during that time to declare war, enacts a specific authorization for use of armed forces, extends the 60- to 90-day period, or is physically unable to meet as a result of an attack on the United States. At any time before the 60 days expire, Congress may direct by concurrent resolution that American military forces be removed by the president.

In one sense the War Powers Resolution has been a failure: It has not been able to remedy the problems of presidents ignoring Congress. President George H. W. Bush, for example, sent troops into action during the Panama Intervention and the Persian Gulf War without formally asking for congressional consent. While Congress, at the last minute (on January 12, 1991), gave him legal authority to commit U.S. forces to combat (which he did on January 15, 1991), he asserted that he didn't really need it—that his authority under the Constitution as commander in chief was sufficient.

On the other hand, the desire to avoid putting their war powers to the test has led presidents to be somewhat more responsive to Congress than they might otherwise have been. The Reagan administration, for example, withdrew U.S. forces from Lebanon when it became clear that there was little congressional or public support for keeping them there. The Clinton administration conducted a major bombing campaign against Serbia to force the Serbian troops out of Kosovo in 1999. But it initially maintained that a ground assault was not an option because it knew that there was slight congressional support for the bombing.

If the president can, as Bush did, send 500,000 troops half a world away to fight for a country with which we had no treaty of obligation to defend, then what, if anything, is left of Congress's constitutional authority to declare war? The answer is that it has never amounted to much. The fallacy of Congress's authority "to declare war" was first exposed by James K. Polk, the president of the United States from 1845 to 1849. When in 1846 Mexico refused a U.S. offer to purchase New Mexico and California, Polk sent the army to provoke a war. The Mexicans obliged with incidents, were conquered, and forfeited (with payment by the United States of $15 million) land comprising the present states of California, Nevada, Utah, and most of New Mexico and Arizona. Former President John Quincy Adams then summed up the implications of this for Congress: "It is now established as an irreversible precedent that the president of the United States has but to declare that war exists, with any nation upon Earth, by the act of that nation's government, and the war is essentially declared."

So it was nothing new when, in the wake of September 11, 2001 attacks, President Bush decided that the United States would be "at war" but that it would not be necessary for Congress to actually declare it. Besides, the traditional declaration of war was designed to be an honorable notice of intent from one sovereign state to another. It hardly made sense to apply it to a criminal gang with branch offices in dozens of states.

Instead of a declaration, the president, on September 18, 2001, signed a joint resolution by Congress entitled "Authorization for Use of Military Force." While he was pleased to have the backing of the members of Congress and promised to "continue to consult closely with them," he also asserted—as did his father before him during the Persian Gulf War—that he didn't need their approval. "In signing this resolution, I maintain the long-standing position of the executive branch regarding the president's constitutional authority to use force."

President Barack Obama demonstrated that he was no different from his predecessors in his disdain for the War Powers Resolution. In 2011 the United States and its NATO allies started military action against Libya in order to help rebels overthrow the regime of Muammar Gadhafi. After the 90 days passed and military operations continued, many members of Congress, both Democrats and Republicans, began publicly complaining that the president was in violation of the Resolution. But the Obama administration refuted this, asserting that the United States had only a supporting role in the NATO operation and that the actions differed from the kind of "hostilities" contemplated in the Resolution's termination provisions.

In effect, the president has always had dictatorial powers concerning military operations. This is only tempered by his political concerns and the ultimate ability of Congress to stop him by cutting off funds. So the answer to the question of who decides if the United States should wage war is very simple: It is the president—alone. And because it is the president alone who makes this decision, it is the president who must accept the political fallout from failed military endeavors that

Back to the future: This photo of U.S. Special Forces in Afghanistan in 2001 shows Americans on horseback riding with our Northern Alliance allies. This new model U.S. Cavalry was so successful in calling in air strikes against the terrorist enemy that the Taliban government of Afghanistan was overthrown in a few weeks. There was an administrative lesson in this for then Secretary of Defense Donald Rumsfeld—perhaps the wrong one. If American technology can use a small group of military personnel suffering few casualties to overthrow one Asian government, then why not try the same strategy with another Asian government deserving to be overthrown? So, in 2003, with fewer forces than many experts recommended, the United States invaded Iraq to liberate it from a tyrant every bit as despicable, but on a smaller scale, as those famous dictators of World War II. While the initial fighting went well and was over in a few weeks, the occupation became a nightmare of guerrilla warfare dragging on for years. Eventually, in 2006, this even cost Rumsfeld his job—but it cost the lives and limbs of thousands of other Americans. The problem here was that the analogy was not apt. Just because high-tech small forces worked in one country doesn't automatically mean that a similar effort will work in another. Differing geographies, cultures, and populations must be taken into account. Rumsfeld and the Bush administration thought they could win the war in Iraq on the cheap with a relatively small expeditionary force still structured for fighting the Russians in Europe. They soon learned that they needed a new mix of forces, new training techniques, new combat doctrines, and new occupation policies. Of course, ideally, these are the kind of administrative problems that should be addressed before you start a war. But who knew beforehand? As it turned out, lots of career experts in the Defense and State Departments did. But neither Rumsfeld nor Bush would listen to them. Sometimes, it can really pay for political executives to heed the advice of professional staff. Even if the career staff disagrees with your policy (such as war), they can often help you do it (wage war) in a smarter way.

eventually disenchant the public because they fail, cost too much, have too many dead and wounded, or simply take too long. Of course, with success, however it is defined, he gets the political credit for foresight and wisdom.

For Discussion: *Why is it that the War Powers Resolution of 1973, Congress's effort to curb the war-making powers of the president, is generally considered a failure? If the American president has, in effect, dictatorial powers in wartime, what has prevented the United States from succumbing to a dictatorial government when this has been the fate of so many other nations?*

WHAT IS PUBLIC POLICY?

In the beginning there was chaos. Then came policy. "Let there be light" (Genesis 1:3) was a policy decision. Policy creates orderly structures and a sense of direction. Public administration cannot exist in a policy vacuum. It must have administrative structures that are directed by leaders who wish to do something—if only to maintain the **status quo.** Thus all of public administration is inherently an instrument of policy—whether that instrument plays well, poorly, or not at all.

Any policy is a decision. A public policy is whatever a government decides to do or not to do. It is what a government does in response to a political issue. A public program consists of all those activities designed to implement the public policy: Often this calls for the creation of organizations, public agencies, and bureaus, which in turn need to create more policies that give guidance to the organization's employees on how to put into practice the overall public policy.

Policy is hierarchical. The broadest, most overarching policy is made at the top. Then increasingly more focused policies must be made at every level on down. For example, the president of the United States sits at the top of the foreign policymaking pyramid. Dozens of layers below him sit thousands of clerks in the **visa** sections of hundreds of embassies and consulates making policy—that is, making decisions—on who may legally enter the United States. To be sure, policy at the bottom is heavily impacted by laws and regulations. But to the extent that these low-level officials—who Michael Lipsky calls **street-level bureaucrats**—have any discretion at all, they are making policy. And if you are on the receiving end of that policy, whether as a visa applicant or a motorist receiving a traffic citation from a police officer, the policy is as real to you as if it were coming from higher levels in the policymaking hierarchy.

Public Policymaking in a Republic

It is the sovereign who makes legitimate policy in a political community. In a traditional society, the sovereign (meaning the monarch) is the sovereign (meaning the boss). In the United States, the people are sovereign and government is considered their agent. In a 1916 speech, President Woodrow Wilson rhetorically asked, "Just what is it that America stands for? If she stands for one thing more than another, it is for the sovereignty of self-governing people." This kind of sovereignty is generally referred to as a democracy.

Status quo ■

The existing state of affairs. This term is often used to describe policies designed to maintain the existng distribution of power.

Visa ■

A document, usually in the form of a stamp in a passport, that allows a citizen of one nation to visit another.

Street-level bureaucrats ■

Those public officials who are literally closest to the people by being in almost constant contact with them. Examples are police officers, welfare caseworkers, and teachers.

But democracy is not a simple or constant concept. Instead, it is an evolving notion regarding the relationship between the people and government. It started, like so many things having to do with government, with the Greeks. Their democracy consisted of rule by an elite group of male citizens, whose well-being was maintained by politically suppressed women and a large slave population (not a desirable situation if you were a woman and worse if you were a slave). The development of popular or universal democracy in the eighteenth century led to revolutionary conceptions of democracy that called for the placing of all power in the hands of the people—at first just white males. The problem remained of constructing a state that could exercise that power not just in the name of, but for all the people. This is what President Abraham Lincoln, a man with strong antislavery credentials, was concerned about in his 1863 Gettysburg Address: ". . . that this government of the people, by the people, for the people, shall not perish from the earth."

The modern problem with "the people" is that so many nasty individuals have done too many despicable things in their name. Because the term *democracy* often has been used by totalitarian regimes and their "people's democracies," one person's democratic regime is too often another's totalitarian despotism. So modern democracy, like the modern contact lens, is in the eye of the beholder. By being used to describe such a large range of institutional possibilities, the term *democracy* has lost its meaning—but not its vitality—in political debate.

The founders of the United States were rightly suspicious of the so-called "pure" democracy of the free male citizens of ancient Athens. As **Aristotle** had warned, time and again throughout history these pure democracies had been captured by **demagogues** and had degenerated into dictatorial tyrannies. As John Adams wrote in an 1814 letter, "Remember, democracy never lasts long. It soon wastes, exhausts, and murders itself. There never was a democracy yet that did not commit suicide." This well-justified fear of "the mob" led the founders to create a **republic**, a form of government one step removed from democracy, which presumably protects the people from their own passions.

While the founders specifically wanted a governing structure that was insulated from a pure democracy, they also wanted a governing arrangement that, unlike the city-states of ancient Greece, could function over a large area. As James Madison wrote in *The Federalist*, No. 14, "In a democracy the people meet and exercise the government in person; in a republic, they assemble and administer it by their representatives and agents. A democracy, consequently, will be confined to a small spot. A republic may be extended over a large region." Yet the founders all knew that many republics in history, such as the Roman republic, had been replaced by despots. Consequently, when Benjamin Franklin was asked what sort of government had been hatched at the **Constitutional Convention of 1787**, he replied, "A republic, if you can keep it." He knew that "keeping it" was far from certain.

In a republic the legislature, whether parliament or Congress, is supreme. After all, it has the greatest number of enumerated powers and the executive and judicial branches must enforce its laws. As Madison wrote in *The Federalist*, No. 51, "In republican government, the legislative authority necessarily predominates." President Franklin D. Roosevelt, in a press conference on July 23, 1937, put it

Aristotle (384–322 B.C.E.) ■
The Greek philosopher who originated much of the study of logic, science and politics.

Demagogue ■
A political leader accused of seeking or gaining power through the use of arguments designed to appeal to a mass public's sentiments, even though critics may consider those arguments exaggerated.

Republic ■
A Latin word meaning "the public thing"; the state and its institutions; that form of government in which sovereignty resides in the people who elect agents to represent them in political decision making.

Constitutional Convention of 1787 ■
The meeting in Philadelphia, held from May 25 to September 18, at which 55 delegates from the various states designed the U.S. Constitution.

another way: "It is the duty of the president to propose and it is the privilege of the Congress to dispose." Yet this system was perverted from World War II until very recently. Because of the necessities of both hot and cold wars, the president has been unusually strong vis-à-vis the Congress. With the end of the Cold War and without the need to rally behind a wartime leader, the power relationship seemed to be returning to its "normal" condition—at least until September 11, 2001, and the war on terrorism.

Executive Powers

Many political executives, whether mayors, governors, or presidents, have tried—often for sound causes relating to the public good—to take more policymaking power unto themselves than may be constitutionally warranted. Just how far can an executive deviate from the legislative will or the letter of the constitution in a republican government? This is usually a function of the political strength of the executive as evidenced by a large electoral mandate, control by the executive's party in the legislature, or public opinion poll ratings. Strong executives are able to put into place more of the policies they espouse. But just how much strength should an executive ideally have or be allowed to have? Fortunately, we can answer this question with the help of three famous statements on executive power, all made by past presidents of the United States—and all equally applicable to any political executive, whether president, governor, or mayor, in any constitutional system: the restricted view, the prerogative theory, and the stewardship theory.

The Restricted View   This is the limited (or literalist) view of presidential power, espoused by President **William Howard Taft**. He, as an archconservative, held that "the president can exercise no power which cannot be fairly and reasonably traced to some specific grant of power or justly implied and included within such express grant as proper and necessary to its exercise." Furthermore (and in direct opposition to President Theodore Roosevelt's stewardship view that follows), "there is no undefined residuum of power which he can exercise because it seems to be in the public interest." Taft viewed the president as the agent of the Congress—in no way a free agent. In a constitutional sense, Taft was a **strict constructionist**. He was disdainful of those who asserted the presence of a "residuum of power" when he clearly saw none. As an administrator, he felt his political hands were tied by the constraints of his office. And he was happy in his bondage. Today he remains a role model for all those public managers who would instantly solve public problems with new public policy if only they had the power. Not having it, they sit back, survey the poor conditions in their administrative realm, and feel quite strongly that they too are victims of "the system."

The Prerogative Theory   This theory of executive power was espoused by President Abraham Lincoln and supported by **John Locke** in his *Second Treatise of Government* (1690). Under certain conditions, they believed that the chief executive possessed extraordinary power to preserve the nation: "Many things there are which the law can by no means provide for; and those must necessarily be left to the discretion of him that has the executive power in his hands." This power, as

William Howard Taft (1857–1930) ■
The only person to be both president of the United States (1909–1913) and chief justice of the Supreme Court (1921–1930). Taft, at 321 pounds, also holds the record as the largest of all presidents.

Strict constructionist ■
One who believes the U.S. Constitution should be interpreted narrowly and literally. A loose constructionist, in contrast, believes that the Constitution should be interpreted liberally in order to reflect changing times.

John Locke (1632–1704) ■
The English physician and philosopher whose writings on the nature of governance were a profound influence on the founding fathers. It is often argued that the first part of the Declaration of Independence, which establishes the essential philosophic rationale for the break with England, is Thomas Jefferson's restatement of John Locke's most basic themes.

Lincoln saw it, might not only exceed constitutional bounds but act against the Constitution. A president, according to this view, could at least for a short while even assume dictatorial powers. Lincoln explained this theory in an 1864 letter:

> [T]hat my oath to preserve the Constitution to the best of my ability imposed upon me the duty of preserving, by every indispensable means, that government— that nation, of which that Constitution was the organic law. Was it possible to lose the nation and yet preserve the Constitution? By general law, life and limb must be protected, yet often a limb must be amputated to save a life; but a life is never wisely given to save a limb. I felt that measures otherwise unconstitutional might become lawful by becoming indispensable to the preservation of the Constitution through the preservation of the nation.

Lincoln's attitude was commendable enough in the middle of a civil war. However, when recent presidents have sought extraordinary powers, even with claims of national security and **executive privilege**, they have been "checked" by the Supreme Court. For example, when President Franklin D. Roosevelt sought to expand the federal government's scope and size during the Great Depression, many of his efforts were rejected by a Supreme Court that viewed his initiatives as exceeding the bounds of executive power established by the Constitution. Similarly, during the Korean War, President Harry S. Truman's attempts to exert executive power over labor and industry were blocked by a skeptical judicial branch. As the war in Korea waged on during the 1950s, Truman issued an executive order directing the secretary of commerce to take possession of and operate the nation's steel mills because of a labor dispute that threatened to disrupt war production. In response, the Supreme Court held, in *Youngstown Sheet and Tube Co. v. Sawyer* (1952), that the president exceeded his constitutional powers. Two decades later the Court in *United States v. Nixon* (1974) rejected President Richard M. Nixon's claim that the Constitution provided the president with an absolute and unreviewable executive privilege—specifically, the right not to respond to a **subpoena** in connection with a judicial trial. The Court held that "neither the doctrine of separation of powers nor the need for confidentiality of high-level communications, without more, can sustain an absolute, unqualified, presidential immunity from judicial process under all circumstances." The Court allowed there was a limited executive privilege that might pertain in the areas of military, diplomatic, or security affairs, and where confidentiality was related to the president's ability to carry out his constitutional mandates. This was the decision that forced Nixon to give the Watergate **special prosecutor** tape recordings of criminal activities in **Oval Office** meetings and, in effect, forced Nixon to resign as president in 1974.

The prerogative approach is not a theory for all seasons. Because it is applicable only in times of extraordinary national emergency, presidents have been able to "get away with it" only during wartime, when Congress has been compliant (as it was during the Civil War) or kept ignorant (as it was during the Vietnam War). Just how much prerogative President Bush should be allowed to exercise during the War on Terror and in Iraq was a major point of contention with the Congress and the public. Similarly, as President Obama confronted the economic crisis in 2009, there was a great deal of criticism that he was overstepping his powers. Despite an economic situation that was described as "the worst since the Great

Executive privilege ■
The presidential claim that the executive branch may withhold information from the Congress or its committees and the courts to preserve confidential communications within the executive branch or to secure the national interest.

Subpoena ■
A written order issued by a judicial officer requiring a specified person to appear in a designated court at a specified time, either to serve as a witness in a case under the jurisdiction of that court or to bring material to that court.

Special prosecutor ■
A prosecutor appointed to consider the evidence in a case and, if necessary, to undertake the prosecution of a case that presents a possible conflict of interest for the jurisdiction's regular prosecutor.

Oval Office ■
The oval-shaped White House office of the president of the United States. Although the office itself was built in the 1930s as part of an expansion of the West Wing of the White House, the term did not come into general usage until the Nixon administration.

Depression," critics of Obama claimed that he was exceeding his prerogative to lead by taking actions beyond the legitimate role of the president. The important thing to remember is that this theory of executive power is quietly reserved to support the efforts of a leader who sees the nation through in a time of crisis, or, alternately, it lurks in the hands of an unprincipled opportunist or demagogue to stifle republican institutions. Only the writers of history get to decide who were the strong leaders and who were the political opportunists.

The Stewardship Theory This is President Theodore Roosevelt's view that the president, because he represents and holds in trust the interests of all the people, should be free to take any actions in the public interest that are not specifically forbidden by the Constitution or statutory law. Although he only articulated this doctrine in his autobiography, published in 1913 after he left office, Roosevelt certainly lived it. For example, he sent the U.S. Navy's battleships on an around-the-world training cruise without congressional permission. He then told members of Congress that if they wanted the ships back, they would have to appropriate funds to buy fuel for the return journey. Roosevelt believed strongly that "every executive officer . . . was a steward of the people bound actively and affirmatively to do all he could for the people." Roosevelt felt, in sum, that he was free to do as he pleased in that twilight zone lying between the prohibitions of the law and the duties required by specific constitutional or statutory enactments.

These three models of executive leadership are all still very much with us. Of course, the prerogative approach of Lincoln and Locke is not much in evidence except in despotic regimes. But the war on terrorism may force a future American president to temporarily suspend some constitutional privileges in the wake of a subsequent disastrous attack. While Lincoln's example remains as a last resort, the more common situation at all political and organizational levels is illustrated by the two ends of a continuum, with a literalist (Taft) at one end, and a steward (Teddy Roosevelt) at the other. The choice for leaders, then, is to be inactive in terms of policy initiation—basically to just maintain what is—or to be proactive in terms of policy and to be at the forefront of continuous change and reform. Or to be where most political and administrative executives are—somewhere in between. That is, they are proactive only on a limited number of issues.

Proactive ■
An administrative style that encourages taking risks on behalf of one's clients or one's moral values; the opposite of a reactive style.

THE POLICYMAKING PROCESS

A new policy proposal is frequently presented to the public as a policy paper—a written argument in favor of (or opposing) a particular public policy. Political candidates typically generate a variety of policy papers on issues of importance to their constituents. Political campaigns often become a "battle" of opposing policy papers. And the modern battleground for these opposing policies is frequently in cyberspace, on political candidates' Web sites. Such Web sites are promoting not only the candidate but the policies of that candidate, as well. Consequently they usually contain white papers about where the candidate stands on various issues and why. In theory, the voters can read these thoughtful papers on a wide range of policy issues. They may even believe the illusion that the papers were actually written by

White paper ■
Any formal statement of an official (or would-be) government policy, with its associated background documentation.

the candidate. In reality, the papers are read by few because most voters are content with the minimally informative **sound bites** that the candidates spit out on TV.

But no matter how astute and detailed the arguments are for or against a particular policy, the media tend to distill them into a few words. Thus an extremely thoughtful review of the utility of capital punishment often comes down to the fact that the candidate is "for" or "against" the death penalty. Voters prefer to think that their favored candidates have given great thought to all the subtle aspects of their policy positions. Consequently, it is more important that such policy papers exist than be read. However, policy papers put out by advocacy groups and academics—and not related to political campaigns—tend to be both more sophisticated and better received.

Policy papers, while currently written, have an ancient unwritten tradition. When, in the Bible, Moses said to Pharaoh "Let my people go!" (Exodus 5:1), and when Ulysses, in Homer's *The Iliad*, told the Greeks besieging Troy to build the Trojan horse, they were presenting policies even before there was paper. There is still a strong oral policy paper tradition. However, the modern version of a would-be Moses or Ulysses is most likely to be found giving a speech on the campaign trail—either running for office or as the representative of a public interest group. The place where you will find this oral tradition flourishing every hour of every day is on TV and radio talk shows. There, the most pressing public policy issues of any given day will be dissected, criticized, and/or supported ad nauseum. Academic policy papers are published in professional journals and read by few. Talk show hosts publish little and may be relatively ignorant—but they can be immensely influential.

Sound bite ■
A political campaign slogan or short statement that summarizes a candidate's beliefs. Such simplistic policies can backfire if they promise more than can be delivered. In 1988 George H. W. Bush became president by shouting, "Read my lips! No new taxes!" But less than two years into his presidency he was forced to eat his sound bite and agree to raise taxes.

▶ BOX 2.1 | How War Studies Became Case Studies

The study of the policymaking process is often undertaken by means of a case study, an in-depth analysis of a single subject. It is a history that offers an understanding of dynamic, constantly moving and changing processes over time. Most traditional news stories use the case study approach. Note that aspiring journalists are taught that a story should contain all the essential elements of a case study: "who, what, why, when, where, and how."

Wars make excellent case studies because they each have a beginning, middle, and end. Indeed, the first case studies examined battles and wars. Thucydides' *History of the Peloponnesian War* (404 B.C.E.) is the progenitor of these military case studies. Military colleges—and general staffs—have long used the case study method to review battles and study generalship. This same technique is now widely used in a civilian context to examine how

policy proposals become law, how programs are implemented, and how special interests affect policy development.

College courses in business and public administration often use a case study approach. An entire course may consist of case studies (frequently combined into a casebook) of management situations to be reviewed. The goal is to inculcate experience artificially. Any manager rich with years of service will have had the opportunity to live through a lifetime of "cases." By having students study many cases, each of which may have extended over many years, the case study course compresses both time and experience. In this way, a relatively young student can gain much of the insight and wisdom of a manager who has had many years of experience. In theory, this makes them so wise beyond their years that employers will eagerly seek them out. ▲

Political Environment

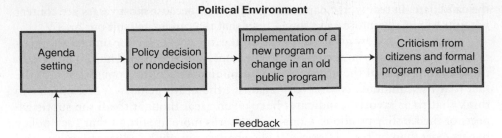

FIGURE 2.1

The public policymaking cycle

Because public policymaking involves so many aspects, so many players, and so many issues, it is difficult to grasp it as one single thing. Of course, it is not a tangible thing; it is a never-ending intangible process. This process can be illustrated by the public policymaking cycle (see Figure 2.1), a conceptual model that views the public policy process as moving through a succession of stages: (1) agenda setting (or the identification of a policy issue), (2) policy decision or nondecision, (3) implementation, (4) program evaluation or impact analysis, and, finally, (5) feedback, which leads to revision or termination. Thus the process comes full circle—which is why it is called a "cycle." A review of this process will show that public administration is both at the heart of the process and a feature of every aspect of it.

Agenda Setting

Agenda setting is the process by which ideas or issues bubble up through the various political channels to wind up for consideration by a political institution such as a legislature or court. We have already mentioned the two greatest sources of agenda items—the executive and the legislators. Their constituents expect that they will seek the enactment into law of the policies that they advocated in their campaigns for elective office. Additionally, the administrative agencies of a government often generate legislative proposals. Sometimes, these are incorporated into the executive's legislative recommendations.

The agenda-setting process often makes extensive use of the mass media to take a relatively unknown or unsupported issue and, through publicity, expand the numbers of people who care about the issue so that an institution, whether it be city hall or the Congress, is forced to take some action. One example can be traced back to 1955, when Rosa Parks, an African-American woman, was arrested for refusing to take a seat in the back of a bus in Montgomery, Alabama. This confrontation sparked the modern civil rights movement. Dr. Martin Luther King, Jr. would later use the tactics of nonviolent confrontation with southern segregational policies to arouse sufficient sympathy and support in the rest of the nation, which would lead to the passage of landmark civil rights legislation in Congress. When these nonviolent demonstrations turned violent, it was all the better—because it made better TV and thus ensured a bigger audience for the message of the cause. Starting in the 1980s, pro-life (meaning antiabortion) groups used demonstrators in front of medical offices providing abortion services to arouse the national consciousness about this issue. These, too, often became spontaneously violent and thus made for better TV. The lesson is clear. "Nonviolent" demonstrations that turn violent or at least contentious once the TV news cameras arrive are more likely to get on the six o'clock news. These approaches to placing issues on the public policy agenda are called pseudo-events by historian Daniel Boorstin because they are "non-spontaneous, planted, or manufactured 'news,' whose main purpose is to gain publicity for the person or cause which arranged the 'event.'"

The importance of TV in propelling an issue onto government's agenda is particularly notable when the policy issue maintains a highly visual element. For example, the stark visual aspects of air and water pollution helped drive environmental protection issues fully onto the federal government's radar in the late 1960s and early 1970s. From oil-covered marine mammals on California's once pristine coast to burning rivers in the petroleum-choked surface water of Cleveland, Ohio, the striking images of environmental destruction directly boosted environmental protection issues into the public consciousness and eventually into the halls of Congress.

Agendas are often set by public policy entrepreneurs, political actors who take a political issue and run with it. Thus certain senators might make particular issues their own by sheer force of expertise that, if respected, "forces" colleagues to take cues on the matter from them. Or a staffer might become such an expert on an issue that he or she can heavily influence legislation dealing with it. Thus, a public policy entrepreneur can be anyone in the political environment whose expertise and actions can affect an issue.

Agenda setting, which is usually confined to professional politicians, is a game that anybody can play. A federal judge could rule that a state prison is unconstitutionally overcrowded and thus force the state's legislature to deal with the issue by appropriating funds for new prisons. A citizens' group could be so concerned about an issue that they gather enough signatures of registered voters to advance the issue

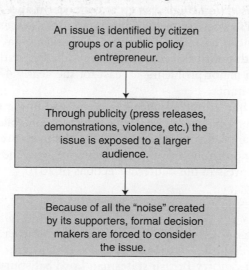

FIGURE 2.2
The agenda-setting process

as a proposition on the next election's ballot. A public interest law firm could challenge the legality of an agency's action and force the courts to ascertain its constitutionality. Or an interest group could get thousands of its members to write (or e-mail) letters to their legislative representatives demanding action on a controversy. While there are only a few places—such as a legislature, court, or regulatory commission—where agendas can be formally enacted, there are infinite numbers of sources from which agenda items spring. And like hope, they spring eternally.

Anthony Downs (1930–) ■
The economist and policy analyst who is generally credited with establishing the intellectual framework for public choice economics in his book *An Economic Theory of Democracy* (1957). His classic book on bureaucracy, *Inside Bureaucracy* (1967), sought to justify bureaucratic government on economic grounds and to develop laws and propositions that would aid in predicting the behavior of bureaus and bureaucrats.

The issue-attention cycle is a model developed by **Anthony Downs** that attempts to explain the way in which many policy problems evolve on the political agenda. The cycle is premised on the notion that the public's attention rarely remains focused on any one issue, regardless of the objective nature of the problem. The cycle consists of five steps:

1. The preproblem stage (an undesirable social condition exists but has not captured public attention)
2. Alarmed discovery and euphoric enthusiasm (a dramatic event catalyzes the public attention, accompanied by an enthusiasm to solve the problem)
3. Recognition of the cost of change (the public gradually realizes the difficulty of implementing meaningful change)
4. Decline of public interest (people become discouraged or bored or a new issue claims attention)
5. The postproblem stage (although the issue has not been solved, it has been dropped from the nation's agenda)

According to policy analyst John Kingdon, "If Anthony Downs is right, problems often fade from public view because a short period of awareness and optimism gives way to a realization of the financial and social costs of action. As people become impressed with the sacrifices, dislocations, and costs to be borne, they lose their enthusiasm for addressing the problem." For example, early in the first Clinton administration there was great enthusiasm and support for a major reform in the nation's system of medical insurance. But as increasing attention was brought to the financial costs and difficulties of implementation, the issue faded from view while both political leaders and the public lost enthusiasm for dealing with what remains a major problem—at least for the nearly 47 million Americans without medical insurance.

By 2009 the public appeared once again engaged in the issue of health care reform with President Obama and the Democratically controlled Congress passing a sweeping health care reform package in 2010. The public reacted to this action with considerable opposition and anger, culminating with the Republicans taking back control of Congress in the midterm elections of 2010.

Decision Making

Public policymaking is the totality of the processes by which a government decides to deal or not to deal with a particular problem or concern. It is a never-ending process. Nineteenth-century British statesman Lord Salisbury is usually credited with first remarking, "There is no such thing as a fixed policy, because policy, like all organic entities, is always in the making."

There are two distinct and opposite theories seeking to explain the mechanisms that produce policy decisions or non-decisions. The first might be called the rational decision-making approach, and it generally has been attributed to Harold D. Lasswell. In his book *The Future of Political Science*, he posited seven significant phases for every decision:

1. The intelligence phase, involving an influx of information
2. The promoting or recommending phase, involving activities designed to influence the outcome
3. The prescribing phase, involving the articulation of norms
4. The invoking phase, involving establishing correspondence between prescriptions and concrete circumstances
5. The application phase, in which the prescription is executed
6. The appraisal phase, assessing intent in relation to effect
7. The terminating phase, treating expectations (rights) established while the prescription was in force

Of course, there is an immediate problem with this and every other such list. It is impossible to complete. No matter how rational we would hope to be, there is no way anyone could gather *all* the facts and take into account *every* consideration. Therefore, decision makers exercise what Herbert Simon, the 1978 Nobel laureate in economics, calls "bounded rationality." The "bounds" are what people put on their decisions. Simon asserts that "it is impossible for the behavior of a single, isolated individual to reach any high degree of rationality. The number of alternatives he must explore is so great, the information he needs to evaluate them so vast, that even an approximation to objective rationality is hard to conceive." Consequently, humans make decisions on satisfactory, as opposed to optimal, information. Inventing a new word, Simon said that decision makers "satisfice" when they accept a satisfactory and sufficient amount of information on which to base a decision. Thus in the real world we are forced to reject the "rational comprehensive" approach and "satisfice" rather than "maximize."

A rejection of this rational approach was urged by Charles E. Lindblom, the leading proponent of the second theory of policy decision making—the incremental approach. In his most famous article, "The Science of Muddling Through," Lindblom took a hard look at the rational models of the decisional processes of government. He rejected the notion that most decisions are made by rational (total information) processes. Instead, he saw such decisions—indeed, the whole policymaking process—as dependent on small incremental decisions that tend to be made in response to short-term political conditions. Lindblom's thesis essentially held that decision making was controlled infinitely more by events and circumstances than by the will of those in policymaking positions. Disjointed incrementalism as a policy course was in reality the only truly feasible route, because incrementalism "concentrated the policymaker's analysis on familiar, better-known experiences, sharply reduced the number of different alternative policies to be explored, and sharply reduced the number and complexity of factors to be analyzed."

The rational and incremental models, often viewed as two ends of a continuum, are useful intellectual tools for conceptualizing the decision-making process. There is even a "split the difference" compromise model that combines the two.

Harold D. Lasswell (1902–1978) ■ One of the most influential and prolific of social scientists. While he made major contributions to the fields of communications, psychology (he pioneered the application of Freudian theory to politics), political science, sociology, and law, his most lasting legacy is probably his pioneering work in developing the concept and methodology of the policy sciences.

Charles E. Lindblom (1917–) ■ The Yale University political scientist who since the 1950s has been asserting that incrementalism is the most viable approach to understanding how public policies are made.

ALTERNATIVE Theories | Rational Decision Making Versus Incremental Decision Making

Rationalism	Incrementalism
All options and means are considered	Only a few options and means are considered
Decisions are the product of structured evaluations	Decisions are the product of negotiated settlements
Major changes can be made on a regular basis	Changes are made gradually over time
Decisions tend to be made proactively	Decisions tend to be made reactively
Decisions should be removed from political pressures	Political considerations are important in determining outcomes

The table above provides a number of the key characteristics associated with the rational and incremental approaches to decision making. While each approach certainly has its advantages and disadvantages, it is interesting to think about the circumstances in which each approach may be more beneficial. In particular, can you identify scenarios where either rationalism or incrementalism would hold a clear advantage as a means of making a public policy decision? ▶

Amitai Etzioni (1929–) ■
The sociologist whose early work on organization theory steered him toward political integration and communitarianism.

Mixed scanning is the decision-making model put forth by **Amitai Etzioni,** which calls for seeking short-term solutions to problems by using both incrementalism and rational-comprehensive approaches to problem solving. For example, a foreign policy analyst responsible for reviewing political developments in Europe might superficially scan all recent developments (the comprehensive approach) but focus only on those political problems that have changed since the last scanning (the incremental approach). In this way the analyst saves time by dealing in detail only with those situations that truly demand attention.

A Single Calculating Decision Maker—Not!

A famous example of a conceptual model of public policymaking is provided by Graham T. Allison's classic study of government decision making, *Essence of Decision: Explaining the Cuban Missile Crisis* (1971). It showed the inadequacies of the view that policies are made by a "single calculating decision maker," such as a president who has complete control over the organizational units and individual officials within his or her government. Instead, Allison—using John F. Kennedy's **Cuban Missile Crisis** of 1962—demonstrated that differing bureaucratic viewpoints (such as those of the State Department, Defense Department, and National Security Council) fight over policy. Although Allison's ideas were not new, he helped crystallize thinking about foreign policymaking by dealing with the different approaches in terms of three models. He argued that the traditionally dominant model, that of the "single calculating decision maker," obscured more than it illuminated. Allison called this the Rational Actor Model or Model One and believed that this model must be supplemented by two other models. Allison's Model Two, the

Organizational Processes Model, basically argued that government action could be understood as the output of large organizations that operated according to standard operating procedures. Allison described Model Three as a Governmental Politics Model, the essence of which was that decisions were the outcome of a bargaining process between different groups and individuals with different bureaucratic perspectives and different political interests. Consequently, foreign policy decisions are not the product of a rational calculation about what is good for the state but a compromise—and often a compromised product of the internal bargaining process.

But in reality, all these models are not much more than mind games for **policy wonks**. The real world of political executives and harried legislators is not so much an intellectual arena as it is a bare-knuckles political arena. Decisions in the political arena are influenced far more by the perception of a situation than by any rational concept of objective reality. It is far more than the difference between a pessimist seeing a glass as half empty and an optimist seeing it as half full. One actor in the decisional drama may view a program as absolutely essential for the national interest, while another is equally certain that it is nothing more than an example of petty bureaucrats wasting the taxpayers' money.

Policymakers bring two kinds of intelligence to bear on their thinking. First is their mental ability to cope with complicated problems. Second is the information and experience they have with the issue at hand. Both kinds of intelligence are then filtered through their ideological predispositions and personal biases before an attitude toward any given problem is set. Thus, political decisions are seldom made on the objective merits of a case because a case only has merit in the eyes of a political decision maker if he or she is intelligent enough to see it and, equally important, is ideologically and politically predisposed to support it.

At the end of the day, the policy processes of government are not only about equity or justice but, fundamentally, about power. But once power is exerted, once a law is enacted, once a program is created, these power brokers—whether democrats or autocrats—turn to their public administrators to make their wishes, to make their power, a reality. Without the administrators of the state to do their bidding, the power brokers are quite literally broke.

Implementation

Implementation is the process of putting a government program into effect; it is the total process of translating a legal mandate, whether an executive order or an enacted **statute**, into appropriate program directives and structures that provide services or create goods. Implementation, the doing part of public administration, is an inherently political process. Architects often say that "God is in the details." So is it with implementation. A law is passed, but the process of putting it into effect requires countless small decisions that necessarily alter it. According to President Carter's National Security Adviser Zbigniew Brzezinski, "Policymakers are overwhelmed by events and information. . . . A great deal of decision making is done through implementation by the bureaucracy, which often distorts it."

"Distort" is a harsh word that implies intentional change. Most administrative implementors, however, act in good faith, with little intentional distortion. But there is substantial friction. This concept has been well expressed by Prussian

Cuban Missile Crisis ■
The 1962 confrontation between the U.S. and the Soviet Union over the Soviet placement of nuclear missiles in Cuba. President Kennedy demanded the removal of the missiles, imposed a naval blockade on Cuba, and waited for the Soviet response. In the end, the Soviets removed their missiles for a U.S. promise not to invade Cuba and an understanding that the U.S. would also remove its missiles from Turkey.

Policy wonks ■
A compulsive analyst of public policy processes. "Wonk" is slang for a student who is a grind or a nerd.

Statute ■
A law passed by a legislature; legislative-made as opposed to judge-made law.

General Karl von Clausewitz, who held that no matter how well planned a large operation is, the reality of delays, misunderstandings, and so forth will make its inevitable execution less than ideal. While military in origin, friction has become a generally recognized phenomenon in all aspects of the administration of public and **international affairs**.

While implementation is obviously at the heart of public administration, it has only recently been self-consciously studied. The first major analysis of implementation as a new focus for public administration was Jeffrey Pressman and Aaron Wildavsky's 1973 study of federal programs in the city of Oakland, California. The unabridged title of their work tells part of the story: *Implementation: How Great Expectations in Washington Are Dashed in Oakland; Or, Why It's Amazing That Federal Programs Work at All; This Being a Saga of the Economic Development Administration as Told by Two Sympathetic Observers Who Seek to Build Morals on a Foundation of Ruined Hopes.* What Pressman and Wildavsky related in their landmark book seems almost simplistic—that policy planners and analysts were not taking into account the difficulties of execution or "implementation." The goal of their book was to consider how a closer nexus between policy and implementation could be achieved. A direct result of this book was a spate of works explaining how policy analysis can accomplish this objective—an objective, it is fair to say, that has yet to be comprehensively implemented.

Pressman and Wildavsky define implementation as "a process of interaction between the setting of goals and actions geared to achieving them" as well as "an ability to forge subsequent links in the causal chain so as to obtain the desired results." This definition usefully calls attention to the interaction between setting goals and carrying them out. This helps clarify that implementation is political in a very fundamental sense. The activities that go on under its banner shape **who gets what** (and when and how they get it) from government. Like lawmakers, administrators and those they interact with during the implementation process exert power over program objectives and influence program inputs and outcomes. Implementation involves administrators, interest groups, and other actors with diverse values mobilizing power resources, forming coalitions, consciously plotting strategies, and generally engaging in strategic behavior designed to ensure that their point of view prevails. The terrain may be different from that found in Congress or other legislatures, but the basic staples of the political process are very much present.

Never forget that the goal of program implementation is necessarily the creation of the myriad details of everyday administrative life. Policy analyst Charles O. Jones maintains that implementation consists of "those activities directed toward putting a program into effect." This involves the "translation of program language into acceptable and feasible directives," as well as creating appropriate organizational structures and routines. A major virtue of Jones's definition is that it explicitly points to the role of routine and other aspects of organizational structure in implementation. In order to conserve time and energy, as well as to promote the equal treatment of clients, organizations develop **standard operating procedures**. These procedures plus other informal **decision rules** greatly simplify choices for administrators. Decisions can be made almost without thinking. Any effort to comprehend how implementation processes affect program

---

International affairs ■
A term that is loosely used as a synonym for international politics. It can include almost anything that is not exclusively domestic in nature.

Who gets what ■
This is the very definition of politics provided by the title of Harold Lasswell's classic 1936 book *Politics: Who Gets What, When, How.*

Standard operating procedures ■
The established routines by which organizations accomplish their objectives.

Decision rule ■
Any directive established to make decisions in the face of uncertainty. For example, a payroll office might be given a decision rule to deduct one hour's pay from an employee's wages for tardiness that exceeds ten minutes but is less than one hour.

outcomes cannot, then, ignore the collective impact of countless procedures and simple decision rules. Implementation is always a mix of the consciously strategic with the daily routine.

Evaluation

Any evaluation is an assessment. A program evaluation is the systematic examination of activities undertaken by government to make a determination about their effects, both for the short term and the long range. Program evaluation is distinguished from management evaluation (also called organization evaluation) because the latter is limited to a program's internal administrative procedures. While program evaluations use management and organizational data, the main thrust is necessarily on overall program objectives and impact. Thus a program evaluation is less concerned with the management of a police department than with that department's overall effect on crime and less concerned with a welfare agency's internal administration than with its effectiveness in dealing with clients.

The concepts of **efficiency** and **effectiveness** are the standard criteria by which programs are evaluated. In addition, these concepts helped to forge a workable distinction between **audits** and evaluations. Audits, primarily financial accounting audits, were traditionally geared to control—to ensure that every dime of public funds is accounted for and that every regulation is complied with. This law enforcement style of management is being increasingly displaced by program evaluation—a far more comprehensive management tool. We still expect programs to be administered efficiently, just as we expect complete fiscal accountability for funds and receipts. But efficiency is not enough. A work unit could be terribly efficient while working toward the wrong goals. Because of this, evaluations, if they are themselves to be effective, must also deal with the questions of effectiveness and relevance. It is not unreasonable to demand that programs have an effect on problems—and the right problems at that. Simply put, the most basic objective of a program evaluation is to assay the impact of a program on its target problem.

Program evaluations, while usually undertaken by the executive and legislative branches of government, are sometimes even done by the courts in response to petitions by client groups. While the three regular branches of government are heavily involved in evaluation, so too is the so-called "fourth branch of government": the press. It conducts evaluations with every exposé of a mismanaged agency. However, journalistic evaluations often tend to be too superficial to serve as instruments of reform, although they do serve to provide impetus for full-scale evaluation efforts by others.

Feedback The public policy cycle comes full circle when evaluative information creates new agenda items for subsequent decisions. This is called feedback because the new information feeds back into its original source. In its purest form feedback can either drive new items onto the policy agenda or reshape issues that are already being considered. But remember, everything about this cycle is impacted by politics. This is because the whole process takes place in a political environment, as shown in Figure 2.1.

Efficiency ■ Competence as well as speed in performance. Americans have historically been suspicious of a too-efficient government, feeling that a truly efficient administration of public affairs could eventually eat into political liberties.

Effectiveness ■ The extent to which an organization accomplishes some predetermined goal or objective; more recently, the overall performance of an organization from the viewpoint of some strategic constituency.

Audit ■ The final phase of the government budgetary process, which reviews the operations of an agency, especially its financial transactions, to determine whether the agency has spent its money in accordance with the law, in the most efficient manner, and with desired results.

Throw the rascals out ■
An oft-heard campaign slogan of the party not in power. Sometimes all it really means is that it is time for a change of rascals.

Feedback is effective to the extent that it is noisy. The people who set the goals and make the decisions must hear it. Sometimes feedback is heard as a complaint about slow service or poor-quality products. Sometimes it is the silent noise of the citizens voting to **throw the rascals out.**

POWER—THE EXTERNAL PERSPECTIVE

Power is the ability or the right to exercise authority over others. Traditionally, according to the founder of the People's Republic of China, Mao Zedong, "Political power grows out of the barrel of a gun." More recently power has been residing in the checkbooks of large corporations and influential lobbyists. Those with traditional power or the power to make large campaign contributions get to make or heavily influence public policy. Whether they do it with a gun or a check is dependent on local conditions. The world is organized into an immense **hierarchy** of power: Political leaders have power over their followers, managers over their workers, and parents over their children. We are all subject to the powers that be that force us to work or school and constrain us from straying too far from what is expected.

Hierarchy ■
Any ordering of persons, things, or ideas by rank or level. The administrative structures are typically hierarchical in that each level has authority over levels below and must take orders from levels above.

One of the best ways to visualize and understand an administrator's power environment is to do a force field analysis of the pressures that bear on any agency. Field theory originated in physics. It was borrowed by psychology to explain how an individual's behavior at any given time is the result of his or her personality interacting with the psychological forces in the environment. Organizational analysts refocused field theory from the individual to the group, the group that made up an organization. By systematically examining all of the forces—all of the powers—in the organization's field (meaning environment)—thus a force field analysis—they were better able to understand why the organization acted the way it did. Those wishing to understand why a government or an agency does seemingly irrational or contradictory things use a force field analysis to arrive at an explanation. For example, the federal government has a variety of laws and programs designed to prevent people from smoking tobacco. It forbids cigarette advertising on television and demands health warnings on tobacco products. But at the same time it encourages the growing of tobacco by American farmers and the sale of tobacco overseas by American companies. Thus the federal government is at the same time both for and against the use of tobacco.

This contradictory policy seems silly on the surface. But the forces of good health work their will on the system to curtail tobacco use at the same time that the forces of commerce work their will on the system to encourage profit from tobacco—and the latter were here first. The obnoxious weed was introduced to Europe by none other than Christopher Columbus. For hundreds of years tobacco has been a major part of the economic foundation of colonial and later republican America. Only in the 1960s did the government "discover" the health hazards related to it. But by then it was just so profitable in terms of **excise tax** yields to both federal and state governments that forbidding the sale on health grounds would mean higher taxes elsewhere. Besides, an illegal market for tobacco would immediately arise in its place, as it did with alcohol during the era of prohibition, thus yielding "tax" revenues only to the smugglers.

Excise tax ■
A tax on the manufacture, sale, or consumption of a product such as gasoline or tobacco.

This all goes to show how governments as well as people get addicted to ad-dictive substances. We as citizens are all addicted in the sense that we depend on smokers to disproportionately pay taxes for their vice and then graciously die pre-maturely without collecting their fair share of Social Security retirement benefits. What self-sacrificing patriots they are! The same can be said of alcoholics. Here we have **public choice economics** in action. The citizen smoker (or drinker), as the sovereign consumer, makes intelligent (or stupid) choices in the marketplace of products and ideas. If you feel this is irrational, you are right—but it is political, too. To understand why administration is so often irrational, we have to look at some of the underlying premises of American government.

Pluralism

The "problem" begins with the fact that American government is inherently pluralistic—composed of multiple elements. First, its constitutional arrange-ment requires a separation of powers, the allocation of powers among the three branches of government so that they are a check on each other. This separation, in theory, makes a tyrannical concentration of power impossible. The U.S. Constitu-tion contains provisions in separate articles for three branches of government—legislative, executive, and judicial. There is a significant difference in the grants of power to these branches: The first article, dealing with legislative power, vests in Congress "all legislative powers herein granted"; the second article vests "the executive power" in the president; and the third article states that "the judicial power of the United States shall be vested in one Supreme Court, and in such in-ferior courts as the Congress may from time to time ordain and establish." Justice Louis D. Brandeis offered the opinion of the U.S. Supreme Court in the 1926 case *Myers v. United States*: "The doctrine of the separation of powers was adopted by the Convention of 1787, not to promote efficiency but to preclude the exercise of arbitrary power. The purpose was not to avoid friction, but, by means of the inevi-table friction incident to the distribution of the governmental powers among three departments, to save the people from autocracy." The "friction" that Brandeis re-fers to is not the friction inherent in implementation that Clausewitz analyzed but the friction of conflict caused by independent power.

Second, American political processes, being inherently pluralistic, emphasize the role of competitive groups in society. Pluralism assumes that power will shift from group to group as elements in the mass public transfer their allegiance in re-sponse to their perceptions of their individual interests. In his book *Who Governs?*, Robert Dahl established key tenets of the pluralist perspective. According to Dahl, pluralism involves varying degrees of political engagement among citizens, with the ability of individuals to impact political decisions in selected areas of public policy. However, according to **power-elite theory**, if democracy is defined as pop-ular participation in public affairs, then pluralist theory is inadequate as an expla-nation of modern U.S. government. Pluralism, according to this view, offers little direct participation, because the elite structure is closed, pyramidal, consensual, and unresponsive. Society is thus divided into two classes: the few who govern and the many who are governed. So pluralism is covert elitism instead of a practical solution to preserve democracy in a mass society.

Public choice economics ■ - An approach to public administration and politics based on microeconomic theory that views the citizen as a consumer of government goods and services. It would attempt to maximize administrative responsiveness to citizen demand by creating a market system for government activities in which public agencies would compete to provide citizens with goods and services.

Power-elite theory ■ - The belief that the United States is basically ruled by a political, military, and business elite whose decisional powers essentially preempt the democratic process. C. Wright Mills (1916–1962) wrote in *The Power Elite* that "the leading men in each of the three domains of power—the warlords, the corporation chieftains, the political directorate—tend to come together to form the power elite of America."

BOX 2.2 | James Madison on Angels and the Separation of Powers

Ambition must be made to counteract ambition. The interest of the man must be connected with the constitutional rights of the place. It may be a reflection on human nature that such devices should be necessary to control the abuses of government. But what is government itself but the greatest of all reflections on human nature? If men were angels, no government would be necessary. If angels were to govern men, neither external nor internal controls on government would be necessary. In framing a government which is to be administered by men over men, the great difficulty lies in this: you must first enable the government to control the governed; and in the next place oblige it to control itself. A dependence on the people is, no doubt, the primary control on the government; but experience has taught mankind the necessity of auxiliary precautions. ◣

Source: James Madison, *The Federalist*, No. 51 (1788)

Those who subscribe to elite theory often have a paranoid political orientation, the belief that there is a nationwide conspiracy against them. Examples include homosexuals who believe that AIDS was "invented" by the government to destroy them, African-Americans who believe that the drug epidemic is encouraged by the government to hurt them, right-wing militia members who believe that the federal government is conspiring to confiscate all firearms in the hands of the citizens, and politicians who—especially during the Cold War—believed that a communist conspiracy was on the verge of taking over the country. In the wake of Hurricane Katrina, there has been considerable discussion that the failure of the levees and the slow government response were part of an intentional plot to eradicate the large African-American population in New Orleans.

This concept was first identified in 1965 by historian Richard Hofstadter in *The Paranoid Style in American Politics*. He found that "there is a vital difference between the paranoid spokesman in politics and the clinical paranoiac: although they both tend to be overheated, oversuspicious, overaggressive, grandiose, and apocalyptic in expression." However, "the clinical paranoid sees the hostile and conspiratorial world in which he feels himself to be living as directed specifically against him, whereas the spokesman of the paranoid style finds it directed against a nation, a culture, a way of life whose fate affects not himself alone but millions of others."

Perhaps the most significant example of the paranoid style in contemporary American politics involves the actions of President Bush leading up to the war in Iraq. President Bush justified the war in Iraq in 2003 partly on the assertion that Iraq had weapons of mass destruction (nuclear, biological, or chemical weapons) and that it was on the verge of using them against the United States or its allies. When no such weapons were found after allied forces occupied Iraq, Bush opponents started to assert with ever-increasing intensity that the president purposely lied to gain public acceptance for the war. Many of them contend that the president knowingly gave false reasons to the Congress and the American public for starting a major war. Bush and his defenders maintained that the problem was just faulty intelligence. Besides, they argued, the war was justifiable on many other grounds as well. Nevertheless, a significant proportion of the U.S. and world population continue to believe that Bush consciously lied about this. Is this an example of the paranoid style at work?

Finally, pluralism has a cultural dimension. Those who espouse this believe that a nation's overall welfare is best served by preserving ethnic cultures rather than by encouraging the integration and blending of cultures. This is in contrast to the assimilationist belief that all immigrants should take their turn in a national melting pot and come out homogenized. But studies have consistently shown this not to be the case. Historian Carl N. Degler wrote, "The metaphor of the melting pot is unfortunate and misleading. A more accurate analogy would be a salad bowl, for, though the salad is an entity, the lettuce can still be distinguished from the chicory, the tomatoes from the cabbage." In recent years the term has become less fashionable and has been replaced in political rhetoric by the image of a mosaic. Without using the term, then Speaker of the House Newt Gingrich resurrected the melting pot concept in 1995 when he asserted that America is a distinct civilization—and that the way for immigrants to become "civilized" is to accept the mainstream "melting pot" values.

Melting pot ■
A sociological term that implies that (1) each succeeding wave of immigrants to the United States blends into the general society and (2) this melting is ideally what should happen.

Group Theory

The importance of pluralism and the significance of groups in the democratic political process has been recognized for more than two thousand years: Aristotle noted that political associations were both significant and commonplace because of the "general advantages" that members obtained. One of the first specific references to groups in the American political process was James Madison's famous discussion of factions in *The Federalist*, No. 10 (1787). In Madison's view, the group was inherent in the nature of people, and its causes were unremovable. Therefore, the only choice was to control the effects of group pressure and power. A more elaborate discussion of group theory can be traced to John C. Calhoun's 1853 treatise *A Disquisition on Government*. While essentially an argument for the protection of minority interests, the treatise suggested that ideal governance must deal with all interest groups, because they represent the legitimate interests of the citizens. If all groups participated on some level of parity within the policymaking process, then all individual interests would be recognized by the policymakers.

Modern group theory has taken greater impetus from the work of **Arthur F. Bentley, David B. Truman,** and **Earl Latham.** Latham viewed the legislature as the referee of the group struggle, responsible for "ratifying the victories of the successful coalitions and recording the terms of the surrenders, compromises, and conquests in the form of statutes." The function of bureaucrats is quite different, however. They are like "armies of occupation left in the field to police the rule won by the victorious coalition." Although Latham's description was aimed primarily at regulatory agencies, he saw the bureaucrat being deluged by the losing coalitions of groups for more favorable actions despite the general rules established. The result is that "agencies are constantly besought and importuned to interpret their authorities in favor of the very groups for the regulation of which they were originally granted."

Arthur F. Bentley (1870–1957) ■
The political scientist who was the intellectual creator of modern interest group theory.

David B. Truman (1913–2003) ■
A political scientist whose principal work, *The Governmental Process* (1951), views group interaction as the real determinant of public policy.

Earl Latham (1907–1977) ■
The group theorist whose *The Group Basis of Politics* (1952) asserted that government itself is a group just like the various private groups attempting to access the policy process.

Latham distinguished three types of groups, based on phases of development: *incipient, conscious,* and *organized.* An incipient group is one "where the interest exists but is not recognized" by the potential members; a conscious group is one "in which the community sense exists but which has not become organized"; and finally an organized group is "a conscious group which has established an objective and formal apparatus to promote the common interest." Latham's incipient and conscious groups are essentially the same as Truman's potential groups, which always exist but do not come together until there is a felt need for action on an issue.

The concept of potential groups keeps the bureaucratic policymaking process honest (or perhaps balanced), given the possibility that new groups might surface or some issues may influence decision making. The potential groups concept also serves as a counterargument to the claim that group theory is undemocratic. Once the concept of potential group is married to the active role of organized groups, the claim can be made, in Truman's words, that "all interests of society by definition are taken into account in one form or another by the institutions of government" (see Figure 2.3).

So much for the theory. The problem is that, according to political scientist Theodore J. Lowi, too much public authority is parceled out to private interest groups, resulting in a weak, decentralized government incapable of long-range planning. Powerful interest groups operate to promote private goals but do not compete to promote the public interest. Government becomes not an institution that makes hard choices among conflicting values but a holding company for interests. These interests are promoted by alliances of interest groups, relevant government agencies, and the appropriate legislative **committees** in each issue area. This is furthered by cozy triangles, the mutually supportive relations among government agencies, interest groups, and the legislative committee or subcommittee with jurisdiction over their areas of common concern. Such coalitions constantly exchange information, services, and money (in the form of campaign contributions

Committee ■
A subdivision of a legislature that prepares legislation for action by the respective house or that makes investigations as directed by the respective house. Most standing (full) committees are divided into subcommittees, which study legislation, hold hearings, and report their recommendations to the full committee. Only the full committee can report legislation for action by the entire legislature.

FIGURE 2.3
Typical outside forces on a public agency manager

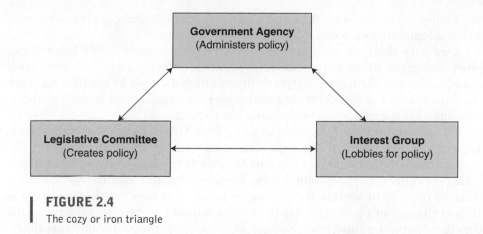

FIGURE 2.4
The cozy or iron triangle

from the interest groups to the members of the legislative committee and budget approval from the committee to the agency). As a whole, they tend to dominate policymaking in their areas of concern. These triangles are considered to be so strong that others elected or appointed to control administrative policy as representatives of the public's interest are effectively prohibited from interfering on behalf of the public (see Figure 2.4).

All government agencies rise and fall, are created or dissolved, in response to an ever-changing external environment made up both of broad historical trends and everyday political maneuvering. NASA is a perfect example of this. It rose in 1958 as the American response to the space race of the Cold War—certainly a broad historical trend. Political maneuvering by cold warriors in the Truman administration allowed Nazi war criminals such as Wernher von Braun, the German rocket scientist, to give American rocketry a decided boost during the early days of the space program. Morality and ethics aside, von Braun and his team of refugees truly were the best rocket scientists available to the United States at the time. Sometimes administrative necessity is as strong a force as **military necessity**. Now that this necessity has lessened in the wake of the Cold War, it is not surprising to find NASA significantly declining in budget and numbers of employees.

POWER—THE INTERNAL PERSPECTIVE

George Orwell was one of the most astute political observers of the twentieth century; however, he was very wrong about one thing. In his book *1984* he wrote that "power is not a means, it is an end" and that "the object of power is power." This highly influential attitude was taken by a man whose only large organizational experience was as a policeman in colonial Burma for a few years in the 1920s, and as the most minor of bureaucrats for little more than a year in the World War II British Broadcasting Corporation (BBC). He loathed the inherent and subtle politics of large bureaucracies—mostly because he saw such wicked ones in the fascist Europe of the World War II era. Indeed, his creation of **Big Brother** in *1984* is the ultimate expression of that loathing. Orwell is a wonderful model for a political writer because he was such a great stylist, but his analysis and disdain of power

Military necessity ■
A justification for actions that violate the laws of war.

Big Brother ■
George Orwell's (1903–1950) symbolization, from his novel *1984* (1949), of government so big and intrusive that it literally oversaw and regulated every aspect of life. The term has evolved to mean any potentially menacing power constantly looking over one's shoulder in judgment.

are hardly useful for would-be and practicing public administrators—because public administration in essence is the exercise of power.

One sure thing about power is that we all understand it. We learn about power in organizations as soon as we go to school. Most of us have a pretty good intuitive grasp of the basic concepts of organizational power by the time we reach the third grade. The newest thing about power in organizations is not our understanding of it but rather our intellectualizing about it.

Discussions of power and politics go back to Aristotle and other writers from antiquity. All of political theory is concerned with the exercise of power. The ancient field of political theory is now frequently applied to the comparatively young concepts of organization theory. Those who would limit themselves to the wisdom of modern writers are putting on intellectual blinders. Remember, it is frequently said of those who rise to rule the nation's largest organizations that they are "natural politicians." Niccolo Machiavelli is the most famous management and political analyst of the Italian Renaissance. His 1513 book of advice to would-be leaders, *The Prince*, is the progenitor of all "how to succeed" books that advocate practical rather than moral actions. In 1967, British Broadcasting Corporation executive Antony Jay reintroduced Machiavelli's concepts to a modern audience with his best selling book *Management and Machiavelli*, which applied Machiavelli's insights for managing a state to the problem of power and politics in organizations. Jay concluded that Machiavelli's principles are as valid now as they were 450 years ago because they are "rooted in human nature." According to Jay, "The new science of management is in fact only a continuation of the old art of government." Consequently, "when you study management theory side by side with political theory, . . . you realize that you are only studying two very similar branches of the same subject."

Ordinary people—as well as scholars—have hesitated to talk about power. For many, power is not a subject for polite conversation. Many of us—including Orwell—have often equated power with force, brutality, unethical behavior, manipulation, connivance, and subjugation. Harvard sociologist Rosabeth Moss Kanter contends that "power is America's last dirty word. It is easier to talk about money—and much easier to talk about sex—than it is to talk about power." Yet we must.

Coalition ■
A temporary joining of political actors to advance legislation or to elect candidates. It is often the case that the actors in a coalition are poles apart on many issues but are able to put their continuing differences aside in the interest of joining to advance (or defeat) the issue at hand.

Organizational Goals

The traditional thinking is that organizations are institutions whose primary purpose is to accomplish established goals. Those goals are set by people in positions of formal authority such as elected officials or appointed agency directors. Thus the primary question for organization managers is how best to design and manage organizations to achieve their declared purposes effectively and efficiently. The personal preferences of organizational members are restrained by systems of formal rules and authority and by norms of rational behavior. But these assumptions about organizations may be naive and unrealistic when organizations are viewed as being complex systems of individuals and **coalitions**, each having its own interests, beliefs, values, preferences, perspectives, and goals. These coalitions—just like the larger group theory of politics—compete with each other continuously for scarce organizational resources. While the battles between groups such as automobile manufacturers and environmentalists over new clean air regulations often play out in the public spotlight, organizational competition is less obvious but every bit as real. The public may not be aware of a deep competition between agencies within the Department of Homeland Security for control over a newly hired group of agents, although such small-scale battles are quite common. Under the reality of scarce resources and individual aspiration, conflict is inevitable. Influence—and the power and political activities through which influence is acquired and maintained—is the primary "weapon" for use in competition and conflicts. Within an organization, this weapon of influence can be based on factors ranging from an employee's knowledge and abilities within a given field to a staff member's skill in "sucking up" to the right people. Therefore, to fully understand an organization, we must get beyond its formally established goals and recognize that power, politics, and influence are critically important and permanent facts of organizational life.

Only rarely are organizational goals established by those in positions of formal authority. Goals result from ongoing maneuvering and bargaining among individuals and transitory coalitions. Just as it is with outside politics in general, coalitions tend to shift with issues. Thus, organizational goals change with shifts in the balance of power among coalitions. Organizational goals are important in the same way organizational power and politics are because they provide the "official" rationale and the legitimacy for resource allocation decisions: who gets which money.

Internal Power Relationships

Power relationships are permanent features of organizations primarily because specialization results in the creation of many interdependent units with varying sizes and degrees of importance that compete with each other for scarce resources. Organization theorist Jeffrey Pfeffer emphasizes this point in his book *Power in Organizations*: "Those persons and those units that have the responsibility for performing the more critical tasks in the organization have a natural advantage in developing and exercising power in the organization. . . . Power is first and foremost a structural phenomenon, and should be understood as such."

Power is related to dependence. Lower-level organizational members have an arsenal of weapons—such as expertise and personal attractiveness—with which to make others dependent on them. Servants who use their cleverness to take advantage of social betters are stock-in-trade in classic drama. This is an intellectualization of something we all know instinctively: that some people are treated like prima donnas or "get away with murder" in organizations because they possess some special skill that gives them power in a specific context. The most ready examples are the characters Hawkeye and Trapper from the *M*A*S*H** movie and television series. If they had not been surgeons badly needed at the battlefront, they would have been court-martialed for their college-boy antics.

Other forms of power and influence often prevail over authority-based power—for example, control over scarce resources (office space, discretionary funds, current and accurate information, and time and skill to work on projects), easy access to others who are perceived as having power (important customers or

◣ IN THE NEWS | Accountability at Walter Reed

All too often, program evaluations come about not as part of the normal process of public administration, but as public scandals exposed by enterprising reporters. This was the case in February 2007 when the *Washington Post* published a series of articles that revealed that some wounded soldiers returning from Iraq for medical treatment were housed in facilities infested with mice and covered in mildew. It seemed all the worse because these facilities, on the grounds of the Walter Reed Army Medical Center, were only a few minute's drive from the White House.

The Congress and the public were outraged. In short order both the general in charge of Walter Reed and the civilian secretary of the U.S. Army were removed from office. For the first time in a war lasting longer than American participation in World War II, a general lost his command for poor performance. While battlefield strategies and tactics are debatable, everybody instantly understood that there was no excuse for housing those honorably wounded in Iraq, many with missing arms and legs, in military slums in suburban Washington, D.C. ◣

clients, members of the board of directors, someone else with formal authority or who controls scarce resources), a central place in a potent coalition, ability to "work the organizational rules" (knowing how to get things done or to prevent others from getting things done), and credibility (believing that one's word can be trusted). Historian Richard E. Neustadt's landmark analysis of the presidency, *Presidential Power*, asserted that a president's real powers are informal, that presidential power is essentially the power to persuade. Neustadt quotes President Harry S. Truman contemplating General of the Army Dwight D. Eisenhower becoming president: "He'll sit here, and he'll say, 'Do this! Do that!' *And nothing will happen.* Poor Ike—it won't be a bit like the Army. He'll find it very frustrating."

Jeffrey Pfeffer defines power as "the ability to get things done the way one wants them done; it is the latent ability to influence people." This definition offers several advantages for understanding organizations. First, it emphasizes the relativity of power. As Pfeffer points out, "Power is context or relationship specific. A person is not 'powerful' or 'powerless' in general, but only with respect to other social actors in a specific social relationship." Pfeffer's phrase "the way one wants them done" is a potent reminder that conflict and the use of power often are over the choice of methods, means, approaches, and/or "turf." They are not limited to battles about outcomes. This point is important because power is often a structural phenomenon—a consequence of organizational specialization. For example, competing organizational coalitions often form around professions: hospital nurses versus paramedics, sociologists versus mathematicians in a university, or business-school-educated staff specialists versus generalists from the "school of hard knocks." Organizational conflicts among people representing different professions, educational backgrounds, sexes, and ages frequently do not involve goals: They center on questions about the "right" of a profession, academic discipline, sex, or age group to exercise its perception of its "professional rights," to control the way things will be done, or to protect its "turf" and status. This point is important because it reemphasizes that organizational behavior and decisions

FIGURE 2.5

Typical inside forces on a public agency manager

frequently are not "rational"—not necessarily directed toward accomplishing the formally stated goals of the organization (see Figure 2.5).

All would-be administrators should be aware of the personal danger in possessing significant power. Say the word "power," and half the people hearing it will immediately think of **Lord Acton**'s 1887 statement that "power tends to corrupt and absolute power corrupts absolutely." Certainly men such as Hitler, Napoleon, Stalin, and Mao all grew more grossly corrupt the longer they held power. But petty tyrants grow proportionately corrupt. Perhaps the best advice on handling power came from Harry Truman in *Plain Speaking*: "If a man can accept a situation in a place of power with the thought that it's only temporary, he comes out all right. But when he thinks that he is the cause of the power, that can be his ruination."

Lord Acton (1834–1904) ■
English historian; original name was John Dahlberg.

THE CULTURES OF PUBLIC ORGANIZATIONS

Administrative institutions are part of the greater culture of their society at the same time that they develop and nurture their own organizational cultures. We learn how to cope in these differing worlds almost instinctively from childhood. How we act in school or at home (each a relatively closed organization) is different from how we act on the street—in the outside world. This is a recognition that each culture demands different behaviors. Thus we talk differently to our friends on the street than we do to our parents or teachers. This literally acculturates us to the fact that each time we join another organization—whether for work, worship, or weight lifting—we expect to—and are usually eager to—learn the new jargon and accepted ways of the new group's culture. To talk of the "two cultures" of public organizations is a gross oversimplification. There is an almost infinite variety of public organization cultures. However, they all have this in common: They interact with the outside environment of the overall culture. In this sense alone it can be said that all public organizations must deal with two cultures: their unique internal culture and the common outside culture.

The Outside Cultural Environment

Citizenship ◼
The dynamic relation between a citizen and his or her nation. The concept of citizenship involves rules of what a citizen might do (such as vote), must do (pay taxes), and can refuse to do (pledge allegiance). Increasingly, the concept involves benefits or entitlements that a citizen has a right to demand from government. In some jurisdictions, citizenship is a requirement for public employment. Citizenship also requires loyalty to and primary residency in one's state.

Police ◼
Paramilitary state and local government organizations whose most basic responsibilities include maintaining public order and safety (through the use of force if necessary), investigating and arresting persons accused of crimes, and securing the cooperation of the citizenry. The term *police*, while referring to all law enforcement officers in general, is usually a reference to municipal law enforcement officers. County officers are sheriffs; state officers are usually called the state police, state troopers, or highway patrol.

Public management is constantly being judged in the wrong context. It is erroneously viewed as a public sector counterpart to industrial management systems. The private sector analogy holds true only for a portion of the total public management function, and the size of that portion depends on the degree to which the administrative operations of the jurisdiction are politicized. Thus public sector operations cannot be properly understood or evaluated outside the political context—the political culture—of the host jurisdiction.

The determinant of any community's attitudes toward the quality and vigor of its governing institutions is the political culture of the geographic area concerned. Political culture is that part of the overall societal culture that determines a community's attitudes toward the quality, style, and vigor of its political processes and government operations. The only way to explain the extreme variations in public bureaucracies is by examining the cultural context of the host jurisdictions. The quality of bureaucratic operations measured by levels of citizen satisfaction, efficiency, or corruption varies for a variety of reasons—not the least of which is the substantial disagreement on just what constitutes a quality operation. But the quality or style of operations is determined only in the lesser part by critics and public officials; the crucial determinant is the political will of the community. It determines the values and resources to be applied to any given public problem, it helps establish the obligations of **citizenship**, and it establishes the parameters of activities in which an official may participate.

Even when corruption is rife, it is the political culture that sets the limits and direction of such dishonesty. For example, James Q. Wilson, in *Varieties of Police Behavior*, demonstrates that the style of **police** operations in eight communities reflected not some abstract standard of quality or professionalism but the expressed and/or implied desires of the community. Thus the police were either exceedingly lenient or exceedingly strict with minor legal violations, depending on the perceived degree of community concern one way or the other. Wilson considers a police department to have a "watchman" style of performance if it is one in which order maintenance is perceived to be the prime function of the department. Such a police operation will tend to ignore law infringements that do not involve "serious" crimes, such as minor traffic violations, bookmaking, and illegal church bingo. Of course, all these activities or nonactivities are subject to occasional crackdowns. The police periodically shut down illegal gambling operations in response to the political needs of the police chief or mayor. The thrust of the "watchman" style is to maintain order, to ensure a smooth, nondisruptive running of the community or bureaucracy. Legal considerations and official operating mandates are paramount only when the "heat" is on. Of course, the standard operating procedures of police will tend to be more legalistic in communities that are so disposed.

Cultural Values and Administration While a community's political culture is seldom articulated, it nevertheless serves as a source of definition. By determining the values to be applied to any given problem, the political culture ensures that the decisional process is filtered through its value system before administrative action is taken. How values influence administrative actions is illustrated by

George Orwell's 1936 essay "Shooting an Elephant." In 1920s Burma, where Orwell was a police officer representing the British colonial administration, trained elephants were used for moving heavy logs. When an elephant suddenly disdained his domesticated labors in the timber industry and went on a rampage, it was the job of the local cop on the beat, in this case Orwell, to shoot him. The problem was that by the time Orwell and the local onlookers caught up with the elephant chronicled in the essay, it was peacefully eating grass and no danger to anyone. But an ever-increasing crowd expected this lone officer, this symbol of imperial presence, to act decisively. "A sahib [a master] has got to act like a sahib; he has got to appear resolute, to know his own mind and do definite things." Orwell was expected by the prevailing culture to shoot the elephant. Orwell says he felt like "an absurd puppet" who was being "pushed to and fro by the will of those" villagers. Despite the fact that there was no public safety reason to do so, he shoots and kills the elephant "solely to avoid looking a fool." The culture made him do it. Of course, today's attitudes are radically different, and it is almost unthinkable that a police officer anywhere in the world would feel pressured to kill any endangered species—let alone a nonthreatening elephant.

The United States is so vast and geographically diverse that while there is an overall American political culture, it is often less influential than the local political subcultures of the individual states and regions. Differing sources of political culture, such as race, ethnicity, and religion, combine with historical patterns of political behavior to yield the distinct political cultures of, for example, the Rocky Mountain West or the Deep South. All political cultures change—some more quickly than others. Germany and Japan have vastly different political cultures today than they did when they were the exemplars of **fascism** prior to and during World War II. In the wake of the Cold War the once communist states of Eastern Europe almost overnight found themselves with new political cultures. The American political culture, with the notable exception of the Civil War of 1861 to 1865, has, in historical terms, been very stable.

The Inside Cultural Environment

An organizational culture—the culture that exists within an organization—is a parallel but smaller version of a societal culture. It is made up of intangible things such as values, beliefs, assumptions, and perceptions. It is the pattern of these beliefs and attitudes that determines members' behaviors in and around the organization, persists over extended periods of time, and pervades all elements of the organization (albeit to different extents and with varying intensity).

An organizational culture is transmitted to new members through socialization (or enculturation) processes; it is maintained and transmitted through a network of rituals and interaction patterns; it is enforced and reinforced by group norms and the organization's system of rewards and controls. It is the unseen and unobservable force that is always behind those organizational activities that can be observed. According to Kilmann and others, "Culture is to the organization what personality is to the individual—a hidden, yet unifying theme that provides meaning, direction, and mobilization."

Fascism ■
A political philosophy that advocates governance by a dictator, assisted by a hierarchically organized, strongly ideological party, in maintaining a totalitarian and regimented society through violence, intimidation, and the arbitrary use of power.

Norms ■
The socially enforced requirements and expectations about basic responsibilities, behavior, and thought patterns of members in their organizational roles.

Organizational culture is created by the attitudes and behaviors of the dominant or early organizational "shapers" and "heroes"; by the nature of the organization's work; and by the attitudes, values, and "willingness to act" of new members. It is transmitted by often-told stories and legends, and by the formal and informal processes of socialization. An organization's culture provides a framework for a shared understanding of events, defines behavioral expectations, serves as a source of and focus for members' commitment, and acts as an organizational "control system" (i.e., through group norms). But while a strong organizational culture can control organizational behavior, it can also block an organization from making those decisions needed to adapt to a changing environment.

Organizational culture is particularly useful as an intellectual construct because it helps us to understand or predict how an organization will behave under different circumstances. A cultural pattern is similar to a genetic inheritance: Once you know the patterns of basic assumptions, you can anticipate how the organization will act in differing circumstances. Most importantly, if it can be deduced that an organizational culture led to poor performance by an agency, it becomes necessary to find ways to break down the problematic elements of that culture. Such a scenario took place during the examination of intelligence breakdowns that allowed the terrorist attacks of September 11, 2001, to succeed. During joint Senate and House hearings in 2002, heavy criticism was targeted at the FBI for creating and fostering an organizational culture where cooperation between varied divisions within the bureau was not valued. More specifically, the hearings called attention to a culture at the FBI, and a similar culture at the CIA, that did not promote interaction between intelligence officers and law enforcement officials.

Like snowflakes, every organizational culture is different. What has worked repeatedly for one organization may not work for another—so the basic assumptions differ. And every organizational culture is shaped by myriad factors—from the societal culture in which it resides to its technologies and competing organizations. Some organizations have strong, unified, pervasive cultures, whereas others have weaker cultures; often "subcultures" evolve in different functional or geographical areas. The most common example of this last phenomenon is the more formal culture of a headquarters office versus the informality of a field office.

Although phrases such as "organizational culture" and "culture of a factory" can be found in a few books on management written as early as the 1950s (for example, *The Changing Culture of a Factory* by Elliott Jaques, and William H. Whyte Jr.'s book about corporate conformity, *The Organization Man*), few students of management or organizations paid much attention to the nature and content of organizational culture until the late 1970s. Nevertheless, today organizational culture is one of the hottest issues in the field of public administration—so much so that whenever there is an organizational breakdown, people start to shout (figuratively if not literally), "It's the culture!"

Professional Socialization

During the 1960s and early 1970s, several books on organizational and professional socialization processes received wide attention. As useful as these earlier works were, they assumed the presence of organizational or professional cultures and proceeded to examine issues involving the match between individuals and cultures. Two of the more widely read of these were *Boys in White* by Howard Saul Becker et al., which chronicled the processes used to socialize medical students into the medical profession, and Herbert Kaufman's *The Forest Ranger*, a study of how the United States Forest Service developed the "will and capacity to conform" among its remotely stationed rangers. Once again, however, these earlier writings did not address important questions such as how cultures are formed or changed, how cultures affect leadership, or the relationship between culture and strategic planning (establishing organizational directions); rather, they focused on the process of socializing employees into existing organizational cultures and the impacts of existing cultures on organizational members. Without attention paid to the effect of culture on outcomes, important issues can be overlooked. For example, while it's important to understand how an FBI agent is socialized into the bureau, it's probably more important to understand how the organization's culture stressed the examination of crimes after the fact rather than stopping terrorism from occurring in the first place.

An entirely different orientation to organizational culture that focused on symbols started to appear in the late 1970s. Symbols are things such as flags and logos, which carry a wider (or different) meaning than their intrinsic content. For example, the "Stars and Stripes" is symbolic because it embodies values, traditions, and emotions. Symbols also can be things such as words (IBM's famous sign "Think"), phrases (*Semper fidelis*, the motto meaning "Always faithful" of the U.S. Marine Corps), and organizational structures. Because the top or seventh floor is the location of the highest officials of the U.S. Department of State, policy is frequently said to come from the "seventh floor"—not from any particular official. Similarly, the White House is a building that can, as a symbol, speak. Reporters and political commentators frequently state that the "White House said" this or that. The building speaks because it is the architectural embodiment of the bureaucratic institution that is the modern presidency. Thus the building speaks through press releases, news conferences, deep as well as shallow background briefings, and **leaks**. While the president is the main and most desired speaker, the few hundred other people who work there also give it voice.

Romanticized stories about organizational heroes and ritualistic ceremonies can also be symbols, if they carry meanings that go beyond their intrinsic content. Military medals and other types of organizational awards for unusual achievement are a major example. When a member of Napoléon's government described military decorations as "baubles," Napoléon replied, "You are pleased to call them 'baubles.' Well, it is with 'baubles' that mankind is governed." Wise managers will create multiple opportunities to use symbols to motivate, inspire, and thank their employees.

Symbolic Management

The manipulation of symbols and the **dramaturgy** of symbolic acts are essential elements of managing people in organizations. While such manipulations may be conscious or unconscious on the part of management, they are invariably there. Frequently, symbolic acts are easily identifiable because of their obvious **beau geste** quality. They form an integral part of everyday manners and courtesies. When an

Leaks ■
The deliberate disclosure of confidential or classified information by someone in government who wants to advance the public interest, embarrass a bureaucratic rival, or help a reporter disclose incompetence or skulduggery to the public.

Dramaturgy ■
The manner in which a person acts out or theatrically stages his or her organizational or political role. Political candidates who make an effort to look or sound senatorial or presidential are engaging in dramaturgy. Of course, if they have to make an effort to look it or sound it, they may not have it. One is reminded of the traditional advice to actors: "Always be sincere. If you can fake that, you've got it made."

Beau geste ■
A noble and/or gracious gesture.

organization's chief executive accidentally meets a lower-echelon employee in a crowded elevator and says, "How's your job coming along?" the executive is not expecting an answer to this question; the words are used simply to communicate sociability—a symbolic ritual. It would be quite out of place and both annoying and surprising to the executive if the employee really answered the question instead of replying with a simple "Fine, thank you." In cases such as these, language ceases being an instrument of communication and becomes a symbol—a thing that carries a different meaning than its intrinsic content.

An act of symbolic management can come in the form of a simple trip by a manager to meet his or her employees. A prime example of symbolic management through appearance is President Barack Obama's visit to the CIA headquarters in 2009. On taking office, Obama had pledged to make public memos that chronicled the use of controversial interrogation techniques by CIA agents, thus causing significant concern among the personnel of the nation's chief spy agency. To help bolster morale at the agency and to reduce anxiety that the new president was making CIA agents scapegoats for past policy failures, President Obama made a trip to the agency's Langley, Virginia, facilities to directly address the agents. While his words to the CIA staff were quite conciliatory, his very presence on their "home turf" sent a symbolic message that he values their work and that he will not desert them as they fight terrorism.

Symbolic management attracted only limited attention during the 1970s. The turning point for the organizational culture (and symbolism) perspective did not arrive until the early 1980s. Then, almost overnight, organizational culture became a very hot topic in books, journals, and periodicals aimed at both management practitioners and academicians. Because of the youthfulness of organizational culture as a perspective, minimal consensus exists about much of anything concerned with it. There are only a few organizational culture issues on which there is widespread agreement, including the following:

1. Organizational cultures exist.
2. Each organizational culture is relatively unique.
3. Organizational culture is a socially constructed concept.
4. Organizational culture provides its members with a way of understanding and making sense of events and symbols.
5. Organizational culture, because of its ability to informally approve or disapprove of behavior, can be a powerful tool for guiding organizations.

Each organization has its own unique culture that determines how it will respond to the same stimuli. At the Pentagon, the story is often told about how the same words can have vastly different meanings in different organizations. A good example is the use of the word *secure* in the U.S. Department of Defense. If the U.S. Army is told to secure a particular building, it will post guards at all the entrances and exits. The U.S. Marine Corps, given the same instructions, will assault the building until everyone inside surrenders. And the U.S. Air Force will achieve its mission to secure the building by negotiating a three-year lease with the owners.

Because the same words used in different organizational cultures can mean radically different outcomes, all would-be managers must be aware that organizational culture is not just something we live in. J. Steven Ott, a professor at the University of Utah, elaborates on this idea in *The Organizational Culture Perspective*. Managers must use organizational culture "as a frame of reference for the way one looks at, attempts to understand, and works with organizations." Thus, even though the vocabulary may be the same, the meaning of words in their organizational context may require a manager to effectively learn a new language. Any manager who doesn't learn to "walk the walk" and "talk the talk" is walking and talking alone—not managing.

A CASE STUDY: | Were the Space Shuttle Astronauts Killed by Fog?

In 1961 President John F. Kennedy told a joint session of Congress, "This nation should commit itself to achieving the goal, before this decade is out, of landing a man on the moon and returning him safely to the Earth." As with much grand policymaking, this was easy enough to say. Few believed that the National Aeronautics and Space Administration (NASA), the federal agency created in 1958 to beat the Soviet Union in the Cold War space race, could achieve this "man on the moon" goal in the allotted time.

NASA not only won the space race, but it became the national exemplar of managerial excellence—at least until a clear day in January 1986 when the space shuttle *Challenger* blasted off into the Florida skies to become a now classic example of managerial incompetence. The shuttle, with six astronauts and New Hampshire schoolteacher Christa McAuliffe aboard, blew up 73 seconds after liftoff because an O-ring seal on one of the booster rockets failed. Yet this was not a complete surprise to anyone who followed the shuttle program in the news media. It was widely reported that such seals nearly failed on earlier shuttle flights. They were most likely to fail when the outside air temperature was close to freezing, as it was on the day of the *Challenger* launch. The problem seems so obvious now. NASA managers had more information than they could adequately process. So while the skies were sunny when the *Challenger* last "slipped the surly bonds of Earth," it can be said that the crew truly died from fog— caused by a blinding array of information that led to a faulty decision by public administrators.

The "fog of war" is the wonderfully descriptive phrase for the confusion and uncertainty that is inherent in combat. Prussian General Karl von Clausewitz originated this meteorological metaphor in his 1832 classic on military strategy *On War*. It is as if a literal fog descends on the battlefield and blinds the combatants to what the enemy and even other elements of their own forces are doing. In the days of black powder, the fog was almost as literal as it was proverbial.

Today, wherever far-flung or large-scale operations have to be coordinated, whether military or managerial, fog or uncertainty is a possibility. The field of management information systems has grown up in recent decades to reduce the inevitable fog to manageable proportions. But the reduction mechanisms

(continued)

A CASE STUDY | Continued

themselves—computer data and memoranda in a seemingly endless stream—often create more problems than the fog they were designed to dispel.

And sometimes the fog is made all the more blinding by political considerations. It was not just that NASA had developed an organizational culture that inhibited bad news from getting to the top in a timely manner. Those who decided to launch that day were under the most exquisitely subtle political pressures as well. If the shuttle had kept its schedule on that ill-fated day, it would have returned in time for Ms. McAuliffe—who had been selected in a highly publicized national search—to sit in the balcony of the chamber of the House of Representatives during the State of the Union speech while President Ronald Reagan pointed her out as an inspiration to the nation and all those desirous of winning lotteries.

Of course, as soon as the accident occurred, all those responsible went into deep denial. Top NASA managers denied having heard of O-ring problems. The White House denied it put any pressure on NASA that would compromise safety. To sort out the denials and gather the facts, the Presidential Commission on the Space Shuttle *Challenger* Accident was promptly appointed. Six months later the commission reported that the failure of the O-ring seals was the physical cause of the *Challenger* explosion. But it also declared that the "decision to launch the *Challenger* was flawed." It further concluded that "if the decision makers had known all the facts, it is highly unlikely that they would have decided to launch." In essence, the commission found that the NASA managers responsible for the launch decision were ignorant—because they were blinded by the fog of competing information.

The commission's report also absolved managers of succumbing to political pressures to prove that shuttle flights were routine and routinely on schedule. It simply denied that there were any political pressures. This was only polite. It certainly would have been unusual for a presidential commission to criticize the president who appointed it. But denial fooled no one and only made them look foolish. According to Barbara Romzek and Melvin Dubnick, writing in *Public Administration Review*, political "pressures existed and came from a variety of sources outside of NASA, including the White House." Charles Peters of *The Washington Monthly* reported that "top NASA officials didn't want to hear the bad news [about the O-rings] because they were determined to launch the next day so that President Reagan could point to this accomplishment in his State of the Union message. They had even written a suggested insert for the speech."

Good managers with the facts before them can make good decisions. However, good managers with an overwhelming volume of data to digest often become unable to make timely or wise decisions; they are reduced to incompetence by the efforts to make them more competent. We live in a contradictory world when the fog does not come in, as poet Carl Sandburg suggests, "on little cat feet," but rides on the crest of an endless wave of computer printouts. The *Challenger* disaster leads an infinite list of things gone wrong despite the best efforts of highly talented and otherwise able individuals—people who have banded together to create an organization that as a whole is less talented than the sum of its very talented human parts.

And just how did NASA respond to this problem of perceived incompetence? A few weeks after the *Challenger* disaster, NASA awarded bonuses to dozens of its top managers for the excellent work they had done. The media made a big joke of this by pointing out the incongruity of giving $10,000 bonuses to members of a team that couldn't "shuttle straight." NASA managers promptly complained that they shouldn't all be punished for the screwups of a few. True, the O-ring failed, but the other 30,000 parts of the shuttle worked just fine!

Even the best-run organization, of which NASA is still an example, can be befuddled by fog. As with real weather, this kind of fog is a sometimes thing. It can be disrupted by more effective management information systems, by supportive organizational cultures, and by determined top managers. The best managers will use a bout of fog as a learning experience—as an opportunity to change their information system, organization culture, and decisional processes so this particular bad weather can never happen again. That is exactly what NASA has proceeded to do. But then NASA failed again, and for the same reason—fog.

Seventeen years passed and shuttle flights once again seemed to be routine. Then on February 1, 2003, the *Columbia* disintegrated while returning from an otherwise successful mission, killing its seven-member crew. The *Columbia* Accident Investigation Board's August 2003 report stated that while the physical cause of the accident was insulating foam from an external fuel tank that damaged a wing during launch, "the organizational causes of this accident are rooted in the Space Shuttle Program's history and culture." It turned out that, as with the O-ring problem, many people also knew of the insulating foam problem, but the fog created by the culture—once again—prevented that information from getting to the appropriate decision makers. In response to the Accident Investigation Board's findings, NASA set out to change its safety culture in order to avoid the fatal errors associated with the *Challenger* and *Columbia* missions. The results of this overhaul could be seen during the 2005 flight of the shuttle *Discovery*. During the first flight since the *Columbia* failure, *Discovery*'s crew was prepared to make in-flight repairs to the shuttle on damage sustained during the launch.

For Discussion: *Why are all large organizations so susceptible to Clausewitz's fog? Are political pressures for performance a common or an uncommon part of public administration?* ▸

SUMMARY

Public administration is an instrument of policy. But public policymaking in republican government is constrained by the very nature of republican institutions. Executive leadership is inherently limited, both by the leader's philosophic views on how to exercise power and the legal constraints of constitutional checks and balances.

Public policymaking is cyclical. As policy decisions are made and implemented, criticism in the form of feedback puts new decisions on the policy agenda. This starts the policymaking cycle all over again. While decisions can be radical departures for the current situation, they are most likely to be incremental.

Public processes, whether public policymaking or public administration, take place within a polity, an overarching political jurisdiction. All public managers have two polities with which to contend—internal (their agency) and external (the outside political world).

Just as public policy and administration exists in two polities, it has a similar double life as a culture. It is part of the greater culture of its society at the same time that it develops and nurtures its own organizational cultures.

REVIEW QUESTIONS

1. What are the major checks on the American president's power to wage war?
2. What are the differences among the three major views of executive power: restricted, prerogative, and stewardship?
3. What are the major elements in the public policymaking cycle and how do they interact?
4. How does the pluralistic notion of the American political process influence public agency managers?
5. What is the difference between the internal and external cultures of public organizations?

KEY CONCEPTS

Agenda setting   The process by which ideas or issues bubble up through the various political channels to wind up for consideration by a political institution such as a legislature or court.

Implementation   Putting a government program into effect; the total process of translating a legal mandate, whether an executive order or an enacted statute, into appropriate program directives and structures that provide services or create goods.

Incremental decision-making model   A view of the public policymaking process that assumes that small decisions made at the margins of problems are the usual reality of change.

Organizational culture   The culture that exists within an organization; a parallel but smaller version of a societal culture.

Pluralism   A theory of government that attempts to reaffirm the democratic character of society by asserting that open, multiple, competing, and responsive groups preserve traditional democratic values in a mass industrial state. Pluralism assumes that power will shift from group to group as elements in the mass public transfer their allegiance in response to their perceptions of their individual interests.

Political culture   That part of the overall societal culture that determines a community's attitudes toward the quality, style, and vigor of its political processes and government operations.

Program evaluation The systematic examination of any activity undertaken by government to make a determination about its effects, both short term and long range.

Public program All those activities designed to implement a public policy; often this calls for the creation of organizations, public agencies, and bureaus.

Rational decision-making model A view of the public policymaking process that assumes complete information and a systematic, logical, and comprehensive approach to change.

Separation of powers The allocation of powers among the three branches of government so that they are a check on each other. This separation, in theory, makes a tyrannical concentration of power impossible.

MySearchLab® EXERCISES

Apply what you learned in this chapter on MySearchLab (*www.mysearchlab.com*).

BIBLIOGRAPHY

The 9/11 Commission. (2004). *The 9/11 Commission Report: Final Report of the National Commission on Terrorist Attacks upon the United States*. United States Government Printing Office: Washington, DC.

Becker, H. S., et al. (1961). *Boys in White: Student Culture in Medical School*. Chicago: University of Chicago Press.

Bell, Daniel. (1960). *End of Ideology: On the Exhaustion of Political Ideas in the Fifties*. Glencoe, IL: Free Press.

Bemis, Samuel Flagg. (1956). *John Quincy Adams and the Union*. New York: Knopf.

Boorstin, Daniel J. (1961). *The Image: A Guide to Pseudo-Events in America*. New York: Atheneum.

Congressional Research Service. (1993). The Intelligence Community and 9/11: Congressional Hearings and the Status of the Investigation. http://www.fas.org/irp/crs/RL31650.pdf.

Dahl, Robert A., and Charles E. Lindblom. (1953). *Politics, Economics, and Welfare*. Chicago: University of Chicago Press.

Degler, Carl. (1970). *Out of Our Past*. New York: Harper and Row.

Downs, Anthony. (1972). "Up and Down with Ecology—The Issue-Attention Cycle." *Public Interest* 28 (summer).

Easton, David. (1963). *A Systems Analysis of Political Life*. New York: Atherton.

Etzioni, Amitai. (1967). "Mixed Scanning: A 'Third' Approach to Decision Making," *Public Administration Review* (December).

Galbraith, John Kenneth. (1956). *American Capitalism*. Boston: Houghton Mifflin.

Gingrich, Newt. (1995). *To Renew America*. New York: HarperCollins.

Hofstadter, Richard. (1965). *The Paranoid Style in American Politics*. New York: Knopf.

Jaques, Elliott. (1951). *The Changing Culture of a Factory*. London: Tavistock Institute.

Jones, Charles O. (1977). *An Introduction to the Study of Public Policy,* 2nd ed. North Scituate, MA: Duxbury Press.

Joseph, Peter. (1974). *Good Times: An Oral History of America in the Nineteen Sixties*. New York: William Morrow.

Kanter, Rosabeth Moss. (1979). "Power Failure in Management Circuits." *Harvard Business Review* (July–August).

Kaufman, Herbert. (1960). *The Forest Ranger*. Baltimore: Johns Hopkins University Press.

Kilmann, R. H., et al., eds. (1985). *Gaining Control of the Corporate Culture*. San Francisco: Jossey-Bass.

Kingdon, John W. (1995). *Agendas, Alternatives, and Public Policies,* 2nd ed. New York: Longman.

Lasswell, Harold D. (1963). *The Future of Political Science.* New York: Atherton.

———. (1936). *Politics: Who Gets What, When, How.* New York: Smith.

Latham, Earl. (1952). *The Group Basis of Politics.* Ithaca, NY: Cornell University Press.

Lindblom, Charles E. (1959). "The Science of Muddling Through." *Public Administration Review* (spring).

Lipsky, Michael. (1980). *Street-Level Bureaucracy.* New York: Russell Sage Foundation.

Lowi, Theodore, J. (1979). *The End of Liberalism,* 2nd ed. New York: Norton.

Markham, Felix. (1964). *Napoleon.* New York: New American Library.

Miller, Merle. (1974). *Plain Speaking: An Oral Biography of Harry S. Truman.* New York: Berkley.

Mills, C. Wright. (1956). *The Power Elite.* New York: Oxford University Press.

Orwell, George. (1946). *Shooting an Elephant and Other Essays.* New York: Harcourt, Brace.

Ott, J. Steven. (1989). *Organizational Cultural Perspective.* Pacific Grove, CA: Brooks/Cole.

Peters, Charles. (1993). "Tilting at Windmills." *The Washington Monthly* 25 (November).

Pfeffer, Jeffrey. (1981). *Power in Organizations.* Marshfield, MA: Pitman.

Pressman, Jeffrey, and Aaron Wildavsky. (1973). *Implementation.* Berkeley: University of California Press.

Romzek, Barbara S., and Melvin J. Dubnick. (1987). "Accountability in the Public Sector: Lessons from the *Challenger* Tragedy," *Public Administration Review* 47 (May–June).

Sheldon, Michael. (1991). *Orwell.* New York: HarperCollins.

Taft, William Howard. (1916). *Our Chief Magistrate and His Powers.* New York: Columbia University Press.

Whyte, William H., Jr. (1956). *The Organization Man.* New York: Simon and Schuster.

Wilson, James Q. (1968). *Varieties of Police Behavior.* Cambridge, MA: Harvard University Press.

Woodward, Bob, and Carl Bernstein. (1974). *All the President's Men.* New York: Simon and Schuster.

RECOMMENDED BOOKS

Barzelay, Michael. (2001). *The New Public Management: Improving Research and Policy Dialogue.* New York: Columbia University Press. How policymakers should treat the denizens of the bureaucracy.

Bratton, William, with Peter Knobler. (1998). *Turnaround: How America's Top Cop Reversed the Crime Epidemic.* New York: Random House. A biographical account of how the author used modern management techniques to change the organizational culture of four major local police agencies (including the police departments of the cities of Boston and New York); this resulted in greater morale, increased productivity, and less crime.

Heady, Ferrel. (2001). *Public Administration: A Comparative Perspective*, 6th ed. Boca Raton: CRC Press. The standard survey of worldwide public administration, providing both historic and contemporary contexts.

Pipes, Daniel. (1999). *Conspiracy: How the Paranoid Style Flourishes and Where It Comes From.* New York: Free Press. An updating of Richard Hofstadter's 1965 *The Paranoid Style in American Politics.* This volume deals with the latest batch of wacky theories as well as the golden oldies.

Simon, Herbert A. (1997). *Administrative Behavior: A Study of Decision-Making Processes in Administrative Organizations*, 4th ed. New York: Macmillan. The fiftieth anniversary edition of the groundbreaking analysis of how organizations make decisions within the context of their social values.

Stone, Deborah. (2001). *Policy Paradox. The Art of Political Decision Making*, rev. ed. New York: W. W. Norton & Co. A clear discussion of the factors that shape policy decisions with a focus on the nexus between politics and governing.

RELATED WEB SITES

www.cbpp.org
Center on Budget and Policy Priorities
The Center conducts research and analysis to help shape public debates over proposed budget and tax policies and to help ensure that policymakers consider the needs of low-income families. In addition, the Center examines impacts of proposed policies on the health of the economy and the soundness of federal and state budgets. The site offers information about this research as well as links to experts in each field and news about changes in policy due to the Center's research.

www.nasa.gov
National Aeronautics and Space Administration
NASA's Web site offers a look at space up close and personal. It has a large multimedia section pertaining to space and aeronautics. The site also offers details on NASA budgets and program designs.

www.public-policy.org
National Center for Policy Analysis
Site allows you to search for information about public policy by providing links that relate to select areas of policy. This Web site also spotlights individual public opinion institutes across the United States and in Canada.

www.nlc.org
National Civic League
The National League of Cities (NLC) is dedicated to helping city leaders build better communities. The site provides information about possible solutions to common problems facing America's urban areas, and provides overviews of the legislative, regulatory, and legal changes that the NCL endorses.

www.publicagenda.org
Public Agenda Online (PAO)
PAO allows viewers to get critical facts and consider the choices and current public opinion on fundamental problems facing the country. The site has research studies in a wide range of topics.

The Continuous Reinventing of the Machinery of Government

KEYNOTE: The New Feudalism

In 1958, economist John Kenneth Galbraith published *The Affluent Society*. This book described American society as one in which scarcity of resources was not a major problem but where "private affluence and public squalor" existed continuously side by side.

Today, this trend is becoming even more pronounced. Journalists such as Michael Lind are observing a "new feudalism" that "reverses the trend of the past thousand years toward the government's provision of basic public goods such as policing, public roads and transport networks, and public schools." Lind concludes that "in the United States—to a degree unmatched in any other industrialized democracy—these public goods are once again becoming private luxuries."

When public services deteriorate—especially in urban areas—those with enough money, increasingly, buy their way out of the problem. They send their children to private schools and hire private police. And in the best feudal tradition, they retire each night behind walled towns where guards at a gate check the identity of all who seek to enter. And we are not just talking about apartment buildings with doormen. We are talking about millions of citizens living in suburban "gated communities" with their own private police, private streets, and private parks.

While most popular in California, Texas, Arizona, Florida, and Virginia, such private residential communities are springing up throughout the United States, patterned after the comprehensive mini-cities that have long been popular with retirees in the Sunbelt. What is new is that middle- and upper-income families of all ages are opting to pay hefty private taxes (community fees) and submit to stringent environmental regulations to lead the good life away from urban ills. It is estimated that more than 7 million Americans already live in such closed-off communities, and that number is expected to double over the next decade. Ironically, according to political analyst Timothy Egan, "The very things that Republicans in Congress are trying to do away with for the nation as a whole—environmental protection, gun control, heavy regulation—are most pronounced in these predominantly Republican private enclaves."

These new-fashioned feudalists, who are decidedly libertarian concerning the outside world, are surprisingly socialistic concerning the private, inside world of their gated mini-cities. They willingly accept a wide variety of community regulations that they would challenge as unconstitutional in other contexts—from gun control to restrictions on exterior paint colors, lawn maintenance standards, and prohibitions on basketball hoops over garages. Homeowners must abide by common mandates, including the carrying of special identification, getting permission for more than a set number of visitors, and paying user fees for a wide variety of services such as trash collection, cable TV connections, and time on tennis courts.

The new feudalism also extends beyond the guarded gates. During the Middle Ages, many of the castles on the Rhine River in Western Europe were built to enforce the collection of tolls on that portion of the river controlled by a local warlord. Today electronic "castles" are enforcing the collection of tolls on a similarly private means of transport. For example, the California Private Transportation Corporation, with state approval, has built a ten-mile, $128 million, four-lane road in the median strip of an existing but highly congested southern California freeway. This new road is certainly a way to avoid the almost daily commuter grid-lock, but it is not free. Users must have a transponder installed on their vehicle's windshield that can be read by an electronic monitor—the "castle"—as they enter the road. Periodically a computer bills the driver's credit card or mails an old-fashioned paper invoice. Anyone seeking to avoid these silent sentries will have their license plates photographed and face state-sanctioned fines of up to $300.

Gerald S. Pfeffer, the managing director of the corporation that owns the new road, explains his company's philosophy: "We're another example of private enterprise filling a gap in government services—the Federal Express of roads." But critics complain that the highway is elitist in that people who can afford the $2.50 rush-hour toll speed along in their luxury cars, while those who can't afford an extra $5.00 a day—more than $1,000 a year—for the round trip must creep along with the poor on the old public freeway. Pfeffer sees nothing wrong with that: "You get what you pay for—the great American way." Besides, toll roads and bridges have long been common in the United States. What is new here is someone collecting tolls for profits and not for governments.

Millions of citizens obviously feel that having private police, roads, and parks are well worth the cost in money and possible personal restrictions. The problem is that the larger sense of community is often lost. Citizens living in their affluent private enclaves are less likely to vote for spending on public services that they do not use, such as traditional public schools, public parks, and public roads. Indeed, the California legislature specifically authorized the private road because it perceived that there was not sufficient public support to pay additional taxes for new public roads.

The result of this trend toward private services is that the needs of citizens who do not have a "going private" option may be ignored. And because these enclaved communities tend to be overwhelmingly white, this leads to a further balkanization of the body politic. The essential question here is: If certain citizens can afford to buy their way out of common public problems, what kind of public services does that leave for the rest of us? It used to be that the "leading" (meaning richer) citizens would make an effort to solve the problems of their communities because, for better or worse, they were part of it. Now they can just hide behind their walls.

Even people living in the heart of a big city can buy better public services for themselves by creating a "business improvement district"—a quasi-government paid for by taxes on property owners within the district. Almost a thousand of these districts nationwide provide extra sanitation, policing, and other services for their residents. Thus many of the richer neighborhoods in New York City are cleaner and safer because their residents can afford to pay for private sanitation services and private police.

The balkanizing of communities in the United States was all too evident in the evacuation of New Orleans before the arrival of Hurricane Katrina. The scenes of the city's poor lining up outside of the Superdome and convention center raised questions about the provision of even the most basic government services. But unlike the moats that kept the masses out of the feudal castles, the masses in the Superdome were trapped by a moat of floodwaters that kept them in.

This new feudalism is just one side of the increasing privatization of the public sector: here, citizens, as is their right, buy the amount of "public" services they can afford. The other side of privatization has government itself contracting for the private provision of public functions. Thus increasingly trash is collected, public buildings are cleaned, and streets are repaired not by public employees but by private sector employees of companies with government contracts. This is often less expensive because such workers are typically paid less than public employees—especially when fringe benefits are considered.

The traditional machinery of government—the administrative structures by which public purposes are achieved—is increasingly being called into question by an angry citizenry that does not always see the contradiction between wanting ever greater government services at ever decreasing costs. Thus privatization, even with its feudal aspects, is seen by some as one means of lowering the overall costs of government, by others as a means of reducing services to the poor, and by still others as a means of eliminating large elements of government altogether. But however it is viewed, and despite the continuing danger of social balkanization, it remains one of the most important tools in reinventing the machinery of government for the twenty-first century.

For Discussion: *Why is it that citizens living in gated communities are less likely to be involved in civic affairs? What does the trend toward gated communities imply for overall public support for increasing taxes and improving public services?*

▶ IN THE NEWS | Selling the Brooklyn Bridge!

Someday soon public sector infrastructure assets such as toll highways and bridges will be appearing in a pension or mutual fund near and dear to you. State and local governments throughout the nation are strapped for cash, anxious to downsize via privatization and increasingly seeing their saleable infrastructure as cash cows waiting to be milked (meaning sold or leased). Just as investment brokers packaged commercial real estate (apartments, office buildings, shopping centers, hotels, etc.) into Real Estate Investment Trusts now readily sold on stock markets, they are currently on the verge of packaging public sector infrastructure (highways, bridges, airports, water systems, etc.) into a new investment option. Tolls or user fees can yield substantial and consistent profits. For example, according to journalist Emily Thornton, "Roads to Riches" (*Business Week*, May 7, 2007), a $3.8 billion deal for a toll road in Indiana concluded in 2006, allows the investors to break even in year 15 of a 75-year lease. Thereafter, they expect to earn "as much as $32 billion in profits." Analysts typically assess the value of infrastructure assets at 40 times annual toll revenues. At this rate, the Golden Gate Bridge at the head of San Francisco Bay could sell for $3.4 billion. Remember that old story about the city slicker having a bridge in Brooklyn to sell to some rube from the country? Well, it is no longer a joke. Thornton concludes: "If permission were granted by New York City to charge the same tolls as the George Washington Bridge, a private owner might shell out as much as $3.5 billion for it." Then part ownership of the bridge could end up in your pension fund—and you could be that proverbial rube from the country. ▶

WHAT IS THE MACHINERY OF GOVERNMENT?

The machinery of government consists of all of the structural arrangements adopted by national, state, or local governments to deliver their legally mandated programs and services. This of necessity includes the central management arrangements of government. In all jurisdictions, the organization and eventual reorganization of executive branch agencies is the everlasting machinery of government issue.

Fine-Tuning the Machinery

In 1733 English poet Alexander Pope wrote the following:

> *For forms of government let fools contest—*
> *That which is best administered is best.*

These two lines from his *An Essay on Man* became so well known that Alexander Hamilton, in *The Federalist*, No. 68 (1788), took the trouble to quote them, denounce the sentiment as "political heresy," and then go on to acknowledge, "Yet we may safely pronounce that the true test of a good government is its aptitude and tendency to produce a good administration." Ever since, one test of governing efficacy has been Hamilton's ideal of "good administration." The machinery that a government creates to work its will must be judged by the quality of public administration that it yields. But many political analysts of Hamilton's generation as well as today would argue that no matter how good the quality, it is the quantity that is the crucial thing. Senator Barry Goldwater's often stated warning during his unsuccessful 1964 presidential campaign still resonates: "a government big enough to give you everything you want is a government big enough to take from you everything you have."

Hamilton's contemporary, Thomas Paine, the pamphleteering propagandist of the American Revolution, wrote in *Common Sense* that "society in every state is a blessing, but government, even in its best state, is but a necessary evil; in its worst state an intolerable one." This certainly reflects the sentiments of the modern Republican Party in the United States. Indeed, this party took control of the U.S. Congress during the 1994 midterm election, running on a platform that differs only in detail with Paine's contention. This can all be summed up in the proposition that "government is best which governs least." New England writer Henry David Thoreau began his famous 1849 essay "Civil Disobedience" with this motto, which has also been attributed to Thomas Jefferson, Thomas Paine, and many other doubting Thomases about government.

But if so many good and wise people believed so strongly that government should be "least," how and why did it grow so large? Has the machine grown too big for its most elemental task of producing Hamilton's "good administration"? The task of this chapter is to examine the machinery of government and its effects on administrations good and bad. Always remember, however, that most of the debate over reinventing government and the best public management practices are not about fundamentally changing the nature of governing institutions but about fine-tuning the machinery. To use a mobile metaphor: It's not about reinventing the automobile; it's about getting more miles per gallon of fuel using fewer and less-expensive parts.

The Rise and Fall of Governmental Machinery

Whenever government seeks to address a major issue, it leaves new machinery in its wake. Thus the civil rights movement that began in the 1950s left the Commission on Civil Rights (created in 1957) and the Equal Employment Opportunity Commission (created in 1964). The environmental movement that began in the 1960s left the Environmental Protection Agency (created in 1970). The war on terrorism that started at the World Trade Center in 2001 has created the Department of Homeland Security. And the economic crisis of 2008 and 2009 left us with the The Recovery Accountability and Transparency Board and Automobile Recovery Task Force. Governmental entities, once established, tend to last a long time and not change easily. They develop constituencies that support their cause. Often they take on new causes that also enhance their support. For example, the Equal Employment Opportunity Commission initially dealt only with cases of workplace discrimination. Today, as federal courts reinterpret the nature of discrimination, it is the nation's prime enforcer of workplace sexual harassment prohibitions as well (see Chapter 12 for more on this).

There is gravity at work in the machinery of government. What goes up can also fall down. For example, the Civil Aeronautics Board, created by the federal government to regulate the airline industry in 1938, was abolished in 1985 as economic deregulation became fashionable. The Office of Technology Assessment, created in 1972 as a support agency of Congress to be an objective source of information on policy alternatives for technology-related issues, was abolished in 1995 as a newly elected Republican-controlled Congress sought to cut costs. In 1996 the Bureau of Mines within the Department of the Interior gave 1,200 of its employees the shaft. This 85-year-old agency was abolished by a Congress less interested in the concerns of **big labor** than in big-budget savings. But even when a piece of the government machine is sliced off, it is seldom completely thrown away. For example, Bureau of Mines' workers engaged in coal mine safety were transferred to the Fossil Energy Division of the Department of Energy. And even the most fervent advocates of abolishing the Department of Commerce believe it would be wise to retain the National Weather Service and the Bureau of the Census, albeit in scaled-down forms.

Big labor ■
The major American labor unions and their federations.

In the United States, the national machinery of government is far more inherently conservative and, in consequence, far more hesitant to change than many other comparable—albeit smaller—democracies, such as Britain, Australia, and New Zealand. However difficult to change, the elements of the machinery of government are not immutable. They can and should be changed as societal needs alter. There is one commonly asked machinery-of-government question. It was posed by Representative Newt Gingrich in a December 1994 speech accepting his party's nomination to be Speaker of the House: "When you see a large government bureaucracy, is it an inevitable relic of the past that can't be changed, or is it an opportunity for an extraordinary transformation to provide better services and better opportunities at lower cost?" This is one of those questions for which there is only one possible answer: Everybody wants "better services" and "lower costs." But are you willing to tinker with your government machine to get them?

THE ADMINISTRATIVE ARCHITECTURE OF THE U.S. GOVERNMENT

A constitution provides the basic political and legal structure, the architecture, that prescribes the rules by which a government operates. James Madison wrote in *The Federalist*, No. 57 (1788), that "the aim of every political constitution is, or ought to be, first to obtain for rulers men who possess most wisdom to discern, and most virtue to pursue, the common good of the society; and in the next place, to take the most effectual precautions for keeping them virtuous whilst they continue to hold their public trust." While Madison asserted that the first aim was to find appropriate "men," he would certainly reconsider that word if he were writing today. To be sure, he would use a sexually neutral term such as *people*, *individuals*, or *persons*. But this does not go far enough—because the primary task of rulers in all modern constitutional systems is administration. So "administrators" should replace "men" in Madison's political philosophy because administrators are those who run a constitution. The echo of Woodrow Wilson's famous statement that "it is getting harder to run a constitution than to frame one" is loud and clear. Madison is generally considered the primary framer of the Constitution. But if he had lived to see what his handiwork had wrought, he would be much more concerned about running it.

The Constitution, with its famous opening words "We the people," asserts that the source of its authority is the people as opposed to the states. It then assigns powers to the various branches of government and in doing so, structures the government. It limits the powers that any branch may have through a system of **checks and balances.** Most significantly, it denies certain powers to the national government by reserving them for the states and the people.

American politics has grown up around the Constitution and has therefore been "constitutionalized." Many domestic political issues are eventually treated in constitutional terms—for example, civil rights, crime, pornography, abortion, and impeachment, to name but some of the more obvious cases. Only the realm of foreign affairs has substantially escaped this tendency, although the war on terror has increasingly brought back questions of the rights of prisoners to the American courts. In addressing matters of government and politics, Americans are likely to pose as the first question, "Is it constitutional?" Only afterward is the desirability of specific policies and government arrangements considered on their own merits. In the 1819 case of *McCulloch v. Maryland*, the Supreme Court explained how to tell if something is constitutional: "Let the end be legitimate, let it be within the scope of the Constitution, and all means which are appropriate, which are plainly adapted to that end, which are not prohibited, but consist with the letter and spirit of the Constitution, are constitutional."

Unlike the British parliamentary machinery of government that evolved over hundreds of years, the American machinery was created at one moment in time for its specific purpose. The Constitutional Convention of 1787 was truly the world's first reinventing-government movement. And the government it invented was designed to be inefficient. Because of their experiences under British rule, Americans have historically been suspicious of a too-efficient government, feeling that an overly efficient administration of public affairs could eventually eat into political

Checks and balances ■ The notion that constitutional devices can prevent any power within a nation from becoming absolute by being balanced against, or checked by, another source of power within that same nation. The U.S. Constitution is often described as a system of checks and balances. For example, it allows the president to check Congress by vetoing a bill and Congress to check the president by overriding a veto or refusing to ratify treaties or confirm nominees to federal office. The Supreme Court can check either by declaring laws passed by Congress or actions taken by the president to be unconstitutional.

liberties. Chief Justice Warren Burger, writing for the Court in *Immigration and Naturalization Service v. Chadha* (1983), offered this opinion:

> It is crystal clear from the records of the [Constitutional] Convention, contemporaneous writings and debates, that the Framers ranked other values higher than efficiency. . . . The choices we discern as having been made in the Constitutional Convention impose burdens on governmental processes that often seem clumsy, inefficient, and even unworkable, but those hard choices were consciously made by men who had lived under a form of government that permitted arbitrary governmental acts to go unchecked.

The modern U.S. Supreme Court then reaffirmed the value of inefficiency when it asserted in the *Chadha* case that "there is no support in the Constitution or decisions of this Court for the proposition that the cumbersomeness and delays often encountered in complying with explicit Constitutional standards may be avoided, either by the Congress or by the president." The Court unanimously declared its support for red tape, the treasured procedural safeguards that protect us even when we do not wish to be protected, and the law's delay. And they have done this as they stated in the *Chadha* case because "with all the obvious flaws of delay, untidiness, and potential for abuse, we have not yet found a better way to preserve freedom than by making the exercise of power subject to the carefully crafted restraints spelled out in the Constitution."

Executive Branch Machinery

One glance at an organization chart of the U.S. government and we can see immediately that the most complex part of the machinery of government lies in the executive branch; the other two branches seem small by comparison, with comparatively few subdivisions (see Figure 3.1). While the inefficiency of the separation of powers is to be highly valued for its protection of basic liberties, this is no excuse for individual agencies to be inefficient as organizations. Indeed, the whole thrust of American public administration reform over the past century has been to create efficient subunits within an overall inefficient system.

Although the executive branch has the most complex structure, the other two branches are also of interest from a machinery-of-government point of view. For example, the U.S. Supreme Court has ultimate administrative responsibility for the entire federal court system. And while most citizens know that the legislative branch contains the Senate and the House of Representatives, not so many realize that other important agencies are located in this branch, ranging from the Architect of the Capitol and the U.S. Botanic Garden to the Library of Congress and the Government Accountability Office (GAO). This last agency is of critical importance, allowing Congress to exercise financial oversight of the executive branch. The GAO would be severely diminished if its functions were located within the executive branch, as it frequently is within democracies based on the British **parliamentary system.** (The GAO's work is discussed in more detail in Chapter 14.)

The executive branch, headed by the president, contains the machinery that serves to implement national policies established by both constitutional and

Parliamentary system ■
A means of governance whose power is concentrated in a legislature, which selects from among its members a prime minister and his or her cabinet officers. The government—that is, the prime minister and the cabinet—stays in power as long as it commands a majority of the Parliament. When the government loses its majority (loses a vote of confidence), elections must be held within a prescribed time period (or at least every five years in British practice).

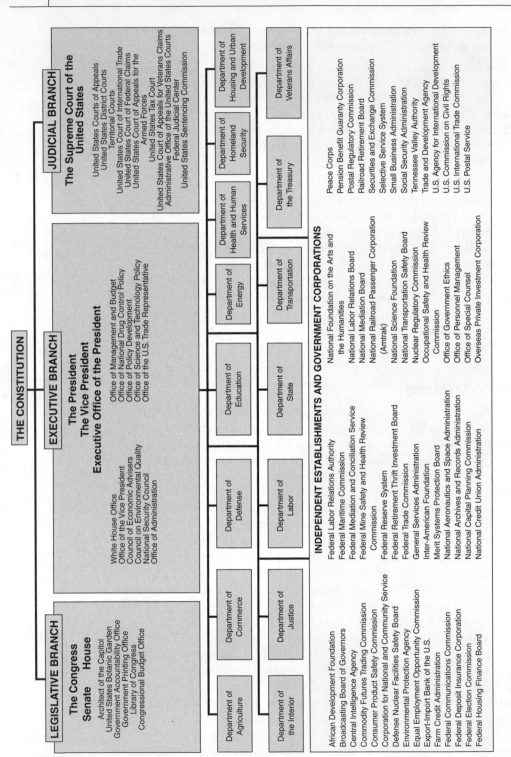

FIGURE 3.1

The government of the united states

Source: *2010–2011 U.S. Government Manual. (IMAGE FOUND AT* http://www.usgovernmentmanual.gov/ReadLibraryItem.ashx?SFN=Myz95sTy04rJRM/nhIRwSw===&SF=VHhnJrOeEAnGaa/rtk/JOg==)

legislative means. There are three main categories of organizations in the structure of the executive branch: (1) executive office agencies, (2) executive departments, and (3) independent public bodies.

Executive Office Agencies   The Executive Office of the President (EOP) is an umbrella office consisting of the top presidential staff agencies that provide the president help and advice in carrying out major responsibilities. These include, as you might expect, some agencies that are concerned with "head office" functions of policy, planning, and resource allocation, such as the Office of Management and Budget, the Council of Economic Advisers, and the National Security Council. But some exist to signify important national priorities, such as the Office of National Drug Control Policy and the Council on Environmental Quality.

Executive Departments   There are 15 executive **departments**. As a group, they constitute the president's cabinet. This is an institution whose existence relies on custom rather than constitutional provision, even though its chief members, the secretaries of the federal executive departments, must be approved by the Senate. It came into being as a single body because President George Washington found it useful to meet with the chiefs of the several executive departments. While all subsequent presidents have considered it necessary to meet with the cabinet, their attitudes toward the institution and its members have varied greatly. Some presidents have convened their cabinet only for the most formal and routine matters, while others have relied on it for advice and support. The president's cabinet differs from the cabinet in the British parliamentary system in that, in the United States, the executive power is not shared by the cabinet as a whole but is constitutionally vested solely in the president. This is famously illustrated by a story about Abraham Lincoln. During the Civil War he called his cabinet together to discuss a pressing matter of war policy. Wanting to get a sense of their feelings, he called for a vote. They all voted "nay." Lincoln alone voted "aye." Yet, as president, he declared, "The ayes have it."

> **Department** ∎
> A confusing word. While it can refer to a cabinet-level agency of the U.S. government, it can also refer to one of the three branches of government: executive, legislative, or judicial. But it is also used as a general term for any administrative subdivision. Thus the Department of the Navy is within the Department of Defense.

At the present time, cabinet membership consists of the secretaries of 15 executive departments, the newest member being the secretary of Homeland Security. But a substantial part of the executive branch is not represented in the cabinet. From the earliest days, presidents have accorded to others the privilege of attending and participating in cabinet meetings. In recent years, the U.S. ambassador to the United Nations and the director of the Office of Management and Budget, among others, have been accorded cabinet rank to symbolize the importance of the functions they represent. However, not all cabinet members are equal. The "inner" cabinet refers to the federal departments of State, Defense, Treasury, and Justice—because they (and their secretaries) tend to be more prominent and influential in every administration than the rest of the cabinet. While all cabinet secretaries are equal in rank and salary, the missions of those in the inner cabinet tend to give them an advantage in prestige, access, and visibility denied to those who head the remaining (the "outer") cabinet.

For better or worse, according to political scientists Edward Weisband and Thomas M. Frank, "Cabinet meetings in the United States, despite occasional efforts

Loyal opposition ■
In a two-party system, the party out of power but loyal to the interest of the nation as a whole.

Corporation ■
An organization formed under state or federal law that exists, for legal purposes, as a separate being or an artificial person. It may be public (set up by the government) or private (set up by individuals), and it may be created to carry on a business or to perform almost any function. It may be owned by the government or by a few persons, or it may be a "publicly owned corporation"—owned by members of the general public who buy its shares on an open stock market such as the New York Stock Exchange.

Commission ■
A group charged with directing a government function, whether on an ad hoc or a permanent basis. Commissions tend to be used (1) when it is desirable to have bipartisan leadership, (2) when their functions are of a quasi-judicial nature, or (3) when it is deemed important to have wide representation of ethnic groups, regions of the country, differing skills, and so on.

to make them into significant decision-making occasions, have, at least in this century, been characterized as vapid nonevents in which there has been a deliberate nonexchange of information as part of a process of mutual nonconsultation." The president's cabinet has never functioned as a unified team. The American machinery of government, which requires cabinet secretaries to be responsible both to the president and the Congress (with its competing interests) makes that virtually impossible.

The structure of U.S. government departments is a reasonably deft selection of topics likely to need a national focus by government. But these topics are not the only ones that could be represented at this level. They represent choices among competing priorities. There is no federal Department of the Environment, for example, which means that environmental issues must be voiced through other departments. While the Clinton administration called for such a new department, its **loyal opposition** in the Congress not only opposed it but made efforts to repeal much of the environmental protection legislation such a department would administer.

Independent Public Bodies   Independent establishments and government corporations form the third main area of the U.S. national machinery of government. They range in purpose from public business **corporations** (such as the U.S. Postal Service, the Export-Import Bank of the United States, and Amtrak—the National Railroad Passenger Corporation) to important regulators and watchdogs (such as the Environmental Protection Agency and the Commission on Civil Rights) to foundations committed to worthy purposes (such as the National Science Foundation and the African Development Foundation).

A regulatory **commission** is an independent agency established by Congress to regulate some aspect of U.S. economic life. Among these are the Securities and Exchange Commission (SEC) and the Federal Communications Commission (FCC). Such agencies are, of course, not independent of the U.S. government. They are subject to the laws under which they operate as these laws are enacted and amended by Congress. Independent agencies and regulatory commissions can be divided into two categories: (1) those units under the direct supervision and guidance of the president, and therefore responsible to him, and (2) those not under such supervision and guidance, and therefore not responsible to him.

Independent executive agencies, with rare exceptions, are headed by single administrators appointed by the president and confirmed by the Senate. These administrators serve at the pleasure of the president and can be removed by the president at any time. In addition, they must submit their budget requests to the Office of Management and Budget (OMB), which is located within the Executive Office of the President, for review and clearance. Examples of independent executive agencies include the Central Intelligence Agency, the Environmental Protection Agency, the General Services Administration, and the Small Business Administration.

Government corporation is the term used for a government-owned corporation or an agency of government that administers a self-supporting enterprise in the following situations:

1. When an agency's business is essentially commercial
2. When an agency can generate its own revenue
3. When the agency's mission requires greater flexibility than government agencies normally have

Examples of federal government corporations include the Saint Lawrence Seaway Development Corporation, the Federal Deposit Insurance Corporation, Amtrak, and the Tennessee Valley Authority. At the state and municipal levels, corporations (often bearing different names, such as authorities) operate enterprises such as turnpikes, airports, and harbors. As we discuss later in this chapter, there has been an increased push, especially under Republican administrations, for many government corporations to be dissolved or sold to private entities.

Separation of Powers

The executive branch organizations discussed in the previous section maintain important powers within their individual spheres. But as even the most casual observer of American government will recognize those powers are significantly constrained by the core principle of separation of powers established by the Constitution. This separation of powers among executive, legislative, and judicial branches, in theory, makes a tyrannical concentration of power impossible. While the Constitution contains provisions in separate articles for the three branches of government, there is a significant difference in the grants of power to these branches: the first article, dealing with legislative power, vests in the Congress "all legislative powers herein granted"; the second article vests "the executive power" in the president; and the third article states that "the judicial power of the United States shall be vested in one Supreme Court, and in such inferior courts as the

---

▶ BOX 3.1 | James Madison on the Separation of Powers

But the great security against a gradual concentration of the several powers in the same department, consists in giving to those who administer each department the necessary constitutional means and personal motives to resist encroachments of the others. The provision for defense must in this, as in all other cases, be made commensurate to the danger of attack. Ambition must be made to counteract ambition. The interest of the man must be connected with the constitutional rights of the place. It may be a reflection on human nature, that such devices should be necessary to control the abuses of government. But what is government itself, but the greatest of all reflections on human nature? If men were angels, no government would be necessary. If angels were to govern men, neither external nor internal controls on government would be necessary. In framing a government which is to be administered by men over men, the great difficulty lies in this:

you must first enable the government to control the governed; and in the next place oblige it to control itself. A dependence on the people is, no doubt, the primary control on the government; but experience has taught mankind the necessity of auxiliary precautions. This policy of supplying, by opposite and rival interests, the defect of better motives, might be traced through the whole system of human affairs, private as well as public. We see it particularly displayed in all the subordinate distributions of power, where the constant aim is to divide and arrange the several offices in such a manner as that each may be a check on the other—that the private interest of every individual may be a sentinel over the public rights. These inventions of prudence cannot be less requisite in the distribution of the supreme powers of the State. ▶

Source: James Madison, *The Federalist No. 51* (1788)

Congress may from time to time ordain and establish." The drafters of the Constitution were very familiar with Sir William Blackstone's *Commentaries on the Laws of England* (1783) which asserted that: "In all tyrannical governments the supreme magistracy, or the right both of making and of enforcing the laws, is vested in one and the same man, or one and the same body of men; and wherever these two powers are united together, there can be no public liberty." Thus Justice Louis D. . Brandeis writes in *Myers v. United States* 272 U.S. 293 (1926): "The doctrine of the separation of powers was adopted by the Convention of 1787, not to promote efficiency but to preclude the exercise of arbitrary power. The purpose was, not to avoid friction, but, by means of the inevitable friction incident to the distribution of the governmental powers among three departments, to save the people from autocracy." Viewing the realtionships between the administration of Barack Obama and the Republican-controlled House of Representatives in 2011 provided observers with a contemporary example of just the types of friction that Brandeis described over 80 years ago.

STATE AND LOCAL GOVERNMENT MACHINERY

American subnational governments are individually smaller than the national government but collectively far larger (see Table 3.1). The number of public employees is a good indicator of this disparity. The federal government, excluding the armed forces, has just about 2.7 million civilian employees. But state and local employment exceeds 17 million. The machinery of government at the state and local levels parallels the national model with legislative, executive, and judicial branches. The Tenth Amendment, the last part of the Bill of Rights, holds that the "powers not delegated to the United States by the Constitution, nor prohibited by it to the states, are reserved to the states respectively, or to the people." This means that whatever the federal government cannot constitutionally do for the people, the states and their subunits must or may do. Significantly, the national

TABLE 3.1

Governments in the United States

Type	Number
National	1
State	50
County	3,033
Municipal	19,492
Townships/Towns	16,519
School Districts	13,051
Special Districts	37,381
Total	89,527

Source: *Statistical Abstract of the United States* (2011) Table 426. http://www.census.gov/compendia/statab/2011/tables/11s0426.pdf

Constitution does not mention cities, counties, or any other type of local government. They are all creatures of their states; their powers are derived from state law; and what a state gives a state may later take away.

The primacy of state over local law is the essence of Dillon's rule—a rule famously formulated by Judge John F. Dillon in his 1911 *Commentaries on the Law of Municipal Corporations*. The rule outlines criteria developed by state courts to determine the nature and extent of powers granted to local governments. It holds that municipal corporations have only those powers (1) expressly granted in the city charter, (2) necessarily or fairly implied by or incidental to formally expressed powers, and (3) essential to the declared purposes of the corporation. "Any fair, reasonable, substantial doubt" about a power is to result in denying that power to the corporation. In some states, the rule has been relaxed, especially in dealing with **home rule** cities. The essence of Dillon's rule was upheld by the Supreme Court in *City of Trenton v. State of New Jersey* (1913).

State Government

The elected chief executive of a state government is the governor. The responsibilities of a governor usually parallel those of a U.S. president, on a smaller scale, but each governor has only the powers granted to the office by the state constitution. Some states severely limit executive powers, while others give their governors powers, such as the **item veto**, that are greater than those possessed by the president of the United States. The term of office for a governor is four years in all states except Arkansas, New Hampshire, Rhode Island, and Vermont, where it is two. Currently, 38 states have limits on the number of terms that their governors can serve, with most allowing two or three four-year terms, and a few, such as Virginia, only allowing a single four-year term. In one sense, it is a misnomer to call a governor the chief executive of a state. The reality is that most state constitutions provide for what amounts to a plural executive, because governors, in marked contrast to the U.S. president, typically must share powers with a variety of other independently elected executive branch officers, such as a secretary of state, an attorney general, a treasurer, and an auditor (or controller). Consequently, a governor's informal powers as a lobbyist for his or her initiatives and as head of his or her party may often be far more useful than the formal authority that comes with the office. Nevertheless, the management job of a governor compares favorably in terms of responsibility to those of the highest-paid corporate executives. For example, in terms of revenues, more than half the states would rank among the top 100 corporations in America. Most would be among the top 200 of the Fortune 500.

The lieutenant governor is the elected state official who would replace the governor should he or she be unable to complete a term of office. The office parallels that of the vice president in the national government but differs in that in many states the lieutenant governor is separately elected and thus may be of a different party from the governor. This can sometimes cause considerable friction when the two officeholders are political rivals—and especially when, as in California, the lieutenant governor assumes some of the governor's powers to act whenever the governor is out of the state. Arizona, Maine, New Hampshire, New

Home rule ■
The ability, the power, of a municipal corporation to develop and implement its own charter. It resulted from the urban reform movement of the early twentieth century, which hoped to remove urban politics from the harmful influence of state politics. Home rule can be either a statutory or a constitutional system and varies in its details from state to state.

Item veto ■
The executive power to veto separate items in a bill. This is also known as the line-item veto.

Fortune 500 ■
A size-ordered (based on gross revenues) directory of the 500 largest U.S. corporations published each year since 1955 by *Fortune* magazine.

Jersey, Oregon, West Virginia, and Wyoming have no lieutenant governors. In four of these states, the president of the state senate would succeed to the governorship; in the other three, the secretary of state would.

The story is often told of Calvin Coolidge, then the lieutenant governor of Massachusetts, who met a woman at a dinner party. She asked him, "What do you do?"

He replied, "I'm the lieutenant governor."

"How interesting, you must tell me all about it," she said.

Coolidge then replied, "I just did." While Coolidge was notoriously tight-lipped, his summation of the limited responsibilities of the office of lieutenant governor was drawn from reality.

County Government

The county is the basic unit for administrative decentralization of state government. Although it is typically governed by an elected board or commission, there is a movement at present toward a county administrator or executive (sometimes elected). In Louisiana, the comparable unit is called a parish; in Alaska, it is a borough. In 2011, the United States had 3,033 county governments. Each state determines for itself how many counties it will have. The elected officials of county government have a bewildering array of titles. According to Dade County, Florida, Commissioner Harvey Ruvin, speaking in 1989, county officials "are supervisors in California, judges in Texas, jurors in Louisiana, freeholders in New Jersey, county legislators in New York, commissioners in Dade. If I tell somebody from New York I'm a commissioner, they think I'm the dog catcher. No wonder the public and the media focus on governors and mayors."

The county seat is the capital of a county, where the courts and administrative offices are located. In much of the United States, the county seat was located in the geographical center of the county so that it would not be more than one day's ride on horseback from the farthest part of the county. This is why there are so many counties. Because few citizens ride horses to government offices today, it would seem to make a lot of sense to combine many counties and thus realize substantial savings from having fewer county clerks, county sheriffs, county courts, and so on. But which clerk, sheriff, or judge is going to quietly resign? The conundrum of reforming the machinery of government can often be summarized by the phrase "You can't get there from here!" Of course, the multiplicity of governing

---

BOX 3.2 | The Meaning of *Gubernatorial*

Gubernatorial is the strange word that refers to things pertaining to the office of governor. It comes from the Greek *kybernan*, meaning "to direct a ship." The Romans borrowed the word from the Greeks as *guberno*. Then the French took it and sent it across the English Channel as *governor*. When the word is used as an adjective, it goes back to its Latin roots: *gubernatorial*. ◤

entities allows for greater democratic control in that government is kept closer to the people. Nevertheless, reformers constantly ask if the benefits derived are worth the extra costs of fragmented government. Numerous consolidations between county and municipal governments have occurred in recent decades. A prominent example is the recent consolidation of Jefferson County, Kentucky, with the city of Louisville into a unified metropolitan (metro) government. We will examine the concept of metro government later in this chapter.

Professor Tanis Janes Salant has classified the forms of county government as follows:

1. *Commission Form.* An elected county commission or board of supervisors, which is the most common form of county government, has legislative authority (e.g., to enact ordinances, levy certain taxes, and adopt budgets), as well as executive and administrative authority (e.g., to administer local, state, and federal policies, appoint county employees, and supervise road work). Typically, however, administrative responsibilities are also vested in independently elected constitutional officers, such as a county sheriff, treasurer, coroner, clerk, auditor, assessor, and prosecutor.

2. *Commission-Administrator.* There are three basic types of this form, some of which also have additional, independently elected constitutional officers. About 786 counties have one type of this form.
   A. *Council Manager.* The county council or board, which is the legislative body, appoints a county manager who performs executive functions, such as appointing department heads, hiring county staff, administering county programs, drafting budgets, and proposing ordinances.
   B. *Chief Administrative Officer.* The county board or commission, as the legislative and quasi-executive body, appoints a chief administrative officer to supervise and coordinate county departments, but not appoint department heads, and to prepare budgets, draft ordinances, and oversee program implementation.
   C. *County Administrative Assistant.* The county board or commission, as the legislative and executive body, appoints an administrative assistant to help carry out the commission's responsibilities.

3. *Council-Executive.* A county executive is independently elected by the people to perform specific executive functions. The county board or commission remains the legislative body, but the county executive may veto ordinances enacted by the commission, with the commission having override power by an extraordinary majority vote. The county executive's authority and responsibilities are much like those of a mayor in a strong mayor-council municipality. About 383 counties have this form.

Municipal Government

Municipal refers to something of local government concern—such as municipal bonds or municipal parks. It implies that the thing it modifies is of internal concern to a state—as opposed to international concern. It comes from the Latin word *municipium*, which was a self-governing body within the ancient Roman Empire.

City charter ■
A document that spells out the purposes and powers of a municipal corporation. To operate, a municipal corporation must have a charter like any other corporation. The municipality can perform only those functions and exercise only those powers that are in the charter. If the particular state permits home rule, a city can develop and implement its own charter. Otherwise, it is limited to statutory charters spelled out by the state legislature.

A city is a municipal corporation chartered by its state. A political subdivision must meet various state requirements before it can qualify for a **city charter**; for example, it must usually have a population above a state-established minimum level.

A city council is the legislative branch, typically **unicameral,** of a municipal government. The duties and size of city councils vary greatly, but in almost all cases the most significant functions include passing ordinances (local laws) and controlling expenditures.

A mayor is the elected chief executive officer of a municipal corporation, the chief ceremonial officer of a city. In most modest-sized and small cities, the office of mayor is a part-time job. He or she may be directly elected. The smaller the city, the more likely that the election will be nonpartisan or that the city council will select a mayor from among its members; then the mayor simply presides as the first among equals on the council. While many big-city mayors such as Rudy Giuliani and Michael Bloomberg have become national figures, no mayor has ever been able to make the leap directly from city hall to the White House—or has even been able to get a major party's nomination for president.

Unicameral ■
A legislature with only one chamber, as opposed to a bicameral one with two—typically a house and a senate. Nebraska is the only state with a unicameral legislature.

Towns and Special Districts

A town is an urban population center—larger than a village but smaller than a city. Typically, its state statutory powers are less than those possessed by cities. The New England town combines the role of both city and county. It usually contains one or more urban areas plus surrounding rural areas. The town meeting is a method of self-government, suitable for only the smallest jurisdictions, where the entire citizenry is eligible to meet to decide local public policy. The town meeting is still the governing body for 88 percent of all New England municipalities. According to journalist Robert Preer, town meetings today are most likely to be controlled by special interests and the town's bureaucracy. Attendance is slight. Even though quorums are set at only 1 or 2 percent of registered voters, meetings are often canceled because of the lack of a quorum. "Raises and promotions pass with ease because meetings are so often packed with employees and their families and friends." Preer concludes that the modern town meeting "is a microcosm of national politics. In both cases, power has shifted from an apathetic and unorganized public to special interests, the mass media, and a bureaucratic-technocratic elite."

A special district is a unit of local government typically performing a single function and overlapping traditional political boundaries. Examples include transportation districts, fire protection districts, library districts, water districts, sewer districts, and so on. Because special districts are such useful devices, they have been multiplying rapidly. In 1942 there were only 8,299 of them in the entire United States. Today there are more than 37,000—not including school districts, and they are the fastest growing governments in the nation. In 2011 they constituted more than 1 out of 3 American government entities.

A school district is a special district for the provision of local public education for all children in its service area. An elected board, the typical governing body, usually hires a professional superintendent to administer the system. School districts often have their own taxing authority. Many are administratively, financially, and politically independent of other local government units. The total number of school districts has been constantly shrinking because of the increasingly common phenomenon of merging two or more districts. There were more than 108,000 school districts in 1942; today there are just over 13,000, with the number shrinking annually.

Local Management Machinery

Local government leadership in the majority of jurisdictions overwhelmingly consists of part-time elected volunteers. Tens of thousands of citizens of middle- and small-sized local governments serve as elected or appointed unpaid (or symbolically paid) council, commission, and board members. Often these amateurs appoint a full-time professional manager. The council-manager plan is a form of municipal government in which an elected city council appoints a professional city manager to administer the city government. A county-manager system offers the same essential structure at the county level.

A city manager is the chief executive of the council-manager system of local government. In contrast to the heads of other types of government, the city manager is an appointed chief executive serving at the pleasure of the council. The concept originated early in the twentieth century by progressive reformers who wanted to replace political bossism with municipal experts. To do this effectively, they created the concept of an administrative chief executive armed with critical administrative powers, such as appointment and removal of administrative officials, but denied any political powers, such as the veto. The city manager concept was sold to the cities as being just like a corporation with its board of directors. The dichotomy between administration and politics (remember Woodrow Wilson) on which the system was premised was implemented by putting all of the policymaking and political functions into the city council, essentially abolishing any separation of powers in the traditional sense at the local level. The decision-making ability of the council was ensured by (1) creating a small council, typically from five to nine members, elected through at-large, nonpartisan elections, and (2) permitting the council to hire and fire the city manager, their expert in the implementation of community policies.

Present council-manager systems often deviate from this traditional model. Many, particularly in bigger cities, have large councils, partisan elections, and separately elected mayors, and some if not all of the council members are elected from a ward or district. In fact, some recent federal court decisions have required ward elections in some cities because at-large elections make it more difficult for minority candidates to be elected. In some larger cities, a variant of the system has evolved, utilizing a chief administrative officer often appointed by the mayor.

The council-manager system has been criticized by some political scientists as being unresponsive to some elements of the community and supported by public administration experts for its effective management in the public interest. Yet even when a city manager delivers effective public management, it is important to remember that he or she is working in an expressly political environment. The best managers are those who are able to neatly balance political pressures with service delivery, thus addressing the real needs of the public.

Bossism ■
An informal system of local government in which public power is concentrated in the hands of a central figure, called a political boss, who may not have a formal government position. The power is concentrated through the use of a political machine, whereby a hierarchy is created and maintained through the use of patronage and government largesse to ensure compliance with the wishes of the boss. It was a dominant system in American city government after the Civil War and was the main target of the American urban reform effort.

Ward ■
A subdivision of a city, often used as a legislative district for city council elections.

At-large ■
An election in which one or more candidates for a legislature are chosen by all of the voters of a jurisdiction. This is in contrast to an election by legislative district, in which voters are limited to selecting one candidate to represent their district.

The mayor-council system is a form of urban government that has a separately elected executive (the mayor) and an urban legislature (the council) usually elected in partisan ward elections. It is called a strong mayor system if the office of mayor is filled by separate citywide elections and has such powers as veto, appointment, and removal. Where the office of mayor lacks such powers, it is called a weak mayor system. This designation does not take into account any informal powers possessed by the incumbent mayor—only the formal powers of the office. Hence, someone can be a strong mayor in terms of actual power in a weak mayor system.

Metropolitan Government

Most larger American cities today cover wide geographical areas. They may have an old urban center with sprawling suburbs extending for many miles, connected to the center by freeways and other forms of urban transportation. The governance of such large conurbations or metropolises presents several options and philosophical choices. There could be a single local government covering the whole area and providing for all. There could be, at the other end of the spectrum, total fragmentation, with many suburban local governments, and even fragmentation within the old center. Or there could be a variety of compromises in between—such as the two-tier government in Miami-Dade County, Florida, where functions are split between an overall metropolitan government and particular localities. The Lakewood Plan, in force in California for many years, offers another option: Local governments remain within the county, but they contract for many of their services from the county.

The adoption of the appropriate machinery of government for a metropolis depends on values. Often, richer and predominantly white residents prefer to withdraw to the suburbs and live under a fragmented local government system, which can avoid the costs of aging urban infrastructure and the social costs of policing and welfare in poorer areas. But fragmented local government lacks the muscle to put investment into social capital that benefits everybody—such as extensive transit systems, museums, parks, and land preserves.

It is also difficult to address regional issues such as transportation and economic development when government authority is highly dispersed among many small governments. A 2003 study by the Brookings Institution attributed many of the state of Pennsylvania's economic and environmental problems to one of the nation's most fragmented systems of local government (see Box 3.2).

Conversely, it's no coincidence that one of the finest transit systems in North America is in Toronto, Canada, where Metro Toronto provides a strong metropolitan government approach. Of course, many wealthier Americans would rather not have any local government at all, but rely instead on private corporations to service their (often gated) communities, distant from urban problems and exempt from both urban costs and urban politics. It's an option some like, but such a degree of civic disengagement is not for everybody.

Continuous State and Local Reform

The progressive reform movement left in its wake some reform institutions that continue to encourage improvements in state and local government machinery.

Government Fragmentation:
BOX 3.3 | The Pennsylvania Story

Pennsylvania is known for many things. From such historical treasures as Independence Hall, Gettysburg, and Valley Forge, to its culinary masterpieces of cheesesteaks and soft pretzels, the Keystone State has many distinguishing qualities. For those interested in the study of local government, Pennsylvania may be most known for its incredibly fragmented system of local governance. According to the Census Bureau, Pennsylvania has 2,630 local governments, amounting to one unit of general government for every 4,760 residents of the state. While the abundance of local governments may provide for an intimate relationship between the government and the governed, the fragmented nature of the system has also come under increased criticism for its inability to deal with many of the problems facing the state.

A 2003 study by the Brookings Institution in Washington, D.C., found that the highly decentralized structure of Pennsylvania's governments works against strategic planning for economic development, transportation, and environmental preservation—thus placing the state at a competitive disadvantage with other states. In particular, the thousands of small governments and authorities stymie planning for business development, open-space conservation,

and growth supported by public infrastructure. The effects of fragmentation are most pronounced in the area of land management, where state law delegates land-use authority to 2,566 municipalities, placing these important decisions at a level of government with very limited capacity to manage them. While many analysts both in and outside the state have brought the problems of fragmentation to the public's attention, there have only been nine municipal mergers since 1956 and very limited changes to the state's planning code. When the Brookings Institution returned to Pennsylvania in 2008 it found that little progress had been made in breaking down the baroque design of government in the Keystone State despite much debate and discussion. Even with evidence accumulating on the disadvantages of fragmentation, Pennsylvanians are very hesitant to make any moves that transfer power from the level of government that is closest to them. ◣

Source: Adapted from Brookings Institution, Back to Prosperity: A Competitive Agenda for Renewing Pennsylvania, December 2003, http://www.brookings.edu/es/urban/publications/pa.htm, and An Economic Plan for the Commonwealth: Unleashing the Assets of Metropolitan Pennsylvania, http://www.brookings.edu/reports/2008/0331_pennsylvania_katz_liu.aspx.

At the beginning of the twentieth century, municipal research bureaus—private nonprofit good government organizations—were established in most major cities. This "bureau movement" emphasized fact finding and the application of the scientific method to urban reform; this was in marked contrast to the simplistic "throw the rascals out" tactics of earlier reform efforts. The New York Bureau of Municipal Research, founded in 1906, pioneered with investigations of wasteful municipal spending (double billing, work paid for but not performed, etc.) that, when it was published, so shocked the community that real administrative reforms followed. The investigatory approach of the New York Bureau (now called the Institute of Public Administration) was then imitated in Philadelphia, Cincinnati, Chicago, Milwaukee, Kansas City, San Francisco, and elsewhere.

The bureau movement was the primary vehicle for developing, and then advocating, the implementation of many administrative innovations that we take for granted today—for example, executive budgeting; uniform accounting standards; merit system selection and staffing procedures; retirement systems; uniform crime statistics; and in-service training. This movement was the source of much of the early scholarly research in public administration. Indeed, it is not an exaggeration to say that academic public administration was almost wholly created in its initial stages by scholars associated with the various bureaus.

REFORMING THE NATIONAL MACHINERY OF GOVERNMENT

It all started with the conquest of England in 1066. William the Conqueror appointed commissioners to make an inventory of the assets of his new kingdom. This report, known as the Doomsday Book (because its findings were as beyond appeal as a Doomsday judgment), is the predecessor of today's royal or presidential commissions and committees. Ever since, prime ministers and presidents have used these devices to investigate a matter of public concern and to issue recommendations for improvement. There is great public satisfaction to be had in bringing together a group of responsible, respected, supposedly objective but knowledgeable citizens to examine and report on a national problem or major disaster.

Such commissions have proven to be handy devices for a modern president who, when faced with an intractable problem such as crime, pornography, or urban riots, can appoint a commission as a gesture to indicate his awareness of constituent distress. Whether that gesture has meaning or sincerity beyond itself is inconsequential for its immediate effect. By the time a commission makes its report—six months to a year later—attention will have been diverted to other issues, and the recommendations can be safely pigeonholed or curtailed.

Often such commissions (or committees) have been used to tinker with the machinery of government. Evolution inexorably marches on. Just as birds are now thought to be all that is left of the dinosaurs, the modern performance review can trace its lineage to the Doomsday Book. Both are efforts by the prevailing regime to assess a present situation so that it can be better repositioned. William the Conqueror used his assessment to restructure England's tax system. A later William— President William Jefferson Clinton—used his to try to reinvent government.

The Brownlow Committee

The advent of the 1990s reinventing-government movement once again made reorganization a fashionable theme in the practice and literature of American public administration. However, the classic example of government reorganization, the one that to this day is still the most significant, is the structuring of the executive branch recommended by the President's Committee on Administrative Management in 1936–1937. This committee was popularly known as the Brownlow Committee, named after its chairman, Louis Brownlow, a major figure in the development of city management as a profession. The two other members of the committee were Charles Merriam of the University of Chicago and Luther Gulick of Columbia University and the Institute of Public Administration in New York City.

BOX 3.4 | How Machinery Begins: Benjamin Franklin Invents the Fire Department in Colonial Philadelphia

I wrote a paper on the different accidents and carelessnessses by which houses were set on fire, with cautions against them, and means proposed of avoiding them. This was much spoken of as a useful piece, and gave rise to a project, which soon followed it, of forming a company for the more ready extinguishing of fires, and mutual assistance in removing and securing of goods when in danger. Associates in this scheme were presently found, amounting to thirty. Our articles of agreement oblig'd every member to keep always in good order, and fit for use, a certain number of leather buckets, with strong bags and baskets (for packing and transporting of goods), which were to be brought to every fire; and we agreed to meet once a month and spend a social evening together, in discoursing and communicating such ideas as occurred to us upon the subject of fires, as might be useful in our conduct on such occasions.

The utility of this institution soon appeared, and many more desiring to be admitted than we thought convenient for one company, they were advised to form another, which was accordingly done; and this went on, one new company being formed after another, till they became so numerous as to include most of the inhabitants who were men of property; and now, at the time of my writing this, tho' upward of fifty years since its establishment, that which I first formed, called the Union Fire Company, still subsists and flourishes, tho' the first members are all deceas'd but myself and one, who is older by a year than I am. The small fines that have been paid by members for absence at the monthly meetings have been apply'd to the purchase of fire-engines, ladders, fire-hooks, and other useful implements for each company, so that I question whether there is a city in the world better provided with the means of putting a stop to beginning conflagrations; and, in fact, since these institutions, the city has never lost by fire more than one or two houses at a time, and the flames have often been extinguished before the house in which they began has been half consumed. ◣

Source: *The Autobiography of Benjamin Franklin* (New York: Washington Square Press, 1791, 1955).

Government grew rapidly during the New Deal period, and there was little time or inclination for planning. It was largely believed that there existed many poorly conceived and poorly implemented organizational designs that were neither economical nor effective. These poor designs were often a reflection of the considerable political conflict between the executive and legislative branches. Both the president's office and the Congress had deliberately contributed to this problem by establishing programs in new organizations or agencies only with regard to political objectives—without taking managerial considerations into account. This persistent struggle over organizational control would be addressed by the Brownlow Committee—which provided the first formal assessment of government organization from a managerial perspective.

The Brownlow Committee submitted its report to President Roosevelt in January 1937. The core proposals of the committee were simple enough. Essentially the report indicated that "the president needs help" and professional staff members who possess a "passion for anonymity." This particular passion seems to have faded in recent years, along with the public's belief that a modern president writes his own speeches.

Frank J. Goodnow (1859–1939) ■
A leader of the progressive reform movement and one of the founders and first president (in 1903) of the American Political Science Association. Goodnow is now best known as one of the principal exponents, along with Woodrow Wilson, of public administration's politics–administration dichotomy.

Overall the committee recommended a major reorganization of the executive branch. The president agreed and appropriate legislation was submitted to Congress in 1938. But Congress, in the wake of the president's efforts to "pack"—to enlarge and thus control—the Supreme Court, and fearful of too much power in the presidency, killed the bill. The president resubmitted a considerably modified reorganization bill the following year, and Congress passed the Reorganization Act of 1939. This law created the Executive Office of the President, brought into it the Bureau of the Budget (later to be the Office of Management and Budget) from the Department of the Treasury, and authorized the president to prepare future reorganization plans subject to an after-the-fact congressional veto.

The Brownlow report, the Executive Office of the President, and many of the other recommendations of the Brownlow Committee that would eventually become law have been sanctified by time. Yet the Brownlow Committee's major proposals initially aroused considerable controversy. Modern scholars now recognize that there were different schools of thought regarding the development of public administration. The executive administration school, espoused by **Frank J. Goodnow,** viewed the roles and functions of government almost exclusively as opportunities for executive actions. In contrast, the legislative administrative school, as espoused by Brookings Institution head William F. Willoughby, viewed the relationship and especially the accountability of administration to the legislative branch as a central focus. This latter school believed that there was a considerable distinction between what was meant by "executive" and "administrative" and that the Constitution gave administrative power mainly to the Congress. The argument over who has more power over the machinery of government, the executive or the legislature, resonated in the mid-1990s with the budgetary struggles between the president and Congress over the size and scope of the governmental machine.

While Congress was considering the Brownlow Committee's various proposals, the forces opposed to an increase in the "administrative" powers of the president at the expense of Congress marshaled their arguments. One of the most eloquent was Lewis Meriam's 1939 *Reorganization of the National Government.* As the Brownlow Committee was arguing for increased presidential power, Meriam was cautioning against it. After "noting Hitler's rise to power within constitutional forms," he warned his readers that "proposals to vest great powers in the executive" might not work "to preserve democracy as we have known it but seriously to endanger it."

Forty years later the only surviving member of the Brownlow Committee would concede a point to Meriam. In considering Richard M. Nixon's abuses of the enhanced powers of the presidency, which the Brownlow Committee helped to create, Luther Gulick is quoted by Stephen Blumberg as saying, "We all assumed in the 1930s that all management, especially public management, flowed in a broad, strong stream of value-filled ethical performance. Were we blind or only naive until Nixon came along?" Nixon's 1970s subversion of constitutional government in the United States during the 1972–1974 Watergate scandal that forced his resignation differed only in degree from the subversion of republican governments that has been the hallmark of twentieth-century dictators.

BOX 3.5 | The Brownlow Committee's Call for a Passion for Anonymity

The president needs help. His immediate staff assistance is entirely inadequate. He should be given a small number of executive assistants who would be his direct aides in dealing with the managerial agencies and administrative departments of the government. These assistants, probably not exceeding six in number, would be in addition to his present secretaries, who deal with the public, with the Congress, and with the press and radio. These aides would have no power to make decisions or issue instructions in their own right. They would not be interposed between the president and the heads of his departments. They would not be assistant presidents in any sense. Their function would be, when any matter was presented to the president for action affecting any part of the administrative work of the government, to assist him in obtaining quickly and without delay all pertinent information possessed by any of the executive departments so as to guide him in making his responsible decisions; and when the decisions have been made, to assist him in seeing to it that every administrative department and agency affected is promptly informed. Their effectiveness in assisting the president, will, we think, be directly proportional to their ability to discharge their functions with restraint. They would remain in the background, issue no orders, make no decisions, emit no public statements. Men for these positions should be carefully chosen by the president from within and without the government. They should be men in whom the president has personal confidence and whose character and attitude is such that they would not attempt to exercise power on their own account. They should be possessed of high competence, great physical vigor, and a passion for anonymity. ◣

Source: President's Committee on Administrative Management, *Administrative Management in the Government of the United States*, January 8, 1937 (Washington: U.S. Government Printing Office, 1937).

Ironically, Nixon sought to enhance the power of the presidency with the creation of the Office of Management and Budget, yet he accomplished just the opposite. Congress, upset by Nixon's budgetary double-dealing, created a parallel Congressional Budget Office so that the legislature had its own number crunchers—who presumably would crunch numbers that could be believed. So, in the game of constitutional checks and balances, new machinery of government is often created to check a would-be king.

The Hoover Commissions

The first Hoover Commission (1947–1949), formally the Commission on Organization of the Executive Branch of the Government, chaired by former President Herbert Hoover, was specifically charged to reduce the number of government agencies created during World War II; it did not, however, do so. Instead, it found that "disorder in the administrative machinery makes the executive branch of the Government work at cross purposes within itself" and focused on strengthening the executive branch by providing for a reorganization of agencies so that there would be a coherent purpose for each department. Instead of calling for a reduction of government agencies, the commission made a vigorous call for increased managerial capacity in the Executive Office of the President (EOP) through (1) unlimited discretion over presidential organization and staff, (2) a strengthened Bureau of the Budget, (3) an office of personnel located in the EOP, and (4) the creation of a staff secretary (what we now call a chief of staff) to provide a liaison between the president and his subordinates. The commission was considered a big success because 72 percent of its recommendations (196 out of 273) were adopted, including passage of the Reorganization Act of 1949 and the establishment of the Department of Health, Education, and Welfare in 1953.

A second Hoover Commission (1953–1955), also chaired by Hoover, is a unique example in the history of American public administration of an important commission being virtually reconvened after four years had passed to continue its work. This second commission recommended the elimination of nonessential government services and activities competitive with private enterprise, based on the assumptions that the federal government had grown beyond appropriate limits and that such growth should be reversed. In contrast to the first commission, the second commission's recommendations accomplished little. In a mere 18 volumes, the former president and his 11 fellow commissioners rigorously argued that a whole host of government activities should be turned over to the private sector. But the U.S. Congress was not so inclined, and this commission's recommendations got essentially nowhere. There was no political will to undertake massive privatization in the mid-1950s. This was a banner in the dust that would not be picked up and held high again until the Reagan administration of the 1980s and, more dramatically, with the Republican capture of Congress in 1994.

The Ash Council

President Richard M. Nixon's Advisory Council on Executive Organization, chaired by Roy Ash of Litton Industries, led to the transformation of the Bureau of the Budget into the Office of Management and Budget. The Ash Council's 1971 recommendations were extraordinarily ambitious in calling for a major restructuring of the cabinet agencies. President Nixon intended to implement this restructuring in his second term, beginning in 1973. But the Watergate scandal (see Chapter 5), which would force his resignation the following year, so dominated his aborted second term that no major domestic policy initiatives were possible.

The President's Private Sector Survey on Cost Control

If the second Hoover Commission is to be measured by 18 volumes of output leading nowhere, the 1982 President's Private Sector Survey on Cost Control (PPSSCC) can be measured by 47 reports from 36 major task forces with approximately similar results. The executive summary alone was 650 pages in two volumes. Like the second Hoover Commission, President Reagan's survey was appointed from an ideological position in which it was assumed that a little private sector know-how was all that it would take to put things right in Washington—an age-old belief that has been applied time and time again with great ardor but to somewhat limited effect. The PPSSCC was chaired by businessman J. Peter Grace, and its various subcommittees were composed of business figures from many large corporations.

It now seems that the PPSSCC, which came to be called the Grace Commission, was ill-fated from the start. The first problem was Grace himself. His true feelings notwithstanding, he came across in countless media interviews as an irascible old corporate patriarch who was condescending enough to disturb his well-earned repose by deigning to advise a misguided government on the multitudinous errors of its ways. The second problem was the commission's ignorance of one of the central precepts of modern management—employee participation. While Grace orchestrated this immense management audit by 2,000 private sector volunteers, the committee's task force largely ignored the expertise that was freely available from within the bureaucracy and the Congress.

Bureaucratic reform historian Donald Savoie reports that both the General Accounting Office and the Congressional Budget Office systematically reviewed the commission's conclusions and "undermine[d] the Commission's credibility" when they demonstrated that too many of the proposed savings were nonexistent and too many of the commission's facts were not factual after all. This however "did not stop the Reagan administration from applauding the findings of the commission and from reporting that it would press ahead with their implementation." But this was largely a public relations exercise of putting a good face on a poor effort. Perhaps the most highly touted recommendation of the commission that was actually implemented was the proposal that federal employees be issued corporate-type credit cards for official travel. While this offered legitimate savings on time previously spent on completing expense reimbursement vouchers, it was hardly worth the estimated $75 million cost (all private sector donated) for the report.

Reinventing Government

The most recent reinventing-government movement was started in 1992 by the David Osborne and Ted Gaebler book with that title. It represents the confluence of two long-standing influences in American public life: the progressive reform movement and management faddism. Reinventing is logically the continuation of the progressive movement's philosophy of continuous improvement. This year's or this generation's most popular management fad is the comprehensive performance audit as a logically prior step in developing a new strategic vision for a business organization or a government operation. Next year, or next generation, there will be a new management fad, but it will still be within the progressive tradition.

Just as every new generation writes its own history, each new managerial generation has its own ideas about the "one best way"—even if that means multiple ways. What has been genuinely new here is that governments at all levels are actually being forced by events to change the fundamental ways in which they operate. They must literally rethink (reinvent) how they operate because they can no longer afford to simply do what they have been doing—with reorganization here and a new public relations effort there—to assuage their critics. The simple overriding impetus to reinventing is a lack of money caused by the dual effects of the tax revolt and the Reagan revolution.

By 1980, the tax revolt movement forced 38 states to reduce or at least stabilize tax rates. Then the Reagan revolution came along and made state and

TABLE 3.2

Major Commissions to Reform Federal Bureaucracy

Name	Chair	Year(s)	President	Result
Brownlow Commission	Louis Brownlow	1936	Roosevelt	Enhanced presidential control of bureaucracy
First Hoover Comission	Herbert Hoover	1947–1949	Truman	Strengthened the Executive Office of the President and enhanced agency management
Second Hoover Commission	Herbert Hoover	1953–1955	Eisenhower	Nothing significant
Ash Council	Roy Ash	1971	Nixon	The Bureau of the Budget became the Office of Management and Budget
Grace Commission	J. Peter Grace	1982	Reagan	A handful of minor bureaucratic adjustments
National Performance Review	Al Gore Jr.	1993	Clinton	A somewhat more streamlined and customer-friendly bureaucracy

local finances even more precarious. The Reagan administration, with its radical changes in the nation's fiscal and tax policies, redefined domestic priorities and curtailed federal programs—especially grants to state and local government—designed to solve social problems. As Reagan often said, "Government is not the solution to our problems. Government is the problem." In other words, the national welfare would be better served with general economic prosperity, brought about by tax cuts rather than with expanded welfare programs.

Necessity being the mother of invention, the next reinventing-government movement began in the early 1980s, to cope with the declining revenues caused by the tax revolt and the Reagan revolution. In 1992 Osborne and Gaebler wrote *Reinventing Government*, a book that essentially categorized many of the things that thousands of state and local governments had been doing throughout the 1980s to cope with this crisis. Bill Clinton, then governor of Arkansas, endorsed the book. As president, he authorized the National Performance Review to seek these same kinds of innovations for the federal government—and for the same reason: money. The federal government was running record deficits. This had to be reduced by reducing (read reinventing) government.

If the federal government was off to the reinventing-government races, Vice President Al Gore was the jockey riding the horse. This was unusual in itself because historically in the United States the vice president's only constitutional responsibility (aside from waiting for the president to die or be removed from office) is to preside over the U.S. Senate (except when it is trying a president for impeachment) and vote in the case of a tie. Recent presidents, however, have tended to give their vice presidents significant domestic and foreign policy assignments. Of course, having the vice president play with a president's **trial balloon** has always been an effective means of insulating a president from critics if the balloon pops.

The Gore Report

When President Bill Clinton launched National Performance Review in 1993—a six-month study, chaired by the vice president, aimed at making the federal

Trial balloon ■
A deliberate leak of a potential policy to see what public response will be. The term comes from the meteorological practice of sending up a balloon to test weather conditions. If public response is hostile, the new policy proposal can be quietly dropped (or deflated).

President Bill Clinton and Vice President Al Gore announce their reinventing-government initiative on the White House lawn in 1993 surrounded by papers representing bureaucratic regulations they promise to discard. This was a truly great photo opportunity. Before most of the cabinet, many members of Congress, and the assembled press corps, Gore then told the president (for the benefit of the press): "Mr. President, if you want to know why government doesn't work, look behind you. The answer is at least partly on those forklifts. Those forklifts hold copies of budget rules, procurement rules, and the personnel code. The personnel code alone weighs in at more than 1,000 pounds. That code and those regulations stacked up there no longer help government work, they hurt it; they hurt it badly. And we recommend getting rid of it." The lesson here is that there is not much political mileage in reinventing government in a closet. Better to do it on the White House lawn and let the whole world watch.

government more efficient—the language he used was familiar: "Our goal is to make the federal government both less expensive and more efficient, and to change the culture of our national bureaucracy away from complacency and entitlement toward initiative and empowerment. We intend to redesign, to reinvent, to reinvigorate the entire national government." In pointed and emphasized contrast to the federal government's last major management reform effort (the Grace Commission), the Gore report would be researched and written largely by the in-house talent of the federal bureaucracy.

Whereas the Grace Report under the Reagan administration—which based its philosophy on the proposition that only private business executives could fix government—was an abject failure, the implementation of reinvention was quite different. The National Partnership for Reinventing Government relied on borrowed federal career officials to do its work. By 1998 it reported savings of $137 billion, a reduction of 351,000 positions in government, and the creation of 340 reinvention laboratories in government agencies. Instead of conflict, partnership was a key theme: between labor and management (occupational health and safety has been a key focus); between regulatory agencies and regulated businesses; and between government agencies. All this was for the common goals of best value for the taxpayer dollar, better service for customers, and better workplaces for employees.

Reinvention in Recess

It must also be said, however, that the Gore report was not unlike its predecessors in that it focused on many specific programs and details, as would a conventional management consultant's report. It lacked the root and branch depth of change achieved in those bureaucracies where new fundamental principles have been adopted. It was an endeavor to fine-tune, but not fundamentally change, the existing system. Some of the recommendations of the National Performance Review—for example, that the Railroad Retirement Board be reinvented—had a familiar ring, while others, such as the recommendation that the management of the Department of Health and Human Services be reviewed, seemed to be like a Russian matryoshka doll—a review that contained a recommendation for another review.

In marked contrast are the machinery-of-government changes that have taken place in the last decades in Britain, Australia, and New Zealand. These have involved fundamental principles and have been more radical than those of the National Performance Review. In fact, the specific machinery-of-government recommendations of the National Performance Review were relatively few—considering that an organization left in place after a review lives to fight another day and to disregard review recommendations it dislikes once the dust has settled.

The defeat of Vice President Al Gore in the 2000 presidential race ended reinvention. But by that time, after eight years of the Clinton administration's reform impetus, the reinventing-government effort badly needed reinventing itself. Its proposals were attacked both by those who felt that its principles didn't fit the traditional values of public administration and by those who felt that its proposals weren't radical enough. During Clinton's second term with a Republican-controlled Congress, reinventing efforts became more rhetoric than reality. The Republicans' idea of reinventing meant two things: devolution and privatization.

Thus the Republican Congress (with Clinton's support) devolved the national welfare program (discussed in Chapter 4), and privatization became the watchword of the subsequent Bush administration. Reinvention became a Clinton-Gore tainted word. While many reforms were achieved by the Bush administration, nothing was "reinvented."

The Obama Revolution—The Return of Big Government

As the end of the Clinton years led to a hiatus for the reinventing-government movement, the election of Barack Obama in 2008 marked a return to the endeavor of government redesign. The combination of vastly expanded government activity as part of the economic recovery effort and enormous fiscal pressures from mounting deficits and debt served as a catalyst for increased attention on redesign of the federal government. While President Obama claimed that his administration's major expansion into areas of the economy such as the auto industry, insurance, and financial securities marked a temporary phase for the federal government, it clearly spelled an end to the idea that the "era of big government" was over. Much to the contrary, government had been placed at the center of steering the nation out of its economic funk, with the Obama administration exerting influence in many spheres of society that at one time might be unimaginable. Perhaps the greatest example of this new order was the 2009 dismissal of General Motors Corporation CEO Rick Wagoner as part of the deal to have the once-proud auto company bailed out by the federal government. President Obama made it clear to GM's board that any financial support from the federal government to keep GM afloat was conditional to Wagoner's dismissal. In essence, the president made GM an offer it couldn't refuse and Wagoner was gone.

After a generation of efforts to make government behave more like business, the failures of major American corporations, banks, and investment firms had many questioning if some of the reforms had gone too far. While it is too early in

---

TABLE 3.3

New Government Organizations Proposed under the Obama Administration

Center for Medicaid and Medicare Innovation

Consumer Financial Protection Agency

Food and Drug Administration Office of Women's Health

President's Economic Recovery Advisory Board

Public Health Workforce Corps

White House Council on Automotive Communities and Workers

White House Office of Cyber Security

White House Office of Health Reform

White House Office of Urban Affairs

Source: http://www.whitehouse.gov

the Obama years to provide a full evaluation of his plans for reinvention of government, it is clear that the structure of American government will look dramatically different after his time in the White House has ended.

The Micromanagers

Woodrow Wilson wrote in his famous 1887 essay "The Study of Administration" that "the field of administration is a field of business . . . a part of political life only as the methods of the counting-house are a part of the life of the society," and "administrative questions are not political questions." This was institutionalized by the Brownlow Committee recommendations for greater managerial capability on the part of the executive. But as Professor David H. Rosenbloom has observed, Congress responded to this stronger, more managerially capable, presidency "in 1946 by establishing the legal and institutional bases for its contemporary role in federal administration." Thus when Truman, a Democrat, was president while the Republicans controlled Congress, a **divided government** brought forth this quartet of laws that sowed the seeds of **micromanagement**:

Divided government ■
A government in which different political parties control the legislative and executive branches.

Micromanagement ■
A pejorative term for too-close supervision by policymakers in the implementation of programs. Congress has been accused of micromanagement when it writes detailed rules governing programs into legislation—thus denying line managers any real administrative discretion. But any manager is a micromanager if he or she refuses to allow subordinates to have any real authority or responsibility.

1. Administrative Procedure Act (APA) of 1946: The basic law governing the way federal agencies operate to safeguard agency clients and the general public. The APA specifies the conditions under which administrative agencies (a) publicize information about their operations, (b) make rules, (c) engage in adjudication, and (d) are subject to judicial review. Thus agencies begin with some form of legislative mandate and translate their interpretation of that mandate into policy decisions, specifications of regulations, and statements of penalties and enforcement provisions. The APA requires that rules be published 30 days before their effective date and that agencies afford any interested party the right to petition for issuance, amendment, or repeal of a rule. In effect, while the APA establishes a process of notice and time for comment, it accords administrative rule-makers the same prerogatives that legislatures have in enacting statutes, as long as the rule enacted is consistent with the enabling statute.
2. Legislative Reorganization Act of 1946: A law that dramatically reduced the number of standing committees in the Senate and House, provided for a major expansion of the Legislative Reference Service (now known as the Congressional Research Service), and promoted the creation of a professional, nonpartisan staff for committees, as well as increased staff for individual members. This was the first attempt by Congress to establish an effective staff system to decrease its dependence on executive agencies for information.
3. Tort Claims Act of 1946: The law that made federal agencies responsible for their torts—legal harms done to another person that can be the cause of a civil court suit.
4. Employment Act of 1946: The law that created the Council of Economic Advisers in the Executive Office of the President and asserted that it was the federal government's responsibility to maintain economic stability and promote full employment.

The combined effect of these laws was to unleash a mob of micromanagers. Members of Congress, once largely limited to policy oversight, now had the opportunity to delve into the minutiae of administration on behalf of their constituents. The APA created a rulemaking process that offered unlimited possibilities for influencing rules for pork barrel motivations. The Legislative Reorganization Act gave Congress the staff it needed to constantly interfere for their specific political purposes. The Tort Claims Act meant that Congress could effectively lobby agencies to redress wrongs to constituents. And the Employment Act meant virtually unlimited justification to pump federal money into selected congressional districts. This process can be seen every time the Department of Defense has been forced into buying more of a weapon than it needs simply because the factory that makes it is in an influential member's congressional district. As Rosenbloom sarcastically noted, "Turning pork barrel politics into a virtuous national economic policy was no small achievement." But while pork by its nature is not kosher, for many Americans the very definition of a member of Congress is one who brings home the bacon. This, however, may be changing.

The importance of all this is that Congress has never drawn—as the Brownlow Committee would have liked—a dichotomy between politics and administration; the two are not separate anyway. So what made anyone think that the reinventing-government movement—the latest effort to take politics out of administration by turning grumpy citizens into happy customers—was going to change the situation?

Now, there is much tinkering that the executive branch can do on its own. It can get the Social Security Administration to answer its phones within a reasonable period. It can force Internal Revenue Service auditors to be polite. But this is minor compared to the power of Congress to determine the amount of Social Security payments and the level of taxes. Members of Congress are hardly likely to give up their ability to micromanage—with all the pork for constituents and re-election prospects that implies—for vague notions of greater efficiency. Members thrive on bureaucratic red tape and the opportunities it creates for constituent service. This is why the **ombudsman/ombudswoman** movement has never gone very far in the United States. This function is happily, even joyously, performed by the elected representatives. It is quite literally what their staffs spend most of their time on—because it is the key to reelection.

The conclusion is in essence quite simple and obvious: To reinvent government, you must also reinvent Congress. And to reinvent state government, you must reinvent the state legislature. Few things are more obvious in the study of public administration than the fact that there exists a strong relationship between the organization of a legislature and that of its executive branch. According to administrative analyst Harold Seidman, "One could as well ignore the laws of aerodynamics in designing an aircraft as ignore the laws of congressional dynamics in designing executive branch structure." Thus "what may appear to be structural eccentricities and anomalies within the executive branch are often nothing but mirror images of jurisdictional conflicts within the Congress. Congressional organization and executive branch organization are interrelated and constitute two halves of a single system." The British and other parliamentary systems have been able to go much further down the reinventing road precisely because they do not have this problem. There the executive and legislature are, for policy purposes, effectively one.

Ombudsman/ ombudswoman ■
An official whose job it is to investigate the complaints of the citizenry concerning public services and to ensure that these complaints will reach the attention of those officials at levels above the original providers of service. The word is Swedish, meaning a representative of the king. Ombudsmen and ombudswomen are now found in many countries at a variety of jurisdictional levels. Many of the functions of ombudsmen in American local, state, and national governments are performed by members of their respective legislatures as casework.

THE PRESSURE FOR PRIVATIZATION

Just as the Clinton administration wanted to reinvent government, the George W. Bush administration sought to privatize much of it through a major commitment to push into the private sector hundreds of thousands of federal jobs. The rationale for this, as explained by Bush OMB Director Mitchell E. Daniels Jr., "is not to move jobs from the public sector to the private sector. The objective is to get the taxpayer the best deal." Notice that the underlying philosophy of this movement toward privatization comes directly from the Second Hoover Commission Report of 1955.

Nothing is more challenging, indeed threatening, to public administration than the now constant specter of privatization. Indeed, to many on the political right, reinventing is virtually synonymous with privatization. There are essentially two kinds of privatization. First, as discussed in the Keynote, there is the private provision of services with a "public" character, such as private police and private parks. These services are public only in the sense that they are available to any who can pay for them. Second, privatization is the process of returning to the private sector property or functions previously owned or performed by government. Conservative Republicans in particular tend to be in favor of privatizing those government functions that can be performed (in their opinion) less expensively or more efficiently by the private sector. Privatization is a broad long-term trend, often fueled with strong and emotional conservative ideology, to reduce government expenditures, to turn (or return) government assets and operations to private enterprise, and, thereby, to increase the effectiveness and efficiency of government.

Privatization is almost always predicated on assumptions about public sector versus private sector efficiency and productivity rates. The burden of proof is often on public sector managers to explain why they are not inferior to private enterprise managers and why they should retain their functions in the face of private sector alternatives. Perhaps no responsibility is greater for public managers today than developing the evaluation and management assessment tools needed to assure critics that public sector programs and enterprises are being managed efficiently and effectively.

Generally there are three basic forms or types of government privatization:

1. The sale of government assets (such as a railroad to a corporation or public housing units to their tenants)
2. The private financing of public facilities (such as toll highways in California or Virginia)
3. The private provision of services (such as trash collection or retirement benefits)

Strategies for Privatization

Privatization is the management ideology for those fearful, suspicious, or skeptical of expanding government. It is equally ideal as a tool for those who wish to reduce the size of government. Done properly, it dovetails with the first principle of the reinventing-government movement: that government should be catalytic and steer (set direction) rather than row (do the work). A review of President

George W. Bush's arguments for partial privatization of Social Security during the 2005 State of the Union address demonstrates the goal of steering rather than rowing. (See the case study in Chapter 13 for excerpts from Bush's address.)

However, privatization sometimes means that government will neither steer nor row. It will simply get out of an activity altogether. For example, some people strongly believe that government should have absolutely no role in birth control, sex education, broadcasting, or the arts. These activities, if undertaken at all, should be undertaken by private citizens at their own initiative. One counterargument was made by playwright **Arthur Miller**. He tells the story of the time he was speaking in defense of government support for theater. A man in the audience asked him, "I manufacture shoes. If the public won't buy enough of them, why shouldn't I demand government support?" Miller couldn't think of a logical and reasoned answer to this perfectly valid question. So he responded with a question: "Can you name me one classical Greek shoemaker?" Of course, Miller was emphatically not in favor of government control of the arts, but he felt, as many do, that government has an obligation to further its notions of civilization—and that this is often done by subsidizing the arts.

Arthur Miller (1915–2005) ■ Pulitzer Prize–winning author of *Death of a Salesman* (1949).

Political analyst E. S. Savas identified four strategies of privatization that together will "halt and reverse the growth of government."

1. Load shedding: A term that refers to government withdrawing from the provision of goods and services and allowing them "to be supplied by the marketplace or by voluntary arrangements."
2. Alternative delivery systems: Arrangements "in which government plays a relatively limited role," including services provided through voluntary or self-service arrangements, competitive markets, franchises, vouchers, grants, and contracts.
3. Imposing user charges for goods and services: Savas argues that government should do this whenever possible in order to expose the true costs of services and, thereby, to increase the chances that alternative delivery systems will evolve.
4. Restoring competition and minimizing government monopolies: Savas maintains that this "requires a conscious strategy of creating alternatives and fostering a receptive climate and mental attitude in favor of giving options to the citizen-consumers of public services."

Privatization is often pursued on the ideological grounds that government should not provide goods and services that firms in the private for-profit or nonprofit sector are able and willing to provide. Government should limit itself to activities that firms in the private sector cannot or will not provide. Policy analyst John Donahue has found that privatization brings both good news and bad news. The good news is that while privatization is not a "universal corrective," it does present some "real opportunities to make public undertakings more efficient and accountable by enlisting the private sector." The bad news is that political pressures could just as easily "tend to retain for the public sector functions where privatization would make sense, and to privatize tasks that would be better left to government."

Privatization in the Military

The military is the most fundamental unit of government—often predating the government it serves. Remember that it was the Continental Army under George Washington that literally enabled the creation of the United States. But the traditional military is fading rapidly. Until recently, the military performed many of its own support functions. From cleaning sheets to digging latrines, basic aspects of military life were handled by members of the armed services. But increasingly, these basic support services are being handled by private, nonmilitary sources. While this "contracting out" of services is often seen as cost effective, there has been considerable criticism of the practice in recent years.

Privatization has been subjected to especially heavy criticism in regard to the war in Iraq. As noted in Chapter 1, the United States has hired private contractors to provide security services for construction workers who are rebuilding Iraq's worn-out infrastructure and oil industry. As the insurgency has continued to mount since 2004, there has been consistent criticism of the role that private security forces have played in the war theater. According to a 2005 PBS *Frontline* report, members of the U.S. military have reported numerous problems with the more than 20,000 individuals who are serving as private security personnel. Among the complaints put forth by U.S. troops are claims that private contractors lack accountability and a clear relationship to the chain of command. There also exists a more emotional disconnect between active military personnel and private contractors that stems from vast differences in pay rates for similar levels of risk and position. Brookings Institution research fellow Peter Singer noted, "There's a bubbling resentment . . . and you're starting to sense a backlash from the military." We explore the use of civilian security forces in more detail in Chapter 11.

Although the potential problems differ somewhat among the various types of privatization, there is evidence that privatization leads to corruption because of its susceptibility to political influence, difficulties in monitoring contract performance and outcomes, reduced control over services, and limited numbers of competitors who are willing or able to provide services. The Halliburton Corporation has been a lightning rod for many of these concerns. This Texas-based construction company has been awarded a number of contracts from the federal government for reconstruction projects in Iraq. In particular, Halliburton was given a contract worth more than $7 billion to help restore Iraqi oil production. The awarding of the contract was controversial not only because Vice President Dick Cheney was once the company's CEO, but because the contract was awarded without inviting bids from other firms. The *Washington Post* reported that Bunnatine H. Greenhouse, the top civilian contracting official at the U.S. Army Corps of Engineers, testified that Halliburton's subsidiary Kellogg Brown & Root (KBR) was given an unusual amount of control over the terms of its no-bid contract to rebuild Iraq's oil infrastructure. Greenhouse stated, "I can unequivocally state that the abuse related to contracts awarded to KBR represents the most blatant and improper abuse I have witnessed during the course of my professional career." To add fuel to the fire, the Defense Contract Audit Agency issued a 2005 report that questioned more than $800 million in expenses that Halliburton charged to the Defense Department.

Indeed, it was exactly these kinds of problems that led to "publicization" of many privately provided services in the first place. The progressive reformers of the municipal research bureaus early in the twentieth century forcefully advocated that the government itself provide services such as street paving and trolley lines as a way of maintaining public accountability.

One of the most vocal opponents of privatization, the American Federation of State, County, and Municipal Employees (AFSCME), has published numerous examples to demonstrate that privatization results in poor performance, fraud, bribery, and graft. AFSCME and other government employee unions are fighting to keep the jobs of their members. In New York, Philadelphia, Indianapolis, and other major jurisdictions, the unions are being forced to prove that they can compete in price and quality with the private sector. The very fact that this is a matter of discussion has had a chilling effect on public employee union militancy and has inhibited demands for wage increases and lessened the likelihood of strikes.

The Nonprofit Gambit

In chess a gambit is a play, such as the sacrifice of a pawn, by which one seeks to gain a later advantage. Governments at all levels are increasingly using nonprofit organizations for just such strategic purposes. Services previously performed by government are being turned over to them—privatized because they are private organizations—so that government can both save money and get rid of perennially troublesome social programs that seek to improve the lot of the poor and unfortunate.

The nonprofit sector is a uniquely democratic phenomenon. In some respects it is the most capitalistic of our economic responses, reacting to **marketplace failure** by filling economic voids with **volunteers** and charitable contributions. In contrast, more socialistic economies tend to meet similar types of community needs through tax-supported government programs and services. Nonprofits provide a flexible alternative to tax-supported government action.

A nonprofit organization is in many respects a concept rather than a specific entity—and it can be defined in many different ways. The primary essence of a nonprofit organization, however, is that it is organized and operated for public or societal purposes (such as alleviation of poverty) rather than private benefit purposes (such as return on shareholders' investments). A second essential element of a nonprofit organization is its reliance on voluntary action for most of its financial and human resources. Despite common misconceptions to the contrary—and within well-defined limitations—nonprofit organizations can realize profits from their activities and programs, and they can engage in commercial-type enterprises. However, such profits must be returned to the operations of the agency.

Nonprofit organizations range in size and structure from large international religious denominations and seminational hospital chains to small, local, nonincorporated associations of people with common interests, goals, or concerns. From a relatively narrow, legalistic point of view, we can argue that a nonprofit organization is, in effect, an organization prescribed by the laws, rules, and codes

Marketplace failure ■
The inability of a society's free markets to provide a needed service.

Volunteer ■
A person who provides a service without compulsion or requirement and typically without compensation. However, with the growth of the voluntary sector, the definition of a volunteer appears to be changing. For example, many volunteer ambulance services and fire departments now pay volunteers for their standby time and/or for making runs. These paid persons are still called volunteers or paid volunteers as long as their work with the ambulance service is not their primary source of income.

of tax exemption. From a tax-exemption viewpoint, there are two basic types of nonprofit organizations:

1. Publicly supported charitable organizations that engage directly in religious, education, and social welfare programs
2. Private foundations, which tend to support other tax-exempt organizations' programs

The Reagan administration refocused the nation on the power of voluntary, nongovernmental responses to community problems. The Reagan agenda was predicated on the assumption that issue identification and action responsibility should be returned to local communities, thus increasing community reliance on nonprofits at a time when the government was simultaneously decreasing the size of, and the sector's access to, its traditional funding sources. Never in the history of the United States had the third sector been called on to do so much more with so much less.

Third sector ■
All those organizations that fit neither in the public sector (government) nor the private sector (business); a generic phrase for the collectivity of nonprofit organizations or organizations that institutionalize activism to deal with issues and problems that are being ignored by the public and private sectors.

The first Bush administration did not signal the arrival of less complex times for the nonprofit sector. In fact, Bush's 1988 presidential campaign may be most remembered for its "thousand points of light," a reference to volunteerism and Bush's belief that a new, more altruistic age had begun throughout the land. Bush first used this metaphor for volunteerism and charity in American life in his acceptance speech at the 1988 Republican National Convention. In his inaugural address he further defined the "points" as "all the community organizations that are spread like stars throughout the nation doing good." Peggy Noonan, who wrote Bush's acceptance speech, said in her memoirs *What I Saw at the Revolution* (1990) that the "thousand points of light . . . became Bush's shorthand way of referring to the network of helping organizations throughout the country, and it became in some circles the object of derision, or at least of good-natured spoofing." The public as well as the press were initially confused about the exact meaning of the "thousand points." The metaphor had to be explained so often that it became a symbol of the fractured syntax of Bush's speech patterns.

Subsequent President Bill Clinton carved out an interesting middle ground between private philanthropic organizations and the federal government. In 1993, Clinton signed the National and Community Service Trust Act, which established the Corporation for National and Community Service. This act brought a wide range of domestic community service programs under the umbrella of one central governmental organization known as AmeriCorps. Members of AmeriCorps serve with more than 3,000 nonprofits, public agencies, and faith-based and community organizations throughout the country. For example, an individual who volunteers with AmeriCorps may be placed with a group such as the Christian Appalachian Project, which builds homes in the impoverished areas of eastern Kentucky.

Despite programs such as AmeriCorps, the national inhibition toward more direct government funding for social programs has continued. The bottom line is that because of their charitable objectives and highly motivated, often volunteer, workforces, nonprofit organizations are a cheap way to fund a legislative mandate. In these instances, the subcontracting relationship to public funders renders the nonprofit organization at least indirectly accountable to the general public. In many cases, nonprofit board decision making is quite similar to that of a public utility: the nonprofit board is free to make decisions within legislative parameters.

The Faith-Based Initiative

The George W. Bush administration was even more enthusiastic than its predecessors about using nonprofit agencies—especially religious organizations—to provide social services. Bush created the Office of Faith-Based and Community Initiatives to further this agenda. And five departments—Health and Human Services, Housing and Urban Development, Justice, Education, and Labor—have created centers to further faith-based efforts. The most controversial element of Bush's initiative was a policy that allowed religious organizations to compete for grants to provide federally funded social services such as drug rehabilitation and health clinics for the poor. This element of Bush's program was criticized for blurring the separation between church and state by providing direct government payment to religious organizations, but most aspects of the faith-based initiative remained intact throughout his administration.

When Barack Obama took over the presidency in 2009, he made it clear that he would not abolish the White House's Faith-Based Initiative, but instead announced major reforms to the program. Obama had spent the earliest part of his career working as a community organizer in Chicago, often interacting with churches on projects aimed at improving the lives of residents in the city's poorest neighborhoods. The president emphasized that those receiving Faith-Based Initiative funds could not proselytize the people they help, nor could they discriminate in hiring practices on the basis of religion. Faith-based groups could only use federal dollars for secular programs. See Figure 3.2.

This issue of federal funding is at the heart of the controversy over faith-based efforts at the federal level. Critics are concerned with a possible breach of the establishment clause, the first part of the First Amendment that asserts that "Congress shall make no law respecting an establishment of religion." The clause is the basis for the separation of church and state in the United States. Yet the Supreme Court has held in *Everson v. Board of Education* (1947) that it is not a violation of the establishment clause for the government to pay for the cost of busing children to religious schools; nor was the tax-exempt status of religious property—at issue in *Walz v. Tax Commission of the City of New York* (1970)—a violation. Increasingly, the Court is taking an attitude of "benevolent neutrality" toward religion. Government activity that has the purpose or primary effect of advancing or inhibiting religion or that results in excessive government entanglement with religion is proscribed.

One continuing problem with the establishment clause is that, traditionally, many welfare and educational services in local communities have been provided by privately funded religious groups. This has posed a problem as far back as the New Deal. This was a potential problem for the Bush administration until the Supreme Court ruled in the 2007 case of *Hein v. Freedom from Religion Foundation* that taxpayers had no standing to sue to stop federal funding that they thought violated the First Amendment's so called "wall of separation" between church and

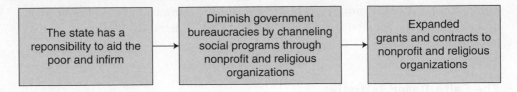

| The state has a responsibility to aid the poor and infirm | → | Diminish government bureaucracies by channeling social programs through nonprofit and religious organizations | → | Expanded grants and contracts to nonprofit and religious organizations |

FIGURE 3.2

A schematic of the faith-based initiative

state. President Obama seems to see a continued coexistence between federal funding of faith-based initiatives and preservation of the divide between church and state. At a 2009 press conference announcing reform of the Faith-Based Initiative he stated, "I believe deeply in the separation of church and state, but I don't believe this partnership will endanger that idea." However, because the case was decided by a five-to-four vote, the Court may have more to say on this issue as its composition changes with the coming years.

Voluntarism and Philanthropy

Nonprofit management, third-sector organizations, and independent-sector programs are only new articulations of the old concepts of charity, philanthropy, and social action. The notions of charity and philanthropy are old, but how they are influencing today's society is new. In a country where the profit motive is supreme, it is both curious and inevitable that there also exists a pervasive nonprofit sector. In most other societies voluntarism does not play as significant a role in the lives of people as it does in the United States.

This Western tradition of voluntarism has roots in two diverse ideological streams:

1. The Greco-Roman heritage of emphasis on community, citizenry, and social responsibility. The Greco-Roman ideology rests on a foundation of social reform to relieve community social problems, in order to improve the quality of life for all in the community.
2. The Judeo-Christian belief that relationships with a higher power affect our choices, our decision making. Thus, our purpose is not to change people's lots but rather to alleviate the (preordained) suffering of others, particularly the poor. Under the Judeo-Christian tradition, one does not help others solely from concern for oneself or one's neighbors but because a deity has given instructions to do so. We have been told to love our neighbors as we love ourselves: One loves one's neighbor because one loves God first and thus seeks to obey.

These two distinct, historical, ideological themes remain clearly evident today. For example, we can distinguish between *cause advocacy*, or leadership for social reform, and *case advocacy*, or individual service to a person or a limited group of persons in need. The influence of the two ideologies has been replayed countless times and in countless ways in the history of the American nonprofit sector. Notice how it is reflected in the following definitions of two types of voluntarism:

- *Philanthropy* is the giving of money or self to solve social problems; it is developmental, an investment in the future, and an effort to prevent future occurrences or recurrences.
- *Charity* is relieving or alleviating specific instances of suffering; it entails acts of mercy or compassion.

We tend to view these two forms of voluntary action as complementary elements in a nonprofit system. We need philanthropy as well as charity. However, this is not always the case. For example, Andrew Carnegie, an ardent philanthropist, abhorred charity. "It were better for mankind that the millions of the rich were thrown into the sea than so spent as to encourage the slothful, the drunken, the unworthy. . . . So spent, indeed, as to produce the very evils which it hopes to mitigate or cure." Yet from the Judeo-Christian charitable tradition, almshouses, charitable hospitals, orphan homes, and charitable organizations such as the Little Sisters of the Poor, the Salvation Army, the International Red Cross, and countless others, have helped relieve untold instances of human suffering.

As this nation was founded on the democratic ideals of both individualism and pluralism, our fundamental notion of how domestic problems (such as poverty, health, childrearing, housing, mental illness, homelessness, and inequitable access to employment opportunities) should be addressed is returning to its historical stable state: community-level problem solving. Our basic approach to dealing with domestic problems has progressed from individual and family-level resolution, to community problem solving (as the country urbanized), to massive state intervention, and back toward community problem solving. In part this return to the past has been a negative reaction to the perceived failure of many New Deal and Great Society social programs. Thus, as we enter a new century, the nexus of responsibility for charity and social action once again shows signs of shifting from a national orientation back to one of local control.

Until recently, philanthropy was largely limited to a leisure-time activity of the rich. In the last century, the great industrialists/robber barons and their families, after making their fortunes, might have donated funds for this or that public improvement. Andrew Carnegie was the most systematic example of this variety of traditional philanthropists. He gave away more than $350 million while he lived. This is equivalent to $6 billion today. But this century's differing attitudes toward social responsibilities and tax laws have transformed philanthropy from the altruistic concern of a single individual or family to a huge enterprise that affects and sustains a major portion of our economy and our society.

To be sure, wealthy people as well as people of all economic means contribute money, time, energy, and property for socially desirable purposes. But the largest share of the available philanthropic dollar goes to endow foundations. There are tax advantages to the donor in doing this. Therefore, using a foundation helps to multiply the total amount of philanthropic funds available for good works.

Now that philanthropy has to a large extent been institutionalized, its role has changed from random charitable or community developmental efforts to systematic efforts to find causes for focused efforts, to alleviate poverty in certain regions, control world population growth, or preserve rare artifacts, to state only three examples. The large-scale nature of philanthropy has caused it to become bureaucratized. No longer will an emotional charitable appeal suffice. A systematic proposal must be written and maneuvered through the various levels of approval of the requesting organization to the granting organization's often equally elaborate bureaucracy. Thus the alternative to government becomes, by trying to do what government has so far failed to do, more like the government than it finds comfortable to admit.

ANDREW CARNEGIE, L.L.D. (lavish library distributor), who believes it a great disgrace to die rich. This sentiment is, however, not taken seriously by his old associates who

A contemporary cartoon of Andrew Carnegie. The popular image of Carnegie is that of an enormously wealthy robber baron giving almost all of his money away before he died. But he is an important philosopher of the movement toward nonprofit organization in twentieth-century America. He sought to create institutions whereby the working classes could better themselves. But they had to be worthy of his largesse. Thus he paid for the construction of 3,000 public libraries—but the local communities had to buy the books and maintain the buildings. He donated organs to 4,000 churches—but only to those that were financially sound and well managed. He created innumerable trusts and foundations as well as museums, institutions for art and music (Carnegie Hall but not the Carnegie Delicatessen across the street), and one of the world's great universities: Carnegie-Mellon. This man who said, "He who dies rich dies disgraced" did not die disgraced. And when he did die, he gave the world the secret to his success by having this engraved on his tombstone:

> Here lies a man
> Who knew how to enlist
> In his service
> Better men than himself

A CASE STUDY: | The Revolution in the British Machinery of Government (1979–2011)

The British machinery of government differs in important respects from that of the United States. It is a system of cabinet, rather than presidential, government. In the British system the cabinet, the collective of ministers, is the ultimate seat of authority, although its existence and role are not provided for in a written constitution. Each minister is an elected member of Parliament, a politician of the ruling party of the day, and is assigned his or her post by the prime minister. The clear division of powers between the executive, legislative, and judicial branches is blurred in the British system, because the executive and the legislature are more closely tied.

Just as the U.S. system puts the three dominant classes of government agencies within the Executive Office of the President, the national executive departments, and independent public bodies, we find in the British system the parallels of Crown agencies, portfolio (cabinet) departments, and public bodies. As in the United States, some of the oldest departments, such as the Treasury and the Foreign Office, have long and independent traditions, and the bureaucracy of "Whitehall" has had a reputation for intransigence and self-serving behavior no less negative than that of the U.S. bureaucracy.

By 1979, the British central machinery of government had evolved into the ideal candidate for substantial reform. It had become large, unwieldy, costly, and secretive. The numbers of public bodies had grown to a point where it was difficult for any one person to understand what they did or to whom they were accountable, much less to assess whether their activities served the public interest or some narrower sectional interest. The legacy of the nationalization of a number of heavy industries that had not been well managed in the 1960s and 1970s represented a serious problem for the country, and their poor performance seemed to play a big part in the overall decline in British economic performance. With this in view, significant reform was necessary. The British system of unitary government, in which there are few of the checks and balances that exist in the U.S. Constitution and in U.S. policymaking behavior, provided circumstances in which far-reaching reform could be undertaken.

The most famous of these reforms, privatization, was not part of Margaret Thatcher's explicit platform when she was elected in 1979, although it was certainly part of the Conservative Party's program. Privatization was particularly focused on the nationalized industries and utilities. In Britain these included the petroleum, aerospace, and automotive industries, as well as gas, electricity, and water. Since the 1980s, these were successively sold to the private sector.

The massive reform of the national government departments, the "Next Steps" program, was launched in 1988. By 1992 more than half the British civil service—290,000 people—was included in the 76 new Executive Agencies. In a

(continued)

Nationalization ■
The taking over by government of a significant segment of a country's private sector industry, land, transportation, and so on, usually with compensation to the former owners. Socialist governments tend to favor extensive nationalization. Indeed, the level of nationalization is an accurate measure of the degree of a nation's socialism. Ironically, even conservative and nonsocialist governments have resorted to nationalization but in an effort to save a collapsing firm or service, rather than in ideological fervor.

Margaret Thatcher (1925–) ■
The conservative prime minister of Great Britain from 1979 to 1990. Elected as the first female prime minister in British history, her championing of free-market economic policies, coupled with an assertive role in world affairs, created an ideological style of leadership that came to be known as "Thatcherism."

U.S. context, this would be comparable to a million federal government employees being reassigned to several hundred new agencies whose executives could be immediately removed if they did not achieve their performance targets. Some former departments, such as Inland Revenue (equivalent to the U.S. Internal Revenue Service), were split into as many as 34 Executive Agencies, and each of these was pursuing stated quantitative performance targets. While these reforms are relatively recent, they do represent a disciplined and systematic program of reforming one of the most difficult parts of the public sector to reach and to manage—that is, the work conducted normally within civil service departments, albeit the "operational" rather than the "policy" aspects of that work. In effect, half of the traditional civil service has been placed in corporate-like structures where they will be treated more like corporate employees than public servants. This is the essence of corporatization—more flexibility for managers and less job security for all.

The results to date are encouraging, although the "arm's length relationship"—meaning no political interference—central to the Executive Agency concept can sometimes break down under sufficient political pressure. Within a decade, the British public sector was changed beyond recognition, with machinery of government changes of the most profound significance taking place. Overall, according to British professor Christopher Pollitt, "in the decade from 1979 to 1990, 800,000 employees were transferred into the private sector, and the share of the gross domestic product accounted for by state-owned industries fell from 11 percent in 1979 to 5.5 percent in 1990." In effect, the Thatcher revolution cut the British public sector in half.

This revolution in the machinery of government continued even after the revolutionary party was voted out of office. In 1997 when the Labour Party led by Prime Minister Tony Blair took over the British government, he declared, to the chagrin of many of the traditionally socialist members of his party, that the reforms would stay. He espoused a "third way" that went beyond the old left's preoccupation with state control but not so far as the far right's "belief that free markets are the answer to every problem." He sought to have his "New Labour" Party "rebrand Britain." And a major part of this "rebranding" was Labour's acceptance of the Conservative Party's radical reforms of the machinery of government.

A key concept in the British reforms is market testing—a process that requires agencies to buy goods and services from the private sector if savings are to be had. This has led to private contractors building and managing prisons, the Passport Agency hiring outside companies to print passports, and the Inland Revenue contracting out the management of its computer databases. According to reinventing guru David Osborne, "The U.K. has gone further in reinventing government than any other country [other] than New Zealand." True, New Zealand has jumped into the deep end of the reinventing pool, but it is so small in population (less than

3.5 million) that its reinventing efforts are more comparable to those of big municipal rather than national governments.

In Britain, the late 1990s saw the headlong dive into privatization slowing a little. The incoming Labour government of Tony Blair in its July 1998 white paper on local government scrapped the compulsory local government outsourcing the Conservatives had insisted on, replacing it with a broader concept of "Best Value." In April 1999, a true watershed was reached when Conservative opposition leader William Hague, in a major public lecture, conceded that privatization should not displace predominant public funding in health, education, and welfare. This does not mean that the pendulum of privatization will swing back to the division between public and private functions that once existed, but it does indicate that, in Britain at least, a practical rather than an ideological stance on these issues is emerging on both sides of the political fence. The practical approach was continued when the Conservative Party, now under Prime Minister David Cameron, came back into power in 2010. While austerity measures have forced the administration to substantially cut government programs, the emphasis has been on reforming, not abolishing, the welfare state.

In the United States, the reinventing-government movement renewed interest in bureaucratic innovation in general, and in aspects of commercialization in particular, but it would be fair to say that the United States has not been a leader in changes in this area. Indeed, if you read the formally stated "Principles of the National Performance Review," espoused by former Vice President Al Gore, you will see that they could easily and honestly be labeled "made in Great Britain."

But the proof of all this is in the implementation. Great Britain is way ahead in this game. Of course, it started a decade earlier and during recent years many have argued that the reinvention movement has run out of steam. Nevertheless, the U.S. machinery of government is radically different, and there is no guarantee that the United States could ever catch up. Different political cultures and different machinery require different administrative solutions.

For Discussion: *How have the British reforms influenced public administration in the United States? What will be the fate of the "third way" espoused by former British Prime Minister Tony Blair and embraced by former Presidents Bill Clinton and George W. Bush under the Obama administration?* ▶

SUMMARY

The machinery of government consists of all of the structural arrangements provided by a constitutional provision or a statute requiring the delivery of government services. These arrangements are not immutable. The functions of public agencies can and should be altered from time to time to reflect emerging needs and changing values.

Executive branch machinery has three main categories of organizations: executive office agencies, executive departments, and independent public bodies. State and local arrangements parallel those of the federal level.

The advent of the 1990s reinventing-government movement made reorganization once again fashionable. But this followed a long tradition of appointed bodies given the task of recommending improvements in governing structures. The Brownlow Committee of the 1930s and the Hoover Commissions of the 1940s and 1950s were followed by the National Performance Review of the 1990s. But because of the micromanagers in the Congress, executive agency reforms can never get too far ahead of the legislative will.

Privatization has two faces: (1) the private provision of services for those who can afford to pay for them and (2) the return to private sector functions previously performed by government. The various aspects of privatization are pivotal to reinventing-government efforts throughout the world. The United States has a uniquely large nonprofit sector that it has been able to use as a vehicle for privatization.

REVIEW QUESTIONS

1. What is the role of the U.S. Constitution in framing the national machinery of government?
2. How do state and local administrative arrangements mirror those of the federal government?
3. Why have the major efforts to reform the administrative machinery of the federal government—from the Brownlow Committee to the National Performance Review—been incomplete successes at best?
4. Why is the privatization of government services usually a more attractive option for Republicans than Democrats?
5. How does the nonprofit sector supplement the government's role in providing social services?

KEY CONCEPTS

Brownlow committee   A committee appointed by President Franklin D. Roosevelt in 1936 for the purpose of diagnosing the staffing needs of the president and making appropriate recommendations for the reorganization of the executive branch.

Bureau movement   The efforts of progressive reformers early in the twentieth century to apply scientific methods to municipal problems. Their efforts led to the creation of research bureaus, which in turn created the academic field of public administration.

Cabinet   The heads of the executive departments of a jurisdiction who report to and advise its chief executive; examples include the president's cabinet, the governor's cabinet, and the mayor's cabinet.

Cabinet government   The British system, whereby the cabinet as a whole, rather than only the prime minister who heads it, is considered the executive, and the cabinet is collectively responsible to the Parliament for its performance. In addition, the cabinet ministers are typically drawn from among the majority party's members in Parliament, whereas in the United States the cabinet secretaries are only from the executive branch.

Constitutional architecture   The administrative arrangements created by a government's constitution—from the separation of powers to the requirement that specific departments be created or services performed.

Dillon's rule   The criteria developed by state courts to determine the nature and extent of powers granted to local governments.

Executive Office of the President (EOP)   The umbrella office consisting of the top presidential staff agencies that provide the president help and advice in carrying out his major responsibilities. The EOP was created by President Franklin D. Roosevelt under the authority of the Reorganization Act of 1939. Since then, presidents have used executive orders, reorganization plans, and legislative initiatives to reorganize, expand, or contract the EOP.

Grace Commission   An attempt made by the Reagan administration to have business leaders study and reform the federal government; much was studied, little was reformed.

Hoover Commissions   The post–World War II efforts to reorganize the federal government.

Nonprofit organization   An organization created and operated for public or societal purposes (such as alleviation of poverty) rather than private benefit purposes (such as return on shareholders' investments).

Privatization   The process of returning to the private sector property or functions previously owned or performed by government.

Regulatory commission   An independent agency created by a government to regulate some aspect of economic life.

Reinventing government   The latest manifestation of the progressive tradition of continuously improving government—this time with an emphasis on privatization.

MySearchLab® EXERCISES

Apply what you learned in this chapter on MySearchLab (*www.mysearchlab.com*).

BIBLIOGRAPHY

American Federation of State, County, and Municipal Employees. (1984). *Passing the Bucks: The Contracting Out of Public Services*. Washington: AFSCME.

Blair, Tony. (1998). "Third Way, Better Way." *Washington Post National Weekly* (October 5).

Blumberg, Stephen. (1981). "Seven Decades of Public Administration: A Tribute to Luther Gulick." *Public Administration Review* 41 (March–April).

Brownlow, Louis. (1958). *A Passion for Anonymity: The Autobiography of Louis Brownlow*. Chicago: University of Chicago Press.

Carnegie, Andrew. (1900). *The Gospel of Wealth*. New York: Century.

Donahue, John M. (1989). *The Privatization Decision*. New York: Basic Books.

Egan, Timothy. (1995). "Many Seek Security in Private Communities." *New York Times* (September 3).

Goodnow, Frank J. (1900). *Politics and Administration: A Study in Governments*. New York: Russell and Russell.

Gore, Al. (1993). *From Red Tape to Results: Creating a Government That Works Better and Costs Less*. Report of the National Performance Review. Washington: Government Printing Office.

Kaufman, Herbert. (1976). *Are Government Organizations Immortal?* Washington: Brookings Institution.

Kettner, P. M., and L. L. Martin. (1987). *Purchase of Service Contracting*. Beverly Hills, CA: Sage.

King, N., and John D. Stoll. (2009). "Government Forces Out Wagoner at GM." *Wall Street Journal* (March, 30).

Lampman, Jane. (2008). "Obama Would Overhaul Bush's Faith-based Initiatives," *Christian Science Monitor* (July 2).

Lind, Michael. (1995). "To Have and Have Not: Notes on the Progress of the American Class War." *Harper's* (June).

Marlin, J. (1984). *Contracting for Municipal Services*. New York: Wiley.

McKenzie, Evan. (1994). *Privatopia: Homeowner Associations and the Rise of Residential Private Government*. New Haven, CT: Yale University Press.

Meriam, Lewis. (1939). *Reorganization of the National Government: What Does It Involve?* Washington: Brookings Institution.

Miller, Arthur. (1995). "To Newt on Art." *Nation* (July 31/August 7).

Morgan, D. R., and R. E. England. (1988). "The Two Faces of Privatization." *Public Administration Review* 48.

Mosher, Frederick C. (1967). *Government Reorganization: Cases and Commentary*. Indianapolis: Bobbs-Merrill.

Nakashima, Ellen. (2001). "Bush Opens 40,000 Federal Workers' Jobs to Competition." *Washington Post* (June 8).

Osborne, David, and Ted Gaebler. (1992). *Reinventing Government*. Reading, MA: Addison-Wesley.

Pollitt, Christopher. (1996). "Antistatist Reforms and New Administrative Directions: Public Administration in the United Kingdom." *Public Administration Review* 56 (January–February).

Preer, Robert. (1986). "Town Meetings Don't Work." *Washington Post* (June 13).

Public Broadcasting System. (2005). *Frontline: Private Warriors*. Airdate: June 21, 2005.

Rehfuss, J. A. (1989). *Contracting Out in Government*. San Francisco: Jossey-Bass.

Rosenbloom, David H. (1993). "Have an Administrative Rx? Don't Forget the Politics!" *Public Administration Review* 53 (November–December).

Ross, Bernard H. (1998). "Metropolitan Organization," *International Encyclopedia of Public Policy and Administration*, ed. Jay M. Shafritz. Boulder, CO: Westview Press.

Salant, Tanis Janes. (1998). "County," *International Encyclopedia of Public Policy and Administration*, ed. Jay M. Shafritz. Boulder, CO: Westview Press.

Savas, E. S. (1982). *Privatizing the Public Sector: How to Shrink Government*. Chatham, NJ: Chatham House.

Savoie, Donald J. (1994). *Thatcher Reagan Mulroney: In Search of a New Bureaucracy*. Pittsburgh: University of Pittsburgh Press.

Seidman, Harold. (1980). *Politics, Position, and Power: The Dynamics of Federal Organization*, 3rd ed. New York: Oxford University Press.

Szanton, Peter L., ed. (1981). *Federal Reorganization: What Have We Learned?* Chatham, NJ: Chatham House.

Wallsten, Peter, and Tom Hamburger. (2006). "The GOP Knows You Don't Like Anchovies," *Los Angeles Times* (June 28).

Weisband, Edward, and Thomas M. Frank. (1975). *Resignation in Protest*. New York: Viking Press.

Witte, Griff. (2005). "Democrats Criticize Payments to KBR. Pentagon Auditors Question More Than $1 Billion in Iraq Costs." *Washington Post* (June 28).

RECOMMENDED BOOKS

Downs, George W., and Patrick D. Larkey. (1986). *The Search for Government Efficiency: From Hubris to Helplessness*. Philadelphia: Temple University Press. An explanation of why efforts to reform government tend to operate in ignorance of previous reform efforts and why all such schemes have only "a minuscule chance of successful implementation."

Ingraham, Patricia W., James R. Thompson, and Ronald P. Sanders, eds. (1998). *Transforming Government: Lessons from the Reinvention Laboratories.* San Francisco: Jossey-Bass. A collection of essays on the lessons for reform derived from the federal government's reinventing-government effort.

Light, Paul C. (1997). *The Tides of Reform: Making Government Work, 1945–1995.* New Haven, CT: Yale University Press. The history of reforming the federal government in the 50 years after World War II.

Osborne, David, and Peter Plastrik. (2005). *Banishing Bureaucracy: The Five Strategies for Reinventing Government,* 2nd ed. New York: Penguin Putnam. More stories of government organization turnarounds; touted as the "sequel" to the 1992 *Reinventing Government* because Osborne is the senior author of both books.

Smith, Steven R., and Michael Lipsky. (1995). *Nonprofits for Hire.* Cambridge, MA: Harvard University Press. The how and why of governmental use of nonprofit organizations.

RELATED WEB SITES

www.americorps.gov

Americorps

Americorps is an organization that offers opportunities for adults of all ages and backgrounds to serve the nation through a network of partnerships with local and national nonprofit groups. This Web site has information about ways for both organizations and indivduals to become involved, with detailed overviews of AmeriCorp programs.

www.brookings.edu

The Brookings Institution

Brookings is a think tank focusing on public policy matters. Brookings research is often cited in policy debates and discussions. Its site offers news and articles on the national and world level as well as the economy. Through its online platform Brookings offers reports about its research and information about how to become involved in the organization and its activities.

www.icma.org

International City/County Management Association

The organization provides technical and management assistance, training, and information resources in the areas of performance measurement, ethics education and training, community and economic development, environmental management, technology, and other topics to its members and the broader local government community. The site also provides information about research, conferences, and career development.

www.napawash.org

National Academy of Public Administration

The National Academy of Public Administration provides insights on key public management issues, as well as advisory services to government agencies. The organization's Web site documents its current research, programs, and publications.

www.gpoaccess.gov/gmanual/

U.S. Government Manual Online

Online access to the *U.S. Government Manual,* which is the official handbook for the federal government. At this site the organizational framework of the federal government is described in detail. It also includes information on quasi-official agencies, international organizations in which the United States participates, and boards, commissions, and committees.

Intergovernmental Relations

KEYNOTE: The Intergovernmental Problem of Marijuana

For many generations the topic of marijuana has been a mainstay of discussions on America's college campuses. This is obvious by the distinctive smell found in the proximity of the nation's institutions of higher education. As students examine their personal freedoms and the limits that may be placed on them by the law, conversations regularly turn to the rules that govern their access to one of the most controversial substances in the United States. It is not unusual to hear a student ask why marijuana, or cannabis as it is more formally known, often remains beyond their legal reach, while alcohol—a substance with a long history of destructive consequences—is legal and readily available to anyone 21 or older.

While the debates regarding marijuana use tend to focus primarily on questions of freedoms and liberties, this substance and its place in contemporary society provides a familiar case study in the complexities and tensions that are inherent in the intergovernmental nature of American federalism.

Marijuana has had a long history of use in the United States. The hemp plant, used in making rope and canvas for sailing ships, from which marijuana is also derived, was a common part of colonial-era agriculture. Proponents of marijuana legalization often point to the fact that George Washington ordered his slaves to cultivate hemp on his Virginia plantation during his years as a gentleman farmer. Indeed, Virginia's original English settlement, Jamestown colony, actually required farmers to plant hemp as one of their crops.

While hemp has been grown for its use in many products (both food and fiber) ever since the colonial period, marijuana's use as an intoxicant in America became prevalent in the late nineteenth and early twentieth centuries. The substance found growing popularity within the expanding Latin American communities of the Southwest and in the African American communities in America's urban areas in the years in and around the turn of the twentieth century. With this growth in use of cannabis in the United States came some real problems, but even more manufactured concerns regarding marijuana's role in American culture.

Marijuana, like many intoxicating substances, can be misused. Excessive use of marijuana by some, during the early twentieth century, did result in incidents where individuals engaged in behaviors that were harmful to themselves or others. However, any real problems associated with its use paled in comparison with the portrayal of marijuana's dangers within the American media. Films such as the 1936 propaganda movie *Reefer Madness* comically (the comedy was inadvertent) dramatized how marijuana use leads to sexual promiscuity, the murder of one's parents, and a liking for jazz music. This was complemented by highly negative stories in William Randolph Hearst's chain of newspapers, which printed sensational and highly questionable stories designed to fuel public fear about marijuana's threat to American society. Many of these so-called threats were crafted as to play on a variety of the nation's worst racial prejudices and fears, including scenarios where minorities perpetrated crimes on whites while under the influence of this poisonous weed.

As the twentieth century began, public fears served to encourage government action on the nation's "marijuana problem." In the earliest stages of the campaign against cannabis, the federal government attempted to tighten regulations on the sale of marijuana throughout the nation. In 1906 Congress passed the Pure Food and Drug Act which, among other things, required the labeling of marijuana when sold without a prescription.

As regulation of marijuana was emerging out of Washington, D.C., the states took the lead in banning marijuana completely. Beginning in California in 1907 and continuing with dozens of other states until the 1930s, marijuana was deemed an illegal substance, with possession and production of the intoxicant ruled as criminal offenses, punishable by fines and jail time.

The patchwork of marijuana laws throughout the nation in the first quarter of the twentieth century and growing public concern with all forms of intoxicants during an age of prohibition helped lead Congress to work on establishing more consistent rules on the sale and trafficking of cannabis. With some states banning marijuana and others taking more of a laissez faire approach, Congress created model legislation for marijuana and other substances under the Uniform Narcotic Act (UNA). At first few states signed on to the voluntary standards of the UNA, but the efforts of the President Franklin D. Roosevelt administration and an impressive propaganda effort on the radio resulted in every state signing on to the standards by 1935.

Even with the adoption of uniform regulations by all states, there was continued pressure in Washington for the federal government to be more aggressive in fighting cannabis use. At the forefront of this campaign for a stronger federal presence was the head of the Federal Bureau of Narcotics (FBN; now merged in the Drug Enforcement Administration), Harry Anslinger (1892–1975). As the first director of the FBN, Anslinger became a crusader for tougher federal narcotics laws. Anslinger, who would serve as the head of the FBN for over three decades (1930–1962), maintained an almost religious zeal for outlawing cannabis, and successfully rallied support from a variety of political and economic sources for his cause. However, without constitutional authority to establish an outright ban of marijuana, Anslinger was forced to find alternative methods to rid the nation of the problem.

As is often the case with federal efforts to change behaviors, the power of taxation was selected as the tool by which the feds could attack marijuana use in America. In 1937 Congress passed the Marijuana Tax Act, which placed taxes on anyone dealing commercially in cannabis and established heavy fines and jail sentences on individuals not in compliance with the act. This act did not criminalize the possession or use of cannabis, but the impact of the law was nonetheless enormous in terms of limiting access to marijuana throughout the nation. Anslinger was a very successful bureaucrat. By expanding his mandate with this new law, he also expanded his agency and his budget—mainly at the expense of minorities and jazz musicians who had little political influence.

States responded to the federal insertion into marijuana matters not with shouts of protest against usurpation of power, but instead cracked down on marijuana even more through their own laws over the following three decades. Anslinger and his allies in the nation's capital had successfully created an environment where any state going against the federal position on cannabis was seen as putting the interests of decadent, drug, induced minorities against the protection of decent, law-abiding white Americans.

It wasn't until the 1960s that both the wisdom and legality of federal marijuana policy began to be challenged in mainstream venues. In the changing American culture of the era it became more fashionable to question the legitimacy of federal incursions into areas of individual freedoms. It was also becoming more apparent that the costs of implementing prohibition of marijuana were rising as the substance grew in popularity during the "hippie" decade.

The federal government under President Richard M. Nixon even reconsidered its hard-line stance on cannabis through a well-publicized commission on drug policy. While Nixon and the federal government opted to continue the hard line against marijuana despite the commission's recommendations to consider other paths, the states began a process of reasserting their control over this policy area.

In 1973 Oregon became the first state to decriminalize marijuana. By decriminalizing consumption and possession of small amounts of cannabis, Oregon made most marijuana use the legal equivalent of speeding. In other words, it was not legal to smoke pot, but doing so would not lead to jail time and a criminal record. By 1978 eight other states had followed Oregon's lead. These states' actions directly contradicted federal policies that identified marijuana as an illegal narcotic. Simply put, the federal government did not recognize the decriminalization efforts and held that federal public administrators, such as those in the Drug Enforcement Agency (DEA), would follow federal standards even if state laws differed. This meant that even if the locals wouldn't arrest you for smoking pot, the feds still might.

The strained relationship between states and the federal government regarding marijuana was exacerbated in the late 1990s when California became the first state to legalize the use of marijuana for medical purposes. Unlike decriminalization, legalization means that the state permits the use of cannabis as long as a prescription for the substance has been obtained. A number of other states quickly followed California's lead, with more than a dozen states providing legal protection for medical marijuana by 2011.

While legalized medical marijuana became popular in the states, the federal government refused to yield on its stance that marijuana has no medical properties and that therefore state laws legalizing the use of cannabis for medical purposes would not be recognized. As is often the case when there is a showdown between the federal government and states, the conflict ended up in the courts.

TABLE 4.1

STATES THAT HAVE "decriminalized" marijuana by treating first-time possession of a small amount for personal use much like a traffic citation

ALABAMA	MISSISSIPPI
CALIFORNIA	NEBRASKA
COLORADO	NEVADA
CONNECTICUT	NEW YORK
MAINE	NORTH CAROLINA
MASSACHUSETTS	OHIO
MINNESOTA	OREGON

Source: National Organization for the Reform of Marijuana Laws.

When federal DEA officials destroyed a number of marijuana plants that were owned by a Californian growing the plant for medicinal purposes under a prescription from a physician, the battle between the states and feds was thrown into the courts.

In the 2005 case of *Gonzales v. Raich*, the U.S. Supreme Court held that Congress may ban the use of marijuana even in cases where states have legalized its use for medical purposes. The Court's decision in this case rested on the position that the federal government's constitutionally delegated power to regulate commerce trumped California's policy on medical marijuana, thus allowing DEA officials the ability to act in the interest of federal laws even if those actions went against state medical marijuana laws.

What is perhaps most interesting about the aftermath of the *Gonzales* case was that the decision did not seem to slow the growth of medical marijuana use in California and other states. In fact the medical marijuana business is booming. Since 2005 more Californians that ever have taken advantage of the state's lax rules on attaining marijuana for medical purposes. It has become almost laughable how easy it is to obtain a prescription for marijuana in the Golden State. Doctors in California have dispensed prescriptions for marijuana by the tens of thousands and pot has become a common sight in storefronts from San Diego to San Francisco.

After California Governor Arnold Schwarzenegger, whose youthful pot smoking was enthusiastically displayed in a 1976 documentary (*Pumping Iron*), signed a 2010 law effectively decriminalizing marijuana, he went on *The Tonight Show* and told Jay Leno and all other citizens of California: "No one cares if you smoke a joint or not"(November 8, 2010). But it is in the nature of the American federal system that governors and criminal justice officials in many other states do care. So beware!

▶ TABLE 4.2

STATES WITH ACTIVE MEDICAL MARIJUANA PROGRAMS: Generally, in these states marijuana can be legally bought and used with a doctor's prescription

ALABAMA	MICHIGAN
ARIZONA	MONTANA
CALIFORNIA	NEVADA
COLORADO	NEW JERSEY
DELAWARE	NEW MEXICO
DISTRICT OF COLUMBIA	OREGON
HAWAII	RHODE ISLAND
MAINE	VERMONT
MARYLAND	WASHINGTON

Source: National Organization for the Reform of Marijuana Laws.

With medical marijuana proliferating in California and beyond, the federal government has been faced with a dilemma. Should DEA agents ramp up their efforts to crack down on the expanding medical marijuana market, or do they turn a blind eye and give their attention to other matters?

In 2009 the answer to this question came in an announcement from U.S. Attorney General Eric Holder that the DEA will no longer raid medical marijuana retail outlets. In effect, the federal government had called a temporary truce with states on this matter. The laws had not changed and the feds continued to have the authority to crack down on medical marijuana use. The desire to do so had simply dissipated with the arrival of the Obama administration.

Although the truce on medical marijuana seems to be holding firm, intergovernmental relations on this matter are far from resolved. With states facing unprecedented fiscal crises, the pressure to legalize and tax marijuana grows. If states turn to pot as a cure for their financial woes, the feds will have to reconsider their marijuana policy. Of course the weight of the federal government's own fiscal troubles may lead future leaders in Washington, D.C., to consider taxation of legalized marijuana as a key to balanced budgets. After all, the estimated number of marijuana users is so large that potential tax revenues would be enormous. While it may be hard to predict the course of federal–state relations in upcoming years, it is fairly certain that those debates on college campuses regarding marijuana will continue on for years to come.

The debate also continues in prisons, where tens of thousands of mostly young men, disproportionately minority, rot because they were caught in possession of minor amounts of marijuana—not for sale but for personal use. They got sucked up by the drug-law enforcement complex. Powerful interest groups wanted the current marijuana legal situation continued. Prison guards want more prisoners. Police officers want to maintain or expand the budgets for drug enforcement. Distillers and brewers who often turn people into alcoholics don't want competition from another legal drug. These manufacturers and law enforcement unions all make major financial contributions to politicians to maintain the status quo. The pot smokers, so often poor, disorganized, and disoriented, have only the slightest political clout.

Ironically, one of these pot-smoking minority young men at loose ends with life got his act together, so to speak, and became president of the United States. Barack Obama, in his bestselling memoir *Dreams from My Father* (2004), confesses to extensive "reefer" experience: "I had discovered that it didn't make any difference whether you smoked reefer in the white classmate's sparkling new van, or in the dorm room of some brother you'd met down at the gym, or on the beach with a couple of Hawaiian kids. . . ." He wrote that the high he got from smoking reefer "could at least help you laugh at the world's ongoing folly and see through all the hypocrisy and bullshit and cheap moralism."

Now he is not only the commander in chief but the chief dispenser of the "hypocrisy and bullshit," not to mention "cheap moralism," concerning marijuana policy. Thousands of young people are having their lives ruined by what he knows to be ill-advised policies that he could change for the better in major ways with the stroke of a pen. Yet, despite the fact that, early in his political career, he called for the decriminalization of marijuana, today he sits atop a bureaucratic criminal justice machine that would have swept him up and thrown him in jail save for the grace of God. Now he has the power to play God in this matter and show grace to so many others. Yet he allows these socially destructive policies to continue. One can only wonder why!

There may be hope on the horizon, not from the executive branch but from the Congress. Appalled at the cruelty and wastefulness of current federal marijuana policy, two leaders in the Congress, one from the far right, Ron Paul, a Republican from Texas, and one from the far left, Barney Frank, a Democrat from Massachusetts, have sponsored a bill in 2011 that could get the federal government out of the marijuana punishment business altogether. The problem would simply be turned back to the states to allow or criminalize marijuana use as they wish. That's one of the nice things about American federalism: the national government can always just dump an intractable problem back on the states. Then it's their problem, and equally important, it is none of the federal government's business.

For Discussion: *Why has the federal government's marijuana policy been treated as a criminal justice problem as opposed to a public health problem as it is in Australia and many European nations? How likely is it that the Obama administration will seek significant reforms if it obtains a second term of office?*

Important Disclaimer

The authors of this text are totally opposed to the use of illegal drugs of any kind because anyone who does so is risking their health, their career, and possibly their personal freedom. For those who feel an urgent need for recreational drugs, we recommend ample portions of dark chocolate, the darker the better, and preferably containing almonds, cashews, or raisins. Then the only thing you risk is the often cited "chocolate high," or getting too fat.

THE EVOLUTION OF FEDERAL SYSTEMS

History indicates clearly that the principal factor in the formation of federal systems of government has been a common external threat. Tribes, villages, cities, colonies, or states have joined together in voluntary unions to defend themselves. However, not all systems so formed have been federal. A true federal system such as that in the United States must have the following features:

1. A written constitution that divides government powers between the central government and the constituent governments, giving substantial powers to each
2. Levels of government, through their own instrumentalities, exercising power directly over citizens (unlike a confederation, in which only subnational units

act directly on citizens while the central government acts only on the subnational governments)

3. A constitutional distribution of powers that cannot be changed unilaterally by any level of government or by the ordinary process of legislation

Alliances and Confederations

In the beginning there was the alliance—a coalition of states agreeing to help each other in the event of war or crises. Alliances do not only involve cooperation and aggregation of capabilities; they are generally directed toward an actual or potential enemy and the actual or potential use of force. The agreement on which an alliance is based is often embodied formally in a treaty, but it can also be based on a tacit or informal understanding. Alliances can exist between states that are relatively equal in power and involve mutual security guarantees, or they can be between unequal states—in which case the more powerful state generally extends a unilateral guarantee to the less powerful one. This is always a dangerous situation for the weaker state. Too often a willingness to protect and preserve has turned into a desire to take over and annex.

Then came the confederation, a group of independent states that delegate powers on selected issues to a central government. In a confederation, the central government is deliberately limited, designed to be inherently weak, and has few independent powers. The United States was a confederation from 1781 to 1789. But the central government was so ineffectual in dealing with problems such as **Shays' Rebellion** and interstate commerce that the Constitutional Convention of 1787 was called to discuss the inadequacies of confederation government. To the great surprise of many who sent them to the convention, the delegates recommended not improvements in the confederation—which was expected—but a whole new form of national government.

Defining Intergovernmental Relations

Finally, when there was a need for even stronger bonding among governments, along came federalism, a system of governance in which a national, overarching government shares power with subnational or state governments. Intergovernmental relations represent federalism in action. It is the complex network of day-to-day interrelationships among the governments within a federal system. It is the political, fiscal, programmatic, and administrative processes by which higher units of government share revenues and other resources with lower units of government, generally accompanied by special conditions that the lower units must satisfy as prerequisites to receiving the assistance.

In essence, intergovernmental relations are the sets of policies and mechanisms by which the interplay between different levels of government serving a common geographical area is managed. Such relations reflect the basic constitutional framework that links the levels of government, as well as dynamic contemporary

Shays' Rebellion ■
A futile armed revolt (1786–1787) led by Daniel Shays (1747–1825), a Revolutionary War officer, in New England to protest the discontent of small farmers over debts and taxes. The rebellion was never a serious military threat, but it raised concern over the inadequacy of the Articles of Confederation to handle internal disorders and thus helped to create support for a stronger national government.

**William Pitt
(1708–1778)** ■
The First Earl of
Chatham, known as
the Great Commoner
for his leadership
in the House of
Commons. The City of
Pittsburgh is named in
his honor. Historians
call him "the elder"
because his son with
the same name was
later prime minister.

Assassination ■
The deliberate murder
of someone, especially
of a politically
prominent personage,
for political motives.
The original assassins
were thirteenth-
century Muslims
whose main goal
was the murder of
Christian Crusaders
and other political
rivals. Assassination is
a time-honored though
dishonorable way
of removing people
from public office.
Presidents Lincoln,
Garfield, McKinley,
and Kennedy were
assassinated;
Presidents Theodore
Roosevelt, Franklin
Roosevelt, Truman,
Ford, and Reagan
all narrowly
escaped death in
various attempted
assassinations.

factors including relative power, financial strengths, ethnic divisions, geographical factors, and so on. The essence of this constitutional framework is well captured by this famous 1763 statement by **William Pitt**, the elder, in the British House of Lords:

> The poorest man may in his cottage bid defiance to all the forces of the Crown. It may be frail—its roof may shake—the wind may blow through it—the storm may enter—the rain may enter—but the King of England cannot enter!—all his force dares not cross the threshold of the ruined tenement!

In the United States today, the "crown"—the federal government—may not interfere unless this "poorest man" commits the proverbial "federal offense" and federal officials obtain a search or arrest warrant. And only local officials can obtain warrants for local crimes. This is why the investigation of President John F. Kennedy's 1963 **assassination** was undertaken by the local police in Dallas, Texas. In the eyes of the law, Kennedy was just the victim of a local murder. In 1963 it was a federal crime to rob a bank if it was insured, as most are, by a federal agency, but it was not a federal crime to murder a president. (It is now!) After the local police so botched the investigation that they inadvertently spawned a conspiracy theory industry, Congress made it a federal offense to threaten or attack a president, vice president, or his or her immediate family. The point here is that within a federal system, different levels of government often perform similar functions, law enforcement in this case, that are constitutionally separate. Each level has constitutional limitations.

An understanding of intergovernmental relations is essential for every public administrator, because this area defines the scope and territory of the administrative world in which he or she lives. It is not just a question of territorial boundaries, though the boundaries of all political units are established by laws, constitutions, and accords, the study of which is central to intergovernmental relations. It is equally a question of functional allocations, because most countries have found it necessary to distinguish among national, regional, and local issues and to allocate them in various ways to different levels of government. This allocation, the question of who does what and with what resources, is the essential core of intergovernmental relations.

THE FUNDAMENTAL SETTLEMENT

The most critical dimension of intergovernmental relations, that which forms and shapes the context of every government, is the fundamental settlement or accord by which the government was created. Such accords can never ultimately be unilateral—they must always involve a settlement between a plurality of communities. Federalism, like most institutional forms, is a solution of, or an attempt to solve, a certain kind of problem of political organization. Viable federal systems accommodate regional or subsystem diversity, thereby enhancing the strength of the greater federation. Both the United States and the European Community offer illustrations of settlements whose terms determine the nature, scope, and powers of the governments involved.

The Constitution

The 1789 Constitution of the United States is the oldest written constitution continuously in force and an enduring example to the rest of the world of the benefits and effectiveness of such a well-crafted document. Its famous beginning, "We the people," asserts that the source of its authority is the people as opposed to the states. It then assigns powers to the various branches of government and in doing so structures the government. It limits the powers that any branch may have and allows each branch to check and balance the others. Most significantly, it denies certain powers to the national government, reserving them for the states and the people. But aside from its legal force as law and its physical existence as a piece of fading parchment in the National Archives, the U.S. Constitution is the national icon, the premier symbol of American freedom and governance; above all, it represents the collective political will of the American people over two centuries to maintain their republican form of government. Nevertheless, because of the nature of judicial review, the Constitution is ultimately, as New York Governor Charles Evans Hughes asserted in 1907, "what the judges [of the Supreme Court] say it is." It is as Thomas Jefferson angrily wrote in a September 6, 1819, letter to Judge Spencer Roane, "a mere thing of wax in the hands of the judiciary, which they may twist and shape into any form they please."

The 85 essays in *The Federalist*, published in 1787–1788, are the classic commentary on the U.S. Constitution and the theories behind it. They are considered by many political scientists to be the most important work of political theory written in the United States—the one product of the American mind counted among the classics of political philosophy. The papers were originally newspaper articles written by Alexander Hamilton, James Madison, and John Jay (all under the pseudonym **Publius**) to encourage New York to ratify the new Constitution.

Jay wrote only a few of the Federalist papers, but he was the first chief justice of the United States—a job he considered so insignificant that he resigned to become governor of New York. His resignation had the beneficial effect of making room for a later chief justice, John Marshall, a Revolutionary War soldier who became the third chief justice of the Supreme Court and, by almost universal agreement, did the most to establish the independent authority of the Court. From 1801 to 1835, he led the struggle for the Court to be the final arbiter of the Constitution and, by sheer force of will and legal cunning, made the federal judiciary a true check on the power of the other two branches.

Marshall, in a wide-ranging series of decisions, helped to create the American style of federalism. For example, in 1819 in *McCulloch v. Maryland* the Court upheld the implied powers granted to the Congress by the **necessary and proper clause** of the Constitution, upheld the supremacy of the national government in carrying out functions assigned to it by the Constitution, and established the doctrine of intergovernmental tax immunity. In stating that "the power to tax is the power to destroy," the Court held that the Bank of the United States was not

Publius ■
An ancient Roman who was famous for his devotion to republican government. It was common in the late eighteenth century for political writers to use a pseudonym of ancient lineage that reflected their political leanings.

Necessary and proper clause ■
That portion of Article I, Section 8, of the U.S. Constitution (sometimes called the elastic clause) that makes it possible for Congress to enact all "necessary and proper" laws to carry out its responsibilities.

subject to taxation by the State of Maryland. And "destroy" is exactly what the Maryland State Legislature wanted to do to the bank. It viewed the "Monster Bank" so much as the tool of the privileged elite and the still-hated British interests that it specifically passed a law taxing the bank's operations in Maryland in the hopes of crippling it.

The European Union

Sometimes the fundamental settlement occurs all at once, as it did with the creation of the American federal system by the U.S. Constitution. Sometimes it evolves over a series of accords, as it has with the European Union, which is still evolving. It may eventually become a "sort of United States of Europe," as Winston Churchill envisioned in 1946; or it could fracture into warring (either hot or cold) camps as it did so often in the twentieth century. Remember, the U.S. experience with federalism was not a ride in a continuous direction. The Civil War was a major setback. Of course, after the war the Union was stronger than ever. Historian James M. McPherson reminds us in his *Battle Cry of Freedom* (1988) that "before 1861 the two words 'United States' were generally rendered as a plural noun: 'the United States *are* a republic.' The war marked a transition of the United States to a singular noun." Only after the Civil War were we "one nation under God, indivisible," as it says in the Pledge of Allegiance. The war had decided once and forever the issue of divisibility.

THE AMERICAN FEDERAL SYSTEM

The U.S. Constitution is the fundamental settlement defining federalism and also defining the permanent features of intergovernmental relations in the United States. Like the constitutions of many countries, the U.S. Constitution is capable both of amendment as to its formal terms and evolution as to its meaning as a result of such things as Supreme Court judgments. Yet, in essence, it represents a relatively unchanging element of the framework within which intergovernmental relations are conducted.

The most fundamental aspects include the Constitution's provisions in three areas:

Bill of Rights ∎
The first ten amendments to the U.S. Constitution. Only a few individual rights were specified in the Constitution that was ratified in 1789. Shortly after its adoption, however, ten amendments— called the Bill of Rights—were added to the Constitution to guarantee basic individual liberties.

1. Its creation of a federal system—that is, one in which there is both a national government and state governments
2. Its allocation of certain functions to the national government
3. Its embodiment of certain principles, particularly through the interpretation of the Constitution and the **Bill of Rights,** which provide scope for Supreme Court judgments that can profoundly alter the respective powers and functions of the national and state governments over time

If we grow up within a federal system and are used to belonging to a state as well as a nation, it is difficult to imagine what it would be like to live in a country without states. Yet this is the case in countries such as France and New Zealand, which have unitary governments, with all significant decisions being made at the national level.

TABLE 4.3

Types of Governments

Type	Examples	
Unitary Governments		
There are no state governments; all important power lies with the national government.	Denmark France	Japan New Zealand
Federal Governments		
There is a national government and a number of state governments; power is shared between them.	Australia Brazil Canada Germany	India Mexico Switzerland United States
Confederations		
Power rests with "sovereign" state governments, and an overarching government has some defined powers.	European Union Commonwealth of Independent States (former USSR)	

Three Categories of Governments

There are three main categories into which we can allocate nations: unitary governments, federal governments, and confederations (see Table 4.3). Each has certain strengths and weaknesses, and it is interesting to consider the effects of altering the system from one of these to another, as New Zealand did in 1879 when it abolished its federal system and moved to unitary government. In Australia today, a significant minority would like to abandon federalism, abolish state governments, and perhaps introduce a new level of less costly, more numerous regional administrations.

Sometimes the reform impetus goes in the other direction. For example, Great Britain, formally the United Kingdom, is on the verge of moving from a unitary government to a federal structure now that Scotland and Wales will have their own legislatures with broad powers.

Unitary Government Advantages   Unitary governments do have some significant strengths. The following are the four key advantages they usually have over a federal system or a confederation:

1. National direction is clear; policies can be made by a single government without the need for negotiation or conflict with subnational states.
2. There can be no confusion as to **accountability**. It is clear to voters which level of government is responsible for a particular problem or function. (Legislators who wish to spend money must raise it; it is not possible for legislators to seek to pass the **buck** for failure to another level of government.)

Accountability ■
The extent to which one must answer to higher authority—legal or organizational—for one's actions in society at large or within one's particular organizational position. Elected public officials are theoretically accountable to the political sovereignty of the voters. In this sense, appointed officials—from file clerks to cabinet secretaries—are less accountable than elected officials. The former are accountable mainly to their organizational supervisors, while the latter must answer to their constituents.

Buck ■
Responsibility. To avoid a problem or a responsibility is to *pass the buck*. President Truman was famous for having a sign on his desk that read "The Buck Stops Here." *Buck,* a term from poker, refers to the marker put in front of the player who next had to deal. Bureaucrats in many jurisdictions refer to the form memos that they use to direct paper from one to another as buck slips.

3. Duplication of legislatures, bureaucracies, and programs is avoided with significant savings in direct costs—and the more subtle but no less real costs of needless duplication.
4. Issues of fairness in raising and spending money between levels of government (vertical fiscal imbalance) simply do not arise.

Federal Government Advantages   Unitary governments also have major drawbacks, which in turn correspond to the major strengths of federal systems. These include the following:

1. A federal system has greater scope for diversity and experimentation in policy.
2. The need to debate issues rather than enact them instantly may provide a more considered and viable policy outcome. This tendency toward incrementalism is seen as integral to democracy.
3. A federal system must consider the different ethnic or cultural groupings that may predominate in a particular state and wish to pursue a distinct cultural or social policy—such as the French Canadians in Quebec. (As the cases of Quebec and Bosnia show, membership in a federation may still fail to fulfill the nationalist aspirations of many people.)
4. The danger always exists in a large country that a unitary government may be too remote for appropriate democratic participation by regional centers located away from the capital; a federal system encourages—indeed demands—regional participation in governance.
5. The danger exists in a unitary government that the stronger regions, the larger racial groups, or more powerful interests will provide insufficient allowance for the needs of minorities or weaker groups.

In *The Federalist*, No. 10, James Madison discusses the problem of such factions and the danger they pose to a political system. Madison feared that the interests of parties and pressure groups could destabilize a government, but he believed that an overarching representative government, with a functional as well as a territorial separation of powers, could prevent this.

Confederations   Confederate systems are inherently weak as central governments. The United States was originally a confederate system. The Articles of Confederation were the original framework for the government of the new United States; they went into effect in 1781 and were superseded by the U.S. Constitution in 1789. The Articles said that the states were entering into a "firm league of friendship" and a "perpetual union for the common defense, the security of their liberties, and their mutual and general welfare." The Articles provided for a weak central government, which could not compel states to respect treaties, could not regulate interstate and foreign commerce, could neither collect taxes directly from the people nor compel the states to pay for the costs of the national government, and could not create a sense of national unity and national purpose. Such absence of central power directly contributed to problems such as a devalued national currency, trade wars between states, and an ineffectual foreign policy. It nonetheless provided the experience of state cooperation out of which the consciousness of the need for a stronger union could emerge.

All confederations such as the present European Union and the Commonwealth of Independent States (the former Soviet Union) pose the same question: Which way are they going? Will they evolve, as the United States did, into a strong federal system? Or will they follow the route of the **Confederate States of America** or the **Confederation of the Rhine** and simply disintegrate, to be replaced by new governing structures?

THE STRUCTURE OF INTERGOVERNMENTAL RELATIONS

There are eternal questions concerning the structure of intergovernmental relations: Which level of government will have overall responsibility for what functions? When functions are shared between levels of government, how will each function be divided among national, state, and local governments? Should the taxes needed to finance local government be raised by the government that is to spend them or by the higher level of government most successful at tax-raising? Should a national government have an objective of redistributing revenues to reduce the differential between the richest and poorest regions of a nation?

As we said earlier, the Constitution itself is the best place to go for answers to these questions. For example, Article I, Section 8, of the Constitution gives the national government the authority to regulate trade "among the several states." Similarly, the Constitution makes explicit the limits of federal intervention in state matters, including restrictions on the federal government's ability to tax interstate commerce (Article I, Section 9). Such direction provides a framework for what governments can and cannot do in relation to each other.

While the Constitution does provide a framework for intergovernmental relations, the document does not provide all the details on how governments should relate to each other. In fact, the Constitution can be particularly vague in laying out the balance of power between the levels of government. Nowhere is this more obvious than in the Tenth Amendment. In this last amendment of the Bill of Rights we are told that "the powers not delegated to the United States by the Constitution, nor prohibited by it to the states, are reserved to the states respectively, or to the people." This amendment, commonly known as the reserved powers clause, has been at the heart of numerous debates on the balance of power between the national and state governments.

Intergovernmental relations structures are almost always designed to accommodate differing communities of interest—social, ethnic, and political—as the boundaries of governments often possess, or soon acquire, symbolic meanings for communities that identify with them. This applies whether we are speaking of what it means to be a European or an American, a Luxemburger or a Texan, a Londoner or a San Franciscan. For example, localities in the United States often create fire, library, and school districts that for obvious reasons of **economies of scale** serve the citizens of small general-purpose jurisdictions, such as boroughs or

Confederate States of America ■
The short-lived confederation formed by the 11 states that sought to secede from the Union. That they could not do so was decided by the Civil War of 1861 to 1865. Those states, in alphabetical order, were Alabama, Arkansas, Florida, Georgia, Louisiana, Mississippi, North Carolina, South Carolina, Tennessee, Texas, and Virginia.

Confederation of the Rhine ■
The 1806–1813 union of the smaller German-speaking states in the Rhine River region.

Economies of scale ■
Cost savings realized by doing things in larger rather than smaller units. This decreases the overall average cost.

towns. These communities may develop a strong sense of identity that is focused on volunteer fire companies or high school sports teams.

The Effects of Pluralism

Sometimes a community is so dominated by one ethnic group that this impacts its relations—its intergovernmental relations—with other levels of government. Thus the people of Quebec, because of their strong French cultural identity, have been able to get special advantages from the Canadian national government. Alternatively, ethnically dominated communities in other countries have complained that they get fewer resources from their national governments because of their minority status. Sometimes national policies even encourage political ghettoization. For example, the United States has long practiced the art of gerrymandering, the reshaping of an electoral district to enhance the political fortunes of the party in power, as opposed to creating a district with geographic compactness. The term first arose in 1811, when Massachusetts Governor Elbridge Gerry reluctantly signed a redistricting bill, creating a district shaped like a salamander.

In 1986 the Supreme Court ruled in *Davis v. Bandemer* that partisan gerrymandering is unconstitutional "when the electoral system is arranged in a manner that will consistently degrade a voter's or a group of voters' influence on the political process as a whole." This encouraged a spate of affirmative gerrymandering, redistricting to consolidate minority votes so that a minority group member will most likely win the next election. This has resulted in more minorities, especially African Americans, being elected to the U.S. Congress than ever before. The effect of this is to give them representation in numbers that approximate their percentage of the population. Just like all other members, they fight the political wars to bring resources to the myriad governments within their legislative districts. However, in the 1995 case of *Louisiana v. Hays*, the Supreme Court seemed to put severe inhibitions on this when it ruled that congressional district lines are unconstitutional if race is the "predominant factor" in drawing them. Nevertheless, the Court did not say that race could not be a factor at all.

The Marble-Cake Metaphor

People who have not worked in or studied public administration are often unaware of the complicated nature of intergovernmental relations. It is not simply a question of dividing the work between the levels—of assigning local issues to local government, and national issues to federal government. The majority of issues have national, regional, and local implications. The popular image of the federal system as a layer cake, with each layer of government neatly on top of the other, is deceptive. The reality is more like a marble cake. This metaphor holds that the cooperative relations among the varying levels of government result in an intermingling of activities; this is in contrast to the more traditional view of layer-cake federalism, which holds that the three levels of government are totally or almost totally separate. Marble-cake federalism is usually associated with **Morton Grodzins**, who made a famous example out of the case of rural county health officials called sanitarians. Sanitarians are appointed by the state government under

Morton Grodzins (1917–1964) ■
A University of Chicago political scientist.

merit standards established by the federal government, and while their base salaries come from state and federal funds, the county provides them with offices and office amenities and pays a portion of their expenses.

According to Grodzins: "It is impossible from moment to moment to tell under which government the sanitarian operates. His work of inspecting the purity of food is carried out under federal standards; but he is enforcing state laws when inspecting commodities that have not been in interstate commerce. . . ."

The essential story of the sanitarian could be told of hundreds of other public sector jobs. Bus drivers, police officers, and teachers are all caught up in the intergovernmental maze. Consequently, mass transit, law enforcement, and education policies, for example, must be subjects of attention at all levels of government. It takes wise legislators at each level to comprehend how their legislation will fit in with that being developed at other levels—and officials working at each level may find it a major task to see that their work is compatible with that of people working on similar topics in other levels of government.

DYNAMIC FEDERALISM

The formal structure of powers, roles, and relationships underlying the intergovernmental relations of a federal system is rather like the trunk and branches of an old tree. It sways in the wind, leaves come and go, and sometimes entire branches are lost in a storm. The more rigid the tree, the greater the possibility that a major storm (such as a civil war) may uproot it entirely. If the tree is more supple, it will adapt and change to withstand the storm—and may be all the stronger for the experience.

Some federations have collapsed entirely in recent political history. The Union of Soviet Socialist Republics and Yugoslavia are leading examples. Others, such as Malaysia, have lost a major branch (Singapore) but survived. Still others, such as Canada, have been close several times to losing a very major branch (Quebec).

In the United States, there has been a series of major phases of intergovernmental relations.

Dual Federalism

This was the nineteenth-century concept, now no longer operational, that the functions and responsibilities of the federal and state governments were theoretically distinguished and functionally separate from each other. With this philosophy—which existed during the nineteenth century, when each level of the government could and did pretend the other level did not exist—rival lawmen rode through the Old West. In the absence of cooperation between jurisdictions, an outlaw could evade capture simply by "crossing the state line."

Some analysts suggest that this kind of federalism, which went out when the New Deal of 1933 came in, is what the Reagan administration sought, at least rhetorically, to eventually get back to. The basic idea of dual federalism was expressed succinctly in 1891 in *The American Commonwealth* by British historian

James Bryce, who visited the United States in the 1880s to observe its political system:

> The characteristic feature and special interest of the American Union is that it shows us two governments covering the same ground yet distinct and separate in their action. It is like a great factory wherein two sets of machinery are at work, their revolving wheels apparently intermixed, their bands crossing one another, yet each doing its own work without touching or hampering the other.

Dual federalism has never really died out. It has just been extensively modified by two centuries of federal legislation and judicial precedents. Indeed, as recently as 1997 the Supreme Court in *Printz v. United States* held that "it is incontestable that the Constitution established a system of 'dual sovereignty.'"

Cooperative Federalism

This is the notion that the national, state, and local governments are cooperating, interacting agents, working jointly to solve common problems, rather than conflicting, sometimes hostile competitors pursuing similar or, more likely, conflicting ends. While some cooperation has always been evident in spite of the conflict, competition, and complexity of intergovernmental relations, cooperation was most prominent between the 1930s and the 1950s. The emergency funding arrangements of the Depression years, known collectively as the New Deal, and the cooperation among federal, state, and local authorities during World War II to administer civilian defense, rationing, and other wartime programs, are noteworthy examples of cooperative federalism in the United States.

The New Deal's scheme of economic reconstruction involved many new federal grants to the states aimed at providing jobs. During this time, the concept of using federal spending to create demand—**pump priming**—led to an entirely new position for federal government as the shaper of programs in the states. This was the economic prescription of the British economist **John Maynard Keynes**, which called for stimulating the economy during a time of economic decline by borrowing money to spend on public works, defense, welfare, and so on. In theory, the prosperity generated by such expenditures would increase tax revenues, which in turn would pay for the borrowing.

Cooperative federalism also has a horizontal dimension: state-to-state interactions and relations. Such interstate relations take many forms, including **interstate compacts** and commissions established for specific purposes: river basin management, transportation, **extradition** of criminals, conservation of forests and wildlife, and administration of parks and recreation. Horizontal relations between local governments also are numerous. Cities frequently contract for services from various neighboring local governments (and even from private providers). The Lakewood plan, established in southern California in 1954, is the best-known example of local contracting for services in the United States. Under this plan, the city of Lakewood contracted for a rather comprehensive package of services from Los Angeles County, where Lakewood is located.

Pump priming ■
Government spending to stimulate an economy during a time of economic decline.

John Maynard Keynes (1883–1946) ■
The English economist who wrote the most influential book on economics of the last century, *The General Theory of Employment, Interest, and Money* (1936). Keynes founded a school of thought known as Keynesian economics, which called for using a government's fiscal and monetary policies to positively influence a capitalistic economy and developed the framework of modern macroeconomic theory.

Interstate compacts ■
Formal arrangements entered into by two or more states, generally with the approval of the U.S. Congress, to operate joint programs.

Extradition ■
The surrender by one nation or state to another of a person accused or convicted of an offense in the second nation or state.

Creative Federalism

This was the Lyndon B. Johnson administration's term for its approach to intergovernmental relations, which was characterized by joint planning and decision making among all levels of government (as well as the private sector) in the management of intergovernmental programs. Many new programs of this period had an urban-metropolitan focus, and much attention was given to antipoverty issues. Creative federalism sought to foster the development of a singular **Great Society** by integrating the poor into mainstream America. Its expansive efforts were marked by the rapid development of categorical grant programs to state and local governments and direct federal grants to cities, frequently bypassing state governments entirely. Great Society programs such as **Head Start** and the **War on Poverty** were all based on the concept of federal grants shaping activities and directions at the state and local levels. However, the idea that all wisdom rested in Washington

Great Society ■
The label for the 1960s domestic policies of the Johnson administration, which were premised on the belief that social and economic problems could be solved by new federal programs. This was Johnson's effort to revive the federal reform presence in social change represented in the Progressive movement, the New Deal, and the Fair Deal.

Head Start ■
The federal program designed to provide early education opportunities for poor children prior to kindergarten. Head Start centers exist nationwide and offer not only preacademic instruction but also health, social, nutritional, and psychological services.

War on Poverty ■
The phrase used by the Johnson administration for those 1960s Great Society programs designed to eliminate the causes and effects of poverty in the United States.

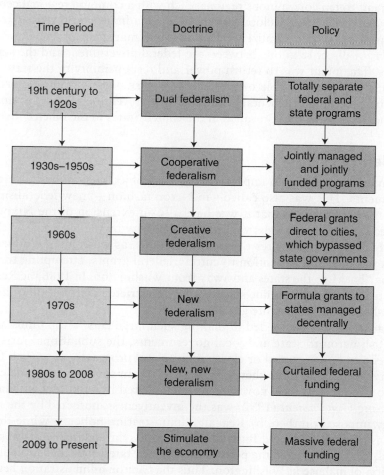

FIGURE 4.1

Evolution of intergovernmental relations doctrine

was not always well received in state capitals or city halls. The Nixon administration's new federalism sought to alter this balance.

New Federalism

This was President Richard Nixon's attempt to return autonomy to the states while maintaining significant levels of federal funding. From 1972 onward, new federalism entailed establishing aggregate grant levels by formula, but allowing state and local governments substantial latitude in applying the funds in their own area. The term has its origins in the liberal Republican effort to find an alternative to the centralized state perceived as having been set up by the New Deal but an alternative that nonetheless recognized the need for effective national government. During the Nixon administration, new federalism referred to the style of decentralized management at the federal level symbolized by such programs as general revenue sharing (see the next section) and the decentralization of federal regional management to ten coterminous regions, each with a common regional center.

New federalism as developed by the Reagan administration disregarded the Nixon approach of decentralized federal regional management and turned to development of direct relations between the federal government and the state governments. The intent was to return power and responsibility to the states and to dramatically reduce the role of the federal government in domestic programs, ranging from community mental health to crime prevention. This was reminiscent of the dual federalism that prevailed in the United States in the nineteenth century.

New, New Federalism

The Reagan administration imposed new policy objectives on intergovernmental arrangements. This was also called—in Nixon fashion—"new federalism." This made sense, however, in that it was basically an extension of the Nixon initiatives. Reagan and his advisers viewed much activity by the national government, especially many expenditures on social programs, as wasteful and unnecessary. Thus they turned their attention to cutting federal grants, attempting to transfer functions "back" to the states and away from Washington. In 1986 the Reaganites also destroyed general revenue sharing, the unrestricted distribution of a portion of federal tax revenues to state governments.

Malaise ■
The medical term for a vague feeling of illness that is used in other contexts to express a lassitude or ineffectiveness not traceable to a specific source and not exhibiting a specific set of symptoms. "Malaise" was President Jimmy Carter's word for the political uneasiness he found in America.

Because Reagan succeeded in making such large cuts in the funds available from Washington to state and local governments, the subnational jurisdictions had no choice but to curtail or close facilities and programs, or to look for energetic ways of funding those they wished to retain. In some respects, the entrepreneurship in state and local government documented by Osborne and Gaebler in *Reinventing Government* (1992) was the inventiveness mothered by the financial necessity imposed on them by Reagan administration policies. While the policy directions of the Reagan and Bush administrations, through their cuts in state and local aid, heavily impacted the poor in the United States, they failed to address the perception of **malaise** in Washington. Thus the Clinton administration began with public confidence in government at record low levels—especially with regard to intergovernmental issues such as welfare and crime.

Then history, as is its wont, repeated itself. The Republican Congress, elected in 1994, declared in 1995 that it was determined to create—what else?—a new federalism. But according to political journalist Alan Ehrenhalt, "It would be more accurate to describe it as the New New New Federalism—the 1995 revival of the Reagan revival of the Nixon revival of some ideas that Dwight D. Eisenhower placed before the country almost 40 years ago." Ehrenhalt views the 1995 Republican version of federalism as "the fourth modern incarnation of the simple-enough notion that Washington ought to be doing less governing and the states ought to be doing more." You may well be thinking by now, "The more things change, the more they stay the same." (This now trite observation was first credited to Alphonse Karr, the nineteenth-century French journalist, in a January 1849 issue of *Les Guépes*, a satirical review of intergovernmental relations in Paris.)

INTERGOVERNMENTAL MANAGEMENT

We cannot usually "see" intergovernmental relations, just as we cannot see other aspects of government machinery. But there are times when intergovernmental management bubbles to the surface and becomes visible. Unfortunately, these times usually involve great tragedies such as a major earthquake in California, the terrorist attack on the World Trade Center in New York, or the bombing of the federal building in Oklahoma City. In each case, the various levels are literally on the scene. First to arrive are local police and fire personnel. They are backed up by appropriate state agencies such as the **National Guard**. The federal government is represented by the FBI (when a crime is suspected, as in a bombing) and the Federal Emergency Management Agency (FEMA), which plans for and coordinates emergency preparedness and response for all levels of government and for all kinds of emergencies—both civilian and military. FEMA is the organization that decides what the various governments should be doing after such a catastrophe.

The political dialogue in American politics is always full of intergovernmental management issues. Politicians running for president or Congress love nothing better than telling the voters what they are going to do about crime or education once elected. But these are only marginal concerns of the federal government. State and local police are responsible for law enforcement. The FBI, while highly visible in the public's crime-fighting imagery, is minuscule in comparison. State and local governments employ more than half a million uniformed police officers. The FBI has only about 13,000 special agents. Education is the province of local school boards. The bottom line is that aside from minor funding for special programs, there is practically nothing the federal government can do about these issues—nothing but talk. But federal officials, and would-be federal officials, spend so much time talking about such hot-button issues that the public often thinks there is something, usually something simple such as mandating more homework for third-graders or telling teenagers not to become sexually active before marriage, that the federal government can do that will make a real difference. While politicians may think the public naive, there are no simple answers to the complex questions of intergovernmental management.

National Guard ■
The military forces of the states, which often are used for civil emergencies, such as major fires or floods. Normally, under the command of each state's governor, any or all of the states' individual guard units may be called (by the U.S. Congress) into federal service at any time. Once a guard unit is called into federal service, it is no longer subject to state control. The National Guard was organized in 1916. Until that time, each state had a volunteer militia.

Picket Fence Federalism

The human body depends on the interplay of a variety of comprehensive systems—from the cardiovascular system to the respiratory system to the nervous system—each one as critical as the next. It is similarly true that a federal system of government is built around several pervasive systems—systems a lot less predictable than those serving the human body but just as pervasive and critical. Picket fence federalism is the metaphor most commonly used for this systemic process. This concept implies that bureaucratic specialists at the various levels of government (along with clientele groups) exercise considerable power over the nature of intergovernmental programs. Bureaucratic or program specialists at national, state, and local government levels for such fields as public housing, vocational education, health and hospitals, and higher education represent the pickets in the picket fence. They communicate with each other in daily work, belong to the same professional organizations, and have similar professional training. They are likely to be in conflict with general-purpose government officials (mayors, governors, the president), who attempt to coordinate the vertical power structures, or pickets. The general-purpose officials are the crosspieces of the fence. The metaphor is credited to Terry Sanford, when he was governor of the state of North Carolina. It was initially presented in his book *Storm over the States*.

Councils of Governments and Intergovernmental Agreements

Any multijurisdictional cooperative arrangement to permit a regional approach to planning, development, transportation, environment, and other problems that affect a region as a whole tends to be known as a council of government (COG), even if the word *council* is not part of its formal title. COGs are typically substate regional planning agencies established by states. They are usually responsible for area-wide reviews of projects applying for federal funds and for development of regional plans and other area-wide special-purpose arrangements. They are composed of designated policymaking representatives from each participating government within the region. Some COGs have assumed a more enterprising role beginning in the 1980s by acting as contractors for, and service providers to, their local governments. For example, the COG for Lee and Russell counties in Alabama helped form a waste management authority to negotiate a single landfill contract with the private company that owns the landfills they use. According to journalist Eileen Shanahan, there is a tendency for COGs to be "transformed into regional entities that amount to multipurpose special districts, with real powers."

The value of councils of government and other cooperative agreements between local governments is becoming particularly noticeable in the area of land-use management. As suburban sprawl has emerged as a significant challenge in many parts of the country, there has been a move on the part of state governments to use incentives to bring counties and municipalities into partnerships to manage growth. For example, local governments in Wisconsin are entitled to state grants for planning only if they enter into intergovernmental agreements with their neighbors. While the best way to effectively manage sprawl-related problems might be to simply merge local governments or shift land-use management completely to the county level, such options are generally a political nonstarter. Thus states will likely continue to rely more on nudging local governments to join forces rather than shoving them together.

Finally, even if states can coax municipalities into councils of government, the voluntary nature of the partnerships makes them only advisory in nature. They have few, if any, independent sources of revenue. Professor Bernard H. Ross has compared them to the General Assembly of the United Nations in that both institutions "can debate, discuss, and suggest, but they cannot enforce action" on any of their members.

Mandate Mania

The key word in the new American thrust toward devolution is *mandate*. Normally this word refers to the perceived popular or electoral support for a public program, political party, or a particular politician. U.S. presidents who win elections by overwhelming majorities may rightly feel the vote was a "mandate" to carry out their proposed policies. But mandate has another equally important meaning: It is one level of government requiring another to offer—or pay for—a program as a matter of law or as a prerequisite to partial or full funding for either the program in question or other programs. It is the federal government ordering, by means of passing a law, state governments to reduce air pollution. Or it is a state government ordering, by means of passing a law, municipal governments to recycle trash collections. Mandates are orders, pure and simple. And the movement toward devolution is spurred on by jurisdictions and constituencies that increasingly resent taking such orders. In the United States these jurisdictions cite the "fact" that they are sovereign states and shouldn't have to put up with this administrative tyranny.

Hypocrisy is what makes it possible for the states to demand federal action and funding on this or that program while complaining that federal regulations on their use of federal funds insult their sovereignty. It is like a grown child demanding his or her parents are obligated to pay for this and that, while at the same time insisting that he or she be treated like an independent adult. Neither the states nor such children can have it both ways. As Shakespeare's King Lear reluctantly learned, "How sharper than a serpent's tooth it is to have a thankless child." But who is the child here? The federal government is the creature (if not the child) of the states. Yet the states, like old King Lear, gave up their sovereign pretensions to "form a more perfect union." Now they complain when things are not perfect enough. But that was not the agreement. The deal made at the 1787 Constitutional Convention was "more perfect"—not perfect. Those who might say to the states, "Quit your whining and act your age" miss the point. The whining, the complaining, and the hypocrisy are an inherent and beneficial part of a never-ending process of intergovernmental give and take. Besides, the complaining often leads to useful change.

Nothing sours intergovernmental relations faster than mandates. It is difficult even to determine how many mandates impact any given jurisdiction. For example, according to journalist Eric Pooley, the New York State Governor's Office of Mandate Relief counted 1,700 state and federal mandates in 1992. But in 1994 the *New York Times* discovered that there were 3,200 from the state alone that affected local government. There is obviously a major problem of definition here. Different things were being counted.

The only way to comprehend the full scope of the mandates problem is to look at their different categories. First, are they direct orders (which imply civil or criminal penalties for disobeying) or merely conditions for receiving aid? If they are the latter, they may not be considered mandates at all, because they do not have any effect unless you want the aid. Then you must also take the strings—the mandates—that come with it. Second, are they programmatic or procedural? Programmatic mandates state the type and quality of program to be implemented—a school lunch program must meet specified national standards for nutrition. A procedural mandate requires jurisdictions to do what they were going to do anyway, but, according to new requirements, personnel must be hired according to equal opportunity provisions; formal meetings and records must be open to the public. While programmatic mandates may cost a great deal, many procedural mandates may cost little or nothing, or have a one-time-only cost.

Some mandates merely constrain. But the constraints can hurt, as they do when state laws specify the kinds of government, religious, and nonprofit organization property that is exempt from local property taxes or when states put limits on property taxes or tax increases for veterans or retired citizens.

Some mandates involve not one but large numbers of programs at once. These so-called crosscutting mandates are found in virtually all state and federal aid programs. For example, if you accept federal funds, you are subject to the Anti-Kickback Act of 1934 (the Copeland Act), which should inhibit you from extorting money from employees or contractors.

While it is possible to classify mandates, they are so integral to all of public policy and administration that it is virtually impossible to accurately count them—without first creating a classification scheme that defines what you mean by a mandate. There is no czar of mandates statistics. There are only countless studies by countless groups, such as the U.S. Conference of Mayors and the **Advisory Commission on Intergovernmental Relations**, that all essentially conclude that there are more mandates than you can shake a stick at!

Mandates and the War on Terrorism

The war on terrorism that started on September 11, 2001, has caused mandates to explode at the same time that state and local governments have had their revenues curtailed because of a poorly performing economy. The Transportation Security Agency, created in 2001, regularly tells airports to raise their security status. However, it hasn't been able to tell the airports where to find the funding to pay for overtime payments to local police. Dale Russakoff and Rene Sanchez reported in the *Washington Post* that when the Department of Homeland Security elevated the terror threat in early 2003, the city of Los Angeles, already spending $1 million a week on extra security and running a high deficit, sought to avoid the additional expense by asking its state to send National Guard troops to the airport. California, already suffering staggering deficits, sent 50 National Guard soldiers to the airport. While the city avoided the expense, the state was stuck with "$100,000 a week more to cut elsewhere."

Czar ■
A former Russian absolute monarch; a nickname for any high-ranking administrator who is given great authority over something—for example, an energy czar, a housing czar.

Advisory Commission on Intergovernmental Relations ■
A national, bipartisan organization created by the U.S. Congress in 1959. The commission sought to address itself to improve cooperation among the levels of government and the function of the federal system. Nevertheless, it became a victim of the budget wars in Congress. It was phased out and shut down by the end of 1996.

In order to address this problem, at least symbolically, Congress passed the Unfunded Mandate Reform Act of 1995. This law holds that any future bill might be out of order if it imposes a financial mandate of more than $50 million on any one state, local, or Native American tribal government. But this requirement could always be rescinded by a majority vote. The law did nothing to end current unfunded mandates. It was basically designed to force Congress to be more aware of the implications of possible future mandates.

Bill ■

A legislative proposal formally introduced for consideration; unfinished legislation. After a bill is passed and signed into law, it becomes an act.

BOX 4.1 | Cyber Sales and Intergovernmental Relations

If you are like a growing number of college students, there is a good chance that you bought this book through an Internet company such as Amazon.com. According to the U.S. Department of Commerce, total Internet sales for 2010 were estimated at $165.4 billion, an increase of nearly 10 percent from 2009 and nearly double the level from 2004. While only amounting to about 4.2 percent of all sales in the nation, the Internet is clearly becoming a cornerstone of the nation's economy. But what about Internet sales as a source of government revenue? When you purchase products or services in most states, you are charged a sales tax. However, when you make Internet purchases, you most likely pay no sales taxes at all. That's because the U.S. Supreme Court ruled in 1992 that online retailers did not need to collect taxes for sales to states where they did not have a physical presence. Thus, if a company doesn't have a store or shipping center in your state, your purchase online should be tax-free. While this scenario is good for you, it places a strain on most states' revenue streams. As of 2008, all but five states (Alaska, Oregon, Montana, New Hampshire and Delaware) collected some form of sales tax. According to the National Governors Association and National Conference of State Legislatures, state and local governments lost approximately 23 billion in 2003 from untaxed Internet sales. Not surprisingly, states have been anxious to find a way to get their money back. However, the states' road to riches must travel through Washington, D.C. That's because the Constitution gives the federal government control over interstate commerce. Without congressional

action, or a change of heart by the federal judiciary, states cannot collect taxes on online sales. In 2000 and 2003 Congress considered legislation to allow state and local governments to tax Internet purchases, but the bills died before ever reaching the Senate or House floors.

Since 2005, 23 states joined together in a consortium under the Streamlined Sales Tax project. Under this initiative the states have been using their numerical strength to try to persuade online retailers to voluntarily collect sales taxes. In October 2005 a large number of Internet vendors began collecting sales taxes based on the rates in effect in the buyer's home states and then remitting the revenue to the states. In return, the e-businesses were to receive a one-year amnesty for taxes they may have owed on past online sales. While the states benefited from the revenue generated from the new system, the project had a broader goal of pressuring Congress to create legislation that allows the states to directly tax online sales. By 2010 this pressure appeared to be bearing some fruit. With fiscal conditions in the states in crisis condition, a bill entitled the Main Street Fairness Act was introduced into both houses of Congress to allow states to collect sales taxes from online purchases, with optimism among the sponsors that the time may have finally arrived for states to have this power. ◣

Source: Adapted from data found in http://www.streamlinedsalestax .org and "The State of the Internet Sales Tax," from *Business- Week* online at www.businessweek.com/the_thread/techbeat/ archives/2009/04/the_state_of_in.html and from "Is an Internet Sales Tax Coming" by Yian Q. Mui of the *Washington Post* at http://voices.washingtonpost.com/political-economy/2010/07/ by_ylan_q_mui_a.html.

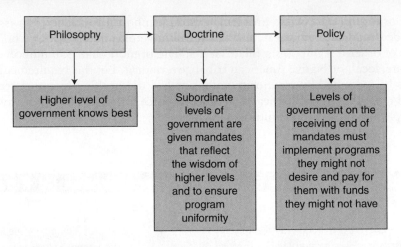

FIGURE 4.2
Doctrine of mandates

The Transformation of Governance

In 1999, the National Academy of Public Administration (NAPA) established a Priority Issues Task Force to identify the key issues in public administration that would face the nation in the first years of the twenty-first century. What the task force found was that governance throughout the United States and around the world was "undergoing a fundamental transformation" that had huge implications for public administrators. In particular, the NAPA group suggested that public administrators would face (1) a growing complexity of relationships between government and society; (2) the shifting of national responsibilities both in the direction of international bodies and systems and in the direction of states, localities, and community-based institutions; and (3) the need for greater capacity to manage these relationships. According to Don Kettl, a leading scholar on the subject, "government at all levels has found itself with new responsibilities but without the capacity to manage them effectively." While government remains the only player in society that has formal authority to act in the name of the "people," it has seen its responsibility distributed to both nonprofit and profit-driven enterprises. Given the increasing importance of public-private partnerships, the already complex nature of intergovernmental relations becomes even more stressed. Not only must a local public administrator work with officials at the state and federal level, but he or she must also coordinate programs with nongovernmental organizations such as private contractors and nonprofit groups. Inevitably, such multidimensional relationships raise questions of accountability and responsiveness, with public administrators receiving blame and credit for actions they really do not have control of.

FISCAL FEDERALISM—FOLLOWING THE MONEY

In the infancy of federalism in the eighteenth century, it may have been grandiose to think of the policy arrangements in national and state government as a system. Geographic separation, painfully slow systems of communication, and a relatively clear differentiation of functions gave each level of government a role that could be carried out with only limited interaction with other levels of government.

Several factors permanently changed this picture during the twentieth century. First, the galvanizing effect of the world wars and the Cold War saw national direction and planning emerge more thoroughly than had ever been necessary before. Second, a revolution occurred in transport and communications that has permanently ended the possibility for states to behave with the completely unilateral autonomy they once had. Third, there emerged with the 1930s New Deal, and with the 1960s civil rights and antipoverty programs, legislation embodying national values that needed to be uniformly implemented across the entire country. The cumulative effect of these fundamental changes gave rise to a concept of national policymaking and state policy implementation overlaid on the traditional and continuing functions of national and state government.

How could a national government bring about actions at the state level that state governments, left to themselves, might find neither palatable nor affordable? Certainly, at times, the federal courts have ordered state governments to adopt policies and actions based on judicial interpretations of the meaning of federal legislation or the Constitution. For example, the courts have ordered states to integrate schools (by **busing** if necessary) and to relieve prison overcrowding if it amounts to **cruel and unusual punishment**. However, the federal government, under the Tenth Amendment to the Constitution, does not have a general power to give directions to the states in their primary areas of power. Consequently, more often than not, financial inducement, through grants of money tied to a particular policy objective, has been the preferred instrument for achieving federal purposes. Financial arrangements have been the predominant vehicle within intergovernmental relations by which national policies have been implemented by and through the states.

The Theory of Fiscal Federalism

Fiscal federalism refers to the fiscal (financial) relationships that exist between and among units of government in a federal system (see Table 4.4). The theory of fiscal federalism, or multiunit governmental finance, addresses the question of the optimal design of governments in a multilevel (or federal) governmental system.

The public sector has three principal economic problems to solve:

1. The attainment of the most equitable distribution of income
2. The maintenance of high employment with stable prices
3. The establishment of an efficient pattern of resource allocation

The theory of fiscal federalism postulates that a federal form of government can be especially effective in solving these problems because of the flexibility it has in dealing with some problems at the national or central level and some at the local or regional levels. It argues that, for a variety of reasons, the first two problems, equitable distribution of income and maintenance of high employment with stable prices, are problems that the national level of government is best equipped to handle. However, according to the theory, the decentralized regional or local units of government can more efficiently deal with the third problem, allocation

Busing ■
The transporting of children by bus to schools at a greater distance than those the children would otherwise attend to achieve racial desegregation. Busing has often been mandated by the federal courts as a remedy for past practices of discrimination. It has been heartily objected to by parents who want their children to attend neighborhood schools and has, in consequence, been a major factor in "white flight" from central cities. Busing is often used as an example of government by the judiciary, because busing, one of the most controversial domestic policies in the history of the United States, has never been specifically sanctioned by the Congress.

Cruel and unusual punishment ■
The criminal penalty prohibited by the Eighth Amendment, which not only bars government from imposing punishment that is barbarous but, as the U.S. Supreme Court has announced, forbids punishment that society's "evolving standards of decency" would mark as excessive.

TABLE 4.4

Federal Aid to State and Local Governments

Year	Total (in millions of dollars)	As a Percentage of Federal Outlays
1980	91,385	15.5%
1985	105,852	11.2
1990	135,325	10.8
1995	224,991	14.8
2000	284,659	15.9
2001	317,250	17.0
2002	351,550	16.9
2003	387,281	17.9
2004	406,330	17.7
2005	426,243	17.2
2006	434,099	16.3
2007	443,797	16.3
2008	466,568	15.9
2009	552,108	15.7

Source: United States Bureau of the Census, http://www.census.gov/prod/2010pubs/fas-09.pdf.

of resources, because such units of government are more familiar than the central or national government with local needs and the desires of citizens for public services. Even so, grants-in-aid from the national level of government to local levels may be needed to stimulate local government spending for national purposes, to provide for uniform or minimum service levels (as in education), or to compensate citizens of one area for benefits from services they finance that spill over to residents of another area. Spillover benefits are especially frequent in such programs as clean water and air pollution control, health, and education.

In theory, an accountable government should involve representatives only voting for programs for which they have voted the taxes. The representatives would be accountable to the voters, who could directly assess whether the "purchase" of services and programs they had made at election time was what they wanted, and whether they got good value for their tax money. But in a large nation, need for services can vary greatly between communities, and the capacity to pay taxes also varies greatly among the categories of those who are taxed. This issue focuses attention on several of the central problems of the federal concept: the difficult notion of two or more governments overlaid on the same geographical territory; the difficulty of persuading voters that they need to pay their taxes twice (or more) to different levels of taxing authority; and the difficulty of persuading taxpayers that it is fair that some of their taxes should produce no direct benefit to them but be used to assist some other community or some ill-defined goal dear to an official in a remote office in another city.

> **TABLE 4.5**

The Politics of Fiscal Federalism: The Case of Federal Stimulus Funds

Who wins and who loses in the game of fiscal federalism is often decided by raw politics. With the passage of the American Recovery and Reinvestment Act of 2009, the federal government sent hundreds of billions of dollars to state and local governments. These two lists illustrate the role of raw politics in this distribution.

Overall Funding (top ten states)	Per Capita Funding (top ten states)
1. California	1. Utah
2. Texas	2. Alaska
3. New York	3. Mississippi
4. Florida	4. North Dakota
5. Illinois	5. Louisiana
6. Pennsylvania	6. California
7. Ohio	7. Michigan
8. Michigan	8. New Mexico
9. Georgia	9. Texas
10. North Carolina	10. Kansas

Note that while the big states get the most money, the small ones get more per person. Why? Is it because they need it more? Not necessarily. While states such as California and Michigan, which were devastated by the recession, received above average per capita stimulus funds, states such as Utah and North Dakota, with the lowest unemployment rates in the nation, got even more funds on a per capita basis. Undoubtedly, other factors such as the political clout and skills of congressional delegations must matter.

Source: U.S. Census Bureau, Congressional Research Service, and U.S. Department of Labor Estimates via the House Appropriations Committee.

Attitudes toward these issues illustrate the level of confidence citizens have in a democratic federation. If confidence is high, and a sense of common national purpose is high—as it was during a "popular" war such as World War II, or during the early days of the Great Society programs, citizens are more prepared to trust politicians and bureaucrats to redistribute taxes to promote national goals elsewhere. If, however, confidence in politicians and the bureaucracy is low, citizens may well take some convincing that spending programs are fair and necessary. A confident, successful federal democracy that has confidence in its political leaders and has honest and efficient bureaucrats and well-articulated national aspirations will be one in which there is more room for redistributive programs—an admirable goal to strive for—or perhaps not!

All too often the same central question of fiscal federalism is asked in countless congressional and presidential elections: Why can't the citizens of the states just keep their money (meaning, have their federal taxes reduced) rather than paying it to the federal government so they can return it in grants and services? The answer is deceptively simple: Not all states are fiscally equal. If there are more poor people in one state, federal welfare funds from other states will in effect subsidize them. Would Delaware and Connecticut, for example, otherwise transfer tax dollars from their citizens to the overall poorer citizens of Mississippi and Alabama? Federal spending for military bases, while concentrated in more southern states for reasons of climate, benefits the entire nation—even if it benefits the local economy of Georgia more. While bases and ports may be concentrated in the South, defense contractors are widely distributed. Indeed, to gain support for many defense systems, the **Pentagon** quite consciously procures goods and services from companies in as many congressional districts as possible. Even NASA once boasted, in order to drum up congressional support, that the parts for the space shuttle were built in most of the 50 states.

Pentagon ■
The building that has become the symbol of the U.S. Department of Defense.

Lobbying by defense contractors aside, the federal government justifies taking its measure of taxes from the states and distributing it in an uneven fashion because this furthers national policies for welfare, for defense, for conservation, for environmental protection, and so on. In this process, some states are winners and some losers. And while no one would deny that any given program could not be better managed or more economically operated, these redistribution programs all exist because lawmakers representing all the citizens thought them to be in the public interest. The members of Congress cannot have it both ways—they cannot argue that the federal government is too full of pork-barrel programs for the congressional districts while at the same time kicking and clawing to bring home the bacon for their constituents. Fortunately this is becoming, though only gradually, a truth more universally acknowledged than before.

Grant Programs

Grants by formula or category are the most significant means by which federal moneys are transmitted to the states. A grant is simply an intergovernmental transfer of funds (or other assets). Since the New Deal, state and local governments have become increasingly dependent on federal grants for an almost infinite variety of programs. From almost the beginning of the republic to the present, a grant by the federal government has been a continuing means of providing states, localities, public (and private) educational or research institutions, and individuals with funds to support projects the national government considered useful for a wide range of purposes. In recent years, grants have been made to support the arts as well as the sciences. All such grants are capable of generating debate over what the public as a whole, acting through the grant-making agencies of the federal government, considers useful and in the national interest.

A "grant-in-aid" is the term used for federal or state payments to local governments for specified purposes and usually subject to supervision and review by the granting government or agency in accordance with prescribed standards and requirements. One function of a federal grant-in-aid is to direct state or local funding to a purpose considered nationally useful by providing federal money on the condition that the jurisdiction receiving it match a certain percentage of it. The federal government actively monitors the grantee's spending of the funds to ensure compliance with the spirit and letter of federal intent. Grants-in-aid have other public policy implications as well, because a jurisdiction that accepts federal money must also accept the federal "strings," or guidelines, that come with it. All federal grantees must comply with federal standards on equal employment opportunity in the selection of personnel and contractors, for example.

Historically, the most common grants have been "categorical"—those that can be used only for specified purposes. But there has been a trend, ever since the Nixon administration, to move toward block grants that give the states more discretion over the funds. This trend decidedly accelerated in the mid-1990s as the Republican-controlled Congress sought to reduce the size and role of the federal bureaucracy by reducing congressional oversight of grant programs—and at the same time permanently removing the federal employees who performed many of the oversight functions. For the public administrator, fiscal federalism refers, first and foremost, to the politics and administration of complex intergovernmental grant-in-aid systems.

The federal government distributes money to the states through hundreds of grant programs, of which about half are related to Medicaid. Some 20 percent are for infrastructure, such as transportation, water, or sewage treatment, and the remainder relate to various social and labor market programs. During the 1970s, the Nixon administration introduced less-specific block grants to counter the criticism that overly restricting the ways federal moneys could be spent tended to reduce state governments to an extremely mechanical role not consistent with their status as governments in their own right. A block grant is distributed in accordance with a statutory formula for use in a variety of activities within a broad functional area, largely at the recipient's discretion. For example, the community development block grant program, administered by the Department of Housing and Urban Development, funds community and economic development programs in cities, counties, Indian reservations, and U.S. territories. The nature of the block grant allows these jurisdictions to allocate the funds to supplement other resources in ways they choose. The

Medicaid ■
The federally aided, state-operated, and state-administered program that provides medical benefits for certain low-income people in need of health and medical care. Authorized by 1965 amendments to the Social Security Act, it covers only members of one of the categories of people who can be covered under the welfare cash payment programs— the aged, the blind, the disabled, and members of families with dependent children where one parent is absent, incapacitated, or unemployed.

► BOX 4.2 | Stimulating the States

In February 2009, President Barack Obama signed a $780 billion stimulus package designed to give a boost to the struggling U.S. economy. As the nation faced the greatest economic downturn in generations, the president and Congress leveraged the financial powers of the federal government to pump more than three-quarters of a trillion dollars into the American economy. While the sheer volume of the government outlays caused considerable debate in the nation's capital, the destinations for all that stimulus cash initiated rancorous arguments among the members of Congress. One of the greatest sticking points in the negotiations involved the transfer of federal money to state governments that were feeling the full force of the recession on their budgets. In 2009 state budgets were being battered by the combination

of dramatically reduced tax revenue and state constitutional requirements that prevented them from running deficits. Unlike the federal government, which more often than not spends more than it takes in, the states must balance their budgets each year because their varied constitutions force them to do so. These conditions forced states to quickly find other sources of revenue and/or cut spending to bring their budgets into balance. Under these pressures, states did make many cuts to programs and services while also coming up with new or enhanced revenue sources to help bring their budgets in line. But even with significant changes to both revenue and spending policies, the absence of federal stimulus dollars in 2011 had left states with some of their deepest deficits ever and more difficult decisions to make. ►

problem with block grants is that Washington loses control and the money may be spent even less wisely than it would if more federal strings were attached.

THE DEVOLUTION REVOLUTION

The dilemmas of intergovernmental relations illustrated so clearly by the problem of federal–state financial relationships have always been critical issues in democratic federations. The only certainty here is that the states have become addicted to intergovernmental funding. The question remains whether their political leaders will gradually wean them from it or feed their habit. On this front there is good news and bad news. The good news is that many state governments seem genuinely caught up in the devolution revolution. In late 1994, all of the Republican governors and governors-elect met in Williamsburg, Virginia—the colonial capital of that state. Representing a clear majority of the states (30) with an overwhelming majority of the population (70 percent), they issued the "Williamsburg Resolve," which called for reversing the power that had been going to Washington since the New Deal. They said grandiose things appropriate to the place where Patrick Henry said in 1775, "Give me liberty or give me death!" California Governor Pete Wilson said that the "states are not colonies of the federal government." Governor Tommy Thompson of Wisconsin said they should no longer have to go to Washington "on bended knee to kiss the ring."

The bad news is that this is somewhat hypocritical. After all, what their "resolve" essentially calls for is the federal money without the federal strings. But these "strings" have important public policy implications—like ensuring the relatively equal treatment of all citizens no matter in which state they may reside. The current movement toward devolution is similar to the Sagebrush Rebellion. This term, first heard in the 1980s, covers any number of dissatisfactions—hardly a rebellion—that some people in the states of the American West have with the federal government's management and use of the federal lands within their borders. In general, they feel that the states should have more control over the lands and how they are used. The counterargument is that such lands are national trusts and can only legitimately be dealt with by representatives of the national government. According to historian Robert Hughes in *The Culture of Complaint*, the American West "is archetypally the place where Big Government is distrusted, the land of the independent man going it alone. Yet much of it—states such as Arizona, for instance—has depended, not marginally or occasionally but always and totally, on federal money from Washington for its economic existence." Consequently, "the Southwestern states could never have been settled at their present human density without immense expenditure of government funds on water-engineering. They are less the John Wayne than the Welfare Queen of American development."

Yet these western states, mostly Republican at that, do not like to be reminded of the role that Washington played in creating and economically developing them. The federal lands within them belong just as much to the rest of the nation. While the political leaders of these western states are quick to assert their "rights" over federal lands, other citizens of other states are just as quick to note that these lands were paid for, indeed fought for, by the entire country.

The latest wrinkle in this Sagebrush Rebellion is to resurrect Gifford Pinchot's definition of conservation as the "wise use" of resources. But this modern wise-use movement is not traditional conservation but a cover for those who advocate greater economic development of public lands. By asserting the legitimacy of multiple uses of public lands, they seek to roll back environmental protections now extant. One legal technique to achieve this rollback is to assert county supremacy by means of local land-use ordinances. This has engendered considerable conflict between local officials and federal land managers. The only certainty here is that as one contemplates the vast expanses of federal land in the West, much litigation can be seen on the horizon.

The web of intergovernmental relations is such a tangled one that there are no easy solutions to the understandable desire for devolution. Even a national administration completely sympathetic to the devolutionist will find it difficult to return powers and lands back to the states. It will take far more than a Williamsburg Resolve and a Sagebrush Rebellion to simply locate, let alone repeal, two centuries' worth of centralizing legislation. In fact, in some cases it may be the states themselves that spearhead campaigns against the weakening of central authority. In an interesting reversal of the dynamic of the Williamsburg Resolve and Sagebrush Rebellion, many state governments in the northeastern United States have joined together not to protest federal intervention but to instead fight against the lack of federal effort in the area of environmental protection. According to the *Christian Science Monitor*, New York, New Jersey, Pennsylvania, and Massachusetts, angered by the EPA's March 2005 mercury emission standards, brought suit against the federal government on the grounds that the new federal rules are not strong enough to meet the intent of the Clean Air Act. Just two years earlier, nine northeastern states banded together to challenge EPA rules that would exempt thousands of industrial air pollution sources, including coal-fired power plants, from the new Clean Air Act standards for emission. In these two instances the states joined forces to encourage the national government to increase its regulation of activities at the state and local levels.

Gifford Pinchot (1865–1946) ■ America's first professional forester, who is credited with coining the term *conservation*. Twice governor of Pennsylvania (1923–1927; 1931–1935), he became internationally famous as President Theodore Roosevelt's partner in making conservation a national issue.

The Public-Choice Solution

The Reagan Revolution of the 1980s, which was continued by the 1990s Republican Congress, coincided with public administration's increasing embrace of public-choice theory. This theory rejected the concept of welfare economics that emerged out of the New Deal: that when private markets failed, the government had to step in to effectively carry out the public interest, and the governmental level best suited to do this was the federal one.

Public-choice theory seriously questioned whether such governmental decisions really represented the wishes of the majority of citizens. More emphatically, public choice denounced governments as being basically inefficient and completely lacking in incentives to perform well unless the expansion of their own programs and the increase of their budgets were involved. The better solution, public-choice advocates argued, was to place governmental action (and expenditures) at the lowest possible levels—that is, at the local government level. The feeling here was that local governments would provide more experimentation, true competition,

IN THE NEWS | Intergovernmental Relations That Work!

As you might have discovered by reading this chapter, there are numerous breakdowns that plague the federalist system of government in the United States. Such is the reality of living in a nation with a highly decentralized political structure. While there are no shortages of problems associated with intergovernmental relations in America, there are also a number of examples when the stars align and the multiple players in the system work efficiently together. This was the case in 2007 when the U.S. State Department and varied state government agencies combined together to deliver assistance to children throughout the nation.

An unfortunate reality of contemporary American life is that many dads, and a few moms, fail to pay financial support to their children. Each and every year hundreds of millions of dollars of court-ordered payments are withheld by "deadbeat" parents who refuse to meet a financial obligation to their children. To force parents to pay their child support payments the states regularly withhold money from individuals' paychecks, but this method cannot fully extract all money due to children. Thus other measures are necessary, and one intergovernmental arrangement paid dividends for the nation's children.

For many years the State Department and state agencies have cooperated on efforts to get delinquent child support payments made. Under the Passport Denial Program (PDP) state governments provided the State Department lists of parents who owed $5,000 or more in child support. This list was then matched up against a list of individuals applying for passports or passport renewals. If a match was found, the passport seeker would have to pay off all overdue child support before he or she could travel abroad. Over the years, the PDP provided a steady but unspectacular amount of back support to children in all 50 states.

But then the State Department decided that Americans would need passports to travel to North American destinations such as Canada and the Caribbean Islands. The new passport rule reflected national security concerns in the post-9/11 global environment. As thousands of Americans began to seek passports in order to honeymoon in the Bahamas or weekend in Montreal, it became clear to State Department officials that some unexpected benefits could be gained from the new rules. In particular, the high volume of people getting passports for the first time provided a windfall of support payments for children throughout the nation. In the first half of 2007 alone the PDP produced almost $25 million in back child support, and some very large one-time payments. For example, a man paid $45,849 in support payments to get his passport for a trip to the Dominican Republic, while a musician paid $46,000 to be allowed to play overseas; then a boxer from Nevada paid $39,000 in back support to get his passport, only to lose it and pay another $8,900 in new child support debts. In the end even the clumsy intergovernmental arrangement of the United States could still find a way to land a pretty good blow against even the meanest of the deadbeat dads and even a few deadbeat moms. ▲

Source: Numerical data from the Associated Press, "Passport Rules Snag Child Support Cash," August 14, 2007.

and innovation. At the local level, citizens could "vote with their feet"—that is, if the citizens had access to appropriate information, they would be able to readily compare the levels of taxation to the quality of services they received. They could then reject inefficient or unresponsive governments by voting down budgets, by voting out big spenders, or even by moving elsewhere—or not moving in at all. Thus the solution to devolution offered by the public-choice advocates is to increase the discretion in the hands of the individual voter by maximizing "user-pay systems" (whether for trash collection or through fees at state park camping grounds) and by placing vouchers (for schools or housing) for spending in the hands of recipients rather than compelling them to use particular government services or institutions.

Welfare Reform

Perhaps the best example of the give-and-take aspect of the federal system is that if a government function is not working at one level, it can be shifted onto another level to see if it can be done any better. A good example of a program that has bounced between the intergovernmental levels is welfare. When the Social Security Act was passed in 1935, it included a small program to help widows and orphans. This was the origin of Aid to Families with Dependent Children (AFDC), the program by which the federal government matched state spending on welfare. AFDC provided federal funds, administered by the states, for children living with a parent or a relative who met state standards of need. The program was controversial because of charges that it not only promoted illegitimacy but also encouraged fathers to abandon their families so they could become eligible for AFDC. In 1995 more than 13 million people were receiving AFDC, up from just over 2 million in 1955 (see Table 4.6).

Claiming that the system had produced "welfare queens"—women conceiving children out of wedlock to qualify for AFDC benefits—and a cycle of generational poverty encouraged by the welfare system, the Republican-controlled Congress in 1995 decided to act. It would change the system by giving the problem back to the states. Welfare was a local problem to begin with. The tradition of the county poor farm or workhouse can be traced back to sixteenth-century England. The money spent on AFDC would be converted to block grants with which the states in their 50 varieties of wisdom would decide who was worthy of the new-style welfare and under what conditions. In essence most of the federal strings would be removed, and the states would overall get less than before, but they would have far greater discretion on how to spend it. Thus a comprehensive welfare reform bill was passed by the Congress in 1996. This repealed the entitlement aspect of AFDC and was signed into law by President Clinton. The states—with the encouragement of the federal government—got busy simultaneously reinventing welfare programs while seeking to discourage the expansion of the welfare rolls by holding fathers more responsible for supporting their children. Simply put, the problem has proved so difficult that Congress is giving up on it and seeking to dump it back on the states. Ah, federalism!

Even without reform we would expect welfare rolls to decrease when jobs are plentiful. But other, more lasting factors are at work as well—factors that suggest that the rolls will not "automatically" go up with a modest economic downturn. First, devolution means that welfare isn't what it used to be; most importantly, it is no longer an entitlement. According to journalists Barbara Vobejda and Judith Havemann, in at least three dozen states welfare managers actively seek to prevent applicants from getting welfare once they apply. "Welfare offices are urging applicants to ask for help from relatives instead of signing up for government assistance, writing one-time emergency checks in place of monthly benefits, or

This 1937 picture, with its juxtaposition of rich and poor, has long symbolized welfare in a land of plenty. But the photo, taken in Louisville, Kentucky, is triply misleading. First, it is not about traditional welfare at all; the people waiting in the bread line were the victims of flooding. Second, it implies that most welfare recipients are black, when almost twice as many welfare recipients are white. This was as true in 1937 as it is today. According to the U.S. Census Bureau figures, about twice as many whites receive welfare as blacks do. However, just about one-third of all blacks receive welfare, while only about 10 percent of whites do (*Charlotte Observer*, September 11, 1997). Finally, the United States does not have the "world's highest standard of living" when judged by overall social indicators such as infant mortality. A United Nations report ranked the United States 4th in overall quality of life (behind Canada, France, and Norway) and 17th in poverty levels behind almost all of the major industrialized states, despite the fact that the United States has the highest per capita income. It is just that this income isn't as evenly distributed as in the 16 other countries with lower poverty rates (*Pittsburgh Post Gazette*, September 9, 1998).

requiring applicants to spend weeks searching for work before they receive their first welfare payment." This raises questions "of whether they have found jobs on their own, never truly needed them in the first place, or have been scared off or intimidated from applying for help that their children genuinely require."

Such diversion tactics are now commonplace. California, Kansas, Florida, Oregon, and New York, among other states, all seek to direct applicants into jobs or one-time cash payments (they cannot then reapply for a prescribed period). This leads to the second major new factor. The traditional welfare office is evolving into a new administrative animal. According to Rachel L. Swarns, in New York City "job centers are replacing welfare offices. Financial planners are replacing case-workers. And the entire bureaucracy is morphing into the Family Independence Administration. In truth the same workers still do business in the same buildings,

TABLE 4.6

Welfare Recipients (in millions) in the United States (1980 to 2006)

Year	Families on Welfare	Individuals on Welfare
1980	3,712	10,774
1990	4,057	11,695
1995	4,791	13,418
1996	4,434	12,321
1997	3,740	10,376
1998	3,050	8,347
1999	2,554	6,828
2000	2,219	5,790
2001	2,110	5,420
2002	2,048	5,069
2003	2,048	4,932
2004	1,978	4,748
2005	1,894	4,471
2006	1,781	4,166
2007	1,730	4,076
2008	1,700	4,001
2009	1,838	4,367
2010	1,909	4,569

Source: The Department of Health and Human Services (2007), http://www.acf.hhs.gov/programs/ofa/data-reports/caseload/caseload_current.htm.

but the city has been infected by a name-changing frenzy that has been sweeping the country. Massachusetts' Department of Public Welfare is now the Department of Transitional Assistance. Florida's welfare program is now the Work and Gain Economic Self-Sufficiency Program." Indicative of this major change in terminology is the 1998 decision of the American Public Welfare Association (which represents social service agencies) to change its name after 66 years to the American Public Human Services Association. Devolution may not yet have killed welfare in fact, but it has certainly killed it in name.

Welfare is just one example of how the age of devolution is bringing us back to the first principles of the age of revolution. Alexander Hamilton, the high priest of an energetic national government among the founding fathers, felt strongly that essentially local issues, as he wrote in *The Federalist*, No. 17 (1787), "can never be desirable cares of a general jurisdiction." Hamilton believed it "improbable that there should exist a disposition in the federal councils to usurp the [local] powers . . . because the attempt to exercise those powers would be as troublesome as it would be nugatory; and the possession of them, for that reason, would contribute nothing to the dignity, to the importance, or to the splendor of the national government." Will a rollback of the welfare state contribute to the "dignity" and "splendor" of the federal government? That depends if it is your welfare that is being rolled back! According to political analyst Gareth G. Cook, at least one thing is certain: "Devolution is the theme that runs through nearly all of the Republicans' high-profile domestic initiatives. . . . Whether it's cops on the street, environmental protection, or school lunches for poor kids, the Republican solution is to devolve it."

But with the election of Barack Obama, a Democrat, to the presidency, all Republican efforts at devolution came to a screeching halt. In a reversal of policy that is as stealthy as it seeks to be comprehensive, welfare reform itself is being reformed with little-noticed additions to economic stimulus laws and revised regulations. The only certainties here are that welfare will increase, that this will be paid for with borrowed money, and that the political drama over the role of welfare rolls will play seemingly forever.

The Race to the Bottom

The ultimate devolution, of course, is to get government out of a particular activity altogether. Certainly, privatization, as discussed in Chapter 3, has a major role to play here. But those who would privatize many aspects of the welfare system are relying on private charitable giving to make up the difference between reduced government spending and the actual life-sustaining needs of the poor. But the very welfare programs that are being criticized were created in the first place because private charity proved insufficient.

Charity notwithstanding, the real issue in the devolution of welfare programs is that of a "race to the bottom." In this race states and their counties increasingly lower their welfare benefits to discourage the out-of-state poor from moving in to collect more generous aid than was possible where they were. "Generous" states increasingly resent the fact that "stingy" states are effectively exporting their poor. But as Minnesota Governor Arne Carlson said, "We do not want to be in the importing business. We will devise a range of policies to make sure we take care of Minnesotans, but we're not in the business of subsidizing Gary, Indiana." This is the crux of the intergovernmental welfare dilemma. A state designs a responsible welfare system to take care of its own only to become a welfare magnet to outsiders. But by "racing to the bottom" in terms of benefits, states discourage the out-of-state poor from moving in. Senator Daniel Patrick Moynihan offered this explanation: "The hidden agenda of the Devolution Revolution is a large-scale withdrawal of support for social welfare, no matter how well conceived. The result would be a race to the bottom, as states, deprived of federal matching funds, compete with one another to reduce spending by depriving their own dependent population of help."

There is already a major differential among the states. The block granting of federal welfare funding that withdraws the federal matching requirement (which was, in effect, an entitlement to the states) may make that differential far worse. Now that welfare eligibility is state (as opposed to nationally) determined, the differential in benefits can vastly increase. Many states now offer a low level of benefits. Conversely, some states have maintained fairly substantial benefits but have dramatically reduced the amount of time one can receive government support. The block grant reforms now allow them to offer no benefits. As this problem shows, the core issues of intergovernmental relations can be reduced to stark realities. It comes down to this: Intergovernmental fiscal arrangements ultimately determine—for a large class of citizens—who eats and who goes hungry.

A CASE STUDY | **Why Illegal Immigration Is an Intergovernmental Mess and Will Remain So**

If you would like to get into a heated debate with someone, illegal immigration would be a good topic. In the United States today there are few issues that draw more emotional reactions than the government's policies for dealing with illegal immigrants. From border security to the provision of social services to illegal residents, there seem to be a countless number of elements to this polarizing issue. And as the nation struggles over the illegal immigration quandary, the issue has become a perennial point of contention within the federal system of government. With the national, state, and local governments all playing key roles in the management of illegal immigration issues, it is inevitable that this topic will illustrate the complexity of intergovernmental relations in the United States today.

As with so many other aspects of public administration, the U.S. Constitution says very little about the subject of immigration. While never mentioning the word "immigration," the Constitution addresses naturalization of citizens in two places: Article I, Section 8, authorizes Congress to "establish a uniform Rule of Naturalization," and the Fourteenth Amendment declares "All persons born or naturalized in the United States . . . are citizens of the United States and of the State wherein they reside." With such scant direction from the highest law in the land it has fallen on generations of public officials to manage the process by which foreign-born individuals enter into citizenship.

While the process of becoming a citizen has been under the federal government's auspices, the management of the flow and treatment of those illegally entering the United States has been much more fragmented. Ports of entry, border-crossing patrols, and customs operations are run by the federal government, with penalties such as incarceration carried out by federal authorities. Although the issue of border security and the prevention of illegal residents from entering the country are the domain of the feds, there is very little satisfaction with the way the powers in Washington, D.C., have dealt with the issue. According to the Pew Hispanic Center, there were approximately 11 million illegal immigrants living in the United States in 2007, with almost 6 in 10 coming from Mexico. But other estimates go as high as 20 million. The situation is so out of control that no one can provide any numbers with certainty.

To deal with this vast population of illegal immigrants, state and local governments have struggled to provide support services. From schools to medical care, illegal immigrants require many of the same services needed by legal immigrants and citizens. However, illegals are likely to have paid less in taxes than citizens because of "under the table" employment options, which often allow them to work for undocumented and untaxed cash as part of the nation's already vast underground tax-evading economy. In addition, their often poor economic conditions, lack of health insurance, and language barriers require more public social services than those needed by average

(*continued*)

A CASE STUDY | *Continued*

Americans. The failure of the federal government to stop the influx of these illegal aliens or to adequately compensate state and local governments for the costs entailed in providing social services for them has led to many initiatives emerging from state capitals, counties, and even cities.

The gut issue here is not so much the immigrants themselves, who tend to be an overall plus for the economy, but the costs of servicing their needs. To the extent that the federal government fails to control its international borders, it is forcing—mandating—state and local governments to provide billions of dollars in educational, medical, and other social services to the illegal immigrants without reimbursement. This is why illegal immigration is the mother of all unfunded mandates.

According to the National Conference of State Legislatures, at least 1,100 immigration bills were submitted by state lawmakers during 2007, a mark that doubled the previous record set in 2006. This flurry of bills came as a major federal immigration overhaul bill that was supported by President Bush failed to emerge from Congress. In the void left by the federal government's inactivity, the state bills have tended to be punitive to illegal immigrants. Among the approaches most commonly employed by states have been policies that deny illegal immigrants access to government programs and laws that penalize employers for hiring undocumented workers. In some cases states have passed laws that strip government funding to charitable organizations if they use the money to provide services to illegal immigrants.

The complexity of this issue can be illustrated by the problem of in-state state university tuition rates for illegal aliens. Out-of-state tuition is often twice as much. But illegal aliens who graduate from local high schools with grades that make them eligible for the less expensive in-state tuition rate say they should be allowed to enroll at that rate. Critics contend that they should not be allowed to enroll at all. Indeed—the critics continue—as they are now adults (being over 18), they no longer need to reside with their parents, and, in consequence, should be immediately deported—as well as their parents, if illegal. Besides, if a state allows the lower tuition rate for illegals, how can the state deny it to perfectly legal citizens of other U.S. states? And if it does, isn't this a violation of Article IV, Section 2, of the Constitution, which states that: "The Citizens of each State shall be entitled to all Privileges and Immunities of Citizens in the several States"?

While the states have thrown themselves headlong into the fracas, the most contentious battles in the immigration tempest seem to be occurring at the municipal level. Surprisingly, many of the most controversial actions are not occurring in major cities or communities on the Mexican border, but in smaller towns far away from the highest concentrations of illegal residents. For example, the small Pennsylvania city of Hazelton drew national attention when it adopted an ordinance that fined businesses and landlords who employ or house illegal immigrants. A recent surge of Hispanic residents to the formerly homogenous city pushed the issue onto the public agenda in Hazelton, but as can be expected in a federal system, Hazelton's laws would not be left to the city's residents to decide. Instead, the Hazelton laws are being challenged in federal court largely on the grounds that municipalities have no right to preempt federal authority on immigration issues, and that the Hazelton laws clash with federal antidiscrimination and fair-housing laws.

While the federal courts did find Hazelton's law unconstitutional in July of 2007, it seems clear that the outcome of the case did not end the intergovernmental mess that engulfs this issue. In 2008 and 2009 several states, including Oklahoma, Colorado, and Virginia, decided to curtail medical care, mortgage loans, and other benefits for illegal immigrants as the national economy soured. And back on the West Coast there were renewed efforts in California to place a question on the ballot that would end public benefits for illegal immigrants, cut off welfare benefits for their children, and impose new rules for birth certificates. It is clear the combination of immense political and economic pressures, changing demographics, and large gray areas within the realm of American federalism will keep intergovernmental relations in the area of immigration very tense for years to come.

For Discussion: *Why have state and local governments become more active in regulating illegal immigrants during recent years? How does the design of American federalism lead to the types of intergovernmental conflicts found in the area of immigration?* ▲

SUMMARY

The process of intergovernmental relations is federalism in action. It is the complex network of day-to-day interrelationships among the governments within a federal system. It is the political, fiscal, programmatic, and administrative processes by which higher units of government share revenues and other resources with lower units of government, generally accompanied by special conditions that the lower units must satisfy as prerequisites to receiving the assistance.

The U.S. Constitution created the permanent features of intergovernmental relations in the United States. The popular image of the federal system as a layer cake, with each layer of government neatly on top of the other, is deceptive. The reality is more like a marble cake, in which the cooperative relations among the varying levels of government result in an intermingling—not a layering—of activities.

The key word in the new American thrust toward decentralization or devolution is mandate: One level of government requires another to offer—or pay for—a program as a matter of law or as a prerequisite to partial or full funding for either the program in question or other programs. Mandates are orders. The movement toward devolution is spurred on by jurisdictions and constituencies that increasingly resent taking such orders.

Fiscal federalism refers to the financial relationships that exist between units of government in a federal system. A central question is frequently asked about fiscal federalism: Why can't the citizens of the states just keep their money (meaning have their federal taxes reduced) rather than paying it to the federal government so that it can be returned in grants and services? The only certainty here is that the states have become addicted to intergovernmental funding. The question remains whether their political leaders will gradually wean them from it or feed their habit.

REVIEW QUESTIONS

1. What are the advantages and disadvantages of a federal system of government?
2. Why is the American federal system considered to be more like a marble cake than a layer cake?
3. Why are mandates such a cause of friction in intergovernmental relations?
4. Why are federal grant programs so important to state and local governments?
5. Is the movement toward devolution more of a threat or an opportunity for national governments in a federal system?

KEY CONCEPTS

Block grant   A grant distributed in accordance with a statutory formula for use in a variety of activities within a broad functional area, largely at the recipient's discretion.

Categorical grant   A grant that can be used only for specific, narrowly defined activities—for example, to construct an interstate highway.

Council of government (COG)   An organization of cooperating local governments seeking a regional approach to planning, development, transportation, environment, and other issues.

Devolution   The transfer of power from a central to a local authority.

Federalism   A system of governance in which a national, overarching government shares power with subnational or state governments.

Federalism, cooperative   The notion that the national, state, and local governments are cooperating, interacting agents jointly working to solve common problems, rather than conflicting, sometimes hostile competitors, pursuing similar or possibly conflicting ends.

Federalism, dual   The nineteenth-century concept, now no longer operational, that the functions and responsibilities of the federal and state governments were theoretically distinguished and functionally separate from each other.

Federalism, marble-cake   The concept that the cooperative relations among the varying levels of government result in an intermingling of activities; in contrast to the more traditional view of layer-cake federalism, which holds that the three levels of government are totally or almost totally separate.

Federalism, new   The Republican efforts begun during the Nixon administration to decentralize governmental functions by returning power and responsibility to the states. This trend was continued in the 1980s by the Reagan administration and culminated in the 1990s movement toward devolution.

Federalism, picket fence   The concept that bureaucratic specialists at the various levels of government (along with clientele groups) exercise considerable power over the nature of intergovernmental programs.

Fiscal federalism   The financial relations between and among units of government in a federal system. The theory of fiscal federalism, or multiunit government finance, is one part of the branch of applied economics known as public finance.

Grant An intergovernmental transfer of funds (or other assets). Since the New Deal, state and local governments have become increasingly dependent on federal grants for an almost infinite variety of programs.

Intergovernmental relations The complex network of interrelationships among governments; the political, fiscal, programmatic, and administrative processes by which higher units of government share revenues and other resources with lower units of government, generally accompanied by special conditions that the lower units must satisfy as prerequisites to receiving the assistance.

Mandating One level of government requiring another to offer—and/or pay for—a program as a matter of law or as a prerequisite to partial or full funding for either the program in question or other programs.

MySearchLab® EXERCISES

Apply what you learned in this chapter on MySearchLab (*www.mysearchlab.com*).

BIBLIOGRAPHY

Arrandale, Tom. (1994). "The Sagebrush Gang Rides Again," *Governing* (March).

Bennett, Clay. (2007). "When Illegal Migrants Flood a City," *Christian Science Monitor* (July 31).

Boyle, Phillip, and Gordon P. Whitaker. (2001). "Educating for the New Public Service: Implications of the Transformation of Governance," *Journal of Public Affairs Education* 7 (October 2001).

Cannon, Angie. (2001). "Final Words from Flight 93," *U.S. News & World Report* (October 29).

Cohen, Richard. (1995). "States Aren't Saints, Either," *Washington Post National Weekly* (April 9).

Cook, Gareth G. (1995). "Devolution Chic: Why Sending Power to the States Could Make a Monkey Out of Uncle Sam," *Washington Monthly* (April).

Ehrenhalt, Alan. (1995). "The Locust in the Garden of Government," *Governing* (March).

Elazar, Daniel J. (1962). *The American Partnership: Intergovernmental Cooperation in the 19th Century United States*. Chicago: University of Chicago Press.

Furtwangler, Albert. (1984). *The Authority of Publius: A Reading of the Federalist Papers*. Ithaca, NY: Cornell University Press.

Greenhouse, Linda. (2007). "Justices Say E.P.A. Has Power to Act on Harmful Gases," *New York Times* (April 3).

Grodzins, Morton. (1966). *The American System*, ed. Daniel J. Elazar. Chicago: Rand McNally.

Helvarg, David. (1994). *The War against the Greens: The Wise Use Movement, the New Right, and Anti-Environmental Violence*. San Francisco: Sierra Club Books.

Hughes, Robert. (1993). *The Culture of Complaint*. New York: Oxford University Press.

Jones, Timothy, and Janine Tyne. (1994). "*Printz v. United States*: An Assault upon the Brady Act or a Tenth Amendment Fortification?" *St. John's Journal of Legal Commentary* 10.

Kettl, Donald F. (2000). "The Transformation of Governance: Globalization, Devolution, and the Role of Government," *Public Administration Review* 60.

Larkin, John. (1995). "Mandate Protesters to Gain Limited Relief," *Public Administration Times* (March 1).

Lloyd, Alan. (1974). *The Scorching of Washington: The War of 1812*. Washington, DC: Robert B. Luce.

Marando, Vincent, and Patricia S. Florestano. (1990). "Intergovernmental Management: The State of the Discipline." In *Public Administration: The State of the Discipline*, eds. Naomi B. Lynn and Aaron Wildavsky. Chatham, NJ: Chatham House.

McCurdy, Howard E. (1984). "Public Ownership of Land and the 'Sagebrush Rebellion,'" *Policy Studies Journal* 12 (March).

McDonald, Forrest. (1985). *Novus Ordo Seclorum: The Intellectual Origins of the Constitution.* Lawrence: University Press of Kansas.

Miller, Sara B. (2005). "Northeast Battles Its Status as US 'Tailpipe,'" *Christian Science Monitor* (April 1).

Moynihan, Daniel Patrick. (1995). "The Devolution Revolution," *New York Times* (August 6).

National Conference of State Legislatures. (2007). "2007 Enacted State Legislation Related to Immigrants and Immigration" (August 15).

Passel, Jeffrey. (2007). "Estimates of the Size and Characteristics of the Undocumented Population," Pew Hispanic Center (March 21).

Pooley, Eric. (1995). "Things That Make Rudy Nuts: The Mayor's Real Top Ten List: Unfunded Federal, State, and Judicial Mandates That Push the City into the Red," *New York Times* (January 30).

Popper, Frank J. (1984). "The Timely End of the Sagebrush Rebellion," *Public Interest* 76 (Summer).

Rainwater, Lee, and William Yancey. (1967). *The Moynihan Report and the Politics of Controversy.* Cambridge, MA: MIT Press.

Ross, Bernard H. (1998). "Metropolitan Organization." *International Encyclopedia of Public Policy and Administration*, ed. Jay M. Shafritz. Boulder, CO: Westview Press.

Russakoff, Dale, and Rene Sanchez. (2003). "Begging, Borrowing for Security: Homeland Burden Grows for Cash-Strapped States, Cities," *Washington Post* (April 1).

Sanford, Terry. (1967). *Storm over the States.* New York: McGraw-Hill.

Shanahan, Eileen. (1991). "Going It Jointly: Regional Solutions for Local Problems," *Governing* (August).

Swarns, Rachel L. (1998). "A New Broom Needs a New Handle: Welfare as We Know It Goes Incognito," *New York Times* (July 5).

Swartz, Thomas R., and John E. Peck, eds. (1990). *The Changing Face of Fiscal Federalism.* Armonk, NY: M. E. Sharpe.

Thompson, Mark. (2005). "Why Did FEMA and Its Chief, Michael Brown, Fail Their Biggest Test?" *Time* (September 19).

Vobejda, Barbara. (1995). "Will There Be a Race to the Bottom on Welfare?" *Washington Post National Weekly* (September 18–24).

Vobejda, Barbara, and Judith Havemann. (1998). "States' Welfare Shift: Stop It before It Starts," *Washington Post* (August 12).

Watanabe, Teresa (2009) "Activists Push Ballot Initiatives to End State Benefits for Illegal Immigrants and Their U.S. Born Children," *Los Angles Times* (July 13).

White, Leonard D. (1948). *The Federalists.* New York: Macmillan.

Wikstrom, Nelson. (1985). *Councils of Governments: A Study of Political Incrementalism.* Chicago: Nelson-Hall.

Wills, Garry. (1981). *Explaining America: The Federalist.* Garden City, NY: Doubleday.

Wright, Deil S. (1988). *Understanding Intergovernmental Relations*, 3rd ed. Pacific Grove, CA: Brooks/Cole.

RECOMMENDED BOOKS

Conlan, Timothy. (1998). *From New Federalism to Devolution: Twenty-Five Years of Intergovernmental Reform.* Washington, DC: Brookings Institution. The history of American federalism from the 1970s through the 1990s.

Dilulio, John, and Donald F. Kettl. (1995). *Fine Print: The Contract with America, Devolution, and the Administrative Realities of American Federalism.* Washington, DC: Brookings

Institution. The story of what happens when Republican Party ideology seeks to cope with and reform the immutable facts of intergovernmental relations.

Filippov, Mikhail, Peter C. Ordeshook, and Olga Shvetsova. (2004). *Designing Federalism: A Theory of Self-Sustainable Federal Institutions.* Cambridge, England: Cambridge University Press. An analysis of the factors that led to the development of successful federalist systems.

Peterson, Paul E. (1995). *The Price of Federalism.* Washington, DC: Brookings Institution. A historical account and optimistic contemporary assessment of the intergovernmental fiscal relationships among the differing levels of government.

Posner, Paul L. *The Politics of Unfunded Mandates: Whither Federalism?* (1998). Washington, DC: Georgetown University Press. The origins and politics of congressional requirements for state and local governments to implement federal policies.

Rabe, Barry. (2004). *Statehouse and Greenhouse: The Emerging Politics of American Climate Policy.* Washington, DC: Brookings Institution Press. An examination of emerging state roles in dealing with international environmental policy.

RELATED WEB SITES

www.naco.org
National Association of Counties
This site presents information from the only national organization that represents county governments. Among the content areas are sections about legislative initiatives at the county level, conferences, and ways for the public to better utilize the resources provided by county governments.

www.narc.org
National Association of Regional Councils (NARC)
The NARC promotes regionalism as the most effective way to provide services and address problems facing local communities. The organization's Web site is a platform for its views and policies and presents legislation that will enhance cooperation between municipal and county governments throughout the United States.

www.ncsl.org
National Conference of State Legislatures (NCSL)
The most comprehensive collection of information regarding state laws and policies, The NCSL site provides comparative data on state policies in a number of areas, including budgetary processes, federal–state and local relations, and regulatory tools. The site also includes many publications provided by the NCSL.

www.nga.org
National Governors Association (NGA)
The organization is a public policy group that represents the nation's governors. The site gives information about the governors as well as current news that deals with their offices. Among the features of the NGA's site is a comprehensive list of the association's positions on major issues related to federal policies toward the states.

www.oxfordjournals.org/our_journals/pubjof/index.html
Publius: The Journal of Federalism
The site allows online access for *Publius,* considered to be the foremost journal on federalism. *Publius* is published quarterly and contains articles exploring all aspects of federalism, both in the United States and around the world.

Honor, Ethics, and Accountability

KEYNOTE: Niccolò Machiavelli, the Preeminent Public Administration Ethicist

It has been more than five centuries since his birth, but Niccolò Machiavelli (1469–1527) remains the most quoted, most read, most interpreted, and most misunderstood public policy adviser who ever lived. By the time William Shakespeare wrote *Richard III* in 1592, he could assume that his audience would be familiar with Machiavelli's diabolical reputation. Thus Shakespeare could have his title character introduce himself as being so evil that he could "set the murderous Machiavel to school." Similar references to Machiavelli as the personification of evil doings abound in the plays and literature of Shakespeare's time and have continued ever since.

But it's a bum rap. Machiavelli was really a nice guy. Indeed, he is an exemplar as a public administrator and policy analyst. Born into a family of ancient nobility but persistent impoverishment, he was educated well enough to become a civil servant and sometime ambassador for Florence beginning in 1498. He was an honest, truthful, and competent employee. But his was a patronage position (there being no merit system then), and he lost his job and nearly his life with a shift in the political winds of 1512. Thereafter, he eked out a living on a meager farm left to him by his father.

His greatest desire was to go back to work for his beloved Florence, now in the control of the Medici family. So, like many a high-level political appointee out of power, he wrote a book (indeed several) to demonstrate his usefulness to potential employers. In his most famous private letter (dated December 10, 1513), quoted by biographer Giuseppe Prezzolini, he expresses hope that "if it [his book *The Prince*] were read, they [the Medici] would see that for . . . fifteen years I have been studying the art of the state." He even offers proof of his honesty as a past and potential employee: "As a witness to my honesty and goodness I have my poverty."

Because Machiavelli, despite constant efforts, never did get the government job he so coveted, after working on his farm all day, he spent his nights working on the most enduring books of political philosophy produced by the Italian Renaissance. *The Prince* (1532) and *The Discourses* (1531) were important political and military analyses that led to the use of the term **Machiavellianism** to refer to cunning, cynical, and ruthless behavior based on the notion of the end justifying the use of almost any means. What Machiavelli actually noted in *The Prince* was that a ruler would be judged by results: "So let a prince set about the task of conquering and maintaining his state; his methods will always be judged honorable and universally praised." Machiavelli, as one of the first policy advisers, developed a set of prescriptions and proscriptions for his prince that were designed to ensure that the prince would flourish politically. His introduction summarizes his methodology: "I have long pondered and scrutinized the actions of the great, and now I offer the results . . . within the compass of a small volume." Machiavelli offers a set of axioms and ideas about obtaining power, holding on to power, and using power to gain advantage:

- Men should either be treated generously or destroyed, because they take revenge for slight injuries—for heavy ones they cannot. [Potential organizational or political rivals should be either made part of your team or "destroyed"—fired or killed—because if left in place, they will, like a snake, bite you in the rear when you least expect it.]
- Princes ought to leave affairs of reproach to the management of others, and keep those of grace in their own hands. [The good news a leader delivers with a maximum of publicity; the bad news is quietly announced by a low-level assistant.]

Machiavellian ■
Referring to Niccolò Machiavelli (1469–1527), the Italian Renaissance political philosopher whose book of advice to would-be leaders, *The Prince* (1532), is the progenitor of all how-to-succeed books. Its exploration of how political power is grasped, used, and kept is the benchmark against which all subsequent analyses are judged. Machiavelli's amoral tone and detached analysis have caused him to be both soundly denounced as well as greatly imitated. While his name has become synonymous with political deception, no other writer has given the world such a brilliant lesson in how to think in terms of cold political power.

- It is necessary for him who lays out a state and arranges laws for it to presuppose that all men are evil and that they are always going to act according to the wickedness of their spirits whenever they have free scope. [It is as James Madison, a reader of Machiavelli, wrote in *The Federalist*, No. 51: "Ambition must be made to counteract ambition." To this extent the U.S. Constitution with its system of checks and balances is reflective of Machiavelli.]
- Princes who have achieved great things have been those who have given their word lightly, who have known how to trick men with their cunning, and who, in the end, have overcome those abiding by honest principles. [This advice may sound familiar to anyone who has been deceived by a leader, such as when President Richard Nixon said, "I am not a crook," or when president Bill Clinton told the nation, "I did not have sexual relations with that woman."]

If lying politicians have a patron saint, it must be Machiavelli, who wrote in *The Prince*, "It is necessary that the prince should know how to color his nature well, and how to be a great hypocrite and dissembler. For men are so simple, and held so much to immediate necessity, that the deceiver will never lack dupes." Machiavelli's ideal prince would not be a traditional man of honor; his word would not be his bond. Machiavelli's advice was "not to keep faith when by so doing it would be against his interest and when the reasons which made him bind himself no longer exist." This was the kind of thing that made people suspect that not only was Machiavelli not a gentleman, but his books were not fit reading for gentlemen either.

Why is this man smiling? Princeton professor Maurizio Viroli titles his biography of Machiavelli *Niccolò's Smile* and then goes to great length—indeed, book length—to explain how the smile in this portrait is indicative of the subtlety of his mind. But because the portrait was painted several years after Machiavelli died, we may surmise that this is not necessarily his real smile. Enigmatic smiles are a hallmark of old portraits. (Remember the *Mona Lisa* by Leonardo da Vinci.) Then remember the reason that practically none of these old portraits have toothy smiles as is common today: bad teeth. Until modern dentistry, even the richest people had terrible teeth—not to mention breath. So it is reasonable to conclude that Niccolò's smile is more dental than mental.

Machiavelli, in his advice, disregarded the issue of morality—apart from those circumstances where it was prudent or necessary for the prince to appear to be moral. Yet this was essentially ethical because the lying was for the good of the state. Machiavelli's theory of lying was a restatement of Plato's noble lie from Book 3 of *Republic*, in which he asserts that the guardians of a society may put forth untruths necessary to maintain social order.

But, alas, Machiavelli's books failed in their initial purpose to get him into a job and out of poverty. While his manuscripts circulated privately among his friends, *The Prince* was not published until five years after his death. Only then did it become a sensation. Posthumously, Machiavelli has been a great success. Much like a modern rapper who becomes more and more famous as critics denounce his vile lyrics, Machiavelli became notorious because he was denounced by all three of the major political factions of his time: the Roman Catholics, the Protestants, and the Republicans.

Because it was so widely denounced, *The Prince* became all the more widely read—or, rather, misread. Readers seeking to find evil found it. But a more subtle and modern reading finds it less and less evil and more and more practical. Machiavelli's book of advice to would-be leaders is the progenitor of all "how-to-succeed" books that advocate practical rather than moral actions. In 1967, British Broadcasting Corporation executive Antony Jay reintroduced Machiavelli's concepts to a modern audience with his best selling book *Management and Machiavelli*, which took Machiavelli's insights for managing a state and applied them to the problem of power and politics in organizations. Jay concluded that Machiavelli's principles are as valid now as they were 450 years ago because they are "rooted in human nature." According to Jay, "The new science of management is in fact only a continuation of the old art of government." Consequently, "when you study management theory side by side with political theory, and management case histories side by side with political history, you realize that you are only studying two very similar branches of the same subject."

For Discussion: *Why is Machiavelli still so critically important for understanding the mechanisms of power in public policymaking and administrative practices? What current public figures have followed Machiavelli's example and have written articles and books specifically so they could influence public policies and/or gain public office?*

THE ORIGINS AND NATURE OF HONOR

Our modern concepts of honor have their origins in ancient Greece and Rome. The classic example of honorable public service was Lucius Quinctius Cincinnatus, the Roman patrician who has become the symbol of republican virtue and personal integrity. In 458 B.C.E., when Rome was threatened with military defeat, Cincinnatus, a farmer, was appointed dictator by the Senate to deal with the emergency. Legend has it that he literally abandoned his plow in midfield to take command. Within 16 days he defeated the enemy, resigned from the dictatorship, and returned to his plow. Ever since, politicians have been insincerely asserting how much they yearn to give up power and return to the farm, as Cincinnatus did. This is a very strong theme in American political history. Until the twentieth century, it was thought politically indecent to publicly lust after political power. Politicians were expected to sit contentedly on their farms, metaphorically behind their plows, until they were called to service.

George Washington is one of the few genuine Cincinnatus figures in world history. Indeed, Lord Byron (George Noel Gordon) in his 1814 *Ode to Napoleon Bonaparte,* called Washington "the Cincinnatus of the West." Garry Wills writes in *Cincinnatus: George Washington and the Enlightenment* (1984), [On December 23, 1783, at the end of the Revolutionary War, General George Washington] "spoke what he took to be his last words on the public stage; 'Having now finished the work assigned me, I retire from the great theater of Action. . . . I here offer my commission, and take my leave of all the employments of public life.' At that moment, the ancient legend of Cincinnatus—the Roman called from his plow to rescue Rome, and returning to this plow when danger had passed—was resurrected as a fact of modern political life."

The example of Cincinnatus is still with us today. It is even unconsciously evoked for a modern public that never heard of the ancient Roman. For example, Ronald Reagan is quoted by E. G. Brown in *Reagan and Reality*: "One thing our founding fathers could not foresee . . . was a nation governed by professional politicians who had a vested interest in getting reelected. They probably envisioned a fellow serving a couple of hitches and then looking forward to getting back to the farm." The modern term limits movement is at its core an effort to legislate Cincinnatus-type behavior—to send them back "to the farm." Of course, both Cincinnatus and Washington were not merely farmers. They both had major estates with slaves to do the heavy lifting. Modern political leaders not only lack slaves, but they also do not even have farms anymore. Having no honorable and luxurious place to which to retreat when recalled from public life, they fight all the harder to stay in the game.

Shakespeare's Marc Antony was right. We are "all honorable men"—and women. Our culture inculcates us with concepts of honor from childhood. Much of our sense of honor comes from observing the actions of family and neighbors. The rest comes from the media. Many people get their first conscious lessons in honor from movies. Westerns directed by John Ford and others taught Americans the "code of the West." They taught you that one's word was sacrosanct and thus was not given lightly, taught you when an insult was so bad that it warranted violence, and taught you, above all, to protect the weak—all notions from medieval chivalry.

Later, space "westerns" such as *Star Trek* and *Star Wars* taught a new generation the intergalactic concept of honor, which, of course, was no different from the medieval concept. Some things have not changed in a thousand years. Thus young people still learn what it means to be honorable by listening to (and watching) the sagas of their culture. *Star Trek* as a transmitter of notions of honor is just a modern version of the eighth-century *Beowulf* or the eleventh-century *Song of Roland.* Honor has been and remains one of the core influences of human behavior. It is often more important than life itself. The founders of the United States in the last sentence of their 1776 Declaration of Independence stated, "And for the support of this Declaration, with a firm reliance on the Protection of Divine Providence, we mutually pledge to each other our Lives, our Fortunes, and our sacred Honor." Their lives were not sacred. Their fortunes were not sacred. But their honor was.

National Honor

Once reserved for the nobility, since the eighteenth century honor has become increasingly democratized. As absolutist governments declined, national honor (once solely the concern of individual monarchs) became a factor that influenced whole peoples. No less a pragmatist than President Woodrow Wilson felt the pull of national honor. In 1916 he asserted that "the nation's honor is dearer than the nation's comfort; yes, than the nation's life itself." Thus a collective democratic citizenry, no less than a defenseless maiden, may espouse the motto "death before dishonor." This notion is more than melodramatic hyperbole. During World War II, the French dishonored themselves by surrendering so quickly to the Germans in the spring of 1940. They were not willing to fight the Nazis in the streets of Paris and see their beautiful city destroyed. But the British, expecting an invasion soon afterward, were willing to sacrifice London.

When Winston Churchill told the House of Commons on June 4, 1940, immediately after the Dunkirk evacuation that "we shall defend our island, whatever the cost may be, we shall fight on the beaches, we shall fight on the landing grounds, we shall fight in the fields and in the streets, we shall fight in the hills; we shall never surrender," he meant exactly that. Indeed, he later wrote in his postwar memoirs, *Their Finest Hour* (1949), that "we were prepared to go to all lengths. I intended to use the slogan 'you can always take one with you.'" Suicidal? Perhaps—but honorable all the same. When General Charles de Gaulle fled to England rather than surrender, he was asked why he was there. He replied, "I am here to save the honor of France." There is still debate about whether he succeeded or not. (At least he tried!)

The U.S. involvement in the Vietnam War can also be viewed through the perspective of national honor. As the costs of the war became more than the American public was willing to bear, the nation's leaders struggled to find a way for the United States to leave Vietnam while maintaining its appearance as a strong and proud world power. Even when the chances of military success in Vietnam became remote, the United States continued to send troops into the field as diplomats tried to negotiate an acceptable peace. In 1973 President Richard M. Nixon addressed a national audience with his announcement that "we today have concluded an agreement to end the war and bring peace with honor in Vietnam and Southeast Asia." Ultimately, it can be argued that Nixon's agreement brought neither real peace nor real honor to the United States, yet the importance of maintaining an appearance of honor was essential to any plan that extricated the United States from its involvement in Vietnam.

As the United States scaled down its military operations in Iraq, the issue of maintaining national honor was once again playing a significant role in the decision-making process on removal of combat troops. During the 2009 presidential campaign then candidate Barack Obama was adamant that if elected he would have American troops out of Iraq within 16 months. Like Nixon before him, Obama would not declare victory in Iraq, but instead attempted to preserve American honor while recognizing the limited success of our efforts there.

Why Honor Precedes Ethics

Honor comes before ethics because a person without honor has no moral compass and does not know which way to turn to be ethical. Honor goes to the essence of public affairs; since ancient times only individuals perceived to be honorable could be trusted with the public's business. Of course, honor always has a context, and it is always influenced by the prevailing organizational and political culture. Melvin M. Belli, the American attorney, relates a story that illustrates this point. In the early 1950s Belli traveled to Paris to represent his client, movie star Errol Flynn, who had a legal tangle with a French firm over the profits from a movie. When Belli arrived, the French lawyer on the case advised him that there was nothing to worry about: "We have given the judge 200,000 francs and the case is in the bag." When Belli wondered aloud what would happen if the other side were to give the judge 300,000 francs, his French associate became indignant and replied, "But Monsieur, we are dealing with a respectable judge. He is a man of honor. He would not think of taking from *both* sides." This French judge's concept of honor was quite unlike the apocryphal American judge who, after taking bribes from both sides in a dispute, decided to try the case on its merits. Which judge is more ethical?

Dimensions of Honor

Honor has many dimensions. The most obvious and superficial kind is *ex officio*. This is the Latin phrase meaning "by virtue of the office." Many people hold positions on boards, commissions, councils, and so on because of another office they occupy. For example, the mayor of a city may be an *ex officio* member of the board of trustees of a university in that city. Thus "honorable" is the form of address used for many public officials, such as judges, mayors, and members of the U.S. Congress. Here honorable does not necessarily imply personal honor or integrity; it merely signifies current (or past) incumbency. Consequently, even after Richard M. Nixon disgraced himself and was forced to resign as president in 1974, he was still formally "The Honorable" in terms of formal address. Other smaller crooks, temporarily in public office, are no less honorable.

Honor is also a function of the outward perception of one's reputation. Reputation in business, whether of an individual or an organization, is a highly valued asset. Indeed, when businesses are sold, they often sell for sums far in excess of their book value because of their intangible **goodwill** or reputation in the community.

Goodwill ■
The reputation and built-up business of a company. It can be generally valued as what a company would sell for above the value of its physical property, money owed to it, and other assets.

True honor begins with personal integrity and honesty. It goes beyond Benjamin Franklin's famous admonition from his *Poor Richard's Almanac* that "honesty is the best policy." Think how cynical Franklin's statement is—it seems to have been derived from Cervantes's *Don Quixote*, anyway. Honesty is not worthwhile for its own sake; it is simply the optimum policy—one choice from among many. But true honesty, as opposed to policy honesty, is the essence of a person of honor. Such people act with integrity. This is at the core of honor. Those who have integrity live up to their stated principles, values, and most importantly, their word. A person whose word is his or her bond gives the full faith and credit of his or her whole being to keeping commitments. Sometimes this is almost frivolous, as it was when the legendary Abraham Lincoln walked miles through the snow to return a book by a promised date. But far more often one's word is the coin of the administrative realm. Things happen because one person tells something to another. This integrity of communication is essential for the smooth functioning of organizations that, in essence, are merely information-processing structures. This is why codes of honor (of integrity) first evolved among the military. Because lives, indeed whole battles, depended on the accuracy of information sent up the chain of command, it was imperative that an ethic of honesty be instilled. This is still true today. If the word of an officer is not known to be good, that officer has lost his or her effectiveness to his or her superior.

A second but more subtle meaning of integrity is integrated strength or character. A building that holds together is said to have structural integrity. Individuals who have character, as demonstrated by an observable long period of acting with integrity, are said to have **gravitas**, or as the British put it, "bottom"—meaning that they are seated firmly enough in their convictions that they are not easily swayed. Thus those who have integrity have a sure sense of right from wrong; they know what their core beliefs are, and what they will or will not do, no matter what the pressure.

Gravitas ■
Intellectual weight. A politician must exhibit a certain degree of gravitas if he or she is to be taken seriously for high office.

Regime Values

Administrators with integrity understand that they have a special moral obligation to the people they serve. They take seriously what John Rohr calls the "regime values" of their jurisdiction. In constitutional systems these values are established by the constitution, whether written, as in the United States, or unwritten, as in the United Kingdom. To a person of honor, an oath to "defend the Constitution of the United States against all enemies, foreign and domestic" is a serious matter. Thus, according to Rohr, the Constitution "is the moral foundation of ethics for bureaucrats." Those senior administrators who gain reputations for being ethical and honorable abide by a new-fashioned *noblesse oblige*. Originally the "nobility obliged" by leading in war and demonstrated their honor and valor by taking physical risks to prove their courage—to demonstrate on the field of honor (a battlefield) just how honorable they were.

Lacking a traditional nobility, republican governments give leadership roles to senior bureaucrats and elected officials. Once in office, their fellow citizens rightly expect them to take moral and career risks, parallel to the traditional risks of combat, to protect their fellow citizens, the regime, and their constitution. And they must be heroic enough to risk not just their lives but their livelihoods as well. Louis Brandeis, later to be an associate justice of the U.S. Supreme Court, argued in the 1910 *Glavis-Ballinger* case that public administrators "cannot be worthy of the respect and admiration of the people unless they add to the virtue of obedience some other virtues—virtues of manliness, of truth, of courage, of willingness to risk position, of the willingness to risk criticism, of the willingness to risk the misunderstanding that so often comes when people do the heroic thing." It is often said that managers are paid more than workers because they are paid to take risks, to make decisions that can cost them their jobs. Public managers live in an even riskier environment. Not only must they take normal management risks, but they must also risk their careers, their reputations, sometimes even their lives, to protect the values of the regime. It is simply a matter of honor.

All too often managers and employees fall from honor—or it may be that they never had it in the first place. Lapses take many forms. The two most common lapses of honor and honesty are corruption and lying.

CORRUPTION IN GOVERNMENT

Scandal ■
In religion, an offense committed by a holder of high office. The term has been popularized to cover the commission of any action considered a demeaning of the responsibilities of office by the holder of that office.

Recurrent scandals and instances of official mischief in government, no matter how much they threaten to cost, pose a great threat to the democratic notions of the rule of law. When a public official misuses his or her office for self-gain, then the rule of law no longer prevails, and there is, in effect, a return to tyranny. By engaging in such self-aggrandizement, corrupt representatives of the people illegally put themselves above the law. Moreover, a public official's act of wrongdoing is destructive of the claim that in a democracy all individuals are equal. Just like the pig in George Orwell's *Animal Farm* who cannot accept the idea that "all animals are equal," these self-interested officials in effect are saying, "but some of us are more equal than others." The porcine imagery continues when you think of them not only feeding at the public trough, but also "hogging" more than their share.

Bribery

Corruption also undermines economic rights. Consider bribery when it occurs within the competitive process of governmental purchasing. When contracts are awarded illegally by means of bribes, the losing competitors can be said to have had their rights to a fair and impartial bidding process abridged. The public's right to have purchases made in the most efficient and least costly fashion is also subverted. This kind of corruption makes a mockery of economic considerations. The few that greedily feed at the public trough deny the rights of others to enter a fair system of economic competition.

Of course, viewed systemically, bribery is an important element in any political system. It supplements the salaries of various public officials. This is especially true in societies where public sector salaries are unreasonably low. Some police officers, customs agents, and building inspectors, for example, would be unable to maintain

TABLE 5.1										
American Government Officials Convicted of Public Corruption under Federal Law										
	1990	**1995**	**2000**	**2001**	**2002**	**2003**	**2004**	**2005**	**2006**	**2008**
Federal Officials	583	438	422	414	429	421	389	390	407	458
State Officials	79	61	91	61	132	87	81	94	116	123
Local Officials	225	191	183	184	262	119	252	232	241	246

Source: *The 2009 Statistical Abstract: The National Data Book,* http://search.creativecommons.org/?q=Statistical+Abstract+of+the+United+States&sourceid=Mozilla-search.

> **TABLE 5.2**

Watergate Chronology

1969	January 20	Nixon inaugurated.
1970	July 23	Nixon approves use of illegal methods to gather intelligence on demonstrators and political enemies.
1971	February	Nixon begins secret taping of all Oval Office conversations.
1972	March 30	John Mitchell, head of Nixon's reelection committee, approves plan for illegal entry into and wiretapping of the Democratic National Committee's Watergate headquarters.
	May 27	The first Watergate break-in takes place.
	June 17	The second Watergate break-in occurs; five agents of the Nixon campaign are arrested.
		Nixon's attorney, Herbert Kalmbach, begins making secret payments to Watergate burglars; over a year's time $450,000 in hush money is paid out of campaign contributions.
	August 29	Nixon announces that White House Counsel John W. Dean has conducted an investigation of the Watergate break-in: "I can state categorically that his investigation indicates that no one in the White House staff, no one in this administration, presently employed, was involved in this very bizarre incident. What really hurts is if you try to cover it up." Dean would later testify that he had not heard of his "investigation" until this announcement.
	September 15	Watergate burglars indicted.
	October 10	*Washington Post* reporters Bob Woodward and Carl Bernstein reveal that the Watergate break-in was part of a massive campaign of political spying and sabotage conducted on behalf of the president's reelection and directed by White House and reelection committee officials.
	November 7	Nixon reelected in a landslide; wins every state but Massachusetts. Shortly thereafter, bumper stickers appear reading, "Don't blame me: I'm from Massachusetts."
1973	January	Watergate burglars tried and convicted.
	February 7	Senate votes to investigate Watergate and other 1972 campaign abuses.
	March 22	Nixon tells John Mitchell, "I want you all to stonewall it—let them plead the Fifth Amendment, cover-up, or anything else."
	April 30	Nixon announces resignations of White House Chief of Staff H. R. Haldeman; White House Domestic Affairs Advisor John D. Ehrlichman; the Attorney General Richard G. Kleindienst; and the firing of White House Counsel John Dean (who had just reported the cover-up to the Justice Department). Nixon tells the nation "We must maintain the integrity of the White House. . . . There can be no whitewash at the White House."
	May 17	Televised Senate Watergate hearings begin.
	May 18	Archibald Cox named Special Prosecutor.
	June 25	John Dean tells the Senate Watergate committee, "I began by telling the president that there was a cancer growing on the presidency and that if the cancer was not removed . . . the president himself would be killed by it."

(Continued)

> **TABLE 5.2 (Continued)**
>
> **Watergate Chronology**
>
> | | | |
> |---|---|---|
> | | July 16 | White House aide Alexander Butterfield reveals existence of White House taping system. |
> | | July 25 | Nixon refuses to release tapes requested by special prosecutor because it would violate executive privilege. |
> | | October 20 | Nixon orders the firing of Special Prosecutor Cox. |
> | | October 23 | Yielding to public pressure, Nixon agrees to hand over some tapes after "firestorm" of criticism. |
> | | October 30 | The House Judiciary Committee begins its impeachment inquiry. |
> | | November 1 | Houston lawyer Leon Jaworski is appointed new Special Prosecutor. |
> | 1974 | March 1 | The grand jury indicts seven former White House aides for Watergate cover-up. |
> | | May 24 | Special Prosecutor Leon Jaworski appeals to the Supreme Court to rule on his subpoena for more tapes. |
> | | July 24 | The Supreme Court in *United States v. Nixon* rules that Nixon must release the tapes. |
> | | July 27 | House Judiciary Committee votes for impeachment. |
> | | August 5 | Nixon surrenders tapes proving he had approved cover-up from the beginning. |
> | | August 9 | Nixon resigns. |
> | | September 8 | Nixon is pardoned by his successor, President Gerald R. Ford. |
> | 2005 | June 1 | Former FBI Deputy Director Mark Felt acknowledges he was Woodward and Bernstein's informant, "Deep Throat." |

their standard of living if it were not for such informal salary increments. Additionally, such income supplement programs forestall the need for politically unpopular, precipitous tax hikes that would bring the legal wages of such officers up to reasonable levels. Systematic bribery allows business operators, dependent on the discretionary powers of public officials for their livelihood, to stabilize the relationships essential for the smooth functioning of their businesses. After all, many regulations that govern safety or conditions of business operation may not be universally applicable, reasonably enforceable, or economically feasible. Bribery's occasional exposure by the press serves to foster the political alienation of the electorate, which in turn encourages cynicism and reduces support for the democratic processes of government. While it is possible to quibble over the particulars of any given instance or non-instance of bribery, its pervasiveness in too many communities is generally not contested except by the most naive or the most corrupt. Bribery is even an important and time-honored tool of foreign policy. Of course, the United States does not have to bribe a foreign government to influence its support on some international issue. It can achieve the same effect by granting or withholding military or economic aid.

Watergate

A society's humor is a good indicator of its political corruption. For example, many analysts predicted that President Nixon would eventually be forced from office because of the Watergate scandal once Johnny Carson, the most popular, most mainstream, and most middle-of-the-road of American comedians, started telling jokes on his *Tonight Show* that were premised on the belief that the president of the United States was dishonest. The jokes were a bellwether because most of the audience—that is, most of mainstream America—accepted the premise. Comedians do not lead public opinion, but they certainly reflect it. The same is true today in Russia. *New York Times* columnist Thomas L. Friedman wrote that "corruption reaches right into the leadership." His indicator of this is the often told joke "about a man who drives into Moscow from the countryside and parks his new car right outside the Kremlin's Spassky Gate in Red Square. A policeman comes along and tells the man, 'Look, you can't park here. This is the gate all our leaders use.' The man answers, 'Don't worry. I locked my car.'"

LYING FOR YOUR COUNTRY

The public officials who have the greatest reputation for lying are ambassadors—the highest ranking of all diplomats, sent as the personal representatives of one head of state to another. Sir Henry Wotton (1568–1639), Queen Elizabeth I's ambassador to Venice, was the first of many wits to write that "an ambassador is an honest man sent to lie abroad for the commonwealth." Often ambassadors are not trusted to lie well enough, so their governments purposely misinform them to ensure that their false representations will seem all the more sincere. Thus the Japanese ambassador to the United States in 1941 did not know of the impending Pearl Harbor attack, the German ambassador to the Soviet Union in 1941 was not

---

▶ BOX 5.1 | The Difference Between Honest Graft and Dishonest Graft

"Everybody is talkin' these days about Tammany men growin' rich on graft, but nobody thinks of drawin' the distinction between honest graft and dishonest graft. There's all the difference in the world between the two. Yes, many of our men have grown rich in politics. I have myself. I've made a big fortune out of the game, and I'm gettin' richer every day, but I've not gone in for dishonest graft—blackmailin' gamblers, saloon-keepers, disorderly people, etc.—and neither has any of the men who have made big fortunes in politics.

There's an honest graft, and I'm an example of how it works. I might sum up the whole thing by sayin': "I seen my opportunities and I took 'em."

Just let me explain by examples. My party's in power in the city, and its goin' to undertake a lot of public improvements. Well, I'm tipped off, say, that they're goin' to lay out a new park at a certain place.

I see my opportunity and I take it, I go to that place and I buy up all the land I can in the neighborhood. Then the board of this or that makes its plan public, and there is a rush to get my land, which nobody cared particular for before.

Ain't it perfectly honest to charge a good price and make a profit on my investment and foresight? Of course, it is. Well, that's honest graft." ▲

Source: William Riordon, *Plunkitt of Tammany Hall* (New York: McClure, Phillips, 1905).

told of the coming invasion, and the U.S. ambassador to the United Nations in 1961, Adlai Stevenson, was not told of the Bay of Pigs landing.

Niccolò Machiavelli wrote in *The Prince* (1532) that "it is necessary that the prince should know how to color his nature well, and how to be a great hypocrite and dissembler." This was the kind of thing that made people suspect that Machiavelli was not a gentleman. A true gentleman had to absolutely keep his word. Not to do so would "prove" that he was not a gentleman—and that he was without honor. Thus lying became as unforgivable an act of moral courage as cowardice was of physical courage. Of course, that was only if you got caught!

The Dirty Hands Dilemma

When do desirable public ends justify the lying means? When is doing evil acceptable to produce a greater political good? The "dirty hands dilemma" is a graphic phrase for this problem. Public officials dirty their hands when they commit an act generally considered to be a wrong to further the common good. This is a dilemma in the sense that doing bad seems to lead to something good. Thus public officials need to decide if they are willing to engage in wrongdoing for the sake of a perceived good deed. Of course, as a general rule they are prohibited from engaging in wrongdoing. Thus the dirty hands dilemma is the product of a tension between perceived professional obligations and long-standing moral obligations that are the standards of everyday life.

Machiavelli did not see this as a problem at all. He held that the rules of morality in everyday life should not be applied to the acts of public officials when they are carrying out their professional roles and responsibilities to further the common good. As Machiavelli expressed it in *The Discourses*, "When the act accuses, the result excuses." But can we divorce the person from his or her administrative role? If any moral judgment is to be made, it must be made about the office or the governmental unit in which the official is housed. We should not apply the ordinary standards of right and wrong to the extraordinary situation of a person who is acting only as a bureaucratic functionary. Others argue that it is a mistake to confuse the role of public official with the person who temporarily holds that role; moral rules are still applicable to the acts of the person who commits wrongs, whether that person be a public official or not.

There can be little doubt that the most common form of the dirty hands dilemma in public administration is lying. Lying can take many forms: direct falsehoods, exaggerations, omissions, evasions, deceptions, duplicity, and so on.

Do public officials have a special obligation to tell the truth? Do their offices permit them special excuses to depart from truth telling? It can be argued that because knowledge is the cornerstone of democracy, an informed public is a prerequisite for a democratic government. Hence, citizens have an inherent right to know the truth of public issues so that they can make intelligent decisions as voters and constituents. When public officials decide to dirty their hands, whether by direct falsehood or by omission, evasion, or whatever, they are abridging the public's right to know. There is, on this account, then, a special obligation for public officials to tell the truth based on this inherent need of democracy.

President Richard Nixon takes time out from subverting the U.S. Constitution (he had already approved illegal methods to gather information on his political enemies) to meet with Elvis Presley in the Oval Office on December 21, 1970. Elvis had a keen interest in public administration and came to offer his services to the country as a part-time, volunteer, federal narcotics agent. After all, few people had more experience with narcotics abuse. Not realizing the irony in this, Nixon was only too pleased to give the even then drug-saturated singer (who was destined to die of drug abuse) the badge and credentials of a special agent of the Bureau of Narcotics and Dangerous Drugs. Elvis was a strong supporter of the administration who had publicly criticized anti–Vietnam War entertainers such as the Smothers Brothers and Jane Fonda. He wanted the credentials so that he would have more credibility as a kind of ambassador to troubled young people. But alas, the only troubled young people with whom he met were teenage girls who had agendas other than politics.

On the other hand, it also can be argued that public officials in a democracy may be excused at times from the general obligation of truth telling. There may be dire situations or times of crises that threaten the government and its people. Under such conditions it may be permissible for a public official to deceive the public for its own good. In other words, when public officials take their oaths of office, they are sworn to do everything in their power to ensure the survival of the government and the safety of the public. It is the very nature of public office, then, that excuses the public official who lies for the public good because the public good is essentially what the official is required to protect. If such protection in times of war or crises entails that officials engage in deception, then so be it. They are only fulfilling the responsibilities of their office. The argument for excusing lies by officials has a long history. The first instance of it appears in Plato's *Republic*, in which the term "royal lie"—referring to lies for the public good—was first coined.

Lying about Sex

When essayist Charles Dudley Warner (1829–1900) wrote in 1871 that "politics makes strange bedfellows," he was referring to the fact that political necessity so often forces unlikely pairs to work together for a common goal—not that politicians must necessarily end up in bed with strangers. Yet those who have a passion for politics all too often have a problem with their passions. American presidents are no exceptions. The multitudinous, miscellaneous trysts of Presidents John F. Kennedy and Lyndon B. Johnson are recent examples that have been thoroughly documented by historians. Johnson even felt competitive with the deceased Kennedy about this. According to biographer Robert Dalleck, Johnson as president bragged that "I had more women by accident than he [Kennedy] ever had by design." President Bill Clinton is unique only in that he has been forced to admit to such infidelities while in office.

Until recently, lies about the sexual activities of consenting adults would not have been of concern to a textbook on public administration. But President Clinton changed that in 1998 when he told one lie after another about his Oval Office encounters with Monica Lewinsky, the White House intern with whom he eventually admitted having a relationship "that was not appropriate." And none of this would have come to public attention, no lies would have publicly been told, except for the involvement of the U.S. Supreme Court.

In what could turn out to be one of the most important modern Supreme Court decisions about the presidency, the Supreme Court ruled in 1998 (*William Jefferson Clinton v. Paula Corbin Jones*) that a sitting president could be sued by a private citizen seeking money damages in a civil suit for conduct alleged to have occurred before the president took office. Jones claimed that she was sexually harassed by Clinton while he served as governor of Arkansas years earlier. President Clinton urged the Court to delay the suit until he left office, claiming that the chief executive should not be burdened and distracted by having to defend against civil suits, except in far more exceptional circumstances.

Writing for the majority, Justice John Paul Stevens rejected Clinton's argument and concluded that that it would be highly unlikely that allowing the Jones case to proceed would generate a flood of other suits against this or other presidents, and, in any event, Stevens noted, the lower court judge could always defer such a case when it appears that to proceed would hamper a president's ability to do his job. What neither the members of the Court nor the public knew at the time was that President Clinton's testimony about Monica Lewinsky in a sworn deposition in the Jones case would set off a political firestorm powerful enough to threaten Clinton's presidency. Whether the Supreme Court's decision to permit civil actions against sitting presidents will result in future political and legal battles for presidents cannot be known. It is possible that the ever-present existence of powerful and well-funded political opponents anxious to "trap" presidents in sworn statements in civil suits was underestimated by the Court.

While Lewinsky's passion for President Clinton has been amply documented, she certainly seems to have lacked the "passion for anonymity" that the Brownlow Committee prescribed for White House assistants (see Chapter 3)—a passion that more mature presidential inamoratas have demonstrated by their silence. Because Lewinsky told so many people about her affair with Clinton, which began in 1995 when she was a 22-year-old, unpaid White House intern, evidence began to appear that she lied in her sworn statement in the Jones case. Jones's lawyers had sought her statement to bolster their contention that Clinton was a persistent and consistent philanderer.

When audiotapes of Lewinsky's telephone conversations about the affair with President Clinton with her "friend" Linda Tripp surfaced early in 1998, two things happened: (1) a special prosecutor (Ken Starr), who had earlier been authorized by Congress to investigate alleged illegalities by the Clintons in other matters, sought and gained the permission of the Clinton-appointed attorney general to expand the investigation into possible perjury by the president in his Jones statements; and (2) many times and before many audiences, the president emphatically denied having had sexual relations with Lewinsky. There is little doubt that he would have continued to lie about the affair had not physical evidence become available that supported Lewinsky's testimony to a grand jury that both she and the president had lied in their Jones case depositions. The evidence was a dress of Lewinsky's that was stained with presidential semen. Prior to the announcement of the existence of the physical evidence, the White House spin on the story was that Lewinsky was delusional about having an affair with the president—that she was just a politically star-struck kid who had lost a firm grasp on reality. But after the DNA of the dress stain was compared with freshly sampled presidential DNA, all doubts were over. After lying about this for seven months, the president, knowing of the DNA evidence of his lying, confessed before the grand jury, and then to the nation in a televised address, that he had had an "inappropriate relationship" with Lewinsky.

What got the president into legal trouble was not his multiple infidelities but the allegations of perjury about them. The party line from the White House after the confession was that because this whole scandal was about sex, it didn't rise to an impeachable offense. As with Watergate, it was not so much the initial "crime" as it was the cover-up—the lies—that forced Nixon from office and brought Clinton to impeachment. While some make the claim that lying about sex between consenting adults is only good manners, such matters are different affairs entirely once the parties have sworn to a grand jury to tell "the truth, the whole truth, and nothing but the truth." What does it say about the American legal system if the president of the United States is held exempt from that legal obligation—the violation of which has landed many of his fellow citizens in federal prison? This question was so troubling and Clinton's behavior was considered so reckless that in the fall of 1998 the House of Representatives impeached him for perjury and obstruction of justice. Clinton was tried by the Senate early in 1999 and was acquitted because there was nowhere near the constitutionally required two-thirds vote needed for his removal from office. Clinton remained president because many senators who believed he was guilty as charged felt that lying about sex was too petty a reason to remove a president.

HIERARCHY OF ETHICS

The public administrator is frequently adrift in a sea of competing duties and obligations. This kind of conflict occurs when an individual is called on to perform mutually exclusive acts by parties having legitimate "holds" on that person. For example, a rising young manager may not make it to the "big" meeting if he must at that moment rush his child to the hospital for an emergency appendectomy. When such conflicts arise, most individuals invoke a hierarchy of role obligation that gives some roles precedence over others. To most fathers, their child's life would be more important than a business meeting—no matter how "big." Real life is not always so unambiguous, however, and role conflict is a common dilemma in the world of work.

The "Nuremberg defense" is the often-used excuse of those caught performing illegal acts for their political or military superiors: "I was only following orders." The term and the tactic comes from war crimes trials in Nuremberg, Germany, of top Nazi leaders in the aftermath of World War II. The fallacy of this defense is that no soldier (or civilian employee) can be required to obey manifestly illegal orders. Indeed, as was even shown in the **My Lai** massacre during the Vietnam War, a soldier (or civilian employee) has a positive obligation to disobey such orders. Fortunately, few officials have to suffer angst over war crimes. But what about fixing traffic tickets, forcing a tax audit on someone, or pressuring employees to buy tickets to political dinners? Same issue, smaller stakes!

My Lai ■
The South Vietnamese village where hundreds of old men, women, and children were murdered in 1968 by a U.S. Army unit commanded by Lieutenant William Calley Jr. Despite complaints by several soldiers, the U.S. Army sought to ignore or cover up this atrocity until congressional inquiries and press reports forced a comprehensive investigation that led to Calley's court-martial.

The Four Levels of Ethics

In public administration there is a hierarchy of levels of ethics, each of which has its own set of responsibilities. First, there is personal morality—the basic sense of right and wrong. This is a function of our past and is dependent on factors such as parental influences, religious beliefs, cultural and social mores, and one's own personal experiences.

Second in the hierarchy is professional ethics. Public administrators increasingly recognize a set of professional norms and rules that obligate them to act in certain "professional" ways. Such guidelines are codified by professional associations such as the American Society for Public Administration and the International City Management Association. However, occupations such as law and medicine, while operating within public administration, also have their own independent professional codes.

A third level of ethics is organizational. Every organization has an environment or culture that includes both formal and informal rules of ethical conduct. Public organizations typically have many such rules. Public laws, executive orders, and agency rules and regulations all can be taken as formal organizational norms for ethical behavior.

Finally, there are social ethics. The requirements of social ethics oblige members of a given society to act in ways that both protect individuals and further the progress of the group as a whole. Social ethics are formal to the extent that they can be found in the laws of a given society, informal to the extent that they are part of an individual's social conscience.

The Iran-Contra Affair

To illustrate the conflicting nature of responsibility and different levels of ethical obligations, let's consider the Iran-Contra affair in general and the actions of Oliver North in particular.

The Iran-Contra scandal arose in the fall of 1986, when it was revealed that the Reagan administration had secretly sold arms to the government of Iran (so Iran would use its good offices to gain the release of American hostages in Lebanon) at higher than normal prices and used the "profits" to fund the Contras in Nicaragua. The controversy grew into a scandal because it was illegal to sell arms to Iran, illegal to fund the Contras beyond limits set by Congress, and against the expressed policy of the United States to negotiate for, let alone trade arms for, the release of hostages. Because the Iran-Contra operation was undertaken primarily by the National Security Council without the formal approval of the departments of Defense and State, the affair called into question the coherence of the Reagan administration's foreign policy.

As the major operative in the scheme, Lieutenant Colonel Oliver North of the U.S. Marine Corps, assigned to the White House National Security Council, serves as a case study in the conflict of responsibility. North has admitted that he found it necessary to lie to Congress about the Iran-Contra arms deal in order to further what he called national security goals. Thus, by overseeing the illegal sales of arms to Iran and channeling profits from the transactions to the Contras in violation of the law, North reached a decision that one set of responsibilities was higher than another. He justified his lies to Congress as necessary for national security. North violated the formal rules of organizational ethics and social ethics in illegally supplying military aid to the Contras and in lying to Congress to cover it up. However, he argued that he upheld his own personal morality and sense of duty to the country by acting as he did. Caught between his own interpretation of what is right and wrong on the personal level and that which his organization and society had deemed to be right and wrong, North chose the former over the latter. For many, he was a hero for doing so. Yet for many others, his actions were criminal and unconstitutional.

Good offices ■
The disinterested use of one's official position, one's office, to help others settle their differences; an offer to mediate a dispute.

Contras ■
The U.S.-backed "democratic resistance movement" in Nicaragua. The Contras opposed the communist Sandinista government. They disbanded in 1990 after the democratically elected government replaced the Sandinista regime.

The Higher Law Defense

When North's secretary, Fawn Hall, was called to testify during the 1987 congressional hearings on the scandal, she asserted, "I felt uneasy but sometimes, like I said before, I believed in Colonel North, and there was a very solid and very valid reason he must have been doing this for and sometimes you have to go above the written law, I believe." In her pedestrian way Ms. Hall defended North by asserting the ancient idea of a higher law: the notion that no matter what the laws of a state are, there remains a higher law to which a person has an even greater obligation.

A higher law is often appealed to by those who wish to attack an existing law or practice that courts or legislators are unlikely or unwilling to change. In a famous speech in the Senate on March 11, 1850, William Henry Seward of New York argued against slavery by asserting that "there is a higher law than the Constitution which regulates our authority." Martyrs throughout the ages have asserted a higher law in defiance of the state, thus earning their martyrdom. The classic presentation of this concept is in Sophocles' fourth-century B.C.E. play *Antigone*, in which the heroine defies the king, asserts a higher law as her justification, and "forces" the king to have her killed. Because the courts of any state will

◣ BOX 5.2 | Thomas Jefferson on Higher Law

A strict observance of the written laws is doubtless one of the high duties of a good citizen, but it is not the highest. The laws of necessity, of self-preservation, of saving our country when in danger, are of higher obligation. To lose our country by a scrupulous adherence to written law, would be to lose the law itself, with life, liberty, property and all those who are enjoying them with us; thus absurdly sacrificing the end to the means. ◣

Source: Thomas Jefferson, letter to John B. Colvin, September 20, 1810.

only enforce the law of the land, appealing to a higher law is always chancy business. Examples of Americans who have appealed to a higher law and wound up in jail as a result are Henry David Thoreau, Martin Luther King Jr., and Vietnam War resisters. Oliver North was convicted and would have gone to jail except that his conviction was overturned on a legal technicality. Thus he had all the glory of being a martyr with none of the pain of serving a prison sentence.

As the North case suggests, responsibilities can conflict because there are multiple levels of ethics and morality, each with its own set of obligations and duties. One of the most difficult aspects of being a public administrator is managing the conflict of responsibilities between the competing claims of stakeholders and the varying levels of ethics.

CODES OF HONOR, CONDUCT, AND ETHICS

It was a code of honor that forced Alexander Hamilton, one of the authors of *The Federalist* and the first U.S. secretary of the treasury, to face Aaron Burr, then vice president of the United States, in an 1803 duel (pistols at ten paces) that ended with Hamilton's death. Duelists have often been occupants of the White House. Andrew Jackson was notorious for it—though not as president. Today, disagreements that once would have warranted duels are decided in the courts or the tabloids. Dueling over honor has not subsided; it has only taken new forms. The one constant factor in affairs of honor, as the Robert McNamara case at the end of this chapter demonstrates, is that they are still often matters of life and death.

The New Face of Dueling

Dueling has never abated. It has only taken on new forms, adapted to new circumstances and new technology. In the classic 1955 film *Rebel without a Cause*, James Dean is challenged to a duel. The weapons are automobiles. He and the challenger drive the cars at high speed toward a cliff. The first one to jump out of his car is "chicken." Afterward, Dean explains to his father what happened: "Dad, I said it was matter of honor, remember? They called me chicken. You know, chicken? I had to go 'cause if I did not, I'd never be able to face those kids again. I got in one of those cars, and Buzz, that—Buzz, one of those kids—he got in the other car, and we had to drive fast and then jump, see, before the car came to the end of this bluff, and I got out okay, but Buzz did not and got killed."

Dueling by hotheaded teenage boys is the stuff of daily newspaper headlines. Teenage gang members, who once would have fought with fists or knives, now have cheap pistols or automatic weapons. A disrespectful comment or even a "look" is, as a matter of honor, all too often repaid with rapid fire. Those who do not act in accordance with gang codes of behavior suffer the consequences. Not all who kill for honor are gentlemen, but no one can be a gentleman if he is not prepared to die for honor.

Honorable Behavior

We still expect that our leaders will act honorably—meaning responsibly—and we disdain them when they do not. Almost everybody has heard of the 1912 *Titanic* disaster, in which many of the richest men in the world quietly went to their deaths when they could have taken the places of women and children in the lifeboats. The *Titanic* followed the tradition of the "Birkenhead Drill." When a British ship, the HMS *Birkenhead*, was sinking in 1852, the captain asked the men to "stand fast" so that the women and children could have the lifeboats. More than 400 men, including the captain, drowned. Ever since, "women and children first" has been the informal law of the sea because no man of honor could dispute it. And a ship's captain, responsible for all souls on board, was, as a matter of honor, traditionally expected to be the last one off of his sinking ship. Thus the world was appalled when Captain Yiannis Avranas was among the first to abandon his sinking Greek cruise ship, the *Oceanos*, off the coast of South Africa in 1991. Hundreds of passengers, many elderly, were left to shift for themselves. (The South African military eventually rescued everyone with helicopters.) As Captain Yiannis cravenly told reporters who asked him why he left his ship so soon, "When I order abandon ship, it does not matter what time I leave. Abandon is for everybody. If some people like to stay, they can stay." But his cowardly act was not morally different from the executive who arranges a golden parachute for himself while hundreds of employees who depended on his leadership are left with only pink slips and barren of financial windfalls. As you will see in this chapter's case study, Robert S. McNamara's dishonor was similar. He bailed out of the sinking ship of the Vietnam War, leaving thousands upon thousands of his country's children, 18- and 19-year-old drafted boys, to die. Leadership, as Shakespeare said of ambition, "should be made of sterner stuff."

More recently, the behavior of members of the New Orleans Police Department in the wake of Hurricane Katrina left many considering the contemporary role of honor. As their city suffered through its bleakest days in September of 2005, many New Orleans police officers either turned in their badges or simply failed to report for duty. Given the police officers' oath to "protect the lives and property" of the citizens of New Orleans, their actions could only be seen as dishonorable in nature. One can only imagine how the officers who continued to work through the deplorable conditions felt when their comrades deserted them in such a time. Desertion in time of crisis is a form of dishonor that strikes at the very heart of a code of conduct. For some, including at least a few New Orleans police officers, their commitment to an ethical code is not strong enough to outweigh other personal interests.

Codes of honor have their origins in ancient precepts about how a person should behave in the face of danger, when confronted with temptation, or before authority figures. Much of what are still considered important elements of honorable behavior is contained in the Bible's Ten Commandments. Thus it is still honorable behavior not to kill, steal, bear false witness, nor covet they neighbor's wife. As life grew more complicated, codes evolved for occupations as varied as clerics, masons, and warriors. The latter is both the most famous and most important, because those who feel a sense of traditional honor in their breasts today ultimately derive these emotions from medieval knights, eighteenth-century military and naval officers, and nineteenth-century British gentlemen.

But the honor of knights and gentlemen was highly stratified. Remember, they were gentlemen in the first place not because they were "gentle" (with women and horses!) but because of their genetic origin (Latin *gentilis*, "of a clan"), their breeding. Even today, polite people, those who ape upper-class manners, are called "well bred"—as if they were! Gentlemen were bound to act honorably only toward others in their own class. Consequently, if an ordinary citizen, having taken a dislike to Alexander Hamilton's face, had challenged him to a duel, he would not have been obligated to accept. There would have been no dishonor in declining. But a gentleman had always to defend his name, his reputation, his honor before members of his own class. According to historian Robin Gilmour, traditional honor to a gentleman "meant paying one's gambling debts, but not the tradesman's bill; deceiving a husband, if need be, but not cheating him at cards; insulting a servant with impunity, but one's equals only at the risk of a duel. The testing ground for one's courage, and therefore the justification for the whole bizarre code, was the gentleman's readiness to defend his honor with his life."

Was "Deep Throat's" Behavior Honorable?

Honorable behavior and ethical actions can sometimes seem at odds with one another. With the 2005 disclosure of Mark Felt as the informant "Deep Throat" in the Watergate scandal, the conflict between maintaining honor and acting ethically received increased public attention. During the investigation of the Watergate break-in, Felt, an FBI deputy director, provided *Washington Post* reporters Bob Woodward and Carl Bernstein with detailed information about the Nixon administration's efforts to cover up its involvement in illegal activities. The information Felt supplied proved essential in helping Woodward and Bernstein to expose the details of the White House's role in Watergate and helped lead to Nixon's unprecedented resignation from the presidency.

While many might think that Felt's role in this historic event was courageous and served the greater interest of the nation, Felt himself harbored misgivings about the honor of his actions. In the process of revealing his long-sought identity to the public, Felt expressed serious concern about how the FBI would regard his role in the Watergate episode. In the *Vanity Fair* article in which the identity of "Deep Throat" was revealed, author John D. O'Connor wrote that Felt "seemed to be struggling inside with whether he would be seen as a decent man or turncoat." He continued, "Deep in his psyche, it is clear to me, he still has qualms about his actions, but he also knows that historic events compelled him to behave as he did: standing up to an executive intent on obstructing his agencies' pursuit of the truth."

Judging from the reaction of many of Felt's contemporaries to his revelation, his concern about being perceived as a "turncoat" was quite warranted. Former Nixon speechwriter and TV pundit Pat Buchanan stated, "I don't think he is a hero at all. . . . Here's a man who has been entrusted with a high honor, deputy chief of the FBI, sneaking around at night, handing out materials he got from a legitimate investigation to the *Washington Post*." Conversely, Terry Lenzner, a senior counsel on the Senate Watergate committee, said, "The reason Felt turned into Deep Throat was that he had a sense that [FBI Director L. Patrick] Gray was participating in the cover-up and that it would destroy the reputation of the FBI. He was a classic FBI guy. His motives were that he had to protect the FBI. And he did." Clearly, one man's traitor is another's hero.

Standards of Conduct

Many civilian government agencies now have standards of conduct, formal guidelines, for ethical behavior. Their objective is to ensure that employees refrain from using their official positions for private gain. Typically, a variety of prohibited activities seek to ensure that employees conduct themselves in a manner that would not offer the slightest suggestion that they will extract private advantage from public employment. All too frequently, standards of conduct are used to say the obvious. For example, the British Cabinet Office created a document meant to be helpful to new cabinet ministers. Paragraph 55 of "Questions of Procedure for Ministers" offers the unsurprising advice that ministers "have a duty to refrain from asking or instructing civil servants to do things they should not do." Standards are often part of a state's formal legal code; thus violations can carry severe penalties—though never as draconian as articles of war. For example, the honest graft described by George Washington Plunkitt earlier in this chapter is now illegal in most jurisdictions in the United States. But because it was once both legal and quite common, we can surmise that ethical progress is being made.

While standards of conduct are always related to a specific organization, codes of ethics are wide in scope and encompass a whole profession or occupational category. A code of ethics is a statement of professional standards of conduct to which the practitioners of a profession say they subscribe. Codes of ethics are usually not legally binding, so they may not be taken too seriously as constraints on behavior. They sometimes become significant factors in political campaigns when questionable behavior by one side or the other is attacked or defended as being within or without a professional code. Professional groups also hide behind codes as a way of protecting (or criticizing) a member subject to public attack. President Ronald Reagan took the attitude "that people should not require a code of ethics if they're going to be in government. They should determine, themselves, that their conduct is going to be beyond reproach." Nevertheless, the problem remains that some people need help in determining just what constitutes ethical behavior. So codes are useful, but standards have the kind of teeth that can put you in jail.

ALTERNATIVE Theories | Standards of Conduct Versus Codes of Ethics

Standards	Codes
Created by government	Created by professional societies
Very specific	Generally general
Applicable to bureaucrats	Applicable to members of a profession
Often enforced	Seldom enforced
Legal penalties for violation	Professional sanctions may apply ◣

THE CHALLENGE OF ACCOUNTABILITY

Accountability is the extent to which one must answer to higher authority—legal or organizational—for one's actions in society at large, or within one's particular organizational position. Elected public officials are theoretically accountable to the political sovereignty of the voters. In this sense, appointed officials—from file clerks to cabinet secretaries—are less accountable than elected officials. The former are accountable mainly to their organizational supervisors, while the latter must answer to the people of their jurisdiction.

Administrative accountability is that aspect of administrative responsibility by which officials are held answerable for general notions of democracy and morality as well as for specific legal mandates. The two basic approaches to administrative accountability were first delineated by political scientists Carl J. Friedrich (1901–1984) and Herman Finer (1898–1969). Friedrich argued that administrative responsibility can be ensured only internally, through professionalism or professional standards or codes, because the increasing complexities of modern policies require extensive policy expertise and specialized abilities on the part of bureaucrats. Finer, on the other hand, argued that administrative responsibility could be maintained only externally, through legislative or popular controls, because internal power or control would ultimately lead to corruption. The tension between these two approaches continues today. Thus the challenge of accountability is to find a balance between completely trusting government officials to use their best professional judgment in the public's interest and watching them so closely through legislative committees or executive review agencies that it inhibits their ability to function.

Because we aspire to a democratic form of government, we need to consider how the links between democratic government and public administration work. What are the things we do, must do, and indeed must avoid if we are to be public administrators in a democracy rather than cogs in a despotic mechanism? Under the totalitarian communism of the former Soviet Union, the Russians had a word for people who served the apparatus of state without question. They were called apparatchiks—a term implying that the individual mindlessly follows orders. What stops us from being apparatchiks in all but name?

The answer to this question is that public administrators in a democracy work within the rule of law—a governing system in which the highest authority is a body of law that applies equally to all (as opposed to the rule of men, in which

Apparatchik ■
This Russian word for a bureaucrat is now used colloquially to refer to any administrative functionary.

the personal whim of those in power can decide any issue). The idea of the desirability of a "government of laws, and not of men" can be traced back to Aristotle. The earliest American reference is in the 1779 Massachusetts Constitution. John Marshall also used this succinct legal description in *Marbury v. Madison* (1803): "The government of the United States has been emphatically termed a government of laws, and not of men. It will certainly cease to deserve this high appellation, if the laws furnish no remedy for the violation of a vested legal right." The rule of law and the concomitant notion that no one is above the law have been continuously critical concepts. When Ford succeeded Nixon (who was forced to resign because of his illegal activities during the Watergate scandal), he told the nation right after taking the oath of office (August 9, 1974), "My fellow Americans, our long national nightmare is over. Our Constitution works; our great Republic is a government of laws and not of men." This was difficult for many citizens to reconcile with his **pardon** of Nixon one month later, so they voted Ford out of office the first chance they got. Now *that's* accountability!

In democratic societies, we require our administrators to work within a system of democratic accountability, respond to a complex system of checks and balances, and be subject to scrutiny by official auditors, by the media, and by community watchdogs and whistleblowers (as Finer advocated). But in the end, they are individually responsible for their own ethical and honorable behavior (as Friedrich believed). We often (but not always) remove from office those public administrators who seek to ignore their responsibilities to democracy. Occasionally, as in the case of J. Edgar Hoover of the FBI, there will be public administrators in democratic societies who seem to be above the law. But they, too, will fall from power in the end—if only because they eventually die.

Sometimes we purposely create public institutions that seem to have an "above the law" status. Security organizations sometimes seem to have this characteristic, best exemplified by the fictional British secret agent James Bond's "license to kill." Intelligence agencies have always had a certain mystical quality—perhaps because they are so associated with fictional exploits. This even affects presidents. Arthur M. Schlesinger Jr., in *A Thousand Days* (1965), quoted President John F. Kennedy: "If someone comes in to tell me this or that about the minimum wage bill, I have no hesitation in overruling them. But you always assume that the military and intelligence people have some secret skill not available to ordinary mortals." The review of the policies and activities of U.S. intelligence agencies by appropriate legislative review committees was not formally done by the Congress until the 1970s, when reports of FBI and CIA abuses of their operating mandates encouraged both houses of the Congress to create committees that would systematically and formally watch over the intelligence operations of the executive branch. Parliamentary systems, which are used in most of the world, have far less opportunity for comparable oversight because prime ministers, who ultimately direct intelligence agencies, lead both the executive and the legislative branches of government.

More generally, however, abuse of authority in public administration is a central target for condemnation in democratic societies and a likely route to disgrace and dismissal. Yet, in many societies around the world, to hold official office, to be a public administrator, is to be able to take **arbitrary** decisions, to confer benefits on family and friends, and to be open to corrupt, unethical—even inhuman—behavior. So we must ask, What legal and institutional arrangements, conventions,

Pardon ■
An executive's granting of a release from the legal consequences of a criminal act. This may occur before or after indictment or conviction. The U.S. president's power to pardon people for federal offenses is absolute except for convictions in impeachment cases. A pardon prior to indictment stops all criminal proceedings. This is what happened when President Gerald Ford pardoned Richard M. Nixon in 1974 for all offenses that he "has committed or may have committed or taken part in while president."

Arbitrary ■
Decided on the basis of individual judgments that do not meet commonly understood rules of procedure and hence may not appear justifiable to those seeking to explain them to others or to replicate them in similar circumstances.

and ethical values essentially distinguish democratic from despotic public administration? In truly democratic societies—as opposed to those that are democratic in name only—there is a framework of constitutional, legal, and procedural requirements that subjects public administrators to rigorous monitoring and oversight by a democratic legislature, independent courts, and other institutions at arm's length from the government. This leads to the expectation on the part of public administrators that, for the most part, they must work in the open, not only expecting, but also welcoming the scrutiny of elected representatives and the others whose task it is to make public accountability work.

Constitutional and Legal Constraints

Like it or not, public administrators always work within some kind of legal framework. In Europe, particularly in Germany, the legal setting of public administration is so all-encompassing that a senior official normally cannot be appointed without a formal law degree. In other parts of the world, a law degree is usually not required, but some understanding of constitutional and administrative law is. For American public administrators, the Constitution serves as an invisible fence surrounding their field of operation. Specific laws deriving from it delineate and regulate in finer and finer detail what public administrators can do to whom and when, and how, they can do it.

David H. Rosenbloom states that there are three reasons why public administrators should understand the Constitution:

1. Public administration must have democratic policy very much at heart so that managerial and political approaches are taken that are compatible with constitutional principles and values.
2. Many public administrators in America take an oath to support the Constitution, and this may be more important than routine administrative functions.
3. Public administrators may be personally liable for civil damages if they act in contravention to the Constitution.

Case law ■
All recorded judicial and administrative agency decisions.

As Rosenbloom emphasizes, it is no easy task to achieve the necessary understanding of the Constitution, because its contemporary meaning extends not only to the letter of the document, but also to case law and extensive interpretation, derived from legal, philosophical, moral, and political considerations as to how the law should be applied.

Public administrators in each policy domain—health, civil defense, education, or whatever it may be—need to maintain an awareness that the Constitution impacts what they can do by virtue of specific judgments and case law in the past, or alternatively because in a general sense what they propose to do may be seen to conflict with the Bill of Rights or some other fundamental constitutional precept. For example, in *Wood v. Strickland* (1975) the U.S. Supreme Court held that a school board member (and by implication other public employees) is not immune from liability for damages "if he knew or reasonably should have known that the action he took within his sphere of official responsibility would violate the constitutional rights of the students affected, or if he took the action with the malicious intention to cause a deprivation of constitutional rights or other injury to the student."

Obsessive Accountability

It was Napoléon's foreign minister Charles-Maurice de Talleyrand who is usually credited with first saying of administrative affairs, "Above all, not too much zeal." Yet it is an excess of zeal, in the form of obsessive attention to minor details, that so often leads to incompetence in modern organizations. Some of this dysfunctional zeal is caused by aberrant personalities, but the real culprit is the formally mandated zeal of governing rules and regulations. Much required zeal is good. No one can argue with requirements for punctuality. But once organization-wide standard procedures are established for major functions, there is an inevitable tendency for minutiae to be covered as well. These minutiae then, quite literally, take more time than they are worth.

For example, in 1993 the U.S. General Accounting Office reported that "each year the military spends some $20 million moving and storing a half-million items worth less than the cost of processing." Thus a U.S. base in Europe returns a few dollars' worth of metal bolts or nylon cord to a Defense Department warehouse in Ohio. But because it costs $40 to process these small items, it would have been far less expensive to give or throw away the stuff. However, there is no provision in the rules for disposing of unneeded items in this way. Such practices would give too much discretion to individual employees. The formal organization, in its zeal to prevent theft, mandates many such wasteful practices.

Peter Drucker maintains that organizations, most typically governments, that are obsessed with accountability are inherently less competent than they might be. New procedures are created in response to possible or previous abuses. Because individuals once showed themselves incapable of being responsible for specified organizational assets, discretion over them was taken out of their hands and given to unemotional, unbending, and, in some circumstances, irrational procedures. Accountability was placed in procedures rather than in individuals, the rationale being that the honest administration was too important a matter to leave to an individual's discretion. It is precisely because of governments' attempts to assign accountability for everything they control that public management operations grow to be outrageously expensive when compared to similar functions in private industry. According to Drucker, government must always tolerate this extra expense—not out of some unwarranted affection for red tape but because a "little dishonesty" in government is a corrosive disease that rapidly spreads to infect the entire polity. To fear such corruption is quite rational. Consequently, government "bureaucracy" and its attendant high costs cannot and should not be eliminated.

While the high costs of accountability can never be totally eliminated, some of the dysfunction of its associated procedures can be mitigated. Such mitigation frequently has organizations bending, ignoring, and subverting regulations in the interests of good management. The discretion that the regulations deny to the executive may be restored by the machinations of administrative operatives. When the flexibility deemed essential for mission accomplishment is formally denied to line managers, it is almost invariably obtained informally through administrative finesse. This is an idea that has not only been demonstrated in countless empirical studies, but also sanctioned and revered in American popular culture. The nation has a tremendous appetite for movies and television programs about war and other violent escapades. As any aficionado with sufficient exposure to this genre of entertainment can explain, you cannot have a successful military operation without a scrounger in your unit—at least not according to Hollywood's version of World War II. A scrounger was that member of the team who was assigned to obtain all the essential requirements of the mission that could not be obtained through official channels. It hardly mattered what methods the scroungers used to secure the needed supplies as long as they succeeded—and there were no official complaints. The war seems to have been won in large measure because our scroungers were better at overcoming organizational constraints than their scroungers.

When mandates from on high reflect neither administrative wisdom nor experience, they are viewed as barriers to managerial effectiveness—which must be overcome. There is even significant evidence that organizational superiors discourage subordinates from reporting fully just how they have accomplished their missions because of concerns for formal or legal culpability. According to public administration scholar Herbert Kaufman, executives "may resort to the strategy of discouraging feedback about administrative behavior because they privately *approve* of the behavior they know they should, according to law and morality, prevent." Thus rookie police officers are told by their more experienced associates that they will have to forget what they learned at the police academy before they can operate effectively—and survive—in a real-world situation. Any new public manager must suffer through an on-the-job acquisition of administrative **realpolitik**. They learn by the unfortunate consequences of violating norms that are discovered only when they are breached.

Avoiding Accountability

The public rightly expects an executive to be accountable for the actions of the subordinates he or she has selected, whether or not the executive had actual knowledge of the actions. It is based on the belief that the selection of subordinates and the monitoring of their behavior is an executive responsibility. Nowhere is primitive ritual or Machiavellian feigning more apparent than in the periodic assumption of full responsibility by an organization's chief executive. Although one of the advantages of delegating a problem is the ease with which the cunning leader can shift the blame for the situation if it sours, modern executives are seldom so crude as to lay blame. The appropriate tactic is to assume full responsibility for the situation. Paradoxically, in assuming full responsibility, the executive is seemingly relieved of it. Political scientist Murray Edelman observed that whenever this ritual is enacted, all of the participants tend to experience "a warm glow of satisfaction and relief that responsibility has been assumed and can be pinpointed. It once again conveys the message that the incumbent is the leader, that he knows he is able to cope, and that he should be followed." In reality, however, this ritual proves to have no substance. It "emphatically does not mean that the chief executive will be penalized for the mistakes of subordinates or that the latter will not be penalized."

This is the tactic that President Richard M. Nixon employed when he first addressed the nation concerning the Watergate scandal in the spring of 1973. He boldly proclaimed that all of the possibly illegal actions of the White House officials were his responsibility and that he fully accepted that responsibility. Certainly, Nixon did not mean to imply—at that point in time—that he should be punished for the transgressions of his underlings. Nor did Ronald Reagan in 1987 when he

Realpolitik ■
A German word, now absorbed into English, meaning the politics of realism; an injunction not to allow wishful thinking or sentimentality to cloud one's judgment. At its most moderate, the word is used to describe an overcynical approach, one that allows little room for human altruism, that always seeks an ulterior motive behind another actor's statements or justifications. At its strongest, it suggests that no moral values should be allowed to affect the single-minded pursuit of one's own self-interest or patriotism. It also makes an absolute assumption that any opponent will certainly behave in this way.

took full responsibility for the Iran-Contra affair. Bill Clinton, during an August 17, 1998, television address to the nation, took full responsibility for lying to his wife, his cabinet, his staff, and his nation about his affair with White House intern Monica Lewinsky. But his hopes that this would be enough to stop an impeachment inquiry were short-lived. Government officials of lesser rank are no less sophisticated with their manipulations of the ritualistic and symbolic aspects of their offices. Of course, the risk they take is that the legislature will investigate the situation thoroughly enough to expose any wrongdoing.

LEGISLATIVE OVERSIGHT

While constitutional and legal frameworks themselves amount to a passive exercise of democratic control over the discretion of public administrators, there is no substitute for active control through energetic elected representatives. The main reason the U.S. Congress (or a state legislature or a city council) monitors the activities of executive branch agencies is to determine if the laws are being faithfully executed. After all, the president has the constitutional obligation (given in Article 2, Section 3) to "take care that the laws be faithfully executed." Congressional oversight is designed in our system of "checks and balances" to check that he does.

Hearings

Oversight takes many forms. The most obvious are the annual congressional hearings on agency budget requests, in which agency activities have to be justified to the satisfaction of the Congress. Both the House and the Senate hold budget hearings. But only the Senate holds hearings on the confirmation of major appointees such as cabinet secretaries and Supreme Court nominees.

Any member of Congress can instigate an investigation. Many of these investigations are small matters concerning the interests of a single constituent (see the following section on casework). But if something significant turns up worthy of a larger inquiry, an appropriate committee or subcommittee always has the right to initiate a further examination. The oversight function is primarily implemented through the process of hearings that often call for sworn testimony from officials, through consultancy reports, and through the publication of findings. Committees that have investigated scandals such as Watergate and the Iran-Contra affair, and issues such as whether gays should be permitted to serve in the military, illustrate how important and central a role this aspect of democratic government can be. In consequence, those who become chair of an influential committee of Congress occupy powerful positions indeed.

The entire Congress is in effect a permanently sitting **grand jury** always waiting to hear of improper acts by executive branch agencies so that **hearings** can be launched and witnesses called. Some members of Congress are so zealous in their oversight concerns that they will go to the trouble of traveling all over the world (at government expense) to see how federal programs and policies are operating. These visits are derisively called junkets, but they are an important part of the oversight process. Some members of Congress simply cannot understand why it is necessary to vote for money for American forces in NATO unless they first visit Europe and make a thorough investigation of the situation.

Grand jury ■
A group of citizens selected to review evidence against accused persons to determine whether there is sufficient evidence to bring the accused to trial—to indict or not to indict. A grand jury usually has from 12 to 23 members and operates in secrecy to protect the reputation of those not indicted. Grand juries have been both criticized for being easily manipulated tools in the hands of prosecutors and praised for protecting the rights of those falsely accused.

Hearings ■
A legislative committee session for hearing witnesses. At hearings on legislation, witnesses usually include specialists, government officials, and representatives of those affected by the bills under study. Subpoena power may be used to summon reluctant witnesses. The public and press may attend open hearings but are barred from closed (executive) hearings.

IN THE NEWS | What's the Matter with New Jersey?

Despite its reputation, New Jersey is really a lovely place to live. Its beautiful beaches, rolling countryside, and quaint towns are often overshadowed by popular images of hazardous waste dumps, refineries, and mob violence. While the Garden State often suffers from an undeserved reputation as an inhospitable place to reside, there is one area where New Jersey's negative image is well deserved—political corruption. Over the years, the number of New Jersey public officials being indicted for corruption has regularly been among the highest of any state. And while the number of cases of corruption is by itself impressive, the details of the cases are what really make New Jersey the epicenter of ethical lapses among public officials.

In their book *Soprano State*, Bob Ingle and Sandy McClure detail a seemingly unending series of ethical violations and outright corruption by the Garden State's elected officials and public administrators. Many of these cases read more like fiction than reality. From a U.S. Senator running for governor who breaks up with his union-leader girlfriend and then gives her a $6 million parting gift without disclosing the information, to a Newark mayor who spends his last days in office on a taxpayer-financed junket to Brazil, the stories are rich in detail about the blatant disregard for ethics among New Jersey's political figures.

Perhaps the pinnacle of New Jersey's tradition of corruption took place in the summer of 2009, when three mayors, two assemblymen, and five rabbis (yes, rabbis!) were among 44 Garden State residents indicted in a bizarre international money-laundering scheme. A two-year federal probe uncovered an array of violations that included illegal sales of freshly harvested body parts for transplant (need a new liver or kidney?), bribes to secure government approval of developments, and the illegal passing of millions of dollars in cash, including nearly $100,000 stuffed into an Apple Jacks cereal box. The corruption plot was so strange that in all likelihood even the producers of HBO's long-running mob saga *The Sopranos* may have passed on the story for fear of being accused of going too far. But in the real world of Garden State governance, this over-the-top corruption scandal was just another example of why New Jersey has earned its reputation for a political culture in which corruption is just another word for doing business. ◤

Source: Data From: Bob Ingle and Sandy McLure (2009), *The Soprano State: New Jersey's Culture of Corruption* (New York: St. Martins Press). David Halbfinger, "44 Charged by U.S. in New Jersey Corruption Sweep," *New York Times* (July 23, 2009).

Of course, the oversight function may be abused, especially when it is done for partisan advantage. Such political oversight often happens when the executive and legislative branches of a government are controlled by opposing parties; then its purpose may be to embarrass the administration. Two famous examples of this are the Democratic Party–sponsored Watergate hearings of 1973–1974, which helped force Republican President Richard Nixon to resign in 1974, and the Republican Party–sponsored Whitewater hearings of 1995–1996, which were designed to embarrass the Democratic President Bill Clinton. Of course, whether an oversight action is simply in the interest of good government or whether it is a play in a game of partisan one-upsmanship is in the eye of the beholder.

Casework

Casework is the term used for the services performed by legislators and their staffs at the request of and on behalf of constituents. For example, a U.S. representative may be asked to discover why a Social Security check has been delayed or why a veteran's claim for benefits has been denied. Casework is an important means by which legislators maintain oversight of the bureaucracy and solidify their political base with constituents.

Casework offers many advantages for legislators. First, it's cheap and isn't controversial. For the price of some minor staff time, a politician can make a voter happy. After dealing with thousands of cases over several years, this can pay back big on election day. Of course, there is always the danger that the legislator will not be able to solve the constituent's problem. But if the situation is handled with promptness and tactfulness, the case can still be a net gain from a public relations viewpoint. Even if the "customer" did not get what was wanted from the bureaucracy, a perception of fair treatment will still go a long way.

Agency administrators can also benefit from good casework service. The responsive handling of constituent problems will tend to make legislators more receptive to next year's budget requests. And a pattern of similar casework complaints could indicate administrative problems that need to be fixed before the numbers explode. Naturally, there is a thin line between administrative troubleshooting and special treatment. This is a line that astute administrators must walk straight—well, almost straight!

A CASE STUDY | Parallel Bloody Hands—Comparing the Administrative Ethics of Secretaries of Defense Robert McNamara and Donald Rumsfeld

Robert S. McNamara and Donald Rumsfeld offer clear examples of government officials in an ethical quandary. Their resolutions of their individual quandries are case studies on the ethics of loyalty. The question here is, to whom must the official be ultimately loyal—to the administration or to the people? Is a patronage appointee's expected loyalty to a mayor, governor, or president greater or lesser than a competing loyalty to the overall interests of the citizenry?

Before World War II, McNamara taught statistics at Harvard Business School. During the war, he served honorably and rose to the rank of lieutenant colonel in the U.S. Army Air Corps, where he helped develop statistical control systems. A civilian again in 1946, he joined the Ford Motor Company, rising to become its president in 1961. It would be only a few months later that President John F. Kennedy would make him secretary of defense. In that position he energetically pursued what was to be by his own admission a futile war in Vietnam. He served as the principal administrative instrument in the deaths of tens of thousands of Americans and more than a million Vietnamese. He consequently was viewed as such a moral and intellectual coward by virtue of his hypocrisy and silence that the *New York Times*, in an unusually personal April 12, 1995, editorial, damned him as someone "who must not escape the lasting moral condemnation of his countrymen."

(continued)

▶ **A CASE STUDY** | *Continued*

How did this man, this Eagle Scout who volunteered for World War II service when he had two legitimate deferments (he was an instructor at an officer training facility—Harvard—and he was a married man with a child), who only wanted to do good in government service, end up doing bad on such a massive scale? What he did was so bad that he was soundly condemned by many on both sides of the issue of whether the war itself was worthy of U.S. involvement. What is undisputed is that McNamara, the archetypal bureaucratic policy analyst and number cruncher, was the architect of American military strategy in Vietnam and the strongest advocate of the war—first for President Kennedy and then, after Kennedy's assassination in 1963, for President Lyndon B. Johnson. In 1964 he even publicly boasted that he was pleased when critics called it "McNamara's War." But gradually, as the war wore on, McNamara became disenchanted with the slaughter, so much so that he began to believe that the war could never be won.

Neil Sheehan wrote in his Pulitzer Prize–winning history of the war, *A Bright Shining Lie* (1988), that by the end of November 1967 President Johnson would complain that "McNamara's gone dovish on me" and had deteriorated into "an emotional basket case" because of the burdens of the war. Thus "McNamara learned through a press leak of his appointment as the new president of the World Bank." According to Senator Max Cleland of Georgia, who lost both legs in the war, "McNamara went to the World Bank, while a lot of other people went to their graves."

For the next quarter-century, McNamara, despite more than a dozen years as head of the World Bank and numerous writings on the inherent evil of nuclear war, was off the public's radar screen. Then in 1995 he published his memoir on the war, *In Retrospect*, which brought a firestorm of condemnation on him. The book essentially said that he knew the war was unwinnable long before he left office and that he continued to pour American blood and treasure into a policy rat hole out of loyalty to President Johnson. Yet this was well known. For more than two decades, history books by the score acknowledged McNamara's disenchantment. And who was the source for all this information on McNamara's true feelings? Why, the man himself! He frequently poured out his anguish to his many influential friends. McNamara's tearful emotions over his role in Vietnam were an open secret. According to popular historian David Halberstam, McNamara "carefully fended off [on-the-record] questions on what he really thought by pointing out that as head of the World Bank, he had no viewpoints, no politics."

More than a quarter-century too late to do any real good, McNamara admitted two explosive things in his book: (1) The Johnson administration did not possess superior knowledge of the situation that was not available to the public (this "you don't know what we know" stance had been used in demanding public deference to their war policies), and (2) he, the secretary of defense, essentially had agreed with the antiwar protesters' belief that the war was futile and unwinnable. If he had said this at the time he left office, if not sooner, it surely would have had a significant effect on the situation and could have saved tens of thousands of American lives.

It is hard today to appreciate the deference in which the American public and members of Congress once held executive branch pronouncements about foreign policy and military issues. The modern cynicism and often-expressed attitude that the government, indeed the president, is lying largely came about because of the lies told during the Vietnam War. If McNamara had rallied the opposition with a timely confession, he could have given political cover to many opinion leaders and officeholders who had doubts but were too fearful to express them. It was literally a matter of life and death. And McNamara chose to sit in his office at the World Bank and let those who were at risk—American soldiers as well as countless Vietnamese—die.

Many questioned McNamara's motives for the book. Some were angered by the thought that he did it for the money. But he was already wealthy enough that money could not possibly have been a motivator. McNamara's motives can best be compared to those of Lady Macbeth trying to wash the blood off her murderous hands ("Out, damned spot!"). Both had a need to come psychologically clean, a need to assuage the guilt for all the spilled blood that was their responsibility ("Who would have thought the old man to have had so much blood in him?"). So Lady Macbeth went mad ("a mind diseas'd"), and McNamara published a *mea culpa*, a public confession, saying that "we were wrong, terribly wrong." Instead of the forgiveness he sought, he got condemned by virtually all sides. Those who protested the war at the time condemned him for not publicly joining their ranks when he first gave them his heart. Those who supported the war condemned him for attacking their strong belief that the war was winnable if only this or that were done. Those who were veterans and families of veterans condemned him for saying in effect that the sacrifices he so often called on them to make were for nothing.

When McNamara was pointedly asked by *Newsweek* (in an April 17, 1995, interview that accompanied an excerpt from his book) whether he put his loyalty to President Johnson over loyalty to the American people, he replied, "I don't think that's the case. We are not a parliamentary government, where ministers can overthrow the prime minister. A minister in our government is there solely as the representative of the president. Therefore, every cabinet officer must do as the president says, or get the hell out. And if he got out, my view is that he cannot attack the president from outside the cabinet, essentially using the power given to him by the president. I recognize this is not a widely accepted view, but I believe it's the correct view—grounded in the Constitution."

However, there is nothing in the Constitution that says former cabinet secretaries lose their rights as citizens to complain about—indeed "attack"—the president they previously served. William Jennings Bryan, President Woodrow Wilson's first secretary of state, resigned in 1915 over Wilson's

(continued)

policy toward Germany. They disagreed on the best way to keep the United States out of the war then raging in Europe. Not only was the policy dispute public at the time, but Bryan continued for months to attack Wilson's policies at every opportunity. There was much noise and debate about who was correct but never a hint of a constitutional crisis. But McNamara did not even have to think back to the Wilson administration for an example of a dissenting former cabinet member. His close friend Robert F. Kennedy, to whom he often confessed his misgivings about the war, resigned his position in the Johnson cabinet as attorney general in 1964 and then proceeded to criticize Vietnam policy as a senator from New York.

There was no constitutional issue that prevented McNamara from speaking out. So why didn't he? Was he so egocentric that his primary loyalty was to himself as opposed to the nation because he wanted to remain a player in the game of power? Or did he, as Colonel David H. Hackworth suggests, "confuse loyalty to his president with a higher loyalty to the country"? As a public official, he was charged with sending fellow citizens to their deaths in a cause he first championed but then labeled both unworthy and impractical. But despite the Lincolnesque "last full measure of devotion" that he had demanded from thousands of Americans, he was unwilling to risk the sacrifice of his public career in an effort to stop the carnage. This is the essence of his moral cowardice and personal dishonor.

Aside from the vital lessons learned about the limitations of mathematical models and systems analysis as aids in decision making, there are two reasons why McNamara's legacy of deceit is important to modern public administration.

First, McNamara's case offers a clear-cut example of one of the most common ethical quandaries facing public officials at all levels—whether political appointees, as McNamara was, or career civil servants. Who deserves our ultimate loyalty—the individual who, by virtue of a public office, employs us or the greater interests of the state? Loyalty is allegiance, but to whom? Mark Twain wrote, "My kind of loyalty was loyalty to one's country, not to its institutions or its officeholders." McNamara's loyalty was bureaucratic—not patriotic. Thus he did not publicly complain about President Johnson's policies. As a good organization man, he did not believe in going over the head of his administrative superior. He silently acquiesced to a policy he knew, and history has proved, to be wrong. This is the kind of loyalty that President Lyndon B. Johnson referred to when he told his staff, according to historian Larry Berman, what he meant by loyalty over Vietnam: "I want him to kiss my ass in Macy's window at high noon and tell me it smells like roses." The strange thing here is that McNamara continued to "smell the roses" long after Johnson was out of office and long after Johnson was dead. It must have been a powerful perfume!

Second, McNamara's most lasting contribution is the cynicism and disaffection so many citizens have toward their governments at all levels in the United States. The Vietnam War made presidential lying to the American public if not normal, then at least an expected part of government. The lying and disinformation machine that McNamara created to "inform" the news media and the American public about the war was continued by and brought into domestic politics and made bipartisan by President Richard M. Nixon. The Nixon administration's lying about the Watergate scandal was just a continuation and extension of Vietnam policy cover-ups. Yet McNamara asserts in his book that one of the reasons he wrote his memoir was because he had "grown sick at heart witnessing the cynicism and even contempt with which so many people view our political institutions and leaders." He should know! It is his legacy to his country—that and many of the names of the dead on the inscribed slabs of the Vietnam War Memorial.

It seems clear that Robert McNamara's experiences as Secretary of Defense would not be soon forgotten by those who followed in his footsteps. The legacy of Vietnam, especially for those who lived through the era, helped define the world view for a generation of Americans who came into public service. Perhaps no one fit this description more than Donald Rumsfeld. In many ways Rumsfeld epitomized a government official who came of age during the Vietnam era. He served in Congress between 1963 and 1969, the heart of the Vietnam War, and then served both Presidents Nixon and Ford in key adminstrative positions as the war came to a close in 1975.

McNamara and Rumsfeld share many parallels in their careers in general and specifically in their tenures as secretaries of defense. They both were sons of the upper middle class who were Eagle Scouts, went to elite colleges, were mid-ranking military officers, were considered brilliant managers by most of their peers, and were generally committed to public service out of a sense of duty and responsible citizenship. Indeed, each assumed office at considerable financial sacrifice. Both McNamara and Rumsfeld, America's two longest serving secretaries of defense, began their tenures with the highest of expectations from those who wanted to see the Pentagon reformed. Nevertheless, despite their best intentions and noblest motives, they both left office in disgrace, both for failing to win their wars and for the strategies they used to fight them. Then they both wrote books explaining themselves that only caused more contempt to be heaped upon them by reviewers, journalists, and their fellow citizens.

Perhaps the essential problem with both of them was hubris, an overwhelming overestimation of their personal competence and judgment that contrasted with reality. At first the public and the presidents under which they served fell for their hubris, their "the secretary knows best" attitude, and cheered them on as they derided their "ill-informed" critics from within and without the professional military. But as the years went on without the anticipated victory and as the numbers of American dead and wounded escalated, their reputations and popularity gradually and continually sank to new lows. The American people overwhelmingly came to judge both of them as outrageous liars, men whose ethics were so corrupted that they should not

(*continued*)

▶ **A CASE STUDY** | *Continued*

be allowed to remain in public office. In the end they were both "fired" by the presidents at whose pleasure they served.

The greatest reproach to Rumsfeld was not contained in the outbursts of his critics, but by the constant example of his successor. Robert Gates, the re-tired CIA director, was serving as President of Texas A & M University in 2006 when President George W. Bush appointed him secretary of defense to put out the firestorm over Rumsfeld's conduct of the continuing wars in Iraq and Afghanistan. In 2011 Gates retired from office with his reputation vastly en-hanced after presenting to the nation an example of competent and honorable ser-vice. Why was Rumsfeld not able to leave under similar circumstances? Hubris!

For Discussion: *Was McNamara ethically justified in keeping silent about his disillusionment with the Vietnam War policies for so many years? Is there ever adequate justification for allowing loyalty to one's administrative supe-rior to outweigh one's overall loyalty to one's country—especially consider-ing that officeholders have usually taken an oath to defend the interests of their country?* ▶

SUMMARY

Honor comes before ethics because a person without honor has no moral compass and does not know which way to turn to be ethical. Honor goes to the essence of public affairs. Since ancient times, only individuals perceived to be honorable could be trusted with the public's business.

Recurrent government scandals, no matter how much they cost, pose a great threat to the democratic notions of the rule of law. When a public official misuses his or her office for self-gain, then the rule of law no longer prevails, and there is, in effect, a return to tyranny.

Do public officials have a special obligation to tell the truth, or do their offices permit them special excuses to depart from truth telling? Because knowledge is the cornerstone of democracy, an informed public is a prerequisite for a democratic government. Hence, citizens have an inherent right to know the truth of public issues. On the other hand, there may be times of crisis when it may be permissible for a public official to deceive the public for its own good.

In public administration there is a hierarchy of levels of ethics: personal mo-rality, professional ethics, organizational ethics, and social ethics. This last level obliges members of a given society to act in ways that both protect individuals and further the progress of the group as a whole.

Codes of honor have their origins in ancient precepts about how a person should behave in the face of danger, when confronted with temptation, or before authority figures. Many civilian government agencies now have parallel standards of conduct, formal guidelines for ethical behavior, which seek to ensure that employees refrain from using their official positions for private gain.

Administrative accountability is that aspect of administrative responsibility by which officials are held answerable for general notions of democracy and morality as well as for specific legal mandates. In democratic societies administrators are required to respond to a complex system of checks and balances and to be subject to scrutiny by official auditors, the media, and community watchdogs and potential whistleblowers.

While a government's constitutional and legal frameworks are a passive exercise of democratic control over the discretion of public administrators, there is no substitute for the active control of energetic elected representatives. This control, known as legislative oversight, takes many forms. The most obvious form is the annual congressional hearings on agency budget requests, in which agency activities have to be justified to the satisfaction of the Congress.

REVIEW QUESTIONS

1. Why is honor, both national and personal, such a critical aspect of public administration?
2. Is corruption in government any worse than in the private sector, or is it just more visible?
3. Is it ever appropriate for a government official to lie to the public?
4. How does a hierarchy of ethics govern the behavior of people holding public office?
5. What means do all legislators have to hold their government's bureaucracy accountable to its legislature?

KEY CONCEPTS

Accountability   The extent to which one must answer to higher authority—legal or organizational—for one's actions in society at large or within one's particular organizational position.

Big lie   An untruth so great or so audacious that it is bound to have an effect on public opinion.

Bribery   The giving or offering of anything of value with intent to unlawfully influence an official in the discharge of duties; a public official's receiving or asking for anything of value with the intent to be unlawfully influenced.

Casework   The services performed by legislators and their staffs at the request of and on behalf of constituents.

Code of ethics   A statement of professional standards of conduct to which the practitioners of a profession say they subscribe. Codes of ethics are usually not legally binding, so they may not be taken too seriously as constraints on behavior.

Common law   The totality of judge-made laws that initially developed in England and continued to evolve in the United States. Whenever this kind of law—which is based on custom, culture, habit, and previous judicial decisions—proved inadequate, it was supplanted by statutory laws made by legislatures. But the common law tradition, based on precedent, is still the foundation of the American legal system, even though much of what was originally common law has been converted into statutes over the years.

Congressional oversight   The total means by which the U.S. Congress monitors the activities of executive branch agencies to determine if the laws are being faithfully executed.

Corruption   The unauthorized use of public office for private gain. The most common forms of corruption are bribery, extortion, and the misuse of inside information.

Dirty hands dilemma   A graphic phrase for the tendency of public officials to commit an act generally considered to be a wrong to further the common good. This is a dilemma in the sense that doing bad seems to lead to something good.

Higher law   The notion that no matter what the laws of a state are, there remains a higher law to which a person has an even greater obligation. A higher law is often appealed to by those who wish to attack an existing law or practice that courts or legislators are unlikely or unwilling to change.

Honor   The internalized moral compass by which individuals ascertain correct behavior in public and private life; the perception by others of one's reputation for integrity.

Integrity   The core of honor. Those who have integrity live up to their stated principles, values, and, most importantly, their word. A person whose word is his or her bond gives the full faith and credit of his or her whole being to keeping commitments.

Rule of law   A governing system in which the highest authority is a body of law that applies equally to all (as opposed to the traditional "rule of men," in which the personal whim of those in power can decide any issue).

Standards of conduct   A compendium of ethical norms promulgated by an organization to guide the behavior of its members. Many government agencies have formal codes (or standards) of conduct for their employees.

Watergate   The scandal that led to the resignation of President Richard M. Nixon. Watergate itself is a hotel-office-apartment complex in Washington, D.C. When individuals associated with the Committee to Reelect the President were caught breaking into the Democratic National Committee Headquarters (then located in the Watergate complex) in 1972, the resulting cover-up and national trauma was condensed into one word: Watergate. The term has grown to refer to any political crime or instance of bureaucratic corruption that undermines confidence in governing institutions.

MySearchLab® EXERCISES

Apply what you learned in this chapter on MySearchLab (*www.mysearchlab.com*).

BIBLIOGRAPHY

Belli, Melvin M. (1973). Review of *The Finest Judges Money Can Buy* by Charles Ashman in the *New York Times Book Review* (November 18).

———— (1976). *My Life on Trial*. New York: Morrow.

Berman, Larry (1982). *Planning a Tragedy: The Americanization of the War in Vietnam*. New York: Norton.

Brown, E. G. (1970). *Reagan and Reality*. New York: Praeger.

Dallek, Robert. (1998). *Flawed Giant: Lyndon Johnson and His Times*. New York: Oxford University Press.

Downs, G., and P. D. Larkey (1986). *The Search for Government Efficiency*. New York: Random House.

Drucker, Peter F. (1969). "The Sickness of Government," *Public Interest* 14 (Winter).

Dynes, Michael, and David Walker. (1995). *The New British State*. London: Times Books.

Feller, Ben (2009). "We Are Leaving Iraq," *Philadelphia Inquirer* (February, 28).

Finer, Herman (1941). "Administrative Responsibility in Democratic Government," *Public Administration Review* 1.

Friedrich, Carl J. (1940). "The Nature of Administrative Responsibility." In Carl J. Friedrich, ed., *Public Policy*. Cambridge, MA: Harvard University Press.

Gillman, Todd J., and Robert Dodge (2005). "Congress Quick to Demand Answers on Response to Katrina," *Dallas Morning News* (September 6).

Gilmour, Robin (1981). *The Idea of the Gentleman in the Victorian Novel*. London: George Allen and Unwin.

Halberstam, David (1972). *The Best and the Brightest*. New York: Random House.

Howard, Philip K. (1995) *The Death of Common Sense*. New York: Random House.

Jos, Philip H., Mark E. Tompkins, and Steven W. Hays (1989). "In Praise of Difficult People: A Portrait of the Committed Whistleblower," *Public Administration Review* 49 (November–December).

Kaplan, Fred (1983). *The Wizards of Armageddon*. New York: Simon and Schuster.

Kearns, Doris (1976). *Lyndon Johnson and the American Dream*. New York: Harper and Row.

Madsen, Peter, and Jay M. Shafritz, eds. (1992). *Essentials of Government Ethics*. New York: Meridian Books.

Miceli, Marcia, and Janet Near (1992). *Blowing the Whistle*. New York: Lexington Books.

Miller, Merle (1973). *Plain Speaking: An Oral Biography of Harry S. Truman*. New York: Berkeley.

Morgan, Arthur E. (1974). *The Making of the TVA*. New York: Prometheus Books.

Mustafa, Husain, and Anthony A. Salomone. (1971). "Administrative Circumvention of Public Policy," *Midwest Review of Public Administration* 5, No. 1.

O'Connor, John D. (2005). "I'm the Guy They Called Deep Throat," *Vanity Fair* (June).

Orwell, George (1946). *Animal Farm*. New York: Harcourt, Brace.

Popkin, James (1993). "Wasteline: By the Book," *U.S. News & World Report* (May 24).

Rohr, John. (1986). *Ethics for Bureaucrats*, 2nd ed. New York: Marcel Dekker.

Romzek, Barbara, and Melvin J. Dubnick (1987). "Accountability in the Public Sector," *Public Administration Review* (May–June).

Rosenbloom, David H. (1993a). "Have an Administrative Rx? Don't Forget the Politics!" *Public Administration Review* 53 (November–December).

———. (1993b). *Public Administration*, 3rd ed. New York: McGraw-Hill.

Sayre, W. (1948). "The Triumph of Techniques over Purpose," *Public Administration Review* 8 (Spring).

Slater, Philip E., and Warren Bennis (1964). "Democracy Is Inevitable," *Harvard Business Review* 42 (March–April).

Steffens, Lincoln (1904). *The Shame of the Cities*. New York: Sagamore Press.

Stevenson, Richard (1992). "U.S. Judge Orders $7.5 Million Award to Whistleblower," *New York Times* (July 7).

Thompson, Dennis F. (1985). "The Possibility of Administrative Ethics," *Public Administration Review* (September–October).

Twain, Mark (1899). *A Connecticut Yankee in King Arthur's Court*. New York: Harper.

Williams, Charles (1993). *The Last Great Frenchman*. New York: Little, Brown.

Wills, Garry (1984). *Cincinnatus: George Washington and the Enlightenment*. New York: Doubleday.

RECOMMENDED BOOKS

Adams, Guy B., and Danny L. Balfour (2009). *Unmasking Administrative Evil*, 3rd ed. Armonk, NY: M.E. Sharpe. Finally, a book that seeks out the evil that lurks within government bureaucracies, and explains how ordinary people doing their normal professional duties can take part in evil without even being aware of it.

Callahan, David (2004). *The Cheating Culture: Why More Americans Are Doing Wrong and Getting Ahead*. Fort Washington, PA: Harvest Books. What happens in government is often an extension of the broader culture. This book nicely examines the types of unethical behavior Americans will embrace in order to succeed.

Kearns, Kevin P. (1996). *Managing for Accountability: Preserving the Public Trust in Public and Nonprofit Organizations.* San Francisco: Jossey-Bass. A strategic management approach to organizational accountability; accountability should not be undertaken as an afterthought—it must be integrated with all aspects of management.

Madsen, Peter, and Jay M. Shafritz (1992). *Essentials of Government Ethics.* New York: New American Library. A collection of writings on government ethics from ancient times to the present.

McMaster, H. R. (1997). *Dereliction of Duty: Lyndon Johnson, Robert McNamara, the Joint Chiefs of Staff, and the Lies That Led to Vietnam.* New York: HarperCollins. The history of the lies and dishonor of America's top military and civilian leadership during the Vietnam War.

Painter, Richard (2009). *Getting the Government America Deserves: How Ethics Reform Can Make a Difference.* New York: Oxford University Press. An articulation of varied approaches to combat corruption in government with a critique of ethics law failures.

Rohr, John A. (1989). *Ethics for Bureaucrats: An Essay on Law and Values.* New York: Marcel Dekker. The original presentation of the concept of regime values, which holds that the most fundamental principles of a polity—such as its constitution—should be the primary guide to ethical behavior.

RELATED WEB SITES

www.factcheck.org
Annenberg Political Fact Check
This site posts articles that point out when politicians or political organizations lie or use misleading facts in their statements and advertisements. Fact Check has been recognized as a non-partisan arbiter of competing claims in elections and policy debates n the United States.

www.ethicsweb.ca/resources/business
Centre for Applied Ethics
This site provides links to organizations that advocate for ethical decision making and presents examples of ethical dilemmas that individuals face in contemporary settings in government and business.

www.accountabilitycircle.org
Citizens' Circle for Accountability (CCA)
The CCA offers information and resources concerning public accountability and why transparent government is essential in a democracy. The organization's Web site includes a blog that allows citizens to express their demand for public accountability as well as primers for civil servants, legislators, academics, and students concerned with government operations.

www.eppc.org
Ethics and Public Policy Center
The Ethics and Public Policy Center is dedicated to applying the Judeo-Christian moral tradition to critical issues of public policy. Its Web site provides information about its issues and legislation, as well as ways to become involved in efforts to promote ethical development in the implementation of public policies.

www.whistleblower.org
Government Accountability Project (GAP)
This organization works to protect the rights of "whistle-blowers" who disclose information that they reasonably believe is evidence of illegality, gross waste or fraud, mismanagement, abuse of power, general wrongdoing, or a substantial and specific danger to public health and safety. The GAP site offers resources for those considering whistle-blowing activities.

The Evolution of Management and Organization Theory

CHAPTER OUTLINE

KEYNOTE: Moses Meets the First Management Consultant

The scene is set as in the Bible: Moses (in Exodus 18) has led the Israelites out of the land of Egypt. Now . . .

> Moses sat to judge the people: and the people stood by Moses from the morning unto the evening.
>
> And when Moses' father-in-law saw all that he did to the people, he said, "What is this thing that thou doest to the people? Why sittest thou thyself alone, and all the people stand by thee from morning unto even?"
>
> And Moses said unto his father-in-law, "Because the people . . . when they have a matter, they come unto me; and I judge between one and another. . . ."

Moses, while certainly an effective and charismatic leader, could not delegate. "The system" he created would not let him let go. He literally had thousands of people reporting to him. The managerial workload became overwhelming. The ancient Israelites by the hundreds were unhappily standing in line "from the morning unto the evening" to confer with him. Finally, Jethro, Moses' father-in-law, became the first-known management consultant when he gave Moses the reengineering advice he needed to create a more competent organization. First he assessed the problem:

> And Moses' father-in-law said, "The thing that thou doest is not good. Thou wilt surely wear away, both thou, and this people that is with thee: for this thing is too heavy for thee: thou art not able to perform it thyself alone.
>
> Hearken now unto my voice, I will give thee counsel. . . . Thou shalt teach them ordinances and laws, and shalt show them the way wherein they must walk.

Here is the beginning of modern bureaucratic structures. A body of laws, a book of regulations, that apply to everyone means that all similar problems are treated alike; the organization does not have to "reinvent the wheel" each time a common problem reoccurs. Jethro next lays out the most basic principles of all hierarchical organizations, the very same principles that are today used in literally all large organizations, whether military or civilian, private or public.

> Moreover thou shalt provide out of all the people able men . . . to be rulers of thousands, and rulers of hundreds, rulers of fifties, and rulers of tens:
>
> And let them judge the people at all seasons: and it shall be, that every great matter they shall bring unto thee, but every small matter they shall judge: so shall it be easier for thyself, and they shall bear the burden with thee.
>
> If thou shalt do this thing, . . . then thou shalt be able to endure. . . ."

In those three verses we have the origins of all large-scale enterprises. Jethro's advice of putting able people to be "rulers of thousands, and rulers of hundreds, rulers of fifties, and rulers of tens" was followed by the ancient Roman army, the early Catholic Church, and every major organization since. Early in the twentieth century, Frederick Taylor, the so-called "father of scientific management," called bringing "every great matter" to the head of the organization "management by exception"—meaning that if all was going well, there was no reason to bother the next-higher layer of management. This is exactly what Jethro advised. He then stated the main advantage of abiding by this advice: "If thou shalt do this thing, . . .

then thou shalt be able to endure." The essential problem of the non-delegating manager is not that he or she is not able and wise, but that in large organizations no one person "is able to endure" without delegating. Thus an otherwise extremely competent manager becomes incompetent by seeking to be supercompetent—by trying to do it all. But what did Moses do with all this good advice?

> So Moses hearkened to the voice of his father-in-law, and did all that he had said.
>
> And Moses chose able men out of all Israel, and made them heads over the people, rulers of thousands, and rulers of hundreds, rulers of fifties, and rulers of tens.

Charlton Heston as Moses in the 1956 film *The Ten Commandments*. Here he demands that Pharaoh (played by Yul Brynner) stop reading his book about Egyptian public administration and "let my people go!" Ever since playing Moses in one of the most successful films of all time, Heston's voice has been the patriarchal voice of authority. This was reinforced by many subsequent films in which he played strong historical characters such as El Cid, Cardinal Richelieu, and Andrew Jackson. Thus, when in 1998 he was elected president of the National Rifle Association (NRA), the preeminent gun lobby, his denunciation of President Clinton in his inaugural speech as head of the NRA had a resonance far beyond these damning words: "Mr. Clinton, America didn't trust you with our health care system . . . America doesn't trust you with our 21-year-old daughters, and we sure, Lord, don't trust you with our guns!" Heston was particularly annoyed that during the course of the Lewinsky affair, the president seemed to have violated at least three of the Ten Commandments (see Chapter 5 for more on this). Consequently, Heston turned the full resources of his organization against Clinton's Democratic Party in the election of 2000 and deserves substantial credit for helping to elect the Republican presidential candidate, George W. Bush.

And they judged the people at all seasons: the hard causes they brought unto Moses, but every small matter they judged themselves.

Moses took his consultant's advice and became a more competent leader. He had to deal only with "the hard causes" because he adopted a system by which "every small matter" would be dealt with by others. Not only did Moses make himself more competent, but his structural reforms also made all of his lieutenants better managers as well. Moses had, to use a modern term, reinvented tribal management.

Now, what happened to Jethro, the consultant who turned Moses from an overcontrolling to an empowering manager? All we know is that Moses "let his father-in-law depart; and he went his way into his own land." He then disappeared from the Bible and from history. It just goes to show that even in biblical times, it was true that all management consultants eventually wear out their welcome. But it gets worse as far as Jethro's reputation is concerned. Later on in the Bible (Deut. 1:9–18), Moses is giving a kind of annual report to the Israelites. He recounts the reorganization plan he adopted with Jethro's advice and, like many a modern executive, does not give any credit at all to the person who had the ideas that he successfully implemented. And this is not unjust. After all, the job of the consultant— the reason he or she is hired in the first place—is to make the person who hires him or her look good. A consultant's final task is to take the money he or she has earned—and run.

For Discussion: Are the organizing principles spelled out by Jethro still valid today? Is it always true that an overcontrolling manager who refuses to delegate authority is destined to fail?

THE ORIGINS OF PUBLIC MANAGEMENT

Municipalities ■
Local governments. The word and concept comes from Latin, in which *municipium* referred to any self-governing body within the Roman Empire.

Management ■
A term that can refer to both (1) the people responsible for running an organization and (2) the running process itself—the use of numerous resources to accomplish an organizational goal.

Profession of arms ■
The practice of the art and science of war; the occupation of a career military officer.

Civilization and administration have always gone hand in hand. Since ancient times, a city was defined by the walls created for its defense. Even today, many **municipalities** will award someone a key to the city in symbolic remembrance of a time when the only way into a city was through a locked gate in the wall. This meant that once primitive tribes gathered in cities—when they literally became *civilized* (meaning *to live in cities*)—they had to be sufficiently organized for war to build their stronghold and defend it from attackers. This necessitated a sophisticated system of administration. Cities without walls only became possible in relatively recent times, when an overarching state authority was able to impose peace over a large area.

Thus the profession of **management** began and developed as the **profession of arms**. To the extent that the history of the world is the history of warfare, it is also the history of public administration—because war at the state level is literally impossible without an effective system of public administration behind it. Military officers were the first public administrators. Societies beyond the extended family only became possible with the rise of an officer class. Thus the first armies were mobs with managers.

Only gradually did these mob managers develop the organizational skills to command large armies and rule large areas. These early martial skills constitute the most basic elements of all administrative processes. Hierarchy, line and staff personnel, **logistics**, and communications were all highly developed by ancient armies. Even *reform* is of military origin. After all, it means to once again ("re") organize the ranks ("form") for an additional assault—whether on another army or on a difficult management problem. And there is hardly any core concept in modern strategic thought that had not been anticipated by **Sun-Tzu** in ancient China. The word *strategy* itself comes from the ancient Greek, meaning "the art of the general."

The vocabulary of public administration is so heavily indebted to its military origins that the field would be literally tongue-tied without it. Next time you see an organization's slogan (such as New Hampshire's "Live Free or Die") printed on a sheet of its letterhead, remember that "quality first" or some other inane would-be motivator had its beginnings as a war cry of the Highland clans of Scotland. If you don't get what you initially want and go for your fall-back position, remember that fall-backs were prepared fortified sites that soldiers ran to once the enemy broke through their first line of defense. If you are in an organization's rear echelon, console yourself with the fact that the French are to blame because they used their word for the rung of a ladder—*échelon*—to describe parallel military formations. And if you cherish a particular tax loophole, remember that a loophole was a small opening in a fort for soldiers to shoot out of, or use as a means of escape, depending on the circumstances. They are still a means of escape—from taxes.

The Continuing Influence of Ancient Rome

In his landmark 1941 book *The Managerial Revolution*, James Burnham contended that as the control of large corporations passes from the hands of the owners into the hands of professional administrators, the society's new governing class would be the possessors not of wealth but of technical expertise. But Burnham was two millennia off in his analysis because this managerial changeover from those of wealth and power to those of professional expertise first occurred in the ancient Roman army. According to military historian John Keegan, "The Roman centurions, long-service unit leaders drawn from the best of the enlisted ranks, formed the first body of professional fighting officers known to history." This middle-management class transmitted from generation to generation the technical skills and discipline by which Rome dominated the world for five centuries. They were the managers who allowed the patrician governing class to exercise actual command. They were motivated by loyalty to their legion, pride in their profession, regular pay, and retirement payments that were an additional inducement to good behavior. Here is the beginning of the modern merit system. The West would not see its like again until Napoléon, espousing the best in French revolutionary idealism, announced "careers open to talent" in both the civilian and military spheres.

The regulating of pay and pensions in ancient Rome was the key to maintaining the army—and to this end the first civil service was created (by the Emperor **Augustus Caesar**) to raise the taxes necessary to support the legions. Thus out of military necessity was born civilian public administration. The same Augustus would boast that "I found Rome a city of bricks and left it a city of marble."

Logistics ■
Traditionally the art and science of moving military forces and keeping them supplied; those inventory, production, and traffic-management activities that seek the timely placement of materiel and personnel at the proper time and in the appropriate quantities.

Sun-Tzu (fourth century B.C.E.) ■
The ancient Chinese writer whose essays, traditionally published as *The Art of War*, have influenced all Western military analysts since they were first available in European editions in the late eighteenth century.

Augustus Caesar (63 B.C.E.–14 C.E.) ■
The nephew of Julius Caesar. He became the first Roman emperor after defeating his rivals Mark Antony and Marcus Brutus in the civil war that followed his uncle's assassination in 44 B.C.E.

Public works ■
Government-sponsored
construction projects.

While spoken by an emperor, these are also the words of a proud municipal **public works** administrator.

While many ancient kingdoms, such as Egypt and China, had sophisticated administrative institutions, the core features of modern public administration in the Western world were first found in the Roman Empire. The Roman state was depersonalized. It had existed independent of any political leader or king; it was not "owned" by anyone. Significantly, the state's public finances were separate from the private funds of its leadership. Second, it made use of a centralized hierarchical structure. At the top was the central government, then the province, and finally the diocese. These structures are still familiar, still in use. Finally, the Romans introduced several units of functional specialization that form the heart of most modern public administrative systems. They had organizational units for military affairs, finance, justice, and police. This last function was so broadly conceived that it included transportation, health, education, agriculture, and commerce.

Ever since the time of ancient Rome, young men have viewed a stint of service as a military officer as a logical prelude to larger public service or to greater political office. Indeed, during the days of the Roman Republic it was a condition of elective office that a candidate have a decade of military service. Not only was this a seasoning period for youths, it also was the only social institution that offered systematic training in administration. It was thought reasonable that those who could demonstrate the ability to command and administer should be considered legitimate candidates. This is still true today. Most U.S. presidents and countless lesser politicians have used their military experience as a springboard for their political careers. Has your member of Congress served in the armed forces?

Police ■
Paramilitary state and local government organizations whose most basic responsibilities include maintaining public order and safety, investigating and arresting persons accused of crimes, and securing the cooperation of the citizenry. But a state's police power goes far beyond the criminal justice system; it is the legal basis by which governments regulate such areas as public health, safety, and morals.

When Governor Bill Clinton of Arkansas announced he would be running in the 1992 presidential race, the very legitimacy of his candidacy was called into question because he not only lacked military experience, but also conspicuously sought to avoid it during the Vietnam War. While many who opposed the war thought that Clinton's legal avoidance of the draft was a more honorable course of action than serving in this unpopular war, the depth of reaction to his lack of prior military service continued to make it difficult for him to function as commander in chief well into his presidency. Even those who did serve in the military may fall prey to criticism regarding the quality of their service. For example, in 2004 John Kerry's bid for the presidency was undermined by a group of his fellow Vietnam veterans, who called his valor into question. Thus the ancient Roman attitude toward the desirability of youthful military service as preparation for later public office still strongly affects modern American politics and administration.

Marcus Tullius Cicero (106–43 B.C.E.) ■
The Roman senator who was killed by henchmen of Augustus Caesar because Cicero was a republican and Augustus was a murderous dictator. This in no way diminishes Augustus's reputation as a fine administrator. Public administrators throughout the ages have used murder as an administrative tool. Only relatively recently has this become less fashionable.

The Military Heritage of Public Administration

The history of the world can be viewed as the rise and fall of public administrative institutions. Those ancient empires that rose and prevailed for a while were those with better administrative institutions than their competitors. Brave soldiers have been plentiful in every society, but they are ultimately wasted if not backed up by administrators who can feed and pay them. Marcus Tullius Cicero, the ancient Roman orator, is usually credited with first saying that "the sinews of war are infinite money." And this was already a trite sentiment when he said it!

► IN THE NEWS | Are We Rome?

In 2007 Cullen Murphy published *Are We Rome?*, his comparison of the ancient Roman empire to the new-style American empire. His answer is essentially yes, with major caveats. After all, few of us speak Latin. But look about you. If architecture indicates a nation's character and destiny, then our traditional public buildings are Rome reincarnated. Until recent decades it was considered out of the question that major courthouses or post offices not look Roman. The founders of the United States were not only quite knowledgeable about Roman history, they quite openly and consciously sought to imitate Rome's best aspects. That's why we are a republic, have a senate, and are wary of would-be Caesars. But the larger question is whether the United States will ultimately have the same fate as Rome. After all, the Roman Empire lasted about a thousand years. We still have a long way to go even if you think we are headed for a fall.

The modern state is built upon the administrative and legal foundations of Rome. For example, contemporary practices in public health, police, welfare, census, public works, and tax administration can be traced back to the Roman army.

Administratively and politically speaking, Rome is in our national blood. We are Rome's children. We are Rome reborn but even better because we have pizza—while the descendants of those ancient Romans had to await the discovery of South America to experience the joys of tomato sauce. ◣

The Roman Empire only fell when its legions degenerated into corps of mercenaries and when its supply and tax bases were corrupted. Napoléon was wrong. Armies do not "march on their stomachs," as he said; they march on the proverbial backs of the tax collectors and on the roads built by administrators. Regular pay allows for discipline. Strict discipline is what makes a mob an army. And a disciplined military, obedient to the leaders of the state, is a precondition for civilization. This is the classic chicken-and-egg problem. Which comes first—effective public administration or an effective military? The rise and fall of ancient Rome proved that you could not have one without the other.

Early bureaucrats in ancient Rome and modern Europe literally wore uniforms that paralleled military dress. After all, the household servants of rulers traditionally wore **livery**. It indicated that the wearer was not free but the servant of another. Government administrators are still considered servants in this sense; they are public servants because they, too, have accepted obligations, which means they are not completely free. Indeed, until early in the twentieth century, many otherwise civilian public officials in Europe—most notably diplomats—had prescribed uniforms.

Both victorious soldiers and successful managers tend to be inordinately admired and disproportionately rewarded as risk takers. True, the specific risks and rewards are different, but the phenomenon is the same. They both may have to put their careers, and sometimes significant parts of their anatomy as well, "on the line" to obtain a goal for their state or organization. Notice again the military language, for "the line" originally referred to the line of battle where you faced the enemy. This is why line officers today are still those who perform the services for which the organization exists. This is the direct link between the Roman centurion and the modern fire captain, chief of detectives, or elementary school principal. Life on the line is still a daily struggle.

Livery ■
The uniform of a servant; any identical and identifying item of dress—such as a necktie, scarf, or blazer—worn by members of the same organization.

THE EVOLUTION OF MANAGEMENT PRINCIPLES

Authoritarian or traditional management is the classic model of military governance applied to civilian purposes. Managers under an authoritarian doctrine value order, precision, consistency, and obedience. To them, the power that flows from structure is supreme. Relationships are hierarchical, based on dominance and dependence. This authoritarian style has gradually given way to less centralized, more participative management styles—not because management developed an altruistic desire to be nice to the workers but because participation has proved to be more competent than authoritarianism when dealing with sophisticated workers. This change takes nothing away from the fact that at earlier times authoritarianism was the most competent management posture. Thus, in judging the competence of an organization at any given time, you must, as with a stock market, learn whether the level of competence (as with the price of a stock) is high or low relative to others in the market.

Since antiquity, the military has evolved principles about how its authoritarian organizations are best managed. While there are many versions of the principles of war that reflect local conditions, they all contain the same basic elements. Those elements having civilian applications have been incorporated into principles of management. Thus concepts once military—such as **span of control** and **unity of command**—are now thoroughly civilian as well.

Span of control ■
The extent of an administrator's or agency's responsibility. The span of control has usually been expressed as the number of subordinates that a manager should supervise.

Unity of command ■
The concept that each individual in an organization should be accountable to a single superior.

Royal road ■
An easy way. The Greek mathematician Euclid in about 300 B.C.E. supposedly told the mathematically challenged Ptolemy I of Egypt that there was no royal road to geometry. There still isn't!

Comparing Military and Civilian Principles

There is no **royal road** to administrative wisdom. There are no generally accepted principles of management, no one list on which there is general agreement. However, there is a principles approach that has its origins in the principles of war. While these precepts can be traced back to ancient times, for comparison's sake it is convenient to use the nine principles of war currently used by the U.S. Army:

1. *Objective:* Direct every military operation toward a clearly defined, decisive, and attainable objective.
2. *Offensive:* Seize, retain, and exploit the initiative.
3. *Mass:* Concentrate combat power at the decisive place and time.
4. *Economy of force:* Allocate minimum essential combat power to secondary efforts.
5. *Maneuver:* Place the enemy in a position of disadvantage through the flexible application of combat power.
6. *Unity of command:* For every objective, ensure unity of effort under one responsible commander.
7. *Security:* Never permit the enemy to acquire an advantage.
8. *Surprise:* Strike the enemy at a time and/or place and in a manner for which he is unprepared.
9. *Simplicity:* Prepare clear, uncomplicated plans and clear, concise orders to ensure thorough understanding.

All nine principles are not always important. But in any large-scale operation they are always all there. Which ones dominate at any given time is a function of context, of the evolving situation. These principles are inherently interrelating and reinforcing. They represent the distilled science of war as it has evolved over thousands of years. But they are merely the colors with which the commander paints. If he or she is artful in execution, then victory, promotion, and acclaim will follow. If clumsy, then removal by death or disgrace will. Note that the principles of war (and management) are not really designed for experienced officers. These are instructions for the inexperienced. Military historian John Keegan even called them "words to the unwise."

There are a large number of formulations of the principles of management from which to choose. The following are from **Catheryn Seckler-Hudson,** who wrote them in 1955 when she was dean of the School of Government and Public Administration at the American University. Her 12 principles, distilled from the literature of business and public administration and presented in her book *Organization and Management,* came with a warning label: "It should never be assumed that principles of organization are immutable laws to be applied automatically."

1. Policy should be defined and imparted to those who are responsible for its achievement.
2. Work should be subdivided, systematically planned, and programmed.
3. Tasks and responsibilities should be specifically assigned and understood.
4. Appropriate methods and procedures should be developed and utilized by those responsible for policy achievement.
5. Appropriate resources (men, money, material) in terms of availability and priority should be equitably allocated.
6. Authority commensurate with responsibility should be delegated and located as close as possible to the point where operations occur and decisions need to be made.
7. Adequate structural relationships through which to operate should be established.
8. Effective and qualified leadership should head each organization and each subdivision of the organization.
9. Unity of command and purpose should permeate the organization.
10. Continuous accountability for utilization of resources and for the production of results should be required.
11. Effective coordination of all individual and group efforts within the organization should be achieved.
12. Continuous reconsideration of all matters pertaining to the organization should be a part of regular operations.

These principles represent the received wisdom of public administration at mid-century by one of its most acknowledged scholars. Yet when they are compared with the principles of war, they seem mushy and vacillating—hardly any guidance for leadership at all. (True, in the book from which these are taken the author includes many pages of additional explanation.) Part of the reason for this is that these are guidelines for administrators, not for leaders. Her guidelines and principles try to be so all-encompassing that they defeat themselves by their complexity. **Herbert Simon** gained much of his early reputation by attacking the principles approach in his 1946 article condescendingly titled "The Proverbs of

Catheryn Seckler-Hudson (1902–1963) ■ A pioneer in developing the "nuts and bolts" of public management technology, she was the author of many groundbreaking works on public sector planning, budgeting, and organization.

Herbert Simon (1916–2001) ■ The winner of the 1978 Nobel Prize in economics for his pioneering work in management decision making.

Administration." He denounced the whole principles approach to public administration that then dominated administrative thinking. He found the management principles of his era inconsistent, conflicting, and inapplicable to too many of the administrative situations facing managers. He concluded that they were little more than proverbs. Simon would later write in his memoirs that this article, which "secured my instant and permanent visibility in public administration," came "almost purely from the logical structure and internal inconsistency of the principles themselves. No experience of organization was required to detect it."

Simon's criticism of these "proverbs" was valid only to a point. Principles of either kind—military or management—were never meant to be dogma. Even Napoléon warned that "no rule of war is so absolute as to allow no exceptions." But rules can be, nevertheless, very useful. As **Bernard Brodie** wrote, "It may be well that the consideration of a catalog of numbered principles (usually fewer than a dozen) with the barest definition of the meaning of each may be necessary to communicate to second-order minds (or minds too busy with the execution of plans to worry much about the specific validity of the ideas behind them) some conception of what the business is all about."

> **Bernard Brodie (1910–1978)** ■
> The American who was the first major academic theorist of nuclear warfare.

What is striking about the two lists is how the military list is more policy oriented, more leadership directed, than the civilian list. The latter seems obsessed with the routines of administration—as opposed to breaking new ground with innovation. The military principles are far more proactive and appropriately aggressive. But strangely enough, aggression is back in fashion in contemporary management thinking. The thrust of the military approach with its emphasis on strategy can be found, for example, in the philosophic underpinnings of the reinventing government and total quality management movements of the 1990s. Far from being of mere historical interest, they seem almost fresh when compared with the staid principles of management—and certainly relevant. When used with common sense and attention to experience, the principles of war can be extremely useful to those public managers who would join the never-ending battle against the evil trinity of waste, fraud, and abuse. This is all the more true for those public sector organizations forced to compete with private sector competitors. Competition by creating "enemies" clarifies objectives. The difference between a lean, mean fighting machine, as the U.S. Marine Corps aspires to be, and a lean, mean management machine is, in essence, one of objectives.

The Principles Approach

The principles approach to management, whether of the civilian or military variety, was a pivotal development in the advancement of management as a profession. Why? Because it seeks to make a science out of what was once considered only art. Antoine-Henri Jomini was the Swiss bank clerk turned Napoléonic era general who wrote dozens of books explaining why some generals (mainly Napoléon) and some armies (mainly the French) were consistently more successful than their rivals. The answer was to be found in scientific principles of strategy. Jomini proved in literally dozens of major books that victory went to those who instinctively followed the principles that he had distilled from historical accounts and years of experience campaigning with Napoléon—simply put, victory went to the general who used massive forces in an offensive action against a decisive point. Yet Jomini was keenly aware that art had a major role to play in this science. As he wrote in *The Art of War*, "It is almost always easy to determine the decisive point of a field of battle, but not so with the decisive moment; and it is precisely here that genius and experience are everything, and mere theory of little value."

While simple enough and mostly common sense, Jomini's principles were enormously influential. Because Jomini was *the* military theorist of the nineteenth century, his ideas were widely disseminated. His basic teaching, his doctrine, was that the management of war could be taught—just study the principles and how they are applied in specific situations. (Today, this technique is known as the case study method.) Because so many of the activities of war—planning, training, logistics, and so on—are more management than fighting, it was not much of a leap of the imagination to apply similar principles to management. The timing was certainly right, because the mid-nineteenth century saw the beginning of large-scale industrial enterprise, especially railroads, the scope of which was similar to managing a large army.

Case study ■
A research design that focuses on the in-depth analysis of a single subject. It is particularly useful for the understanding of dynamic processes over time.

By the time business administration emerged as an academic field toward the end of the nineteenth century, it seemed only natural to take a principles approach to teaching management. But these early efforts at developing and teaching principles were authoritarian in that they were premised on the notion that all direction and innovation came from the top—that the people in power, while not necessarily having a monopoly on brains in the organization, had the only brains that mattered. Thus success or failure was a function of how smart the boss was. Bosses would certainly be more effective if they adopted principles, but they were inherently limited by their own abilities.

The explosion of textbooks, self-improvement, and "how-to-succeed" books on management that take a principles approach began early in the twentieth century and has never abated. Next time you see a best seller offering a new management system, remember that while the author may never acknowledge it, he or she is an intellectual disciple of Jomini—because the authors of these best- and would-be best sellers all premise their works on the belief that management is a skill that can be taught.

WHAT IS ORGANIZATION THEORY?

An "organization" is a group of people who jointly work to achieve at least one common goal. A "theory" is a proposition or set of propositions that seeks to explain or predict something. The something in the case of organization theory is how groups and individuals behave in differing organizational arrangements. This is critically important information for any manager or leader. It is not an exaggeration to say that the world is ruled by the underlying premises of organization theory. This has been true ever since humankind first organized itself for hunting, war, and even family life. Indeed, the newest thing about organization theory is the study of it.

Only since the twentieth century has intellectual substance and tradition been given to a field that was the instinctual artistic domain of adventuresome entrepreneurs and cunning politicos. It was artistic in the sense that it was done naturally without formal learning. Leaders in every field during every age used organization theory as naturally as they used their oratorical powers. In neither case did they need to intellectualize about it. Thus the pirate captain in the seventeenth-century Caribbean, the revolutionary leader in eighteenth-century colonial America, and the suffragist leader in late-nineteenth-century America were all organization theorists—because none of them could have made it as leaders without understanding, if only subliminally, how to structure and motivate a group.

Organization theory was always there in the authoritarian model offered by the military. While many of its premises were understood by the ancients, it did not coalesce as a self-conscious field of knowledge until society found a practical use for it—to help manage the ever-burgeoning national (as opposed to local) industries and institutions brought about by the **industrial revolution**. When the problems of managing an organization grew to be more than one head could cope with, the search for guidance on how to manage and arrange large-scale organizations became as noble a quest as the secular world of business could offer. If a commercial society ever had prophets, it was those pioneers of industrial engineering who claimed that the path to ever-greater prosperity was to be found in the relentless search for the "one best way." They were offering society a theory—abstract guidance for those who knew where they wanted to go but did not quite know how to get there. They already knew what social psychologist Kurt Lewin would assert years later: "There is nothing so practical as a good theory." What was once said of the first atomic bomb has also been said of the first U.S. voyage to the moon: It was as much an achievement of organization as it was of engineering and science. Have our more recent theories of organization kept pace with our industrial and technical achievements? Maybe. But certainly yes when they are compared with the "primitive" authoritarian management. Yet many of the basics remain the same—remain as givens. The laws of physics and gravity do not change with intellectual fashions or technological advances, nor do the basic social and physical characteristics of people. Just as those who would build spaceships have to start by studying the physics of Isaac Newton, those who would design and manage organizations must start with Frederick Taylor, Scottish economist Adam Smith, and French executive engineer Henri Fayol. The future will always build on what has endured from the past.

It was T. E. Lawrence (of Arabia) who wrote, "With 2,000 years of examples behind us, we have no excuse when fighting, for not fighting well." The same, even double, can be said of organization theory: With 4,000 years of examples behind us, we have no excuse when organizing, for not organizing well.

While it is always great fun to delve into the wisdom of the ancients, most analysts of the origins of organization theory view the beginnings of the **factory system** in Great Britain in the eighteenth century as the birth point of complex economic organizations and, consequently, of the field of organization theory.

Classical Organization Theory

Classical organization theory, as its name implies, was the first theory of its kind, is considered traditional, and continues to be the base on which other schools of organization theory have been built. Its basic tenets and assumptions, however, which were rooted in the industrial revolution of the 1700s and the professions

Industrial revolution ■
A very general term that refers to a society's change from an agrarian to an industrial economy. The Industrial Revolution of the Western world is considered to have begun in England in the eighteenth century.

Factory system ■
Any production process that has individual workers specializing in the varying aspects of a larger task.

of mechanical engineering, industrial engineering, and economics, have never changed. They were only expanded on, refined, and made more sophisticated. Thus an understanding of classical organization theory is essential not only because of its historical interest, but also, more importantly, because subsequent analyses and theories presume a knowledge of it.

The fundamental tenets of organization theory can be summarized as follows:

1. Organizations exist to accomplish production-related and economic goals.
2. There is one best way to organize for production, and that way can be found through systematic, scientific inquiry.
3. Production is maximized through specialization and division of labor.
4. People and organizations act in accordance with rational economic principles.

The evolution of any theory must be viewed in context. The beliefs of early management theorists about how organizations worked or should work were a direct reflection of the societal values of their times. And the times were harsh. It was well into the twentieth century before the industrial workers of the United States and Europe began to enjoy even limited "rights" as organizational citizens. Workers were not viewed as individuals but as the interchangeable parts in an industrial machine whose parts were made of flesh only when it was impractical to make them of steel.

The advent of power-driven machinery and hence the modern factory system spawned our current concepts of economic organizations and organization for production. Power-driven equipment was expensive. Production workers could not purchase and use their own equipment as they once had their own tools. The memorable phrase for being fired—"get the sack"—comes from the earliest days of the industrial revolution, when a dismissed worker literally was given a sack in which to gather up his tools. Increasingly, workers without their own tools and often without any special skills had to gather for work where the equipment was—in factories. Expensive equipment had to produce enough output to justify its acquisition and maintenance costs.

Under the factory system, organizational success resulted from well-organized production systems that kept machines busy and costs under control. Industrial and mechanical engineers—and their machines—were the keys to production. Organizational structures and production systems were needed to take best advantage of the machines. Organizations, it was thought, should work like machines, using people, capital, and machines as their parts. Just as industrial engineers sought to design "the best" machines to keep factories productive, industrial and mechanical engineering-type thinking dominated theories about "the best way" to organize for production. Thus the first theories of organizations were concerned primarily with the anatomy or structure of formal organizations. This was the milieu, or the environment, the mode of thinking, that shaped and influenced the tenets of classical organization theory.

Adam Smith and the Pin Factory

Centralization of equipment and labor in factories, division of specialized labor, management of specialization, and economic paybacks on factory equipment all

BOX 6.1 | The Invisible Hand

Every individual endeavors to employ his capital so that its produce may be of greatest value. He generally neither intends to promote the public interest, nor knows how much he is promoting it. He intends only his own gain. And he is in this led by an invisible hand to promote an end which was no part of his intention. By pursuing his own interest he frequently promotes that of society more effectually than when he really intends it. ◣

Source: Adam Smith, *The Wealth of Nations* (1776).

were concerns identified by the Scottish economist Adam Smith (1723–1790) in his work *An Inquiry into the Nature and Causes of the Wealth of Nations*. Smith and James Watt (1736–1819), the inventor of the steam engine, are the two people who are most often named as being responsible for pushing the world into industrialization.

Smith, considered the "father" of the academic discipline of **economics**, provided the intellectual foundation for **laissez-faire** capitalism. But Smith's *The Wealth of Nations* devotes its first chapter, "Of the Division of Labour," to a discussion of the optimum organization of a pin factory. Why? Because specialization of labor was one of the pillars of Smith's "invisible hand" market mechanism in which the greatest rewards would go to those who were the most efficient in the competitive marketplace.

Economics ■
The study of how people or states use their limited resources to satisfy their unlimited wants; how scarce resources are allocated among competing needs.

Laissez-faire ■
A hands-off style of governance that emphasizes economic freedom so the capitalist invisible hand can work its will.

Traditional pin makers could produce only a few dozen pins a day. When organized in a factory with each worker performing a limited operation, they could produce tens of thousands a day. Smith's chapter, coming as it did at the dawn of the Industrial Revolution, is the most famous and influential statement on the economic rationale of the factory system, even though factory systems had been known since ancient times. For example, in 370 B.C.E., Xenophon described the division of labor in a shoe factory. But it was not until centuries later that the popularity of Smith's 1776 book revolutionized thinking about economics and organizations. Hence, 1776 is the year that is traditionally considered the starting point of organization theory as an applied science and academic discipline. Besides, 1776 is easy to remember as it was a good year for other events as well.

All formal organizations, whether Smith's eighteenth-century factory or the most sophisticated modern corporation, are *force multipliers* in the sense that they allow the combined individual efforts to be far greater than the sum of their parts. Smith's pin makers acting individually could make a few dozen pins a day at best; as a team, they could make many thousands. Proper organization thus means that two plus two does not equal four; it can "equal" many thousands.

The military uses the term *force multiplier* to refer to any new technology that makes a soldier more effective on the battlefield. Thus the machine gun is a force multiplier because it means that one soldier with it is as effective as, say, a hundred soldiers with traditional rifles. Modern computers and word processors are force multipliers in a civilian context because one word processor operator can be as effective as dozens of traditional typists. But as Smith has shown, it is not just

BOX 6.2 | Adam Smith on the "Division of Labour"

The way in which this business [pin making] is now carried on, not only the whole work is a peculiar trade, but it is divided into a number of branches. . . . One man draws out the wire, another straights it, a third cuts it, a fourth points it, a fifth grinds it at the top for receiving the head; to make the head requires two or three distinct operations; to put it on, is a peculiar business, to whiten the pins is another; it is even a trade by itself to put them into the paper; and the important business of making a pin is, in this manner, divided into about 18 distinct operations. . . . I have seen a small manufactory of this kind where ten men only were employed, and where some of them consequently performed two or three distinct operations. But though they were very poor, and therefore but indifferently accommodated with the necessary machine, they could, when they exerted themselves, make among them about 12 pounds of pins in a day. There are in a pound upwards of 4,000 pins of a middling size. Those ten persons, therefore, could make among them upwards of 48,000 pins in a day. Each person, therefore, making a tenth part of 48,000 pins, might be considered as making 4,800 pins in a day. But if they had all wrought separately and independently, and without any of them having been educated to this peculiar business, they certainly could not each of them have made 20, perhaps not one pin in a day. . . . In every other art and manufacture, the effects of the division of labour are similar to what they are in this very trifling one. ◣

Source: Adam Smith, *The Wealth of Nations* (1776).

technology that can be a force multiplier. Good organization is a technology in its own right, is as powerful a force multiplier as any machine—and far cheaper, too!

THE ORIGINS OF SCIENTIFIC MANAGEMENT

The basic problem with the traditional hierarchical organization was that it was dependent on the proper enculturation of individual supervisors at every level for its success. Under stable conditions, properly trained military officers and factory supervisors performed well. But as military affairs and factory production became increasingly unstable during the French Revolution, the Age of Napoléon, and the industrial revolution, mechanisms had to evolve to compensate for the inherent rigidity of the traditional hierarchy. Individual officers and supervisors, competent enough under stable conditions, became less competent under revolutionary conditions. Whether on the "field of honor" or the factory floor, they could not cope with the competition—organizations that adopted the major structural innovation of that era, the staff concept.

While traditional hierarchical organizations allowed leaders to extend their reach, the organization was still dependent on the necessarily limited intellectual energy at the top. But even the greatest mind with the best advisers has limits. The staff concept evolved to overcome the inherent limitations of a single mind and ever-fleeting time.

French Revolution ■
The political convulsions that began in Paris when the citizens stormed the Bastille (a prison) on July 14, 1789. These convulsions have continued ever since.

The Staff Concept

"Staff" refers to two mutually supporting ideas that gradually evolved in both military and civilian contexts. As the management function became increasingly complex and differentiated, managers started using assistants—secretaries and clerks at first, later personnel and purchasing specialists. This traditional use of staff was followed by the staff principle (or staff concept), which created a specific unit in the larger organization whose primary responsibility was to think and plan, to ponder over innovations and plan for their implementation. Under the factory system that emerged from the industrial revolution, business success resulted from well-organized production systems that kept machines busy and costs under control. Industrial and mechanical engineers—and their machines—were the keys to production. Organizational structures and production systems needed constant tinkering and refining to take best advantage of ever-evolving technology. Organizations, it was thought, should work like machines, using people as their parts. Just as industrial engineers sought to design "the best" machines to keep factories productive, industrial and mechanical engineering-type thinking dominated theories about "the best way" to organize people for their role as part of the overall industrial machine.

Beginning with the industrial revolution (and Napoléonic-era military organizations), the staff concept has made ever-increasing inroads into the public and private sector. The concept was first formally instituted in the military, and it can be traced back to the ancient Greek armies of Alexander the Great. While generals have always had **aides-de-camp**, the modern military general staff principally originates from the Prussian military reforms that transformed an inefficient army into the foremost military machine in Europe by the middle of the nineteenth century. The Prussian, later German, general staff has been admired for its efficiency (if not its ethics), though seldom fully imitated, by military analysts ever since. It consisted of a small group of the most intellectually able officers, drawn from the main officer corps relatively early in their careers, who then spent their professional lives in the central planning unit known as the general staff. The general staff then developed the strategies and tactics that Germany would use in future wars. By the end of the nineteenth century, all of the major military powers, including the United States and Japan, had adopted a variant of the German general staff for their militaries.

The general staff concept, modified to reflect local conditions, was increasingly adopted by burgeoning industrial and governmental organizations. In the latter part of the nineteenth century, American industrial engineers began asserting that factory workers could be much more productive if their work was designed scientifically. And who would these designers be? They would be the civilian counterparts of the military general staff. Their job was to conduct the research and do the planning that would make the organization more competitive relative to other organizations. Thus scientific management grew out of engineering—which brings up another connection to our old friend Jomini. The greatest single source of the nineteenth-century American engineers who built the railroads, canals, harbors, and bridges was one school, West Point, where the principles espoused by Jomini were and are still taught. The professional paper that management historians considered to be the first call for scientific management was entitled "The Engineer as an Economist," and it was presented by **Henry R. Towne** at the 1886 meeting of the American Society of Mechanical Engineers. Those nineteenth-century engineers, whether educated at West Point or not, tended to know good principles when they saw them.

Aide-de-camp ◼
A young officer serving as a personal assistant to a general.

Henry R. Towne (1844–1924) ◼
An early scientific management advocate whose efforts predated and influenced Frederick W. Taylor.

The Influence of Frederick W. Taylor

Frederick Winslow Taylor became the acknowledged father of the scientific management movement. He pioneered the development of **time-and-motion studies**, originally under the name "Taylorism" or the "Taylor system." Taylorism, or its successor, scientific management, was not a single invention but rather a series of methods and organizational arrangements designed by Taylor and his associates to increase the efficiency and speed of machine shop production. Premised on the notion that there was "one best way" of accomplishing any given task, Taylor's scientific management sought to increase output by using special staff to discover the fastest, most efficient, and least-fatiguing production methods.

Scientific management emerged as a national movement in the United States during a series of events in 1910. Some eastern railroads filed for increased freight rates with the **Interstate Commerce Commission (ICC)**. Louis D. Brandeis, the populist lawyer who would later be a Supreme Court justice, took the case against the railroads. He called in **Harrington Emerson**, a consultant who had "systematized" the Santa Fe Railroad, to testify that the railroads did not need increased rates: They could "save a million dollars a day" by using what Brandeis initially called "scientific management" methods. According to historians Harold Smiddy and Lionel Naum, this "sudden realization among business leaders everywhere that the then proudest industrial achievement, the system of railroads, was actually something less than the flawless gem of American enterprise, brought at last the needed widespread attention and support the management movement had lacked." It was a managerial epiphany similar to, but less nationwide in effect than, the shock of *Sputnik* in 1957. It was, as the saying went, "a hell of a way to run a railroad!"

At first Taylor was reluctant to use the phrase "scientific management" because it sounded too academic. But the ICC hearings meant that the national scientific management boom was under way, and Taylor was its leader. Taylor had a profound—indeed revolutionary—effect on the fields of business and public administration. His work and fame gave ever-increasing credence to the notion that organizational operations could be planned and controlled systematically by staff experts using scientific principles.

Taylor echoed Jomini when he asserted that "the remedy for . . . inefficiency lies in systematic management, rather than in searching for some unusual or extraordinary man." Jomini's goal was to make any would-be Napoléon as skillful as the legendary general if they adopted Jomini's principles. Taylor sought "to prove that the best management is a true science, resting upon clearly defined laws, rules, and principles, as a foundation." Taylor—indeed all the scientific managers of his generation—took Jomini's approach to teaching war and applied it to management.

Many people unfamiliar with Jomini think that Clausewitz was *the* greatest nineteenth-century theoretician of war. After all, his classic *On War* was published in 1832. Yes, but being published is not the same as being read. Clausewitz had to wait for the beginning of the twentieth century and good translators to become influential. Fortunately, Taylor had better luck. His classic book *The Principles of Scientific Management* was an instant success when it was published in 1911 and has been in print ever since. Unfortunately, Taylor died in 1915, so he had only a few years to enjoy his success. Still, he fared better than Clausewitz, whose great

Time-and-motion studies ■ Various techniques for establishing time standards for the performance of manual work.

Interstate Commerce Commission (ICC) ■ The federal agency that regulated interstate surface transportation. Established in 1887, it was abolished in 1996.

Harrington Emerson (1853–1931) ■ One of the first management consultants in the United States; known as the "high priest of efficiency" because of his advocacy of eliminating "wanton, wicked waste."

book was published a year after he died. Posthumous publication is a much overrated joy!

Taylor's greatest public sector popularity came in 1912 after he presented his ideas to a Special Committee of the House of Representatives to Investigate the Taylor and Other Systems of Shop Management. Taylor's comprehensive statement of scientific management principles was focused on what he called the "duties of management":

1. Replacing traditional, rule-of-thumb methods of work accomplishment with systematic, more scientific methods of measuring and managing individual work elements.
2. The scientific study of the selection and sequential development of workers to ensure optimal placement of workers into work roles.
3. Obtaining the cooperation of workers to ensure full application of scientific principles.
4. Establishing logical divisions within work roles and responsibilities between workers and management.

Taylor's duties seem so obvious today, but they were revolutionary in 1912. Taylor himself even insisted in his *Principles of Scientific Management* that "scientific management does not necessarily involve any great invention, nor the discovery of new or startling facts." Nevertheless, it did "involve a certain combination

Frederick W. Taylor, a strange man. Born to wealth, he graduated from Phillips Exeter Academy in Exeter, New Hampshire, and passed the entrance exam to Harvard with honors but declined to go. Instead, he had family friends arrange a job for him as an apprentice pattern maker and machinist at the Enterprise Hydraulic Works of Philadelphia. In the following years he led a double life: a genuine member of the working class by day, who, on any night he wished, could be found in Philadelphia's most exclusive clubs. Indeed, in 1881 he won (with his brother-in-law) the first U.S. Lawn Tennis Association doubles championship—at a time when tennis was the most upperclass of sports. Meanwhile, he earned an engineering degree through correspondence at the Stevens Institute of Technology of Hoboken, New Jersey. As he advanced into management jobs, he never lost his understanding of workers, his hostility to poor supervision, and his profound belief that labor should be paid for performance, not mere attendance. Thus was formed his religious zeal to measure output as a means toward greater productivity and more equitable pay.

of elements which have not existed in the past, namely, old knowledge so collected, analyzed, grouped and classified into laws and rules that it constitutes a science."

Fayol's General Theory of Management

While the ideas of Adam Smith, Frederick Winslow Taylor, and others are still dominant influences on the design and management of organizations, it was Henri Fayol (1841–1925), a French executive engineer, who developed the first comprehensive theory of management. While Taylor was tinkering with the technology employed by the individual worker, Fayol was theorizing about all of the elements necessary to organize and manage a major corporation. Fayol's major work, *Administration Industrielle et Générale* (published in France in 1916), was almost ignored in the United States until Constance Storr's English translation, *General and Industrial Management*, appeared in 1949. Since that time, Fayol's theoretical contributions have been widely recognized, and his work is considered fully as significant as that of Taylor.

Fayol believed that his concept of management was universally applicable to every type of organization. While he had six principles—(1) technical (production of goods); (2) commercial (buying, selling, and exchange activities); (3) financial (raising and using capital); (4) security (protection of property and people); (5) accounting; and (6) managerial (coordination, control, organization, planning, and command of people)—Fayol's primary interest and emphasis was on his final principle: managerial. His managerial principle addressed such variables as division of work, authority and responsibility, discipline, unity of command, unity of direction, subordination of individual interest to general interest, remuneration of personnel, centralization, scalar chains, order, equity, stability of personnel tenure, initiative, and esprit de corps.

Fayol was the first to explain why principles beyond the golden rule and other moral precepts were needed: "Surprise might be expressed at the outset that the eternal moral principles . . . are not sufficient guide for the manager. . . . The explanation is this: the higher laws of religious or moral order envisage the individual only, or else interests which are not of this world, whereas management principles aim at the success of associations of individuals and at the satisfying of economic interests. Given that the aim is different, it is not surprising that the means are not the same."

Scalar chain ■
The chain of supervisors from the top of an organization to the bottom.

Esprit de corps ■
The spirit or morale of a group; traditionally, the pride that soldiers take in their military units.

THE PERIOD OF ORTHODOXY

It is hardly possible to exaggerate the influence that scientific management has had and continues to have on the intellectual development of public administration. Those who have traced the historical evolution of public administration, such as Dwight Waldo, Vincent Ostrom, Nicholas Henry, and Howard McCurdy, would describe the pattern of development within public administration between the world wars as a "period of orthodoxy." The tenets of this orthodox ideology held that the work of government could be neatly divided into decision making and execution (the politics–administration dichotomy of Woodrow Wilson) and that administration was a science with discoverable principles (scientific management). This dichotomy, which played such an important part in the historical development of public administration, would hardly have been possible if scientific management had not evolved when it did.

The notion that politics could, let alone should, be separated from administration was quickly disposed of by the New Deal and World War II. While those wars against depression and oppression were primarily economic and military operations, they were also immense managerial undertakings. The experience of those years called into question much of what was then the **conventional wisdom** of public administration. The politics–administration dichotomy of the progressive reform movement lost its viability amid the New Deal and the war effort because it was increasingly seen that it simply was not possible to take value-free processes of business and apply them to government. Government, in spite of the best efforts of many reformers, was not a business and was not value-free.

The attack on the politics–administration dichotomy came from many quarters at once. David E. Lilienthal, writing of his experiences as chairman of the Tennessee Valley Authority—the federal government's flood control and electric power corporation for the Tennessee River Valley—found the planning process of government to be a blatantly political enterprise. One that was, not incidentally, both healthy and beneficial for a democratic society.

Paul Appleby's Polemic

But it remained for Paul Appleby, a prominent New Deal administrator and dean of the Maxwell School at Syracuse University, to write the most skillful polemic of the era, which asserted that this theoretical insistence on apolitical governmental processes went against the grain of the American experience. In his book *Big Democracy,* Appleby emphatically shattered public administration's self-imposed demarcation between politics and administration. He held that it was a myth that politics was separate and could somehow be taken out of administration. This was good—not evil, as many of the progressive reformers had asserted—because this political involvement in administration acted as a check on the arbitrary exercise of bureaucratic power. In the future, those who would describe the political ramifications and issues of administration would not begin by contesting the politics–administration dichotomy as incorrect or irrelevant, but they would begin from the premise, as Appleby put it so succinctly, that "government is different because government is politics."

Luther Gulick's POSDCORB

The second tenet of the interwar "orthodoxy," that administration was a science with discoverable principles, has never left us. The influence of scientific management continues to be pervasive. Taylor's scientific management sought to increase output by discovering the fastest, most efficient, and least-fatiguing production methods. The job of the scientific manager, once the "one best way" was found, was to impose this procedure on his or her organization. Classical organization theory derives from a corollary of this proposition. If there was one best way to

Conventional wisdom ■

That which is generally believed to be true. However, any writer who uses the phrase is setting something up to be knocked down; so conventional wisdom really means that which most people believe to be true but is not. The phrase first gained currency after John Kenneth Galbraith used it in *The Affluent Society* (1958): "Only posterity is unkind to the man of conventional wisdom, and all posterity does is bury him in a blanket of neglect."

accomplish any given production task, then correspondingly, there must also be one best way to accomplish any task of social organization—including organizing firms. Such principles of social organization were assumed to exist and to be waiting to be discovered by diligent scientific observation and analysis. Thus the methodology used to divine the "one best way" to accomplish physical tasks was increasingly applied to the problem of social organization.

Luther Gulick's "Notes on the Theory of Organization" is without doubt the best-known statement of this "principles" approach to managing organizations. In 1937, he and Lyndall Urwick edited a collection entitled *Papers on the Science of Administration*. Originally this was intended to be a staff report for the Brownlow Committee (see Chapter 3). Overall, these *Papers* were a statement of the "state of the art" of organization theory. It was here that Gulick introduced his famous mnemonic, POSDCORB, which stands for the seven major functions of management:

- Planning, which is working out in broad outline the things that need to be done and the methods for doing them to accomplish the purpose set for the enterprise
- Organizing, which is the establishment of the formal structure of authority through which work subdivisions are arranged, defined, and coordinated for the defined objective
- Staffing, which is the whole personnel function of bringing in and training the staff and maintaining favorable conditions of work
- Directing, which is the continuous task of making decisions and embodying them in specific and general orders and instructions and serving as the leader of the enterprise
- Coordinating, which is the all-important duty of interrelating the various parts of the work
- Reporting, which is keeping those to whom the executive is responsible informed as to what is going on, which thus includes keeping him- or herself and his or her subordinates informed through records, research, and inspection
- Budgeting, with all that goes with budgeting in the form of fiscal planning, accounting, and control

Gulick helped shape a critical distinction in orthodox public administration: that the study of management and administration was to be focused on the role of upper-level management. Its organizational outlook, as demonstrated by POSDCORB, took the point of view of the top. But this narrow focus was to be increasingly challenged. Even as Gulick wrote, his "scientific" approach to management was being confronted by the more humanistic focus that would increasingly challenge it. Although this was not immediately apparent, the theoreticians of the human relations and **behavioral science** approaches to management were very much contemporaries of Gulick; they were simply prophets before their time.

THE MANY MEANINGS OF BUREAUCRACY

The bureaucratic institutions of the modern state with their hierarchies of officials have their origins in ancient times, as the keynote story about Moses illustrated. Ever since, most large organizations, both in the public and private sectors, have

Luther Gulick (1892–1993) ■ Perhaps the most highly honored reformer, researcher, and practitioner of public administration in the United States. Often called the dean of American public administration, Gulick was intimately involved with the pioneering development and installation of new budget, personnel, and management systems at all levels of government. He was a founder of the Institute of Public Administration, the American Society for Public Administration, and the National Academy of Public Administration.

Behavioral science ■ A general term for all of the academic disciplines that study human and animal behavior by means of experimental research. The phrase was first put into wide use in the early 1950s by the Ford Foundation to describe its funding for interdisciplinary research in the social sciences and by faculty at the University of Chicago seeking federal funding for research—and concerned in an era of McCarthyism that their social science research might be confused with socialism.

been hierarchical structures. Thus bureaucracy has always been one of the central concerns of organization theory. But before we can deal with this concern, we must explore the many meanings of the word itself.

All Government Offices

First, "the bureaucracy" is the totality of government offices or *bureaus* (a French word meaning "office") that constitute the permanent government of a state—that is, those public functions that continue irrespective of changes in political leadership. Modern Western-style bureaucracies originated in Europe when the governing affairs of centralized autocratic regimes became so complicated that it became necessary to delegate the king's authority to his representatives. American bureaucracy has never fully recovered from its nondemocratic European origins. This has allowed politicians to continually rejoice in attacking the "unresponsive" bureaucracy. At the same time, "good government" groups often contend that, once in office, politicians make the bureaucracy all too responsive to special interests instead of leaving it alone to impartially administer the programs for which it was originally established.

Interests ■
A group of persons who share a common cause, which puts them into political competition with other groups or interests. Thus, the oil interests want better tax breaks for the oil industry, and the consumer interests want new laws protecting consumer rights vis-à-vis the business interests, who want fewer laws protecting consumer rights.

All Public Officials

Second, "the bureaucracy" refers to all of the public officials of a government—both high and low, elected and appointed. Thus the secretary of the treasury is a bureaucrat, but so is a lowly secretary in the Treasury Department. We typically think of a bureaucrat sitting at a desk shuffling papers on behalf of the citizenry. But most bureaucrats lead far more active lives. They are police officers, teachers, firefighters, scientists, and astronauts. While many fit the image and do sit behind a desk all day— somebody has to shuffle the papers—they are no more representative of bureaucrats as a whole than are other major categories such as trash collectors and street maintenance workers. However, the paper shufflers often finish the day cleaner.

A General Invective

Third, bureaucracy is often used as a general invective to refer to any inefficient organization encumbered by red tape. We've all heard the jokes. There was the malfunctioning rocket that was named "the civil servant" because it would not work and you could not fire it. When a voter registration card arrived in the mail for her recently deceased husband, the bereaved widow dutifully informed the Bureau of Elections of his passing and promptly received an absentee ballot for him. Then there is the story of the spy sent to discover which Washington agencies could be sabotaged. He reports back, "Suggested plan hopeless. Americans brilliantly prepared. For each agency we destroy two more are already fully staffed and doing exactly the same work." There is a germ of truth in all these stories and their ilk. Some rockets do not work. Some agencies send letters (and even checks) to the dead. And duplication of efforts is not uncommon. This does not mean that the government organization involved is always inefficient. Many government agencies have long-standing reputations for efficient operations. We do not hear much about them because normal everyday efficiency does not generate much publicity—and bad publicity is a long-lasting stain. For example, NASA (as the case study in Chapter 2 showed) has an extraordinary reputation for efficient operations. But the space shuttle disasters of 1986 and 2003 have been long-lasting stains. Nevertheless, efficient operations, whether in NASA, the Postal Service, or your municipality, are the norm in government. But widespread perceptions of inefficiency have given an additional meaning to the word *bureaucracy*.

Max Weber's Structural Arrangements

Fourth, bureaucracy refers to a specific set of structural arrangements. The dominant structural definition of bureaucracy—indeed, the point of departure for all further analyses on the subject—is that of the German sociologist **Max Weber**, who used an "ideal type" approach to extrapolate from the real world the central core of features that would characterize the most fully developed bureaucratic form of organization. This ideal type is neither a description of reality nor a statement of normative preference; it is merely an identification of the major variables or features that characterize bureaucracy. The fact that such features might not be fully present in a given organization does not necessarily imply that the organization is not bureaucratic. It may be an immature rather than a fully developed bureaucracy. At some point, however, it may be necessary to conclude that the characteristics of bureaucracy are so lacking in an organization that it could neither reasonably be termed bureaucratic nor be expected to produce patterns of bureaucratic behavior.

Weber's ideal type of bureaucracy possesses the following characteristics:

1. The bureaucrats must be free as individuals; they can only be bossed around with respect to the impersonal duties of their offices.
2. The bureaucrats are arranged in a clearly defined hierarchy of offices, the traditional scalar chain wherein every bureaucrat has an unambiguous place—and knows his or her place!
3. The functions of each office are clearly specified in writing.
4. The bureaucrats accept and maintain their appointments freely—without duress. Slave bureaucrats, while once fashionable in the Ottoman Empire and Imperial China, are an inherent contradiction except within military or prison organizations.
5. Appointments to office are made on the basis of technical qualifications, which ideally are substantiated by examinations administered by the appointing authority, a university, or both.
6. The bureaucrats receive money salaries and pension rights, which reflect the varying levels of the hierarchy. While the bureaucrats are free to leave the organization, they can be removed from their offices only under previously stated, specific circumstances.
7. The office must be the bureaucrat's sole or at least major occupation.
8. A career system is essential; while promotion may be the result of either seniority or merit, it must be premised on the judgment of hierarchical superiors.
9. The bureaucrats do not have property rights to their office nor any personal claim to the resources that go with it.
10. The bureaucrat's conduct must be subject to systematic control and strict discipline.

Max Weber (1864–1920) ■ The German sociologist who produced an analysis of an ideal-type bureaucracy that is still the most influential statement—the point of departure for all further analyses—on the subject. Weber also pioneered the concepts of the Protestant ethic, charismatic authority, and a value-free approach to social research.

While Weber's structural identification of bureaucratic organization (first published in 1922) is perhaps the most comprehensive statement on the subject in the literature of the social sciences, it is not always considered satisfactory as an intellectual construct. For example, Anthony Downs, in *Inside Bureaucracy*, argued that at least two elements should be added to Weber's definition. First, the organization must be large. According to Downs, "Any organization in which the highest-ranking members know less than half of the other members can be considered large." Second, most of the organization's output cannot be "directly or indirectly evaluated in any markets external to the organization by means of voluntary **quid pro quo** transactions." This latter element is what economist Ludwig von Mises meant when he said that the work of a government bureaucracy had "no cash value." It is not that the "successful handling of public affairs has no value, but that it has no price on the market, that its value cannot be realized in a market transaction and consequently cannot be expressed in terms of money."

Definitions of bureaucracy apply equally to organizations in the public as well as the private sector. However, public sector bureaucracies tend to operate in a somewhat different climate from those in the private sector. What has come to be known as the "third sector"—not-for-profit organizations such as hospitals, universities, and foundations—would analytically be classed with public organizations because of the lack of free-market forces on them. In short, bureaucracy is best conceptualized as a specific form of organization, and public bureaucracy should be considered a special variant of bureaucratic organization. Yet in the popular imagination a bureaucracy is any organization in which people arranged in hierarchical ranks have to obey lots of rules.

Quid pro quo ■
A Latin phrase meaning "something for something"— initially meaning the exchange of one thing for another. In politics it suggests actions taken because of some promised action in return.

NEOCLASSICAL ORGANIZATION THEORY

There is no precise definition for *neoclassical* in the context of organization theory. The general connotation is that of a theoretical perspective that revises and/ or is critical of classical organization theory—particularly for minimizing issues related to the humanness of organizational members, coordination needs among administrative units, internal-external organizational relations, and organizational decision processes. The major writers of the classical school did their most significant work before World War II. The neoclassical writers gained their reputations as organization theorists by attacking the classical writers after the end of the war. They sought to "save" classical theory by introducing modifications based on research findings in the behavioral sciences.

The neoclassical school was important first because it initiated the theoretical movement away from the oversimplistic mechanistic views of the classical school. The neoclassicists challenged some of the basic tenets of the classical school head on—and they did so when the classical school was the only school. Organization theory and classical organization theory were effectively synonymous.

Second, in the process of challenging the classical school, the neoclassicists raised issues and initiated theories that became central to the foundations of most of the schools or approaches to organization theory that have followed. Thus the neoclassical school was a critically important forerunner to the "power and

TABLE 6.1

Classical Organization Theory: A Chronology

1776   Adam Smith's *The Wealth of Nations* discusses the optimal organization of a pin factory. This becomes the most famous and influential statement on the economic rationale of the factory system and the division of labor.

1832   Charles Babbage's *On the Economy of Machinery and Manufactures* anticipates many of the notions of the scientific management movement, including "basic principles of management" such as the division of labor.

1855   Daniel C. McCallum, in his annual report as superintendent of the New York and Erie Railroad Company, states his six basic principles of administration; the first was to use internally generated data for managerial purposes.

1885   Captain Henry Metcalfe, the manager of an army arsenal, publishes *The Cost of Manufactures and the Administration of Workshops, Public and Private,* which asserts that there is a "science of administration" that is based on principles discoverable by diligent observation.

1886   Henry R. Towne's paper "The Engineer as an Economist," read to the American Society of Mechanical Engineers, encourages the scientific management movement.

1903   Frederick W. Taylor publishes *Shop Management.*

1904   Frank B. and Lillian M. Gilbreth marry; they then proceed to produce many of the pioneering works on time-and-motion study, scientific management, and applied psychology, as well as 12 children.

1910   Louis D. Brandeis, an associate of Frederick W. Taylor (and later a U.S. Supreme Court justice), coins and popularizes the term "scientific management" in his Eastern Rate Case testimony before the Interstate Commerce Commission by arguing that railroad rate increases should be denied because the railroads could save "a million dollars a day" by applying scientific management methods.

1911   Frederick W. Taylor publishes *The Principles of Scientific Management.*

1912   Harrington Emerson publishes *The Twelve Principles of Efficiency,* which put forth an interdependent but coordinated management system.

1916   In France, Henri Fayol publishes his *General and Industrial Management,* the first complete theory of management.

1922   Max Weber's structural definition of bureaucracy is published posthumously; it uses an "ideal type" approach to extrapolate from the real world the central core of features that characterizes the most fully developed form of bureaucratic organization.

1931   James Mooney and Alan Reiley in *Onward Industry* (republished in 1939 as *The Principles of Organization*) show how the newly discovered "principles of organization" have really been known since ancient times.

1937   Luther Gulick's "Notes on the Theory of Organization" uses a mnemonic device (POSDCORB) to draw attention to the functional elements of the work of an executive.

politics" and the "organizational culture" perspective discussed in Chapter 2 and the "systems theory" school discussed later in this chapter.

Herbert A. Simon's Influence

Herbert A. Simon was the most influential of the neoclassical organization theorists. He was the first to seriously challenge the principles approach proposed by Fayol, Gulick, and others. (His assertion that those principles were more like proverbs was discussed earlier in this chapter.) Simon was also a firm believer that decision making should be the focus of a new "administrative science." He wrote that organization theory is, in fact, the theory of the **bounded rationality** of human beings who **satisfice** because they do not have the intellectual capacity to maximize. He was also the first analyst to draw a distinction between "programmed" and "unprogrammed" organizational decisions; he highlighted the importance of the distinction for management information systems. His work on administrative science and decision making went in two major directions: First, he was a pioneer in developing the "science" of improved organizational decision making through quantitative methods such as operations research and computer technology. Second, and perhaps even more important, he was a leader in studying the processes by which administrative organizations make decisions.

Bounded rationality ■
The "bounds" that people put on their decisions. Because truly rational research on any problem can never be complete, humans make decisions on satisfactory as opposed to optimal information.

Satisfice ■
Accept a satisfactory and sufficient amount of information on which to base a decision. Herbert Simon invented this word to help explain his theory of bounded rationality.

The Impact of Sociology

One of the major themes of the neoclassical organization theorists was that organizations did not—indeed, could not—exist as self-contained islands isolated from their environments. As might be expected, the first significant efforts to "open up" organizations (theoretically speaking) came from analysts whose professional identity required them to take a broad view of things—from sociologists. One such analyst was Philip Selznick, who in his 1948 *American Sociological Review* article, "Foundations of the Theory of Organization," asserted that while it is possible to describe and design organizations in a purely rational manner, such efforts can never hope to cope with the nonrational aspects of organizational behavior. In contrast with the classical theorists, Selznick maintained that organizations were made up of individuals whose goals and aspirations might not necessarily coincide with the formal goals of the organization—as opposed to consisting of just a number of positions for management to control. Neoclassical writers such as Simon and Selznick opened up the field of organization theory. Thereafter, it would be inherently interdisciplinary and open to the perspectives of sociology, cultural anthropology, political science, business administration, economics and, of course, public administration.

"MODERN" STRUCTURAL ORGANIZATION THEORY

Usually when someone refers to the structure of an organization, that person is talking about the relatively stable relationships among the positions and groups of positions (units) that comprise the organization. Structural organization theory is concerned with vertical differentiations—hierarchical levels of organizational authority and coordination, and horizontal differentiations between organizational units—for example, between product or service lines, geographical areas, or skills. The organization chart is the ever-present "tool" of a structural organization theorist.

Basic Assumptions

The label "modern" is used to distinguish the more recent writers of structural organization theory from the pre–World War II classical theorists such as Taylor and Weber. Management analysts Lee Bolman and Terrence Deal identified the basic assumptions of the "modern" structural school:

1. Organizations are rational institutions whose primary purpose is to accomplish established objectives; rational organizational behavior is achieved best through systems of defined rules and formal authority. Organizational control and coordination are key for maintaining organizational rationality.

2. There is a "best" structure for any organization—or at least a most appropriate structure—in light of its given objectives, the environmental conditions surrounding it (for example, its markets, the competition, and the extent of government regulation), the nature of its products and/or services (the "best" structure for a management consulting firm probably is substantially different than that for a certified public accounting firm), and the technology of the production processes (a coal mining company has a different "best structure" than the manufacturer of computer microcomponents).

3. Specialization and the division of labor increase the quality and quantity of production—particularly in highly skilled operations and professions.

4. Most problems in an organization result from structural flaws and can be solved by changing the structure.

Mechanistic and Organic Systems

The most immediate issue in the design of any organization is the question of structure. What should it look like? How should it work? How will it deal with the most common structural questions of specialization, departmentalization, span of control, and the coordination and control of specialized units? A famous example of structural organization theory in action was provided by two British researchers: Tom Burns and G. M. Stalker of the Tavistock Institute in London. They developed a widely cited theory of "mechanistic" and "organic systems" of organization, while examining rapid technological change in the British and Scottish electronics industry.

Burns and Stalker found that stable conditions may suggest the use of a mechanistic form of organization, where a traditional pattern of hierarchy, reliance on formal rules and regulations, vertical communications, and structured decision making is possible. However, more dynamic conditions—situations in which the environment changes rapidly—require the use of an organic form of organization where there is less rigidity, more participation, and more reliance on workers to define and redefine their positions and relationships. For example, technological creativity, an essential ingredient in an organic system, requires an organizational climate and management systems that are supportive of innovation. The impacts of these two organizational forms on individuals are substantially different. Supervisors and managers find that the mechanistic form provides them with a greater sense of security in dealing with their environment than the organic form, which introduces much greater uncertainty. Thus either form may be appropriate in particular situations.

SYSTEMS THEORY

Systems analysis ■
The methodologically rigorous collection, manipulation, and evaluation of data on social units (as small as an organization or as large as a polity) to determine the best way to improve their functioning and to aid a decision maker in selecting a preferred choice among alternatives.

Since World War II, the social sciences have increasingly used **systems analysis** to examine their assertions about human behavior. The field of management, which to the extent that it deals with human resources can be said to be a social science, has been no exception.

Systems theory views an organization as a complex set of dynamically intertwined and interconnected elements, including its inputs, processes, outputs, feedback loops, and the environment in which it operates and with which it continuously interacts. Any change in any element of the system causes changes in other elements. The interconnections tend to be complex, dynamic (constantly changing), and often unknown. Thus, when management makes decisions involving one organizational element, unanticipated impacts usually occur throughout the organizational system. Systems theorists study these interconnections, frequently using organizational decision processes and information and control systems as their focal points for analysis.

Whereas classical organization theory tends to be one-dimensional and somewhat simplistic, systems theories tend to be multidimensional and complex in their assumptions about organizational cause-and-effect relationships. The classicalists viewed organizations as static (unchanging) structures; systems theorists see organizations as continually changing processes of interactions among organizational and environmental elements. Organizations, not being static, are in constantly shifting states of dynamic equilibrium. The maintenance of this dynamic equilibrium was the task referred to in the title of the 1938 classic *The Functions of the Executive*, by **Chester I. Barnard**. Barnard viewed organizations as cooperative systems where "the function of the executive" was to maintain the dynamic equilibrium between the needs of the organization and the needs of its employees. In order to do this, management had to be aware of the interdependent nature of the formal and informal organization. Barnard's analysis of the significance and role of informal organizations provided the theoretical foundations for a whole generation of empirical research.

Chester I. Barnard (1886–1961) ■
The Bell System executive closely associated with the Harvard Business School, best known for his sociological analyses of organizations that encouraged and foreshadowed the post–World War II behavioral revolution.

Cybernetics

Because organizations are adaptive systems that are integral parts of their environments, they must adjust to changes in their environment if they are to survive; in turn, virtually all of their decisions and actions affect their environment. Norbert Wiener's model of an organization as an adaptive system, from his 1948 book *Cybernetics*, epitomizes the basic theoretical perspectives of the systems perspective. *Cybernetics*, from a Greek word meaning "steersman," was used by Wiener to mean the multidisciplinary study of the structures and functions of control and information processing systems in animals and machines. The basic concept behind cybernetics is self-regulation—biological, social, or technological systems that can identify problems, do something about them, and then receive feedback to adjust themselves automatically. Wiener, a mathematician, developed the concept of cybernetics while working on antiaircraft systems during World War II. Variations on this simple model of a system have been used extensively by systems theorists for many years—particularly around the development and use of management information systems.

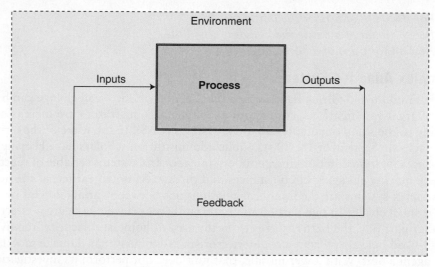

FIGURE 6.1

Norbert Wiener's model of an organization as an adaptive system, from *Cybernetics*

The systems approach is strongly cause-and-effect oriented (logical-positivist) in its philosophy and methods. In these respects, systems theories have close ties to Taylor's scientific management approach. Whereas Taylor used quantitative scientific methods to find "the one best way," the systems theorist uses quantitative scientific methods to identify cause-effect relationships and to find optimal solutions. In this sense, the conceptual approaches and purposes between the two perspectives are strikingly similar. Thus systems approaches are often called management sciences or administrative sciences. However, one should never make the unpardonable error of calling them scientific management!

Systems thinking is critically important because the whole world, in essence, is a collection of interrelated systems. Nothing happens in isolation. Your reading of this page is made possible by your visual system. Your turning to the next page is a function of your nervous system and muscular system—which is also related to your visual system. How else would you know when to turn the page? The systems of the world seem so infinite that another theory—chaos theory—has evolved to explain why they are often unexplainable. This theory postulates that the tiniest change in the smallest part of a system can eventually produce enormous effects. In weather forecasting this has become known as the butterfly effect. According to James Gleick, this is "the notion that a butterfly stirring the air today in Peking can transform storm systems next month in New York." All of chaos theory seeks to explain how the smallest elements of a system, whether weather or organizational, can have the biggest consequences. Yet all this was summed up by Benjamin Franklin in a 1758 issue of *Poor Richard's Almanac*:

For the want of a nail the shoe was lost,
For the want of a shoe the horse was lost,
For the want of a horse the rider was lost,

For the want of a rider the battle was lost,
For the want of a battle the kingdom was lost—
And all for want of a horseshoe-nail.

Complex Adaptive Systems

While Franklin and Gleick have pushed the theory that one small change can have much larger ramifications, contemporary public administrators are increasingly turning to the study of complex adaptive systems (CAS). In the wake of the terrorist attacks on September 11, 2001, public administration scholars have become increasingly interested in thinking about organizations as systems capable of reacting to very quickly changing circumstances and threats. As noted earlier, at the heart of complex systems are the nonlinear relationships between variables. This means that a small change in one part of an organization may have a very great effect on another part (i.e., the butterfly effect). In the area of homeland security, removing a well-liked field agent from a counterterrorism assignment may damage morale in that agent's unit. With lower morale, that unit does not perform its investigations as well, thus missing critical leads that could have uncovered a terrorist plot that caused major loss of life. This example demonstrates how a relatively minor and well-meaning act can end up causing significant negative results. But how can we foresee such seemingly unpredictable outcomes? While difficult, methods such as laboratory experiments and computer modeling have showed promising results in predicting what will happen when even the smallest changes occur. Of course, such approaches to organization management are not easy to complete, so their use in many organizations may just have to wait.

> **A CASE STUDY | The Critical Importance of Administrative Doctrine**
>
> All organizations are guided by a doctrine of management that reflects basic values. Doctrines and values may be stated or unstated, conscious or unconscious, advertent or inadvertent, but they are always there. Without a guiding doctrine and compatible behavioral techniques for implementing it, no management program can be viable. The first administrative doctrine was that contained in the brutality of military discipline: "Do this or die." Indeed, one of the main reasons officers traditionally carried pistols was to shoot their own men if they were not sufficiently enthusiastic about obeying an order—especially one involving great danger. As Edward Gibbon wrote in *The Decline and Fall of the Roman Empire* (1776), "It was an inflexible maxim of Roman discipline that a good soldier should dread his own officers far more than the enemy."
>
> A more modern example of a doctrine is **Henry Ford's** famous simplistic dictum: "All that we ask of the men is that they do the work which is set before them." With Ford there was an underlying assumption that employees who do not respond adequately to the "work which is set before them" should be dismissed. (A much better alternative than being shot!) The

Henry Ford (1863–1947) ■ The founder of Ford Motor Company, which first mass-produced automobiles on a moving assembly line.

behavioral technique used here is the same as that applied to those small experimental animals who have spent generations running through mazes for
psychologists. The more work, the more cheese.

More sophisticated doctrines are needed when meaningful and fulfilling work for its employees is a central goal of the organization. Here the
underlying assumptions are radically different. Wages are not the only reason
for working! Strategies that emerge from this management value and philosophy
are more conducive to long-term organizational effectiveness and productivity.
Just as religious doctrine often defines an individual's attitude toward life, a
managerial doctrine defines management's values and attitude toward work
and people at work. By the exercise of its doctrinal philosophy, management
earns a reciprocal attitude from others toward their responsibilities. This is
why doctrines, values, and attitudes on the part of management so often become self-fulfilling prophecies. Employees and managers, like students and
teachers, tend to live up (or down) to expectations.

But doctrine and attitudes do far more than affect the morale and performance of individual employees; they are part of the culture of the organization, and the organizational culture affects the overall competence or
incompetence of an organization. When managers are heavily constrained
by official doctrine, by standard operating procedures, and by "the book,"
they cannot use discretion to respond to changing circumstances. Faced with
an obvious right decision that is contrary to formal policy, they all too often
dutifully make the wrong decision, feeling that they have no choice. This is
a faulty conception of managerial responsibility. Any organization that does
not allow its managers to appropriately respond to changing conditions is
headed for a fall. It is this conception, this philosophy, this doctrine of leadership as expressed by the organization's culture and as manifest in the organization's policies that ultimately determines success or failure, victory or
defeat, competence or incompetence.

Administrative doctrines resemble the paradigms of Thomas S. Kuhn. In
his landmark 1962 book *The Structure of Scientific Revolutions*, Kuhn explained that as the natural sciences progressed, they amassed a body of ever-
changing theory. Scientific advances were based not on the accumulation of
knowledge and facts but rather on a dominant paradigm (or model) used in
any specific period to explain the phenomena under study. Rather than refuting previous theories, each paradigm would build on the body of relevant
knowledge and theories. Once a paradigm was accepted by consensus among
current scholars, it would last as long as it was useful. Ultimately, it would be
replaced by a more relevant and useful paradigm; this process of replacement
was Kuhn's "scientific revolution."

While paradigms have their own timeframes and contents, they overlap
both in time and content because they are constantly evolving. In a parallel
sense, doctrinal development in administration has been inherently cyclical.

(*continued*)

Effectiveness ■
Traditionally, the extent to which an organization accomplishes some predetermined goal or objective; more recently, the overall performance of an organization from the viewpoint of some strategic constituency. Effectiveness is not entirely dependent on the efficiency of a program because program outputs may increase without necessarily increasing effectiveness.

Productivity ■
The measured relationship between the quantity (and quality) of results produced and the quantity of resources required for production. Productivity is, in essence, a measure of the work efficiency of an individual, a work unit, or a whole organization.

Morale ■
The collective attitude of the workforce toward their work environment and a crude measure of the organizational climate.

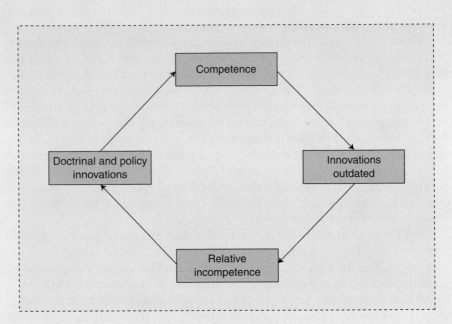

FIGURE 6.2

The cyclical nature of doctrinal and policy development

A successful innovation by reformers is followed by a period of increased effectiveness, at least until competing organizations adopt similar reforms. But over time, advancing technologies and changing environments allow the innovation to deteriorate relative to other arrangements—first to become less competent, then to become incompetent. After an innovative change remedies the problem, the cycle of competence and incompetence repeats. This "time lag" phenomenon is similar to the traditional boom-and-bust business cycle, with incompetence occurring when the cycle is in recession. Thus maintaining organizational competence is a never-ending struggle.

This is why competing organizations tend to look like each other over time. Whenever an innovation earns a reputation for being successful, it is copied by others wishing to be equally successful. But equality in structure and equipment is not always enough to ensure being a successful competitor. A famous example will illustrate. During the spring of 1940, Nazi Germany conquered France using tanks and troops in a **blitzkrieg** formation. Germany won despite the fact that France not only had more troops, but also significantly more tanks that were of better quality. What made the difference was the fact that the Germans had a better tactical doctrine for the use of their tanks—in massed assaults as opposed to piecemeal support for infantry.

Remember that the military, the seminal administrative institution of all societies, only has to be led in battle a relatively few days of any year. But it

Blitzkrieg ■
German for "lightning war," the tactical method used by the German army in the invasion of Poland, France, and the Soviet Union during World War II. The classic blitzkrieg campaign involves swift strikes with tanks and planes and a series of army columns exploiting weak spots in the enemy line. Advance units pass behind the enemy, destroying its lines of communication and disrupting unit cohesion.

has to be administered every day. Societies may be protected by their standing armies or navies, but armed forces cannot stand or float without administrative institutions to support them. It is often true, as Mao Zedong famously said, that "political power grows out of the barrel of a gun." But political power is empty and meaningless without concomitant economic and administrative power. Historian Paul Kennedy in his *The Rise and Fall of the Great Powers* demonstrated how in modern times ultimate victory went to the state that was economically strong. Those that were merely militarily strong—Austria, France, Great Britain, Germany, Spain, and the Soviet Union—all suffered from "imperial overstretch" and declined as great powers.

Revolutionaries with their guns can start a revolution, but only the administrators who follow in their wake can solidify and complete it. Thus all conquering armies have necessarily been followed by hordes of bureaucrats. Napoléon solidified the French Revolution of 1789 with the administrative reforms embodied in the Code Napoléon and the creation of a merit-based civil service. The U.S. Constitution of 1787, which followed the Revolution of 1776, still provides the administrative framework of American government. The Russian Revolution of 1917 led to the administrative apparatus of a socialist state that, with its **command economy**, was so cumbersome and inefficient that a subsequent revolution in 1991 replaced it with a regime that had greater hopes for efficiency. All the political revolutions in Eastern Europe during the late 1980s, while initially politically motivated, increasingly became administrative revolutions to secure for their people the blessings of a new administrative doctrine that allows a state's economy to function with the greater efficiency offered by a free market.

Every major political revolution—from the American to the French to the Russian—can be said to have been caused by the same thing—poor public administration. Remember that the large middle section of the American Declaration of Independence is a list consisting largely of administrative complaints against George III, the British king. For example, the Declaration asserted that the king "has obstructed the administration of justice," has imposed "taxes on us without our consent," and "has erected a multitude of new offices and sent hither swarms of officers to harass our people, and eat out their substance." Simply put: Happy and prosperous people do not revolt. Revolutions are caused by incompetent public administration, and they are made by disgruntled consumers of government services. This is why an effective public administration doctrine is so important—because no society can live in peace and prosperity, or prevail in war, without it. It is a matter of national security!

For Discussion: *Why is an effective administrative doctrine essential for the successful public administration of a state? Why is the competence/incompetence cycle of large organizations so much like the boom and bust of the traditional business cycle?* ◢

Command economy ∎
The traditional economic model offered by communism wherein all industry is controlled by a central government that makes all decisions and appoints all managers.

SUMMARY

Modern management has its origins in the military institutions of the ancient world. While many ancient kingdoms, such as Egypt and China, had sophisticated administrative institutions, the core features of modern public administration in the Western world were first found in the Roman Empire.

All organizations are guided by a doctrine of management that reflects the basic values of the cultural environment. No management program can be viable without such guiding doctrines and compatible behavioral techniques for implementing them. The first doctrines were authoritarian and paralleled the brutality of military discipline. Since antiquity the military has evolved principles about how its authoritarian organizations were best managed. Those elements having civilian applications have been incorporated into principles of management. Thus concepts once military—such as span of control and unity of command—are now thoroughly civilian as well.

Advances in organization theory are not based on the accumulation of knowledge and facts but rather on a dominant paradigm (or model) used in any specific period. Rather than refuting previous theories, each paradigm builds on the body of relevant knowledge and theories. Once a paradigm is accepted by consensus, it lasts as long as it is useful. Ultimately, it is replaced by a more relevant and useful paradigm.

Classical organization theory (which includes bureaucracy), as its name implies, was the first theory of its kind, is considered traditional, and continues to be the base on which other schools of organization theory have been built.

In the latter part of the nineteenth century, American industrial engineers began asserting that factory workers could be much more productive if their work was designed scientifically; their job was to conduct the research and do the planning that would make the organization more competitive relative to other organizations. Thus scientific management grew out of engineering. The progressive reformers were able to use scientific management as the core rationale for their call to separate politics from administration.

The pattern of development within public administration between World Wars I and II became known as a "period of orthodoxy." This ideology held that the work of government could be neatly divided into decision making and execution (the politics–administration dichotomy) and that administration was a science with discoverable principles (scientific management). This dichotomy would hardly have been possible if scientific management had not evolved when it did.

All the subsequent perspectives on organization theory—for example, the neoclassical, the "modern" structuralists, and systems theory—are essentially revisions and expansions of the classical writers. There is no consensus on what constitutes knowledge in organization theory. Anyone who studies this subject is free to join the school of organization theory of his or her choice and is free to accept the philosophic boundaries of one group of serious thinkers over another. No single perspective may deserve your loyalty because each contains important information and insights that are useful in differing circumstances.

REVIEW QUESTIONS

1. Why is it that so many of the principles and practices of public administration have their origin in military organizations?
2. Why are classical organization theory and scientific management still relevant today?
3. What is the essence of Max Weber's concept of bureaucracy?

4. How can systems theory be used to explain the workings of a government organization?
5. How does the concept of administrative doctrine help to explain the success or failure of any given organization?

KEY CONCEPTS

Administrative doctrine   The rules, procedures, and ways of doing things that reflect the basic values of an organization.

Bureaucracy   The totality of government officers; all of a government's employees; a general invective to refer to any inefficient organization encumbered by red tape or a specific set of structural arrangements.

Classical theory   The original theory about organizations that closely resemble military structures.

Neoclassical theory   Theoretical perspectives that revise, expand, or are critical of classical organization theory.

Organization   A group of people who jointly work to achieve at least one common goal.

Organization theory   A set of propositions that seeks to explain or predict how groups and individuals behave in differing organizational arrangements.

Paradigm   An intellectual model for a situation or condition.

POSDCORB   The mnemonic device invented by Luther Gulick in 1937 to call attention to the various functional elements of the work of a chief executive.

Principles of management   Fundamental truths or working hypotheses that serve as guidelines to management thinking and action.

Scientific management   A systematic approach to managing that seeks the "one best way" of accomplishing any given task by discovering the fastest, most efficient, and least fatiguing production methods.

Systems theory   A view of an organization as a complex set of dynamically intertwined and interconnected elements, including its inputs, processes, outputs, feedback loops, and the environment in which it operates and with which it continuously interacts.

MySearchLab® EXERCISES

Apply what you learned in this chapter on MySearchLab (*www.mysearchlab.com*).

BIBLIOGRAPHY

Appleby, Paul (1945). *Big Democracy*. New York: Knopf.

Barker, Ernest (1944). *The Development of Public Services in Western Europe, 1660–1930*. London: Oxford University Press.

Bolman, L. G., and T. E. Deal (1984). *Modern Approaches to Understanding and Managing Organizations*. San Francisco: Jossey-Bass.

Brodie, Bernard (1973). *War and Politics*. New York: Oxford University Press.

Burnham, James (1941). *The Managerial Revolution*. New York: John Day.

Burns, T., and G. M. Stalker (1961). *The Management of Innovation*. London: Tavistock Publications.

Byrne, John A. (1993). *The Whiz Kids: The Founding Fathers of American Business—and the Legacy They Left Us*. New York: Doubleday.

Downs, Anthony (1967). *Inside Bureaucracy*. Boston: Little, Brown.

Drucker, Peter F. (1950). *The New Society: The Anatomy of the Industrial Order*. New York: Harper.

Gerth, H. H., and C. Wright Mills, eds. (1946). *From Max Weber: Essays in Sociology*. New York: Oxford University Press.

Gladden, E. N. (1972). *A History of Public Administration*, 2 vols. London: Frank Cass.

Gleick, James (1987). *Chaos: Making a New Science*. New York: Viking.

Grant, Michael (1991). *The Founders of the Western World: A History of Greece and Rome*. New York: Charles Scribner's.

Gulick, Luther, and Lyndall Urwick (1937). *Papers on the Science of Administration*. New York: Institute of Public Administration.

Handel, Michael I. (1992). *Masters of War: Sun-Tzu, Clausewitz, and Jomini*. London: Frank Cass.

Henry, Nicholas (1975). *Public Administration and Public Affairs*. Englewood Cliffs, NJ: Prentice Hall.

Jomini, Antoine-Henri (1862). *The Art of War*. Philadelphia: Lippincott.

———. (1805). *Treatise on Great Military Operations*. New York: Van Nostrand.

Keegan, John (1993). *A History of Warfare*. New York: Knopf.

Kennedy, Paul (1987). *The Rise and Fall of the Great Powers*. New York: Random House.

Kuhn, T. S. (1970). *The Structure of Scientific Revolutions*, 2nd ed., enlarged. Chicago: University of Chicago Press.

Lilienthal, David E. (1944). *TVA: Democracy on the March*. New York: Harper & Bros.

Livingston, J. Sterling (1969). "Pygmalion in Management." *Harvard Business Review* (July–August).

Marini, Frank E. (1971). *Toward a New Public Administration*. San Francisco: Chandler.

Marrow, Alfred J. (1969). *The Practical Theorist: The Life and Works of Kurt Lewin*. New York: Basic Books.

McCurdy, Howard E. (1986). *Public Administration: A Bibliographic Guide to the Literature*. New York: Marcel Dekker.

Mises, Ludwig von (1944). *Bureaucracy*. New Haven, CT: Yale University Press.

Osborne, David, and Ted Gaebler (1992). *Reinventing Government*. Reading, MA: Addison-Wesley.

Ostrom, Vincent. (1974). *The Intellectual Crisis in American Public Administration*, rev. ed. Tuscaloosa: University of Alabama Press.

Ott, J. Steven (1989). *The Organizational Culture Perspective*. Pacific Grove, CA: Brooks/Cole.

Seckler-Hudson, Catheryn. (1955). *Organization and Management: Theory and Practice*. Washington, DC: The American University Press.

Shaw, George Bernard (1944). *Everybody's Political What's What*. New York: Dodd, Mead.

Simon, Herbert A. (1991). *Models of My Life*. New York: Basic Books.

———. (1946). "The Proverbs of Administration." *Public Administration Review* (Winter).

Smiddy, Harold F., and Lionel Naum (1954). "Evolution of a Science of Managing in America," *Management Science* 1 (October).

Taylor, Frederick W. (1911). *The Principles of Scientific Management*. New York: Harper.

Waldo, Dwight (1948). *The Administrative State: A Study of the Political Theory of American Public Administration*. New York: Ronald Press.

Wiener, Norbert (1948). *Cybernetics*. Cambridge, MA: MIT Press.

Wilson, John A. (1951). *The Culture of Ancient Egypt*. Chicago: University of Chicago Press.

Wren, Daniel A. (1987). *The Evolution of Management Thought*, 3rd ed. New York: Wiley.

RECOMMENDED BOOKS

Bovaird, Tony, and Elke Loffer (2009). *Public Management and Governance*. New York: Oxford University Press. An examination of public management under changing conditions and within a mixed economy structure.

Kanigel, Robert (1997). *The One Best Way: Frederick Winslow Taylor and the Enigma of Efficiency.* New York: Viking. More than you ever wanted to know about the man, his times, his movement, and his continuing influence.

Merkle, Judith A. (1980). *Management and Ideology: The Legacy of the International Scientific Management Movement.* Berkeley: University of California Press. A highly readable historical analysis of the continuing influence of Frederick Taylor and scientific management in business and public administration.

Shafritz, Jay M., J. Steven Ott, and Yong Suk Jang, eds. (2010). *Classics of Organization Theory*, 7th ed. Boston, MA: Wadsworth. A comprehensive collection of the most important writings on organization from ancient times to the present, from Socrates to postmodernism.

Wren, Daniel A., and Ronald G. Greenwood (1998). *Management Innovators: The People and Ideas That Have Shaped Modern Business.* New York: Oxford University Press. A collection of minibiographies of all the major thinkers on and experimenters with management techniques, from Eli Whitney to Peter Drucker.

RELATED WEB SITES

www.psy.cmu.edu/psy/faculty/hsimon/hsimon.html
Herbert A. Simon
Simon earned an international reputation as one of the founders of artificial intelligence. Simon's research extended from computer science into the realm of public administration and government. The Web site contains many of his key writings, lectures, and biographical background.

www.ispi.org
International Society for Performance Improvement (ISPI)
The ISPI works to improve productivity in the workplace. The site is dedicated to raising awareness of performance enhancement efforts.

www.faculty.rsu.edu/~felwell/Theorists/Weber/Whome.htm
Max Weber's home page
Weber's many accomplishments, including theories, writings, and research, are neatly organized in this web site. Among the highlights are thorough online resources on the rise of bureaucracies and civil service systems.

www.napoleonguide.com/leaders_napoleon.htm
Napoleonic Guide
The career, accomplishments, and quotes from the life of one of the world's most influential leaders are organized in this Web site. Napoléon's contributions to the deveopment of modern organizational structures and management are chronicled.

www.stevens.edu/library/collections/fwtaylor.html
Fredrick Taylor Archive
Taylor, often known as the founder of scientific management, had a great influence on developing methods to improve the efficiency of administration and public policy. This Web site maintains his archives, which consist largely of Taylor's personal and work-related correspondence, including his communications with companies interested in implementing scientific management.

Organizational Behavior

KEYNOTE: Henry II of England, Archbishop of Canterbury Thomas Becket, and Rufus Miles of the U.S. Bureau of the Budget: How a Medieval King, a Martyred Saint, and an American Bureaucrat Illustrate Miles's Law

Laws are enacted by governments to regulate our behavior in a seemingly infinite number of ways. Thus, citizens are obligated to stop at traffic lights when they turn red, pay their taxes on time, and not impose violence on fellow citizens who are merely rude or dishonorable.

Laws also govern the physical world. Isaac Newton (1642–1727) wrote that "To every action there is always opposed an equal reaction." This is known as Newton's "third law of motion." Because Newton discovered so many laws of the physical universe, he is widely considered to be the founder of modern physics.

Then there are laws that are not of the legal world or of the physical realm but that merely explain human behavior. This last category has a long tradition in both literature and the social sciences. For example, Jane Austen wrote as the first sentence in her novel *Pride and Prejudice* (1813) that "It is a truth universally acknowledged, that a single man in possession of a good fortune, must be in want of a wife." If you believe that, maybe you'll also believe what Leo Tolstoy (1828–1910) wrote in his novel *Anna Karenina* (1875): "Happy families are all alike; every unhappy family is unhappy in its own way." Hardly! Nevertheless, "laws" such as these have formed the plot of countless other novels, plays, films, and real-life adventures. But in their essence, they are not laws, but merely observations.

The observatory nature of such laws is their chief commonality and characteristic. A law, to be truly a law, must be universal; this is the chief characteristic of the laws of science and the goal of laws enacted by governments. Observational laws as offered by literature, however great, invariably fail this test of universality. Surely you have heard of single men "in possession of a good fortune" who are most decidedly not "in want of a wife."

For greater, if not universal, consistency in observational laws we must turn to the social sciences. The Austrian-born British philosopher Karl R. Popper (1902–1994) is generally credited with being the first to promulgate the law of unintended consequences, that conscious human efforts to accomplish one goal will lead to "as a rule, the indirect, the unintended and often the unwanted by-products of such actions." Thus, in 1964 the U.S. Congress passed the Civil Rights Act with its Title VII equal employment opportunity provisions intended to help African Americans; but the most immediate beneficiaries of this new law were white women. Not a bad result and not an "unwanted by-product," but unintended and unexpected.

Another observational law is Laurence J. Peter's (1919–1990) law from his book *The Peter Principle* (1969) that "In a hierarchy every employee tends to rise to his level of incompetence." Corollaries of the Peter principle hold that "in time, every post tends to be occupied by an employee who is incompetent to carry out its duties." In answer to the logical question of who then does the work that has to be done, Peter asserts that "work is accomplished by those employees who have not yet reached their level of incompetence."

The problems with observational laws is that they are, of course, not laws at all, merely strong tendencies, just as Peter suggests when he asserts in his principle that "every employee tends to rise." Nevertheless, even if such laws or principles are not to be depended on for all occasions, they remain extraordinarily useful in explaining and understanding human behavior.

The preceding discussion has been the preamble to our main story that "proves" one of the best-known observational laws in public policy and administration, Miles's Law. It was first put into words in the middle of the twentieth century in the United States, but it has always been applicable. We'll prove this by using a famous example of the law taking effect from England in the twelfth century.

Miles's Law

It is often said in relation to real estate that three things are critical in arriving at a sale price: location, location, and location. Of course, other factors enter into consideration. But none comes even close to location in importance. It's the same with the location of public policy studies, attitudes, and decisions. Nothing is more important in determining the nature of a public policy study, proposal, or decision than its source of origin.

This phenomenon is commonly known as Miles's Law, after a manager in the Bureau of the Budget (now the Office of Management and Budget) who first observed, "Where you stand depends on where you sit." Rufus E. Miles Jr. (1910–1996) chronicled the history of his law in a 1978 *Public Administration Review* article after it had been folk wisdom among federal bureaucrats for many years.

While admitting that his "concept was as old as Plato," the "phraseology" evolved from a specific sequence of events that occurred when Miles was supervising a group of budget examiners in the 1940s. One of the examiners was offered a higher-paying new job as a budget analyst at one of the agencies he had been reviewing. Because he had been particularly critical of this agency in his capacity as a reviewing budget examiner, he told Miles (his boss) that he would prefer to stay in his present job if his salary could be raised. Miles, ever concerned about federal expenditure levels, refused to support a raise of his subordinate's salary. So the subordinate resigned his position with the Bureau of the Budget to accept a higher-paying job with an agency he believed was not very efficient with its use of public funds.

Miles then remarked to the remaining workers under his supervision that soon the former employee would be defending the new budget policies that he had so vociferously criticized. His fellow budget examiners found this incredulous. After all, the exiting analyst was a man of strongly held judgments and great personal integrity. But Miles insisted this would happen and was proven correct by events. As his law states, "Where you stand depends upon where you sit."

Because the former employee was sitting elsewhere, his views would naturally evolve to reflect his new position. It wasn't a matter of ethics so much as it was a matter of perspective. In effect, no employee can be separated from the perspective of the particular responsibilities of his or her current position. Revised stances on issues and policies can be, and often are, the opposite of those previously held. This is not so much hypocrisy as it is loyalty to, and greater understanding of, one's new employer. World history offers no better example of this common phenomenon than the events that led up to the death and martyrdom of Thomas Becket during the reign of England's Henry II in the twelfth century.

The Rise of Thomas Becket

England's Thomas Becket (1118–1170) is one of those historical figures, such as ancient Rome's Julius Caesar and Victorian London's Jack the Ripper, almost as well known for how they have been treated by legend and literature than for what they did in real life. While Becket was a high achiever in what many consider to be a bad cause (that clergy should be above the common law), he remains a superb example of an extraordinarily successful bureaucrat. So successful that he earned the highest possible promotions (first as chancellor of England and then as archbishop of Canterbury); and so loyal that he willingly died for his agency (the church), was sainted for his sacrifice, and thus became the world's most famous example of Miles's Law in action. His rise and fall, and its relevance for today, is our story.

There are surprising commonalities between Becket's rise and that of Alexander Hamilton (whose face is on the $10 bill), who would come to be the first U.S. Secretary of the Treasury under President George Washington. Although Becket and Hamilton lived six centuries apart, on different continents, and in radically contrasting political cultures, consider that they both rose to prominence despite their middling births and modest prospects because of essentially the same set of circumstances. Mainly, they were handsome, brilliant boys with such intrinsic charm that they attracted the attention of wealthy men who gratuitously saw to it that they received the best education available. In both cases the precocious boys more than lived up to the expectations of their sponsors.

Hamilton, born in 1755, was sent from an obscure island in the West Indies (Nevis) to study at King's College (now Columbia University) in New York City in 1772, just in time to be a Revolutionary War agitator, an artillery officer in that war, and eventually General George Washington's most indispensable aide-de-camp. Becket was sent to the best monastic schools in England and later to the budding universities of Europe to study civil and canon law. His natural skills as an administrator and diplomat eventually led to his appointment as chancellor, the highest office in England after the king.

To complete this comparison, note that both Hamilton and Becket were physically brave: each excelled in combat on many occasions. While Hamilton as an American fought the English, Becket in full knightly armor had many occasions to literally charge on horseback into the frequently troublesome French. Eventually, each would die a violent death, but not in war: Hamilton was shot in 1804 in a duel with Aaron Burr, then the vice president of the United States; Becket by assassins sent by his king.

Which King Henry?

Literature has been extremely kind to the King Henrys of England. Henry VIII, with his six wives (two of whom he had executed), has been the subject of countless films and historical novels, plays, and real histories. Henry IV warranted two plays by Shakespeare. His son, Henry V, has the title role in Shakespeare's most popular history. (The Bard even wrote a three-play saga of Henry VI. The trilogy is such a lesser effort, however, that it's rarely performed. But it does contain one of Shakespeare's most famous public policy quotes: "Let's kill all the lawyers" [Part II, Act 4, Scene 2].)

Henry II (1133–1189), was the great-grandson of William the Conqueror, the Norman bastard (earlier known as "William the Bastard"), who brought his army from France and conquered England in 1066 by killing the then-resident king, Harold, during the Battle of Hastings. Henry II had to wait until the twentieth century to become a permanent fixture on the English-speaking stage in plays such as T. S. Eliot's *Murder in the Cathedral* (1935) and Jean Anouilh's *Becket or the Honor of God* (1960); and in big-budget Hollywood extravaganzas such as *Becket* (1964) and *The Lion in Winter* (1968). This is the Henry of our concern.

To place Henry II in his historical era, just remember that he was the father of (1) Richard I, the "Lion-hearted," who was the famous crusader, and (2) King John (who doesn't get a number, being the only John ever to sit on the English throne). John, Richard's younger brother, was the decidedly nasty antagonist of

Robin Hood. John, when his time came to rule, proved to be such a bad king that his nobles forced him to sign the Magna Carta in 1215, which limited his powers and started England down the road to a constitutional monarchy. Becket would have known both these future kings as young men.

Without Henry II there would have been no Becket, at least, no Becket who would be remembered today. Henry II was Becket's friend and patron, he appointed Becket to his highest offices, and he was the direct instrument in Becket's sudden rise and spectacularly martyr-making fall. Thomas Becket and Henry II are the two sides of the same story.

The land ruled by Henry II was not only England, but half of France as well. The rest of Western Europe (what is now Germany, Italy, and Spain) was still fragmented into relatively tiny political entities. Consequently, Henry's realm was Europe's largest and richest kingdom. Becket as its chief administrator and chief tax collector used his office, as was considered appropriate at the time, to make himself the richest man in the kingdom after the monarch.

Becket's lavish lifestyle and sumptuous hospitality to his friends became as famous as his ample charity to the poor. His penchant for extravagant dining, the finest most elegant clothes, and vast numbers of horses and servants contrasted sharply with the king's comparatively Spartan ways. But the king didn't begrudge him these indulgences because Becket, a workaholic, got the job done and was great company.

Becket's Predicament

As the two men spent more and more time together, Henry increasingly relied on Becket's competence and judgment. To the extent it was ever possible to be so with an absolute monarch, Becket became Henry's best friend, both socially and professionally. This friendship was key to the events that followed because it was what earned Becket his new appointment as archbishop of Canterbury and what doubled Henry's sense of betrayal when Becket's later actions were decidedly unfriendly to the king.

The problem was the church. The church in twelfth-century England was not the Church of England that exists today; that was created in the sixteenth century by Henry VIII when he had England break away from the Roman Catholic Church so that he could more conveniently arrange for a divorce from his first wife. In the twelfth century there was only one Christian church in England, and it considered itself loyal to the doctrines espoused by the pope in Rome. Problems arose when church practices came into conflict with mandates of the secular rulers, the kings, to whom the churchmen also owed loyalty.

Henry's problem with the church as an institution was that it considered itself above or beyond the law of the land. Thus, priests could, and frequently did, rape or murder innocent peasants without answering to the king's justice. And Henry II took his justice very seriously. He practically invented the modern criminal justice system by first using 12-man juries and creating different courts for different types of legal cases.

Nevertheless, the church held that its members, its priests, were answerable only to canon or church law. And this law was notoriously unsympathetic to the interests of aggrieved peasants. The essence of the conflict between Henry II and the church could be summed up in one question: Should clerics accused of crimes be tried in royal (civil) or ecclesiastical (church) courts?

The leaders of the church believed that church law outranked all other laws, that God's concerns were more important than those of any individual king. Consequently, the church also believed that neither the king nor his representatives should interfere with church affairs even if the affair was the rape and/or murder of an innocent peasant. The church also held that if the king did interfere, church leaders had the God-given right to resist him. But Henry, a king of remarkably modern sensibilities in this regard, was equally adamant that all church members in his land, from an archbishop on down, should be subject to his will and the laws he promulgated—especially if criminal acts were at issue.

A New Archbishop of Canterbury

By 1162 the king and the church, led by the archbishop of Canterbury, were at an impasse over this issue. The king was hesitant to push too hard on his goal of a unified criminal justice system because the English churches could always appeal to the pope in Rome to announce an unpleasant edict or threaten the excommunication (meaning eternal damnation) of any civil officer who sought to arrest church personnel.

Just as this issue was about to become very nasty, God seems to have intervened. The archbishop of Canterbury, the king's major opponent on this issue, died. Score one for Henry, because it is the king (or queen) of England, then as well as now, who appoints the next archbishop whenever God creates a vacancy. Henry thought he could resolve this church-versus-state impasse once and for all by making his most trusted friend and his most intimate adviser, Becket, the next archbishop of the church in England.

Becket had never been a priest, but this was a mere technical detail that could be, and was, quickly attended to. After all, he already was the archdeacon of Canterbury, and had been for some years. This meant that he was the second in command to, the chief administrator for, the archbishop. Even if he had not been the king's dearest friend, he would have been an obvious choice to be on the short list of realistic appointees for the new vacancy. It was common in those days for influential courtiers to hold multiple positions with multiple incomes. And Becket held many. This was one of the means by which he became so wealthy—all with the king's blessing. This wasn't corruption; merely good fortune. But Becket's fortunes were about to change.

The king assumed that Becket would continue as chancellor in addition to being archbishop. With the two offices held by one man, and that man the king's best friend, Henry assumed there would be no more conflict between church and state because the king's friend would see to it that the state prevailed. But Becket saw things differently and surprised the king by resigning as chancellor, feeling that his duty to God was greater than his duty to his king. The king wasn't pleased.

Very soon, the new archbishop showed how serious he took his new position. Well known for fine wining and dining, Becket reverted to simple fare and gave up wine for water. He gave away his exquisite wardrobe and adopted priestly garb. He even took to wearing a hair shirt underneath his robes of office. The hair shirt, made of coarse, itchy horsehair, was traditionally worn by religious ascetics as a self-imposed penance. Furthermore, on a daily basis, Becket washed the feet of a dozen or more poor men, in imitation of Jesus Christ's cleansing the feet of his followers. If this didn't demonstrate holiness enough, he frequently had himself stripped and whipped as penance for past transgressions. It amazed all observers that the man who had been the richest playboy in the realm suddenly got religion with a vengeance.

Miles's Law in Action

As the king's chancellor, Becket naturally sided with his monarch on the issue of civil-versus-church courts for errant priests. Miles's Law was in effect: Where he stood depended on where he sat. And he sat at the king's side. But after his appointment as archbishop, he suddenly had a new seat; he then sat as head of the church in England. Consequently, his stands, his policy positions, on errant priests and a host of other issues reversed themselves. The new archbishop became the king's new arch foe, and a far more brilliant, tenacious, and dangerous foe than the previous occupant of his seat. After all, Becket was still the ablest bureaucrat and most eloquent advocate in the land. Only this time, his client was the church, not the king.

Henry was bitterly disappointed in Becket's new attitude as well as by the loss of a dear friend. A kind of bureaucratic civil war ensued. Becket refused to surrender either his policy positions or his appointment, which was for life. Fearing for his life, he fled England and took refuge under the protection of the King of France for six years. Eventually, a reconciliation was arranged, and in 1170 Becket returned to England and his duties as archbishop.

The Martyr-Making Murder

When he returned, the old problems flared up. The breaking point came when Becket refused to lift the excommunication orders on several churchmen who had previously supported the king. Then came Christmas Day of 1170, when Becket, back in Canterbury Cathedral for the first time in six years, shocked his congregation by telling them that he would soon die, possibly as a martyr. Then he confirmed the excommunication orders, which he had already issued, and excommunicated another half-dozen of the king's supporters.

When Henry learned of this, shortly thereafter, he was furious. Once again he felt betrayed by Becket. In a bout of frustration, he supposedly shouted words to this effect: "Will nobody rid me of this turbulent priest?" No one knows the exact words generated by Henry's uncontrolled anger, but they were clear enough to trigger two actions: (1) send four knights—who believed they were acceding to the king's wishes—into the night to murder Becket in Canterbury Cathedral; and (2) provide Henry with plausible deniability when he asserted that he wasn't complicit in the death of England's leading churchman.

The murder itself, and the heated discussion that preceded it, has been extremely well documented by Becket's attendants. The knights, thinking they were on the king's business, felt no need to also murder the witnesses to the most famous murder in a cathedral. On December 29, at dusk, the knights found Becket enjoying his evening meal in a building near the cathedral. They sought to reason with him.

They demanded on behalf of the king that Becket reverse his orders of excommunication. Becket told them it was now a matter for the pope.

The knights argued that because Becket had issued the orders, he should be able to reverse them. Becket refused. The knights implied that he was insulting the king. Becket angrily responded that anyone who challenged the church might also be excommunicated. This was a direct threat to the knights as well as the king. To excommunicate a king is to absolve his subjects from the requirement to obey him: It was equivalent to inciting revolution. Becket was careful with words, so his use of such language can lead one only to conclude that he was asking for his death.

The knights, who had approached Becket unarmed, left to gather their weapons, while Becket walked into the cathedral. He knew what was coming. The knights found him at prayer and took turns slashing this willing martyr. One knight specifically cut open Becket's skull, scooped out his brains and spilled them on the cathedral floor. All this was seen by many unarmed monks and attendants, some of whom were notable historians.

As with Shakespeare's Hamlet, there was method in Becket's madness, his seeming unreasonableness. He knew that the only way he could defeat the king on the issue of church supremacy in its own sphere was to "force" the king to kill him, by becoming a bloody martyr for his cause, for his church. He knew the result would be universal condemnation of the king.

Henry immediately sent a message to the pope declaring his innocence in Becket's murder. At the same time he told the four knights to hide out in Scotland. His deniability existed in absence of a direct order on his part; but everyone believed that the king was complicit. To further atone for his role in the murder, however unintentional, Henry volunteered to perform any penance the pope might require. As might be expected, the pope wanted just what Becket wanted. In addition to a shopping list of church benefits, Henry agreed that royal courts would be powerless to try any member of the clergy; only church courts could try churchmen.

The church won. Becket won at the cost of his life. But it was only a tactical—and, from a historical perspective, temporary—victory, because the idea of a common law for all wouldn't die. It took hundreds of years, but the secular courts gradually gained jurisdiction over all subjects of the king. Henry was right. Becket was wrong.

Nevertheless, it was Becket the martyr who is remembered. It was Becket who was made a saint in 1173. It was Becket's bones at Canterbury Cathedral that immediately became the biggest tourist attraction in England. Pilgrims from throughout Europe would go to stand on the floor where Becket's blood had dripped, believing that the experience would cure their ills. Becket's severed skull was on display for hundreds of years, until all his holy relics (bones) disappeared during Henry VIII's reign in the early sixteenth century. Finally, it is Becket who is the star of plays and movies. Henry II, the absolute monarch and criminal justice system reformer, lives on through the ages only as a supporting player to Becket's story.

Occupational socialization is the process by which an individual absorbs and adopts the values, norms, and behavior of the occupational role models with whom he or she interacts. Occupational socialization is complete when an individual internalizes the values and norms of the occupational group. By that time, where he or she sits has long determined where he or she will stand. In the long history of the Western world there is no better, nor better known, example of occupational socialization in general and Miles's Law in particular than that of Thomas Becket, the martyred archbishop of Canterbury.

For Discussion: *A worker who has been extremely critical of management is made a supervisor and immediately changes his or her attitude; is this an example of Miles's Law? What are the parallels between Becket's efforts to make church law dominant and current efforts by some Islamic religious leaders to impose elements of Sharia law in the Western world?*

ORGANIZATIONAL BEHAVIOR

The study of organizational behavior includes those aspects of the behavioral sciences that focus on the understanding of human behavior in organizations. Students of public administration have always been interested in the behavior of people in government organizations. But fundamental assumptions about the behavior of such people at their work did not change dramatically from ancient efforts at organization until only a few decades ago. Using the traditional authoritarian, militaristic, and "Papa knows best" set of attitudes toward work organizations, **Hugo Münsterberg** pioneered the application of psychological findings from laboratory experiments to practical matters. He sought to match the abilities of new hires with a company's work demands, to positively influence employee attitudes toward their work and their company, and to understand the impact of psychological conditions on employee productivity. Münsterberg's pre–World War I approach was typical of how the behavioral sciences tended to be applied in organizations well into the 1950s.

In contrast to Münsterberg's traditional perspective on organizational behavior, a new style of applied behavioral science emerged in the 1960s. It focused attention on seeking to answer questions such as how organizations could encourage their workers to grow and develop. The belief was that organizational creativity, flexibility, and prosperity would flow naturally from employee growth and development. The essence of the relationship between organization and people was redefined from dependence to codependence. In contrast, managers in Münsterberg's day did not believe (assume) that codependence was the "right" relationship between an organization and its employees.

There has long been considerable interest in the behavior of people inside bureaucracies. After all, the whole purpose of organization theory, as discussed in the previous chapter, is to create mechanisms for regulating the behavior of people in organizations. However, it was not until about 1960, with the publication of Douglas McGregor's *The Human Side of Enterprise*, that our basic assumptions about the relationship between organizations and people truly began to change. This new approach to analyzing organizations focused on people, groups, and the relationships among them and the organizational environment. It was built around the following assumptions:

1. Organizations are created to serve human ends.
2. Organizations and people need each other (organizations need ideas, energy, and talent; people need careers, salaries, and work opportunities).

Hugo Münsterberg (1863–1916) ■
The German-born psychologist whose later work at Harvard would earn him the title of "father" of industrial or applied psychology.

3. When the fit between the needs of the individual and the organization is poor, one or both will suffer: Individuals may be exploited or may seek to exploit the organizations, or both.

4. A good fit between individuals and organizations benefits both because people gain meaningful and satisfying work—and organizations receive the talent and energy they need to thrive.

It is instructive to contrast these assumptions with the paternalistic authoritarian attitudes that preceded them. Previously, when new technology was to be introduced, new orders were given for its installation and operation. There was no concern about what the workers would think about such changes. They simply had no say. Once in a while some **Luddites** might surface, but they were quickly suppressed. Compare this "orders is orders" approach to how modern organizational behaviorists contemplate the introduction of a new technology. They immediately start thinking about and planning a specific approach:

1. Minimize fear of change by involving people at all levels in designing the introduction of the changes.

2. Minimize the negative impacts of the change on groups of workers at risk (such as older, less-skilled, or younger workers).

3. **Co-opt** informal and formal (usually union) leaders, especially those who might become antagonistic.

4. Find alternatives for employees who do not see the changes as consistent with their personal goals.

Because the modern perspective places a high value on the individual, employees are provided with maximum amounts of accurate information, so they can make informed decisions about their future.

The assumptions of the Münsterberg traditional perspective continue to be alive and well in many less-sophisticated organizations—where it is still assumed that people should be fitted to the organization. With the classical organization theory of Frederick Taylor and others, the organizational role of the applied behavioral sciences largely consisted of helping organizations find and shape people to serve as human replacement parts for the organizational machine.

Yet, under the right circumstances, people and organizations will grow and prosper together. Individuals and organizations are not necessarily antagonists. Managers can learn to unleash previously stifled energies and creativities. Two of the most important "tools" for doing this are group dynamics and organization development.

Group Dynamics

Since the earliest days of the Industrial Revolution, workplace organizations have been constructed on the foundation principles of specialization and division of labor (remember Adam Smith's pin factory). In our complex organizations of today, few jobs can be done from start to finish by one person. Specialization allows an organization to use people's skills and efforts more systematically and to focus their knowledge and energy on a limited number of tasks. Employee **learning curves** are minimized.

Luddites ■
Originally English workers in the early nineteenth century who destroyed new textile machinery that was displacing them in factories; now the term, after the legendary Ned Ludd, refers to anyone who sabotages high-tech equipment to protect jobs.

Co-opt ■
To include potentially dissident group members in an organization's policymaking process to prevent such elements from being a threat to the organization or its mission. The classic analysis of co-optation is found in Philip Selznick's *TVA and the Grass Roots* (1949).

Learning curve ■
The time it takes to achieve optimal efficiency in performing a task. When workers repeatedly do a new task, the amount of labor per unit of output initially decreases according to a pattern that can be plotted as a curve on a graph.

Most employees who perform sets of specialized functions are organizationally clustered in work groups, which are organized into units or branches, which are organized into divisions or departments, which are organized into agencies, and so forth. Work groups attract people with similar backgrounds—for example, professional training, socialization, and experience as accountants, teachers, engineers, or computer programmers. All such shared backgrounds involve the socialization of people into common value/belief/behavior systems. We learn how to think and act like lawyers, teachers, or accountants—and like Virginians or Southern Californians.

Practically all groups, and particularly purposeful, specialized, organizational groups, develop their own sets of norms of behavioral assumptions about things such as the nature of their organizational environment and appropriate relations with other groups. All groups expect their members to conform to their norms. By rewarding activities the organization wants done and punishing counterproductive behavior, managers engineer the accomplishment of organizational goals. Virtually all organizations attempt to motivate employees through combinations of rewards and punishments. **Reinforcement** theories of motivation assume that people at work seek rewards and try to avoid punishments.

Reinforcement ■
An inducement to perform in a particular manner. Positive reinforcement occurs when an individual receives a desired reward that is contingent on some prescribed behavior. Negative reinforcement occurs when an individual works to avoid an undesirable outcome.

Acceptance of and adherence to group norms permits people to know what to expect from each other and to predict what other members will do in different circumstances. Norms cause people to behave in patterned and predictable ways. Thus, by institutionalizing common expectations, they stabilize the organization. Always remember, though, that too much adherence to norms causes excessive conformity. This can hurt or destroy individualism—and even lead to groupthink (see the section on groupthink in this chapter). The potential damage here is not limited to individuals who work in organizations. Excessive conformity may result in so much organizational rigidity that the organization's overall ability to achieve its mission is degraded.

When a group becomes institutionalized in an organization, such as a production unit or a branch office, these shared beliefs, values, and assumptions—these norms—become the essence of a cohesive group and of an organizational subculture. Most group subcultures have a resemblance to the overall organizational culture but also contain unique elements that form through the impacts of events, circumstances, and personalities. Considering the normal loyalties that groups demand and the affiliational needs they meet, it becomes easy to understand why in-groups and out-groups and feelings of we-and-they and we-versus-they are so characteristic of life in organizations.

Group dynamics is the subfield of organization behavior concerned with the nature of groups, how they develop, and how they interrelate with individuals and other groups. Usually the term "group" refers to what is more technically known as a primary group—a group small enough to permit face-to-face interaction among its members that remains in existence long enough for some personal relations, sentiments, and feelings of identification or belonging to develop. There are two basic kinds of primary groups: formal and informal.

Formal groups are officially created by a larger organization, usually for the purpose of accomplishing tasks. Employees are assigned to formal groups based on their position in the organization. There are two basic types of formal groups.

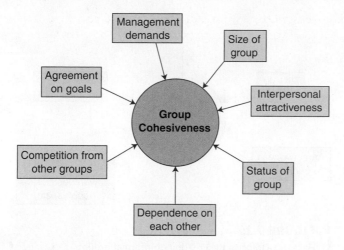

FIGURE 7.1

Factors contributing to group cohesiveness

First, there are command groups that are specified in a formal organization chart. These include both supervisors and the people who report directly to them. Groups of this type are the essential building blocks of organizational structure. They vary from a mail room staff to the employees of a small branch office to an entire headquarters staff. Second, there are task groups, formally sanctioned job-oriented units with short lives. Here you will find employees who work together to complete a particular project or task and then are disbanded. Any ad hoc ("for this") **task force** or temporary ("for this") committee is an example.

Informal groups are made up of individuals who have spontaneously developed relationships and patterns of interactions in work situations. Included here are employees who associate voluntarily, primarily to satisfy social needs. Although informal groups at work may have goals and tasks (for example, ethnic support groups, bowling clubs, and luncheon speaker groups), their primary reasons for existence are friendship, affiliation, and shared interests. Although informal groups seldom are formally sanctioned, they are extremely important to the working of organizations. Their norms, values, beliefs, and expectations have significant impacts on work-related behavior and attitudes. Chester I. Barnard in *The Functions of the Executive* has provided the classic statement on the vital significance of informal groups:

> Informal organization, although comprising the processes of society which are unconscious as contrasted with those of formal organization which are conscious, has two important classes of effects: (a) it establishes certain attitudes, understandings, customs, habits, institutions; and (b) it creates the condition under which formal organization may arise.

Groups in organizations of all types are of high importance and interest to students and practitioners of organizational behavior, both for what happens in them (and why) and what happens between them.

Task force ■

A temporary interdisciplinary team within a larger organization charged with accomplishing a specific goal. Task forces are typically used in government when a problem crosses departmental lines.

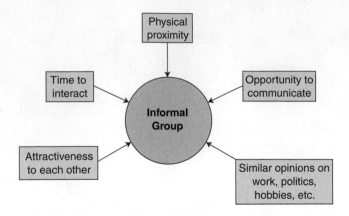

FIGURE 7.2
Factors leading to the creation of informal groups

Organization Development

The French Foreign Legion, when it occupied most of the North African desert early in the twentieth century, had the slogan "march or die"—which meant that a legionnaire could not survive unless he kept his place in the moving column. A similar slogan should be on the walls of all organizations: "Change or die." The message here is that without constant change, renovation—indeed reinventing—this social organism will die just as surely as the solitary legionnaire of old.

Organization development (OD) is planned organizational change. Organizations exist in a dynamic environment, both internally and externally, to which they must respond or become ineffectual. The responsibility of OD advisers, specialists on applied behavioral science, is to facilitate change—to use their knowledge of the behavioral sciences for organizational improvement. These advisers can be internal in that they already work for the organization or external independent consultants. A frequently desired change is the installation of a beneficent managerial philosophy. More modest goals might be the creation of an atmosphere of trust in order to facilitate communications or the development of participatory mechanisms that would stimulate productivity. Any organization that wishes to survive or simply to remain healthy must periodically divest itself of those parts or characteristics that contribute to its malaise.

OD itself is not a philosophy. It is an approach or strategy for increasing organizational effectiveness. As a process, it has no value biases, but it is usually associated with the idea that effectiveness is found by integrating the individual's desire for growth with organizational goals. There is no universal OD model that can easily be plugged into a troubled organization. The basic task of the OD adviser is to adapt appropriate portions of the generally available OD technology to the immediate demands of his or her organizational problem. This is why the OD adviser must be thoroughly conversant with the findings of the behavioral technology of modern management. Because no textbook will have a case study of the exact organizational problem to be remedied, these advisers must be prepared to draw on their backgrounds to improvise. OD advising, like much of the rest of public administration, contains a large element of art.

The OD process is made all the more difficult to implement in the public sector because top management, which must first be sold on the OD process, is fractured, consisting of political and career executives, legislative committees, client groups, and so on. Hostility can also be expected from line management. As an OD role for the personnel department implies a greater involvement with management's traditional line prerogatives, it may take some time before personnel's agitation in this regard is viewed as supportive instead of threatening.

A decision on the part of top management to suddenly replace a highly structured authoritarian organizational climate with an atmosphere of greater employee participation and collaboration probably would create a great sense of shock and suspicion among employees. All changes in organizational climate or culture must be well planned in advance and implemented gradually. OD is not something that can be accomplished in an afternoon. It is a slow process that extends, at the very least, over many months and requires the commitment and cooperation of all of the principal actors in the organizational drama. The first phase of almost all OD models is the education of top management in basic OD objectives and strategies. OD as a process is one that must flow from the top down. As leadership sets the tone of organizational life, it is futile to seek to change the pace and quality of that life without uninhibited cooperation from the top down.

OD is concerned with deep, long-lasting organization-wide change or improvement—not in superficial changes in isolated organizational pockets. This concern for broad-based and long-term change led OD practitioners to an interest in the concept of organizational culture long before it became a fashionable management topic in the 1980s. OD advisers have developed numerous strategies and techniques for improving organizations: Most of them utilize **interventions** facilitated by outsiders (often called change agents). Some of the most common strategies include organizational diagnosis, **process consultation,** team building (in many forms), action research, data feedback, **job enlargement, job enrichment,** and conflict management. But each adviser has his or her own preferred tactics.

The origins of the organization development movement can be generally traced to the Hawthorne studies (discussed later in this chapter). But the specific understandings of organizational behavior-oriented change processes came out of the sensitivity training (or **T-group**) movement that started in 1946 when Kurt Lewin and associates collaboratively conducted a training workshop to help improve racial relations and community leadership in New Britain, Connecticut. During their evening staff meetings, they discussed the behavior of workshop participants and the dynamics of events. Several workshop participants asked to join the night discussions, and the results of the process eventually led to the initiation and institutionalization of T-group technology. Although the early T-groups focused primarily on individual growth and development, they quickly were adapted for organizational application. T-groups became the method by which organizational members learned how to communicate honestly and directly about facts and feelings. (From the human relations perspective, feelings are facts.) Thus T-groups became a keystone strategy for increasing organizational effectiveness by

Intervention ■
The entering of an outsider into an ongoing system of relationships, such as an organization, to help make it perform better.

Process consultation ■
The interventionist activities of an organization development adviser.

Job enlargement ■
Adding additional but similar duties to a job.

Job enrichment ■
Adding different kinds of duties so that the work is both at a higher level and more personally satisfying.

T-group ■
A training group. According to Chris Argyris, a leading authority on OD techniques, the T-group experience is "designed to provide maximum possible opportunity for the individuals to expose their behavior, give and receive feedback, experiment with new behavior, and develop everlasting awareness and acceptance of self and others."

improving interpersonal communications (e.g., feedback), reducing defensiveness (and thus rigidity), and otherwise helping organizations achieve greater effectiveness through the development of coping processes. The meaning of coping here is twofold: coping with the job and coping with fellow workers.

But the T-group needed to be part of a larger overarching methodology. Survey research methodology, when combined with feedback/communication (T-group) techniques and applied to planned organizational change, resulted in the development of the action research model of organizational change—the mainstay of OD practitioners and theorists. The action research model is a process for identifying needs for organizational improvement through the use of external consultation but also through fostering **psychological ownership** of problems and solutions by organizational members. Briefly, action research involves the following:

Psychological ownership ■
Emotional involvement with, and commitment to, an intangible something, such as an organizational reform effort.

1. Collecting organizational diagnostic data (ascertaining the problem) usually either through written questionnaires or interviews
2. Systematically feeding back information to the organization members who provided input
3. Discussing what the information means to members and its implications for the organization in order to be certain if the "diagnosis" is accurate and to generate psychological ownership of the need for actions to improve the situation
4. Jointly developing an improvement plan, using both the knowledge and skills of the consultant and the insider perspective of members
5. Repeating all of the preceding as needed

The key to long-term OD success is this very last step: repeat as needed. Lewin is well known for his assertion that social change must be viewed as a three-step process of unfreezing, change, and refreezing. If one focuses only on the change process per se, change will be short lived at best. The organization must put the change in place to see if it takes. The process is called action research because the thing being experimented on, the organization, is constantly in action. When Lewin says "unfreezing," he means opening up the organization to change. The "refreezing" process is installing the new change, then watching it to see if the "refreezing" is an improvement. This OD effort toward continuous improvement is a precursor to the total quality management (TQM) movement discussed in Chapter 8.

The ultimate question here is not whether organizations should change. They are constantly changing in response to the dynamic environments in which they all exist. Of course, some environments are more dynamic than others. But change, fast or slow, is inexorable. The best line Thomas Wolfe ever wrote was the title of his 1940 novel *You Can't Go Home Again*. The home you left, because of the simple passage of time, is no longer the home to which you return. The home in which you once lived, just like the office in which you once worked, changes every day. People get older, attitudes evolve, and new skills are learned no matter what we do. So the question for would-be managers of organizations is not change: yes or no, but unplanned change or planned change. OD as planned change is just a tool for managers to gain control of and give direction to the inevitable changes within their organizations.

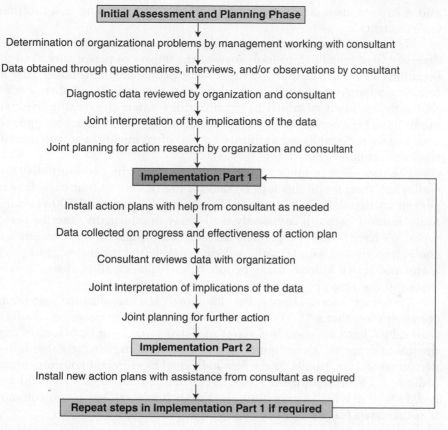

FIGURE 7.3

The organization development action research model

The Impact of Personality

Chris Argyris, a preeminent analyst of organizational phenomena for more than four decades, first became noteworthy with the publication of his 1957 book *Personality and Organization*. In it he claimed that there was an inherent conflict between the mature adult personality and the needs of modern organizations. The problem, simply put, was that most organizations were treating adults like children. As the truth of this finding was made increasingly evident, ways of treating employees changed. A new dogma evolved that organizations should give their citizens all the responsibilities they could handle—and then some.

While this nicely dovetailed with concerns for greater productivity and effectiveness, the inherent problem of personality was not so much superseded as ignored. After all, in the era of equal employment opportunity and workforce diversity, efforts to address the impact of individual personalities on organizations could be dangerous. Who needs lawsuits claiming that an employee's cultural heritage is being "attacked" by an inherently oppressive organization and a supervisor insensitive to the subtleties of managing in a multicultural environment?

Nevertheless, organizational analysts have once again begun, despite the diversity issue minefield, to look anew at the impact of personality. And they are beginning to say things that will make some people uncomfortable. They are not rejecting what Argyris said about adults and organizations. But they are saying that different kinds of adults fit organizations differently, that individuals who might have been heroes in an earlier age because of their inherent aggressiveness and disdain for established authority are too often misfits in a contemporary bureaucratic culture.

The issue here is inherent temperament. According to journalist Winifred Gallagher, there is still much to be said for the validity of four basic human temperaments first described in ancient Greece by Hippocrates 2,500 years ago. His four "humors" are still commonly used today to informally describe personality types. We have all seen people who are sanguine (optimistic and energetic), melancholic (moody and withdrawn), choleric (irritable and impulsive), and phlegmatic (calm and slow). Indeed, many people have displayed all of these "humors" or moods at one time or another.

Even if we discard Hippocrates' "humors" as a classification system, it is just common sense that a "Dirty Harry" (the archetypal aggressive police officer portrayed by Clint Eastwood in a series of films) should not be placed in charge of the police department's computer system. Similarly, an extremely shy, soft-spoken person would not usually be the best individual to represent your organization on radio and TV. And someone prone to constant anxiety and worry will probably not do well in a high-stress position. Yet such mismatches are so commonplace that they are a leading cause of organizational incompetence.

THE IMPACT OF BUREAUCRATIC STRUCTURE ON BEHAVIOR

Organization chart ■
The visual representation of the structure of an organization, usually in the form of a diagram.

Peer group ■
People at the same organizational level in terms of rank, title, or salary.

The impact of bureaucratic structure on the behavior of its denizens results from their unique personalities interacting with the organizational structures in which they must function. Each organization has structures that define the unique ways labor is divided, how specialized roles and functions are coordinated (related to each other and to other organizational levels and functions), how information flows among people and groups, and how the system of controls (how tasks are measured, evaluated, and altered) is to work. These structures, often visualized in the form of an **organization chart**, establish how roles, expectations, and resource allocations are determined for people and groups in any given organization. Structure is a primary reason why organizational behavior differs from behavior in everyday life and thus why organizational behavior developed as a separate field of study within the applied behavioral sciences. Structure, however, is only one of a variety of forces that affect the behavior of people in organizations. Attitudes and behaviors are also shaped by **peer group** pressure, shared group norms of behavior, social and technical aspects of work tasks, and the organization's internal and external cultures (discussed in Chapter 2).

The structures of a large bureaucracy are inherently conservative in that they are slow to change. Thus one of the perennial complaints about bureaucracy is its lack of responsiveness to changing conditions. But this notorious slowness to change is very often a function of its legal mandate. No public bureaucracy in a democratic government does anything that is not provided for by its enabling legislation. This alleged slowness, from another point of view, is simply its obedience to the law. What a chief executive would streamline and make more efficient, the power brokers of the legislature would just as often keep bloated and inefficient. And if government jobs for their constituents are at stake, efficiency and economy in government suffer even more. This is exactly what members of the U.S. Congress must confront every time the Department of Defense seeks to close military bases. Congressional doves suddenly turn into defense hawks when the jobs of the voters in their district are at stake.

As organizations grew from small offices and shops into large corporations and government agencies, the disciplined hierarchies and unambiguous functional assignments of bureaucracy evolved as the ideal structural form. This structure allowed for pervasive control from the top of an organizational pyramid. But tight control is a good news/bad news story. The good news is that it is possible to centrally monitor and regulate the behavior of the employees. The bad news is that there are high costs involved with excessive control and the line between tight control and excessive control is a thin one. Employees in organizational straitjackets are unlikely to exercise initiative. Like automatons—human robots—they perform their prescribed duties until appropriate bureaucratic authority tells them otherwise. A properly designed bureaucratic organization can be impressively efficient even though none of its individual bureaucrats are in any way exceptional individuals. This is why Herman Wouk in his 1951 novel *The Caine Mutiny* called the U.S. Navy "a machine invented by geniuses, to be run by idiots." These machines, whether governmental or industrial, can be extraordinarily impressive in performance even when run by mediocre people. Thus the French novelist Honoré de Balzac called bureaucracy "the giant power wielded by pygmies." In this sense bureaucracy, far from being incompetent, is a bastion of super-competence—its overall performance far exceeding the quality that could otherwise be expected from its miscellaneous human parts.

Dove ■
A peaceful bird in metaphor; a symbol of peace since ancient times.

Hawk ■
Person inclined toward military action. Its antithetical term is *dove*.

Bureaucratic Dysfunctions

Unfortunately, bureaucracies often have within them the seeds of their own incompetence, like a bad genetic inheritance. Contemporary writers such as Robert K. Merton and Victor A. Thompson have argued that bureaucracies have inherent dysfunctional and pathological elements that make them inefficient in operations. Merton found that bureaucracies have a "trained incapacity." This refers to a "state of affairs in which one's abilities function as inadequacies or blind spots. Actions based on training and skills that have been successfully applied in the past may result in inappropriate responses under changed conditions." According to Merton, bureaucracy exerts constant pressures on people to be methodical and disciplined, to conform to patterns of obligations. These pressures eventually cause people to adhere to rules as an end rather than a means—as a matter of blind conformance.

It is this blind conformance that gives bureaucracy its catch-22 quality, its trained incapability to respond to contradictory requirements. This "catch," from Joseph Heller's 1961 novel of the same name about American bomber crews in World War II, meant that you could get out of flying combat missions if you were insane. All you had to do was ask. But if you asked, you demonstrated that you were not insane because seeking to avoid combat was a rational, not insane, act. In Heller's words a pilot "would be crazy to fly more missions and sane if he didn't, but if he was sane, he had to fly them. If he flew them, he was crazy and didn't have to, but if he didn't, he was sane and had to." The "catch" is beautifully circular in its perversity. Because the book was such an enormous best seller, "catch-22" entered the language as the code word for the essence of bureaucratic dysfunctionalism, for being trapped between contradictory bureaucratic regulations. A common example of catch-22 is this double bind: A person can't get a job without experience but can't get experience without first having a job.

Bureaucratic structure also stresses depersonalized relations, and power and authority gained by virtue of organizational position rather than by thought or action. Thus ideas and opinions are valued not according to their intrinsic merit but according to one's rank. This would be perfectly fine if the bosses truly were always smarter than the workers. Without question, Merton sees bureaucratic structure as more than affecting organizational behavior and thinking: It also determines and controls. It determines that not all of the organization's brain power will be used and that the objectively less deserving may remain in control. Of course, there is always the bright, aspiring bureaucratic leader who holds his tongue or her brains in check while climbing the bureaucratic career ladder. But the danger here is that he or she suffers from "evaporation." Historian B. H. Liddell Hart observed in his *Why Don't We Learn from History?* that "ambitious officers when they came in sight of promotion [to high rank] would decide that they would bottle up their thoughts and ideas, as a safety precaution, until they reached the top and could put these ideas into practice. Unfortunately the usual result, after years of such self-repression for the sake of their ambition, was that when the bottle was eventually uncorked the contents had evaporated."

As a form of organization, bureaucracy has many advantages: order, predictability, stability, professionalism, and consistency. Nevertheless, the behavioral consequences of bureaucratic structure are often negative. To illustrate this, Thompson combined "bureaucracy" with "pathological" to describe the all-too-familiar "bureaupathic official." Such a person "usually exaggerates the official, nontechnical aspects of relationships and suppresses the technical and the informal." Being insecure, he or she "may be expected to insist on petty rights and prerogatives, on protocol, on procedure—in short, on those things least likely to affect directly the goal accomplishment of the organization." This is the classic stereotype of "the bureaucrat." Thus an otherwise "functionless reviewing officer will often insist most violently on his right to review and scream like an injured animal if he is bypassed." Moreover, "if he has a counterpart at a higher organizational level, he will probably insist on exclusive contact with that higher clearance point. By controlling this particular communication channel, he protects his authority and influence." This stereotype has been around, quite literally, for ages. In *Measure for Measure* (Act II, Scene 2) Shakespeare writes of the "petty officer," the "proud man, dress'd in a little brief authority, most ignorant of what he's most assur'd." This "petty officer" with his or her "little brief authority" is also probably performing at a bureaucracy near you—right now!

Bureaucratic Impersonality

Max Weber referred to bureaucracy's "special virtue" as "dehumanization." Hardly anyone would argue that bureaucracy does not have dehumanizing consequences for its employees and, to a lesser extent, for its clients as well. By dehumanization, Weber meant the elimination "from official business [of] love, hatred and all purely personal, irrational, and emotional elements." In Weber's view, formalization, hierarchy, and the other central features of bureaucracy render the individual bureaucrat "only a single cog in an ever-moving mechanism which prescribes to him an essentially fixed route of march." Consequently, "the individual bureaucrat is forged to the community of all functionaries who are integrated into the mechanism." He cannot "squirm out of the apparatus in which he is harnessed." Today the term *impersonality* is generally used in referring to this aspect of bureaucratic behavior. Viewed against a historical background of administrative organizations characterized by such "irrational" elements as **nepotism**, personal subjugation, and capricious and uninformed judgment, impersonality can be seen as a step in the direction of greater rationality; a step further in the direction of Aristotle's ideal of "**a government of laws**; not of men."

Bureaucratic impersonality has three major advantages. First, it increases organizational effectiveness by enabling administrators to do things that are otherwise difficult for people to do. In the course of their normal functioning, organizations may create considerable hardships for individuals. This is especially true of public organizations, which are often engaged in punishment, taxation, and the withholding of benefits such as food stamps, unemployment compensation, or welfare funds. Impersonality creates a desirable moral insensitivity. For example, it is much easier—emotionally speaking—for military planners on a general staff to select targets for bombardment than it is for a rifleman to shoot an enemy soldier who is a few yards ahead of him and whose face is clearly visible. Similarly, it is far easier for welfare agency budget analysts to cut school lunch funding for poor students than for a food service worker at a school cafeteria to see children go hungry when they cannot pay for lunch.

A second advantage of impersonality flows from the fact that as Peter Blau and Marshall Meyer observed in *Bureaucracy in Modern Society*, "Efficiency also suffers when emotions or personal considerations influence administrative decisions." If, for example, recruitment and promotions within an organization are based on personal preference, or ascriptive criteria (such as race or class), rather than competence, that organization's administrative processes will over time become less efficient.

Finally, impersonality tends to produce relatively evenhanded rule application. Thus procedural, if not necessarily actual, justice is ensured. "By the book" behavior requires equal treatment of those in the same categories, regardless of their social status. While this attitude may cause hardship for some, there has long been great philosophic support for it. For example, eighteenth-century philosopher Jean

Nepotism ■
Any practice by which officeholders award positions to members of their immediate family. It is derived from the Latin *nepos*, meaning "nephew" or "grandson." The rulers of the medieval church were often thought to give special preference to their nephews in distributing churchly offices—at that time, "nephew" being a euphemism for an illegitimate son.

Government of laws ■
A governing system in which the highest authority is a body of law that applies equally to all (as opposed to the rule of men, in which the personal whim of those in power can decide any issue). The idea of the desirability of a "government of laws, and not of men" can be traced back to Aristotle. The earliest American reference is in the 1779 Massachusetts Constitution. John Marshall also used this succinct legal description in *Marbury v. Madison* (1803): "The government of the United States has been emphatically termed a government of laws, and not of men. It will certainly cease to deserve this high appellation, if the laws furnish no remedy for the violation of a vested legal right."

Jacques Rousseau denied that it was an abridgment of anyone's freedom to do the general will. Rousseau defined freedom in this context as simply being treated the same as everyone else. He would have loudly applauded modern bureaucracy's institutionalized lack of respect for a person's station in life.

Although impersonality may further procedural justice, it may at the same time fail to provide substantive or actual justice. The decisions bureaucrats reach may fail to fit the individual cases in terms of providing a just resolution. Many people fail to accept that their case is no different from those of others. They resent being treated on the basis of categories to which they do not feel they rightly belong. This tendency of bureaucracy has often aroused considerable hostility—sometimes even violence—on the part of clients. But the nature of impersonal organization is such that bureaucrats must apply established rules and procedures, even when they realize that these will not provide a reasonable or just resolution of a specific problem. Consequently, it has frequently been argued that a characteristic pathology of bureaucracy is an inversion of ends and means whereby the rules become more important than the objectives underlying their creation.

While impersonality is acknowledged as a central feature of bureaucratic behavior, there is disagreement over its desirability. Given that it has both advantages and dysfunctions, it would appear that the most sensible approach is to try to maximize the former while minimizing the latter. At the very least, this requires that students and practitioners of public administration avoid sweeping generalizations about bureaucratic behavior. The focus of concern ought to be the operations of individual bureaucratic units. By the same token it is imperative that the serious student recognize that some popular analyses of bureaucratic behavior—for example, **Parkinson's Law** that "work expands so as to fill the time available for its completion" and the **Peter principle** that "in a hierarchy every employee tends to rise to his level of incompetence"—are generally more amusing than descriptive of reality.

Bureaucrat Bashing

Bashing is extreme and public criticism (often unwarranted and irrational) of a person, policy, or nation. Domestically, bashing has often followed the word *bureaucrat*. During the 1980s, the constant complaints and jokes about the competence of government employees—led by President Ronald "Government Is the Problem" Reagan—helped to create an acceptance of bureaucrat bashing. Following his 1964 campaign for governor of California, Reagan was constantly complaining that "government is like a big baby—an alimentary canal with a big appetite at one end and no sense of responsibility at the other."

The term *bureaucrat bashing* has been used so frequently in so many contexts that it has taken on two meanings that are the opposite of each other. Those on the ideological right who tend to oppose big government use it to refer to justified criticism of "lazy and incompetent" government employees. At the same time, those on the ideological left, who tend to be more supportive of big government, use it to refer to the political right's "unnecessary and inappropriate" condemnation of public employees. But the meaning goes beyond rhetoric. The term now also refers to widespread support for specific policies that adversely impact or demean public

General will ■
Jean Jacques Rousseau's ideal from *The Social Contract* (1761) that there is a collective will or consensus among the people, which is the ultimate locus of all political power.

Parkinson's Law ■
The title of a 1957 best seller by C. Northcote Parkinson (1909–1993), an otherwise serious British naval and economic historian. Parkinson also "discovered" that any public administrative department will invariably increase its staff an average of 5.75 percent per year. In anticipation of suggestions that he advise what might be done about this problem, he asserted that "it is not the business of the botanist to eradicate the weeds. Enough for him if he can tell us just how fast they grow."

Peter principle ■
The 1969 best seller of the same name by Laurence J. Peter (1919–1990), then an obscure professor of education, who offered the corollary that "in time, every post tends to be occupied by an employee who is incompetent to carry out its duties."

employees. For example, monitoring phone calls to prevent personal use, reducing office sizes, and curtailing free parking privileges all reduce the quality of bureaucratic life on the job. And being asked to take a urine test to detect drug use or to sign an anti-leak (of information) pledge may be personally demeaning.

The problem with bureaucracy from the point of view of the cultural conservatives is that the values they most cherish seem to be under attack by bureaucratic institutions. They see a red flag in both the literal (meaning danger) and political senses when a government agency such as the National Endowment for the Arts subsidizes works of art they consider to be obscene or when a government welfare agency takes the social stigma out of illegitimacy by making no distinction between widowed (or divorced) women with dependent children in financial need and never-married mothers. The bureaucratic grouping of them together as simply "single mothers" is morally offensive to many cultural conservatives who view it as a policy that only encourages a continual rise in the number of children born outside of marriage (38 percent of all U.S. births in 2006). Thus the bureaucracy with its subsidizing of single motherhood is castigated by conservatives as seeking to destroy the traditional family, the indispensable weaver of the social fabric.

Red ■
A communist; the red flag is the international symbol of communism. This is why someone thought to be leaning toward communism might be called *pink* or a *pinko.*

There is really nothing new in American politics about attacking the bureaucracy. Indeed, the middle of the Declaration of Independence of 1776 contains a major assault on the bureaucracy of King George's colonial government. But what is new is that the people running the bureaucracies, not just their political opposition, are also on the attack. Ronald Reagan won election in 1980 by running against the federal bureaucracy. After four years of being responsible for it, he successfully ran against it again in 1984. Bill Clinton pledged in his successful 1992 presidential campaign to reinvent federal bureaucracy. His reinventing cost 200,000 federal bureaucrats their jobs by 1996. The bureaucracy is an easy political target to bash because, being largely politically neutral, it does not bash back.

The Case for Bureaucracy

Despite widespread berating of "the bureaucracy" and a constant stream of jokes about the efficiency of government employees, Americans often like their bureaucrats and think highly of the quality of the services they receive. Charles T. Goodsell, a professor of public administration at Virginia Polytechnic Institute and State University, got so enraged about the popular "vision of a failed bureaucracy" that he wrote a book, *The Case for Bureaucracy*, exploring what he called "the great falsehood about American government." After reviewing a wealth of research reports, he found "satisfactory citizen treatment as the *norm* rather than the *exception.*"

Moreover, Goodsell argued, "The commonly accepted view of political conservatives that government never performs as well as business is also shown to be a patent falsehood." In addition, "a comparison of American bureaucracy to that of other countries reveals that we experience one of the best levels of service in the world, light years ahead of that endured by most national populations." Goodsell's book is a perennial rebuttal to all those misguided or malicious bureaucrat bashers.

MOTIVATION

Theatrical lore has it that as a famous actor struggled to find just the right characterization for a scene, he turned to his director and asked, "What's my motivation?" The director sarcastically replied, "To keep your job!" And so it is with most work done off the stage as well. "Keeping the job" has been the primary goal of industrial workers ever since they abandoned their farms to find work in the factories of the city. The perennial problem for managers is to motivate the workers to do more than is minimally necessary to keep that job.

While there always has been consensus about the need for motivated employees, the same cannot be said for beliefs about how to induce higher levels of motivation—and concomitant productivity. Not only have prevailing views (or theories) of motivation changed radically over time, but incompatible theories usually have competed with each other at the same points in time. Some theories assume that employees act rationally: Managers simply need to manipulate rewards and punishments logically, fairly, and consistently. Other theories start from the position that managerial assumptions about employees—which undergird such systems of rewards and punishments—actually stifle employee motivation. This section summarizes some of the more important theories.

The Hawthorne Experiments

It was during the late 1920s and early 1930s that the Hawthorne experiments were undertaken at the Hawthorne Works of the Western Electric Company near Chicago. This study, consisting of the most famous management experiments ever reported, was conducted by Elton Mayo and his associates from the Harvard Business School. The decade-long series of experiments started out as traditional scientific management examinations of the relationship between work environment and productivity. But the experimenters, because they were initially unable to explain the results of their findings, literally stumbled on a finding that today seems so obvious: that factories and other work situations are first of all social situations. The workers, as **Mary Parker Follett** had suggested a decade earlier, were more responsive to peer pressure than to management controls. The Hawthorne studies are generally considered to be the genesis of the human relations school of management thought, providing the first major empirical challenge to the scientific management notion that the worker was primarily an economic animal who would work solely for money.

Mary Parker Follett (1868–1933) ∎
An early social psychologist who anticipated, in the 1920s, many of the conclusions of the Hawthorne experiments of the 1930s and of the post–World War II behavioral movement.

It is important to note that the Mayo team began its work trying to fit into the mold of classical organization theory thinking. The team phrased its questions in the language and concepts that industry was accustomed to using in order to see and explain certain problems, among them productivity in relationship to such factors as the amount of light, the rate of flow of materials, and alternative wage payment plans. The Mayo team succeeded in making significant breakthroughs in understanding only after it redefined the Hawthorne problems as social psychological problems—problems conceptualized in such terms as interpersonal relations in groups, group norms, control over one's own environment, and personal recognition. It was only after the Mayo team achieved this breakthrough that it became the "grandfather"—the direct precursor—of the field of organizational behavior and human resource theory. The Hawthorne experiments were the emotional and intellectual wellspring of modern theories of motivation. They showed that complex, interactional variables make the difference in motivating people— things such as attention paid to workers as individuals, workers' control over their own work, differences between individuals' needs, management's willingness to listen, group norms, and direct feedback.

A particularly notable discovery that came out of the Hawthorne experiments was the Hawthorne effect: the discovery that production increases were due to the known presence of benign observers. The researchers' concern for and attention to the workers led the workers, who naturally wanted to be reciprocally nice, to increase production. This "effect" caused great confusion at first because the changing physical conditions (lighting, rest breaks, etc.) seemed to make no difference. Output just kept going up. Once they realized that the workers' perception of participation was the true "variable," the effects of the "effect" were understood.

The Needs Hierarchy

Abraham H. Maslow, a psychologist, took the basic Hawthorne finding that workers are as much social as economic creatures a step further when he first proposed his famous "needs hierarchy" in his 1943 *Psychological Review* article, "A Theory of Human Motivation." Maslow asserted that humans had five sets of goals or basic needs arranged in a hierarchy of prepotency: (1) physiological needs (food, water, shelter, etc.), (2) safety needs, (3) love or affiliation needs, (4) esteem needs, and (5) self-actualization needs. After fulfilling these needs, an individual theoretically reaches self-fulfillment and becomes all that he or she is capable of becoming. Once the lower needs are satisfied, they cease to be motivators of behavior. Conversely, higher needs cannot motivate until lower needs are satisfied. Simply put—a person will risk being eaten by a hungry lion if that risk is the only way to get food and water. Only after the body is sustained can thoughts turn to safety and the other higher needs.

According to Maslow, "It is quite true that man lives by bread alone—when there is no bread. But what happens to man's desires when there is plenty of bread and when his belly is chronically filled? At once other (and higher) needs emerge, and these, rather than physiological hungers, dominate the organism." When these in turn are satisfied, new, even higher needs will emerge. Maslow's psychological analysis of motivation proved to be the foundation for much subsequent research. While other researchers, such as Herzberg, McGregor, and Bennis (all discussed on the following pages), would take Maslow's concepts and develop them into more comprehensive theories of motivation and organizational behavior, Maslow's work remains the point of departure.

The Motivation-Hygiene Theory

One of the first extensive empirical demonstrations of the primacy of internal worker motivation was the motivation-hygiene theory put forth by Frederick Herzberg, Bernard Mausner, and Barbara Snyderman, in a landmark 1959 study entitled *The Motivation to Work*. Five factors were isolated as determiners of job

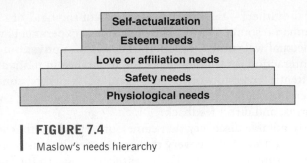

FIGURE 7.4
Maslow's needs hierarchy

satisfaction: (1) achievement, (2) recognition, (3) work itself, (4) responsibility, and (5) advancement. Five factors associated with job dissatisfaction were similarly realized: (1) company policy and administration, (2) supervision, (3) salary, (4) interpersonal relations, and (5) working conditions. The satisfying factors were all related to job content, the dissatisfying factors to the environmental context of the job. The factors that were associated with job satisfaction were quite separate from those factors associated with job dissatisfaction. Herzberg later made this observation in "The Motivation-Hygiene Concept" in *Personnel Administration*:

> Since separate factors need to be considered depending on whether job satisfaction or job dissatisfaction was involved, it followed that these two feelings were not the obverse of each other. The opposite of job satisfaction would not be job dissatisfaction, but rather NO job satisfaction; and similarly the opposite of job dissatisfaction is NO job dissatisfaction—not job satisfaction.

Because the environmental context of jobs, such as working conditions, interpersonal relations, and salary, served primarily as preventatives, they were termed hygiene factors, as an analogy to the medical use of hygiene meaning preventative and environmental. The job-content factors such as achievement, advancement, and responsibility were termed motivators because these are the things that motivate people to superior performance. Herzberg wrote in *Work and the Nature of Man* "that the hygiene or maintenance events led to job dissatisfaction because of a need to avoid unpleasantness; the motivator events led to job satisfaction because of a need for growth or self-actualization."

Since its original presentation, a considerable number of empirical investigations by a wide variety of researchers has tended to confirm the motivation-hygiene theory. Its chief fault seems to be its rejection of the view that pay is a unique incentive capable, in differing circumstances, of being a hygiene factor as well as a motivator. But the theory's main holding—that worker motivation is essentially internal—remains largely unchallenged.

Toward a Democratic Environment

According to Warren Bennis, a preeminent sage of organizational futures, democracy in an organization context "is inevitable." Its inevitability has been determined by its empirically proven effectiveness when compared with the more traditional, autocratic methods of organizational management. While the evidence is not complete, the whole thrust of behavioral research concerning employee motivation and productivity supports the notion of extending democracy to the lowest levels of the organizational hierarchy. That extension includes sharing power and policy decisions.

Three basic stratagems have evolved to meet the demands for a more democratic environment in the workplace. First—and historically the most common in the public as well as the private sector—top management tries to meet an expressed need for greater participatory management with a symbolic sop rather than with a meaningful program. When an employee "crisis" erupts because of the general alienation of the workforce or because of some specific reason such as perceived racism or the dehumanizing nature of the work, management seeks to mollify the situation. If it is unable to make any substantial changes, it can often defuse a present crisis by providing a limited upward mobility program or employee representation on the decisional councils of the organization. However, this tactic can only mitigate or alleviate the current problem; there is no real change. There is only an increase in what Frederick Herzberg has called the "hygiene" factors of work—salary, working conditions, interpersonal relations, and so forth. These in turn lead to an insatiable appetite for still more "hygiene." Like heroin, it soon takes more and more to produce less and less effect. In such a context, a manager is called on to play the morally corrupt role of a narcotics pusher, rather than the more beneficial role of an organizational physician.

Yet this is not all dysfunctional. It is a gross misunderstanding to view symbolic rewards as mere deception. In redressing a real or imagined grievance with a symbolic gesture, management, perhaps unwittingly, is taking its first step toward actually resolving the grievance. Responding to an employee demand with a symbolic reward simultaneously acknowledges the appropriateness of the demand and establishes its legitimacy. Once the legitimacy of a demand is established, its eventual achievement is practically preordained, though it may be many years in coming.

To attempt to deal with the question of employee participation in decision making on the plane of symbolic action, however, is not to deal with the question at all. It is merely a delaying tactic, and delay becomes less and less of an option as public sector unions take ever-increasing interest in participatory management. Therefore, the manager sincerely interested in increasing productivity and decreasing turnover will adopt one of the remaining two stratagems: participation implemented by management from above or participation implemented in cooperation with an employee organization such as a union.

Theory X and Theory Y

Psychologists have long been noted for their studies of human and animal motivation. Why else have so many rats gotten so lost in so many mazes? But the operative discipline in organizational motivation is philosophy. The sincerity and rigor of the motivation of employees toward their duties is a direct reflection of management's philosophy toward them. That an operative philosophy is neither written down nor formally stated is irrelevant to its existence. Many organizations have commendable formal managerial philosophies. Ream upon ream of paper have been dedicated to

Alienation ■
A term adopted by Marxism to describe the inevitable feeling of dissociation of industrial workers because of their lack of control over their work (thus making them ripe for revolution). The word has largely lost its Marxist meaning and now refers to any feelings of estrangement from one's work, family, government, society, and the like. In the context of politics and voting behavior, alienation refers to a voluntary dropping out of the political process, to nonvoting, to feelings of contempt or indifference toward government.

Turnover ■
The rate at which employees leave an organization— usually expressed as a percentage of all workers who resign or are fired each year.

espousing an official view of what an idyllic place the jurisdiction is in which to work. The only problem with these fine-sounding philosophies is that they are seldom operational, tending to exist only on paper. Subordinates soon perceive the reality of the situation.

All managerial philosophies are premised on a set of assumptions about human behavior. Douglas McGregor, through his 1960 book *The Human Side of Enterprise*, popularized the contending concepts of managerial philosophy with his now famous Theory X and Theory Y sets of assumptions. McGregor hypothesized that a manager's assumptions about human behavior predetermined his administrative style. Because of the dominance of traditional theory in managerial thought, many managers had long accepted and acted on a set of assumptions that are at best true of only a minority of the population. McGregor labeled as Theory X the following assumptions:

1. The average human being has an inherent dislike of work.
2. Most people must be coerced or threatened with punishment to get them to put forth adequate effort.
3. People prefer to be directed and wish to avoid responsibility.

Theory X sounds very much like a traditional military organization, which is in fact where it comes from. While McGregor's portrait of the modern industrial citizen can be criticized for implying greater pessimism concerning human nature on the part of managers than is perhaps warranted, Theory X is all the more valuable as a memorable theoretical construct because it serves as such a polar opposite of Theory Y, which assumes the following:

1. The expenditure of physical and mental effort in work is as natural as play or rest.
2. A person will exercise self-direction and self-control in the service of objectives to which he or she is committed.
3. Avoidance of responsibility, lack of ambition, and emphasis on security are generally consequences of experience, not inherent human characteristics.
4. The capacity to exercise a relatively high degree of imagination, ingenuity, and creativity in the solution of organizational problems is widely, not narrowly, distributed in the population.

Of course, these differing philosophic orientations are extremes for purposes of example. Most work situations would require a mix rather than a simplistic acceptance of either construct. Nevertheless, assumptions shape destiny; they tend to create self-fulfilling prophecies. Just as it has been shown in experiments with schoolchildren that a teacher's attitude toward any given child helps to determine that child's classroom performance, so it has been shown in similar studies that management's attitude toward workers has the same effect. Simply put, if management assumes that employees are "no damn good" and acts on these assumptions, employees are going to live down to management expectations.

Different philosophies are appropriate to differing organizational environments and work situations. The philosophy appropriate to a military combat unit would hardly be suitable for a research program in computer science. Unfortunately, the environment in which a public sector personnel program tends to operate frequently mitigates against the development of a coherent managerial philosophy. The most basic reason for this is external to the nature of the individuals comprising the organization. While private organizations typically exist in response to a specific goal, the objectives of public organizations are seldom as definite. It has frequently been shown that the professed objectives of a public organization are only vaguely related to its actual mission. For example, the goal of a correctional institution may be reform, but the organization's specific mission is more likely to be simply that of detention. The goal of a police department may be to enforce all of the laws of the community, but its specific mission is more likely to be the maintenance of public order. One goal of a public personnel unit may be to find the best-qualified managers for its agency, but its specific mission in some cases may be limited to processing the papers of those candidates with prior political clearance. When the public policy process is so schizophrenic, it is little wonder that it is difficult or impossible for coherent managerial philosophies to emerge.

Political clearance ■
The process by which qualified applicants for both patronage and merit system appointments are hired only after there is an appropriate indication of partisan political sponsorship. While it is illegal to require political clearance for merit system appointments, it remains a common practice.

BOX 7.1 | Tom Sawyer Anticipates Theory X and Theory Y

Tom went on whitewashing [the fence].

Ben said: "Hello, old chap, you got to work, hey?"

Tom wheeled suddenly and said. . . . "What do you call work?"

"Why, ain't *that* work?"

Tom resumed his whitewashing, and answered carelessly:

"Well, maybe it is, and maybe it ain't. All I know is, it suits Tom Sawyer."

"Oh come, now, you don't mean to let on that you like it?"

The brush continued to move.

"Like it? Well, I don't see why I oughtn't to like it. Does a boy get a chance to whitewash a fence every day?"

That put the thing in a new light. . . . Tom swept his brush daintily back and forth—stepped back to note the effect—added a touch here and there— criticized the effect again—Ben watching every move and getting more and more interested, more and more absorbed. Presently he said:

"Say, Tom, let me whitewash a little."

Tom considered, was about to consent; but he altered his mind:

"No—no—I reckon it wouldn't hardly do, Ben. You see, Aunt Polly's awful particular about this fence—right here on the street, you know—but if it was the back fence I wouldn't mind and she wouldn't. Yes, she's awful particular about this fence; it's got to be done very careful; I reckon there ain't one boy in a thousand, maybe two thousand, that can do it the way it's got to be done."

"No—is that so? Oh come, now—lemme just try. Only just a little—I'd let you, if you was me, Tom. . . ."

Tom gave up the brush with reluctance in his face, but alacrity in his heart. And . . . the retired artist sat on a barrel in the shade close by, dangled his legs, munched his apple, and planned the slaughter of more innocents. There was no lack of material; boys happened along every little while; they came to jeer, but remained to whitewash. . . .

Tom said to himself that it was not such a hollow world, after all. He had discovered a great law of human action, without knowing it—namely, that in order to make a man or boy covet a thing, it is only necessary to make the thing difficult to attain. If he had been a great and wise philosopher, like the writer of this book, he would now have comprehended that Work consists of whatever a body is obliged to do, and that Play consists of whatever a body is not obliged to do. ◢

Source: Mark Twain, *The Adventures of Tom Sawyer* (1876).

> ### TABLE 7.1
>
> **Alternatives to the Bureaucratic Paradigm**
>
> | The Bureaucratic Agency | The Customer-Driven Agency |
> | --- | --- |
> | Focuses on own needs | Focuses on customer needs |
> | Defined by the resources it controls | Defined by results it achieves for customers |
> | Controls costs | Creates value |
> | Sticks to routine | Responds to changing customer demands |
> | Fights for turf | Competes for business |
> | Follows standard procedures | Builds choice into operating systems |
> | Separates thinking from doing | Empowers all front-line employees |
>
> Source: Adapted from Michael Barzelay, *Breaking through Bureaucracy* (Berkeley: University of California Press, 1992).

By the end of the 1960s, the basic relationship between people and the organizations they work in was being redefined from the old world of dependence to the new world of codependence. The whole focus of organization management began to shift from executive control to executive nurturing of the people, groups, and relationships in the organizational environment. The new goal of management was less leadership than the unleashing of the previously stifled energies and creativities of the organization. This trend was fine as far as it went. But a happy organization is not necessarily the most productive one.

THE FUTURE OF ORGANIZATIONS

Be assured—organizations have a future. What that future will be is far more difficult to predict. But change is inevitable. Here are the major trends that will have impact on government organizations in the years ahead.

Postbureaucratic Organizations

In 1952 administrative historian Dwight Waldo prophesied a future society in which "bureaucracy in the Weberian sense would have been replaced by more democratic, more flexible, though more complex, forms of large-scale organization." Waldo called such a society "postbureaucratic." However, it remained for Warren G. Bennis, in the 1960s, to make the term particularly his own with a series of articles and books predicting the "end of bureaucracy." In its place, Bennis wrote in *The Temporary Society*, "There will be adaptive, rapidly changing temporary systems. These will be task forces composed of groups of relative strangers with diverse professional backgrounds and skills organized around problems to be solved." The various task forces would "be arranged in an organic, rather than mechanical, model, meaning that they will evolve in response to a problem rather than to present programmed expectations." Thus employees would "be evaluated not vertically according to rank and status, but flexibly according to competence. Organizational charts will consist of project groups rather than stratified functional groups."

Bennis wasn't a voice in the wilderness. Many other organization analysts of the time (such as Leonard Sayles, George Berkley, and Victor Thompson) were making similar noises. But it remained for **future shock** theorist Alvin Toffler, in his 1970 worldwide bestseller *Future Shock,* to give the popular name to the postbureaucratic lack of structure: "ad hocracy"—a contraction of **ad hoc** and bureaucracy—for "the fast-moving, information-rich, kinetic organization of the future, filled with transient cells and extremely mobile individuals."

Is the bureaucratic form of organization on an inevitable road to extinction? Is it being replaced by systems of temporary democratic networks or structures without hierarchical layers of authority, responsibility, and accountability? If so, the trend is not apparent yet. The announcement of bureaucracy's death seems, once again, to be premature—or at the very least, as in Mark Twain's case, "greatly exaggerated." Actually, bureaucracy appears to be holding its own quite well in practice—even if not in the mainstream literature of organization theory. Within the discipline of public administration, defenders (such as Kaufman, Krislov, and Goodsell) have emerged who justify the bureaucratic form of organization both for its efficiency as well as for its promotion of equity and representativeness.

Elliott Jaques emerged as the foremost defender of the hierarchical-bureaucratic form of organization in the 1990s. Jaques contends that those who argue against hierarchy are "simply wrong, and all their proposals are based on an inadequate understanding of not only hierarchy but also human nature." Hierarchical layers add value to organizations by separating tasks into manageable series of steps: "What we need is not some new kind of organization. What we need is managerial hierarchy that understands its own nature and purpose." According to Jaques, hierarchy is *the* best alternative for large organizations: "We need to stop casting about fruitlessly for organizational Holy Grails and settle down to the hard work of putting our managerial hierarchies in order." Well said!

The enduring strength of the hierarchical structure is elegantly illustrated by Leon E. Panetta, a U.S. representative from California who became President Clinton's first director of the Office of Management and Budget. After the president realized that there was much validity in the widespread criticism about how the White House was managed, he promoted Panetta to chief of staff in 1994. Panetta thereupon set about creating the most ancient of organizational structures for the White House. According to *New York Times* reporter Alison Mitchell, "Panetta set about creating a hierarchy, with himself and his two deputies . . . at the top. He instituted a 7:30 A.M. meeting for a handful of senior staff members—the restrictiveness of the meeting sending a message about the chain of command." There's nothing like a chain of command for creating organizational order out of chaos—even at the White House.

So if the traditional hierarchy (which is all that most people think of when they hear the word "bureaucracy") continues to hold its own, what will happen to all these highly structured government agencies aching for reinvigoration? After the polemical bashing of bureaucracies by angry politicos and "end of bureaucracy" futurists subsides, what will remain is a kernel of reform that calls for traditional

Future shock ■
Alvin Toffler's term, from his book *Future Shock,* for the "distress, both physical and psychological, that arises from an overload of the human organism's physical adaptive systems and its decision-making processes. Put more simply, future shock is the human response to overstimulation."

Ad hoc ■
A Latin term meaning "temporarily, for this one time." It is sometimes used to criticize methods that substitute for standard procedures.

bureaucracies to be transformed into customer-driven service organizations. In *Breaking through Bureaucracy*, Michael Barzelay outlines the new-style government organization that offers "responsive, user-friendly, dynamic, and competitive providers of valuable services" as the alternative to traditional Weberian bureaucracy. In essence, modern government bureaucracies are fighting a two-front war. They are being denounced from without at the same time they are being reformed from within.

Postmodernism

Nothing is changing bureaucracies—both public and private—faster than postmodernism, an "ism" that embraces constant change and accepts as a new fact of life that large organizations today are living on the edge, on the boundary between order and chaos. In this context, however, "chaos" is not synonymous with "anarchy." Instead, it refers to a pervasive condition of unpredictability and complexity. The chaos and uncertainty of this approaching postmodern era has been accompanied by—and accelerated by—rapidly advancing information technology, particularly information networks. In the space of only a few years, information technology has evolved from mainframes to personal computers, local area networks, remote bulletin boards, information networks, and the Internet.

We have been experiencing technological advancement, however, almost since time began. Is something different happening now? The answer is a resounding yes. Information—and information technology—can extend human mental capability. We are not certain, though, what effects information technology will have on interpersonal relations, working teams, and thus organizations as we know them. Emerging forms of communication technology already are spanning time and space. The differences between information technology in premodern, modern, and postmodern organizations can be illustrated by examining the changing nature of the passport. This ubiquitous document is of ancient origins. It is essentially an instruction from the ruler (the state) to allow the bearer to "pass" through the "port"—the gateway to a city, whether on a waterway or a highway. In the modern period it became a small printed book with pages for visa stamps and personal information about the bearer (address, next of kin, etc.). A suspicious-looking traveler might have his or her passport closely inspected to see if the seals on it were authentic or forgeries. The traveler's name might be checked against a list of undesirables. But today's postmodern passports may contain encrypted information on an attached plastic strip allowing immigration officials access to much of the bearer's life and medical history. Or the document can be matched with information from a worldwide network of data that reveal even more about the bearer. What do officials do with all this information? What implications are here for the abuse of civil liberties? The postmodern passport illustrates both the potentialities as well as the dangers of a total information age.

Information networks that tap into (and simultaneously update) real-time databases are providing empowered, self-managing work teams with the information they need to schedule and coordinate their own tasks as well as discipline their own members. Layer upon layer of supervisors and middle managers that are no longer needed are being eliminated. The traditional hierarchy (remember

Moses in Chapter 6) was created in the first place so that information could be efficiently communicated up and down the line (often, the line of battle). If all of the organization members now (because they are each online in the computer sense) instantly have the same information, the traditional communicators—the hoards of middle managers—are, at the very least, less necessary if not totally superfluous.

Information networks in the postmodern era are raising vexing questions that tax existing theories of organization. Those postmodernists who consider themselves deconstructionists (because they intellectually take things apart to analyze their parts) like to think of organizations not as entities in their own right but just simply as a web of relationships. To them an organization can have no goals; it is simply the vehicle by which individuals pursue their personal goals.

Technology and postmodernism also raise questions about the experience of people who work in—or around—organizations. Will Warren Bennis's prediction finally come true? Will bureaucratic organizations as we know them disappear because they are unable to adapt to rapidly changing environments? Will working at home and "telecommuting" become the norm for some public service occupations? If so, how will government employees be held accountable for their time? Can trusting relations be established through interpersonal communications along the information highway in cyberspace?

The Problem of Technocracy

Organizations today must wrestle with complex dilemmas about participating in this "new world" where the workers who once interacted face to face with other people now "float in space" and stare at computer screens instead of faces. In 1965 Don K. Price formulated a new hypothesis on the impact of decisional authority. In his book *The Scientific Estate*, he posited that decisional authority inexorably flowed from executive to technical offices. Consequently, a major distinction had to be made between the legal authority to make a policy decision and the technical ability to make the same decisions. Price's work predated John Kenneth Galbraith's *The New Industrial State* (1967), in which Galbraith made a similar claim for the decisional processes of the large corporations. This theme is destined to be a continuing one in the study of public administration, involving the dilemmas of control of power, information, and technical expertise—what many writers have called the problem of technocracy.

The postmodern world can be extremely frightening to people of traditional bureaucratic sensibilities. There is something comforting about knowing, quite literally, where you stand in your organizations and what your duties are. The premodern, modern, and postmodern organizational worlds will continue to live side by side for the foreseeable future—sometimes even in the same overall organization. The post office, for example, has premodern door-to-door mail delivery, it has modern automated mail-sorting operations, and somewhere in the depths of its research and development operations it has postmodern units trying to discover a role for the Postal Service on the Internet. In the premodern world land was the dominant form of capital. In modern times money and buildings became more important. In the postmodern world information is the new capital. This is why Bill Gates of Microsoft, the world's leading computer software company, is now the richest person in America.

Postmodern Public Administration

So far we have been discussing postmodernism within the context of organizations. But there also exists another context for postmodernism under the rubric of postmodern public administration. This perspective takes the view that the logical-positivism of the social sciences that has evolved since the enlightenment is, according to H. George Frederickson and Kevin Smith "simply misguided." After all, facts, the building blocks of logical-positivism, are mute. They do not really speak for themselves. "Facts represent propositions or hypotheses derived from observation. In the telling of facts, therefore, the observer is not only an active shaper of the message sent but also an active shaper of the likely image received." This frame of reference whereby a fact exists on two planes at the same time, in reality and in the mind of the person perceiving it, is known as phenomenology. This is why the essence of postmodern public administration is a concern for the semantics of a situation (or the "text," both as written and as perceived). This means that postmodernists must study both the real facts and the facts as perceived—which may be unreal but real to the observer.

Postmodern public administration represents a bundle of theories about perceptions and the social construction of reality. It offers a unique way of thinking about social and administrative problems rather than a bundle of techniques for resolving them. Such issues as the transformation of governance structures that we discussed in Chapter 3 are a prime focus of postmodern public administration. Given the complexities of relationships between multilevel governments and nongovernmental organizations, postmodern public administration attempts to provide resolution to the problems brought on by transforming systems. But understanding is the first step in resolution.

A Feminist Perspective

Viewing organizational behavior from a feminist perspective is important for two reasons. First, there is an ever-increasing body of literature on the different ways that the genders operate in organizations. Any managers, whether male or female or from the private or public sector, who are ignorant of this perspective are figuratively walking into an unmarked minefield. No matter how careful they try to be, they will eventually step on something that will do them great harm. Reinforcing the importance of this first reason is the simple fact that women in the United States are an ever-increasing majority of public sector workers. Women constituted 24 percent of all public officials and administrators in 1970. By 2005 they constituted 45 percent. The growth of women in government is not only at low-level positions, but also in professional and administrative capacities. The Office of Personnel Management (OPM) found that between 1992 and 2002 the percentage of women in management-level jobs increased by 15 percent. While the current gender makeup of government employment demonstrates the increasing role of women, the future appears to hold even greater promise for the presence of women in the field of public administration. According to U.S. Department of Education data published in the *Chronicle of Higher Education* (June 9, 1995), women are earning bachelor's degrees in public administration and related service

Logical-positivism ■
An approach to scientific explanation that emphasizes empirical methods and uses quantitative analysis wherever appropriate to logically create formal explanations for the phenomena under study.

Enlightenment ■
The seventeenth- and eighteenth-century European intellectual movement that advocated reason, as opposed to God, as the prime means by which the human condition could be understood and improved.

areas at more than three times the rate of men. More recently, the Council of Graduate Schools found that in 2001, three out of every four public administration graduate students were women. However, if you deduct the number of foreign students in these degree fields, who are almost all men, then the percentage of female predominance in America is even greater. So we may conclude that a feminist perspective on public administration is important because this profession is being feminized in the most literal sense possible.

Feminist organizational analysts such as Joan Acker have argued that long-standing male control of organizations has been accompanied and maintained by male perspectives of organization theory. Thus it has been mainly through male lenses that we see and analyze organizations. At least four sets of gendered processes perpetuate this male reality of organizations:

1. Gender divisions that produce gender patterning of jobs
2. Creation of masculine organizational symbols and images
3. Interactions characterized by dominance and subordination
4. "The internal mental work of individuals as they consciously construct their understandings of the organization's gendered structure of work and opportunity and the demands for gender-appropriate behaviors and attitudes"

Ordinary activities in organizations are not gender-neutral. They perpetuate the "gendered substructure within the organization itself and within the wider society"— as well as in organization theory. So what do we do about this? One option is to do nothing. Just wait—and consider lung cancer. It used to be that lung cancer was pretty much a male problem. Then women started smoking as much as men. Because lung cancer takes a few decades to develop, it takes a while to catch up. But "progress" is slowly being made. Complete equality, thanks to continued cigarette advertising and government subsidies of tobacco farmers, is approaching ever nearer.

What happened with women and lung cancer is also happening today in organizations. As women increasingly climb the organizational ladders, they leave their mark—they gradually change the culture. Substantial research has already shown that women tend to have different management styles from men. For example, Judy B. Rosener, an expert in the area of women and men at work, has shown women to be more cooperative and to share leadership; they are less apt to use the traditional authoritarian "command and control" militaristic style so favored by men. The greatest beneficiaries of the last three decades of affirmative action hiring policies have been women. The seed has been planted. Organizations, as they are increasingly impacted by feminine management styles, will gradually change their operating styles to reflect ever-increasing female influences. The alternative hypothesis is that instead of making their organizations more hospitable to feminine management culture, the women managers—subject to the same stimuli for increased production as men have traditionally been—will become more like the men, will adapt more masculine attitudes because that is the way to thrive in the competitive environment of organizational life.

According to Camilla Stivers, in her book *Gender Images in Public Administration*, "As long as we go on viewing the enterprise of administration as genderless, women will continue to face their present **Hobson's choice**, which is either to adopt a masculine administrative identity or accept marginalization in the bureaucratic

Hobson's choice ■
A dilemma; a difficult decision; a choice of only the lesser of two evils. No choice at all is the original meaning. Thomas Hobson (1544–1631) ran a stable in England. When someone came to rent a horse, Hobson made him take the next horse in line.

hierarchy." So the leaders of today's organizations have three options: (1) do nothing and wait for the problem to resolve itself over time, (2) intervene to consciously create organizations more hospitable to women, or (3) hope that managerial women will be content to become more like men. These options are not mutually exclusive.

For a point of reference on the role of gender in public administration, Stivers examines the effect of strict gender roles during the progressive era in her book *Bureau Men, Settlement Women: Constructing Public Administration in the Progressive Era*. During the government reform movement of the early twentieth century, the policy innovativeness of women social workers was not brought into the emerging field of public administration, thus making the field unnecessarily rigid. Stivers argues that the reliance on the scientific management approach that was part of the traditional male-dominated public administration limited the growth of the field and we should be careful not to let such situations repeat themselves.

| A CASE STUDY | The Dangers of Groupthink from Pearl Harbor to the War in Iraq |

In a classic 1951 article "Effects of Group Pressure upon the Modification and Distortion of Judgments," social psychologist Solomon Asch described his investigations into the ways individuals cope when a group's majority opinion is contrary to the facts of a situation. Asch put lone experimental subjects in rooms with people who had been instructed to give blatantly wrong answers to factual questions—for example, saying a chair was green when it was obviously blue. Only the experimental subjects did not know what was going on. Although a slim majority of subjects retained their independence and reported the facts accurately, a sizable minority of them altered their judgment to match that of the majority. When faced with a group opinion that was obviously wrong, they were not willing to report what they saw. They changed their minds.

Asch's experiments provided dramatic evidence of group impacts on people in organizations. From a managerial perspective, they showed why it is extremely important to focus attention on a work group's beliefs, values, and composition. But for the most part, informal groups are outside of the formal organization's direct sphere of influence.

Twenty years after Asch's experiments, psychologist Irving Janis published his now even better-known study on "groupthink." Like Asch, Janis explored pressures for conformance—the reason why social conformity is encountered frequently in groups. But unlike Asch's experimental use of college students, Janis looked at high-level decision makers at the time of the following major fiascoes:

- The 1941 failure to prepare for the Japanese attack on Pearl Harbor. This brought the United States into World War II.
- The 1950 decision during the Korean War to send General Douglas MacArthur to the Yalu River, the boundary between North Korea and China. This provoked Chinese intervention and expanded the war.

- The 1961 decision to allow an American-sponsored invasion of Cuba by expatriate Cubans trained by the CIA to overthrow the government of Fidel Castro. The landing at the Bay of Pigs was a total failure and a major embarrassment to the Kennedy administration.

Groupthink is "the mode of thinking that persons engage in when concurrence seeking becomes so dominant in a cohesive in-group that it tends to override realistic appraisal of alternative courses of action." Thus a "desperate drive for consensus at any cost . . . suppresses dissent"—and information that might encourage or support dissent as well. The organizational culture that allows groupthink also stifles information. Janis identified eight easily observable symptoms of groupthink that lead to incompetent—and sometimes disastrous—decisions:

1. An illusion of invulnerability
2. Collective construction of rationalizations that permit group members to ignore warnings or other forms of negative feedback
3. Unquestioning belief in the morality of the in-group
4. Strong, negative, stereotyped views about the leaders of enemy groups
5. Rapid application of pressure against group members who express even momentary doubts about virtually any illusions the group shares
6. Careful, conscious, personal avoidance of deviation from what appears to be a group consensus
7. Shared illusions of unanimity of opinion
8. Establishment of mind guards—people who "protect" the leader and fellow members from adverse information that might break the complacency they shared about the effectiveness and morality of past decisions

The groupthink phenomenon is hardly limited to high-level decision makers in the government. Groupthink tends to occur when individuals value membership in a group and identify strongly with their colleagues. It may also occur because the group leader does not encourage dissent or because of stressful situations that make the group more cohesive. In essence, group members suppress doubts and criticisms about proposed courses of action, with the result that the group chooses riskier and more ill-advised policies than would otherwise have been the case. Groupthink, because it refers to a deterioration of mental efficiency and moral judgment due to in-group pressures, has now developed an invidious connotation.

Janis concluded that groupthink has a negative influence on executive decision making because it leads to an overestimation of the group's capabilities and a self-imposed isolation from new or opposing information and points of view. Note that there is nothing new about groupthink. For example, what happened at the Bay of Pigs in 1961 is in groupthink essence no different from what happened to the Spanish Armada's attempted invasion of England in 1588. In both cases leaders (John F. Kennedy and Philip II of Spain) expected small landings of hostile forces to lead to a general uprising against the established regime. False intelligence led to false premises that,

(continued)

> ▶ **A CASE STUDY** | *Continued*
>
> in turn, led to failed invasions. In the cases concerning the Pearl Harbor attack and the Korean War, false intelligence was not the issue. Here there was plenty of intelligence. The failure was to accurately interpret and act on it.
>
> What's really new about groupthink is that we can now label it with an official social science word. Kennedy speechwriter Theodore C. Sorensen, in his biography of his old boss, quotes the president in assessing his judgment on the Bay of Pigs: "All my life I've known better than to depend on the experts. How could I have been so stupid, to let them go ahead?"
>
> Groupthink seems to have played a major role in the decision to go to war with Iraq in 2003. The major justification for the war was the fallacious assumption that Iraq had weapons of mass destruction. This was something that "everybody" believed. The few dissenting voices were ignored or dismissed as uninformed. Nevertheless, after it became evident that the dreaded weapons did not exist, the Bush administration simply took the view that while it was wrong on this point, the war was still more than justified on other grounds. This attitude, as well as the ever-increasing number of American dead and wounded in the war, led to a steady decline in public opinion support of the war as well as a concomitant decline in President Bush's personal popularity.
>
> **For Discussion:** *What are the major factors that lead to groupthink in any organization? Is groupthink only of historical interest, or is it still a common occurrence in government?* ▶

SUMMARY

Organizational behavior examines individuals, groups, and the relationships among them within their organizational environments. Typically, people are clustered in work groups; when a group, such as a branch office, becomes institutionalized in an organization, it evolves shared beliefs, values, and assumptions—norms that become the essence of a cohesive group and of an organizational subculture. Formal groups are officially created by a larger organization. Informal groups are formed through spontaneously developed relationships.

Organization development is planned organizational change necessitated by the fact that organizations exist in a dynamic environment, both internally and externally, to which they must respond or become ineffectual. This process is especially difficult to implement in the public sector because top management, which must first be committed to the process, is so fractured.

As a form of organization, bureaucracy has many advantages; nevertheless, the behavioral consequences of bureaucratic structure are often negative. Because structure stresses depersonalized relations and authority gained by virtue of position, individual ideas and opinions are often valued not according to their intrinsic merit but according to rank.

While there always has been consensus about the need for motivated employees, the same cannot be said for beliefs about how to induce higher levels of motivation. The Hawthorne experiments provided the first major empirical challenge to the scientific management notion that the worker was primarily an economic animal who worked solely for money. Abraham H. Maslow took these findings a step further with his "needs hierarchy." Based on this, Douglas McGregor developed his Theory X and Theory Y sets of managerial assumptions.

Postbureaucratic organizational theorists predict a future society in which traditional bureaucracy is replaced by more flexible forms of large-scale organization. Nevertheless, the hierarchical-bureaucratic form of organization is still highly defended because of its ability to add value to organizations by separating tasks into manageable series of steps.

Two new forces are rapidly changing the organizational world. Postmodernism, with its acceptance of unpredictability and complexity, is being accelerated by rapidly advancing information technology. And as women increasingly climb organizational ladders, they are changing organizational cultures, causing them to be more cooperative and less militaristic.

REVIEW QUESTIONS

1. How does an understanding of group dynamics help managers motivate their subordinates more effectively?
2. How do the organizational change techniques called for by the action research model facilitate more capable organizational arrangements?
3. What are the pros and cons of bureaucratic impersonality?
4. Why is Maslow's needs hierarchy considered to be the foundation for all subsequent research on organizational motivation?
5. In terms of overall policy and management practices, how much difference would it make if women were in charge of all major government organizations?

KEY CONCEPTS

Bureaucrat bashing   Either justified criticism or inappropriate condemnation of public employees.

Bureaucratic impersonality   The dehumanizing consequences of formal organizational structures eliminating personal and emotional consideration from organizational life so that the individual bureaucrat functions only as a cog in an ever-moving machine.

Group dynamics   The subfield of organization behavior concerned about the nature of groups, how they develop, and how they interrelate with individuals and other groups.

Hawthorne experiments   The late 1920s and early 1930s management studies undertaken at the Hawthorne Works of the Western Electric Company near Chicago. Conducted by Elton Mayo and his associates from the Harvard Business School, they became the most famous management experiments ever reported.

Motivation   An amalgam of all of the factors in one's working environment that foster (positively or negatively) productive efforts.

Needs hierarchy   Abraham H. Maslow's five sets of goals or basic needs arranged in a hierarchy of prepotency: physiological needs (food, water, shelter, etc.), safety needs, love or affiliation needs, esteem needs, and the need for self-actualization.

Organization development   An approach or strategy for increasing organizational effectiveness. As a process it has no value biases, but it is usually associated with the idea that effectiveness is found by integrating the individual's desire for growth with organizational goals.

Postbureaucratic organization Constantly changing temporary organizational systems; task forces composed of groups of relative strangers with diverse skills created in response to a special problem rather than to a continuing need.

Postmodernism The belief that constant change is a new fact of life for large organizations that are living on the edge, on the boundary, between order and chaos.

Technocracy A contraction of "technical" and "bureaucracy," which refers to the high-tech organizational environments of the postmodern world.

Theory X The assumptions that the average human being has an inherent dislike of work, that most people must be threatened to get them to put forth adequate effort, and that people prefer to be directed and to avoid responsibility.

Theory Y The assumptions that work is as natural as play, that workers can exercise self-direction and self-control, and that imagination, ingenuity, and creativity are widespread.

MySearchLab® EXERCISES

Apply what you learned in this chapter on MySearchLab (*www.mysearchlab.com*).

BIBLIOGRAPHY

Acker, Joan (1992). "Gendering Organizational Theory." In *Gendering Organizational Analysis*, A. J. Mills and P. Tancred, eds. Newbury Park, CA: Sage.

Argyris, Chris (1964). "T-Groups for Organizational Effectiveness." *Harvard Business Review* (March–April).

————. (1957). *Personality and Organization*. New York: Harper and Row.

Asch, S. E. (1951). "Effects of Group Pressure upon the Modification and Distortion of Judgments." In *Groups, Leadership, and Men*, H. S. Guetzkow, ed. Pittsburgh, PA: Carnegie Press.

Barnard, Chester I. (1938). *The Functions of the Executive*. Cambridge, MA: Harvard University Press.

Barzelay, Michael (1992). *Breaking through Bureaucracy*. Berkeley: University of California Press.

Bennis, Warren G. (1966). *Changing Organizations*. New York: McGraw-Hill.

Bennis, Warren G., and Philip E. Slater. (1969). *The Temporary Society*. New York: Harper Colophon Books.

Berkley, George E. (1971). *The Administrative Revolution*. Englewood Cliffs, NJ: Prentice Hall.

Bernstein, R. J. (1992). *The New Constellation: The Ethical-Political Horizons of Modernity/Post-modernity*. Cambridge, MA: MIT Press.

Blau, Peter, and Marshall Meyer (1971). *Bureaucracy in Modern Society*. New York: Random House.

Clegg, S. (1990). *Modern Organizations: Organizational Studies in the Postmodern World*. Newbury Park, CA: Sage.

Drew, Elizabeth (1996). *Showdown*. New York: Simon & Schuster.

Drucker, Peter F. (1988). "The Coming of the New Organization." *Harvard Business Review* (January–February).

Durant, Will (1950). *The Age of Faith*. New York: Simon & Schuster.

Guiler, Jeffery K. (1998). "Miles's Law." In *International Encyclopedia of Public Policy and Administration*, Jay M. Shafritz, ed. Boulder, CO: Westview Press.

Hillman, David (2005). *Thomas Becket: English Saint and Martyr*. New York: Rosen Publishing Group.

Fox, Charles J., and Hugh T. Miller (1995). *Postmodern Public Administration: Toward Discourse*. Thousand Oaks, CA: Sage.

Frederickson, H. George, and Kevin B. Smith (2003). *The Public Administration Theory Primer*. Boulder, CO: Westview Press.

Gallagher, Winifred (1994). "How We Became What We Are." *Atlantic Monthly* (September).

Goodman, P. S., and L. S. Sproull, eds. (1990). *Technology and Organizations*. San Francisco: Jossey-Bass.

Goodsell, Charles T. (1994). *The Case for Bureaucracy*, 3rd ed. Chatham, NJ: Chatham House.

Guy, Mary (1992). "The Feminization of Public Administration." In *Public Management in an Interconnected World*, Mary Timney Bailey and Richard T. Mayer, eds. New York: Greenwood Press.

Hayles, N. I., ed. (1991). *Chaos and Order: Complex Dynamics in Literature and Science*. Chicago: University of Chicago Press.

Herzberg, Frederick (1964). "The Motivation-Hygiene Concept." *Personnel Administration* (January–February).

———. (1966). *Work and the Nature of Man*. Cleveland, OH: World.

Hoesterey, I., ed. (1991). *Zeitgeist in Babel: The Post-Modernist Controversy*. Bloomington: Indiana University Press.

Janis, Irving L. (1972). *Victims of Groupthink*. Boston: Houghton Mifflin.

Jaques, Elliott (1990). "In Praise of Hierarchy." *Harvard Business Review* (January–February).

Kaufman, H. (1977). *Red Tape*. Washington: Brookings Institution.

Keil, L. Douglas (1995). *Managing Chaos and Complexity in Government*. San Francisco: Jossey-Bass.

Kellert, Steven H. (1993). *In the Wake of Chaos: Unpredictable Order in Dynamical Systems*. Chicago: University of Chicago Press.

Krislov, S., and D. H. Rosenbloom (1981). *Representative Bureaucracy and the American Political System*. New York: Praeger.

Kurtz, Howard (2005). "Dressed for Success, Primed for Failure." *Washington Post* (November 4).

Liddell Hart, B. H. (1972). *Why Don't We Learn from History?* New York: Hawthorn Books.

Mayo, Elton (1933). *The Human Problems of an Industrial Civilization*. New York: Viking.

Miles Jr., Rufus E. (1978). "The Origins and Meanings of Miles's Law." *Public Administration Review* (September–October).

McGregor, Douglas M. (1960). *The Human Side of Enterprise*. New York: McGraw-Hill.

Merton, Robert K. (1957). *Social Theory and Social Structure*. New York: Free Press.

Mitchell, Alison (1995). "Panetta's Sure Step in High-Wire Job." *New York Times* (August 17).

Osborn, Alex F. (1953). *Applied Imagination*. New York: Scribner's.

Pain, Nesta (1964). *The King and Becket*. London: Eyre and Spottiswoode.

Peter, Laurence J. (1969). *The Peter Principle: Why Things Always Go Wrong*. Boston: Houghton Mifflin.

Popper, Karl R. (1945). *The Open Society and Its Enemies*. New York: Routledge.

Price, Don K. (1965). *The Scientific Estate*. Cambridge, MA: The Belknap Press of Harvard University Press.

Rheingold, H. (1993). *The Virtual Community*. Reading, MA: Addison-Wesley.

Roberts, Rand, and James S. Olson (1995). *John Wayne: American*. New York: Free Press.

Rosener, Judy B. (1995). *America's Competitive Secret: Utilizing Women as a Management Strategy*. New York: Oxford University Press.

Sayles, Leonard R., and Margaret Chandler (1971). *Managing Large Systems*. New York: Harper and Row.

Schein, Edgar H. (1969). *Process Consultation: Its Role in Organization Development.* Reading, MA: Addison-Wesley.

Sorensen, Theodore C. (1965). *Kennedy.* New York: Harper and Row.

Sproull, L. S., and P. S. Goodman (1990). "Technology and Organizations: Integration and Opportunities." In *Technology and Organizations,* P. S. Goodman and L. S. Sproull, eds. San Francisco: Jossey-Bass.

Stivers, Camilla (1993). *Gender Images in Public Administration: Legitimacy and the Administrative State.* Newbury Park, CA: Sage.

——— (2002). *Bureau Men Settlement Women: Constructing Public Administration in the Progressive Era.* Lawrence, KS: University of Kansas Press.

Thompson, Victor A. (1961). *Modern Organization.* New York: Knopf.

Toffler, Alvin (1970). *Future Shock.* New York: Random House.

Truman, David B. (1951). *The Governmental Process.* New York: Knopf.

Villa, D. R. (1992). "Postmodernism and the Public Sphere." *American Political Science Review* 86.

Waldo, Dwight (1952). "Development of Theory of Democratic Administration." *American Political Science Review* 44 (March).

Weick, Karl E. (1990). "Technology as Equivoque: Sensemaking in New Technologies." In *Technology and Organizations,* P. S. Goodman and L. S. Sproull, eds. San Francisco: Jossey-Bass.

Wilson, James Q. (1989). *Bureaucracy.* New York: Basic Books.

RECOMMENDED BOOKS

French, Wendell L., and Cecil H. Bell (1998). *Organizational Development: Behavioral Science Intervention for Organization Improvement,* 6th ed. Englewood Cliffs, NJ: Prentice Hall. Everything you always wanted to know about how to do organizational development.

Kaufman, Herbert (1977). *Red Tape: Its Origins, Uses and Abuses.* Washington, DC: Brookings Institution. A very engaging account of the bureaucratic origins of red tape; after defining this elusive term, Kaufman assesses its pros and cons.

Lipsky, Michael (2010). *Street-Level Bureaucracy: Dilemmas of the Individual in Public Services. Expanded Edition.* New York: Russell Sage Foundation. Many were genuinely surprised when the author first asserted that public employees who interacted directly with the public—police, social workers, and so on—were also, by default, the makers of bureaucratic policy, albeit on a small scale but with vast implications for accountability.

Ott, Steven J., Sandra J. Parks, and Richard B. Simpson. (2007). *Classic Readings in Organizational Behavior,* 4th ed. New York, NY: Wadsworth. A thorough collection of the key works in the field of organizational behavior.

Wilson, James Q. (2000). *Bureaucracy: What Government Agencies Do and Why They Do It.* New York: Basic Books. A now-classic analysis of bureaucratic behavior in a wide variety of institutional settings. This book could be retitled "everything Max Weber would have said about modern bureaucracy if he were still alive and working as an American professor of public administration."

RELATED WEB SITES

www.asq.org
American Society for Quality
A global community of experts on quality in all fields, organizations, and industries. The Web site includes case studies of efforts to improve the overall quality of services and management.

www.peoplemanagement.co.uk/index.html
People Management
An online magazine that focuses on various aspects of human resource (HR) management. It includes articles on legal and legislative activities that affect HR management and the latest in research related to the advancement of best practices for HR efforts.

www.pmn.net
Performance Management Network (PMN)
The PMN's mission is to add value to public and private sector enterprises through the exchange of ideas and insights on performance management.

www.siop.org
Society for Industrial and Organizational Psychology
This site has information about jobs, graduate programs, research, and news in this subfield of psychology.

www.aspaonline.org/swpa/
Section for Women in Public Administration
This organization is dedicated to working with women and men on projects and programs promoting participation and recognition of women at all levels and areas of the public sector.

Managerialism and Information Technology

KEYNOTE: Socrates Discovers Universal Management

In ancient Greece, Socrates was busy establishing the intellectual foundations of modern educational testing when he discovered that "the unexamined life is not worth living." Still, he found time to argue for the universality of management, that a successful business leader could be an equally effective general. Universal or generic management refers to management practices that are equally applicable in the public, private, and nonprofit sectors. The underlying doctrine holds that a properly trained manager will be effective in any type of organization, whether public or private, whether in service or manufacturing.

In a dialogue recorded by Socrates' disciple Xenophon, an experienced soldier named Nicomachides complains to Socrates about being passed over for promotion to general despite "having received so many wounds from the enemy" (as he says this, he opens his cloak to reveal his scars) in favor of a businessman "who has never served in the heavy-armed infantry and who indeed knows nothing but how to get money."

Socrates tells the brave soldier that a leader who "knows what he needs, and is able to provide it, [can] be a good president, whether he have the direction of a chorus, a family, a city, or an army."

"By Jupiter, Socrates," cried Nicomachides, "I should never have expected to hear from you that good managers of a family [business] would also be good generals."

"Come, then," proceeded Socrates, "let us consider what are the duties of each of them, that we may understand whether they are the same, or are in any respect different."

"By all means."

"Is it not, then, the duty of both," asked Socrates, "to render those under their command obedient and submissive to them?"

"Unquestionably."

"Is it not also the duty of both to entrust various employments to such as are fitted to execute them?"

"That is also unquestionable."

"To punish the bad, and to honor the good, too, belongs, I think to each of them."

"Undoubtedly."

"And do you think it is for the interest of both to gain for themselves allies and auxiliaries or not?"

"It assuredly is for their interest."

"Is it not proper for both also to be careful of their resources?"

"Assuredly."

"And is it not proper for both, therefore, to be attentive and industrious in their respective duties?"

"All these particulars," said Nicomachides, "are common alike to both; but it is not common to both to fight."

"Yet both have doubtless enemies," rejoined Socrates.

"That is probably the case," said the other.

"Is it not for the interest of both to gain the superiority over those enemies?"

"Certainly; but to say something on that point, what, I ask, will skill in managing a household avail, if it be necessary to fight?"

"It will doubtless in that case, be of the greatest avail," said Socrates, "for a good manager of a house, knowing that nothing is so advantageous or profitable as to get the better of your enemies when you contend with them, nothing so unprofitable and prejudicial as to be defeated, will zealously seek and provide everything that may conduce to victory, will carefully watch and guard against whatever tends to defeat, will vigorously engage if he sees that his force is likely to conquer, and, what is not the least important point, will cautiously avoid engaging if he finds himself insufficiently prepared."

Socrates, in listing and discussing the duties of all good leaders—of public as well as private institutions—emphasized their similarities. He then states that "the conduct of private affairs differs from that of public concerns only in magnitude; in other respects they are similar." Socrates concludes that "those who conduct public business make use of men not at all differing in nature from those whom the managers of private affairs employ; and those who know how to employ them conduct either public or private affairs judiciously, while those who do not know will err in the management of both." His is the first known statement that managerial competence was transferable. Thus a manager who could cope well with one type of organization would be equally adept at coping with others, even though their purposes and functions might be widely disparate. Ever since, the generalist manager has been an ideal.

Socrates was not the only ancient Greek to provide significant insights into modern management. Plato, a student of Socrates, is often considered to be the first political scientist. His *Republic* (360 B.C.E.) is the Western world's first systematic analysis of the political process. There he provided an intellectual rationale for the "divine right of kings" even before Christianity sanctioned the notion. To Plato, only an elite of philosopher kings or "guardians" had the political wisdom necessary to govern; he would not have been an equal opportunity employer. His just society was one where each person had a predetermined place—with the guardians on top. Yet, in essence, Plato's elitism is a call for professionalism—a challenge to his contemporaries who thought that no training or aptitude was necessary to manage public affairs.

In his *Politics*, Aristotle, a student of Plato, wrote of the division of labor, departmentalization, centralization, decentralization, and delegation of authority. But most importantly he presented the first comprehensive analysis of the nature of a state and any other political community. To Aristotle, the state was a natural development because "man is by nature a political animal." The state was even more important than family because, while a family exists for comfort, the state can be a vehicle for glory and the good life.

Perhaps Aristotle's most famous analytical construct is his classification of the three basic forms of government. He found that every political community had to be governed by either the one, the few, or the many. This corresponds to his three governing types: kingship, aristocracy, and polity (majority rule). Unfortunately, each of these had its perversions, the conditions to which it degenerated when the rulers ceased ruling in the interests of the whole community. Kingship often degenerated into tyranny; aristocracy (rule by a talented and virtuous elite) into an

In the Bible it is written that "greater love hath no man than this, that a man may lay down his life for his friends" (John 15:13). In this 1787 depiction of *The Death of Socrates* by French artist Jacques-Louis David, Socrates is explaining to his followers why he is expressing love for them by laying down his life (by drinking hemlock, a poison) for the public administrative institutions of his state, the city of Athens. Socrates, as the inventor of the Socratic method of seeking truth by a constant, nagging questioning of facts and values, had so annoyed most of his fellow citizens that they condemned him with the expectation that he would then voluntarily exile himself—and pester citizens of another city with his questions. Socrates always took pride in his service to the state as a sometimes soldier and as a citizen gadfly and critic. He was too respectful of the institutions of his government to disdain them by exiling himself. So he tells his distraught followers that he is about to drink the hemlock as his final duty as a citizen. Or maybe he was just ravaged by the illnesses of old age and tired of living. All we know for sure is that Socrates remains the archetype of a great teacher—even when he quite literally (as in this picture) points out his final lesson: that government-mandated suicide is an acceptable way of dealing with adverse administrative edicts.

oligarchy (rule by a small group in its own interest); and a polity or constitutional system (where a large middle class rules for the common interest) into democracy (mob rule in the interests of the lower classes). Overall, Aristotle favored a mixed constitution—one in which all citizens "rule and are ruled by turn," where no class monopolizes power and a large middle class provides stability.

It is only in this last situation that administrative institutions evolve to be responsive to the needs of the mass of the citizenry. Still the Greeks limited citizen participation. Manual workers, merchants, and other "disreputable" types (including large numbers of slaves) were excluded from citizenship. Because work itself was disdained, no professional corps of administrators emerged. The relatively few citizens, competent or not, took turns managing the public's business. As Pericles

PPBS ■
Planning,
programming,
budgeting systems;
a budgeting process
that requires agency
directors to identify
program objectives,
to develop methods of
measuring program
output, to calculate
total program costs,
to prepare detailed
multiyear program
and financial plans,
and to analyze
alternatives.

**Zero-based
budgeting ■**
A budgeting process
that is, first and
foremost, a rejection
of the incremental
decision-making
model of budgeting.
It demands a
rejustification of
the entire budget
submission (from
ground zero).

Internal control ■
The sum of the many
diverse procedures
that management
uses to administer
an agency, from
accounting systems to
training programs.

**James Burnham
(1905–1987) ■**
The professor of
philosophy at New
York University who,
after an early career
as a communist of
the anti-Stalinist,
Trotsky type, became
a leading conservative
writer who advocated
defeating the Soviet
Empire.

said in his funeral oration over the Athenians who died in the Peloponnesian War, "We are called a democracy, for the administration is in the hands of the many and not of the few." The Athenians assumed that all citizens would participate in government. Pericles proudly asserted that "we are the only people to regard the man who takes no interest in politics not as careless, but as useless." Thus it made sense to them that most offices were filled by lot for short terms. Effectively, the gods decided who did what. However, some offices such as treasurer or military commander were elected—they were simply too important to give the gods free rein. As any student of Greek mythology knows, the gods often proved to be perverse.

Aristotle's most famous student was Alexander the Great. He did not write any books; he just used what Aristotle taught him and conquered the world. But because he never created an institutional foundation for his empire, it dissipated shortly after his death. The Greeks simply lacked the knack—lacked the doctrine—for large-scale administrative structures. They never got beyond the city-state. So it was relatively easy for the better organized Romans to take them over in the middle of the second century B.C.E. It just goes to show that in the game of chutes and ladders that is the rise and fall of civilizations, the better organized—those who have the best public administration doctrine—win. And it has been that way since the beginning of recorded history. Aristotle might just as well have said that "man is an administrative animal" because states do not get very far politically or militarily unless they also develop administratively.

For Discussion: *What is the validity of Socrates' core argument in favor of the universality of management? Is management as universal and generic today as it was at the time of Socrates?*

MANAGERIALISM

In the 1960s and 1970s there was a vast expansion in the intellectual development and technical capabilities of public administration. The new tools of program evaluation and policy analysis, with quantitative precision, called into question the efficacy and utility of long-standing public programs—especially those having to do with social services and education. New budgeting techniques—from **PPBS** to **zero-based budgeting**—meant that political executives and legislators could better see, if not better control, where money was spent. The traditional management focus was expanded to include greater emphasis on strategic planning (see Chapter 9), and **internal control** and ethical responsibility (see Chapter 5). Nevertheless, in spite of all these advances in the art and science of public administration, the 1980s became a period of decline in the public service—declining budgets, declining productivity, declining quality of services, and the declining reputation of the public service itself. In response a new doctrine—managerialism—would emerge and ride, if not to the rescue, then at least into the fray.

Managerialism as a term has long been used by sociologists as referring to the economic and bureaucratic elites that run an industrial society. **James Burnham**, in his 1941 *The Managerial Revolution*, announced that the world was in transition "*from* the type of society which we have called capitalist or bourgeois *to* a type of society which we shall call *managerial*." Burnham asserted that as control of large businesses moved from the original owners to professional managers, society's new governing class would be not the traditional possessors of wealth—but those who have the professional expertise to manage, to lead, those large organizations. The same phenomenon was occurring at roughly the same time in the communist world. **Milovan Djilas** wrote in his 1957 *The New Class* that instead of producing a classless society, the communists had developed a new class system consisting of party officials, managers of the nationalized industries, and bureaucrats. These people, especially those near the top, were the only ones in the communist states to have any power. They used the repressive forces of the state, especially the secret police, to ensure total obedience. This enabled them to enjoy a standard of living vastly higher than that of ordinary members of society. And they were able to pass on this privilege to their children. Even though they could not legally own much more than ordinary citizens, access to high-quality education and easy entrance to prestige jobs guaranteed their children the same status that they possessed themselves. Thus they constituted an upper social class, albeit a nontraditional one.

In the 1980s managerialism, now a well-established sociological "ism," took on new connotations. When Margaret Thatcher began her 11-year stint as British prime minister in 1979, she immediately sought to refocus the civil service from policy toward management. Thus she tried to force the bureaucracy to be more responsive to the needs of its customers (into which citizens were to be transformed). Managerialism, entrepreneurial management that goes beyond participative management to unleash the creative abilities of public managers at all levels, became the prevailing public sector doctrine. As a philosophy of continuous reform, it seeks to prevent an organization from ever degenerating into incompetence. Paradoxically, managerialism is also a retreat from participative management in that it romantically assumes that a managerial elite can radically change and control the direction, culture, and purpose of organizations. The romance of managerialism would not be possible if there were not heroes to romanticize. Who are these new-style heroes? The answer is, the managers themselves, who have come to revitalize the public service by slaying the dragons of self-serving unions and inefficient bureaucrats. Plato would have felt right at home with these modern philosopher-kings.

A New Managerial Revolution

The core theme of managerialism is management rights—giving managers enough room to maneuver so that they can accomplish their goals. This additional managerial room is necessarily taken from the **rank-and-file**. Thus managerialism is quite comfortable with authoritarian management styles and a new version of scientific management—except the search for the "one best way" has been updated to the constant installation of the latest in behavioral and mechanistic technologies. In an effort to gain maximum control of personnel costs, and minimal problems with introducing labor-saving technologies, managerialism seeks to contract out to the private sector as much of the public's business as it can. The techniques of administrative improvement advocated by managerialism, such as management audits and program evaluations, are comparatively old. What's new is that these same old techniques, like the same old tanks (remember the 1940 blitzkrieg discussed in Chapter 6), are being reinvigorated by a new doctrine or guiding philosophy.

Milovan Djilas (1911–1995) ■
The Yugoslavian vice president whose writings attacking European communism cost him his job and earned him a lengthy stay in jail.

Rank-and-file ■
A colloquial expression for the masses. When used in an organizational context, it refers to those members of the organization who are not part of management; those who are the workers and have no status as officers. *Rank-and-file* was originally a military term referring to the enlisted men who had to line up in ranks, side by side, and files, one behind the other. Officers, being gentlemen, were spared such indignities.

It is no longer sufficient for a public manager to be the traditional "neutral gun for hire" passively performing the tasks set by political masters. In 1923 Charles G. Dawes, the first modern budget director of the U.S. government (and later vice president from 1925 to 1929), explained the traditional concept of neutral competence thusly: "If Congress . . . passed a law that garbage should be put on the White House steps, it would be our regrettable duty, as a bureau, in an impartial, nonpolitical and nonpartisan way to advise the Executive and Congress as to how the largest amount of garbage could be spread in the most expeditious and economical manner."

Policy Entrepreneurs

Today such an attitude by a senior administrator would find him or her in bad odor—and not just because of the garbage. Modern public managers are expected to be policy entrepreneurs who forcefully develop, argue for, and, yes, sell creative solutions to vexing problems. Current thinking calls for the most aggressive actions on the part of administrators to fight the never-ending threats of waste, fraud, and **abuse**. These modern crusaders go into the administrative battles shouting their slogans in the same manner that the French revolutionaries of 1789 chanted, "Liberty, Equality, Fraternity." But today's administrative chant, also of French etymological origin, is reengineering, empowerment, and entrepreneurialism.

The current horde of administrative revolutionaries preach as if they are the first to ever see the light of divine bureaucratic guidance. But none of this is new. Franz Kafka, the preeminent novelist of bureaucratic oppression, warned us that "every revolution evaporates, leaving behind only the slime of a new bureaucracy." In a parallel sense, every revolution in management thinking and dogma leaves in its wake only the slime of a new vocabulary.

Abuse ■
The furnishing of excessive services to beneficiaries of government programs, violating program regulations, or performing improper practices—none of which involves prosecutable fraud. Fraud, a more serious offense, is the obtaining of something of value by unlawful means through willful misrepresentation.

REENGINEERING

Reengineering is an old-fashioned reorganization with a college education. Traditional reorganization calls for changes in the administrative structure or formal procedures of government that do not require fundamental constitutional change or the creation of new bodies not previously established by the legislature. Many reorganizations are undertaken for the purposes of departmental consolidation, executive office expansion, budgetary reform, and personnel administration—primarily to promote bureaucratic responsiveness to central executive control and, second, to simplify or professionalize administrative affairs. Of course, all those contemplating a major reorganization should first heed John Kenneth Galbraith's timeless advice: "When things are not good, it is usually imagined that a review, or possibly a reorganization, will make things better. No one ever asks whether the best is being made of a lousy situation."

Radical as Opposed to Incremental Change

The "message" of reengineering is that all large organizations must undertake a radical reinvention of what they do, how they do it, and how they are structured. There is no room for incremental improvement—for small and cautious steps.

Organizations need to quit asking, "How can we do things faster?" or "How can we do our current work at the lowest cost?" The question needs to be "Why do we do what we do—at all?" In *Reengineering the Corporation*, reengineering proselytizers Michael Hammer and James Champy claim that reengineering "is to the next revolution of business what the specialization of labor was to the last." It is the process of asking, "If I were recreating this company today, given what I know and given current technology, what would it look like?" More formally, reengineering is the "fundamental rethinking and radical redesign of business processes to achieve dramatic improvements in critical, contemporary measures of performance, such as cost, quality, service, and speed." Thus reengineering is the search for new models for organizing work.

Reengineering takes reorganization beyond its traditional focus by seeking to totally rethink and refocus how programs are managed and to take maximum advantage of new technology—especially computers. Laudable intentions, indeed! But neither reorganization nor reengineering happens in a political vacuum. Harold Seidman, in *Politics, Position, and Power*, warns that all potential reengineers should be aware of the strong relationship between the organization of a legislature and its executive branch. "One could as well ignore the laws of aerodynamics in designing an aircraft as ignore the laws of congressional dynamics in designing executive branch structure. What may appear to be structural eccentricities and anomalies within the executive branch are often nothing but mirror images of jurisdictional conflicts within the Congress." Legislative and executive branch organizations are "interrelated and constitute two halves of a single system."

The most famous warning on reorganization applies equally to reengineering. It is usually attributed to Petronius Arbiter, a Roman writer of the first century: "I was to learn later in life that we tend to meet any new situation by reorganizing; and a wonderful method it can be for creating the illusion of progress while producing confusion, inefficiency, and demoralization."

Note that Hammer and Champy's best seller contains a reformulation of what has been known since ancient times. Remember the story of the Trojan horse, about how the besieging Greeks finally defeated the defenders of Troy in Asia Minor? For years the Greeks used conventional siege tactics to no avail. Then Ulysses said that the Greeks had to completely rethink what they were doing. With the help of Minerva—the goddess of wisdom, no less—Ulysses reengineered the siege. The new approach was to feign abandoning the siege while leaving behind a wooden horse large enough to contain a squad of Greek soldiers inside. The Trojans, thinking the horse was a tribute from the fleeing Greeks, took it within their city's walls and had a party. Later that night the Greeks who were hiding inside the horse came out and opened the gates for their returning comrades. Then they sacked and looted Troy in the classic manner. Hammer and Champy could not offer a better example of a "fundamental rethinking and radical redesign" of a business effort. Ever since, Ulysses the reengineer has retained his reputation for cunning.

Becoming a Reengineer

Reengineering is as much a mental discipline and a philosophy as it is a process. The reengineer's primary skill is an ability to look at things such as work processes and organizational structures with new eyes. Reengineering is a radical change strategy, not an incremental "grass-roots" employee involvement approach. Reengineering literally means what its name implies. According to Hammer and Champy, "When someone asks us for a quick definition of business reengineering, we say that it means 'starting over.' It *doesn't* mean tinkering with what already exists or making incremental changes that leave basic structures intact. . . . It involves going back to the beginning and inventing a better way of doing work."

While there are various paths to reengineering, they all usually include the following three steps:

1. *Process mapping:* The flowcharting of how an organization presently delivers its services and products as a process. This emphasis on process is why reengineering is often called "process reengineering."
2. *Customer assessments:* The evaluation of the organization's customers' needs, both presently and in the future, by means of **focus groups**, surveys, and meetings with consumers of the organization's products and services.
3. *Process visioning:* A total rethinking of how the work processes ought to function, keeping in mind the latest available technology.

Focus group ■
A relatively small number (6 to 20) of people with a common characteristic brought to a neutral setting to participate in a discussion on products or politics led by a trained researcher. Focus groups are a major tool of marketing research. They allow analysts to delve deeply into the motivations for buying a product or voting for a politician.

Barriers to entry ■
Impediments to further competition in an industry, whether they be legal (critical patents owned by others), economic (start-up costs too high), political (unstable government), or social (the market has established brand preference).

The key to successful reengineering efforts is the ability to challenge the assumptions underlying the current system. Just as there are **barriers to entry** that face all new business ventures, there is a parallel set of barriers to reengineering. Barriers include bureaucratic turf concerns, employee resistance to change, lack of incentives, and general skepticism about just another in a long line of reform efforts. But with a strategic commitment from top management, these barriers can be overcome. For example, a 1994 International City/County Management Association report illustrates how Charlottesville, Virginia, reengineered its process for issuing new business licenses to take less than a half-hour instead of two days; how Merced County, California, reengineered its social service eligibility process to take less than 3 days instead of the previous 40 days; and how Phoenix, Arizona, reengineered the time it took to get city property maps from five days to five minutes.

Robert M. Melia, as first deputy commissioner of the Massachusetts Department of Revenue, became a famous reengineer to many "deadbeat dads" in the early 1990s when he reengineered how past-due child support payments are collected. According to journalist John Martin, because "there was no money for throwing more caseworkers at the problem . . . [Melia] forced the department to rethink child-support enforcement from the ground up—the essence of reengineering." Consequently, "these days, it's a computer, rather than expensive caseworkers, that handles the bulk of the commonwealth's child-support cases. The computer issues a single warning before proceeding to collect overdue child support anywhere it can: garnishing wages, raiding bank accounts, and intercepting tax refunds, unemployment benefit checks, and lottery winnings." Collections have gone up 30 percent. But, more important, the average number of families leaving the welfare rolls because of improved child support is now double its previous monthly rate.

Reengineering, thinking from the ground up, is hardly new. In the nineteenth-century operetta *The Mikado* by Gilbert and Sullivan, the Mikado's (the emperor of

Japan) efforts at reengineering the Japanese judicial system are explained in Act 1: "Our logical Mikado, seeing no moral difference between the dignified judge who condemns a criminal to die, and the industrious mechanic who carries out the sentence, has rolled the two offices into one, and every judge is now his own executioner." Then as now, reengineering is merely a combination of applied logical and strategic will.

EMPOWERMENT

Power is the fuel of organizational life. It is what makes things go. It is relatively easy for managers to get the traditional authoritarian powers of domination that allow them to control and punish subordinates. What is far more difficult is obtaining the power needed for positive accomplishment. This kind of power is less formally given than informally earned—often by empowering others. Thus the paradox that managers can often make themselves more powerful by giving power away. By empowering others, leaders actually acquire more "productive power"—the power truly needed to accomplish organizational goals.

Managers who cannot delegate, who will not trust or empower subordinates, become less and less powerful, and correspondingly more and more incompetent, as they increasingly seek to hoard power. Remember power, much as with money—a variant of power—is like manure: you have to spread it around for it to do any good. Perhaps the most common example of the dysfunctional withholding of power concerns the way managers are punished for not spending all of their budgeted funds. The typical punishment is to take away the money by reallocating the funds and then, to add insult to injury, budget less money during the next budget cycle. No wonder managers have become adept at spending their allocations down to virtually the last penny. Not only is this wasteful, but it also discourages cost-cutting to achieve real savings and greater productivity. Empowering managers to control their budget savings is one of the main thrusts of the entrepreneurial management movement in the United States.

Nor are universities immune from this problem. University administrators seem constantly surprised when academic departments vote tenure for mediocre or marginally competent professors. This tends to happen when the administration maintains a policy of automatically taking budget authority for professional positions away from departments whenever a position becomes vacant. Thus, from the point of view of the department, a faculty slot filled by a mediocrity is better than being understaffed. So the department's tenure decision all too often is based not on merit or competence but on whether the individual in question is better than nothing.

Empowering Teams

Virtually all of the "new" approaches to management that are being advocated—the attempts to find solutions to the "productivity problem"—have blended traditional management methods with new forms of employee involvement and participative management. For the past two decades, we have witnessed a never-ending series of "new" management approaches, particularly approaches that

Empowerment ■
Giving a person or organization the formal authority to do something.

Job satisfaction ■
The totality of an employee's feelings about the various aspects of his or her work; an emotional appraisal of whether a job lives up to an employee's values.

TQM ■
Total quality management; processes to ensure that all aspects of an organization are performing at an optimal level.

emphasize organizational flexibility through the development and empowerment of individuals and work groups.

All of these team-based approaches assume that groups provide individuals with opportunities for personal and professional growth and self-expression and job satisfaction. They also assume that these opportunities cannot become available to workers in traditional hierarchical organizations. Groups provide structure and discipline for individuals at work. Therefore, organizations that permit empowerment do not need multiple levels of supervisors to coordinate, control, and monitor production.

While empowerment is a proven means of enhancing productivity, professor Marc Holzer warns, "One danger in employee involvement, especially within the TQM envelope, is the extent to which it will parallel or bypass the union. In those cases the gains to be made through participation may run up against the losses resulting from political alienation of the union hierarchy." It is reasonable to conclude that the "most effective systems might involve both union and workplace committees. In both sectors the most effective organizations are those which treat unions as real partners, not imagined enemies. Excellent union relationships are especially important in the more heavily unionized public sector."

ENTREPRENEURIALISM

The last and potentially most powerful element of the revolutionary credo is entrepreneurialism. This calls for managers to be transformational leaders who strive to change organizational culture. Each must develop a new vision for the organization—and then convert that vision into reality.

President George H. W. Bush was not a man to inadvertently create many new phrases. But "the vision thing" inadvertently became uniquely his own after he first complained about it in 1988 because he seemed to lack it, knew he seemed to lack it, and couldn't get it. This lack of vision created an image of domestic-policy incompetence that greatly contributed to his failure to win reelection in 1992. Perhaps President Bush should have paid more attention to the biblical Moses. There was a man with vision. He took a people who were slaves in Egypt and transformed them into an independent nation. Now we cannot all be a Moses and get our vision from a burning bush, but we can all avoid being a Bush with no vision.

Entrepreneurial vision cannot and should not be limited to the top. At every organizational level managers need vision and dreams, need the ability to assess the situation and plan for a better future. Those who cannot do this, who cannot visualize and plan for change, are by definition incompetent. After all, organizations that do not change must eventually die—even in the public sector. Besides, if you don't have a dream—a vision—how will you ever know if it comes true?

But be aware that the true believers of any philosophic system or ideology are often headed for a fall. This is nowhere more true than with theories of management. We constantly fool ourselves into thinking we're onto something really new until we discover that, for example, Socrates in ancient Greece espoused the merits of generic management, that Aristotle anticipated the underlying premises of organizational culture, and that during the Italian Renaissance Niccolo Machiavelli wrote *The Prince*, the first of an endless series of "how-to-succeed" books of management advice.

Too many organizations become infatuated with every new management fad and slick-talking consultant that comes along. They buy books for their managers, send them to training programs, and then expect them to manage by **MBO**, **OD**, **ZBB**, **QC**, **TQM**, and a host of other acronyms submerged in a bowl of alphabet soup.

But be careful of swallowing any of this soup whole. Both you and your organization could get a bad case of indigestion because management philosophy taken to extremes is one of the leading causes of incompetence. For example, the scientific management of Frederick Taylor was premised on the notion that there was "one best way" of accomplishing any given task. The job of the line manager, then—once the "one best way" was found by the staff—was to impose this procedure on the organization. The problem with traditional scientific management is its paternalistic "Papa knows best" attitude. It presupposes that the managers have a monopoly on brains, that input from the workers is a distraction to be avoided. But every worker comes with a brain. Only an incompetent organization wastes or ignores this resource. Thus scientific management, a good idea in principle, becomes scientific incompetence when taken to extremes.

Public administration, and management in general, is newly concerned—indeed, newly obsessed—with an issue variously described as quality, competence, more bang for the buck, or meeting the needs of your customers. The whole thrust of this trend toward managerialism is with instilling a newfound sense of competence in organizations—to ward off the evils of incompetence. Unfortunately, competence and incompetence are two sides of the same trick coin. It is a trick coin because there is no common agreement on which side wins—no universal agreement on what constitutes either competence or incompetence. This problem is much like Supreme Court Justice Potter Stewart's famous dilemma over defining pornography. He asserted that while he could not define it, he nevertheless knew it when he saw it. Competence suffers from a similar problem of perception. After all, while one person may see obstructing red tape, another, looking at the same thing, may see a treasured procedural safeguard.

Perhaps the greatest example of the dangers associated with the entrepreneurial spirit in public administration can be found in Orange County, California, during the 1990s. Back in the soaring days of the stock boom, Orange County Treasurer Robert Citron attempted to cash in on the vibrant market through investing public funds in a particularly risky form of investments called derivatives. While Citron was responsible for the decision to invest in derivatives, he did so with the tacit consent of the county government. Citron had established a strong track record of robust returns from his investments. Those earnings had become an increasingly important part of the Orange County budget since the late 1970s. With such success at raising funds without raising taxes, it's not surprising that there came a relaxation of the rules surrounding how funds could be invested. For local government officials, the steady supply of investment revenue allowed them to "have their cake and eat it, too." However, in 1994 Citron's investment strategies began to fail, eventually leading to a loss of $1.6 billion and the bankruptcy of one of the most prosperous counties in the nation. In essence, the county was relying on Citron's entrepreneurial skills in making money and ignoring the risks that such entrepreneurial behavior entails.

MBO ■
Management by objectives; an approach to managing, the hallmark of which is a mutual setting—by both organizational subordinate and superior—of measurable goals to be accomplished by an individual or team over a set period of time.

OD ■
Organization development; a process for increasing an organization's effectiveness. As a process it has no value bias, yet it is usually associated with the idea that maximum effectiveness is to be found by integrating an individual's desire for personal growth with organizational goals.

ZBB ■
Zero-based budgeting.

QC ■
Quality circles; small groups of employees working in the same organizational unit who, with the approval of management, voluntarily meet on a regular basis to identify and solve problems that directly affect their work.

Toward a Competitive Public Administration

The great flaw in managerialism is the logic by which it approaches reform. The problem is not so much the fine people who populate the public service but the systems under which they must work. Just bring in hardheaded managers, presumably with considerable private sector experience, and they will whip things into shape in no time. While it is always true that public service operations can be improved, it does not necessarily follow that the wholesale adoption of private sector tactics will do the job. What the would-be reformers so often forget is that government operations are not inefficient because stupid people work there; they are inefficient because they have been designed by the legislature to reflect the competing interests of patronage, representativeness, and due process. Efficiency has to take its turn with these other factors. And no upstart executive most recently from some hotshot corporation is going to push these other factors out of line—because they are just as much a part of the agency's legal mandate as efficiency.

This is why the managerialist impulse initially rode into town on the back of conservative or right-of-center governments such as the Reagan (U.S.) and Thatcher (U.K.) administrations of the 1980s. They both talked a better managerial game than they played. Nevertheless, their influence has been both lasting and ultimately bipartisan in politically center and left-of-center governments. In the early 1990s the United States, Australia, and New Zealand, for example, also adopted the essence of managerialism. As the guru of managerialism Christopher Pollitt has argued, "Managerialism is the 'acceptable face' of new-right theory concerning the state. . . . [It] provides a label under which private sector disciplines can be introduced to the public services, political control can be strengthened, budgets trimmed, professional autonomy reduced, public service unions weakened, and a quasi-competitive framework erected to flush out the 'natural' inefficiencies of bureaucracy."

The myriad managerialist initiatives have been favorably received by the public because of the general antipathy toward "the bureaucracy," the increasing reluctance of citizens to pay more taxes, the widespread belief (which is often erroneous) that privatization will cost the public less, and the fact that reform of whatever ilk is often good politics.

Nearly all the managerialists' goals can be achieved by what has come to be known as **competitive public administration**. At all levels of government under regimes of vastly differing political philosophies, self-standing bureaucratic components such as building-maintenance staffs or trash-collection operations are being forced to compete in price with private sector contractors that are ready and willing to put the jobs in question into the private sector. Various **voucher systems** allow this same strategy to be applied to public education and housing—even free meals for the homeless. This Darwinian atmosphere of the "survival of the cheapest" is indeed introducing private sector discipline, strengthening political control, trimming budgets, and curtailing unionism and professionalism. What was once right wing is now mainstream. In the United States this is often referred to as the "reinventing-government" movement after the book of that same title by David Osborne and Ted Gaebler.

A perennial theme in American politics is that government's administrative problems will be solved just as soon as some successful business leaders show those

Competitive public administration ■ Public sector policies that force different organizations to compete with each other for the opportunity to do the public's work. Thus private contractors compete with a government agency, government agencies compete with each other, and so on.

Voucher systems ■ A government program that issues redeemable vouchers to eligible citizens to purchase services on the open market. For example, housing vouchers have been suggested as an alternative to public housing, and education vouchers have been suggested as an alternative to public education. The idea of using vouchers was popularized by economist Milton Friedman in *Capitalism and Freedom* (1962).

bureaucrats what's what. Yet managerialism's doctrine of transferability, this genericism that goes back to Socrates, when tried, has usually been far less successful than initially anticipated. Within private corporations, a parallel genericism has been equally destructive. As managers skilled in finance increasingly gained control of manufacturing corporations, products and eventually sales suffered. This problem of a top-management cadre skilled in juggling numbers but ignorant of how their products are made has become so great as to call into question the core beliefs of genericism. Indeed, there is now talk of what economist Robert Samuelson calls the "death of management," the death of the notion that a manager with an MBA (master of business administration) degree "should be able to manage any enterprise, anywhere, anytime."

The New Public Management

As a doctrine, managerialism continues to evolve, its essence having been distilled under the label "the new public management," which, according to Christopher Pollitt, has four main aspects:

1. A much bolder and larger-scale use of market-like mechanisms for those parts of the public sector that could not be transferred directly into private ownership (quasi-markets)
2. Intensified organizational and spatial decentralization of the management and production of services
3. A constant rhetorical emphasis on the need to improve service "quality"
4. An equally relentless insistence that greater attention be given to the wishes of the individual service user/"consumer"

The new public management is ambitious. It is far more ambitious than the traditional management aspects of public administration (which can be called the "old" public management), and, according to Owen Hughes in *Public Management and Administration*, it is a "new paradigm" that heralds a major change in the role of government in society. Like any good paradigm, it seeks to replace the earlier model of public administration because that model "has been discredited theoretically and practically." While one can admire Hughes's intensity of feeling, it is difficult not to figuratively shout, "Don't throw out the baby with the bathwater!"

All reform movements seek vehicles for proselytizing, for educating new converts. The most prominent vehicle for this has been Osborne and Gaebler's *Reinventing Government*. This 1992 surprise best seller has become the bible of the new public management movement. And just as the original Bible warns us that "there is no new thing under the sun" (Ecclesiastes 1:9), the Osborne and Gaebler bible preaches its gospels using ten principles, the most important being the first—"steering rather than rowing"—that is, getting others (such as other levels of government, nonprofit organizations or private business), to perform tasks that you want done. Other principles call for the now old standbys of empowerment, competition, and meeting the needs of the customers. Sounds familiar?

Will these new principles "solve the major problems we experience with bureaucratic government," as their authors intend? To find out, stay tuned to another exciting chapter in the history of public administration! There is no official "new public management." No government has formally sanctioned a group of practices with that title. There only exists a disparate group of structural reforms and informal management initiatives that reflect the doctrine of managerialism and can usefully be grouped under the rubric of the "new public management."

Subsequent chapters will constantly return to these themes not because they are supplanting a "discredited" public administration, but because they are an almost expected revitalization of public administration in the tradition of the progressive movement that started more than one hundred years ago. The progressives got their name from the fact that they believed in the doctrine of progress—that governing institutions could be improved by bringing science to bear on public problems. It was a disparate movement, with each reform group targeting a level of government, a particular policy, and so on. Common beliefs were that good government was possible and that "the cure for democracy is *more* democracy." To achieve this, they only had to "throw the rascals out." And it was the progressive influence that initially forged the fledgling discipline of public administration.

Doctrines come and doctrines go, but public administration is always and inherently progressive. Managerialism, the new public management, and the reinventing government movements are just the latest landmarks on the yellow brick road of progressivism. All these reforms are like Macbeth's "poor player that struts and frets his hour upon the stage and then is heard no more." In 1933 Leonard D. White, the preeminent historian of American public administration, published *Trends in Public Administration*, in which he devoted several chapters to "the new management" that had evolved since 1900. In 1971 Frank E. Marini published his highly influential edited volume *Toward a New Public Administration*. New! New! New! But all this new stuff is just the reaffirmation of the progressive doctrine. There can be no end to the doctrine of public administration; there is only continuous doctrinal reform.

WHAT IS PERFORMANCE MANAGEMENT?

Performance management is what leaders do, it is the primary responsibility of an organizational leader. It is the systematic integration of an organization's efforts to achieve its objectives. What makes performance management different from mere management is this emphasis on systematic integration. Thus it includes the comprehensive control, audit, and evaluation of all aspects of organizational performance. The components of performance management are long-established management tools that encompass most of the other senses in which the term performance is used in the language of public sector management. These components include:

1. the specification of clear and measurable organizational objectives (i.e., management by objectives), which is the essence of strategic management (discussed in Chapter 9);
2. the systematic use of performance indicators, measures of organizational performance, to assess organizational output (this is closely linked to concepts of performance standards to allow the performance measured in one

organization to be compared with industry averages, **best practice**, and benchmarking—the systematic comparison of performance between or among organizations);

3. the application of the performance appraisal of individual employees to assist in harmonizing their efforts and focusing them toward organizational objectives;

4. the use of performance incentives, such as **performance pay**, to reward exceptional personal efforts toward organizational goals;

5. the linking of human and financial resource allocation to an annual management or budget cycle; and

6. regular review at the end of each planning cycle of the extent to which goals have been achieved and the reasons for performance that is better or worse than planned. This creates the feedback that helps start the cycle anew.

Best practice ■
The generally recognized optimal way of performing a task.

Performance pay ■
Extra compensation for extraordinary efforts on the job.

The Politics of Performance Management

Performance management begins with a plan. It is tempting to think of planning as a rational, linear, straightforward process of collecting and analyzing data, establishing and assigning priorities to strategic targets, assessing alternative methods for achieving ends, designing implementation programs, and evaluating programs so as to use the information to improve program and agency impact and performance. However, this is an illusion. Planning is neither straightforward nor linear. Planning never occurs in a vacuum; it is an inherently political process. Consequently, the success of a plan of any kind is often a function of the political astuteness of the planner. Things are still the same as they were in 1788, when Alexander Hamilton advised in *The Federalist*, No. 70, "Men often oppose a thing merely because they have had no agency in planning it, or because it may have been planned by those whom they dislike."

In the public sector, plans often begin out of political necessity. The citizens literally vote for the plans espoused by elected political executives in their campaign promises. For example, Jimmy Carter promised, if elected president, to implement zero-based budgeting. He was, and he did—but then his successor, Ronald Reagan, used an executive order to abolish zero-based budgeting for the federal government on his first day in office. Rudolph W. Giuliani ran for mayor of New York in 1993 and promised to reduce crime. During his first year in office, crime—especially the murder rate—declined. Whether this was caused by changing demographics or better police management, nobody really knows. What is certain is that the mayor—as any mayor would—took credit for the decrease. In 1994 the Republican Party offered a "contract with America" that would radically affect federal budgeting practices. Because of the party's electoral victory, many federal agencies had to begin planning for downsizing. And opposition party President Bill Clinton was no less ambitious with his reinventing-government plans to significantly reduce federal employment.

Performance management plans do not have to wait on elected officials. In the early 1990s the postmaster general did not have to run for office to hear the political winds blowing. All he had to do was read the newspaper accounts of increasing criticisms of mail services, of members of Congress calling for the dismemberment of the Postal Service, and of business leaders calling for an end to the government's first-class-mail monopoly. He got the message. Performance, meaning on-time mail delivery, started going up; complaints and calls for dismemberment started going down.

The most comprehensive adoption of performance management by the U.S. government to date has been the Government Performance and Results Act of 1993—sometimes known as just the "Results Act." This legislation is a typical performance management system in that it seeks to link resource allocations and results; improve program performance; provide better information for congressional policymaking; force agencies to specify their missions, objectives, and strategies; and require them to advise Congress on just how they've gone about this.

Management Control

Control ■
That aspect of management concerned with the comparison of actual versus planned performance as well as the development and implementation of procedures to correct substandard performance. Control, which is inherent to all levels of management, is a feedback process that ideally should report only unexpected situations.

Management information and **control** systems are instituted in public agencies for two primary reasons: (1) to allow administrators to find out what is going on in an organization (and in the environment as the result of an agency's activities) and thereby to manage the activities of others, and (2) to respond to the need to report (to be accountable) to external groups. Control systems are employed to see whether plans are being executed as intended, to monitor goal-oriented behavior, and to make corrections when behavior or results veer from planned goals. This monitoring is essential because organizational goals, quite simply, often get lost. This happens in part because organizations, as artificial entities, cannot have true goals; only people can. And people, despite the fact that they create or join organizations with professed goals, all too often have goals of their own that do not coincide with the ostensible goals of the organization.

The more an organization's stakeholders—the people affected directly or indirectly by the organization's activities—work toward their own separate goals, as opposed to the "official" goals of the organization, the more incompetent the organization must necessarily become. Organizational goals get displaced when employees become more concerned with what they can get out of, as opposed to what they must contribute to, the organization. Thus, the most essential task of a manager—indeed, the "function of the executive," as organization theorist Chester I. Barnard asserted—is to maintain the "dynamic equilibrium" between the needs of the organization and the needs of its employees.

PRODUCTIVITY IMPROVEMENT

Productivity in private and public sector organizations has become the overriding issue in top-management suites as well as in the legislative corridors of power. The ultimate aim of all performance management efforts is greater productivity. Productivity is a measured relationship between the quantity (and quality) of results produced and the quantity of resources required for the production of goods or services. Productivity is, in essence, a measure of the work efficiency of an individual, a work unit, or a whole organization.

Productivity Measurement

Measuring the productivity of any jurisdiction, organization, program, or individual is particularly problematic in the public sector because of the problem of defining outputs and of quantifying measures of efficiency, effectiveness, and impact.

Organizations that provide public services often have multiple and sometimes intangible outputs. In evaluating efficiency, selecting from among the many possible input/output ratios is troublesome. A considerable danger exists in selecting only certain input and output variables because a single efficiency measure may be, in truth, a meaningless or oversimplified measure of performance.

The productivity measurement issue is further complicated by the fact that different efficiency and effectiveness measures must be selected, depending on certain organizational variables: highly routine work versus nonroutine work, high or low degrees of employee discretion, and outputs that are standard, novel, or simple, as opposed to complex work processes. Another way of stating this problem is that from the variety of available productivity measures, those selected must differentiate between intermediate outputs (outputs used by other members of the organization) and final outputs (those absorbed by the outside environment) and between staff and line functions (some individuals/units perform support functions whose impact can be assessed only in terms of increased performance of line departments). Productivity measurement is beset by many obstacles, not the least of which is the insecurity felt by managers attempting to undertake productivity assessments.

And none of this is new. In 1776 Adam Smith in his *Wealth of Nations* wrote, "The labor of some of the most respectable orders in the society is, like that of menial servants, unproductive of any value, and does not fix or realize itself in any permanent subject or vendible commodity, which endures after that labor is past." The eternal problem is that in some areas, when government produces a service, the labor that goes into it cannot be measured as to impact and evaluated as to quality as if it were a manufactured product. Thus it is easy to measure and even improve government productivity when factory-like operations lend themselves to engineered work measurement standards. But service workers such as police officers, social workers, and grade school guidance counselors do not always create a product that is directly measurable except by broad social indicators.

Barriers to Productivity Improvement

The barriers to increased public employee productivity are legion. They can often appear insurmountable: cumbersome and rigid civil service procedural rules that prevent management from reallocating and reorganizing work; a public personnel management approach that has created endless, cumbersome, inflexible systems of position descriptions, job classifications, testing, and equal employment opportunity and affirmative action requirements, which in combination have resulted in what Wallace Sayre called a "triumph of techniques over purpose"; union intransigence; and combinations of procedural and structural rules that inhibit management's ability to reward and punish workers for performance or lack thereof.

The public sector productivity problem also ties directly into the privatization debate. Again, there are assumptions about inferior public sector versus private

Work measurement standard ■
A numerical value applied to the units of work an employee or group can be expected to produce in a given period of time.

Social indicators ■
Statistical measures that aid in the description of conditions in the social environment (e.g., measures of income distribution, poverty, crime, health, physical environment).

sector productivity rates. Although researchers such as George W. Downs and Patrick D. Larkey have gone to great lengths to explain why these comparisons cannot be made, are not made correctly, and should not be made in the first place, the simple truth remains that the burden is on public sector organizations to demonstrate that they are not inferior in terms of their productivity. This is doubly difficult because productivity in the public sector frequently involves multiple client groups and conflicting objectives and priorities. In comparison, private sector counterparts like to make single horizontal comparisons and to stack one set of products or services against another.

Public sector organizations can certainly be faulted for not being willing to do productivity measurements, but one should be clear about both the context and reasons for that unwillingness. There are far too many system "disincentives" built into productivity measurement—from fears of having budgets cut, personnel levels trimmed, or other penalties for producing above-budgeted levels to the serious measurement problems that are inherently biased against public sector goods and products.

Because it traditionally has been so difficult for government organizations, already fiscally strapped, to find the funds to invest in productivity improvement efforts (especially new technology), many jurisdictions have created "innovation funds" to finance such ventures. For example, both the Internal Revenue Service and the state of Florida use this approach. The city of Philadelphia uses savings from cost-cutting for productivity improvement. Mayor Ed Rendell told the National Performance Review Staff, "We tell a department, 'You go out there and do good work. You produce more revenue. You cut waste. And we'll let you keep some of the savings of the increased revenue.'"

Traditionally, the mayor said, "Every nickel that they would have saved would have gone right back to the general fund. . . . They would have gotten a pat on the back, but nothing else." Now municipal departments can keep some of the money they save to finance productivity improvement projects. For example, when Philadelphia's Department of Licenses and Inspection generated $2.8 million more than expected in 1992, the city let the department keep $1 million of the savings to hire more inspectors, which in turn led to increased collections in subsequent years.

Total Quality Management

Although comprehensive productivity improvement movements have taken different shapes, developed much jargon, and took off in many directions in the 1980s and 1990s, the origins of all of them can be traced back to W. Edwards Deming and his 1950 trip to Japan. Deming, a New York University professor, was invited by Japanese executives to teach them his approach to statistical quality control. Joseph Juran, who emphasized the "management" part of "quality," followed Deming to Japan in 1954. In turn, Armand V. Feigenbaum followed Juran with "total quality control" (TQC), a management approach that required all employees to participate in quality improvement activities—from the chair of the board to hourly workers.

By 1975 Japan had developed into the world leader in quality and productivity. In contrast, "quality teachings" were mostly ignored in the United States.

W. Edwards Deming (1900–1993) ■

The professor of management who developed his philosophy of customer service and statistical quality control while working at AT&T's Hawthorne plant (see Chapter 7) in the 1920s and 1930s.

Statistical quality control ■

A statistical technique for maintaining product quality at the desired level without 100 percent inspection. Statistical quality control uses acceptance sampling to determine whether a large lot of finished products meets preset quality levels. Using statistical techniques, a random sample is taken from a lot of goods and the sample is inspected. From this analysis, an inference as to the quality level of the entire lot is made. This technique is often used in conjunction with periodic inspection along the production line that permits corrective action to be taken before final assembly of the product.

According to Keki Bhote in *World Class Quality*, "Deming's popularity in Japan was in contrast to an almost total ignorance about him in the United States. . . . Deming remained in the quality wilderness of America for a whole generation."

If any one event can be said to have triggered the total quality movement in the United States, it was a June 24, 1980, NBC television documentary, "If Japan Can . . . Why Can't We?" The program documented Deming's experiences and successes in Japan. The response was overwhelming. Within months, hundreds of major U.S. corporations and government agencies had scrambled aboard the quality bandwagon. Quality circles—voluntary work groups that cut across organizational layers and boundaries to analyze and recommend solutions to organizational problems—appeared everywhere as if by magic. In 1991 the U.S. Government Accounting Office defined "quality management":

> A leadership philosophy that demands a relentless pursuit of quality and the stamina for continuous improvement in all aspects of operations: product, service, processes, and communications. The major components of quality management are leadership, a customer focus, continuous improvement, employee empowerment. . . .

"How to Do It" TQM materials are now abundant, but Deming's 14 points of management is its most famous formulation. Note how Deming's "theory of TQM" is the intellectual descendant of Jomini's (see Chapter 6) principles of war—a road map for organizational, as opposed to military, victory. In *Out of the Crisis* Deming provides this 14-point guide, which we have paraphrased, for would-be quality managers:

1. Create constancy of purpose for improvement of products and services. (A long-term focus is thus essential.)
2. Adopt the new philosophy. (Be prepared for a total transformation.)
3. Cease dependence on mass inspections. (Quality must be built in; defects must be prevented rather than detected.)
4. End the practice of awarding business on the basis of price tag alone. (Low bids lead to low quality. Long-term relationships must be established with single suppliers.)
5. Improve constantly and forever the system of production and service. (Continuous improvement becomes a philosophy, not just a goal.)
6. Institute training. (Training at all organizational levels is a necessity, not an option.)
7. Adopt and institute leadership. (Managers must lead, not supervise.)
8. Drive out fear. (All employees must feel secure enough to express ideas and ask questions.)
9. Break down barriers between staff areas. (Work in organizations is inherently teamwork.)
10. Eliminate slogans, exhortations, and targets for the workforce. (Problems are caused by the system, not by individuals. Posters and slogans tend to create resentment.)
11. Eliminate numerical quotas for the workforce and numerical goals for people in management. (Production quotas yield defective products; replace work standards with intelligent leadership.)

12. Remove barriers that rob people of pride of workmanship. (The individual performance appraisal is a barrier, not an aid, to productivity.)
13. Encourage education and self-improvement for everyone. (Education never ends—for anybody at any level of the organization.)
14. Take action to accomplish the transformation. (Both top-management and employee commitment is essential.)

Deming, being a quantitative type, loved to make lists. So while he offered 14 points to transform an organization, he also warned of 7 deadly diseases and 16 obstacles that tended to inhibit or altogether prevent such transformation. As Steve Wall, the director of Ohio's Office of Quality Services, told Jonathan Walters in *Governing*, "This [TQM] isn't about hitting home runs. This is about hitting single after single after single after single. You score a lot more runs that way." The problem is that too many managers want to use TQM just to hit a few home runs so they can look good and go on to higher positions.

TQM is further hampered by an emphasis on short-term profits (in the private sector) or short-term "looking-good" results (in the public sector). The whole thrust of TQM is to change the organizational culture to one that values long-term, long-lasting effectiveness. This is why Deming finds short-term numerical ratings of productivity or individuals to be ineffective. Deming believes the effects of annual performance appraisals or management by numbers to be devastating. "Management by fear would be a better name." Such systems force managers to manage defects rather than lead toward constant quality.

Still the question must be asked, as Albert C. Hyde of the Brookings Institution puts it, "Is it a fad, or is it for real?" Hyde laments the fact that "for over two decades the public management experience seems to replicate one management fad after another, each promising more and delivering less. Little wonder that there is so much cynicism about quality management." Yet quality seems to be a major movement now. *Quality Is Free* shouts the title of a book by Philip Crosby, urging organizations to constantly do their best and focus on the needs of the customers. It's "free" because it doesn't really cost any more to do your best as an individual or as an organization.

INFORMATION TECHNOLOGY

In many ways public administration reflects the broader society in which it operates. From the women and men who carry out the laws to the types of tools that they employ, there are striking similarities between the work of government and the larger world that it occupies. Therefore it should not come as a surprise when many of the defining features of contemporary American life find their way into the work of public policy and its administration. Most notably, in a nation that's increasingly defined by the prevalence of technology in the daily lives of its citizens, it can be expected that technology would play a major role in the work of those executing the nation's laws. With global positioning systems (GPS) in our automobiles and high-speed Internet in our homes, it is hard to escape the wired landscape of the nation. Not surprisingly, public administrators have embraced technology to improve their performance in delivering services to citizens. With GPS units in police cruisers and Blackberries in the hands of everyone from road crew workers to the president, government employees have fully joined the technology-addicted American populace. As we'll see in the upcoming discussion, the proliferation of technological tools in government has been beneficial in helping government to be more effective in performing its core function of serving the people, but also has entailed significant costs to both citizens and public administrators themselves.

Social Networks and New Media: Government 2.0

How long has it been since you last sent a text message? When was the last day that you didn't update your Facebook page? How often do you view material on YouTube? Have you sent a text while reading this book? If you're like most college-age individuals, the answers to the above questions probably indicate that you interact very heavily with the most popular technology of the day. From texting to tweeting, Americans have become an increasingly wired, or shall we say wireless, people. While government often lags behind the public and private businesses in adopting various forms of information technology, it eventually catches up. Thus it should not be surprising to find that government agencies have created their own Facebook pages, upload content to YouTube, and send daily tweets and text messages to the world. Such actions are not born out of the government's desire to be trendy, but instead stem from their desire to connect with the public they serve. Among the technologies that government officials have become most enamored with are Facebook, Twitter, YouTube, and texting. As the following sections will demonstrate, these tools are quickly becoming major communication tools for government organizations seeking to reach a diverse citizenry.

Facebook   Since it was launched from a Harvard dorm room in 2004 by the now-famous Mark Zuckerberg, Facebook has become one of the biggest communications phenomenon in contemporary times. From serving a small population of students in Cambridge, Massachusetts, to reaching more than 750 million active users in 2011, Facebook has become a part of everyday life for a large portion of the American population. More than 10 billion minutes per day are spent on Facebook on the average day, with 35 million users updating their status at least once daily. At its core, Facebook provides its users with the ability to more easily communicate with others. This primary focus of Facebook has made it extremely attractive to government organizations and officials who are always in search of better ways to reach the public that they serve.

One problem for federal government agencies seeking to use Facebook was limits from the General Service Administration (GSA) in terms of permitted uses. Without GSA approval, federal agencies or employees who used Facebook for official purposes could find themselves facing problems related to liability, public endorsements, or freedom-of-information violations. To provide agencies with protection on these matters the GSA negotiated a terms-of-service agreement with Facebook in 2009 that made it easier for agencies to create Facebook pages and to disseminate information through the popular social networking site. Since this agreement, federal government Facebook pages have flourished.

A great example of government use of Facebook is the Centers for Disease Control and Prevention's (CDC's) eHealth Marketing Division. This division of

TABLE 8.1	
Selected Examples of Government Facebook Pages	
Centers for Disease Control and Prevention	www.facebook.com/CDC
New York City Department of Education	www.facebook.com/NYCschools
The U.S. Army	www.facebook.com/USarmy
The White House	www.facebook.com/WhiteHouse

the CDC is responsible for much of the Center's AIDS-prevention efforts, with its signature outreach effort being the AIDS.gov Web site. To further the reach of AIDS.gov, the CDC created a Facebook presence that includes a forum for discussion on AIDS-related topics, imbedded videos regarding AIDS education, and widgets that allow for easy access to AIDS facts and information.

Even the centuries-old U.S. Army has established a presence on Facebook. The U.S. Army's Facebook page allows recruits to form bonds before they ever meet at basic training and provides a source of information for individuals considering a career in the military. For example, a discussion forum thread from 2011 involved the types of tattoos that are acceptable for men and women serving in the armed services. Of course, the U.S. Army also uses its Facebook page to help it recruit new soldiers with neatly embedded recruiting videos and discussion groups focusing on the benefits of "army life."

Twitter   Not long ago a tweet was a sound a bird made and twitter meant nothing more than a short burst of fairly meaningless information. Of course these terms mean much more today, with business professionals, government officials, and celebrities sending out millions of tweets each day. Since its creation in 2006, Twitter has quickly become one of the most widely used forms of social networking in the world. At its core, Twitter is a communications service that allows its users to send and receive each other's updates, known as tweets, through e-mail accounts, smartphones, and Web sites. What helped make Twitter so popular was that it limited the size of each post to only 140 characters. Unlike Facebook, which provides a full multimedia experience, Twitter's character limit keeps communications short and sweet. Thus the network is perfect for anyone sending a quick update regarding timely events, and is the reason that so many government agencies have turned to Twitter to help them more effectively do their jobs. In particular, for government agencies with a major focus on disseminating information quickly, Twitter has become an attractive tool.

Public safety and emergency service providers have been especially interested in Twitter's capacity to get quick messages out to millions of subscribers. In Southern California, where cutting-edge technology and natural disasters (e.g. earthquakes, wild fires) are abundant, Twitter has become a favorite tool of the Los Angeles Fire Department (LAFD). Each day the LAFD sends tweets to its fans (a.k.a. subscribers) to let them know of emergencies that may affect their lives. For example, the LAFD issued numerous tweets in September of 2008 when a commuter train derailed, killing dozens and injuring hundreds. And because Twitter

TABLE 8.2

Selected Examples of Government Twitter Feeds

U.S. Department of State	@dipnote
The Environmental Protection Agency	@greenversations
The Transportation Security Administration	@TSABlogTeam
National Aeronautic and Space Agency (NASA)	@nasa

IN THE NEWS | Twit for Tat

Debates over budgets are as old as government itself. When resources are scarce the fights on how those resources will be allocated can be intense. In the past these debates and verbal sparring would occur on the floor of legislative chambers or in the form of competing press releases that would be channeled through the media to the public. As with most areas of American life, the arrival of social networks has changed the way budget debates take place, and in 2011 the combination of deep budget cuts and Twitter made for some very interesting exchanges. Perhaps none was better than this one that took place in Pennsylvania, the home of some of the most famous debates in American history. This time the debates were not made in stately Independence Hall, but instead they were conducted over Twitter, 140 characters at a time.

In 2011 Pennsylvania Governor Tom Corbett proposed a budget that called for significant cuts in state spending in areas that included education and social welfare. To help sell these cuts to the public, the Corbett administration announced over Twitter that it would announce the "Top 12 Facts About the 2011–2012" budget in the form of tweets. As the governor sent out his messages via @GovernorCorbett, the Pennsylvania Democratic Party head quarters decided that it would play a game of twit-for-tat with Corbett through its feed @PaDems. Here is an example of the twitter exchange.

@GOVERNOR CORBETT

Here it is! The #1 fact of the Top 12 Facts about the #PaBudget: The budget does not raise or include any new taxes. #keepingpromises

29 Jul

@PADEMS

And here it is, #RealBudgetFact #1: @GovernorCorbett's #PABudget decimated K-12 education funding for PA's children. #BleakFuture

29 Jul

For those unfamiliar with the language of Twitter the number signs (know as hashtags) before some of the words are links used by those sending the tweet to connect followers to the previous feeds on the subject matter. In this case the @PADems, use of the hashtags #BleakFuture took a follower to all previous feeds that explained why Corbett's budget was damaging public schools in the state.

The 2011 Twitter debate between Tom Corbett and the Democratic Party in Pennsylvania pales in comparison with the eloquent debates that the founding fathers engaged in during the hot Philadelphia summer of 1776. However in our on-demand world those drawn-out debates of long ago may not play well with an impatient public. It makes one wonder how @ThomasJefferson or @JohnAdams might have justified the Declaration of Independence in 140 characters or less if Twitter was available to them. Maybe it would have been something like this:

@THOMASJEFFERSON

Without protecting rights of the people, government is not legitimate. #BritishAbuses Time for a fresh start. #RevolutionTime ◢

communication is a two-way street, citizens have used the network to help fire-fighting efforts, as in the case of the Griffith Park wildfires in 2007. During these wildfires citizens tweeted to the LAFD to report "hot spots" and changes in wind direction, thereby contributing to the eventual containment of the fires.

Another important asset that Twitter brings to government operations is that it can provide continuity of operations when other methods of communication break down. During a crisis or an emergency, a government agency's Web site may be overwhelmed by traffic, and consequently its Web servers can crash. Such was the case at the Washington State Department of Transportation (WSDOT), whose Web site had buckled under spikes in hits during heavy snowstorms. To overcome the problem, the WSDOT turned to Twitter for answers. As WSDOT spokesperson Lloyd Brown told *Government Technology* in 2009, "If we get into an emergency situation, we can update Twitter with our handheld BlackBerry."

While Twitter is emerging as a powerful communication tool for some government agencies, it can fail to deliver results if not used properly. Because of its focus on brevity, Twitter doesn't work well for transmitting policy details. If tweets become too heavily laden with details, this may turn off Twitter users who expect the communications to be more engaging. Twitter's focus on fast transmission of information can also bump up against government's need to prevent disclosure of confidential information. Such was the case in 2009, when Republican Congress-man Pete Hoekstra tweeted during his trip from Iraq. Hoekstra's tweets may have been interesting, but they were also very ill advised, given the fact that his trip was supposed to be secret. Luckily for the good congressman, anti-American insurgents in Baghdad were not yet Twitter users.

YouTube "Check out this YouTube video." Chances are you have heard these words repeated many times by friends and family as YouTube has become part of daily life in the United States and beyond. On the average day, over 3 billion videos are watched by viewers throughout the world, with the total growing dramatically since the video-sharing Web site was introduced in February 2005. From clips of old television shows to videos shot at elementary school concerts, YouTube has provided a clearinghouse for countless hours of video footage. Amid the vast array of music videos, movie clips, and home videos that inhabit You-Tube, government agencies and officials have seen an opportunity to use this technology to make them more effective in carrying out their work. Because it's cheap, easy to use, and reaches a very large audience, YouTube has become a popular tool for public administrators at all levels of government. Importantly, in a world that's increasingly dominated by images, YouTube is perfectly positioned to help government deliver messages to target audiences.

The U.S. government has established its own channel on YouTube, and it contains videos from the White House, the National Aeronautics and Space Agency (NASA), the Food and Drug Administration (FDA), and other federal agencies. One of the best and most developed government presences on YouTube is the NASA site. The amazing visuals associated with space exploration and travel have made YouTube the perfect vehicle for the nation's space agency. While it might seem that it isn't urgent or important to keep the public informed of its operations, for NASA public outreach is critical. In an era of very tight government budgets,

> ## BOX 8.1 | Best Practices for Government Agency Use of Twitter
>
> 1. Use Twitter as a point of customer service. Set a designated time for agency reps to log onto the organization's Twitter account to conduct a question-and-answer session.
> 2. Use Twitter to attract individuals to more detailed content on other platforms such as Web sites and YouTube, but don't use it as the primary means of sharing details.
> 3. Be conversational when using Twitter. People will be more likely to follow tweets if the agency representatives use @ replies and retweet as much as possible.
>
> 4. Have fun and be human! Give people following agency activities a firsthand and personal perspective about government work.
> 5. Don't share classified information on Twitter. The fast pace of the communication may increase the chances that classified material is inappropriately released. ◣
>
> Source: Adapted from the GovTwit Directory, govtwit.com, and Ethan Klapper's "Twitter in Government Agencies: Best Practices" at open.salon.com.

NASA is perpetually looked at as a place where government expenditures can be trimmed. With the budget axe perpetually hovering over it, NASA needs strong public support to help it make the case that its work is relevant. Thus the striking visuals from Mars and the edges of the solar system that reach viewers through YouTube help build a loyal fan base among Americans, and this popularity can help NASA keep its funding during even the most fiscally tight times.

Of course government can also use a visually friendly tool such as YouTube to soften its image in areas where the public may be less than enamored with government activities. Such is the case with the Internal Revenue Service's YouTube channel. The IRS channel contains dozens of clips with smiling IRS agents giving citizens helpful tips on how to lower their tax burden. For example, a 2011 posting on the IRS channel included a pleasant agent named Diane explaining how Americans can file their taxes for free, thus avoiding the cost of paying a preparer. Taxpayers may still hate the IRS, but at least those who have seen Diane have a friendly face to help them through the onerous tax process.

Texting If you are like most college students you have probably just finished sending one of the 50 text messages that individuals in your group send daily. In fact, texting has become the single most common form of communication for the youngest generation of Americans and is quickly surpassing phone calls as the most common form of communication for the entire population of the United States. Texting, with its shorthand language (e.g., LOL, OMG, WTF), offers users a fast, discrete, and cheap way to communicate. According to a 2010 Pew Research Center study, about three out of four adult Americans text, averaging about ten text messages per day. With such a fertile landscape of communication to dig into, it's not shocking that governments at all levels have entered into the realm of texting.

It's sometimes easy to forget that many of the nation's colleges and universities are part of state governments, and thus the staffs of these institutions are

IN THE NEWS | Government Has an App for That

Smartphone owners love to compare the number of apps that they have downloaded to their devices. From apps that allow individuals to track the arrival of their flights to apps that turn your phone into a flashlight, apps have become a passion for tech-loving Americans of all ages. While apps can do many things for their users, it has been less obvious what role if any apps can play for government. In 2010 it became much clearer that if government offered a service, there was going to be an appropriate app for it. Below are just a few of the apps that you can find on the federal government's online home for government services, USA.gov. And of one thing you can be sure, there are apt to be more.

- The Transportation Safety Administration (TSA) created the My TSA app to allow travelers to check the wait time at the security gates at American airports.

- The Consumer Product Safety Commission developed the RECALLS.GOV app, which provided mobile phone users with the ability to check if a product has been recalled because of safety concerns.
- The U.S. Department of Energy introduced the Alternate Fueling Station locater app, which provides users with the ability to locate the closest place to fuel up with biodiesel, electricity, or natural gas.
- The Federal Bureau of Investigation came out with the FBI's Most Wanted app that allows smartphone users to quickly identify criminals and missing children.
- The Bureau of Engraving and Printing created the Eye Note app to allow blind and visually impaired individuals to determine the denomination of the bills that they are holding.

Source: http//:apps.usa.gov.

public administrators. In the wake of the tragic shootings at Virginia Tech University in 2007, college administrations at both public and private institutions turned to text messaging as a way of protecting the safety of students on their campuses. It is now common practice for colleges to ask students to sign up for emergency notification texts from their institutions. For example, when an armed man was found at Purdue University in 2009, it took only seven minutes for students to receive notification from university officials to stay indoors until the "all-clear" text arrived.

On the broader level, the Federal Emergency Management Agency (FEMA) has developed a national-level emergency alert texting system known as PLAN, the Personalized Localized Alerting System. Under PLAN, which began with pilot programs in New York City and Washington, D.C., in 2011, individuals can sign up for the system, which will send geographically targeted emergency alerts to everyone with an enabled device in the area where the emergency is taking place. The four major wireless phone companies in the United States partnered with FEMA on this system, with any phone entering the market by 2011 automatically equipped to receive the alerts.

The use of text messaging by government entities has grown with the expansion of texting as a means of communication, but its rise to prominence has been hindered by a number of factors—most notably difficulties in getting citizens to provide their cell numbers to government officials. Individuals don't like to give away their cell phone numbers for fear of loss of privacy and annoyance. Even when citizens might be willing to part with their phone numbers for the right texting service, there is no guarantee that they would be aware of the government service. Thus strong outreach efforts are necessary on the part of government to get citizens to turn over their prized numbers. A good example of how this is done comes from the Orange County Transportation Authority (OCTA) in California

For years OCTA received thousands of phone calls about schedules and delays for its fleet of buses. The process of answering those calls was both costly and slow, and thus OCTA was optimistic that a text messaging system could address the problems it faced. In 2009 OCTA introduced a system called "OCTAGO," in which riders would receive text updates about schedules and arrival times of buses. While the technical aspects of the system were fairly easy to figure out, the process of getting riders to sign up for the text service was more challenging. To get subscribers to the text service, OCTA came up with a campaign around the message, "When's your next bus? OCTAGO knows." The message was delivered through a coordinated campaign that involved advertisements on the OCTA Web site, posters on the inside and outside of buses, and a group of OCTA representatives called the "Text4Next Street Team" traveling around the county demonstrating the ease in getting signed up for the service. The result was growth in the number of monthly texts from 7,000 in November of 2009 to nearly 200,000 in November of 2010. The cost savings to OCTA were substantial, with phone calls that cost an average of $2 to respond to replaced by texts that cost about 10 cents each.

FROM E-COMMERCE TO E-GOVERNMENT

E-commerce has arrived. The simple proof of this is that you can now buy almost anything over the Web—from automobiles to zippers. And things that can't be bought directly on the Web, such as real estate, can be researched so that any eventual purchase is made by a better-informed buyer. And e-commerce is not only retail; it is also wholesale—business to business. While there are quibbles over which e-commerce activities and individual businesses will thrive and which will decline, there is no doubt that e-commerce is BIG and here to stay.

Another major aspect of e-commerce is the ease with which the Internet facilitates conveying information to customers about their accounts. On any given day millions of citizens can access their accounts with various vendors and see the exact status of their orders—when they were shipped, what has been backordered, and how much is owed or has been charged to a credit card. Similarly, clients can access their checking and retirement accounts to see what checks have cleared and how their 401(k) stock portfolios are faring in a volatile market. This technological wonder begs a very serious question: If a mutual stock fund holding many hundreds of different securities can at the close of each business day tally up the values of its assets and within several hours tell (on the Web) each client the value of his or her accounts to the penny, why can't governments do the same with their myriad accounts? The answer is, of course, that they could. But, as we know, for the most part, they don't. So the question to be answered is "Why don't they?"

Government organizations are inherently and properly conservative—not necessarily in the political sense of tending toward the political right but in the legal sense of having a fiduciary responsibility to manage government assets and programs in a prudent manner. Consequently, governments cannot undertake

▶ TABLE 8.3	
Citizen Interaction with Government Online in 2010	
Looked for Information about a pubic policy or issue online	48%
Looked up what services a government agency provides online	46%
Downloaded government forms	41%
Renewed a driver's license or auto registration online	33%
Received information or applied for government benefits online	23%
Paid a ticket or fine online	15%

Source: How Americans Interact with Government Online. Pew Internet & American Life Project, April 27, 2010, http://pewresearch.org/pubs/1575/how-americans-interact-with-government-online, accessed on Nov 18, 2011.

the kinds of risks with evolving technologies that businesses routinely do. Governments cannot "bet the firm" on a new technology because, quite literally, it wouldn't be prudent. Therefore, in terms of customer service, government will always tend to offer older technologies because they must wait until the newest technologies have proven themselves. Only then can a "prudent" public manager pay for and install them. This is why e-government is much later in arriving than e-commerce. So the answer to the question "Why don't they?" is "They will—it just takes a bit longer to institutionalize innovations in government."

The Two Faces of E-Government

There are two faces to e-government: internal and external. The internal face refers to the operations of government itself—for example, using the Web for electronic procurement, electronic forms, and Web-based management information systems. The external face refers to the online services offered to citizens and businesses—for example, community calendars, bill payment portals, and application forms for employment. While there are two distinct faces to e-government, they seldom represent independent initiatives. *E-government*, then, is in essence the overarching term for all efforts to use the Internet to simplify governmental activities for both the public and the public's employees.

WIRED CITIZENS

Since its arrival as a part of mainstream culture, the Internet has been hailed as a major stimulus for American democracy. With "the Net's" capacity for information sharing and dialogue, the technology seemed primed to play a beneficial role in connecting the government with the governed. Some of the connections enabled by the development of the Internet were fairly straightforward, with government Web sites providing information on meetings, services, and procedures. But as time has gone by, the government's use of the Internet has grown to include much more interactive uses. Public administrators have begun to employ technologies that allow citizens to lodge complaints, pay fees, request services, and submit applications in electronic formats. From paying traffic tickets online in Philadelphia to registering for police officer exams in Seattle over the Web, America's governments have fully embraced electronic government.

Of course the ability of government to electronically interface with citizens is predicated on citizen access to electronic tools such as the Internet. While just a decade ago only one in four Americans used the Internet, in 2007 nearly three in four were online. And not only have Americans increasingly found Web access, more than half now maintain broadband capabilities, thus allowing them to navigate the Net in a quick and efficient manner. To be certain there remain some barriers to entering cyberspace. The ability of an octogenarian grandfather in a Florida retirement village to surf the Web is most likely less developed than that of a 20-year-old student at UCLA, but in general, Americans of all backgrounds are increasingly capable of going online as part of their daily lives.

The growing breadth and quality of Internet access among the U.S. population may underlie its interest and confidence in utilizing e-government. A survey by the Pew Internet & American Life Project found that 82 percent of Internet users (61 percent of all Americans) went to government Web sites or e-mailed government officials in 2010 alone. With the Internet continuing to grow in almost all areas of contemporary American life, it seems very likely that its role in government will further develop in upcoming years. Of particular interest to public administrators will be how the Internet can be packaged with other technologies to produce efficient delivery of public services.

One-Stop Government

The utilization of general technologies such as the Internet and e-mail has opened the door for more integrated technological efforts to connect citizens and government. But how can all the communications technology be brought together in a way that allows citizens to get what they need from government? For many, the answer to this question lies in the idea of one-stop government. *One-stop government* refers to an integration of public services from the point of view of the citizens of the community. Under the one-stop principle, a person should never be given "the runaround" when seeking help from government. Instead, public administrators can overcome many of the built-in hurdles to public service delivery by calling on the technological tools at their disposal.

Perhaps the most publicized example of a one-stop government initiative is the 311 system that many U.S. municipalities are now employing. As almost any American over the age of five can tell you, 911 is the number to call when you need emergency services. But what number do you call when the storm drains on the street are clogged with leaves, or the swings on the playground have rusted? In the past, there were hundreds of possible numbers that you could dial to contact a municipality for services. Other than a name attached to those phone numbers, it was likely that citizens were fairly unsure of which office could best meet their needs. The all-too-common experience of being pushed from agency to agency often prevented government help from being rendered in a timely manner, while it also injected the public with unfavorable thoughts toward their government.

TABLE 8.4	
New York City 311 System Statistics for Fiscal Year 2009	
Total Incoming Calls	18.7 Million
Average Weekday Call Volume	51,200
Average Wait Time	7 Seconds
Average Time to Handle a Call	3 minutes and 48 seconds

Source: © 2012 New York City Department of Information Technology and Telecommunications. All rights reserved. Chart used with permission of the City of New York.

Under the 311 approach, the easy-to-remember number becomes an ingrained part of a citizen's knowledge base. As a call to 911 has become an instinctual aspect of an American's life when faced with an emergency, the hope is that 311 will become a beacon of government responsiveness. Under 311, individuals are placed in contact with a municipal employee who is familiar with the array of city services and programs available to meet the citizen's needs. The employee directs the citizen to the appropriate office or agent and then creates a record of the transaction in order to track the government's performance in addressing the issue. The resulting database gives elected officials and public administrators valuable information on the needs, wants, and concerns of residents, thus helping policymakers make more informed and efficient decisions. According to a 2007 report by the International City/County Management Association (ICMA), the government of San Antonio, Texas, doubled the number of customer service calls received by the city, while simultaneously improving efficiency in service delivery.

New York City's 311 system is perhaps the most noted example of this system. If there's any one municipality where citizens can be overwhelmed by the complexities of municipal government, it's certainly the Big Apple. On his election as Gotham's mayor, Michael Bloomberg noted that his city was operating 40 individual call centers and that the phone book contained *14 pages* of contact numbers for city offices. With his background in business and a strong desire to make New York government more efficient, Bloomberg made the adoption of a citywide 311 system the first initiative of his administration. In March 2003, New York's 311 system went online in service of nearly 8 million residents. In 2007, 400 call center representatives were answering thousands of additional calls daily, with an average wait of just seven seconds. In June 2007, the NYC 311 system received its 50 millionth call, and Mayor Bloomberg announced plans for enhancing the system. In 2008, the city began providing New Yorkers with the choice to manage their interactions with 311 by phone or Web, via NYC.gov. By 2011 the NYC 311 system was receiving over 50,000 calls a day and the 311 web portal had links to Twitter feeds, I-phone apps, and blogs.

Technology and Government Productivity

For public administrators, budget constraints are a part of daily life. With elected officials opposing tax increases but still demanding excellent government services, there is constant pressure on public administrators to do more with less. Under these constraints government employees have often turned to technological fixes in order to maintain the quality of services without increased revenue generation. Just consider the potential savings from having citizens pay their taxes and user fees online. If a jurisdiction needs fewer clerks at front-office windows where citizens can walk in to pay their bills, and fewer back-office clerks to open envelopes and process checks, their personnel costs go way down. And if you need fewer clerks, then you also need fewer staff supporting them, such as guards and cleaning staff again—a cut in personnel staff. And fewer staff requires less office support, and means more savings.

But bill paying online is just the tip of the proverbial iceberg. Big savings are also to be had in a great variety of other areas. For example, occupational licenses can be renewed online. Architectural review of building plans can be done without having to send blueprints across town. Health and building inspection reports can be sent to those concerned the moment they are written—saving on postage and handling. E-government does not, cannot, and will not replace human interaction. But with less interaction come more savings and a greater increase in productivity. And when government increases its productivity, that means stable or lower taxes. This is why President George W. Bush, in his 2002 federal budget proposal, recommended $20 million as the first installment on a $100 million fund for an intra-agency e-government initiative to be managed by the General Services Administration. Despite the fact that Bush wanted to cut taxes and reduce the size of government, he recognized that this increase in spending was seed money that would produce big returns. The president's recommendations helped to pass the E-Government Act of 2002. This Act formally established federal infrastructure to assist in the evolution of e-government throughout the nation. According to the Office of Management and Budget (OMB), the E-Government Act achieved a gross cost savings of $508 million in fiscal year 2007, helping to secure its reauthorization in 2008.

With the federal government increasingly turning to technology, municipalities have followed. Law enforcement is a particular area where technology has been seen as a key to productivity improvements. As law enforcement officers in U.S. cities have come under the heavy demands of increased levels of violent crime and the constant threat of terrorist attacks, technology has offered an important means of assistance. From cameras at busy intersections to streaming video from public parks, police personnel survey the city landscape. In New York alone there are nearly 3,000 cameras scanning the city for illegal activity. And it's not only in megacities such as New York where the cameras are on. In small cities such as Allentown, Pennsylvania, where tight budgets and increasing crime have strained the capacity of police forces, surveillance cameras are being hailed as crucial elements in the area of public safety. To be sure, the arrival of public surveillance cameras has drawn the ire of civil liberty groups, such as the ACLU, which view the cameras as an invasion of privacy. But short of Supreme Court orders to remove the cameras from the streets, it appears that video surveillance cameras will become an increasingly common aspect of the American landscape.

All great leaders have been spinners—public opinion manipulators—to some extent. Was there ever any greater spin than that of the ancient divine right of kings? The Vikings called a frozen island in the North Atlantic "Greenland" and their foothold in what is now eastern Canada "Vineland." While there was not much green and fewer vines, some settlers were initially encouraged by the sharply spun names.

Propaganda is spin in action. At its core is the manipulation of people's beliefs, values, and behavior by using symbols (such as flags, music, or oration) and other psychological tools. In effect, it is the management of public opinion. Propaganda is the older term for what we now call public relations, a government's mass dissemination of true information about its policies and the policies of its adversaries—or alternatively, similar dissemination that is untruthful (sometimes called black propaganda). The term itself stems from the Congregation of Propaganda set up by the Roman Catholic Church in 1622 to propagate its views and to refute the views of Protestants and those considered heretics.

The growth of democracy and mass political awareness presented new possibilities for propaganda. So too has the development of the mass media, which all governments use to influence their publics. The concept was introduced into American political science after World War I when British news reports of German atrocities (both real and imagined) were indicted as having influenced American attitudes toward entry into the war. This fostered Harold D. Lasswell's landmark analysis *Propaganda Technique in World War I* (1927). Ever since World War II, when the German Ministry of Propaganda under Joseph Goebbels broadcast one lie after another, the term has taken on a sinister connotation. Goebbels musically advised to: "Think of the press as a great keyboard on which the government can play" (*Time* March 27, 1933). While Goebbels has been dead since 1945, his example still inspires modern governments—especially those of corrupt dictators. But even democratic governments use the "great keyboard" as Goebbels so helpfully suggested.

Propaganda today is no longer presented with the heavy hand of the mailed fist. It is subtle, delicate, almost subliminal. Modern propaganda is offered to a TV-addicted public as a media event, an activity undertaken as a means of generating publicity from the news media. The defining criterion for a media event is that it would not be done if cameras and reporters were not present. Examples include an orchestrated news leak, the releasing of trial balloons, protest demonstrations scheduled for the convenience of the early evening television news programs, or a walk through a poor or ethnic neighborhood by a candidate for public office to demonstrate meaningful (meaning photogenic) concern. These pseudo-events, historian Daniel J. Boorstin's term for nonspontaneous, planted, or manufactured "news," are designed to gain publicity for the person or cause which arranged the "event."

Mailed fist ■
A tightened hand in chain mail armor, a traditional symbol of military might and oppression.

Leak ■
The deliberate disclosure of confidential or classified information by someone in government who wants to advance the public interest, embarrass a bureaucratic rival, or help a reporter disclose incompetence or skullduggery to the public. As *New York Times* reporter James Reston (1909–1995) often said: "The government is the only known vessel that leaks from the top."

Trial balloon ■
A deliberate leak of a potential policy to see what public response will be. The term comes from the meteorological practice of sending up a balloon to test weather conditions. If public response is hostile, the new policy proposal can be quietly dropped (or deflated).

Cunning politicos throughout the ages have instinctively practiced effective public relations. Some techniques are timeless. When William Shakespeare's Richard III wanted to enhance his seeming worthiness to be king among the masses, he conspicuously went about carrying a Bible. President Bill Clinton did the same when the Monica Lewinsky scandal broke in 1998. The following Sunday he went hand in hand with his wife to church while conspicuously carrying his Bible. The Bible, in addition to its other uses, is a time-honored public relations prop.

But it was only in the twentieth century that public relations advanced beyond politics to become a self-conscious management art, even a profession. Edward L. Bernays (1891–1995) is generally considered to be its founding practitioner. He was the first to make big money selling his ideas on how to influence public opinion on products as well as politicians. He took his skills as an experienced New York theatrical press agent and his understanding of psychology from being **Sigmund Freud**'s nephew (his mother was Freud's sister) and sought to mold public attitudes. For example, in the 1930s Procter & Gamble wanted to sell more Ivory soap. But children didn't like soap. So Bernays came up with the National Soap Sculpture Contest, an annual event whereby a million children got their hands dirty carving Ivory soap.

The American Tobacco Company, makers of Lucky Strike cigarettes, wanted to sell more cigarettes to women. But respectable women didn't smoke and certainly not in public. How to encourage them? In answer to Uncle Sigi's (as he called Freud) famous question, "What does a woman want?" Bernays decided that a woman wants to be thin. So he came up with an advertising campaign that featured slender women smoking as the ad copy read: "Reach for a Lucky instead of a sweet." He then associated smoking with women's rights by having fashionable ladies puffing away on their "torches of freedom," as he called their cigarettes, during the 1929 Easter Parade in New York City. Finally he arranged for experts such as doctors to endorse the benefits of smoking. Women eventually achieved equality with men in smoking—and in lung cancer. Meanwhile, Uncle Sigi, a famous cigar smoker, was gradually dying of throat cancer. All the while Bernays knew enough about the dangers of smoking that he did not smoke himself (he lived to the age of 103) and insisted that his wife and children not smoke as well.

Bernays always sought quite consciously to associate what he was selling with powerful symbols. Smoking was liberating for women. When President Calvin Coolidge, a politician who had an image as a sourpuss, needed help getting elected president in 1924, Bernays very publicly associated him with cheerful smiling people from the New York Broadway theaters. When in the early 1950s a client, the United Fruit Company, was having its banana plantations expropriated by the new leftist government in Guatemala, he made the issue a part of the Cold War by announcing that this **banana republic** had become a bastion of Soviet influence. This encouraged the CIA in 1954 to

(continued)

Sigmund Freud (1856–1939) ■
The Austrian medical doctor who became the founder of psychoanalysis.

Banana republic ■
A frivolous unstable republic; one that changes its laws, leaders, and constitutions too casually. The phrase is a pejorative way of referring to Latin American countries because of the historically unstable nature of their regimes.

◣ A CASE STUDY | *Continued*

sponsor a coup that brought in a government that was friendly to the United Fruit Company. Bernays's tactics earned him the title "father of spin."

If Bernays is the "father of spin," then all current practitioners are his disciples—whether they have ever heard of him or not. They all seek for their candidate or incumbent a defining moment that will symbolically etch their man (or woman) into the minds of the public. Sometimes it occurs in a speech, as when President Franklin D. Roosevelt during his 1933 inaugural address at the height of the Great Depression told the nation: "We have nothing to fear but fear itself." Or when President John F. Kennedy told a joint session of Congress on May 25, 1961: "I believe that this nation should commit itself to achieving the goal, before this decade is out, of landing a man on the moon and returning him safely to the earth." This the United States achieved in 1969.

Perhaps the best-known defining moment in recent history occurred on September 11, 2001. As the fires were still burning in the rubble of the World Trade Center, New York City's mayor, Rudy Giuliani, stood before the world's news cameras and announced in a commanding yet compassionate voice that the "number of casualties will be more than any of us can bear." For his actions on that day, when he truly had to run for his life to escape falling debris, he became "America's mayor" and, eventually, a viable presidential candidate. Yet, if you look closely at his management efforts before and after that day you may find more public relations that substance. Yes, crime went down in New York City; but it also went down in almost every other major American city as well. Fiscally, his city was in great shape; but this was mainly the result of the economic boom of the 1990s. Tellingly, many of his city's firefighters do not feel he was such a great manager. In July of 2007, the International Association of Firefighters released a video denouncing "America's mayor" as an "urban legend." One reason: because so many more firefighters than police officers died on September 11. Why? Because most of the police, who had radios that worked, were told to exit the Twin Towers in time to reach safety. The firefighters, who were carrying obsolete and/or defective radios, didn't get the word in time. Budget priorities are ultimately the responsibility of the mayor, and they often turn out to be matters of life or death.

Probably the leader who has been most defined by a historical moment than any other in recent memory is President George W. Bush. In 2003 he told his nation that he was using his authority as commander in chief of the armed forces of the United States to invade Iraq to forestall its use of weapons of mass destruction (WMDs). When it turned out that no such weapons were to be found, he was branded a liar by his critics. It didn't matter whether he believed that WMDs were there or not. The fact that they could not be found defined him as a liar. There seemed no way—despite his best efforts—that he could spin himself out of the contention that he took his country to war under false premises.

Great Depression ■
The period between the stock market crash of October 29, 1929, and World War II, when the United States and the rest of the Western world experienced the most severe economic decline in the twentieth century. The main focus of the New Deal was to lessen privations caused by the Depression and to create regulatory structures and economic policies that would modify the severity of the normal business cycle. It would cause President Franklin D. Roosevelt to say in his second inaugural address, January 20, 1937, that: "I see one third of a nation ill-housed, ill-clad, ill-nourished." Because the Great Depression started during the Republican Hoover administration, the Democrats have ever since blamed Republicans in general for it.

The ultimate lesson here is that major management decisions must always be made with an eye to public relations—with an eye to how the public will perceive your efforts. This is cynically illustrated by the organization that decides to spend a million dollars on pollution control and 10 million to advertise it. Obviously, the public relations benefits available are perceived to be far greater than the actual pollution controlled. Thus many of the most visible "management" initiatives of governments and corporations must be scrutinized carefully enough to ascertain if they are for real or really just public relations.

Public relations is a tool with no inherent values. It is used by despicable tyrants to hide their villainy, by incompetent managers to cover up their ineptitude, and by honest administers to inform the public about how that public's business is being run. Thus it becomes the obligation of astute citizens to learn to see behind the public relations veil to determine if they are being tyrannized, mismanaged, or properly served by their public servants. The propaganda of the modern age spews forth from the benign face of a press secretary whose job may be as much to obscure as to reveal the truth. But you, dear reader, have no more important job than to ascertain the facts of the situation so that you may function better as an administrator and as a citizen.

For Discussion: *Is public relations as practiced by government leaders a new management skill or just one that is newly analyzed? Can you offer recent examples of "defining moments" by public officials or candidates for public office?* ▶

SUMMARY

Managerialism as a term has long been used by sociologists as a reference to the economic and bureaucratic elites that run an industrial society. In the 1980s this well-established sociological "ism" took on new connotations when the British government sought to refocus the civil service from policy toward management. Now "managerialism" is used worldwide to refer to efforts to force the bureaucracy to be more responsive to the needs of its customers. Thus it is no longer sufficient for public managers to be the traditional "neutral guns for hire." They are now expected to be policy entrepreneurs who forcefully develop creative solutions to vexing problems.

There are three major aspects to managerialism: (1) reengineering, which takes reorganization beyond its traditional focus by seeking to totally rethink and refocus how programs are managed and to take maximum advantage of new technology—especially computers; (2) empowering others, which reflects the paradox that managers can often make themselves more powerful by giving power away; and (3) entrepreneurialism, which calls for managers to be transformational leaders who strive to change organizational culture—to develop a new vision for the organization and then convert that vision into reality.

Performance management, the primary responsibility of an organizational leader, is the systematic integration of an organization's efforts to achieve its objectives. It includes the comprehensive control, audit, and evaluation of all aspects of organizational performance. Closely associated with this is the concept of contracting, because individual or organizational goals are often embodied in quasi-commercial contracts.

Measuring the productivity of any jurisdiction, organization, program, or individual is particularly problematic in the public sector because of the problems of defining outputs and quantifying measures of efficiency, effectiveness, and impact. Total quality management programs require all employees to participate in quality improvement activities; the thrust is to change the organizational culture to one that values long-term, lasting effectiveness. A customer service orientation is inherently part of the workplace quality movement. This means not just good service in the present but a constant striving for better service.

Governments have been increasingly turning to technology, including social networks, to help them meet the demands of citizens. By introducing various forms of e-government, public officials have sought to make government more accessible to the public while simultaneously increasing productivity. Such advancements as one-stop government have helped to simplify the complexities of massive bureaucracies by leveraging the power of contemporary information technologies such as the Internet.

REVIEW QUESTIONS

1. Does managerialism represent a new managerial revolution or a sophisticated new version of scientific management?
2. Why is the reengineering of an organizational unit considered a radical rather than an incremental approach to making it more efficient?
3. How does competitive public administration and the new public management seek to deal with the traditional inefficiencies of public bureaucracies?
4. Will the total quality management movement become a long-standing management approach, or will it fade away as the latest management fad?
5. What are the forces encouraging the implementation of e-government operations within established government bureaucracies?

KEY CONCEPTS

E-commerce Selling and buying over the Internet, whether wholesale or retail.

E-government Conducting any aspect of government business operations over the Internet—from providing information by government to paying bills to government.

Management control That aspect of management concerned with the comparison of actual versus planned performance, as well as the development and implementation of procedures to correct substandard performance.

Managerial revolution James Burham's concept that as control of large businesses moved from the original owners to professional managers, society's new governing class became not the traditional possessors of wealth but those having the professional expertise to manage, to lead, large organizations.

Managerialism An entrepreneurial approach to public management that emphasizes management rights and a reinvigorated scientific management.

New public management A disparate group of structural reforms and informal management initiatives that reflects the doctrine of managerialism in the public sector.

Performance management The systematic integration of an organization's efforts to achieve its objectives.

Productivity A measured relationship between the quantity (and quality) of results produced and the quantity of resources required for production. Productivity is, in essence, a measure of the work efficiency of an individual, a work unit, or a whole organization.

Reengineering The fundamental rethinking and redesign of organizational processes to achieve significant improvements in critical measures of performance, such as costs or quality of services.

Self-directed work team A work group that will accept responsibility for its processes and products—as well as for the behavior of other group members.

Total quality management (TQM) A new phrase for quality control in its most expanded sense of a total and continuing concern for quality in the production of goods and services.

MySearchLab® EXERCISES

Apply what you learned in this chapter on MySearchLab (*www.mysearchlab.com*).

BIBLIOGRAPHY

Abramson, Mark A., and Grady E. Means, eds. (2001). *E-Government 2001*. Latham, MO: Rowman & Littlefield.

Aristotle (1952). *Politics*, B. Jowett, trans. Chicago: Great Books, Encyclopedia Britannica.

Barnard, Chester I. (1938). *The Functions of the Executive*. Cambridge, MA: Harvard University Press.

Barzelay, M. (1992). *Breaking through Bureaucracy: A New Vision for Managing in Government*. Berkeley: University of California Press.

Beizer, Doug (2009). "Looking for a Few Good Friends." *Federal Computer Week Magazine* (April 17). http://fcw.com/Articles/2009/04/20/Facebook-and-government-agencies.aspx.

Bhote, Keki R. (1991). *World Class Quality*. New York: Amacom.

Boorstin, Daniel J. (1961). *The Image: A Guide to Pseudo-Events in America*. New York: Atheneum.

Borick, Christopher (1998). "Going to Market: The Relationship between Fiscal Constraints and State Investment Management Policies." *State and Local Government Review* 30, No. 3.

Bowen, D. E., and E. E. Lawler III. (1992). "The Empowerment of Service Workers: What, Why, How, and When." *Sloan Management Review* (Spring).

Burnham, James (1941). *The Managerial Revolution*. New York: John Day.

Coates, Breena E. (2001–02). "Smart Government Online, Not Inline." *The Public Manager* 30, No. 4 (Winter).

Congressional Research Service (2003). A Primer on E-Government: Sectors, Stages, Opportunities and Challenges of Online Government. http://www.fas.org/sgp/crs/RL31057.pdf (January 28).

———. (2008) Reauthorization of the E-Government Act: A Brief Overview. http://www.fas.org/sgp/crs/secrecy/RL34492.pdf (May 14).

Cornwell, Elmer E. (1965). *Presidential Leadership of Public Opinion*. (Bloomington, Indiana: Indiana University Press).

Crosby, P. B. (1979). *Quality Is Free*. New York: McGraw-Hill.

———. (1984). *Quality without Tears*. New York: McGraw-Hill.

Dawes, Charles G. (1923). *The First Year of the Budget of the United States.* New York: Harper & Brothers.

Deming, W. E. (1986). *Out of the Crisis.* Cambridge, MA: MIT Press.

———. (1993). *The New Economics.* Cambridge, MA: MIT Press.

Djilas, Milovan (1957). *The New Class.* New York: Praeger.

Downs, G., and P. D. Larkey. (1986). *The Search for Government Efficiency.* New York: Random House.

Dynes, Michael, and David Walker (1995). *The New British State.* London: Times Books.

Feigenbaum, Armand V. (1983). *Total Quality Control.* New York: McGraw-Hill.

Galbraith, John Kenneth (1998). *Letters to Kennedy*, James Goodman, ed. Cambridge, MA: Harvard University Press.

Gallup, George (1939). *Public Opinion in a Democracy.* Princeton, NJ: Princeton University Press.

Goodwin, Doris Kearns (1994). *No Ordinary Time.* New York: Simon & Schuster.

Halachmi, Arie, and Geert Bouckaert, eds. (1995). *Public Productivity through Quality and Strategic Management.* Amsterdam: IOS Press.

Hammer, Michael, and James Champy (1993). *Reengineering the Corporation.* New York: HarperCollins.

Holzer, Marc. (1995). "Productivity and Quality Management." In *Handbook of Public Personnel Administration*, Jack Rabin, et al., eds. New York: Marcel Dekker.

Horrigan, John (2006). "Home Broadband Adoption 2006: Home Broadband Adoption Is Going Mainstream and That Means User-Generated Content Is Coming from All Kinds of Internet Users." *Pew Internet and American Life Project* 9 (March 26).

Hughes, Owen (1994). *Public Management and Administration.* London: Macmillan.

Hyde, Albert C. (1991). "Productivity Management for Public Sector Organizations." In *Public Management: The Essential Readings,* J. S. Ott, A. C. Hyde, and J. M. Shafritz., eds. Chicago: Lyceum Books/Nelson-Hall.

———. (1992). "Implications of Total Quality Management for the Public Sector." *Public Productivity and Management Review* 16 (Fall).

International City Management Association. (1986). *1985 Municipal Year Book.* Washington: ICMA.

Juran, J. M. (1992). *Juran on Quality by Design.* New York: Free Press.

Juran, J. M., and F. M. Gryna, eds. (1988). *Juran's Quality Control Handbook*, 4th ed. New York: McGraw-Hill.

Katzenbach, J. R., and D. K. Smith. (1993). *The Wisdom of Teams: Creating the High-Performance Organization.* Boston: Harvard Business School Press.

Lasswell, Harold, D. (1927, 1971). *Propaganda Technique in World War I.* Cambridge, MA: MIT Press.

Lawler, E. E. III, S. A. Mohrman, and G. E. Ledford Jr. (1992). *Employee Involvement and Total Quality Management.* San Francisco: Jossey-Bass.

Lemov, Penelope (1995). "Managing Cash in a Post-Orange County World." *Governing* 8, No. 8.

Linden, Russ (1994). *MIS Report: Re-Engineering Local Government.* Washington: International City/County Management Association.

Lippmann, Walter (1922). *Public Opinion.* New York: Macmillan.

Lueck, Thomas, J. (2005). "City's 311 Help Line Plans to Add Data on Social Services." *New York Times* (November 11).

Marini, Frank E. (1971). *Toward a New Public Administration.* San Francisco: Chandler.

Martin, John. (1994). "Robert M. Melia: The Soul of a Child Support Machine." *Governing* (December).

M.I.T. Commission on Industrial Productivity. (1989). *Made in America: Regaining the Productive Edge*. Cambridge, MA: MIT Press.

Mitroff, I. I. (1987). *Business Not as Usual*. San Francisco: Jossey-Bass.

Osborne, D., and T. Gaebler. (1992). *Reinventing Government: How the Entrepreneurial Spirit Is Transforming the Public Sector*. Reading, MA: Addison-Wesley.

Pascale, R. T., and A. G. Athos. (1981). *The Art of Japanese Management*. New York: Simon and Schuster.

Peters, T. J., and R. H. Waterman Jr. (1982). *In Search of Excellence*. New York: Harper and Row.

Plato. *The Republic* (1925). Oxford: Clarendon Press.

Pollitt, Christopher. (1993). *Managerialism and the Public Services*, 2nd ed. London: Blackwell.

Pollitt, Christopher, and Geert Bouckaert, eds. (1995). *Quality Improvement in European Public Services*. London: Sage.

Samuelson, Robert J. (1993). "The Death of Management." *Newsweek* (May 10).

Sayre, Wallace S. (1948). "The Triumph of Techniques over Purpose." *Public Administration Review* 8 (Spring).

Seidman, Harold (1980). *Politics, Position, and Power*, 3rd ed. New York: Oxford University Press.

Tichy, N. M., and D. O. Ulrich. (1984). "The Leadership Challenge—A Call for the Transformational Leader." *Sloan Management Review* 26.

Tye, Larry (1998). *The Father of Spin: Edward L. Bernays & The Birth of Public Relations* New York: Crown.

United States General Services Administration. (2009) "GSA Signs Agreement with Facebook." http://www.gsa.gov/Portal/gsa/ep/contentView.do?noc=T&contentType=GSA_BASIC&contentId=26065.

U.S. General Accounting Office. (1997). "Performance Budgeting: Past Initiatives Offer Insights for GPRA Implementation." Washington: GAO (March).

Walters, Jonathan (1994). "TQM: Surviving the Cynics." *Governing* (September).

Weisbord, M. R. (1991). *Productive Workplaces: Organizing and Managing for Dignity, Meaning, and Community*. San Francisco: Jossey-Bass.

Wendt, Theodore Otto Jr. (1986). "Presidential Rhetoric: Definition of a Field of Study." *Presidential Studies Quarterly* 16, No. 1 (Winter).

White, Leonard D. (1933). *Trends in Public Administration*. New York: McGraw-Hill.

Williams, Matt (2009). "Governments Use Twitter for Emergency Alerts, Traffic and More." *Government Technology* (Jan. 7). http://www.govtech.com/gt/579338?topic=117680.

Xenophon (1859). *The Anabasis or Expedition of Cyrus and the Memorabilia of Socrates*, J. S. Watson, trans. New York: Harper and Row.

RECOMMENDED BOOKS

Hammer, Michael (1996). *Beyond Reengineering: How the Process-Centered Organization Is Changing Our Work and Our Lives*. New York: HarperCollins. What to do after you reengineer, by the author who first popularized the concept.

Hilmer, Frederick G., and Lex Donaldson (1996). *Management Redeemed: Debunking the Fads That Undermine Our Corporations*. New York: Free Press. An exposé on how the latest management trends all too often lead managers down "false trails."

Holzer, Marc, and Kathe Calahan (1998). *Government at Work: Best Practices and Model Programs*. Thousand Oaks, CA: Sage. After presenting a model for comprehensive productivity improvement, the authors offer a number of good examples in which such "best practices and model programs" are succeeding every day.

Pollitt, Christopher (1993). *Managerialism and the Public Services*, 2nd ed. London: Blackwell. The first major work applying managerialism to public administration. Unfortunately, it has decidedly difficult diction—a book more to be aware of than to read.

RELATED WEB SITES

www.apqc.org
American Productivity and Quality Center
This organization is a member-based nonprofit specializing in benchmarking, knowledge management, measurement, and process improvement. This site offers information about methods to enhance productivity and ways to improve interactions between service providers and their clients.

www.ctg.albany.edu
Center for Technology and Government
The site has information about locating current and past research related to the application of technology in the field of public administration, as well as results and analysis on these studies.

www.govtech.com
Government Technology Magazine (GTM)
GTM is a clearinghouse for news and information about technology use in government. The site provides updates on any legislation at the federal and state levels that affects the use of technology by public organizations and administrators; features examples of cutting-edge use of technology by governments.

www.quality.nist.gov
National Institute of Standards and Technology Quality Program (NISTPQ)
The NISTQP site offers information about job opportunities, news, and other facts pertaining to keeping organizations in the United States competitive on the world stage.

www.performanceweb.org
The Performance Institute
This institute, a think tank focused on performance measurement in government, uses its Web site to present information and research conducted by the institute about performance in government, including case studies that highlight advancements in performance at all levels of government.

Strategic Management and Government Regulation

KEYNOTE: Using Government Regulations of Business to Strategically Manage the Environment

Strategic management, the achievement of long-term organizational goals, is not a tidy business. It is not that managers do not want to be neat; it is just that the managerial environment, especially in the public sector, is inherently and notoriously lacking in neatness. It is not exactly what the Scottish poet Robert Burns (1759–1796) had in mind when he said that the "best laid schemes of mice and men" often go awry; it is rather that these plans are seldom presented in comprehensive documents, if they exist at all. Often the overall strategy exists only as a campaign speech, a vague document, or an unwritten philosophy. The full implementation of a strategic plan usually takes many years, sometimes decades or even more. The usefulness of a strategic plan is that it provides a long-term doctrine, the overall guidance, so essential for short-term, or tactical, management decisions.

Strategic management is hardly new. For example, ancient Rome was into strategic management in a big way. Of course, there was no one single document entitled "The Strategic Plan for the Roman Empire," but all of its elements lay scattered about in various laws, policies, and proclamations. It was much like the British Constitution of today, unwritten but nevertheless thoroughly understood by all those with the responsibility for its implementation. Indeed, the essence of strategic planning—the heart of strategic management—has always been done, especially in a military context, where it began. However, the Romans of old were among the first to apply strategic concepts to the large-scale nonmilitary aspects of government as well.

As with their predecessors in the Roman and British empires, Americans have incorporated strategic approaches to manage many of the largest and most persistent problems that have faced the nation. Since the onset of the Industrial Revolution in the nineteenth century, the issue of environmental degradation has been one of the most widespread challenges for policymakers and has provided the stimulus for the development of strategic management of environmental conditions in the United States. From the beginning of the Industrial Revolution there was pollution. And it was good. Good? Yes, because it was a byproduct of all the mass-produced things that make modern life longer and more fun than it was in the pre-industrial era. The additional cost we increasingly paid for cheap food, cheap kitchen utensils, cheap clothing, and cheap transportation was environmental degradation.

The first efforts of American governments to "save" the environment were the conservation and preservation movements of the early twentieth century. As it became more and more obvious that the toll of economic prosperity was a landscape that showed the scars of unchecked industrialization, the need for a strategy to manage the environment became obvious. However, there was not a single dominant strategy that guided government efforts to manage the nation's natural bounty. Instead, the nation adopted two broad strategies to protect environmental resources—preservation and conservation. Under the preservationist management doctrine, government used its powers to set aside land from the waves of development and industrialization that were engulfing the nation. Under this strategy large tracts of land were placed "off limits" to industrial exploitation. Thus many of our national and state parks came into existence during this period.

In contrast to the preservationist strategy that kept lands out of the destructive hands of despoiling industrialists, the conservationist approach sought to manage land exploitation in a way that would continue to allow socially responsible industrialists to produce the things most desired by the citizens of the nation. Conservationism stressed scientific management as the key to the efficient use of America's forests, rivers, and farm lands. The strategy recognized the fact that if Americans wanted to continue to improve their quality of life with bigger houses and more productive farms, they could no longer think of resources as inexhaustible. Instead, conservation meant considering the long-term condition of the environment as part of the broader drive to economic prosperity.

While the conservation and preservation movements have shaped natural resource policy ever since, the next major effort to strategically manage the environment came in the 1960s when the government turned its attention to the burgeoning problem of pollution. With city air darkened by dense smog and the nation's rivers so clogged with chemicals and oil that some actually caught fire, the public began to clamor for greater government efforts to control pollution. As the 1970s began, the federal government embarked on a 10-year period of tremendous legislative and administrative efforts that targeted the environmental degradation that was enveloping the nation. The trademark of these efforts was the utilization of policies that set mandatory standards that citizens and businesses would have to meet. This command-and-control approach did enable some improvements in environmental quality. But it also drew the ire of many government officials—and even more business leaders—who saw such efforts as excessively intrusive and burdensome to the national economy—as well as to personal profits.

Now a third wave of a strategic management of the environment is at hand that uses economic incentives to encourage businesses to do right by their environment. With problems such as global warming straining the capacity of government to regulate solutions, other strategic approaches have become necessary. And as is the American way, the use of financial incentives has arrived as the driving force behind the latest route to environmental salvation. If you just tell Americans they must not do something, it's often likely they will do it anyway. Remember prohibition! But if you offer them a way to save money, their natural sense of thrift may encourage them do the things you want them to do. In the area of environmental protection, incentives to buy hybrid cars, energy-efficient light bulbs, and solar water heaters have become the preferred route to a greener world. This approach is a victory for classical liberalism, for the public choice approach to public administration, and for the logic of going back to the future.

The environment is just one example of the government's strategic approach to regulation. Similar analyses could be made for the curtailment of smoking by regulating advertising, sales locations, public education, and taxation on cigarettes. All government regulation is a combination of legal controls, advertised sanctions, taxation, education, and moral suasion. Of course, an occasional highly publicized jail sentence helps as well. Ideally it is all wrapped up in one comprehensive strategic plan. But more likely it is the product of the fits and starts of the policymaking process stretching over many decades. Regulation, like sausage and legislation, is often sloppy in production, but delicious in effect.

WHAT IS STRATEGIC MANAGEMENT?

Strategy, the ancient art of generalship, is the employment of—the management of—overall resources (classically soldiers) to gain an objective. Tactics are the use of a subset of these resources to gain a part of the overall objective. Strategic management is the modern application of this ancient art to contemporary business and public administration. It is the conscious selection of policies, development of capability, and interpretation of the environment by managers in order to focus organizational efforts toward the achievement of preset objectives. These objectives necessarily vary. In the private sector it could be the doubling of annual dividends to stockholders within so many years. In the nonprofit sector it could be the creation of a repertory theater or a significant increase in attendance at symphony orchestra concerts. In the public sector it could be a reduction in the crime rate, an increase in the high school graduation rate, the defeat of worldwide communism, or victory in the war against terrorism.

All strategic management efforts take an essentially similar approach to planning where an organization wants to be by a future target date. These are the six features that identify a strategic, as opposed to a nonstrategic, management approach:

1. The identification of objectives to be achieved in the future (these are often announced in a vision statement)
2. The adoption of a time frame (or "planning horizon") in which these objectives are to be achieved
3. A systematic analysis of the current circumstances of an organization, especially its capabilities
4. An assessment of the environment surrounding the organization—both now and within the planning horizon
5. The selection of a strategy for the achievement of desired objectives by a future date, often comparing various alternatives
6. The integration of organizational efforts around this strategy

The overall strategy chosen is in essence the package of actions selected after analyzing alternatives, assessing the outside environment, and determining the internal capabilities of an organization to achieve specified future objectives through the integration of organizational effort. The strategic management process is often conducted by a strategic planning unit within the organization. Eventually, its findings are presented in a detailed document known as the strategic plan. Many of the core elements of strategic management just listed have unique considerations when they are applied to public sector organizations.

Objectives

Objectives-based thinking in management has become so pervasive that it is as hard to think of management without objectives as living rooms without television sets. Originally, objectives were part of military thinking. The Swiss-born Napoléonic era general Henri Jomini, in his 1838 book *The Art of War*, taught how battles should be conducted, with soldiers' moves being planned either for strategic benefit (a qualitative improvement in the long-term position, particularly vis-à-vis the enemy) or tactical benefit (that is, a shorter-term move designed to win the problems—the fighting—of the day and create a better position for the next day's battle).

In this context, we can think of a tactical objective such as "Hill 45"—a specific location that must be taken from the enemy to further the purpose of the overall plan of battle. A strategic objective might be victory on the whole of a battlefront or theater of war. This military vocabulary is now commonly applied to business. For example, when Honda, the Japanese company, started selling

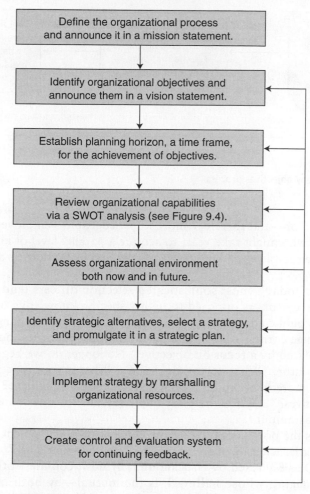

FIGURE 9.1

The strategic management process

motorcycles in the United States in the early 1960s, it secured a tactical objective. When it forced British motorcycles out of the American market, however, it secured a strategic victory.

The public sector was slower than the private sector in embracing strategic management notions. This is because, traditionally, public administrators were expected to focus not on their objectives—what they were trying to achieve—but on their functions and responsibilities—that is, the duties assigned to them by law. Indeed, public administration was traditionally defined as the enforcement or implementation of public policy—that is, the law. This emphasis on the responsibility to discharge ongoing functions set down by law has been the focus of traditional public administration. The seniority principle in promotions often accompanied this attitude. After all, if detailed knowledge of how to administer the laws in a certain functional area were critical, it logically followed that it must be better to

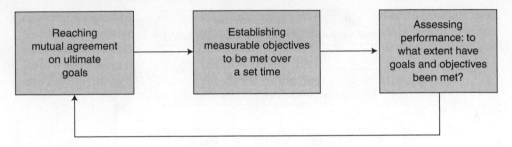

FIGURE 9.2

The management-by-objectives process

have a more senior—and therefore more knowledgeable—employee than to hire someone fresh, who might take years to acquire a parallel level of knowledge. Job descriptions even emphasized knowledge of laws and regulations as a key selection criterion.

In contrast, today's most sophisticated selection officers tend to look for a record of achievement, as opposed to highly specific knowledge of this kind. A world in which public administrators take responsibility for unchanging functions still exists in some corners of the public sector in most countries, but it is increasingly being replaced by a focus on objectives. No longer do we begin by asking a public administrator, "What do you do?" (i.e., "What is your function?"). Today the question is more likely to be "What are you trying to achieve?" (i.e., "What are your objectives?"). While there are many reasons for this change in perspective, three are paramount.

The first is the popularization of the concept of management by objectives (MBO) by Peter Drucker through his pioneering 1954 work *The Practice of Management*. MBO as espoused by Drucker and, by now, countless others, is an approach to managing whose hallmark is the mutual—by both organizational subordinate and superior—establishment of measurable goals to be accomplished by an individual or team over a set period of time. The widespread adoption of the MBO concept across the world has aided in the distinction between a function and an objective. It is now widely understood that an emphasis on the latter can stimulate a focus on performance and effort as opposed to the more traditional custodial focus toward one's organizational obligations.

Second, the ever more rapid pace of change in the communities served by the public sector is such that there are now few functions that can go on unchanged from year to year and decade to decade. The public organizations of today must generally fight and compete in a less-sheltered environment—where the luxury of just "administering" timeless functions rarely exists. The objectives of public sector organizations have become moving targets—and public sector managers must move with them.

Third, the ideas of strategic management and the use of objectives are pervasive in the private sector. Since there is no **Berlin Wall** dividing the sectors, and staff move increasingly in and out of each sector, there is an ever-increasing unification of language, concepts, and standards between the sectors.

Peter Drucker (1909–2005) ■
The preeminent philosopher of management during the post–World War II era.

Berlin Wall ■
The concrete and barbed-wire wall built by East Germany in 1961 to divide East and West Berlin. The wall became the symbol of the division of Eastern and Western Europe. It was dismantled in 1989.

Nonetheless, many public sector organizations still produce separate statements of their functions (or responsibilities) and objectives. You can broadly distinguish the language of each. Since a statement of functions is about what an organization is responsible for under law, it broadly answers the question "What do we do?" The answer is normally a static description, timeless and without directionality. A statement of objectives (often called a mission statement), however, answers the question, "What are we trying to achieve?" Instead of a static description, this normally implies a direction being pursued, along with specific measures so that we will know when we get there. A statement of functions might say, "We are in charge of child care"; a statement of objectives might say, "We intend to provide a preschool place for every child in the community by 2012." A statement of objectives should be the following:

1. Succinct, and limited to the organization's sphere of influence
2. Directional, with specific future states to be achieved
3. Time limited, with indications of when each objective is to be achieved
4. Measurable, so that achievement or progress can be evaluated

The Planning Horizon

Sometimes when you apply for a job, the recruitment officer or selection committee may ask you, "Where do you see yourself in ten years' time?" This is often perceived to be a silly question, and, with respect to the structure of women's careers, it is possibly a discriminatory one. But in asking this question, a selection committee is trying to see whether the applicant for the job has a personal career strategy or is drifting in an opportunistic way without a strategy, without personal objectives, and without a career plan.

The same question is most decidedly not silly when addressed to public sector organizations. It is of the utmost importance to assess whether or not they have strategic intent—that is, the will to shape their future, rather than merely reacting to changes driven by others. Any organization's planning horizon, the time limit of organizational planning beyond which the future is considered too uncertain or unimportant to waste time on, is an important factor in assessing its short- as well as long-term viability. While private corporations have the luxury of determining their own planning horizons, severe obstacles are put in the path of those who advocate the most rational possible planning in the public sector. The inherently political nature of public administration can place a premium on short-term thinking. It was the late British Prime Minister Harold Wilson who said, "A week is a long time in politics." By this he was drawing attention to the fickle nature of the public's awareness, to the fact that an issue of premier significance one week may be forgotten the next. Political leaders may lose power—and even office—in a very short time, often unexpectedly. "Today a rooster, tomorrow a feather duster" sums up the uncertain job prospects of those who would lead the political barnyard. Thus the reigning administrations in developed democracies feel they must be very sensitive to the results of very short-term opinion polling. These factors and all others that bring a short-term focus to bear on public policymaking work—and work very hard—against strategic management efforts.

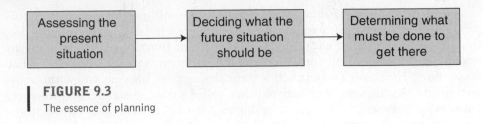

| Assessing the present situation | → | Deciding what the future situation should be | → | Determining what must be done to get there |

FIGURE 9.3
The essence of planning

Public budgeting procedures, because of their annual nature, reinforce this tendency toward short-term thinking. National, state, and local legislators are accustomed to exercising oversight authority during the annual rituals of the budget formulation and review process. To them, biennial and multiyear budgeting represent immediate threats to their political powers and patronage prerogatives. Aaron Wildavsky discussed this problem in a famous article, "A Budget for All Seasons: Why the Traditional Budget Lasts." It lasts because it is the basis of the political power of so many legislators. Otherwise, rational reforms leading to multiyear budgets are simply not in their personal political interests. Despite the many efforts that have been made over the years to introduce longer budget cycles, success has been limited. Thus short-term budgeting continues to reinforce short-term policymaking and inhibit the inherently long-term nature of strategic planning.

Despite the preceding constraints, long-term planning is inescapable in some areas of public sector activity. Some endeavors clearly require long-term planning horizons because they need both gradual development and enormous capital investment. Publicly owned power, water, and transit utilities must operate in this way. They must have long forward plans and multiyear lead times to complete a new transit system, power station, or water purification plant. Here, the constraints of traditional short-term government planning cannot apply. Often, such utilities, if they are not already in the private sector, are placed in semi-autonomous public corporations or commissions. There they have more freedom to think, plan, and operate within a longer-term time horizon than if they were to operate as traditional government departments. Government-owned utilities, with their heavy investment and long lead times, illustrate areas of the public sector where long-term strategy and concomitant long-term planning are inescapable.

When strategic management is adopted in a corporation, municipality, or bureau, or in a presidential initiative, a choice is made for rational decision making. In this sense, there is now a greater commitment to rational planning in American institutions than ever before. For example, the Government Performance Results Act of 1993 requires that "federal agencies must prepare and submit strategic plans to the Office of Management and Budget and Congress." The states are increasingly passing similar legislation. For example, according to House Bill 2009, passed by the Texas State Legislature in 1991, all state agencies must use strategic plans as the basis for developing their "requests for legislative appropriations, and measure agency effectiveness by the outcomes and outputs they achieve."

Capabilities

Strategic management has been described, most notably by strategic analyst H. Igor Ansoff, as "a matching process" in which the variables of strategy, capability, and environment are matched as the organization seeks to manage change through strategy. As the environment moves from stable to turbulent, Ansoff argues, the required capability moves from "custodial" toward "entrepreneurial." In a stable environment, a custodial, unchanging capability may suffice. But as the environment becomes surprising and turbulent, a more entrepreneurial and risk-taking capability is needed.

When mismatch exists between environment and capability, management must take action to better match its human resources capability with the emerging environment. The actions required may include hiring new employees who are better oriented by disposition or training to a new entrepreneurial environment. Existing employees could be given additional training. Unfortunately, it is often the case that some employees may no longer be suited to what the present environment requires. For example, a juvenile correctional institution moving toward a counseling and support model may find difficulties if its staff capability exclusively consists of tough custodial officers. Similarly, many organizations in the public sector whose strengths have traditionally been in technical or professional excellence may find that new requirements for customer orientation require, at the very least, extra training programs, but more likely the hiring of some new staff with new attitudes and skills.

What is true of human resources capability is also likely to be the case with systems capability, or financial capability—indeed, capability in whatever dimension is critical to the organization's ability to adapt to an emerging environment. For example, years ago, the task of servicing lighthouses—traditionally a public sector function—was viewed as requiring a capability to maintain a fleet of tough little ships that could reach remote areas. This capability later gave way to a

---

Strengths
- Delivery network that reaches virtually all possible customers
- Established branch office in every significant locality
- An ongoing capability to complete its core mission (deliver the mail) every day

Weaknesses
- Inferior top-management core
- Poorly motivated and alienated workforce
- Large organization with difficulties maintaining service of consistent quality
- Public perception of massive incompetence

Opportunities
- Every citizen is a potential customer
- Expand services into new technologies
- Alliances with private deliverers

Threats
- Forced privatization by Congress
- Competition from private sector (Federal Express, United Parcel Service, etc.)
- Hostile labor unions

FIGURE 9.4

SWOT analysis for the U.S. Postal Service

capability to service remote locations by helicopter. Eventually, as global positioning systems developed, that capability in turn became obsolete.

The SWOT analysis—a review of an organization's strengths, weaknesses, opportunities, and threats—is a technique widely used to provide another test of strategic viability. SWOT analysis is often conducted by consultants or senior management groups in an interactive, brainstorming mode, in which the group turns its attention sequentially to each aspect of the organization's position. Analysis of strengths and weaknesses highlights capability issues, while attention to opportunities and threats turns attention to the opportunistic as well as the predatory aspects of organizational survival. A SWOT analysis is often undertaken as part of a situation audit, an assessment of an organization's performance in absolute terms or in comparison to a competing or parallel organization.

Game Theory

In recent years public administrators have begun to embrace game theory as a key component of strategic management. Game theory has been a major tool for scholars for many decades, with applications in fields such as international relations, business management, and economics. At its core, game theory deals with cooperation and conflict in the context of decision making. It assumes that individuals who behave rationally will seek to maximize their benefits whenever they make a decision. Thus if one can identify the goals of the other players in the game, he or she can strategically adapt his or her decisions.

For managers in public agencies and organizations, this approach to decision making may have many applications. One area where a public manager may apply game theory is in budget negotiations with elected officials. By recognizing that the primary goal of most politicians is to be reelected to political office, a public administrator can craft budget requests in a way that puts pressure on the elected officials. For example, through framing of a budget request in an "all-or-nothing" form, a manager may place the members of Congress in a difficult situation. If Congress supports full funding of a program, government resources will be strained. However, no funding of a program (i.e., Amtrak rail service) may cause anger among constituents depending on a service. By making the decision an all-or-nothing proposition, the public manager is structuring the "game" between him- or herself and Congress in a manner that seeks to optimize the probability of full funding.

STRATEGIC MANAGEMENT TOOLS

The level of analysis is one of the classic issues in the study of politics because it poses an eternal question: Should the focus of political analysis be the individual political actor, a local government, a national government, or the international political system as a whole? The forces at play and the linkages that are made within and between these levels make single-level analysis problematic at best. Thus there is no point in undertaking a political analysis of a political actor in isolation—because that actor is never in isolation. He or she is always a citizen of a state and/or a member of other large groups. Thus there are always a large number of linkages and interactions among the various levels of government and other social groupings.

Strategy presents a similar level-of-analysis problem. It is inherently hierarchical. The most general notions come down from the top to be implemented at various stages leading to the bottom. When the president orders "justice" for America's enemies, that order travels down the chain of command until a soldier pulls the trigger on his rifle and administers a full measure of such justice to a deserving person. Strategy sets into action the ways and means by which people are ultimately shot, or given food stamps, or provided health care. Whether the end result is bullets or bedpans, the strategy involved will travel a similar route toward implementation—from the grand strategic (the national policymaking) level to the strategic (the highest organizational level) to the operational (the planning or administrative) level to the tactical (the service delivery) level. Each level accepts strategy from above but uses discretion to create substrategies or level-specific strategies that facilitate implementation. At the same time each level develops measurement and reporting techniques to assess how well the overall strategy is being implemented. Three of these tools for measuring effectiveness are best practices, benchmarking, and management scorecards.

Best Practices

This may be the oldest idea in war and management—look at what your competitors are doing and imitate their successful innovations. Long before the age of patents and copyrights, organizations—whether military or industrial—would simply steal, borrow, or copy the best ideas of others. Remember that the whole thrust of the scientific management movement (see Chapter 6) was to find the "one best way." But "best" is inherently temporary. A successful innovation by reformers is followed by a period of increased effectiveness—at least until competing organizations adopt similar reforms. But over time advancing technologies and changing environments allow the innovation to deteriorate relative to other arrangements,

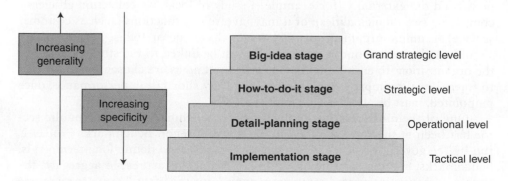

FIGURE 9.5
The hierarchy of strategy

first to become less competent and then to become incompetent. Thus installing and maintaining best practices is quite literally a matter of organizational life and death.

This critical question must always be asked: Is this organization efficient by industry standards? For public sector managers, the challenge to maximize operational efficiency is critical because public organizations may lose their credibility or even their right to exist if their managers cannot operate them in such a way as to demonstrate acceptable standards of competence. In past years, managers could sometimes obfuscate discussion of the efficiency of public sector organizations by references to unique characteristics, measurement difficulties, and the complexity of public sector life. While there is a measure of truth in all of these as reasons for why assessing the efficiency of public sector organizations is difficult, it is also true that we now have, through benchmarking and studies of comparative performance, a good deal more data to consider—especially in those parts of the public sector where measurements and comparisons are easiest—that is, where "hard," measurable outputs exist.

Despite the problems and subtleties of measuring performance and productivity in the public sector, an objective baseline is indispensable if any manager or government wishes to bring about better performance. Almost as indispensable is a systematic way of comparing how you are doing with the efforts of others working in the same sphere. This latter problem is not unique to public sector management; it is a problem all managers face. This technique of comparison, known as benchmarking, was developed by the Xerox Corporation just for this purpose. It has now spread around the world and is widely used in the public sector.

Benchmarking

Benchmarking systematically compares work processes with those of competitors or with best practices in an industry. It involves choosing and studying key performance areas in an organization and often involves entering into cooperative arrangements with partner organizations. The process may be carried out internally (perhaps comparing how the organization's regional offices perform); it may be carried out externally (for example, a study of local tax collection efficiency comparing two municipalities); or it may involve like functions (such as customer service) in unlike organizations. Whatever the scope or focus, benchmarking should not be carried out in isolation. It must be linked to the strategic plans of the organization (to ensure that the most relevant areas are chosen for study) and to formal quality improvement efforts, since any shortfall in performance, once pinpointed, must be attacked and improved.

One of the most creative applications of benchmarking in the public sector has been in the state of Oregon, where the Oregon Benchmarks Project is run by the governor's office. Each agency is required to define long-term goals, benchmarks, mission statements, and performance measures. In aggregate, the process achieves integrated strategic planning for the state. (You can see these benchmarks on the Internet at www.oregon.gov/DAS/OPB/obm.shtml.) Oregon has used this concept very creatively; it even has detailed (and quantified) benchmarks for "civic engagement."

In Australia, benchmarking was first promoted heavily within industry in the 1980s by the federal government as a means of encouraging private enterprise to become more internationally competitive. Then it was used in the struggle to make public enterprises more efficient. In the 1990s, a number of benchmarking studies compared the performance of Australian public enterprises (like railroads, ports, and electricity undertakings) with each other and with those overseas. Then benchmarking was extensively applied in local government. Benchmarking can be a valuable aid in judging the efficiency of a public organization. However, the technique is susceptible to misuse and poor application if inappropriate comparisons are made and if sufficient explanation of variances is not provided in published results.

Where public and private sector organizations are able to compete with one another on a "level playing field"—that is, under circumstances where regulatory controls, policy latitude, and other key determinants are impartial—public sector organizations often compare well with private sector counterparts. This has been demonstrated in Australia, where public/private competition in the airline and banking industries existed for many years and where the large public operators often defeated large private operators under comparable operating conditions. Such examples reinforce the proposition that competition is a more important precondition of organizational efficiency than ownership as such.

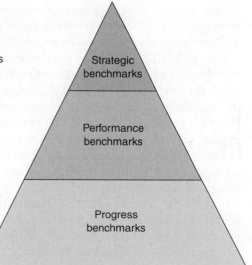

Focus

How public, private, and nonprofit organizations compare with each other. Strategic benchmarking is seldom industry focused. It moves across industries and cities to determine the best-in-class strategic outcomes.

Strategic benchmarks

How public, private, and nonprofit organizations compare with each other in terms of product and service. Performance benchmarking usually focuses on elements of price, technical quality, ancillary product or service features, speed, reliability, and other performance features.

Performance benchmarks

How public, private, and nonprofit organizations compare, through the identification of the most effective operating practices of many organizations that perform similar work processes.

Progress benchmarks

FIGURE 9.6

Three types of benchmarks

Source: Benchmarking to Become Best in Class, Anthony Rainey, Government Finance Review (February 1997).

Management Scorecards

In essence, a management scorecard is a tally sheet, just as are scorecards in golf or bowling. However, what is being tallied is the performance not of individual players, but of the individual units or functions of a large organization. This allows the managers at the top to get an overview of how well their tactical managers are playing the "game." The whole point of the scorecard approach is to allow executives to instantly scan, by looking at the scores, the status of their organization units.

In the early 1990s "balanced scorecards" first became fashionable in the private sector as a means to evaluate a company's performances from several perspectives simultaneously. Traditionally the emphasis had been on financial performance (the bottom line), but a balanced scorecard complemented financial performance with data on customer satisfaction, internal processes, and ability to learn—among other measures. While report cards of this nature are as old as school, the scorecard approach suddenly became "hot" in government once it was introduced in 2002 as part of the president's management agenda. All of the major federal agencies (more than 50 in all) are now being graded on their progress in these five government-wide management initiatives:

1. Strategic management of human capital
2. Competitive sourcing
3. Improving financial performance
4. Expanded electronic government
5. Budget and performance integration

The grades are color coded so each department is rated red, yellow, or green for the level of success in implementing each of the preceding initiatives. The first scorecard, the 2001 Baseline Evaluation, gave out mostly red circles. As the Office of Management and Budget explained, "The initial scorecard shows a lot of poor scores, reflecting the state of government this Administration inherited." Every six months, acting for the president, OMB issued new grades. At the end of March 2007 the OMB report showed that only the Departments of Labor and State met the standards for all five management initiatives. Meanwhile, the Departments of Defense (DoD) and Veterans Affairs (VA) ranked at the low end of federal performance, with the DoD possessing unsatisfactory scores in three areas and the VA failing to meet standards in four of five rating categories. Given the problems in Iraq and at VA facilities throughout the nation during that time period, these poor ratings do not seem very surprising.

With the arrival of Barack Obama in the White House in 2009, management scorecards took on a different format. A priority interest for the Obama administration was sustainability and renewable energy development. The president had the OMB enact a scorecard system that rated federal agencies in several sustainability areas, including: energy intensity; water intensity; fleet petroleum use; greenhouse gas pollution; green building practices; and renewable energy use. The scorecard employs a simple evaluation system: green for success, yellow for mixed results, and red for unsatisfactory.

So what's the point of these exercises in score keeping that have been employed by the Bush and Obama administrations? It is mainly a way of artificially creating the competitive forces inherent in the private sector. To a large degree this is management by shame—no organization wants to be ashamed of its rankings. Not surprisingly, the scores have been going up. OMB has also introduced directional arrows within the circles. Thus a yellow circle with an upward-pointing arrow is like a B-plus. While the red, yellow, and green circles may seem silly on the surface, underneath they facilitate three key objectives:

1. To focus attention on what top management considers its key priorities
2. To motivate organizational units to improve
3. To provide timely assessments of progress

It would be hard to argue against the Bush administration's five government-wide initiatives. Worthy goals all! But will they be achieved with a management scorecard system that employs "getting to green"? Or will managers, like students, work mainly for the grade at the expense of real learning or real reform? Only two things are certain: (1) nothing will be reinvented, as that was the goal of the previous administration, and (2) the Obama administration will have a new set of strategic management tools. Early in his tenure as the nation's chief executive Obama signaled that he would have a focus on performance management that would include a number of specific initiatives:

1. The creation of a new Chief Performance Officer who reports directly to the president.
2. Reconfiguration of the OMB's Program Assessment Review Tool (PART) to make it more accessible to the public.
3. Implementation of consequences for success or failure in meeting objectives.

Many of these initiatives sound as if they've been tried in some form in the past. Time will tell if they work any better during the Obama years in the nation's capital.

GOVERNMENT REGULATION FOR HEALTH, SAFETY, AND ECONOMIC EQUITY

Among the most important roles of government is its ability to regulate society in order to preserve and enhance the public welfare. As the protector of the public interest, public administrators maintain substantial power to set and enforce rules that govern many aspects of life within America. To bring this point home, just think about the way government regulation affects each and every day of your life.

Consider the simple act of going to McDonald's to buy a hamburger or a salad. You leave your house or apartment, which has been built according to local building codes—regulation. You get into your car, which has many safety features required by the federal government—regulation. You drive to an intersection and stop at a red light—regulation. Once at McDonald's, you notice a sticker on the door from the local public health agency indicating that the establishment has been inspected and found free of insect and rodent infestation—regulation. On the wall is a framed certificate from the local municipality indicating that the property is licensed to operate as a business—regulation. Then you give your order to a person whose minimum wages and maximum working hours are set by legislation—regulation—and whose supervisor is required by guidelines issued by the Equal Employment Opportunity Commission to maintain a workplace free of sexual harassment—regulation—and whose wages are reduced by mandatory deductions for income tax and Social Security—regulation. If after your meal you feel the need to visit one of the restrooms, you will find one oversized toilet stall designed for the physically handicapped—regulation.

As the above scenario demonstrates, regulation is everywhere in your life, whether you notice it or not. This should not come as a surprise. To facilitate the strategic management of government objectives (e.g., clean air, safe roads), regulation stands as one of the most potent tools available to public administrators and as a cornerstone of contemporary public policy in the United States. But when regulation fails, as it did when Minnesota's Interstate 35 Bridge collapsed in 2007, the public quickly takes notice and demands answers for why regulations did not perform. Perhaps it is most useful to think of regulation in the same way you think about a baseball umpire. During a game you rarely notice the ump until a call is blown and your team pays the price on the field. Similarly, we rarely think of regulations until they fail to do their job.

While we tend to see regulation in its myriad details from restaurant inspection to zoning enforcement, it is always part of a larger strategic effort such as improving public health. Figure 9.8 illustrates how the various aspects of regulation reflect the strategic management process discussed previously in this chapter. Note that a regulation does not exist for its own sake; it is always part of a larger strategic goal.

In the remainder of this chapter we explore some of the key players, processes, and tools that form regulatory efforts at the federal, state, and local levels. This necessarily entails an examination of the strategies and weaknesses of varied regulatory approaches employed by the different levels of government.

Independent Regulatory Agencies

Modern-day regulation is so pervasive and so commonplace that we see it every day and accept it without thinking. As a general rule of thumb, the more crowded and economically developed a place is, the more regulations it has. Society needs rules so that people don't inadvertently bump into each other's cars, live in houses that fall down because they are structurally unsound, or get food poisoning from contaminated meat. Such catastrophes were common before government regulations—at least in the developed world—made them relatively rare.

Consider that in December 2003 both central California and southern Iran had earthquakes of similar magnitude. Yet, while just two people died in California, tens of thousands died in Iran. Erik Kirschbaum quotes Iranian officials as reporting that "poor design, primitive materials, and widely ignored building codes were prime causes of the high death rate." Government regulations in California requiring architectural approval, strict adherence to building codes, and building inspections saved lives.

Regulation has its origin in legislation. But since legislation can never be totally comprehensive on any subject, rules are typically needed to address the details that have not been specified in the written law. Thus rulemaking authority is necessarily exercised by administrative agencies; it is a power that has the full force of law. Agencies begin with some form of legislative mandate and translate their interpretation of that mandate into policy decisions, specifications of regulations, and statements of penalties and enforcement provisions. The exact process to be followed in formulating regulations is only briefly described in the federal Administrative Procedure Act (APA). The APA does distinguish between rulemaking that requires a hearing and rulemaking that requires only notice and the opportunity for public comment. Whether the formal or informal procedure is to be used is determined by the enabling statute: the Supreme Court's decision in *United States v. Florida East Coast Railway* (1973) held that formal rulemaking need only be followed when the enabling statute expressly requires an agency hearing prior to rule formulation. The APA also requires that rules be published 30 days before their effective date and that agencies afford any interested party the right to petition for issuance, amendment, or repeal of a rule. In effect, while the APA establishes a process of notice and time for comment, it accords administrative rule makers the same prerogatives as legislatures in enacting statutes. There is, of course, the additional requirement that the rule enacted be consistent with the enabling statute directing the rulemaking.

All new federal rules must be published in the *Federal Register*, the daily publication (begun in 1935) that is the medium for making available to the public the forthcoming rules and regulations of federal agencies—as well as other legal documents of the executive branch, such as presidential proclamations and executive orders. Of course, any controversial proposed rules will quickly find their way into the mainstream press, especially since the *Register* began issuing online publications in 1992. All the states have similar rulemaking procedures involving the publication of proposed rules, mechanisms for receiving comments, and final action.

The Rulemaking Process

A large share of regulatory work in the United States is completed by the many agencies that form the federal bureaucracy. While all federal level agencies play some role in regulating the nation, there have also been numerous governmental organizations established primarily for the purpose of regulating many aspects of American society. These organizations are categorized as independent regulatory commissions, and include prominent government entities such as the Federal Communication Commission (FCC) and the Securities and Exchange Commission (SEC). Independent regulatory commissions are headed by several commissioners, directors, or governors who are also appointed by the president and confirmed by the Senate. But unlike administrators of independent executive agencies, they serve for fixed terms and cannot be removed at the pleasure of the president. When

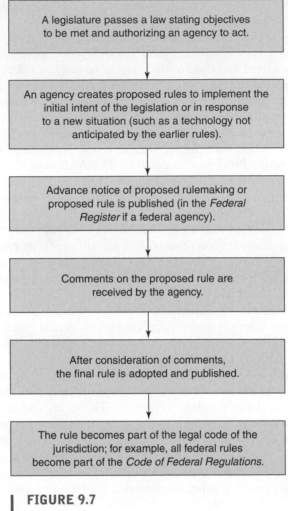

A legislature passes a law stating objectives to be met and authorizing an agency to act.

An agency creates proposed rules to implement the initial intent of the legislation or in response to a new situation (such as a technology not anticipated by the earlier rules).

Advance notice of proposed rulemaking or proposed rule is published (in the *Federal Register* if a federal agency).

Comments on the proposed rule are received by the agency.

After consideration of comments, the final rule is adopted and published.

The rule becomes part of the legal code of the jurisdiction; for example, all federal rules become part of the *Code of Federal Regulations*.

FIGURE 9.7
The rulemaking process

Franklin Roosevelt sought to dismiss commissioners of the Federal Trade Commission (FTC) for disagreements over policy, the Supreme Court ruled in *Humphrey's Executor v. United States* (1935) that the FTC "occupies no place in the executive department." Thus all such commissioners can serve to the end of their fixed terms unless impeached by Congress. This independence from direct executive control can serve as a source of considerable strength for individuals serving on regulatory boards and commissions. Nowhere is this power more evident than with the Federal Reserve Board and its panel of governors. The "Fed," as it's commonly known, has the authority to regulate monetary policy in the United States, and therefore can directly impact the performance of the nation's economy. Not surprisingly, the chair of the Fed's Board of Governors, currently held by Benjamin Bernanke, is generally considered one of the nation's most powerful government officials.

> **BOX 9.1 | Why Regulation Came to the Meatpacking Industry**
>
> There was never the least attention paid to what was cut up for sausage. . . . There would be meat that had tumbled out on the floor, in the dirt and sawdust, where the workers had tramped and spit uncounted billions of consumption germs. There would be meat stored in great piles in rooms; and the water from leaky roofs would drip over it, and thousands of rats would race about on it. It was too dark in these storage places to see well, but a man could run his hand over these piles of meat and sweep off handfuls of the dried dung of rats. These rats were nuisances, and the packers would put poisoned bread out for them, they would die, and then rats, bread, and meat would go into the hoppers together. This is no fairy story and no joke; the meat would be shoveled into carts and the man who did the shoveling would not trouble to lift out a rat even when he saw one—there were things that went into the sausage in comparison with which a poisoned rat was a tidbit. There was no place for the men to wash their hands before they ate their dinner, and so they made a practice of washing them in the water that was to be ladled into the sausage. There were the butt-ends of smoked meat, and the scraps of corned beef, and all the odds and ends of the waste of the plants, that would be dumped into old barrels in the cellar and left there. Under the system of rigid economy which the packers enforced, there were some jobs that it only paid to do once in a long time, and among these was the cleaning out of the waste barrels. Every spring they did it; and in the barrels would be dirt and rust and old nails and stale water—and cart load after cart load of it would be taken up and dumped into the hoppers with fresh meat, and sent out to the public's breakfast. ▄
>
> Source: Upton Sinclair, *The Jungle* (1906). This novel caused such a sensation that President Theodore Roosevelt authorized an investigation of the meatpackers. This led to the Pure Food and Drug Act of 1906, which provided for federal inspection.

Note that many regulatory functions are also performed by traditional cabinet departments. For example, the Food and Drug Administration (FDA) is located within the Department of Health and Human Services, and regulates such things as the approval of new pharmaceutical products. Once again the public rarely thinks about the work of the FDA until it approves a new drug that turns out to cause more health problems than it cures. The well-publicized dangers from major drugs such as Vioxx and Celebrex exposed significant problems within the FDA's regulatory system and increased public unease about the safety of the pharmaceuticals they rely on to make their lives better.

STATE GOVERNMENT REGULATION

Although public attention is often focused upward to the federal level, state governments should not be ignored in terms of their regulatory functions. With the Tenth Amendment reserving powers to the states, there are many policy areas where state governments play preeminent roles. From transportation to education, the states have primary responsibility for many areas of regulatory policy, including many of the standards that govern the provision of services to the public from professionals such as doctors, dentists, teachers, and accountants.

Occupational Licensing (Who Puts the "Certified" in CPA?)

Do you trust your doctor? How about your dentist or pharmacist? Because of your personal experiences over years of contact with these individuals, you probably have built up a relationship. But who certifies the credibility of these professionals for the public at large? In most cases it's the state government that provides the licensing and regulations that govern most professionals. Remember that a certified public accountant (CPA) is "certified" by a state only after the accountant has demonstrated specified educational and experience requirements and then passed a state examination.

As with the U.S. Constitution, almost every state constitution makes some explicit mention of the government's role in protecting the public welfare. While you may immediately think that protecting the public welfare involves police officers rounding up criminals, it also includes measures that protect the public from the very people that are hired to help them. Through their regulatory powers states set the standards under which individuals can be granted licenses to practice select professions—from big-rig truck drivers to brain surgeons.

And though you may not be surprised to discover that states grant licenses to doctors, nurses, and accountants, there are many more occupations that are also overseen by the states. For example, such professions as athletic trainer, interior designer, and massage therapist may not be the type of careers you would expect to find on a list of regulated professions, but in many states you will find just such a rich array of occupations under government watch.

Regulation of professionals does not end at their licensing; it continues throughout their careers. To protect the public, state regulators establish the conditions under which services can be rendered. From requiring massage therapists to keep records of transactions to mandating that pharmacists transfer prescriptions at a customer's request, states set the operating procedures for many professions. When those providing services noticeably fail to abide by the rules of business, they come under the regulatory wrath of administrative agencies. Now you may be wondering what kind of wrath a government agency can bring down on a massage therapist for failure to abide by the rules. It can be a revoked or suspended license, a mandatory continuing education course, or a monetary fine. And before the massage therapist lays hands on another patient, the controlling hand of public administration must give the okay for the therapist to continue with his or her ministrations.

LOCAL GOVERNMENT REGULATION

As we noted in Chapter 4, local governments play a major role in providing many of the most obvious forms of government services. From plowing roads after a snowstorm to teaching children calculus, local governments deliver key public services on a daily basis. But not only do county and municipal governments provide services, they also regulate many aspects of the lives of their citizens. On an ordinary day local governments regulate the size of the pool in your backyard, the food that you eat at the Chinese restaurant down the street, and the speed of your car as you drive back from work. While there are hundreds of different ways that local government regulates your life, we have selected three areas of particular interest to examine more deeply in the remainder of the section.

Zoning

One of the most prized rights of an American citizen is his or her ability to own and develop land. Since the first land claims on the continent nearly five centuries ago, individuals have taken ownership of land and shaped their property in ways that they desire. While prized, the right to own and develop land is one of the most regulated aspects of life in the United States. Over the last century, states and municipalities have increasingly used their powers to limit the way private land is used. In particular, through the process of zoning, governments tell landowners what they can use their land for, when they are permitted to build structures, and what type of buildings can occupy a piece of property. Given the importance of land regulation, it's not surprising that it has been one of the most controversial aspects of government regulation.

When land was plentiful and population density was low, the need to regulate land use was not a major priority for policymakers. But as the nation grew and Americans were brought closer together, the need for government regulation of land use became clear. Imagine buying a beautiful house on a pretty piece of land and settling your family down to enjoy the "American Dream," only to discover that the owner of an adjacent property has decided to use his land to house a meat packing plant. Or picture your beautiful view of a sunrise over the mountains blocked by a 20-story apartment building that was built right next to the century-old farmhouse that you inherited from your parents. Such scenarios became more and more prominent by the end of the nineteenth century and pushed governments deep into the realm of land regulation and zoning beginning in the early twentieth century.

Not surprisingly, the first major zoning ordinance was passed in the nation's most populous and densely packed metropolis—New York City. As the city grew both outward and upward, conflicts between landowners became more and more common. Finally, the construction of the mammoth (for its day) Equitable Building on Broadway triggered city action on the matter. The Equitable Building covered every square inch of the property that it sat on and rose 36 stories into the sky. Its height and placement blocked windows of adjacent buildings and prevented sunlight from ever reaching many nearby properties. In reaction, in 1916 the city government developed a set of regulations that restricted the types of construction that can take place in New York, limiting such aspects of development as building size and placement on lots. And as is often the case, what starts in New York quickly spreads to all reaches of the nation. By the 1920s the use of zoning was widespread throughout the United States, with the number and specificity of land-use regulations increasing annually. However, the growth of zoning was by no means universally accepted or embraced. If there is one thing about Americans that is universally accepted, it is that they do not want to be told what they can and can't do with their lives or property. Thus the expanding role of government land regulation was challenged in many ways, which included the introduction of legal suits.

In the most important zoning case in history, the U.S. Supreme Court was asked to decide if zoning laws conflicted with the individual protections of the U.S. Constitution. When Euclid, Ohio, introduced a zoning plan that segregated land uses into specialized districts (e.g., residential, commercial), a local developer

Zoning ■
The process by which local government can designate the types of structures and activities for a particular area. Zoning began in the 1920s to protect neighborhoods from the encroachments of business and industry and to preserve their economic and social integrity. It involves a highly complex legal process, which is often impacted by local politics.

challenged the law on the grounds it violated the Fourteenth Amendment's protection of due process and equal protection under the law. In the case of *Ambler Reality Co. v. Village of Euclid* (1924) the Supreme Court upheld the legality of zoning, with the majority opinion holding that "regulations, the wisdom, necessity and validity of which are so apparent that they are now uniformly sustained, under the complex conditions of the day." In essence the *Ambler* decision gave the Court's stamp of approval to land regulation, recognizing that the realities of the modern world require such government intervention. To be sure there have been many cases since *Ambler* that have helped define what can and can't be regulated, but **Euclidian zoning** has become an established part of American life.

Building Codes

A man's home may be his castle, but the castle better meet code if he wants to live in it. Just like zoning can tell us what we can and can't do with our property, building codes establish what the inside of our homes and buildings must look like. As the realities of an increasingly congested society pushed municipalities into zoning, the development of taller and bigger buildings led to the creation of building codes. A building code or control is a set of regulations that establish the minimum accepted level of safety for a constructed object. The use of building codes has a long history, dating back as far as 1760 B.C.E. and the **Code of Hammurabi**. Under Hammurabi's Code, the following rules were established:

- If a builder builds a house for someone, and does not construct it properly, and the house which he built falls in and kills its owner, then that builder shall be put to death.
- If it ruins goods, he shall make compensation for all that has been ruined, and in as much as he did not construct properly this house which he built and it fell, he shall re-erect the house from his own means.
- If a builder built a house for someone—even though he has not yet completed it: if then the walls seem toppling, the builder must make the walls solid from his own means.

While good enough for Hammurabi, building codes were not quickly embraced in the United States. Even though both Washington and Jefferson encouraged the adoption of building codes to protect health and property, there were few codified standards for buildings until the early twentieth century. A number of noteworthy disasters helped push municipalities to adopt building standards. Most notably, the 1911 Triangle Shirtwaist Factory fire in New York City called attention to dangerous building conditions in the United States. In this horrific fire, 146 workers died when a fire trapped them on the ninth floor, forcing many women to make fatal jumps to the city streets below. The outrage in the aftermath of the Triangle fire led to increased efforts to establish better building safety standards. In 1915, code enforcement officials from throughout the country met to develop standard safety codes for buildings. Out of these meetings came the formation of the Building Officials and Code Administrators (BOCA) building regulations, which became the standard for many municipalities throughout

Euclidian zoning ■
A zoning policy that keeps apartments and businesses out of single-home residential areas. This kind of zoning was adopted by Euclid, Ohio, and the subject of the Supreme Court case of *Village of Euclid v Ambler Realty Company*, 272 U.S. 365 (1926), which asserted that zoning was a valid exercise of local government powers.

Code of Hammurabi ■
The Code of Hammurabi was created in approximately 1760 B.C.E. in Mesopotamia and is one of the earliest sets of laws to govern a society. The code contains an enumeration of crimes and their various punishments as well as settlements for common disputes and guidelines for citizens' conduct.

North America. Through the years the formulation of standards has continued to increase, with **The International Code Council** now serving as the primary governing body for building regulations in the United States and beyond. In addition to requiring basic safety features such as fire escapes and sprinkler systems, building codes now include standards for energy efficiency and accessibility for individuals with special needs.

Public Health (Do You Want Roaches with Those Fries?)

Perhaps no area of government regulation is more indicative of the age that we live in than public health policies. In a world where threats to our health are broadcast into our homes on a daily basis, the issue of public health inhabits a prominent place in American society. From the spread of the avian flu to *E. coli*–laced hamburgers, there are no shortages of public health concerns facing the nation. Sometimes the need for government intervention in public health is obvious to everyone, as when roach-invested restaurants are shut down or in instances of preventing contaminated food products from reaching consumers. But in other areas the role of government regulation is less clear and far more controversial. Let's look at an example to clarify the point.

The issue of obesity has become one of the greatest threats to the health of Americans over the past quarter century. According to the Centers for Disease Control (CDC), about 33 percent of individuals living in the United States are clinically obese. This level of obesity is more than double the mark of 13 percent reached in 1960. The high prevalence of obesity has an enormous impact on many aspects of life in the United States. The CDC estimates that obesity is responsible for more than 112,000 excess deaths per year in the United States and nearly $100 billion a year in additional health care expenses. While it's clear that obesity is a major threat to the nation's health, regulating the problem is quite difficult. With other health risks—such as tobacco and alcohol—the government has regulated the products through means such as restricted access and **sin taxes**. However, such regulatory tools are not easily applied to the root causes of obesity—overeating and lethargic lifestyles. Could you imagine an age requirement for buying a Whopper at Burger King or a tax of one dollar on every sale of McDonald's French fries? Such options are politically infeasible, forcing public health officials to be more creative in their approaches to the problem.

One approach to regulating obesity is to require restaurants to post nutrition information next to prices on menus. For example, in July of 2007 the King County, Washington, board of health created a regulation that requires any restaurant with 10 or more locations to put nutritional information next to the menu item's name and price in the same font and size as the price. And while it may be politically difficult to ban the sale of French fries and deep-dish pizza in restaurants, city governments have begun to regulate the unhealthiest items that are used in fast foods. In cities such as New York and Seattle, local governments have banned the use of trans fats at restaurants in order to limit consumption of one of the greatest contributors to obesity and heart problems. These bans have drawn

The International Code Council ■
An association dedicated to building safety and fire prevention that develops the codes used to construct residential and commercial buildings, including homes and schools. Most U.S. cities, counties, and states that adopt codes choose the International Codes developed by the International Code Council.

Sin tax ■
A tax specifically levied on certain behaviors that are deemed to be contrary to the societal good. Primary examples of sin taxes include levies on smoking, alcohol consumption, and gambling.

the ire of restaurants and some citizens who feel such regulations are an assault on personal freedoms and choice. New York Mayor Michael Bloomberg countered criticisms by arguing that "Nobody wants to take away your French fries and hamburgers, but if you can make them with something that is less damaging to your health, we should do that." Not everyone appreciates the mayor's attitude; many believe that it is an example of the "nanny state" getting too much in our faces—or, more specifically, in our mouths.

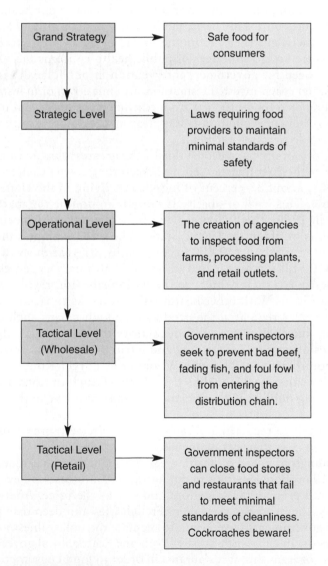

FIGURE 9.8

The strategic approach to government regulation of food

IN THE NEWS | China Kills for Good Government Regulation

A sound program of government regulation of consumer products is not just to ensure that citizens get their money's worth; it is literally a matter of life and death. The integrity of a nation's food and medicine is maintained by inspection, which is necessarily limited, and prosecution, which is rare but often highly publicized. The free market is in essence its own regulator. After all, if you as a drug manufacturer or food distributor poison your customers, you have lost your market. It is simply good business to sell wholesome products.

If a company or country loses its reputation for food and drug safety, it may suffer an economic catastrophe. This is why China is so concerned about the early 2007 scandals concerning poisons found in ingredients for pet food and toothpaste. More recently the U.S. government has rejected imports of toxic fish, fruit juice with unsafe color additives, defective automobile tires, and toys with lead paint. Nevertheless, China is determined to solve its problem concerning the safety of its exports. Consequently, its regulatory efforts are growing apace. Too much is at

stake for it not to make an extraordinary effort to redeem its products and its reputation.

To demonstrate its sincerity on this issue to its own citizens as well as to those of the larger world, China has executed—put to death—the former head of its State Food and Drug Administration (Associated Press, July 10, 2007). It seems that he was approving untested and/or phony medicines for substantial cash bribes during his tenure from 1998 to 2005. His execution was not necessarily inappropriate, as many people died because they took the fake drugs he approved for malaria and other deadly ills. While the Chinese government secretly executes large numbers of people every year, this execution was given maximum publicity. The Chinese government wants its people to know that life-threatening corruption isn't worth your life. And China wants the world to know that it will kill to maintain the integrity of its food and drug exports. But the question remains: how many more people will get sick or die before China implements a rigorous regulatory regime? ◣

A CASE STUDY | Opportunity Lost: The Story of Bernie Madoff and the Securities and Exchange Commission

Independent regulatory agencies may not be in the everyday thoughts of most Americans, but when such agencies fail to do their job, they can quickly draw the ire of an angry public. Such was the scenario in 2008 when the nation was introduced to Bernie Madoff and his elaborate multibillion-dollar scheme to defraud thousands of investors.

As is always the case, Madoff's fall was preceded by his ascendancy. For decades, he was considered a star in the investment world. He regularly provided his clients with returns on their investments that surpassed market averages, and he was known throughout New York City as a philanthropist and community leader. What wasn't well known was that Madoff was conducting one of the largest Ponzi schemes in the history of the United States. In other words, Madoff was using money from new investors to pay old investors, a process that gives the appearance of providing high rates of return

(*continued*)

▶ **A CASE STUDY** | *Continued*

when, in fact, the schemer isn't investing any money at all. Like any Ponzi scheme, Madoff's scam was eventually exposed when it became impossible for him to pay all the investors he owed. However, before his scheme was found out, Madoff had defrauded investors of an estimated $65 billion. Among those defrauded by Madoff were many charities, colleges, and non-profit organizations—many of which lost their entire investment portfolios.

At this point, you may be asking, "Wasn't anybody from government watching Madoff as he perpetrated this elaborate scheme?" The answer, unfortunately, is no. The investment activities of Madoff were under the regulatory jurisdiction of the Securities and Exchange Commission (SEC). The SEC is charged with ensuring that investments are legitimate through enforcing the regulations that govern markets in the United States. In essence, the SEC is designed to make sure that fund managers such as Madoff are playing by the rules of the game. The Madoff case, therefore, exposed the many weaknesses in how the SEC oversees and manages the investment world. These weaknesses became all too apparent during 2009 congressional hearings that examined the conditions that allowed Madoff to perpetrate his crime.

During the February 2009 hearings before the House Financial Services Subcommittee on Capital Markets, Insurance and Government Sponsored Enterprises, witnesses brought forth strong evidence that the SEC was tipped off about Madoff's activities on numerous occasions, but for various reasons failed to act on the information. Harry Markopolis, an independent financial fraud investigator, told the subcommittee that he "gift wrapped and delivered the largest Ponzi scheme in history to them and somehow they couldn't be bothered to conduct a thorough and proper investigation because they were too busy on matters of higher priority." Indeed, Markopolis had sent detailed letters to the SEC listing numerous red flags in Madoff's actions and establishing a route by which the agency could completely expose Madoff's scam. So, why didn't the SEC act on this information?

The answer is multifaceted and demonstrates the importance of organizational design and personnel. First, the SEC's relationship with the firms that it is supposed to regulate has proven problematic. During the subcommittee hearings, claims were made that the SEC is too "chummy" with prominent Wall Street investment houses and that the agency was reluctant to take on the well-known players in the financial world. This phenomenon is commonly referred to as *agency capture*. Under agency capture, regulators are hesitant to challenge some of the "celebrity" names in the financial world. Individuals such as Bernie Madoff, with their incredible wealth and social prominence, are imposing figures for agency officials who may have to bring charges against these "stars."

Consider, for example, Meghan Cheung, the branch chief of the SEC's enforcement division in New York City. Cheung was the SEC official who signed the commission's 2006 investigation that cleared Madoff to continue doing business. In 2006, she was a 34-year-old public administrator who had to decide whether she wanted to challenge one of the most well-known and powerful names in New York's financial community. Despite the compelling evidence provided by Markopolis, Cheung never brought charges against Madoff and effectively allowed him to continue his Ponzi scheme. While Cheung claimed that Madoff's stature did not affect her decision in the case, her comments on the matter suggest this may not be the case. In 2009, she asked a *New York Post* reporter who was interviewing her, "Why are you taking a mid-level staff person and making me responsible for the failure of the American economy?" Cheung's description of herself as a mere "mid-level staff person" demonstrates some of the disadvantages that the SEC faces when it decides whether or not to take on investment "giants" such as Madoff. In Cheung's case, it's reasonable to believe that a mid-level bureaucrat didn't relish going head to head with one of the biggest players in the game.

In addition to issues of agency capture, the SEC's failure to stop Madoff appears to be the product of interagency rivalries. During Markopolis's testimony to Congress regarding the Madoff scandal, he noted that when he first approached the SEC's Boston office with his allegations against Madoff, he received a warm reception from the Bureau Chief, Edward Manion. However, the SEC's New York City office, which supervises the Boston branch, made the decision to block further investigation into the matter. Why didn't the New York branch take the lead from Boston and vigorously pursue Madoff? One answer to this question is that the Boston and New York branches don't like each other. According to Markopolis, Manion felt the relationship between the New York and Boston regional offices "was about as warm and friendly as the Yankees-Red Sox rivalry and that New York does not like to receive tips from Boston."

Finally, the failure of the SEC to stop Madoff raised questions about the agency's personnel. It's often said that you need a fox to catch a fox: In other words, if you're trying to discover fraud on Wall Street, you need the assistance of individuals who've spent many years in the investment game. Seasoned Wall Street veterans should be able to recognize scandals because they know how things work. Unfortunately, the SEC hasn't brought experienced Wall Street players into its ranks. Instead, the SEC has relied more on a group of young attorneys and lifelong government employees to do its business. This situation becomes even worse when some of its best employees are hired away by the very investment houses the agency is monitoring.

Under most circumstances, the work of the SEC may not interest the average American. But after Bernie Madoff stole millions from many average citizens, most citizens were outraged by the agency's failure to do its job. The outrage brought increased public pressure on Congress to make changes in the SEC to prevent this type of crime from occurring again. If such changes aren't made, Bernie Madoff may someday have a rival for the unofficial title as America's most notorious con artist.

On a positive note, however, the American legal system has forced some changes in Bernie Madoff's lifestyle. He's been ordered to repay billions, yes

(continued)

> ▲ **A CASE STUDY** | *Continued*
>
> billions—to investors and to spend 150 years in prison. He will probably not be able to repay the billions he owes; but he is currently spending the rest of his life in prison.
>
> **For Discussion:** *Why did the SEC respond so slowly to tips about Bernie Madoff's Ponzi scheme? Will the failure to stop Bernie Madoff lead to major changes in the way SEC officials do their job?* ▲

SUMMARY

Strategy is the employment of resources to gain an objective. Tactics are the use of a subset of these resources to gain a part of the overall objective. Strategic management is the application of this ancient art to contemporary business and public administration. Strategic planning should not be equated with strategic management because strategic management often occurs without formal strategic planning. Strategic planning, however, is meaningless without strategic management.

All strategic management efforts entail all the following:

1. The identification of objectives to be achieved
2. The adoption of a time frame
3. An assessment of the organization's capabilities
4. An assessment of the organization's environment
5. The selection of a strategy from among alternatives

Overall, strategic management approaches in the public sector can more readily be adopted (1) the further a public organization is from the heart of its political leadership, (2) the more the organization undertaking strategic management is self-contained and autonomous, (3) the smaller it is (providing that it has the minimum critical mass), and (4) the more its results are consistently measurable.

Strategic management has become an indispensable perspective for many public sector managers. Such perspectives do not displace traditional management concerns but rather add a new dimension. And to facilitate the strategic management of government objectives (e.g., clean air, safe roads), regulation stands as one of the most potent tools available to public administrators, and as a cornerstone of contemporary public policy in the United States. Regulation allows public administrators the ability to take broad legislative directives and create specific rules that are designed to deliver desirable societal conditions.

REVIEW QUESTIONS

1. What are the differences between strategy and tactics for an overall national government or for an individual government agency?
2. Why must strategic planning be fully integrated with strategic management?

3. Is management by objectives more of a planning technique or more of a management control technique, or is it both?

4. Select any major government agency and explain how a SWOT analysis of it would usefully contribute to its strategic planning processes.

5. What are the key limitations that public administrators face when developing regulations?

KEY CONCEPTS

Objective   A short-term goal; something that must be achieved on the way to a larger overall achievement.

Planning horizon   The time frame during which the objectives of a strategic plan are to be achieved.

Strategic management   A philosophy of management that links strategic planning with day-to-day decision making. Strategic management seeks a fit between an organization's external and internal environments.

Strategic plan   The formal document that presents the ways and means by which a strategic goal will be achieved.

Strategic planning   The set of processes used by an organization to assess the strategic situation and develop strategy for the future.

Strategy   The overall conduct of a major enterprise to achieve long-term goals; the pattern to be found in a series of organizational decisions.

SWOT analysis   A review of an organization's strengths, weaknesses, opportunities, and threats. This technique is widely used to examine the viability of strategic plans.

Tactics   The short-term immediate decisions that in their totality lead to the achievement of strategic goals.

Vision   A view of an organization's future. The purpose of strategic management is to make such a vision a reality.

Vision statement   The identification of objectives to be achieved in the future.

MySearchLab® EXERCISES

Apply what you learned in this chapter on MySearchLab (*www.mysearchlab.com*).

BIBLIOGRAPHY

Appelbaum, Binyamin, and David S. Hilzenrath (2008). "SEC Didn't Act on Madoff Tips," *Washington Post* (December 16).

Ansoff, H. Igor (1965). *Corporate Strategy*. New York: McGraw-Hill.

Bryson, John M. (1995). *Strategic Planning for Public and Nonprofit Organizations*, 2nd ed. San Francisco: Jossey-Bass.

Dickson, Paul (1971). *Think Tanks*. New York: Atheneum.

Dror, Yehezkel (1964). "Muddling Through—'Science' or Inertia," *Public Administration Review* 24 (September).

Drucker, Peter F. (1954). *The Practice of Management*. New York: Harper.

Goldfarb, Zachary A. (2009). "Staffer at SEC Had Warned of Madoff," *Washington Post* (July 2).

Gordon, Gerald C. (1993). *Strategic Planning for Local Government*. Washington: International City Management Association.

Kamensky, John M. (2009). "Building Obama's Performance Management Approach," IBM Center for the Business of Government (December 2009).

Keegan, John (1993). *A History of Warfare*. New York: Knopf.

Kennan, George F. ("X") (1947). "The Sources of Soviet Conduct," *Foreign Affairs* (July).

Kim, Jane J. (2009). "Hunt Goes on for Missing Madoff Money," *Wall Street Journal* (June 29).

Lindblom, Charles E. (1959). "The Science of Muddling Through," *Public Administration Review* 19.

Lueck, Thomas, and Kim Severson (2006). "New York Bans Most Trans Fats in Restaurants," *New York Times* (December 6).

Luttwak, Edward N. (1976). *The Grand Strategy of the Roman Empire*. Baltimore: Johns Hopkins University Press.

McMillan, John (1996). *Games, Strategies, and Managers*. Oxford, England: Oxford University Press.

Mintzberg, Henry (1994). *The Rise and Fall of Strategic Planning*. New York: Free Press.

Osborne, David, and Ted Gaebler (1992). *Reinventing Government*. Reading, MA: Addison-Wesley.

Ostrom, Carol M. (2007). "New Rules: Menus Must Say What's in Your Meal," *Seattle Times* (July 20).

Pascale, Richard T. (1993). "The Honda Effect." In *The Strategy Process*, James Brian Quinn, Henry Mintzberg, and Robert M. James, eds. Englewood Cliffs, NJ: Prentice Hall.

Porter, Michael E. (1980). *Competitive Strategy*. New York: Free Press.

Pressman, Jeffrey L., and Aaron Wildavsky (1973). *Implementation: How Great Expectations in Washington Are Dashed in Oakland; Or, Why It's Amazing That Federal Programs Work at All*. Berkeley: University of California Press.

Roberts, Nancy C. (1993). "Limitations of Strategic Action in Bureaus," In *Public Management: The State of the Art*, Barry W. Bozeman, ed. San Francisco: Jossey-Bass.

Rumelt, Richard (1992). "The Evaluation of Business Strategy." In *The Strategy Process*, James Brian Quinn, Henry Mintzberg, and Robert M. James, eds. Englewood Cliffs, NJ: Prentice Hall.

Wettenhall, Roger, and Colm O. Nuallain, eds. (1990). *Public Enterprise Performance: Seven Country Studies*. Brussels: International Institute of Administrative Studies.

Wildavsky, Aaron (1978). "A Budget for All Seasons: Why the Traditional Budget Lasts," *Public Administration Review* 38, No. 6 (November–December).

RECOMMENDED BOOKS

Bryson, John M. (2004). *Strategic Planning for Public and Nonprofit Organizations*, 3rd ed. San Francisco: Jossey-Bass. A comprehensive guide to all aspects of strategic leadership, with an emphasis on planning, implementation, and strategy evaluation.

Crowley, Steven (2007). *Regulation and Public Interests*. Princeton, NJ: Princeton University Press. The book defends regulation in an era of deregulation through the use of both theory and examples.

Dixit, Avinash, and Barry Nalebuff (1993). *Thinking Strategically*. New York: W. W. Norton. An accessible introduction to game theoretical approaches to decision making.

Kellar, Morton (1998). *Regulating a New Society: Public Policy and Social Change in America, 1900–1933*. Cambridge, MA: Harvard University Press. An insightful examination of how regulation was used to manage the dramatic changes in American society during the first third of the twentieth century.

Koteen, Jack. (1997). *Strategic Management in Public and Nonprofit Organizations in Managing Public Concerns in an Era of Limits*, 2nd ed. Westport, CT: Praeger.
A comprehensive how-to-do-it manual on creating, installing, and evaluating strategic management systems.

Mitchell, Jerry (1998). *The American Experiment with Government Corporations*. Armonk, NY: M. E. Sharpe. A survey of the organizational form that incorporates the best features of public and private management to accomplish tasks that are deemed unsuited for commercialization or traditional bureaucracy.

Moore, Mark, H. (1995). *Creating Public Value: Strategic Management in Government*. Cambridge, MA: Harvard University Press. A call for public managers to go beyond being competent bureaucratic technicians; they must retool as strategic managers who "search for public value"—that is, more bang for the buck, better quality or quantities for each dollar spent.

RELATED WEB SITES

www.csis.org
Center for Strategic and International Studies (CSIS)
CSIS provides strategic insights and policy solutions to decision makers in government, international institutions, the private sector, and civil society. The site provides information and guidance to policymakers on the subjects of foreign policy and national security issues.

www.csmweb.com
Center for Strategic Management (CSM)
This center strives to transform slow-moving, bureaucratic organizations into high-performing groups that deliver more meaningful results. The site provides information about CSM's services, including speakers and teams to help improve efficiency.

www.hoover.org/
Hoover Institution on War, Revolution and Peace at Stanford University
This think tank, through its goals of collecting knowledge, generating ideas, and disseminating both, seeks to secure and safeguard peace, improve the human condition, and limit government intrusion into the lives of individuals.

www.rand.org
Rand Corporation
This organization, the world's archetypal think tank, strives to improve policy making and decision making through research and analysis. Rand's Web site has information about all of its current research initiatives, past research findings online, information about its locations worldwide, and graduate program offerings.

http://pimsonline.com
Strategic Planning Institute
This site enables business managers to "reality test" and strengthen their strategic thinking by comparing their thinking with the experience of comparable businesses drawn from the actual business cases documented in the PIMS (Profit Impact of Market Strategy) database. This Web site allows access to the experiences of more than 3,000 businesses.

Leadership

KEYNOTE: The Hedgehog, the Fox, Henry V, or the "Hidden-Hand" Golfer

The hedgehog is a small animal similar to a porcupine. When threatened, it rolls up into a ball so it is protected by the sharp quills covering its body. The fox is a notoriously clever, shrewd, and ingenious creature—so much so that "foxy" has become a synonym for these traits. One fine day in ancient Greece the poet Archilochus wrote, "The fox knows many things, but the hedgehog knows one big thing." Twenty-six hundred years later Isaiah Berlin (1909–1997), the British political philosopher, used Archilochus's brief poetic fragment as the basis for *The Hedgehog and the Fox*, his now-famous essay on intellectual style, on how leaders think, and on the utility of animal similes for describing human traits.

Berlin's essay has inspired a popular parlor game in political circles: classifying leaders as either hedgehogs or foxes. Hedgehogs are those who are single-minded about a concept. They know, like the hedgehog, "one big thing." President Ronald Reagan was a hedgehog. He knew that capitalism was better for the prosperity of the peoples of the world than socialism. This basic belief guided both his domestic policies (lower taxes, less government regulation) and his foreign policies (defeat communism wherever possible). As a hedgehog he was notorious for not bothering with the details of policy implementation. But that, of course, was what helped define him as a hedgehog. Hedgehogs are big-picture, not small-detail, leaders.

Now contrast Reagan with the Democratic presidents who preceded and followed him. Both Jimmy Carter and Bill Clinton were policy wonks obsessed with the details. They were both brilliant foxes. They knew all the excruciating details on all the policies before them. The problem was that they were men who knew too much. They were so obsessed with details that they never gave their subordinates in the administration, let alone the American people, a clear vision to follow. They thought and acted too much tactically and not enough strategically. Foreign policy to them was essentially a collection of improvisations. In contrast, Reagan's foreign policy could be summed up in two words: beat communism. And he did!

A hedgehog leader is one who imbues the organization with his or her overall philosophy of action. It is Elizabeth I heaping "foul scorn" on the 1588 Spanish armada that unsuccessfully sought to invade England. It is Admiral Horatio Nelson telling his captains before the 1805 Battle of Trafalgar, "No captain can do very wrong if he places his ship alongside that of the enemy." It is President Abraham Lincoln in 1863 dedicating the cemetery at Gettysburg, Pennsylvania, and demanding of the nation "that from these honored dead we take increased devotion to that cause for which they gave their last full measure of devotion; that we here highly resolve that these dead shall not have died in vain." Fancy words for "Let's win the war." It is President Franklin D. Roosevelt telling the nation in a radio address (December 19, 1940) that "we must be the great arsenal of democracy." And it is President Ronald Reagan telling a Republican congressional dinner (May 4, 1982), "We're the party that wants to see an America in which people can still get rich."

"Hedgehogic" visions all. These are calls to action that, while simple, are not simplistic, that offer specific instructions, and that are ultimately inspirational. After all, the job of a leader is to inspire—and hedgehogs do it better than foxes because they are more focused, more on target. People will not rally around a laundry list of little things no matter how worthy each item may be. Foxes may be brilliant managers and organizers of all the policy details, but management is not leadership. The original managers, etymologically speaking, were horse trainers. The word's meaning was gradually extended to any kind of skillful handling. So while a fox's skill in handling situations is generally acknowledged, handling is not leadership. All the attention to details may not add up to "Follow me!" A leader with a hedgehogic vision inspires others, while a manager merely delegates.

The presidential election of 2000 offered a direct contrast between a hedgehog and a fox. Then Governor George W. Bush knew a few big things: cut taxes, strengthen the military, and reform education and Social Security. His opponent, then Vice President Al Gore, wallowed in details like the class know-it-all. Despite Gore's obviously better grasp of the facts at hand, Bush seemed to win the presidential debates because he stayed on message with his hedgehogic vision. According to columnist Dick Morris, "It wasn't that Bush didn't know the details, but that he didn't much care. He knows, instinctively, that details don't matter as much as big ideas do" (New York Post, January 2, 2001). So President Bush got to be a hedgehog in the White House. He showed every sign of following in the hedgehogic tradition of Ronald Reagan—except that while the elderly Reagan sought a nap every afternoon, the energetic Bush headed off to the gym for a workout. Remember that leaders may have a detached management style and still be strongly focused on objectives. They just see things differently. They see to it that their staff deals with the foxy details.

Note that it is Reagan that Bush is imitating here, not his father. The first President Bush, despite being understudy to hedgehog Reagan for eight years, became too foxy for his own good. He got off his own message domestically ("Read my lips—no new taxes") when he raised taxes. Then his foreign policy of forging a "new world order" was so vague and complicated—not to mention reminiscent of Nazi phraseology—that what he meant by it remains elusive to this day. The best proof that the son will not imitate the father is the glaring fact that the father lost his 1992 bid for reelection to the fox from Arkansas. Bill Clinton was the ultimate fox. He put forth one detail after another with no overarching vision. So the public is all the more ready to follow a presidential hedgehog—especially if there are no sex or financial scandals that demean the presidential office.

There is no better example in the world's literature of tactical rhetoric supporting a strategic objective than Shakespeare's *Henry V*. President George W. Bush has often been analyzed as a modern Henry V. While still a prince, young Henry led a degenerate life as a hard-drinking associate of fun-loving ne'er-do-wells—thieves, prostitutes, and worse. His father despairs that his son, destined to inherit the throne, will never amount to much. As he approaches death, King Henry IV advises the prince to cope with his forthcoming domestic problems by making an effort to "busy giddy minds with foreign quarrels." The youthful Prince Hal, when crowned Henry V on his father's death, takes exactly that advice. Shakespeare has the new king order his officials to find a legal justification for waging war on France. Henry then assembles his "band of brothers" and forces them to listen to some of the most famous, most inspirational, and most quoted lines in all of Shakespeare. With poetry he rallies them to go "once more into the breach," compares them to "greyhounds in the slips, straining upon the start," and has them attack on the shout of "the game's afoot!" Thanks to Shakespeare's stirring words and to the 1415 Battle of Agincourt, Henry conquers France, thus becoming history's and literature's greatest example of how someone turns out to be a great national hero after a misspent youth.

Ever since George W. Bush became a serious contender for president, political commentators have compared him to Henry V as a leader. (Nobody has compared him to Henry for eloquence.) Like Henry, Bush has a father who led a great nation, logged a misspent youth replete with frequent alcoholic binges, and ascended to power. All this links the forty-third president with the legendary English ruler. Yet the question remains, did Bush end up as much of a hero as Henry V? He certainly followed Henry in busying "giddy minds with foreign quarrels" with wars in Afghanistan and Iraq. But Henry V won his wars. In contrast, when Bush left office in January 2009, he handed off two unfinished wars to his successor, he left the American economy in the worst shape since the Great Depression, he departed with record-low approval ratings, and, finally, he left the nation in the hands of an ascendant left determined to reverse his right-wing agenda. Henry V remains one of England's great heroes. George W. Bush, despite his unwavering focus on the war in Iraq for most of his two terms, is overwhelmingly considered if not a failure, then less than a success as a president.

President Barack Obama's leadership style seems to be a hybrid of the hedgehog and the fox. In his first few months in office, he laid out a hedgehogic list of big things to accomplish: conclude two wars, reform health care, stimulate an economy in deep recession, develop new energy policies, reform education, install new regulatory regimes for business and banking, reform immigration policies, and facilitate peace in the Middle East. He seeks to be an everything-at-once, a hedgehog with a fox's control of details.

But perhaps there is another model at work here—that of the "hidden-hand" golfer. This was Fred I. Greenstein's description of President Dwight D. Eisenhower's management style. Outwardly Eisenhower appeared to the public to be an amiable golfer, a president who would rather spend his days chasing after golf balls than chasing after legislators to get them to implement his agenda. He left office in 1961 with a reputation as a nice man, truly a beloved figure, who didn't accomplish very much as president except to play a lot of golf. That image changed radically two decades later when Greenstein published the first edition of *The Hidden-Hand Presidency*. Greenstein had gone into the archives and discovered that Eisenhower's fingerprints, so to speak, were figuratively all over every major policy issue dealt with by the Congress or the cabinet departments. Eisenhower believed in working behind the scenes, with what Greenstein termed a "hidden-hand," to bend the legislature and bureaucracy to his will. Greenstein's analysis started a major upward reassessment of Eisenhower's presidency.

Are there parallels here with the Obama administration? The most obvious is that President Obama also plays so much golf, so publicly, that he is criticized for it now as Eisenhower was then. But political observers also complain that Obama is not as engaged in the policy process as he should be, that he is too laid back. As a result he has been accused by Ryan Lizza (*The New Yorker*, May 2, 2011) of "leading from behind" in foreign and domestic policy. Other journalists have picked up on the phrase and claimed that "leading from behind" is not leading at all. But this all sounds very much like an Eisenhower-like "hidden-hand." Whether Obama's "hand" turns out to be as effective as Eisenhower's remains to be seen. Stay tuned!

For Discussion: *Why are the hedgehog and fox analogies so useful as shorthand ways of referring to leadership styles? Have you seen leaders in organizations with which you are familiar who fit the hedgehog and fox analogies?*

LEADING FOR PERFORMANCE

There are many characteristics of public sector management that call for knowledge and skills somewhat distinct from those required in private sector management. We have seen how the political context and governance arrangements that exist in the public sector present constraints and frameworks of decision making that must be understood and in many respects "managed" by public officials. We have discussed the special problems in public sector strategic management of converting political programs and managerial imperatives into a well-sequenced path to be followed. We have examined how the external and internal structures through which government is managed—intergovernmental relations and the machinery of government—give a framework that public sector managers must acknowledge and accommodate if they are to work effectively.

BOX 10.1 | The Lion and the Fox

Beastly descriptions of leaders have a long lineage in political analysis. Perhaps the best known is Niccolò Machiavelli's comparison of the lion and the fox in *The Prince* (1532):

> A prince being thus obliged to know well how to act as a beast must imitate the fox and the lion, for the lion cannot protect himself from traps, and the fox cannot defend himself from wolves. One must therefore be a fox to recognize traps and a lion to frighten wolves.

The most famous recent political leader with both of these animalistic traits was President Franklin D. Roosevelt (1882–1945). Roosevelt reached the height of political power despite the fact that, after 1921 when he contracted polio, he was basically confined to a wheelchair. Yet, because he was able to stand (with braces) to give speeches and because reporters were not allowed to take pictures that made him appear to be disabled, much of the American public was unaware of his handicapped condition— even though it was not a secret. His critics attacked him and his wife, Eleanor, as being either socialist or fascist. But he was just being pragmatic in response to his times. He was the president of the United States (1933–1945) whose New Deal policies are often said to have saved the capitalistic system; who led the nation through the Great Depression of the 1930s and to victory in World War II; and who is on every leading historian's list, along with Abraham Lincoln and George Washington, as one of the best U.S. presidents ever. So it was not surprising that historian James MacGregor Burns entitled his 1956 biography of him *Roosevelt: The Lion and the Fox* ◣.

All of these areas, however fundamental, really amount to parts of the context in which the public sector manager is to operate. It is as though we have examined a theater—its lighting, its marketing arrangements, its ownership, the way the supporting cast of actors and dancers are hired and fired. But we have now to turn to the heart of the question: how good is the performance going to be? What do the producer and director, the managers, have to do to exact from the cast the best performances of which they are capable?

The word *performance* is shared here by the world of management and the theatrical world—it also permeates the sporting world. There, too, the task is to exact a personal best from an athlete or a supreme performance from a team. There, too, issues such as training, team functioning, leadership, comparison with the best, total quality in the sense of trying never to miss a trick, and of course strategy are central ideas. *Performance*, above all, means the demonstration of a skill, the display of competence. In public sector management there are now many senses in which the term is applied. There are so many because knowing what kind of performance we are getting and setting up means for individuals and teams to do better are central concerns of public sector leaders. Thus performance management really does begin with leadership.

Defining Leadership

As a callow youth, one of the authors of this book took an undergraduate course in medieval history. Having seen dozens of films in which castles were stormed by a cast of thousands, this student asked the professor, "How do they get large numbers of men in real life to storm castles and the like when it appears to be, and indeed often is, certain death?" The professor's answer was memorable: "That's leadership for you!"

And so it is. The job of the leader of any organization is to get people to do things they have never done before, to do things that are not routine, and to take risks—and sometimes even to die—for the common good. Once the organization accepts the credo of Alexander Dumas's three musketeers—"One for all and all for one"—then they have been led, and only then have they been molded into an organization. In essence, that is the most basic task of a leader—to create organization out of disorder, to make people more capable as a cohesive group than they are as unorganized individuals.

Leadership is the exercise of authority, whether formal or informal, in directing and coordinating the work of others. The best leaders are those who can simultaneously exercise both kinds of leadership: the formal, based on the authority of rank or office, and the informal, based on the willingness of others to give service to a person whose special qualities of authority they admire. It has long been known that leaders who must rely only on formal authority are at a disadvantage when compared with those who can also mobilize the informal strength of an organization or nation. Shakespeare observed this when in *Macbeth* (Act V, Scene 2) he has Angus describe Macbeth's waning ability to command the loyalty of his troops:

Those he commands move only in command,
Nothing in love: now does he feel his title
Hang loose about him, like a giant's robe
Upon a dwarfish thief.

Macbeth had become the very definition of an incompetent leader. Once he lost the respect and admiration of his followers, his organization was as doomed as he was.

The power that a leader possesses implies a hierarchy of control of stronger over weaker. J. R. P. French and B. Raven, in "The Bases of Social Power," suggest that there are five major bases of power: (1) expert power, which is based on the perception that the leader possesses some special knowledge or expertise; (2) referent power, which is based on the follower's liking, admiring, or identifying with the leader; (3) reward power, which is based on the leader's ability to mediate rewards for the follower; (4) legitimate power, which is based on the follower's perception that the leader has the legitimate right or authority to exercise influence over him or her; and (5) coercive power, which is based on the follower's fear that noncompliance with the leader's wishes will lead to punishment. Subsequent research on these power bases has indicated that the first two (expert and referent power) are more positively related to subordinate performance and satisfaction than the last three (reward, legitimate, and coercive power).

Leadership and Management

We need to distinguish between leadership and management. The two functions and roles overlap substantially. Management involves power (usually formal authority) bestowed on the occupant of a position by a higher organizational

BOX 10.2 | Leading Through Public Relations

Napoléon Bonaparte (1769–1821) was a master of modern propaganda. The horsey example in this picture has Napoléon gloriously pointing the way to victory in Italy. Life-sized pictures such as this were commissioned for public display to influence popular feelings and perceptions of Napoléon. Of course, this picture by Jacques-Louis David (1748–1825) is a lie. Note that the rider has a great-looking long leg. But if Napoléon had legs that size, he would not have been the subject of so many "short" jokes. And, unlike generals such as George Washington and Ulysses S. Grant, who were among the best horsemen of their age, Napoléon was a notoriously poor rider—often falling off his horse, especially if it had reared up as in the picture. This is why he much preferred traveling by coach. But the greatest misrepresentation here is that Napoléon crossed the Alps not on a fleet-footed steed but on a sure-footed mule. Thus this picture is a good example of Napoléon's policy of never telling the truth when a lie would do him more good. After all, a diminutive Napoléon on a rearing mule would hardly have had the same emotive punch. The French wouldn't have it. The only people ever to be inspired by mules are members of the Democratic Party in the United States.

Of course, American presidents don't do propaganda. They do photo opportunities. This President George W. Bush action figure toy was not authorized by the White House. But it was inspired by President Bush's visit to the aircraft carrier *Abraham Lincoln* on May 1, 2003. He landed on the flight deck as a passenger in a military aircraft so all the world would see him exit in full "top gun" regalia—just like the action figure. While the photos were optimal, he was severely criticized for imitating a real warrior when it was totally unnecessary. After all, the carrier was within sight of the California coast and his regular helicopter could have transported him without the need of a photogenic costume. While he also gave an internationally televised speech to the crew of the carrier, the "warrior" photos of the commander in chief in wartime were the major reason for the trip. Unfortunately, the photos also reminded his critics that when Bush had the opportunity to be a real warrior as a young man during the Vietnam War, he conspicuously avoided combat by joining the National Guard. Nevertheless, both Bush and Napoléon knew that whatever their critics said, all that mattered was their posturing pictures. And pictures never lie—or do they? ▶

authority. With the power of management comes responsibility and accountability for the use of organizational resources. In contrast, leadership cannot be bestowed on a person by a higher authority. Effective managers must also be leaders, and many leaders become managers, but the two sets of roles and functions differ.

The subject of leadership raises many complex issues that have plagued the behavioral sciences for generations. For example, what gives a manager or a leader legitimacy? Simply put, legitimacy is a characteristic of a social institution, such as a government, a family, or an organization, whereby it has both a legal and a perceived right to make binding decisions. Thus managers presumably have legitimacy because of the legal and perceived rights that accompany their organizational positions. In contrast, the legitimacy of a leader—separate and distinct from the legitimacy of a manager—cannot be addressed without introducing the concept of charisma, leadership based on the compelling personality of the leader rather than on formal position.

This last concept was first articulated by our old friend Max Weber—he wasn't called a universal genius for nothing—who distinguished charismatic authority from the traditional authority of a monarch and the legal authority one receives by virtue of law, such as the authority that legitimizes organizational executives. The word *charisma* is derived from the Greek word for divine grace. Charismatic leadership, if it is to survive, must eventually be institutionalized or routinized. Thus the founder of a movement or organization may be a charismatic spellbinder, but his or her successors are often, of necessity, comparatively dull bureaucrats.

Despite the differences and the unresolved questions, two things are evident: First, leadership involves a relationship between people in which influence and power are unevenly distributed on a legitimate basis; and second, a leader cannot function in isolation. In order for there to be a leader, someone must follow.

Perhaps the most accepted pure definition of the organizational leadership function comes from Chester I. Barnard. In his 1938 study *The Functions of the Executive*, he defines three essential functions of leaders or executives:

1. To provide a system of communication
2. To promote the securing of essential efforts
3. To formulate and define the purposes and goals of an organization

Note how he was decades ahead of his time in arguing that the most critical function of a chief executive is to establish and communicate a system of organizational values among organizational members. "The formulation and definition of purpose is then a widely distributed function only the more general part of which is executive. In this fact lies the most important inherent difficulty in the operation of cooperative systems: the necessity for indoctrinating those at the lower levels with general purposes." Here Barnard is referring to the necessity for top management to develop and instill a strategic vision for the organization. "Without that up-and-down-the-line coordination of purposeful decisions, general decisions and general purposes are mere intellectual processes in an organization vacuum, insulated from realities by layers of misunderstanding. The function of formulating grand purposes and providing for their redefinition is one that needs sensitive systems of communication, experience in interpretation, imagination, and delegation of responsibility." Barnard knew, in part because he was a real executive, that if the value system of the organization was clear and strong, the day-to-day concerns would take care of themselves.

Trait Theories

The trait approach to leadership assumes that leaders possess traits—personality characteristics—that make them fundamentally different from followers. Advocates of trait theory believe that some people have unique leadership characteristics and qualities that enable them to assume responsibilities not everyone can execute. Therefore they are "born" leaders.

It is no longer fashionable to contend that people will be effective leaders because they possess certain traits—without also considering other variables that influence leadership effectiveness. The arguments against trait theory are persuasive and come from a number of points of view. First, trait theory has largely fallen out of favor because reality never matched the theory. Instead, starting in the late 1950s, it has become standard practice to view leadership as a relationship, an interaction between individuals. The interaction was called a transaction, so that the term *transactional leadership* has become the umbrella label encompassing many theories of leadership. Second, the situation strongly influences leadership. The situation is now viewed as an enormous influence in determining the qualities, characteristics, and skills needed in a leader. There is even a **law of the situation** that deals with this.

Probably the most damaging criticism of trait theory, however, has been its lack of ability to identify which traits make an effective leader. Even among the traits that have been most commonly cited—intelligence, energy, achievement, dependability, and socioeconomic status—there is a lack of consensus across studies. The most obvious proof that leadership involves more than possessing certain traits is the simple fact that a leader may be effective in one setting and ineffective in another. It all depends on the situation.

Transactional Approaches

While the central question for the trait approach was who was a leader, transactional approaches sought to determine how leadership was established and exerted. Leadership-style-oriented **transactional approaches** all follow in the tradition of the famous K. Lewin, R. Lippitt, and R. K. White (1939) studies of the effectiveness of leadership styles on the group efforts of 10-year-old children engaged in hobby activities. The leader in each group was classified as having an authoritarian, a democratic, or laissez-faire orientation.

Authoritarian leaders determined all policies, set all work assignments, were personal in their criticisms, and were product (or task) oriented. Democratic leaders shared decision-making powers with subordinates, left decisions about assignments up to the group, and participated in group activities but tried not to monopolize. They exhibited high levels of consideration for others. Laissez-faire leaders allowed freedom for individual and group decision making, provided information (or supplies) only when requested, and did not participate in the group except when called upon. They functioned more as facilitators.

Law of the situation ■
A notion developed by social psychologist Mary Parker Follett (1868–1933) that one person should not give orders to another person, but both should agree to take their orders from the situation. If orders are simply part of the situation, the question of someone giving and someone receiving does not come up.

Transactional approaches ■
Any means of analyzing leadership style that focuses on how leaders interact and how they treat those they seek to lead.

Groups with democratic leaders were the most satisfied and productive. The authoritarian-led groups showed the most aggressive behavior and were the least satisfied, but they were highly productive (possibly because of fear of the leader). The groups with laissez-faire leaders showed low satisfaction and low production, and they were behaviorally aggressive toward group members and other groups. Thousands of subsequent studies have essentially presented the same findings. Democracy, meaning participative management, works.

Managers with authoritarian personalities and styles value order, precision, consistency, obedience, rules, law, and organization. To them, the power that flows from structure is supreme. Relationships are hierarchical, based on dominance and dependence. Authoritarianism, control through structure, is rigidly unbending. Yet authoritarians, while often initially successful, cannot survive over the long term. Whether large scale (such as Hitler or Stalin) or pint sized (such as an oppressive supervisor), authoritarians will ultimately fail because "democracy is inevitable." It is inevitable not just because it is good but because it is more effective—especially in the modern world, with its high-tech workforce. In the meanwhile, however, authoritarians cause considerable psychic damage in individuals and generate lost productivity in the internal organizational polity while often sustaining **authoritarianism** in the outside polity.

Because it is so easy and tempting for authoritarian personalities to rise to power, they must be all the more resisted because of their inherent tendencies toward destruction. People, groups, and organizations must evolve and adapt to their environment. Authoritarians do not adapt willingly to changing circumstances and new ideas. They are conservative in the worst sense of the word. Thus their need to protect and preserve the past and to inhibit constructive change leads to organizational rigidity and incompetence. Authoritarians dominate; their disciples obey. Organizational authoritarians and democrats cannot coincide; they are mutually exclusive.

Democracy, whether it takes the form of representative government or participative management, is in marked contrast. It allows for a peaceful evolution and change. Dissent is not suppressed; it is instead used as a creative force leading to greater effectiveness and less incompetence. The Soviet Union and its Communist Party disintegrated in 1991 because its authoritarian command economy was increasingly unable to provide its citizens an adequate standard of living. Democratic institutions are more competent because they allow for inevitable mistakes to be corrected in an evolutionary manner—before they lead to revolution.

Authoritarian rigidity is an important structural cause of organizational incompetence. It inhibits an organization's ability to learn and adapt to its environment. It concentrates decision making and responsibility in too few places and individuals. It denies others the right and opportunity to influence or to grow as employees and as people. Rigidity is illustrated by the British contingent of soldiers continuing to march in formation between Lexington and Concord, Massachusetts Colony, in 1775 despite colonial sharpshooters diminishing their ranks. Why did the dedicated targets keep on marching in file? Because the structure (the rules, lines of authority, the policies and procedures) said that was how wars were to be fought and soldiers were to behave. British structural rigidity—in all aspects of its eighteenth-century relationships with its American colonies—not only caused the American Revolution, but also led to the British defeat as they tried to suppress it.

Authoritarianism ■
Rule by an individual whose claim to sole power is supported by subordinates who sustain control of the system by carrying out the ruler's orders and by a public that is unwilling or unable to rebel against that control. The ruler's personality may be a significant element in maintaining the necessary balance of loyalty and fear. Authoritarianism differs from totalitarianism only in that the latter may have a specific ideology that rationalizes it, although it may require a leader who embodies that ideology to sustain public support. An authoritarian state may be further distinguished from a totalitarian one by the fact that under some circumstances an authoritarian state could allow limited freedom of expression and political opposition, as long as the regime does not feel threatened.

Transactional leadership approaches assumed that leaders could be trained to act in the appropriate way as called for by their organization. This has proved to be wishful thinking. When leaders return to their organization after leadership training sessions, they seldom exhibit behavior changes. Despite training, department heads will not necessarily act considerately toward subordinates if their own supervisors do not act supportively toward them. One obvious implication is that changes must be introduced into an organization as a whole—not just to certain employees. In practice, leaders apply different styles in different situations. Thus the "pure" leadership style emphasis has given way to contingency approaches.

Contingency Approaches

We have all seen examples of the heroic leader: The general who leads troops from the front lines is the managerial cousin to the supervisor who leads from the assembly line. Each finds it almost impossible to delegate responsibility and, by trying to do it all alone, ultimately fails. This inherently theatrical style of leadership was appropriate for ancient armies when an Alexander the Great, sword in hand, would be the first to engage the enemy. This lead worker (or lead killer) approach had by the middle of the twentieth century become discredited. True, there will always be organizational heroes, but their heroism will be more situational, a response to an urgent need or crisis—not a way of organizational life.

Heroic-style managers are stress carriers. They create high levels of stress for themselves and transmit it to others around them. Such managers typically will give a secretary a handwritten letter to type and then stand there and *watch*, with ever-increasing nervousness, as it is typed. He will give an assignment to subordinates and then tell them exactly how to do it. She will insist on being the center and controller of all organizational communications, creating information bottlenecks and corresponding organizational incompetence. When heroic leadership is allowed by the organization's top managers, it is reinforced and imitated by lower-level managers. While no organization would advocate self-destructive leadership styles, tolerating them amounts to the same thing. Modern organizational leadership is inherently more situational or contingent than heroic.

▶ BOX 10.3 | Oligarchic Leadership

"Who says organization says oligarchy." This is Robert Michels's "iron law of oligarchy," stated in his *Political Parties*, which holds that organizations are by their nature oligarchic because majorities within an organization are not capable of ruling themselves:

> Organization implies the tendency to oligarchy. In every organization, whether it be a political party, a professional union, or any other association of the kind, the aristocratic tendency manifests itself very clearly.

The mechanism of the organization, while conferring a solidity of structure, induces serious changes in the organized mass, completely inverting the respective position of the leaders and the led. As a result of organization, every party or professional union becomes divided into a minority of directors and a majority of the directed. ▶

Source: Robert Michels, *Political Parties* (Glencoe, IL: Free Press, 1915, 1949).

Unlike the trait theory and transactional leadership approaches, contingency approaches take into consideration the many factors that may influence a leader's style. There is a recognition that a successful leader in one type of organization may not be successful in another simply because it differs from the previous one. Its situation (or context) is different, and the choice of a style needs to be contingent on the situation. As leadership historian Ralph Stogdill notes, the contingency theories stress:

1. The type, structure, size, and purpose of the organization
2. The external environment in which the organization functions
3. The orientation, values, goals, and expectations of the leader, his or her superiors, and subordinates
4. The expert or professional knowledge required of the position

The contingency approaches assert that different leadership styles will differ in their effects in different situations. The situation (not traits or styles themselves) determines whether a leadership style or a particular leader will be effective. Thus, contingency theorists maintain that there is no "one best way"—as in the scientific management of Frederick Taylor—of effective leadership. Just think of Ulysses S. Grant, the victorious general of the American Civil War. On the basis of his war record, he was elected president in 1868, but as good as he was a general, he was bad as president. He is rated among the best generals in American history, but historians almost universally concede that he was one of the very worst presidents. Other American generals were able to make the leap from military to civilian leadership: George Washington, Andrew Jackson, and Dwight D. Eisenhower being the most famous examples. But poor President Grant just did not have it in him. He wasn't able to spontaneously retool his mind as a civilian leader. While Grant himself was honest, he consistently showed blind loyalty to corrupt friends.

Professors Robert Tannenbaum and Warren Schmidt conducted one of the first studies that actually indicated a need for leaders to evaluate the situational factors prior to the implementation of a particular leadership style. They concluded that "the successful manager . . . can be primarily characterized neither as a strong leader nor as a permissive one." Indeed, he or she "is one who maintains a high batting average in accurately assessing the forces that determine what his most appropriate behavior at any given time should be and in actually being able to behave accordingly."

While Tannenbaum and Schmidt assert that leaders should adjust their styles to accommodate followers, University of Washington professor Fred Fiedler found that the opposite was often true. It is sometimes easier to change the work environment, the situation, to fit a leader's style. The underlying leadership style depends on personality. According to Fiedler, a leader's personality is not likely to change because of a few lectures or a few weeks of intensive training. Therefore, an organization should not choose a leader who fits a situation but should change the situation to mesh with the style of its leader. But this is easier said than done. The choices are clearly expressed by the new boss who tells the staff, "We can do things my way, your way, or the company's way. If you do things my way, we'll get along just fine."

Transformational Leadership

A transformational leader is one with the ability to change an embedded organizational culture by creating a new vision for the organization and marshalling the appropriate support to make that vision the new reality. The best-known transformational leader is General George S. Patton Jr., who during World War II took charge of a defeated and demoralized American Army in North Africa and transformed it into a winning team. The task was different but no less difficult for Lee Iacocca when he took charge of a Chrysler Corporation on the verge of bankruptcy and disintegration in the late 1970s and brought it back into profit. Similar challenges faced the leadership of AT&T in 1984 when it went from a monopoly public utility to a company that had to change its corporate culture to compete in the open market.

Edward G. Rendell faced a similar problem (but different in its content) when he became mayor of Philadelphia in 1992. Philadelphia was a "loser"—in just about every way—in the eyes of employees, potential employers, bondholders, suppliers, and citizens. It was simply *assumed* that the city could not compete head-on with comparable cities. Rendell had to change not only an organizational culture, but also just about *everybody's perception* of that culture. He effectively told the municipal unions to get with the plan or "kiss off." After a brief strike that was notable for its lack of public support, they got with the plan. Philadelphia needed and got in Rendell a transformational leader, a person who could totally transform an embedded organizational culture by creating a new vision of and for the organization, and successfully selling that vision—by rallying commitment and loyalty to make the vision become a reality.

Social scientists Noel Tichy and David Ulrich describe transformational leaders as those rare individuals who can lead employees through their fears and uncertainties to the realization of the new vision. This requires strategic leadership that successfully changes people's perceptions of the organization. Transformational change is more than a rational, technical, incremental approach to change. The leader's primary function is to lead and support through carefully conceived change stages, acting as a cheerleader and as a belief model—verbally and nonverbally communicating belief in the benefits to all that will accrue from the changes.

Whereas the transactional theories of leadership apply primarily to leadership roles, functions, and behavior within an existing organizational culture,

BOX 10.4 | Machiavelli on Leadership Style

From this arises the question whether it is better to be loved more than feared, or feared more than loved. The reply is, that one ought to be both feared and loved, but as it is difficult for the two to go together, it is much safer to be feared than loved, if one of the two has to be wanting. . . . And men have less scruple in offending one who makes himself loved than one who makes himself feared; for love is held by a chain of obligation which, men being selfish, is broken whenever it serves their purpose; but fear is maintained by a dread of punishment which never fails. ◤

Source: Niccolò Machiavelli, *The Prince* (1513).

transformative leadership is about leadership to change a culture. Transactional leadership focuses on incremental change. Transformative leadership is about radical change. Sometimes the radical changes call for co-optation, the inclusion of new, potentially dissident group members into an organization's policymaking process to prevent such elements from being a threat to the organization or its mission. More often it is the implementation of a new strategic vision.

It is interesting to observe that transformational leadership theories have many similarities with the trait theories of leadership. Transformational leadership borders on "great man" theory—the belief that leaders are born, not made. In many ways, leadership theory is once again involved in seeking to find the basis of leadership in traits—rather than in relational and cultural factors. We have come full circle!

The Importance of Optimism

At the beginning of the World War II Battle of the Bulge the Americans were reeling from a German counterattack and things seemed quite desperate. As matters went from bad to worse General Dwight D. Eisenhower (later to be president) called a meeting of his leading commanders and announced: "The present situation is to be regarded as one of opportunity for us and not of disaster. There will only be cheerful faces at this conference table." His newly "cheerful" commanders went on to win the battle.

Historian Stephen E. Ambrose wrote that Eisenhower felt it was critical that he, no matter what his personal feelings at the time, maintain an air of absolute confidence. He knew that confidence, or "cheerleading," at the top would permeate down through every level of his immense organization. Eisenhower instinctively knew, as social science now proves, that a confident organization is far more likely to succeed than a doubtful one—even if its leader in reality has doubts. Optimism or positive thinking works—even when the leader has to fake it.

Throughout history the most successful leaders—whether generals, managers, or football coaches—have been those who were the most optimistic. Was there ever a more optimistic politician than President Franklin D. Roosevelt who in the depths of the Great Depression told his nation in his 1933 inaugural address that "the only thing we have to fear is fear itself"? Here was a man who in his prime was crippled by polio. Yet he only succumbed to physical paralysis. He didn't let his affliction prevent him from becoming governor of New York and then president of the United States. His optimism was infectious. People around him caught it. This was a communicable "disease" that was good for the country.

Effective leaders have long known the importance of instilling a winning optimism in their followers. Even though it may not be warranted by circumstances, it is a far more potent force in leading than logic would dictate. What is certain is that the opposite of optimism, pessimism, depression or what social psychologist Martin E. P. Seligman has called "learned helplessness," will tend to lead to failure both of the mission at hand and eventually of health. When people find themselves in situations where they feel that they have no control and that their best efforts are futile, they "learn" from this repeated experience that they are "helpless" and thus become pessimistic and depressed. Seligman uses the example of American prisoners of war in Korea. Those who retained an optimistic outlook were far more likely to survive their ordeal. Those who felt helpless and consequently depressed were far more likely to die in captivity even though they got the same food and treatment as the others.

Optimistic attitudes on the part of leaders often become self-fulfilling prophecies. This Pygmalion effect, causing something to happen by believing it will, has been often demonstrated with both teacher/student and manager/worker relationships. If the teacher or manager believes his or her students or workers are capable (or not capable), they will tend to live up (or down) to expectations. This helps to explain why optimistic leaders are more likely to have successful followers. And why pessimistic leaders tend to wind up with a bunch of losers.

Remember the advice traditionally given to actors: Always be sincere—once you can fake that, you've got it made. It's the same with leadership. Always be optimistic and fake it if you don't feel it. New York City Mayor Rudy Giuliani admitted as much when discussing his inspiring leadership after the terrorist attacks that destroyed the Twin Towers of the World Trade Center on September 11, 2001: "I wonder how much of it [his leadership] was bluff. A lot of it had to be bluff. . . . Look, in a crisis you have to be optimistic. When I said the spirit of the city would be stronger, I didn't know that. I just hoped that" (*Time*, December 31, 2001). And do you think President Franklin D. Roosevelt really thought that the only thing we had "to fear was fear itself"? All who knew him agree that he was a great actor. Of course, all politicians are actors. Some just get better reviews than others.

TOO MUCH LEADERSHIP

Structural rigidity often causes managers to overmanage—to lead too much. *Micromanage* is the pejorative term for supervising too closely. Any manager may be guilty of micromanagement for refusing to allow subordinates to have any real authority or responsibility, thereby ensuring that subordinates can neither function as, nor grow into, effective managers. Furthermore, the managers are kept so busy micromanaging that they never have time to do what managers are supposed to do—like develop long-term strategy and overall vision. Legislators at all levels of government are frequently practitioners of micromanagement. By writing detailed rules for programs into legislation, by demanding that particular items be procured from suppliers in their districts, or by mandating that certain employees be hired or promoted for patronage purposes, they deny public managers a large measure of the real administrative discretion that all effective managers need.

Micromanagement

An apt example of legislative micromanagement is provided by Philip Howard. In *The Death of Common Sense*, his denouncement of governmental micromanagement, he recounts the story of Mother Teresa's Missionaries of Charity's attempts to build a homeless shelter in New York City. A group of nuns from the organization proposed refurbishing an abandoned four-story building that would house 64 residents. But all four-story buildings in New York must, by law, have an elevator—which would have added $100,000 to the cost. This lack of amenities did not deter the nuns, who shun modern conveniences and did not want an elevator anyway. It was to be a no-frills basic shelter. But regulations are regulations. When the Mother Teresa group could not find anyone who had the authority to waive the elevator requirement after 18 months of navigating the hallways of the municipal bureaucracy, they gave up and went on to other good works.

While there is some legitimate justification for micromanagement by legislators and directors (after all, they are the legitimate representatives of the owners of the government or corporation), there is no justification for micromanagement along the traditional chain of hierarchical authority. While close supervision is appropriate for a trainee, it is insulting and disabling for any employee who is presumably able. And it can be dangerous. Micromanagement can drive employees over the edge into violence. For example, in recent years the U.S. Postal Service has had a spate of enraged workers go berserk and murder their supervisors. These tensions are common in many industries. But according to journalist Peter Kilborn, in post offices they "fester[ed] within an archaic, Army-like culture in which many top managers communicate by directive, and front-line supervisors often hover over their charges, waiting for a mistake and timing workers' trips to the bathroom." Shootings killed three dozen people in U.S. post offices from the mid-1980s to the mid-1990s. In 1994 the Federal Centers for Disease Control and Prevention found that murder was the second leading cause of death on the job for postal workers.

Micromanagement will not make a competent employee more competent; it only makes things worse by wasting time, by damaging interpersonal relationships, by demonstrating that the micromanagers themselves are not competent supervisors, and by distracting managers from the kinds of activities that can prevent organizational incompetence. Instead, micromanagement—and overmanagement—lead to overcommitment and bureaucratic overcontrol, two of the classic symptoms of organizational incompetence.

Overmanagement

Having too many managers for the nature of the organization or task—overmanagement—is related to and inevitably leads to micromanagement and organizational rigidity. Overmanagement has become a particularly important problem in recent years as computer-driven information systems render once-useful layers of middle management obsolete. These threatened managers struggle to find new roles for themselves and ways to retain their long-standing sources of authority, which have depended on their exclusive control of organizations' knowledge bases. They get in the way of more productive organizational units until periodic downsizing efforts permanently remove them. But until they are sought out and expelled, they are among the major structural causes of organizational incompetence.

MORAL LEADERSHIP

Political scientist Garry Wills in the *Atlantic Monthly* warns that "if the leader is just an expediter of what other people want, a resource for their use, the people are not being *led* but *serviced*." Thus it is moving people in new directions—taking them to places where they did not know they wanted or needed to go—that is the essence of leadership and has been since ancient times. Thucydides, in his *History of the Peloponnesian War*, describes Pericles, the leader of ancient Athens, as someone who, because he was so "clearly above corruption, was enabled, by the respect others had for him and his own wise policy, to hold the multitude in a voluntary restraint." Thus "he led them, not they him; and because he did not win his power on compromising terms, he could say not only what pleased others, but also what displeased them, relying on their respect."

The Bully Pulpit

Pericles exercised moral leadership. He was able to send people in new directions of action and thought because it was the right and decent thing to do. During the presidential campaign of 1932, then New York Governor Franklin D. Roosevelt spoke for all political executives when he said, "The presidency is not merely an administrative office. That's the least of it. It is more than an engineering job, efficient or inefficient. It is preeminently a place of moral leadership. All our great presidents were leaders of thought at times when certain historic ideas in the life of the nation had to be clarified." Presidents have traditionally used what President Theodore Roosevelt called their "bully (meaning "first-rate") pulpit" to provide this clarification.

Rhetorical Leadership

Political scientists James Caeser, Glen Thurow, Jeffrey Tulis, and Joseph Bessette, in their article "The Rise of the Rhetorical Presidency," argue that, historically, leadership through rhetoric was suspect, that presidents rarely spoke directly to the people, and that, in any event, presidents relied much more heavily on party and political leadership in the Congress for their electoral and programmatic support. But today's presidents attempt to move mass opinion by speeches that exhort the public to support their policies and programs. Presidents are obliged to do this for three reasons: (1) the modern doctrine of the presidency, which avers that the presidency is a place of moral leadership and should employ rhetoric to lead public opinion; (2) the advent of the modern mass media, especially television, which facilitates the use of rhetoric; and (3) the modern presidential campaign, which blurs campaigning and governing.

According to Caeser et al., "Popular or mass rhetoric, which presidents once employed only rarely, now serves as one of their principal tools in attempting to govern the nation. Whatever doubts Americans may now entertain about the limitations of presidential leadership, they do not consider it unfitting or inappropriate for presidents to attempt to 'move' the public by programmatic speeches that exhort and set forth grand and ennobling views." But just as it was with ancient Pericles, their views are only accepted as "grand and ennobling" if they themselves are perceived as noble, worthy, and above corruption.

The "two-presidencies" phenomenon is telling here. This is Aaron Wildavsky's division of the presidency into two differing spheres of influence: foreign policy and domestic policy. Wildavsky contended that presidential leadership in foreign policy will, generally speaking, find greater support among the public than

Theodore Roosevelt charging toward the bully pulpit. His heroism during the 1898 Spanish-American War made him a national icon. Within a year he was elected governor of New York. Within another year he was elected vice president of the United States. Then less than a year after he was inaugurated, his president, William McKinley, was assassinated and the leader of the "Rough Riders" who charged up San Juan Hill had his bully pulpit. But this contemporary picture is a lie. While Roosevelt's cavalry charged, they did so on foot. The U.S. Army's administration of the war was so poor that their horses were left behind in Florida.

President Roosevelt was such an energetic speaker—really a civil preacher—that once in 1912, when a would-be assassin shot him in the chest, he refused medical treatment until he had finished his speech. He told his Milwaukee audience, "I have just been shot, but it takes more than that to kill a Bull Moose!" They looked on in shocked admiration as he continued to bleed and talk. What saved Roosevelt's life was the fact that the bullet went into his breast pocket and through a folded piece of paper on which his speech was written and a metal eyeglass case before hitting him. While the event was dramatic and bloody, Roosevelt, with his extensive combat experience during the Spanish-American War, knew that he had suffered only a flesh wound. And why let that ruin a good speech on an otherwise fine day?

leadership in domestic policy. To test his hypothesis, Wildavsky examined congressional action on presidential proposals from 1948 to 1964. For this period, the Congress approved 58.5 percent of the foreign policy bills; 73.3 percent of the defense policy bills; and 70.8 percent of general foreign relations, State Department, and foreign aid bills and treaties. During this same period, the Congress approved only 40.2 percent of the president's domestic policy proposals. Thus the two-presidencies thesis was confirmed. Wildavsky's work has spawned a bevy of research articles. While Wildavsky himself in "Reconsidering the Two Presidencies" would in 1989 concede that his thesis was decidedly "time and culture bound," nothing has materially diminished the essence of his original thesis put forth in 1966. The reason the president is so much more successful in foreign policy is that he comes to the table with cleaner hands. He is less the conniving politician and more the noble statesman.

But more people than presidents can offer moral leadership. For example, Secretary of Health and Human Services Louis W. Sullivan was considered one of the most ineffectual members of the Bush administration until 1990, when he started attacking cigarette companies for targeting the marketing of cigarettes to minorities and women. His popularity and stature immediately soared. More important, he was effective. R. J. Reynolds, one of the largest U.S. tobacco companies, was test-marketing a new brand called "Uptown," which was specifically aimed at African-Americans. Sullivan said, "This brand is cynically and deliberately targeted toward black Americans. . . . At a time when we must cultivate greater responsibility among our citizens, Uptown's slick and sinister advertising proposes instead a great degree of personal irresponsibility." After Sullivan's attack, the brand was withdrawn. While moral leadership may not move mountains, it can sometimes move cigarette companies.

▶ A CASE STUDY | Transforming the Postal Service

Ever since the nineteenth century when stamps were first used as postage on letters, people have collected them for their artistic merit and their investment value. The United States first issued adhesive postage stamps in 1847. These stamps had portraits of Benjamin Franklin and George Washington. Governments have produced a multitude of commemorative stamps for the collectors' market. After all, a stamp purchased and saved is almost pure profit to the post office.

When the U.S. Postal Service decided to issue a stamp commemorating the rock 'n' roll star Elvis Presley, it created publicity by asking Americans to "vote" on stamp designs featuring either the young or old Elvis. When the "polling" was complete, the young Elvis design won by four to one. More importantly, this created a ready audience—a ready market—for the stamp when it was released in 1992. Nevertheless, the Postal Service was surprised at the depth of the public's enthusiasm. People who had never saved stamps before suddenly become collectors—at least of this stamp. The Postal Service could barely keep up with the initial demand for the Elvis stamp. Because hardly anyone bought the first Elvis stamps to use on letters, the Postal Service, from its point of view, was almost literally printing money.

Taken by surprise by the public's tremendous response to the Elvis stamp, the Postal Service was determined that the next time it would be ready—ready with more stamps to sell. But stamps of what? Most commemorative stamps are issued, bought by collectors or people who prefer stamps with some distinction, and then forgotten. The Postal Service searched for another dead national icon with a following comparable to Elvis's. "Dead" was an important consideration here. Contrary to the philatelic policies in monarchies and dictatorships, only the likenesses of the deceased are allowed on American stamps. Marilyn Monroe, dead since 1962, had never faded from the public's mind. As with Elvis, her face and persona were instantly recognizable. Both had died prematurely of drug overdoses when they were still enormously popular.

Realizing the market potential, the Postal Service gave the Marilyn stamp a lavish publicity send-off. Postmaster General Marvin Runyon made the rounds of the TV and radio talk shows as if he were hawking a book. He scheduled visits to shopping malls where he would judge Marilyn Monroe look-alike contests. They even advertised her on TV. Over old news clips of Marilyn, an announcer asks, "When is a stamp not just a stamp? The Marilyn stamp [picture of stamp replaces news film] now at your post office." Many people give great patriotic service to their government when they are alive; to do so after death as Marilyn has done—and is still doing—is patriotism indeed.

Today's Postal Service was created by the Postal Reorganization Act of 1970. This federal statute converted the Post Office Department into an independent establishment—within the executive branch of the government—to own and operate the nation's postal system, thereafter known as the U.S. Postal Service. The old Post Office Department was "reinvented" (before this term was in common usage in government) as a public enterprise because the Nixon administration was unhappy with its poor management and constant need for public subsidies.

Amid a dramatic postal strike in the spring of 1970, the government for the first time in history agreed to allow wages, which hitherto had always been set through the legislative process, to be negotiated between union and government representatives. That ended the strike. Subsequently, the Postal Reorganization Act was passed, establishing the corporate framework sought by Nixon and providing for collective bargaining with postal employees in the future. The Postal Service remains the only federal agency whose employees are governed by a collective-bargaining process that permits negotiations over wages.

The chief executive officer of the Postal Service, the postmaster general, is appointed by the nine governors of the Postal Service, who are appointed by the president, with the advice and consent of the Senate, for overlapping nine-year terms. The ambiguous legal status of the Postal Service has been the source of political controversy since it was established in 1970. It does not report to the president and is only indirectly responsible to Congress. Even though it is an "independent" government corporation, it cannot even set its own prices for services. A Postal Rate Commission, created by the 1970 Reorganization Act, must approve all postage rates, fees, and mail classifications. The commission also has appellate jurisdiction to review Postal Service determinations to close or consolidate small post offices. There have been a number of bills introduced in recent congresses to return the Postal Service to the status of a regular executive department—and to greater political control. Such proposals tend to increase dramatically whenever local post offices are forced to merge or close.

(*continued*)

▶ **A CASE STUDY** | *Continued*

Despite perennial criticism, what the Postal Service (USPS) does is impressive: In 2006 more than 213 billion pieces of mail were delivered to 146 million residences and businesses by almost 700,000 career employees in 37,000 post offices. With annual revenues of more than $72 billion, and the largest civilian fleets of vehicles on the planet, it delivers more than 46 percent of the world's card and letter mail each day. But the USPS is changing rapidly. Because of the decline in mail volume due largely to the Internet and text messaging, by 2011 there were 5,000 fewer post offices. Employees were down to 532,000. Physical mail peaked in 2006 with 213 billion pieces; by 2010 it was 20 percent lower and declining.

While most Americans do not realize it, their daily mail is cheap, comparatively speaking. The United States has the lowest first-class postage of any industrialized state. For the price of a first-class stamp, even one with Marilyn or Elvis on it, the Postal Service will take your letter—if properly addressed—to the bottom of the Grand Canyon by mule, to the Arctic Circle in Alaska by bush pilot, or to ships on America's remote rivers by mail boat. The current motto of the Postal Service is "We Deliver for You." It knows that if it doesn't, that if there are too many complaints, Congress may change its mandate.

The Postal Service's worst nightmare is that Congress will jeopardize the service's solvency by allowing others—maybe Federal Express (FedEx) or United Parcel Service (UPS)—the right to deliver first-class mail. Such totally private corporations could then easily skim off the easy and profitable urban delivery routes and leave the Postal Service with all the unprofitable and difficult ones. Thus "express mail" overnight delivery was created in 1977 specifically to compete with Federal Express, and the Postal Service has conducted quarterly performance evaluations since 1990 to monitor the timeliness of its first-class mail delivery. And with perpetual fears of losing its monopoly and viability, the Postal Service is hustling to improve its core services, to create new products, such as the 2005 Muppet stamps and the 2006 "Forever" stamp that can be used to mail a standard first-class letter anytime in the future.

The Marilyn and Elvis stamps are indicators of a major new trend in public administration in general, and the Postal Service in particular: the concern for marketing. Marketing, entrepreneurship, and promotional management are relatively new areas of interest in the public and nonprofit sectors. The first published argument (that we have been able to locate) that nonprofit organizations should engage in marketing even though they face somewhat unique circumstances is in Philip Kotler and Sidney Levy's 1969 article "Broadening the Concept of Marketing." The first textbook on the subject, also by Kotler, was not published until 1975. Although some nonprofit organizations have engaged in business-enterprise-type activities at least since the beginning of the twentieth century—for example, the Metropolitan Museum of Art in

New York City opened its first official sales store in 1908—only scattered attention was paid to such income-generating activities prior to 1980.

Entrepreneurial-type business ventures by agencies of the public sector are not limited to the Postal Service. Creating and capitalizing on chances to make money—the core of entrepreneurship—are becoming increasingly fashionable. Thus organizations as diverse as the Chicago Public Library and the Los Angeles County coroner's office sell a wide range of memorabilia.

The result of entrepreneurial forays by the Postal Service and other public sector entities is to raise revenue through non traditional methods rather than increasing taxes or user fees (or stamp prices). Entrepreneurship is a frame of mind, a willingness to create and to be receptive to opportunities, an orientation toward risk-taking ventures. But nonprofit organizations cannot allow the current interest in entrepreneurship to allow them to forget their traditional purposes. Business ventures can be dangerous when they compromise the organization's original mission. Marilyn and Elvis stamps, pins, and other souvenir items are like best selling books. They generate tremendous income when first offered for sale and even have comfortable backlist sales, but they are no substitute for the organization's core function: selling a service.

So what's the lesson here? The public sector can benefit from some entrepreneurial techniques. If stamps with Washington, Franklin, and other dignitaries do not sell well enough as collectibles, then sell what sells. Sell Marilyn, Elvis, and even Miss Piggy. The Postal Service, by being made a public enterprise, has simply used its discretion to branch out into the entertainment industry. In so doing, it has found a way to improve its financial health so as to better fulfill its primary purpose: delivering the mail. While its long-term survival is still very much in question, the USPS appears to be making a good-faith attempt to keep itself a player in the twenty-first-century world of communication.v

For Discussion: *What steps has the U.S. Postal Service taken to transform itself? How has the fear of increased competition from FedEx and UPS motivated the Postal Service to reform?* ▸

SUMMARY

Leadership is the exercise of authority, whether formal or informal, in directing and coordinating the work of others. The best leaders are those who can simultaneously exercise both kinds of leadership: the formal, based on the authority of rank or office, and the informal, based on the willingness of others to give service to a person with special qualities of authority.

There is a difference between leadership and management: management involves power (formal authority) bestowed on the occupant of a position by a higher organizational authority. Leadership, in contrast, cannot be bestowed by a higher authority but must be earned.

REVIEW QUESTIONS

1. What is the difference between leadership and management?
2. Which leadership style is more likely to be successful over the long term: authoritarian or democratic?
3. Why are transformational leaders so essential in times of organizational crisis?
4. Why is micromanagement a trap into which so many leaders fall?
5. Under what circumstances can moral leadership be effective?

KEY CONCEPTS

Charisma Leadership based on the compelling personality of the leader rather than on formal position. The word *charisma* is derived from the Greek word for divine grace. The concept was first developed by Max Weber, who distinguished charismatic authority from both the traditional authority of a monarch and the legal authority given to someone by law.

Contingency theory An approach to leadership asserting that leadership styles will vary in their effects in different situations. The situation (not traits or styles themselves) determines whether a leadership style or a particular leader will be effective.

Leadership The exercise of authority, whether formal or informal, in directing and coordinating the work of others.

Moral leadership Leading people in specific directions of action and thought based on morals and decency.

Rule of law A governing system in which the highest authority is a body of law that applies equally to all (as opposed to the traditional "rule of men," in which the personal whim of those in power can decide any issue).

Trait theory An approach to leadership that assumes leaders possess traits that make them fundamentally different from followers. Advocates of trait theory believe that some people have unique leadership characteristics and qualities that enable them to assume responsibilities not everyone can execute. Therefore they are "born" leaders.

Transformational leadership Leadership that strives to change organizational culture and directions. It reflects the ability of a leader to develop a values-based vision for the organization, to convert the vision into reality, and to maintain it over time.

MySearchLab® EXERCISES

Apply what you learned in this chapter on MySearchLab (*www.mysearchlab.com*).

BIBLIOGRAPHY

Ambrose, Stephen E. (1994). *D-Day*. New York: Simon and Schuster.

Barnard, Chester I. (1938). *The Functions of the Executive*. Cambridge, MA: Harvard University Press.

Berlin, Isaiah (1953). *The Hedgehog and the Fox*. New York: Simon and Schuster.

Caeser, James, Glen Thurow, Jeffrey Tulis, and Joseph Bessette (1981). "The Rise of the Rhetorical Presidency," *Presidential Studies Quarterly* (Spring).

Cohen, Jeffrey E. (1982). "A Historical Reassessment of Wildavsky's 'Two Presidencies,'" *Social Science Quarterly* (September).

Dynes, Michael, and David Walker (1995). *The New British State*. London: Times Books.

Edelman, Murray (1967). *The Symbolic Uses of Politics*. Urbana: University of Illinois Press.

Edwards, George C., III. (1986). "The Two Presidencies: A Reevaluation," *American Politics Quarterly* (July).

Fiedler, F. E. (1967). *A Theory of Leadership Effectiveness*. New York: McGraw-Hill.

Fielder, F. E., and M. M. Chemers (1974). *Leadership Style and Effective Management*. Glenview, IL: Scott, Foresman.

Fielder, F. E., M. M. Chemers, and L. Mahar. (1976). *Improving Leadership Effectiveness: The Leader Match Concept*. New York: Wiley.

Fink, S. L. (1992). *High Commitment Workplaces*. New York: Quorum Books.

French, J. R. P., and B. Raven (1959). "The Bases of Social Power." In D. Cartwright and A. Zander, eds., *Studies in Social Power*. Ann Arbor: University of Michigan, Institute of Social Research.

Greenstein, Fred I. (1994) *The Hidden-Hand Presidency: Eisnehower as Leader*. Baltimore, MD: Johns Hopkins University Press

Howard, Philip K. (1995). *The Death of Common Sense*. New York: Random House.

Ignatieff, Michael (1998). *Isaiah Berlin: A Life*. New York: Henry Holt.

Kilborn, Peter T. (1993). "Inside Post Offices, the Mail Is Only Part of the Pressure," *New York Times* (May 17).

Kotler, Philip (1982). "The Responsive Organization: Meeting Consumer Needs." In D. Gies, ed., *Marketing for Nonprofit Organizations*, 2nd ed. Englewood Cliffs, NJ: Prentice Hall.

Kotler, Philip, and Sidney J. Levy (1969). "Broadening the Concept of Marketing," *Journal of Marketing* (January).

Lewin, K., R. Lippitt, and R. K. White (1939). "Patterns of Aggressive Behavior in Experimentally Created Social Climates," *Journal of Social Psychology* 10.

Levitz, Jennifer (2011). "Postal Service Eyes Closing Thousand of Post Offices," *Wall Street Journal* (January 24).

Light, Paul C. (2005). "Rumsfeld's Revolution," Govexec.com (August 8). www.govexec.com/dailyfed/0805/080805ol.htm.

Livingston, J. Sterling (1969). "Pygmalion in Management," *Harvard Business Review* (July–August).

Marinucci, Carla (2001). "Gingrich Says GOP Has a Handle on High Tech," *San Francisco Chronicle* (January 27).

Metcalf, Henry C., and Lyndall Urwick, eds. (1940). *Dynamic Administration: The Collected Papers of Mary Parker Follett*. New York: Harper.

Morgan, Arthur E. (1974). *The Making of the TVA*. New York: Prometheus Books.

Mustafa, Husain, and Anthony A. Salomone (1971). "Administrative Circumvention of Public Policy," *Midwest Review of Public Administration* 5, No. 1.

Myers, Steven Lee (1995). "City Hall's Going Retail in Wholesale Fashion," *New York Times* (July 9).

Oldfield, Duane M., and Aaron Wildavsky (1989). "Reconsidering the Two Presidencies," *Society* 26 (July–August).

Popkin, James (1993). "Wasteline: By the Book," *U.S. News & World Report* (May 24).

Rosenbloom, David H. (1993*a*). "Have an Administrative Rx? Don't Forget the Politics!" *Public Administration Review* 53 (November– December).

——— (1993*b*). *Public Administration*, 3rd ed. New York: McGraw-Hill.

Sayre, W. (1948). "The Triumph of Techniques over Purpose," *Public Administration Review* 8 (Spring).

Slater, Philip E., and Warren Bennis (1964). "Democracy Is Inevitable," *Harvard Business Review* 42 (March–April).

Stogdill, Ralph M. (1974). *Handbook of Leadership: A Study of Theory and Research*. New York: Free Press.

Tannenbaum, Robert J., and Warren H. Schmidt (1973). "How to Choose a Leadership Pattern," *Harvard Business Review* 51 (May–June).

Tichy, N. M., and D. O. Ulrich (1984). "The Leadership Challenge—A Call for the Transformational Leader," *Sloan Management Review* 26.

Wildavsky, Aaron (1966). "The Two Presidencies," *Trans-Action* (December).

Wills, Garry (1994). "What Makes a Good Leader?" *Atlantic Monthly* (April).

RECOMMENDED BOOKS

Barnard, Chester I. (1968). *The Functions of the Executive*, 30th anniversary ed. Cambridge, MA: Harvard University Press. The classic analysis of organizations as cooperative systems wherein the function of the executive was to maintain the "dynamic equilibrium" between the needs of the organization and the needs of its employees.

Burns, James MacGregor (1982). *Leadership*. New York: Harper & Row. Uses history and biography to distill the essential elements of leadership.

Goleman, Daniel, Richard Boyatzis, and Annie McKee (2002). *Primal Leadership*. Boston: Harvard Business School Press. A demonstration of how current behavioral science research validates the doctrine of optimism for leaders.

Harari, Oren (2002). *The Leadership Secrets of Colin Powell*. New York: McGraw-Hill. How-to-do-it advice from one of America's most successful leaders.

Klitgaard, Robert, and Paul Light (2005). *High Performance Government: Structure, Leadership, Incentives*. Washington, DC: Rand Corporation. An examination of the contemporary role of leadership in relation to organizational structure.

Wren, J. Thomas (1995). *The Leader's Companion: Insights on Leadership through the Ages*. New York: Free Press. Sixty-four selections of the best writing on leadership, from ancient classicists to modern social scientists.

RELATED WEB SITES

www.gsb.stanford.edu/cldr/
Center for Leadership Development and Research at Stanford University
The center promotes learning and scholarship in the area of organizational leadership and based on the premise that leadership is something that is learned best through experience.

www.ccl.org
Center for Creative Leadership
The center provides executive education that develops leaders through its focus on flexible work styles, leadership for sustainability, and high-impact succession development.

www.leadership.opm.gov
OPM Leadership Development and Training
This site from the federal government's Office of Personnel Management provides an array of information on developing leadership positions, including details about training, programs, and certificates.

www.ntl.org
NTL Institute for Applied Behavioral Science
NTL Institute (National Training Laboratories Institute) provides organizations, leaders, and practitioners with research and guidance related to individual, team, and organization effectiveness.

Personnel Management and Labor Relations

KEYNOTE: The Adventures of a Young Man as a Personnel Technician

I didn't mean to discover the netherworld of personnel administration in 1965. I was just looking for a job. This was complicated by the fact that I had no skills. A bachelor's degree in English from Temple University and a decidedly undistinguished academic record did not suggest any immediate directions. I thought it might be fun to be a librarian, so off I went to the Free Library of Philadelphia. I asked a bored circulation clerk, "Could you please tell me whom to see about becoming a librarian?" She sent me to Mr. Greenberg in the personnel office.

I bounded into his office and politely inquired if he could advise me on how to get a job as a librarian. Never in 30 subsequent years of going in and out of other people's offices have I been greeted with such genuine warmth and solicitude. And I didn't even have an appointment! But I had something going for me that Mr. Greenberg needed very badly—my gender; that is, I was a male college graduate and thus met all of his needs in a new librarian trainee. Even today, careers as professional librarians attract a disproportionate number of females. It was much more so in the mid-1960s. This caused a very particular staffing problem for the library because it had recently purchased a new bookmobile. But the female librarians were exceedingly reluctant to work on a bookmobile that traveled through Philadelphia's poorer neighborhoods. They felt, and with good reason, that it was too dangerous. This accounts for Mr. Greenberg's immediate warm regard for me. He was very much in need of a brave young man to take literacy into the neighborhoods of the inner city.

There was just one minor technicality to attend to before I could gain the command of a municipal bookmobile. I had to pass a civil service examination. Mr. Greenberg was almost apologetic about the inconvenience as he told me where in City Hall I would find the continuous testing room of the Civil Service Commission. There I would take a general entrance examination for new college graduates desiring a variety of entry-level professional positions. The test, he assured me, would be scored immediately after I completed it, and he would be able to formally put me on the payroll and in the bookmobile within a few days. He was very pleased to have solved a personnel problem using the much unappreciated but classic technique of sitting at his desk waiting for someone to walk in the door.

But I was fated never to be a librarian, never to ride the bookmobile, and never to see Mr. Greenberg again. Yet this was my start in the world of personnel. The examination I took was used by the city for a dozen different professional trainee positions. On the first page I was asked to check off the names of all the jobs for which I wished to be considered. I checked every one. After being told by the examinations proctor that I had easily passed the hour-long, multiple-choice examination, I went home to await my call to the bookmobile. Instead it was Mrs. Margolis, a certification clerk for the Civil Service Commission, who called. It was her job to take the names of job applicants who passed various civil service examinations and officially certify them as eligible for appointment. Whenever a municipal department had a vacancy in a given job category, she would contact the highest scorers on the list of eligibles to see whether they were still interested in employment with the city. If so, she would arrange a job interview. I told her of my meeting with Mr. Greenberg and how anxious I was to get started on my new career on the bookmobile. She immediately and emphatically responded with these immortal words of career advice: "Don't be an idiot! That's not for you."

She went on to explain that I ought to take the highest paying of all the entry positions for which my test score now qualified me. The job for me, she insisted, was management trainee. This paid a whopping 20 percent more than librarian trainee, $6,000 a year as opposed to $5,000. I told her that I didn't know anything about management but knew lots about books. She assured me that it didn't matter. They would train me; that's why the job was called management *trainee*. A 20 percent raise even before I started working for the city and not being an idiot were pretty powerful inducements. So I agreed.

"Good," she said. "I'll schedule you for an oral exam at three o'clock tomorrow afternoon."

"What oral exam?" I asked in amazement.

"All management trainee applicants must take an oral exam. You put on your suit and come to the sixth floor of the Municipal Services Building at three," she demanded of me as if she were my mother. To this day I still wonder how she knew that I had only one suit.

The next day I put on that suit, as ordered, and having never taken an oral exam before, and not knowing what to expect, I also brushed my teeth very carefully. On my arrival at the designated place at the designated time, a receptionist ushered me into a small room in which three men were seated behind a table. I would later learn they were all personnel officers for the city. They each wore a dark suit with a thin tie atop a white shirt. They could easily have been mistaken for the FBI agents or IBM salesmen of those days, who were all required to wear white shirts, thin ties, and short hair. After a round of handshakes, they offered me a chair and proceeded to ask me a series of questions that I could not possibly answer. I had never given any thought to the problems of perpetually tardy employees and clogged typing pools. I didn't even know that typists were allowed to swim! So I responded to their questions by just making up stuff off the top of my head all the while thinking, "Bookmobile, here I come."

To make matters worse, one of my examiners took an immediate dislike to me. He was unusually rude and kept badgering me with questions phrased in a hostile manner. He would constantly interrupt my sentences and often call my answers stupid. I soon realized that the situation was hopeless; so I relaxed and took what Californians would call a mellow approach to the examination. I calmly answered all questions as best I could and didn't let the badgerer upset me, no matter what his antics. Consequently, I exhibited a degree of self-confidence that was as convincing as it was artificial.

A few weeks later I would learn that the oral exam had no purpose except to size up the physical deportment and extemporaneous speaking ability of the applicant. One member of the examining board was always hostile to see if the examinee could be emotionally shaken by a disagreeable exchange. My badgerer didn't dislike me after all; it was simply his turn to be the bad guy. Nevertheless, I left the Municipal Services Building confident that the bookmobile was my destiny. Shortly after nine the next morning Mrs. Margolis called again. Before I could tell her how sorry I was that I did so poorly on the oral exam, she said, "Congratulations, you've passed the oral."

"You've got to be kidding," I said in contradiction. "I was terrible."

"No. You got a very high score. They even want you for personnel. You have to come to an interview this afternoon at two."

"But I did the interview yesterday," I complained.

"No, that was the oral exam. The job interview is today. Put your suit back on."

The subsequent job interview was my first introduction to position classification. Two nice, elderly senior supervisors in the Department of Personnel (which is administratively under the Civil Service Commission) spent an hour asking me about my whole life. At 21, there wasn't much to tell. When they seemed on the verge of ending the discussion and offering me a position, I bluntly asked what the duties would be. They said I would start in the Division of Position Classification and Pay doing reports that would ultimately determine how much city employees would be paid.

"But I thought the mayor did that," I explained in honest ignorance.

"No," I was corrected, "the city has more than 30,000 employees. He couldn't possibly do it all. That's why we have position classification."

"Oh," I responded, still not really sure what they meant by *classification*.

They seemed to understand my discomfort about the strange nature of the work they were describing. To conclude, they said they had only one final question: "If we forced you to state the one area that you really know well, what would it be?"

I quickly thought about all that I had studied in college and replied with great seriousness and complete honesty, "The only thing I really know well is modern American fiction."

They thereupon hired me to write job descriptions for the employees of the City of Philadelphia. I would report to work on the following Monday and be a management trainee in the personnel technician series, meaning that I would later be eligible for promotion to Personnel Technician I, Personnel Technician II, and so on. By going to the library to seek a job that would allow me the leisure to write fiction, I stumbled onto a job for which I would be paid to write fiction—although I wouldn't be allowed to call it that.

I started my new job with every intention of doing well and pleasing my superiors. It was my first real job after college, and I was determined to be a success. Unfortunately, within eight weeks I had become such a problem for my employers that I was about to be dismissed.

The Division of Classification and Pay occupied one-quarter of the sixth floor of the Municipal Services Building. There were two private offices for the division chief and his deputy. Everyone else, a dozen professionals and four clerk-typists, had desks in one large, open area whose walls were lined with file cabinets. Promptly at 8:30 Monday morning I reported to Mrs. L., the deputy chief, who introduced me to everyone and assigned me a desk directly in front of her door. She then told me that my first week would be spent in training. She handed me a very thick book with small print that she described as "the bible" of position classification—Ismar Baruch's *Position Classification in the Public Service*, written in 1940. This was my training—to sit at my desk under the helpful eye of Mrs. L. and read. It was just like the library except that I could read only one book.

The theory underlying position classification is quite rational and logical. In the bad old days the salaries of public employees were determined by whatever entity had authority over the budget, usually the legislature. Any individual salary was a function of that individual's influence with the legislature. Vast disparities in pay grew up over the years as public servants worked the political system; one clerk would often be paid twice as much as another in the same job, all because an uncle or sugar daddy was on an appropriate legislative committee. Position classification was put forth by reformers early in the twentieth century as a way of curbing the corruption inherent in the old system. Jobs would be grouped according to their duties and responsibilities so that all similar positions would be paid the same.

After a week of reading "the bible" of classification, I spent another week following an experienced classifier around as he did desk audits—that is, as he traveled to the "desk" or workstation of an employee to interview him or her about his or her job to ascertain if it was properly classified. After talking to the incumbent and the incumbent's supervisor, the classifier would write an elaborate report, which was technically a memorandum to the Civil Service Commission. Only one of three recommendations was possible: that the job be reclassified to a higher level or a lower level, or that it remain the same. Because the whole point of classification was ultimately to determine salary levels, everybody wanted to be reclassified upward. Consequently, much of the work of the Division of Classification and Pay consisted of dealing with reclassification requests by means of desk audit reports.

Finally, my several weeks' training complete, I was let loose to play in the fields of municipal administration. Assigned to do a desk audit on a variety of relatively uncomplicated junior clerk-typists who wanted to be senior clerk-typists, I became the boy investigative reporter I was fated to be.

A few days later, Mrs. L. was quite annoyed. She held up my report and asked in a tone of controlled fury, "Just what do you think you are doing?"

"What do you mean, 'Just what do you think you are doing?'" I asked back in all innocence. But this only agitated her further.

"You know very well what I mean," she insisted in a loud voice.

"No, I don't," I replied, suddenly realizing I must be in a lot of trouble for something.

"Where did you get the information that went into your desk audit report?"

"I did just what you told me to do. I spoke to the incumbent and to the incumbent's supervisor."

"But they didn't tell you all this?"

"No. Much of the information came from coworkers and other people around the office such as the security guards, the mail room guy, and the other secretaries."

"But you weren't supposed to speak to them," she lamented.

"Whom was I supposed to speak to?"

"Just to the incumbent and to the supervisor."

"But they lied," I said in explanation.

"That's none of your business," she responded in exasperation.

"You mean I'm just supposed to take down their lies and write them up as if they were the truth? You've got to be kidding!"

"I never joke about classification."

"And I don't write lies, with all due respect, for you or anyone."

"No one's asking you to lie," she explained. "We just don't want you talking to the wrong people and getting the wrong idea about things."

"But it's a good thing that I did speak to those additional people. Otherwise I would never have been able to write up the whole story."

"You just don't understand. Your job is to interview just the people we tell you to. Then write up what they say."

"But what if they lie?" I asked.

"That's not for you to determine."

"Then who does?"

"This is getting us nowhere. Please wait outside."

"Should I continue with my work?"

"No. Just sit at your desk."

I sat and tried to figure out what went wrong. As an idealistic youth I genuinely wanted to do well by my city but had only managed to get myself into trouble. A short while later the ax fell. The deputy director of personnel came by and told me that it had been decided that I wasn't quite ready for the arduous life of a position classifier. I assumed that his next words would herald the end of my life in municipal administration. I wondered if the bookmobile was still available. But to my astonishment he offered to transfer me to the Division of Recruitment and Examinations. So I was only half fired. What a break! My budding career in public administration had been salvaged by the kindness of strangers. For my sins, such as they were, I would spend the next year writing civil service examinations for such exciting jobs as morgue attendant and sewer crawler.

It would be several years before I fully realized what had happened to me in classification. I had stumbled on the netherworld, but hadn't seen it. Of course nobody calls it that. "The netherworld" is just my term for the underground or black market in personnel decision making that exists in all large governmental organizations. It was just an accident that I first discovered it in Philadelphia. It exists almost everywhere. It exists whenever a government manager wants to reward an unusually productive employee but cannot because the system denies managers any real discretion over salaries. So they play the position classification game to informally win the discretion that they are formally denied.

Suppose you have a secretary who is the best ever. You are going to lose her if you cannot get her salary raised. What's worse, she would then be replaced by someone not half as good. That was the quality of secretary—"not half as good"—that you could typically expect to come from civil service lists. Consequently you'll do anything to keep your current secretary happy—even lie, cheat, and steal. Fortunately, that is exactly what you must do to win the position classification game.

But all this I would discover later. At the time, all I knew was that I had bumped into some strange ethics. And I felt extremely fortunate to be exiled into the world of civil service examinations, where I would spend the next year writing multiple-choice tests and avoiding the moral mazes of position classification. But it was a dull life for an adventurous soul. The library would have been more exciting. I yearned for something more and found it in the *New York Times*. I came on an advertisement that graduate assistantships were available at the Baruch School of Business and Public Administration of the City University of New York. I applied in October 1966. Before Christmas I received a letter congratulating me on the scholarly attainments that had earned me a research assistantship beginning in January. I felt like a fraud. But I was equally determined to take full advantage of my ill-deserved appointment. So off I went to the Big Apple to earn a master's degree in public administration.

Years later, after I had earned my Ph.D. and was a new assistant professor attending a professional conference, I chanced to come on Professor Samuel Thomas, then still dean of the Baruch School. It was he who awarded me the graduate research assistantship that started my academic career. We exchanged a few pleasantries, and when the moment seemed right, I popped the question: Why had I been awarded the assistantship when my record was so undistinguished and comparatively undeserving? "Oh, that's easy to recall," he said with an impish grin. "You, Dr. Shafritz, were the only one to apply." It seems that Woody Allen was right: "Eighty percent of success is showing up."

For Discussion: *Why is the public personnel netherworld such an important, and often beneficial, part of public personnel practices? Have you seen the netherworld in operation, for good or ill, in organizations with which you have been associated?*

THE PERSONNEL FUNCTION

The function of a personnel staff, or even an entire personnel agency, is to service line management. Typical services include recruiting, selection, training, evaluation, compensation, discipline, and termination. *Personnel* is a collective term for all of the employees of an organization. The word is of military origin—the two basic components of a traditional army being materiel and personnel. Personnel is also commonly used to refer to the personnel management function or the organizational unit responsible for administering personnel programs. While the terms *personnel administration* and *personnel management* tend to be used interchangeably, there is a distinction. The former is mainly concerned with the technical aspects of maintaining a full complement of employees within an organization, while the latter concerns itself as well with the larger problems of the viability of an organization's human resources—how motivated and productive they are.

Not very long ago, it would have been absurd to refer to the occupation of the public personnel administrator as a *professional* practice. The traditional professions all presupposed a large measure of formal training in preparation for the ensuing professional practice—a practice that was highlighted by the personal autonomy and independent judgments of the practitioner. Just as the repugnant caterpillar evolves into the graceful butterfly, personnel management is undergoing a similar metamorphosis. From its origins as a clerical function, it has gradually been evolving into an in-house consultant to management on labor relations, job redesign, Equal Employment Opportunity (EEO) provisions, organization development, productivity measurement, and other pressing concerns. Top management values and seeks out the professional opinion of the personnel practitioner because that opinion is backed up by expertise that is essential if the organization is to thrive. Unfortunately, in the majority of U.S. jurisdictions this metamorphosis is only just beginning. The in-house expertise either does not yet exist or is ignored by political executives. Butterfly status is many years away. All the more reason to now begin raising the consciousness of the occupation.

As with many questions in public administration, the issue of how the overall public personnel function should be organized has been plagued by an attempt to realize several incompatible values at once. Foremost among these values have been those of "merit" or neutral competence, executive leadership, political accountability, managerial flexibility, and representativeness. The main problem of the structure and policy thrusts of central personnel agencies has been that maximizing some of these values requires arrangements ill-suited for the achievement of others. Thus achieving neutral competence requires the creation of a relatively independent agency to help insulate public employees from the partisan demands of political executives. Yet the same structural arrangement will tend to frustrate executive leadership and the ability of political executives to manage their agencies. To facilitate executive leadership, on the other hand, the central personnel agency should be an adjunct of the president, governor, or other chief executive. Similarly, maximizing the value of representativeness may require less emphasis on traditional merit concepts and examinations, and the placement of personnel functions having an impact on EEO in an equal employment or human rights agency. So doing, however, will also complicate the possibilities of achieving a high degree of executive leadership and neutral competence, as traditionally conceived.

Codetermination ■
Union participation in all aspects of management, even to the extent of having union representatives share equal membership on an organization's board of directors.

Matters are further confused by the rise of public sector collective bargaining, which emphasizes employee–employer **codetermination** of personnel policy and the creation of independent public sector labor relations authorities. The desire to maximize simultaneously these incompatible values accounts for many of the problematic aspects of the organization of the central personnel function. Arrangements satisfying some values inevitably raise complaints that others are being inadequately achieved.

Recruitment

Recruitment is the process of advertising job openings and encouraging candidates to apply. It is designed to provide an organization with an adequate number of viable candidates from which to make its selection decision. One indicator of the economic health of a community is the number of applicants for public employment. In poor economic times, government agencies are flooded with applications from the qualified and unqualified alike.

The main objective of recruitment is the generating of an adequate number of qualified applicants. An applicant is any individual who submits a completed application form for consideration. Indeed, it is often said that the first phase of the examining process consists of filling out the application form. If applicants do not provide the necessary information documenting their minimum qualifications, they are not given any further consideration—they are not permitted to take the formal examination. However, it is not uncommon for applicants who qualify in every respect for a position to be refused consideration. Many positions above the entry level are open only to individuals already employed within the jurisdiction. Outsiders, no matter how qualified, may not be admitted to such promotional examinations. For example, only currently employed police officers may be permitted to take the police sergeant's examination; only police sergeants may take the police lieutenant's examination.

Merit Selection

Selection is the oldest function of public personnel administration. The 1883 Pendleton Act, which put the federal government on the road to widespread, merit system coverage, foreshadowed the character of the examinations process when it mandated that "examinations shall be practical in their character." As the British civil service was the greatest single example and influence on the U.S. reform movement, there was considerable concern that a merit system based on the British system of competitive academic examinations would be automatically biased in favor of college graduates. Because higher education in the United States was essentially an upper-class activity at that time, this was reminiscent of the aristocratic civil service that the Jacksonian movement found so objectionable only 50 years earlier. Mandating that all examinations be "practical in their character" presumably neutralized any advantage that a college graduate might have, for in those days there was little that was "practical" taught in most U.S. colleges. Indeed, it would not be until 1934 that the U.S. Civil Service Commission offered its first entrance examination designed especially for liberal arts graduates.

Over the years, the primacy of examination practicality was often breached. However, that primacy was loudly reaffirmed by the U.S. Supreme Court in the *Griggs v. Duke Power Company* decision of 1971—the most significant single decision concerning the validity of employment examinations. The Court unanimously ruled that Title VII of the Civil Rights Act of 1964 "proscribes not only overt discrimination but also practices that are discriminatory in operation." Thus, if employment practices operating to exclude minorities "cannot be shown to be related to job performance, the practice is prohibited." The ruling dealt a

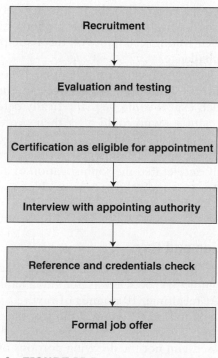

FIGURE 11.1
The selection process

Restrictive credentialism ■
A general term for any selection policy adversely affecting disadvantaged groups because they lack the formal qualifications for positions that, in the opinion of those adversely affected, do not truly need such formal qualifications.

Equal Employment Opportunity Act of 1972 ■
An amendment to Title VII of the 1964 Civil Rights Act strengthening the authority of the Equal Employment Opportunity Commission and extending antidiscrimination provisions to state and local governments and labor organizations with 15 or more employees, and to public and private employment agencies.

blow to **restrictive credentialism**, stating that, while diplomas and tests are useful, "Congress has mandated the commonsense proposition that they are not to become masters of reality." In essence, the Court held that the law requires that tests used for employment purposes "must measure the person for the job and not the person in the abstract." The *Griggs* decision applied only to the private sector until the **Equal Employment Opportunity Act of 1972** extended the provisions of Title VII to cover public employees.

Job relatedness is now the paramount consideration in developing a selection device. The legality of any test hinges on its capability in predicting job success, and validation is the process of demonstrating how well the testing device actually can predict success on the job. While examinations were once simply technical and administrative problems of the personnel department, they are now of equal concern to a jurisdiction's legal office. The thrust of the Equal Employment Opportunity Act of 1972 is to stop discrimination, by providing legal remedies for acts of discrimination in hiring, assignments, promotional opportunities, or any other benefits or conditions of employment. Theoretically, there is no inherent conflict between a merit selection program and EEO laws. Each requires selection without regard to race, color, religion, sex, quotas, or compensatory hiring (although the courts retain discretion to impose remedies for proved past patterns of discrimination). While there are no legal limits on an organization's use of tests, all examining tools may now be challenged as discriminatory in effect. Job success is a complex matter and not generally attributable to any single factor. To ensure job relatedness, organizations must identify the appropriate criteria that "contribute" to job success and must ensure that the testing devices used accurately measure those criteria. Those responsible for the preparation of examinations have no choice but to develop their testing techniques on the assumption they will have to be defended in a court challenge.

In the United States every important public issue becomes a legal problem. Such an issue is the central question of civil service examinations—test validity. While the validity of such exams could be theoretically determined by psychologists and other social scientists who could offer their professional opinions, the opinion of a federal judge provides binding social legitimacy. When the historians of personnel operations look back at the last few decades, they no doubt will write that the courts markedly accelerated the sophistication of aptitude examinations, which became so sophisticated and valid they were able to withstand considerable litigation.

Position Classification and Pay

A fable is sometimes told about position classification. Once upon a time, a new tiger was brought to a municipal zoo. He was put into a habitat, cages being passé, next to another tiger. At mealtime, 10 pounds of raw red meat was thrown into the habitat of the tiger next to him. "Yummy," thought the new tiger as he eagerly awaited the first meal in his new home. You can imagine his surprise, however, when the zookeeper tossed him not the decaying portions of a bloody carcass but 20 pounds of bananas. After a few days of enforced vegetarianism, the tiger finally asked the zookeeper why his neighbor got meat and he only got yellow finger food. "Well," said the zookeeper, "this is a government zoo, and we didn't have money in our budget that was authorized for another tiger. But we did have approval to buy more monkeys. Because we bought you instead, you get the food for six monkeys."

While this is but a fable, it does contain a large germ of truth. For example, it is true that a large municipal hospital on the East Coast of the United States once employed a janitor to perform brain surgery. Just as with the tiger/monkey story, the hospital was authorized to hire an additional full-time janitor, but it really needed a part-time brain surgeon. So they hired the brain surgeon to work one day a week but paid him the full-time salary of the janitor—and kept him on the official books as a janitor. While the personnel staff thought it was a very funny way of solving a very real management problem, it also illustrates—and reinforces our keynote adventure about—how position classification systems create much dysfunctional and sometimes silly activity.

Position classifications are formal job descriptions that organize all jobs in a civil service merit system into classes on the basis of duties and responsibilities, for the purposes of delineating authority, establishing chains of command, and providing equitable salary scales. The principles and practices of position classification that are generally used in the public service are throwbacks to the heyday of the scientific management movement. They were conceived at a time—before 1920—when this school of management thought held sway, and they have never really adapted to modern currents of management thought. Reduced to its essentials, a classification plan is nothing more than a time-and-motion study for the governmental function. The duties of the larger organization are divided into positions in order to prevent duplication and promote efficiency. In this schema, a position merely represents a set of duties and responsibilities, not a person. While position classifications tend to be universally recognized as essential for the administration of a public personnel program, their allegiance to notions of the past causes them to be frequently denounced as unreasonable constraints on top management and sappers of employee morale, or for being little more than polite fictions in substance.

Because the most basic doctrines of position classification were established prior to World War II, current practices ignore many of the advances in management science and theory that have occurred since then. In addition, the kind of workforce that classification plans were originally designed to accommodate no longer exists. Classification principles assume, in the best scientific management tradition, that work can most efficiently be organized by imitating industrial machinery and creating a system of human interchangeable parts. Thus one person in any given class was considered absolutely equal to any other person in that class. However, because of advances in the social sciences and radical changes in the nature of the workforce, conventional classification systems are obsolete for many categories of employees, in terms of simply not being as efficient as other modes of organization. They have also proved themselves to be frequently counterproductive in achieving the organizational mission.

Because of the ever-increasing rise in U.S. educational levels, the bulk of the labor force now consists of highly skilled technical and professional employees. Such workers should not be treated as if they were semiskilled laborers, menials, or clerical functionaries. Yet classification systems, designed to meet the needs

BOX 11.1 | Position Classification Principles

Here are basic principles of position classification that constitute the foundation of most position classification systems in government. They were promulgated by the 1919 Congressional Joint Commission on Reclassification of Salaries:

1. Positions and not individuals should be classified.
2. The duties and responsibilities pertaining to a position constitute the outstanding characteristics that distinguish it from, or mark its similarity to, other positions.
3. Qualifications in respect to education, experience, knowledge, and skill necessary for the performance of certain duties are determined by the nature of those duties. (Therefore, the qualifications for a position are an important factor in the determination of the classification of a position.)

4. The individual characteristics of an employee occupying a position should have no bearing on the classification of the position.
5. Persons holding positions in the same class should be considered equally qualified for any other position in that class. ◣

Source: *Report of the Congressional Joint Commission on Reclassification of Salaries,* 66th Cong., 2nd sess., 1920, H. Doc. 686.

of these latter employees, are being imposed on administrative, professional, and technical employees for reasons that are hardly defensible in light of what is known today about organizing and motivating a workforce. The old dichotomy between managers and workers is no longer valid. Workers in the traditional sense are an ever-decreasing minority. They are being replaced by technical and professional employees. This group is more likely to consider itself part of management than of the oppressed proletariat.

Even employees at the bottom of the organizational hierarchy are at such a level of education and consciousness that they cannot be casually treated as so many human, interchangeable spare parts. Relying on a management tool—position classification—that has not changed in two generations is akin to relying on a pre–World War I Model T Ford for transportation in the supersonic age. Is there another field of endeavor in the United States that is so backward? An engineer or architect could not design very much for today's world if limited to the technology of the 1930s. This is exactly what public personnel administrators are doing to the employees of their jurisdictions: engaging in a presumably professional practice using a technology that predates World War II.

Performance Appraisal

Performance appraisal is the title usually given to the formal method by which an organization documents the work performance of its employees. An employee evaluation process is essential for managerial decisions on retention, advancement, and separation. Lamentably, most performance evaluation systems have not been very successful. The main reason may be that supervisors have a great deal of difficulty writing useful and objective performance reports. They submit appraisals that tend to be very subjective, impressionistic, and not comparable with the reports of other raters.

Performance appraisals are designed to serve a variety of functions, among them (1) changing or modifying dysfunctional work behavior, (2) communicating to employees managerial perceptions of the quality and quantity of their work, (3) assessing the future potential of an employee in order to recommend appropriate training or developmental assignments, (4) assessing whether the present duties of an employee's position have an appropriate compensation level, and (5) providing a documented record for disciplinary and separation actions:

There are five basic types of appraisals:

1. *Supervisory ratings:* This is the most common type of appraisal, whereby the supervisor evaluates the performance of subordinates.
2. *Self-ratings:* Individuals rate themselves by completing a standard form, writing a narrative report on their work, or submitting a work product as documentation of performance.
3. *Peer ratings:* Each individual rates every employee in his or her division or office at a parallel level in the organization.
4. *Subordinated ratings:* Subordinates rate the performance of a supervisor.
5. *Group ratings:* An independent rater, usually a qualified expert, rates the performance of an entire work unit based on selected interviews or on-the-job visitations.

When significant numbers of employees must be evaluated, rating forms often offer multiple choices to the evaluator. Then all the evaluator must do is check the appropriate boxes. Typically, these forms are behaviorally anchored—that is, they are premised on varying levels of performance. Here is an example of a behaviorally anchored numerical rating scale for tennis players:

Rating	Behavioral Anchor
1	Knows rules of tennis, can bounce ball and hit it over the net
2	Hits forehand strokes with consistency, backhand weak
3	Hits both forehand and backhand strokes with consistency
4	Can place ball accurately, including serves, volleys, and half volleys
5	All strokes are accurate, firm, and consistent; topspin and underspin strokes can be employed as required

Strong-minded supervisors with very high standards will do their better employees an injustice when their reports are compared with those of supervisors who have low standards or are less professional. The result is a vast quantity of inflated reports filled with superlatives so that any review of performance appraisals will boil down to a consideration of who wrote the report, what other reports they have prepared, and what was left unsaid. More often than not, reports submitted on employees will primarily reflect the strengths and weaknesses of the rater. The impact of this factor substantially limits the validity and use of an individual performance appraisal. To complicate matters even further, supervisors are often not sure of "what" is really being rated—their subordinates' work performance,

Critical-incident method ■
Identifying, classifying, and recording significant examples—critical incidents—of an employee's behavior for purposes of performance evaluation. The theory behind the critical-incident approach holds that there are certain key acts of behavior that make the difference between success and failure. After the incidents are collected, they can be ranked in order of frequency and importance and assigned numerical weights. Once scored, they can be as useful for employee development and counseling as for formal appraisals.

or their own ability to use the **critical-incident method** of evaluative narration. Nevertheless, appraisal systems will always be with us if only because so many civil service laws and regulations require them as a precondition to annual salary increases. Employees without at least a satisfactory rating may be denied even "automatic" wage increases based on longevity.

The question remains: Why do so few employees receive poor evaluations—the first step toward dismissing them? The answer is that there is seldom adequate incentive for a line supervisor to be held accountable for his or her lack of punitive action toward deserving employees. Why should a supervisor risk creating a difficult interpersonal situation with all other subordinates for some vague notion of the public interest? Unless there is some extraordinary pressure for productivity, there is simply no incentive to take the hard action that is occasionally the duty of all managers. The public manager is not, after all, the proprietor of his or her own small business; the actions or inactions of employees, unless they exhibit some gross misconduct, do not directly affect his or her own interests. Why should he or she be the one manager in the jurisdiction to take the waste of public funds seriously enough to take concrete action? Does it not take an individual of intense ideological conviction to act on his or her beliefs when all others indicate contrary attitudes? Before interfering with a system that tolerates marginally performing employees, a reasonable person would have to be sure of the legitimacy of his or her actions. Precedence creates legitimacy. To upset what has evolved as the natural order of things may be socially and morally illegitimate, and simultaneously legally appropriate.

Training

Training has frequently been a victim of organizational neglect. In a budget squeeze, training funds have tended to be cut in favor of the examination and the classification functions frequently mandated by legislation or charter. Training was considered to be an option, a luxury, or, even worse, illegal. Prior to the 1950s, many jurisdictions operated on the premise that employees hired via the merit system were fully qualified for their duties. Training almost by definition was superfluous. Why should a jurisdiction suffer the expense of training individuals to do a job that they had to have a proven capability of performing before they were employed? Attitudes changed as merit systems grew stronger, as more and more occupations became limited to the public service, and as public jobs came to be thought of as career positions requiring continuous upgrading rather than as sets of static duties.

It wasn't until 1958 that Congress passed the Government Employees Training Act that required federal agencies to provide for employee training. It would be yet another decade before the U.S. Civil Service Commission would be authorized to create the federal government's first in-residence management training facility: the Federal Executive Institute in Charlottesville, Virginia. And it was not until the Intergovernmental Personnel Act of 1970 that the federal government was able to provide any funds for state and local government training programs. But this was only temporary. The Reagan administration discontinued such grants in the mid-1980s. With such a recent history as a serious concern for personnel, it's no wonder that the state of the training art is, at the very least, immature.

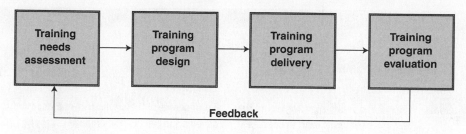

FIGURE 11.2
The training system

A training program is not complete without an evaluation of its effectiveness and usefulness. Yet most government training efforts that do not simply stop at the training itself are given only the most cursory of evaluations. While evaluation is the last phase of a training program, preparations for it must be made prior to the commencement of the program. If base points of performance aren't established prior to training, subsequent attempts to measure progress are likely to yield spurious results.

The essential question is whether or not a training effort has met its objective. While this is relatively easy when you are dealing with word processors, the matter becomes vastly more complicated when your training population consists of police officers, research scientists, or administrators. The measurement and evaluation of training programs for these latter classes require a great deal of subtlety, technical skill, and time. A word processor training program can be evaluated immediately thereafter, but it could easily take months and in some cases years to objectively measure the effectiveness of training for police officers, administrators, and scientists.

Although there is a great variety of training formats, almost all will fall into one of the following categories:

1. *Skills training:* Teaching specific skills such as word processing, welding, or computer operation.
2. *Coaching:* Personal instruction in which an expert oversees the efforts of a learner and provides continual advice.
3. *Formal or informal classroom instruction:* Traditional classroom instruction, including courses at nearby academic institutions, whereby groups of employees are instructed (with jurisdictions often providing subsidies for job-related college courses).
4. *Sensitivity or "T-group" training:* Assembling small groups of employees to deal with the problems of interpersonal relationships (usually requiring a professional "facilitator" and relying heavily on the willingness of individuals to confront the emotional aspects of their behavior).
5. *Job rotation:* Providing employees with differing work activities in order to increase their experience (a variant of this being cross-training, where each job, and thus the entire work of an office, is learned by each employee).
6. *Special conferences and seminars:* Meetings of employees or professional groups to discuss and exchange ideas about common processes, problems, and techniques.

TABLE 11.1		
Training and Development Compared		
	Training	**Development**
Time Frame	Short term	Long term
Goals	To learn specific techniques, behaviors, and processes	To understand the context of management, develop judgment, and enlarge personal abilities
Measures of Effectiveness	Performance appraisals, testing, and/or certification	Promotion of those developed; an overall organization with a competent managerial corps

7. *Modeling, games, and simulation training:* Simulated real-life situations providing employees with various experiences.
8. *Exchange and sabbatical programs:* Getting the individual out of the organizational environment and into a totally different one for a substantial period of time—several months to a year.

All the training options just listed are limited by the availability of funding. While all large organizations have training budgets, these are among the most tempting targets to cut during times of financial strain. Nevertheless, annual reports frequently boast of the number of employees who have been trained during the past year. But such statistics must be looked on with great suspicion. It is a common mistake to assume that the number of people who have been subjected to training is equal to the number that have actually been trained. No statement of training accomplishment can honestly be made unless it is supported by sophisticated measures of evaluation.

Management Development

Management development is a hybrid of training and selection. Any conscious effort on the part of an organization to provide a manager with the skills needed for future duties such as rotational assignments or formal educational experiences constitutes management development. The semantic difference between *training workers* and *developing managers* is significant. Workers are trained so that they can better perform their present duties; managers are developed so that they can be of greater organizational value in both present and future assignments. In such a context, the development investment made by the organization in a junior manager may pay off only if and when that individual grows into a bureau chief. One common method of developing managers is to provide them with the kinds of assignments and experiences that will allow them to grow professionally. Unfortunately, rank-in-position personnel systems—the norm in the U.S. public service—very much inhibit such efforts.

The secondary focus of management development is selection. The range of experiences, both on and off the job, that managers are exposed to over the years leaves records in terms of specific scores or subjective evaluations on which future advancements may be based. While it is not overly difficult to make promotional decisions based on this array of information, what criteria should an organization use in selecting relatively inexperienced managers in whom to invest its development resources? **Assessment centers** have proved to be an increasingly popular way of establishing the criteria on which to base management-development program selection. The assessment-center process typically consists of the intense observation of a subject undergoing a variety of management simulations and stress situations over a period of several days. The resulting evaluations have proved to be remarkably accurate in indicating capability and potential.

Assessment center ■
Not a particular place but a process consisting of the intense observation of a person undergoing a variety of simulations and stress situations over a period of several days.

The assessment-center concept is far from new. Assessment-center techniques were used by the German army for selecting officers in World War I, and the Office of Strategic Services used them for selecting secret agents in World War II. However, the assessment-center concept did not reach U.S. industry until the mid-1950s, when AT&T pioneered a program. The practice spread during the 1960s, but it was not until 1969 that a U.S. government agency, the Internal Revenue Service, used assessment-center methodology on a large scale. Today such techniques are being rapidly adopted by government agencies at all jurisdictional levels.

Mentoring as Management Development

The word *mentor* predates English, coming from ancient Greek. When Odysseus (or Ulysses) in Homer's *Odyssey* left home for the war in Troy, he left his estate and family in the care of a trusted friend, Mentor. When things got rough at home for Odysseus's family, Athena, the goddess of wisdom, assumed the shape of Mentor and provided Telemachus, the son of Odysseus, with some very helpful advice about how to deal with the problems of his most unusual adolescence.

While mentoring relationships have always existed, there was not much analysis of them as an organizational phenomenon until the advent of the modern women's movement that began in the late 1960s. Organizational analysts, concerned with the limitations on the careers of women, noticed that many successful men had their careers advanced by informal mentoring. This has a more experienced worker or manager take under his wing, so to speak, a more junior member of the organization. Then through the processes of friendship and informal interaction (lunches, golf dates, after-hours drinks, etc.), the mentor shares with the mentee the "tricks of the trade" by which he can eventually advance in his career.

The key here is that mentoring has traditionally been a spontaneous process. Friendship cannot be ordered. You cannot be told to "take pleasure" in someone's company. Senior people can be directed to train their juniors. But mentoring, which may include training for specific tasks, goes far beyond training to become a unique variant of management development. This can only truly happen when there is an element of genuine affection at work, when the mentor finds joy in the company of a gifted apprentice. It is the same kind of joy, love if you will, that a teacher finds with the best students. All teachers, including college professors, know that instructing—mentoring—eager and capable students is the greatest joy of their professional life.

THE BITTERSWEET HERITAGE OF CIVIL SERVICE REFORM

The perversion of most civil service merit systems for private, administrative, and especially partisan ends is one of the worst kept, yet least written about, secrets in government. It is one of the dirty little secrets of life. ("Dirty" because it is less than honorable, and "little" because it is not really a secret at all—just a much-neglected topic of conversation.) Books on government management tend to deal with this subject as if it were an abnormal malignancy instead of an inherent and frequently beneficial part of civil service systems. But this is a faulty perspective. The perversion of merit systems is a normal, even healthy, condition. Indeed, such perversions are essential if actual merit is often to be rewarded within the merit system.

"Civil service" and "merit system" are concepts that are frequently confused. A civil service consists of all those civilians who work for a government. Any government employee who is not in the military is part of the civil service. A jurisdiction's merit system, if it has one, consists of all those members of the civil service who are selected by a formally established merit process. Of course, to be intellectually honest, "merit system" should always be proceeded by the phrase "so-called" because merit may or may not be an integral part of any given "so-called merit system." Because of the netherworld of personnel administration, determining the true level of merit in any given merit system is almost impossible.

The Netherworld of Public Personnel Administration

Throughout the United States, public personnel merit systems tend to operate on three different planes within the same jurisdiction. In effect, parallel administrative universes, invisible to the untrained eye, occupy the same physical space. This notion of parallel universes was a plot device used on the *Star Trek* television series during the late 1960s. It seemed that the "good" starship *Enterprise* had a parallel but "evil" twin operating in a hidden dimension. The personnel netherworld is much the same in that both good and bad occupy the same space but on different planes. The vast majority of civil service employees within the merit system enter, perform, and advance on the basis of their own talents and the design of the system. However, at the same time and within the same system there are two groups of employees who enter the system and advance according to criteria other than those provided for by merit system regulations.

The first group consists of all those employees who were appointed for considerations other than personal fitness. Here are hidden the political appointees in excess of those policymaking and confidential positions that are legally the chief executive's prerogative. These positions are obtained only after months of diligent effort performing political good works, such as aiding the mayor's, the governor's, or the president's election campaign or playing up to some other influential political actor. *Washington Post* columnist Mike Causey wrote that both the White House and Congress "all too often defend the career civil service system up to the point where a friend or brother-in-law needs a job badly." The same can be said of governors and state legislators, of mayors and city councils.

> ### TABLE 11.2
>
> **A Few Examples of How Civil Service Systems Are "Fudged"**
>
> | Model | Process |
> |---|---|
> | "Tailoring" | "Preferred" candidate is identified. Qualifications for position in vacancy announcement tailored to skills of preferred candidate. Preferred candidate hired or promoted. This practice is technically legal but it goes beyond the spirit of civil service law. |
> | "Bridging" appointment | Agency targets highly qualified (i.e., "preferred") candidate. To avoid a hiring delay, a permanent candidate is hired on a temporary line, which is later converted, or bridged, to a permanent line. This practice is technically legal, but it goes beyond the spirit of civil service law. |
> | Provisional appointment | This practice is technically legal, but it goes beyond the spirit of civil service law. |
> | "Soliciting" a declination | Convince persons ranked high on civil service list to turn job offer down. To do so, candidate must be convinced that the work is undesirable and unpleasant. Or a bargain will be made whereby the candidate is promised a "helping hand" for some other current or future job vacancy. This practice is clearly illegal. |
>
> Source: Adapted from Carolyn Ban, "The Realities of the Merit System." In *Public Personnel Management: Current Concerns, Future Challenges,* eds. Carolyn Ban and Norma M. Riccucci (White Plains, NY: Longman Press, 1991).
>
> NOTE: This represents just a sample of techniques, all of which have been employed at least at the federal level of government.

It is a time-honored practice for a limited number of such politicos to be fudged into presumably merit system positions. "Fudge," meaning to cheat or grossly exaggerate, is one of the most important words in personnel management. Indeed, it can be said that the whole public personnel netherworld only exists because of the ability of personnel administrators to produce a seemingly endless supply of fudge. The extent of such placements depends on such factors as the strength and longevity of the merit system, the political culture of the community, and the personal integrity of a chief executive who, having taken an oath to uphold all of the laws of the jurisdiction, can only make such appointments in violation of the spirit, if not the letter, of that oath.

While the merit system is frequently perverted for traditional political purposes, it is similarly abused for more scrupulous purposes. The excessively rigid procedures for entering and advancing in most merit systems have long been recognized as being hindrances to effective management practices. In order to compensate for the lack of management discretion caused by these rigidities, career civil servants as well as other highly qualified individuals from outside the system have been advanced or initially installed through a fudging of the civil service regulations similar to the processes by which politicos are foisted on the merit system. The formal system with its attendant procedural morass simply does not allow for the timely promotion or placement of such meritorious individuals.

Consequently, what frequently exists in fact, although nowhere is it officially recognized, is a first-class and a second-class civil service. This is not an indicator of the quality of any individual or of the productive value of each class; it is merely a reference as to how people are treated by the merit system. While the politically uninfluential who comprise the civil service proletariat must be content with careers bounded by the full force of the frequently unreasonable and always constraining regulations, others—fortunate enough to be recognized for their talents or in spite of their talents—benefit markedly by having these same regulations waived, fraudulently complied with, or simply ignored.

From Spoils to Merit

Of course, all this—the formal merit system and the informal netherworld—was brought about by the civil service reform movement. While federal civil service reform is generally dated from the post–Civil War period, the political roots of the reform effort go back much earlier—to the beginning of the republic. Thomas Jefferson was the first president to face the problem of a philosophically hostile bureaucracy. While sorely pressed by his supporters to remove Federalist office-holders and replace them with Republican partisans, Jefferson was determined not to remove officials for political reasons alone. He maintained that only "malconduct is a just ground of removal: mere difference of political opinion is not." With occasional defections from this principle, even by Jefferson himself, this policy was the norm rather than the exception down through the administration of Andrew Jackson. President Jackson's rhetoric on the nature of public service was far more influential than his administrative example. In claiming that all men, especially the newly enfranchised who did so much to elect him, should have an equal opportunity for public office, Jackson played to his plebeian constituency and put the patrician civil service on notice that they had no natural monopoly on public office. The spoils system, used only modestly by Jackson, flourished under his successors. The doctrine of rotation of office progressively prevailed over the earlier notion of stability in office.

Depending on your point of view, the advent of modern merit systems is either an economic, a political, or a moral development. Economic historians would maintain that the demands of industrial expansion—a dependable postal service, a viable transportation network, and so on—necessitated a government service based on merit. Political analysts could argue rather persuasively that it was the demands of an expanded **suffrage** and democratic rhetoric that sought to replace favoritism with merit. Economic and political considerations are so intertwined that it is impossible to say which factor is the true midwife of the merit system. The moral impetus behind reform is even more difficult to define. As moral impulses tend to hide economic and political motives, the weight of moral concern undiluted by other considerations is impossible to measure. Nevertheless, the cosmetic effect of moral overtones was of significant aid to the civil service reform movement, because it accentuated the social legitimacy of the reform proposals.

With the ever-present impetus of achieving maximum public services for minimum tax dollars, business interests were quite comfortable in supporting civil service reform, one of a variety of strategies they used to have power pass from the politicos to themselves. The political parties of the time were almost totally dependent for financing on **assessments** made on the wages of their members in public office; with the decline of patronage, the parties had to seek new funding sources,

Suffrage ■
The right to vote. Property ownership was commonly required for voters in the early years of the United States, but, by the time Andrew Jackson became president in 1829, universal white male suffrage had been effectively achieved. Since then, various constitutional amendments have been devoted to expanding the suffrage. In 1870, the Fifteenth Amendment held that suffrage shall not be denied "on account of race, color, or previous condition of servitude." In 1920, the Nineteenth Amendment held that citizens of either sex had the right to vote.

Assessment ■
The contributions to political parties determined according to a schedule of rates and made in order to retain a civil service patronage appointment.

and American business was more than willing to assume this new financial burden—and its concomitant influence.

The Pendleton Act

There is no doubt that civil service reform would have come about without the 1881 assassination of President James A. Garfield; there is also no doubt that the assassination by a disappointed office seeker helped. Garfield was shot by Charles Guiteau, an insane, self-styled attorney who had worked for Garfield's election and was angry about not receiving a patronage appointment. While the twentieth president's death was certainly instrumental in creating the appropriate climate for the passage of the Pendleton Act, historians maintain that the Republican reversals during the midterm elections of 1882 had the more immediate effect on enactment. Civil service reform had been the deciding issue in a number of congressional contests. Thus, when President Chester A. Arthur signed the Pendleton Act into law on January 16, 1883, and created the U.S. Civil Service Commission, it was essentially a gesture by reluctant politicians to assuage public opinion and the reform elements.

The Pendleton Act or "An Act to Regulate and Improve the Civil Service of the United States" has been a remarkably durable piece of legislation. Within it is the framework for personnel management that is still the heart of the federal civil service system. The act created the U.S. Civil Service Commission as the personnel management arm of the president. While it was termed a **commission,** it was by no means independent. It was an executive agency that for all practical purposes was subject to the administrative discretion of the president. Written into the act were requirements for open competitive examinations, probationary periods, and protection from political pressures. While the personnel program was to remain decentralized and in the control of the departments, the commission was authorized to supervise the conduct of examinations and make investigations to determine the degree of departmental enforcement of its rules.

The Pendleton Act was hardly a total victory for the reformers. It only covered just over 10 percent of the federal service. Actually the reformers were not at all anxious for near-universal merit system coverage. They recognized the problems of creating the appropriate administrative machinery and were concerned that the reform program would be overburdened and subject to failure if complete reform were attempted all at once. Over the years, federal employees were brought more and more under the jurisdiction of the Civil Service Commission or of other federal merit systems, such as those of the Foreign Service, Tennessee Valley Authority, and so forth.

American presidents during the reform period typically entered office taking full advantage of their patronage prerogatives and left office with extensions of the merit system to their credit. This was the case with every president from Arthur to Wilson. Merit system coverage went from 10 percent in 1884 to more than 70 percent by the end of World War I. Generally, lame-duck presidents being succeeded by someone of a different party would **blanket-in** large numbers of employees in order to reduce the amount of patronage available to the opposition party. One of the ironies of civil service reform brought about by such blanketing-in is

Commission ■
A group charged with directing a government function, whether on an ad hoc or a permanent basis. Commissions tend to be used (1) when it is desirable to have bipartisan leadership, (2) when their functions are of a quasi-judicial nature, or (3) when it is deemed important to have wide representation of ethnic groups, regions of the country, differing skills, and so on.

Blanket-in ■
A term for the large-scale importation of previously noncareer jobs into the regular civil service merit system. In the short run, blanketing-in can be (and has been) used to protect political favorites from the next administration. In the long run, blanketing-in is one of the major means through which the civil service merit system has been enlarged.

that such initial reforms had a tendency to benefit employees who were the least meritorious.

State and Local Reform

Influenced by the example of the 1883 Pendleton Act, state and local jurisdictions began to institute civil service commissions. But this was a very slow process. While New York adopted a merit system that same year and Massachusetts did so during the following year, it was more than 20 years before another state did so in 1905. By 1935, only 12 states had formally instituted merit systems. These early efforts were not all successes. Connecticut had its first civil service law repealed, while Kansas kept the statute as law but "made it innocuous by refusing to vote appropriations." Nor were these laws necessarily effective even when kept on the books. For example, New York State, which since 1883 had the most stringent prohibitions against political assessments on the salaries of public employees, had widespread "voluntary" contributions to the party at least through the 1930s. It wouldn't be until well after World War II that most states would install merit systems—initially, in many cases, only to qualify for federal grants. Today, almost all states have general merit system coverage for their employees.

Only 65 cities had created civil service commissions by 1900. By 1930, that number had risen to 250. Today, less than 12 percent of cities with populations exceeding 50,000 do not have merit systems. The percentage lacking merit-system coverage is almost double that for all cities in the 25,000 to 50,000 population range. Only 6 of the more than 3,000 counties had adopted merit systems by 1933. Even today, less than half of all county government have instituted general merit systems.

It's important to note that all statistics concerning merit system coverage are inherently deceptive. While such figures may be numerically accurate, they merely indicate that merit systems are "on the books," not that they exist in practice. The surveys of merit system coverage that are annually undertaken by a variety of good-government groups are typically administered by mailed questionnaire. These statistics are by no means ascertained by empirical investigation. Consequently, while the arithmetic of these surveys may be impeccable, the resulting summaries frequently belie the true extent of merit system coverage. Remember, the city of Chicago has an excellent merit system on the books, yet it manages to retain its well-earned reputation as the American city with the most notorious patronage abuses.

The Rise and Fall of the Civil Service Commission

Subnational jurisdictions followed the federal merit system example in many respects: Bipartisan civil service commissions became common, examining methods and related administrative detail were frequently similar, and prohibitions concerning assessments and other varieties of political interference were legally binding many years before a general pattern of compliance appeared. In some areas, such as position classifications programs and retirement provisions, a variety of local jurisdictions were many years ahead of the federal service. However, at the local level the pattern of reform that evolved contained a crucial difference—the civil service commission was made administratively and presumably politically independent of the jurisdiction's chief executive officer.

The commission format was mandated by political, not administrative, considerations. Then, as now, the illogic of divorcing the control of personnel from programmatic authority was recognized. Nevertheless, the more immediate goal of defeating the influences of spoils was paramount. With this in mind, the rationale for the commission device was quite reasonable. Not only would it be independent from the party-controlled government, but its three- or five-part membership would be in a better position to resist political pressures than could any single administrator. Appellate functions, especially, are better undertaken by a tribunal than by a solitary judge. Not insignificantly, a commission provides a political safety valve by making room for representatives of special interests such as racial or employee groups.

Appellate ■
Any court that considers appeals concerning a lower court's actions.

It was not very long before the rationale for the independent commission was seriously challenged. As the city manager movement developed early after World War I, managers—nonpartisan reform-type managers at that—found themselves burdened with the same kinds of restrictions on their authority over personnel that had been designed to thwart the spoilsmen. They felt, quite reasonably, that the

---

George Washington Plunkitt on "The Curse
BOX 11.2 |of Civil Service Reform"

This civil service law is the biggest fraud of the age. It is the curse of the nation. There can't be no real patriotism while it lasts. How are you goin' to interest our young men in their country if you have no offices to give them when they work for their party? Just look at things in this city to-day. There are ten thousand good offices, but we can't get at more than a few hundred of them. How are we goin' to provide for the thousands of men who worked for the Tammany ticket? It can't be done. These men were full of patriotism a short time ago. They expected to be servin' their city, but when we tell them that we can't place them, do you think their patriotism is goin' to last? Not much. They say: 'What's the use of workin' for your country anyhow? There's nothin' in the game.' And what can they do? I don't know, but I'll tell you what I do know. I know more than one young man in past years who worked for the ticket and was just overflowin' with patriotism, but when he was knocked out by the civil service humbug he got to hate his country and became an Anarchist.

This ain't no exaggeration. I have good reason for sayin' that most of the Anarchists in this city to-day are men who ran up against civil service examinations. Isn't it enough to make a man sour on his country when he wants to serve it and won't be allowed unless he answers a lot of fool questions about the number of cubic inches of water in the Atlantic and the quality of sand in the Sahara desert? There was once a bright young man in my district who tackled one of these examinations. The next I heard of him he had settled down in Herr Most's saloon smokin' and drinkin' beer and talkin' socialism all day. Before that time he had never drank anything but whisky. I knew what was comin' when a young Irishman drops whisky and takes to beer and long pipes in a German saloon. That young man is to-day one of the wildest Anarchists in town. And just to think! He might be a patriot but for that cussed civil service. ◢

Source: William C. Riordon, *Plunkitt of Tammany Hall* (New York: McClure Phillips, 1905).

personnel function should be integrated with the other administrative functions under the executive.

While this line of reasoning made considerable headway where the city manager concept was firmly entrenched, it had little applicability for most of the larger cities where merit system provisions implemented only a few years earlier had degenerated into a sham. This was achieved by the dual process of appointing persons unsympathetic to merit system ideals as civil service commissioners and by restricting the work of the commission by denying adequate appropriations. In response to such "starve 'em out" tactics, many jurisdictions later enacted **ordinances** providing that a fixed percentage of each year's budget would be for the administration of the merit system.

Despite these rather inauspicious beginnings, the merit system has now taken a firm hold on most sizable public jurisdictions. Two basic factors have accounted for the continued growth of merit systems at the state and local level. First, as the scope and nature of state and local employment changed, it was almost inevitable that patronage appointees would have to give way to those with greater technical training and an interest in public service careers. It should be remembered in this context that even in the federal government at its worst, the spoils system never substantially abused positions requiring technical skills. For the most part, then, the complex functions of government, rather than the ideals of civil service reformers, have led to the relative demise of spoils practices.

Second, the federal government threw its weight in favor of the development of forceful merit systems at the state and local levels. Beginning in the 1930s, it has adopted a variety of measures to coerce or induce states to use merit procedures where federal funding is involved. Federal standards for this purpose were first issued in 1939 and have been periodically revised ever since.

Ironically, at the same time that the federal government has been pressuring state and local governments to adopt and strengthen merit systems, the commission form of administering them has been on the wane for reasons similar to the abolition of the commission format at the federal level. Put simply: Independent, structurally and politically isolated personnel agencies of a regulatory nature have great difficulty in serving the needs of elected executives and public managers.

The advent of the civil service commission as a political device was not synonymous with the development of personnel administration as such. The commission impetus was decidedly negative and heavily moralistic. Its goals were to smite out "evil" as personified by the spoils system. Viewed historically and dispassionately, one could argue that considerable good in the guise of executive discretion also got washed away with the evil. Administrative historian Frederick C. Mosher saw two lasting efforts from the widespread implementation of civil service commissions. They not only "perpetuated the association of public personnel and its administration with morality," but they also "divorced personnel administration from general management—from the executives responsible for carrying out the programs and activities of governments." Unlike its private sector counterpart, the personnel function in government has two frequently conflicting roles. Of necessity, it must attend both to service and to control. Is it possible to be both an integral member of the management team and the organization's policeman at the

Ordinances ■
Regulations enacted by a local government that have the force of law but must be in compliance with state and national laws. They are issued under the authority derived from a grant of power (such as a city charter) from a sovereign entity (such as a state).

same time? In its various manifestations, this is the central dilemma of public personnel administration today.

The Civil Service Reform Act of 1978

On March 2, 1978, President Jimmy Carter, with the enthusiastic support of his Civil Service Commission leadership, submitted his civil service reform proposals to Congress. On that same day, before the National Press Club, he further called his proposals to the attention of the Congress by charging that the present federal personnel system had become a "bureaucratic maze which neglects merit, tolerates poor performance, and permits abuse of legitimate employee rights, and mires every personnel action in red tape, delay, and confusion."

The reform bill faced considerable opposition from federal employee unions (which thought the bill was too management oriented) and from veterans' groups (which were aghast at the bill's curtailment of veterans' preferences). The unions lost. The veterans won. The bill passed almost intact, thanks in great measure to the efforts of Alan K. "Scotty" Campbell, the last chairman of the U.S. Civil Service Commission, who was both the architect of the reform act and its most fervent advocate before Congress. (Campbell would then serve as the first director of the new Office of Personnel Management during 1979–1980.)

The Civil Service Reform Act of 1978 mandated that the U.S. Civil Service Commission would be divided into two agencies: an Office of Personnel Management (OPM) to serve as the personnel arm of the chief executive and an independent Merit Systems Protection Board (MSPB) to provide recourse for aggrieved employees. In addition, the act created the Federal Labor Relations Authority (FLRA) to oversee federal labor–management policies.

Was the OPM nothing more than the old commission with a facelift? A case can be made that the whole Civil Service Reform Act was not much more than reorganization for cosmetic effect—that is, much changed on the surface but essentially the same underneath. While some criticize the act as too little too late, others concede their misgivings and say "better a symbolic act than no act." The show must go on! For if the act fails in substance, it is an overwhelming success as a symbol. Because of the scandals that arose during the Nixon–Ford years, the U.S. Civil Service Commission grew to symbolize corruption and incompetence. Of course, only a minority of individuals engaged in corrupt behavior or exhibited incompetent tendencies. But that was enough to ruin a reputation.

The commission's "good name" could not be salvaged. Only a new name could remove the stigma of past indiscretions. The stigma was so great that the reformers went so far as to formally assert that it was not the giant Office of Personnel Management that would be the successor agency to the commission but the little Merit Systems Protection Board. OPM would be a totally new entity—an organization without a history starting with a clean slate. It's a nice thought. But quite untrue except as a symbolic purging of the evils of the past. Yet on this plane of symbolic action it has been a considerable success. Alan K. Campbell and company deserve a lot of credit. You cannot help but admire a federal manager who, on inheriting a troubled and demoralized agency, destroys it only to find himself and practically all of his previously troubled agency born again on the White House organization chart.

REINVENTING PUBLIC PERSONNEL ADMINISTRATION

Personnel management in government has been heavily impacted by the reinventing-government movement. Indeed, civil service reform was a major theme of the 1993 National Performance Review (the Gore Report), which stated that "to create an effective federal government, we must reform virtually the entire personnel system: recruitment, hiring, classification, promotion, pay, and reward systems." If one word sums up the overall focus of the reform agenda, that word is *decentralization*. Accordingly, the federal government did the following:

1. Deregulated personnel policy by phasing out the 10,000-page Federal Personnel Manual and all agency-implementing directives
2. Gave all departments and agencies authority to conduct their own recruiting and examinations for all positions, and abolished all central registers and standard application forms
3. Dramatically simplified the current classification system to give agencies greater flexibility in how they classify and pay their employees
4. Allowed agencies to design their own performance management and reward systems, with the objective of improving the performance of individuals and organizations
5. Sought to reduce by half the time required to terminate federal managers and employees for cause

Cause ■
The reason given for removing someone from an office or job (short for just cause). The cause cited may or may not be the real reason for the removal.

For more than 100 years, the concept of merit employment progressively spread across U.S. governments. However, in 1996, Georgia introduced Senate Bill 635 to "eliminate" the merit system the state had introduced in 1943. In practice, the legislation drew on common themes of increasing decentralization, employment flexibility, and ease of hiring and firing. But it went further and abolished the state's merit system as well, including employment protections and grievance appeal processes.

Was this an aberration or a turning point? Advocates of the change noted greater simplicity and ease of personnel action by management, especially simplicity of firing. But the way was opened for the return of a political spoils system, and it is doubtful whether a regime with no due process rights for employees and a capacity to diminish minority rights will withstand constitutional scrutiny.

Attrition ■
The reduction in the size of a workforce that naturally occurs through voluntary resignations, retirements, and deaths.

Nevertheless, it is difficult to usher in the brave new world of reinvented government in an era of downsizing and privatization. Downsizing is reducing the total number of an agency's employees by **attrition**, buy-outs (financial incentives to retire or resign), and layoffs—often called "reductions-in-force." Privatization entails sending both a function and the employees who performed it to a private company. With this, the U.S. Office of Personnel Management has led the way. (The Clinton administration's first major privatization of a federal program took place in 1995, when about 125 former employees of the Office of Personnel Management's Workforce Training Service started work for the U.S. Department of

Agriculture's Graduate School. While affiliated with the Department of Agriculture, this "graduate school" is a nonprofit organization that receives no federal funds; it supports itself through tuition fees.)

The ultimate goal of the reinventors of public personnel administration is to force government personnel offices to always remember the customer, as stated in the Gore Report: "Personnel officers must shift from reactive processors of paperwork to responsive consultants and advisors." This new focus requires personnel officers to look at the federal manager "as a customer" with needs that must be anticipated and met with responsive service.

Note the significant change here. The manager is the customer, the manager is the priority. The traditional public personnel agency concerns of protecting the rights of employees and maintaining the integrity of the merit system have been relegated to the appeals agencies such as the Merit Systems Protection Board and to the public employees' unions.

Privatizing Public Personnel

The push to make government personnel more efficient and responsive to "customer" demands has produced an increased government reliance on the practice of privatization. Privatization entails sending both a function and the employees who performed it to a private company. With this, the U.S. Office of Personnel Management has led the way. This harkens back to the romance of managerialism discussed in Chapter 8. Starting in a limited way with the Clinton administration's reinventing government efforts spearheaded by then Vice President Al Gore, this romance has become even more torrid during the George W. Bush administration because the Republicans are so much more enamored of anything that smells of privatization and reduces the total number of government employees.

Since 1995 privatization has become a much more common practice at all levels of government in the United States. Ironically, one of the most significant privatizations of government services and personnel has come in the area of human resource management. In 2004 the OPM awarded a contract to the company TMP Worldwide Government Services to operate the federal career Web site "USAJobs." This company is best known for its service Monster.com, the largest and most popular online job search site. TMP personnel, and not OPM staff, are now responsible for managing the "help wanted" needs of the federal government. These needs amount to about 17,000 job postings each month. The reasoning behind the shift of USAJobs to a private firm rested in the belief that the services could be performed both cheaper and better in the hands of a private company. The same reasoning has been behind the privatization of jobs in the areas of education, corrections, and security.

While growing in popularity, the practice of hiring nongovernment employees to perform government functions is not without controversy. First, contracting out jobs to private firms has taken on qualities of a new political patronage system. Contracts for public services may be used as rewards for campaign supporters, just as political jobs once were. Second, it is unclear if contracting out government jobs to private firms really saves the taxpayer money. Numerous studies have tried to measure the cost effectiveness of contracting out policies, with significantly varied findings. A detailed GAO examination of contracting out during the 1990s provided no conclusive evidence of the financial benefits of this practice. As the GAO report noted, "We cannot convincingly prove nor disprove that the results of federal agencies' contracting out decisions have been beneficial and cost-effective." Finally, questions of accountability have surrounded the privatization of government employees. More specifically, while government employees work directly for the taxpayer, contracted employees are only indirectly linked to the citizens whose interest they are supposedly serving.

Contracting Out Personnel

Even with the controversy that surrounds privatization of personnel, the practice found a strong supporter in the administration of George W. Bush. The Bush administration introduced its competitive sourcing initiative on taking office in 2001, establishing a policy in which government agencies had to provide evidence that their functions are better off being carried out by government employees rather than contracted out to private employers. Under competitive sourcing, the OMB classified more than 800,000 federal government positions as "commercial," thus requiring government agencies to provide evidence that their employees could do their work more efficiently than private contractors or risk having the work outsourced. In 2006 the OMB released a report on competitive sourcing that showed federal agencies completed 1,060 job competitions, putting more than 40,147 full-time federal jobs up for competition from contractors. The OMB calculated that those contests produced a net savings of $5.5 billion for the federal government between fiscal years 2003 and 2005. These savings were realized despite the fact that 83 percent of the time an agency's employees were found to be a more efficient option than the private contractors they were competing against.

The most notable example of contracting out has taken place in the defining issue of the Bush administration—the Iraq War. Like the war itself, the use of contracted civilian laborers in the theater of conflict has been an ongoing source of debate. In 2007 there were more than 125,000 government contractors in Iraq, performing a large variety of functions. Among the most controversial functions performed by military contractors were combat-related activities. The Pentagon has identified 20,000 security contractors that have been intimately involved in the military operations in Iraq. These modern-day mercenaries provided security for logistical operations such as truck conveys, but they also worked in conjunction with the U.S. military in field operations.

As the war in Iraq became a prolonged engagement, the Defense Department became more and more dependent on security contractors. With perpetual troop shortages and escalating insurgent attacks, private contractors became a significant component of tactical efforts. The private security forces allowed military brass a fairly high degree of flexibility in bolstering military operations with a quick supply of personnel, but this raised many concerns. Most notably, the industry is basically unregulated by the U.S. and Iraqi governments, and therefore the "hired warriors" are not governed by the same standards that military personnel must follow. According to Joshua Partlow and Walter Pincus of the *Washington Post*, there have been major concerns raised regarding both the quality of training received by the private security forces and their behavior and performance in the field. While a private catering firm's failure to deliver appetizing food to military personnel might not draw great attention, the failure of contractors to provide support for American soldiers in the field will.

Even for the harshest critics of big government, the work of soldiers has been seen as one of the truly necessary functions of the state. To protect the public good it is important to have individuals willing to put their lives on the line for their country. And over the last two centuries, millions of Americans have given the last full measure to ensure the survival of the nation. Conversely, very few individuals are willing to die for their company. You simply won't see a man taking a bullet for Microsoft or a woman throwing herself on a grenade for General Motors. Therefore, when a company such as Blackwater hires individuals to work alongside troops in the field, it is reasonable to be concerned that when things get hot, the private contractors might not be as committed to the cause as their counterparts in the armed forces. Even an executive of one of the private security firms had reservations about some aspects of the work that the "hired guns" perform in Iraq. Crescent Security Group managing partner Franco Picco told Steve Fainaru of the *Washington Post* in 2007 that "We protect the military. Isn't that mind-boggling?" and "I'm talking about escorting soldiers, as well. Isn't that frightening?"

While competitive sourcing has been embraced by many aspects of the federal government, such as the Defense Department, it has been ignored seemingly by many more. The OMB's 2004 report found that more than one out of four major federal agencies didn't complete any studies at all in 2003. How could agencies ignore a directive that came from the president himself? The answer is, things move slowly in federal personnel management. Government employee unions have been strong adversaries of competitive sourcing, helping to prevent its adoption. In addition, there are numerous statutory or legislative constraints that actually prevent the federal government from introducing competition in many situations. For example, many appropriation bills contain provisions that limit the amount of funding available for competitive sourcing actions.

Even the Bush administration itself recognized the difficulties in bringing competition to the federal bureaucracy, abandoning the aggressive overall goal for competitive sourcing tests, and allowing agencies to set more modest targets. In the end, even this glacial change in federal personnel policy that has occurred under this initiative may be considered an accomplishment. As Bush's former head of competitive sourcing at OMB, Angela Styles, noted in an interview with *Government Executive* magazine, "If you get some, then you've made progress. In some respects, that's better than anyone else has done in 50 years."

PATRONAGE APPOINTMENTS

At exactly noon on January 20, 2001, George W. Bush took the oath of office as president of the United States. That same day a memorandum was sent to all the heads and acting heads of executive departments and agencies by Andrew H. Card Jr., the new president's chief of staff. Card observed that "the President's appointees have the opportunity to make personnel decisions consistent with his goals."

Therefore, he ordered, "Effective immediately, no decision relating to hiring shall be made unless and until such decision is reviewed and approved by a department or agency head appointed by the President after noon on January 20, 2001." This was the new administration's first step in taking control of the federal bureaucracy. But the same order could have been issued by a new governor or mayor—because the way any new administration takes control of its bureaucracy is to first control its patronage positions.

Patronage is the power of elected and appointed officials to make partisan appointments to office or to confer contracts, honors, or other benefits on their political supporters. While subject to frequent attack from reformers, patronage has traditionally been the method by which political leaders ensure themselves a loyal support system of people who will carry out their policies and organize voters for their continued political control. The patronage appointments process is more commonly known as the spoils system. The spoils system got its name in 1832 when Senator William L. Marcy (1786–1854) asserted in a Senate debate that "that the politicians of the United States . . . see nothing wrong in the rule, that to the victor belongs the spoils of the enemy."

While modern civil service reforms have curtailed many of the excesses of the spoils system, there remains at the top of all government bureaucracies a thin veneer of spoils that goes by the name of "policy and supporting positions" or "policy and confidential positions." Whenever there is a change of administration—whether in Washington, a state capital, or a city hall—there is a concomitant patronage feeding frenzy over these positions. When the national government changes administrations, this frenzy is encouraged by "the Plum Book." Formally *United States Government: Policy and Supporting Positions*, this book is published by the Government Printing Office every four years, right after the presidential election. It lists most of the jobs that a new president can fill at his or her discretion.

The 2000 edition of the Plum Book, for the first time sporting a plum-colored cover, lists 6,722 high-level policy jobs for both political and career appointees. Fewer than half of this number are clearly available to the new administration. The rest are either part of the merit-based Senior Executive Service or are of such a scientific or technical nature that traditional political considerations cannot apply to them. However, that still leaves a healthy number of jobs for the party faithful. And, according to *Washington Post* reporter Stephen Barr, many Senior Executive Service jobs that are filled by career federal employees "can be flipped to political status when a career employee leaves the position, if an administration wants to expand the number of patronage slots."

The man President George W. Bush designated to determine just how faithful and deserving the party faithful have been is Clay Johnson. His qualifications: He was the president's college roommate at Yale and his chief of staff when Bush was governor of Texas. As director of Presidential Personnel, Johnson candidly told *New York Times* reporter Mark Lacey, "I didn't know anything about government or politics when I joined the governor in Austin. I didn't know anything about the federal government when I came up here. I know I don't have very good political instincts, but I know people who do, and I'm not here to be the political manager. I'm here to help identify people and let others make sure the politics are right." Here is a man happy in his ignorance. Effectively, what he has said is that he gets to consider an applicant only if the "politics are right," if the candidate has already been politically vetted.

The process Johnson so obliquely describes is the same with every new administration. In response to the fact that jobs such as "Confidential Assistant to the Executive Assistant to the Secretary of Agriculture" and "Commissioner, Inter-American Tropical Tuna Commission" are now open, thousands of patriotic citizens send their résumés to the White House. For most it will be a totally futile effort. In 1993, according to *Washington Monthly* editor Charles Peters, "The Clinton administration dumped 25,000 unread, unprocessed résumés out of the 40,000 it received from citizens hoping to serve as a part of the new administration." And the earlier Bush and Reagan administrations did the same. Despite the fact that every new administration states it is seeking to hire the best people the nation can offer, don't think that just submitting a résumé—however impressive it might be—will land you a plum job from the Plum Book. The brutal political fact is that no one will even look at unsolicited credentials for high-level patronage jobs unless they are politically sponsored. Only phone calls and letters from influential people will get you serious consideration. The reason they call it *patronage* is that you need a *patron*.

Has the Obama administration brought about any changes in patronage appointment practices? Well, yes. The Plum Book is now available online. You can also apply electronically for the high-level jobs you find therein. This has created greater efficiency in the rejection process for those without a patron. The applicant saves paper and postage just as the incoming administration's transition team can reject them without even the traditional effort it took to throw the unsolicited résumés into the wastepaper basket. The cast of characters may have changed but they are singing the same old song.

The Constitutionality of Patronage

Patronage has always been one of the major tools by which executives at all levels in all sectors consolidate their power and attempt to control a bureaucracy. In the 1990 case of *Rutan v. Republican Party*, the U.S. Supreme Court ruled that traditional patronage in public employment is unconstitutional. Writing the majority opinion, Justice William J. Brennan Jr. said, "To the victor belongs only those spoils that may be constitutionally obtained." In earlier cases, *Elrod v. Burns* (1976) and *Branti v. Finkel* (1980), the Court held that the First Amendment forbids government officials to discharge or threaten to discharge public employees solely for not being supporters of the political party in power, unless party affiliation is an appropriate requirement for the position involved.

In the *Rutan* case, the Court was asked to decide the constitutionality of several related political patronage practices—"whether promotion, transfer, recall and hiring decisions involving low-level public employees may be constitutionally based on party affiliation and support. We hold that they may not." In a stinging dissent, Justice Antonin Scalia said, "The new principle that the Court today announces will be enforced by a corps of judges (the members of this Court included) who overwhelmingly owe their office to its violation. Something must be wrong here, and I suggest it is the Court." The Supreme Court notwithstanding, patronage will turn out to be like prostitution: It can be outlawed, but it cannot be stopped. Laws barring either will merely drive the practice underground—into the netherworld.

Veterans Preference

Patronage appointments are essentially a means of implementing a society's values. The United States has always sought to advance the interests of its military veterans. Thus veterans preference—special influence earned by honorable military service—has become a special variant of patronage. While veterans have always been given special benefits by their governments, the formal concept dates from 1865, when the Congress, toward the end of the Civil War, affirmed that "persons honorably discharged from the military or naval service by reason of disability resulting from wounds or sickness incurred in the line of duty, shall be preferred for appointments to civil offices, provided they are found to possess the business capacity necessary for the proper discharge of the duties of such offices." The 1865 law was superseded in 1919, when preference was extended to all "honorably discharged" veterans, their widows, and wives of disabled veterans. The Veterans Preference Act of 1944 expanded the scope of veterans preference by providing for a 5-point bonus on federal examination scores for all honorably separated veterans (except for those with a service-connected disability, who are entitled to a 10-point bonus). Veterans also received other advantages in federal employment (such as protections against arbitrary dismissal and preference in the event of a reduction in force).

All states and many other jurisdictions have veterans preference laws of varying intensity. New Jersey, an extreme example, offers veterans absolute preference; if a veteran passes an entrance examination, he or she must be hired (no matter what the score) before nonveterans can be hired. Veterans competing with each other are rank-ordered, and all disabled veterans receive preference over other veterans. Veterans preference laws have been criticized because they have allegedly made it difficult for government agencies to hire and promote more women and minorities. Although the original version of the Civil Service Reform Act of 1978 sought to limit veterans preference in the federal service, the final version contained a variety of new provisions strengthening veterans preference.

In *Personnel Administrator of Massachusetts v. Feeney* (1979), the Supreme Court held that a state law operating to the advantage of males by giving veterans lifetime preference for state employment was not in violation of the equal protection clause of the Fourteenth Amendment. The Court found that a veterans preference law's disproportionate impact on women did not prove intentional bias.

Patronage Gone Bad

While patronage is almost as old as the nation itself—and a useful tool for rewarding political loyalty—it can be damaging to elected officials when patronage appointments go bad. The 2005 case of Federal Emergency Management Agency Director Michael Brown reminded the nation that patronage can come with both political and performance costs. Brown's less than impressive handling of the

Hurricane Katrina disaster, coupled with his vastly limited experience in the field of emergency management, drew high levels of scrutiny from both the media and Congress in the wake of the destruction along the Gulf Coast. While this scrutiny was bad for Brown himself (he resigned under pressure), it also ended up damaging President Bush. After all, it was Bush who personally appointed Brown to the position, and it's the president who is ultimately accountable for the performance of the federal bureaucracy. While the case of Michael Brown may not end the long history of ill-prepared political appointees, it may serve as a cautionary tale that leads future elected officials to place their least-skilled patronage appointments in offices that don't have substantial responsibilities.

Although patronage hirings often draw the most public attention and criticism, patronage firings can also raise concern about public personnel management. Such was the case in 2007 when a major uproar followed the dismissal of eight U.S. attorneys by the Bush administration. The eight attorneys were serving as federal prosecutors within the Justice Department when, on December 7, 2006, they were notified that they would not be retained in their positions. Importantly, their dismissal was completely within the legal purview of President Bush, for prosecutors serve at the pleasure of the chief executive. But sometimes legal protection of patronage decisions does not equate to political protection from patronage practices.

In this case, at least six of the eight fired lawyers had recently received positive reviews by the Justice Department, but were fired by Attorney General Alberto Gonzalez anyway. While there is no legal protection of a prosecutor's job even if he or she is doing it well, the dismissals placed the Bush administration in a very awkward position. It became clear that the firings were based on the desire of the White House to have more loyal Republicans serving as federal prosecutors, and that, in this case, loyalty was more important than competence. And it seemed that the Bush administration's idea of loyalty could only be demonstrated by prosecuting Democrats. Such highly publicized priorities for the Bush administration did not jive very well with the popular, if naïve, notion that the law should be above politics. Bush and Gonzalez held the legal powers to make these personnel decisions in the prosecutors' case, but the court of public opinion got to render the verdict on the acceptability of the practice.

Ironically, as the firings were being investigated by Congress and the Attorney General was defending his decision to replace the prosecutors, it was discovered that Gonzalez had made contradictory statements about his role in the dismissal of the attorneys. These inconsistencies led to even greater scrutiny by members of the Senate Judiciary Committee, and the calls for Gonzalez's resignation or firing became louder throughout the summer of 2007. Of course attorney generals serve at the pleasure of the president and thus his fate came down to yet another patronage decision for President Bush. So Gonzalez "voluntarily" resigned.

PUBLIC SECTOR LABOR RELATIONS

Unions are groups of employees who create a formal organization (the union) to represent their interests before management. *Labor relations* is the term for all of the interactions between the union leaders (representing the employees) and

Blue flu ■
An informal strike by police officers, who all call in sick on the same day; the "blue" refers to their uniforms.

management (representing the corporation or jurisdiction). The importance of labor relations in the public sector is painfully evident to anyone who has ever sniffed through a garbage strike, walked through a transit strike, or suffered through the **blue flu**. A reasonable person would seem to have adequate cause to be alternately optimistic or pessimistic concerning the emergence of militant public employee unions. Job actions notwithstanding, the extraordinary ability of such unions to gain fiscally crippling pay raises from their jurisdictions without exchanging corresponding increases in productivity is certainly adequate cause for pessimism. On the other hand, the future of unions as vehicles to replace part of the merit system's worn-out regalia and as a source of leadership in the fight for greater productivity is exceedingly hopeful.

Why have the unions been so successful in so many instances? Simply put, union leaders have been better politicians than the elected political executives. Their acceptance of a militant posture directly followed their recognition that non-traditional forms of political behavior had been exceedingly productive for other interest groups—especially the civil rights advocates of the early 1960s whose use of civil disobedience was exceedingly effective.

Public personnel departments have traditionally had the dual function of simultaneously representing management while enforcing and interpreting civil service regulations. This institutionalized degree of conflict over what role personnel should play on what occasion has often been noted, but the problem is reaching its resolution. Unions, opting for the pluralistic conflictive model of ascertaining the public interest, reject the proposition that personnel departments in the public sector have as equal a responsibility to employees as they do to management. No less an authority than the longtime public employees union chief Jerry Wurf has flatly stated that the "civil service is nothing more—and not much less—than management's personnel system." The unions see their prime role as representing the public employee. Any remaining pretensions on the part of personnel that this is not the case will eventually be negotiated away. Even the sacrosanct, independent civil service commission will gradually see its duties considerably narrowed by the more vigilant and better staffed unions. This situation begs a significant question. If the civil service commissions are not to play a role in the collective bargaining process, how are they to remain relevant? The National Civil Service League—the organization that drafted the original 1883 Pendleton Act, which established the U.S. Civil Service Commission—has concluded that other forces have so lessened the significance of the independent civil service commission that the league's current Model Public Personnel Administration Law now recommends the abolition of such commissions.

The AFL-CIO

The American Federation of Labor-Congress of Industrial Organizations is a voluntary federation of more than a hundred national and international labor unions operating in the United States and representing in total more than 13 million workers. The AFL-CIO is not itself a union; it does no bargaining. It is perhaps best thought of as a union of unions. The affiliated unions created the AFL-CIO to represent them in the creation and execution of broad national and international policies and to coordinate a wide range of joint activities. The American Federation of Labor (organized in 1881 as a federation of craft unions, the Federation of Organized Trade and Labor Unions) changed its name in 1886 after merging with those craft unions that had become disenchanted with the more idealistic national labor organization, the Knights of Labor. In 1955, the AFL merged with the Congress of Industrial Organizations to become the AFL-CIO. Each member union of the AFL-CIO remains autonomous, conducting its own affairs in the manner determined by its own members. Each has its own headquarters, officers, and staff. Each decides its own economic policies, carries on its own contract negotiations, sets its own dues, and provides its own membership services. Each is free to withdraw at any time. Such was the case in July 2005 when three of the AFL-CIO's largest unions—Service Employees International Union (SEIU), International Brotherhood of Teamsters (IBT), and United Food and Commercial Workers (UFCW)—officially split from the AFL-CIO. While it is unclear what effect the split will have on the bargaining position of labor in the United States, the AFL-CIO shakeup has raised questions about the future of organized labor groups in representing the interests of workers. But through such voluntary participation, the AFL-CIO, based in Washington, plays a role in establishing overall policies for the U.S. labor movement, which in turn advances the interests of every union.

Administrative Agencies

In the context of labor relations, an administrative agency is any impartial private or government organization that oversees or facilitates the labor relations process. The contemporary pattern of labor relations in both the public and private sectors relies on administrative agencies to provide ongoing supervision of the collective bargaining process. While generally headed by a board of three to five members, these agencies make rulings on unfair labor practices, on the appropriateness of bargaining units, and sometimes on the proper interpretation of a contract or the legitimacy of a scope of bargaining. They also oversee **authorization elections** and certify the winners as the exclusive bargaining agents for all of the employees in a bargaining unit. The National Labor Relations Board (NLRB), created in 1935 by an act of Congress, is the prototype of administrative agencies dealing with labor relations. The NLRB seeks to protect the rights of employees and employers, to encourage collective bargaining, and to eliminate practices on the part of labor and management that are harmful to the general welfare. The NLRB establishes procedures by which workers can exercise their choice at a secret ballot election and determines whether certain practices of employers or unions are unfair labor practices. The NLRB model has been adapted to the public sector by the federal government and several states.

The equivalent agency for federal employees is the Federal Labor Relations Authority (FLRA), created by the Civil Service Reform Act of 1978 to oversee the creation of bargaining units, supervise elections, and otherwise deal with labor–management issues in federal agencies. The FLRA is headed by a three-member panel—a chair and two members—who are appointed on a bipartisan basis to staggered five-year terms. The FLRA replaced the Federal Labor Relations Council (FLRC). A general counsel, also appointed to a five-year term, investigates alleged

Authorization election ■
Polls conducted by the National Labor Relations Board (or other administrative agency) to determine if a particular group of employees will be represented by a particular union or not. Authorization election is used interchangeably with certification election (because, if the union wins, it is certified as the representative of the workers by the administrative agency) and representative election (because a winning union becomes just that: the representative of the workers).

TABLE 11.3		
The Labor Relations Legal System		
Sector	**Legal Base**	**Administrative Agency**
Private industry	National Labor Relations Act, as amended	National Labor Relations Board
Railroads and airlines	Railway Labor Act, as amended	National Mediation Board
Postal Service	Postal Reorganization Act of 1970	National Labor Relations Board
Federal government	Civil Service Reform Act of 1978	Federal Labor Relations Authority
State and local government	Public employees relations acts	Public Employment Relations Boards

unfair labor practices and prosecutes them before the FLRA. Also, within the FLRA and acting as a separate body, the Federal Service Impasses Panel (FSIP) acts to resolve negotiation impasses.

In the states, such agencies are generally called Public Employment Relations Boards (or PERBs). Typically, their functions parallel those of the NLRB, as do the methods by which they are appointed, their terms of office, and their administrative procedures. One important difference in the public sector is that binding arbitration over questions of contract interpretation may be used instead of strikes as the final means of resolving disputes. When this is the case, the PERB may have a role in overseeing the use of arbitration and even the substance of the arbitrators' rulings when they raise serious issues about the scope of bargaining or public policy.

Collective Bargaining

Collective bargaining is bargaining on behalf of a group of employees, as opposed to individual bargaining, in which each worker represents only himself or herself. Collective bargaining is a comprehensive term that encompasses the negotiating process that leads to a contract between labor and management on wages, hours, and other conditions of employment as well as to the subsequent administration and interpretation of the signed contract. Collective bargaining is, in effect, the continuous relation between union representatives and employers. There are four basic stages of collective bargaining:

1. The establishment of organizations for bargaining
2. The formulation of demands
3. The negotiation of demands
4. The administration of the labor agreement

Collective bargaining is one of the keystones of the **National Labor Relations Act** (the Wagner Act) of 1935, which declares that the policy of the United States is to be carried out "by encouraging the practice and procedure of collective bargaining and by protecting the exercise by workers of full freedom of association, self-organization, and designation of representatives of their own choosing, for

National Labor Relations Act ■ In common usage, the National Labor Relations Act refers not just to the act of 1935 but to the act as amended by the Labor-Management Relations (Taft-Hartley) Act of 1947 and the Labor-Management Reporting and Disclosure (Landrum-Griffin) Act of 1959.

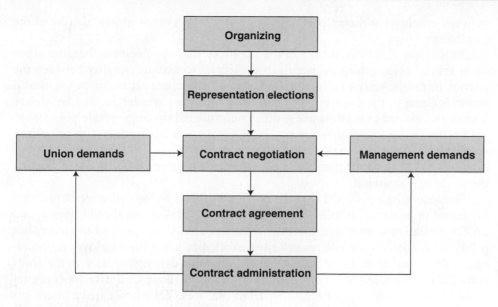

FIGURE 11.3

An overview of the collective bargaining cycle

the purpose of negotiating the terms and conditions of their employment or other mutual aid or protection".

The predominant public sector labor relations model comes from the private sector. But this fit has been long recognized as far from perfect. This is one reason why public sector labor relations were at first opposed and then organized as **meet-and-confer discussions** rather than as a collective bargaining process. The term "collective negotiations" was often used to further avoid the suggestion of actual bargaining. But today those jurisdictions with well-developed labor relations programs rely on the private sector model. The ramifications are considerable.

Instead of accepting the "public interest" or some equally saccharine goal as the watchword of the negotiating process, they have tended to adopt the adversary model of negotiations so common in the private sector. This model assumes that for one side to win the other must lose. Essentially, each party is haggling over its share of the organization's profits. There being no legal profits as such in government, has the private sector model based on conflict and individual acquisitiveness been appropriately applied to the public sector?

This private sector model of labor relations was consolidated by the National Labor Relations Act. It provides for negotiations between workers and management on the assumption that the outcome will reflect the inherent **bargaining strength** of each. Rules for fair labor relations practices were established, and the National Labor Relations Board was created to adjudicate disputes over their application. Workers retain the right to strike and to bargain as equals with management over virtually all employment-related issues not constrained by law. Although relations are assumed to be adversarial, the model is based on the belief that the free market imposes an ultimate harmony of interest

Meet-and-confer discussions ■
A technique used mostly in the public sector for determining conditions of employment whereby the representatives of the employer and the employee organization hold periodic discussions to seek agreement on matters within the scope of representation. Any written agreement is in the form of a nonbinding memorandum of understanding. This technique is often used where formal collective bargaining is not authorized.

Bargaining strength ■
The relative power each party holds during negotiation. Management has greater bargaining strength than labor if it believes that a short strike would be desirable. Final settlements often reflect the bargaining power of each side.

between employer and employee: Neither party favors the economic demise of the employer.

Employing this basic model in the public sector is problematic because some of its crucial assumptions do not fit. It is difficult to assume equality between the parties in public sector collective bargaining. What does it mean to say that a union is equal to the government or to the people as a whole? Elected legislative bodies and elected executives are generally considered the appropriate policymaking bodies in American government. Public managers bargaining with organized employees are not. The basic adjustment to the inequality of the parties in labor disputes has been to recognize the government's greater authority by restricting the scope of bargaining.

Because it isn't assumed that the parties in public sector collective bargaining are equal in principle, it follows that the outcome of disputes should not depend on their relative strengths; consequently, there should be no need to strike. But public sector strikes are not necessarily intended to harm the employer economically. They tend to do more political than economic damage, at least in the short run. This is because the governmental employer is likely to derive its revenues from taxation, rather than exclusively from user fees. Yet when a strike interrupts a government service, tax dollars are not refunded, nor are they paid out in compensation to striking employees. So a strike may temporarily enhance a government's economic position. In short, the function of a strike in the public sector is substantially different from that in the private sector.

Overall, the public sector is incredibly fragmented in terms of collective bargaining. There is no national law on the subject. States and cities vary widely in their practices. In 2010 and 2011 the collective bargaining rights of public sector employees was severely curtailed in states such as Wisconsin, Indiana, and Ohio and the unions representing government workers protested mightily, with mixed results. The reduction of collective bargaining powers in the states highlighted the tenuous place that public employees unions find themselves in. The disparities from one political jurisdiction to another places substantial burdens on national labor unions and dispute-resolution personnel who work in different jurisdictions. While the opportunity to experiment and to adapt to local conditions is valuable, such fragmentation makes it hard to speak of "public sector collective bargaining" without engaging in overgeneralization.

Scope of bargaining ■
Those issues over which management and labor negotiate during the collective bargaining process.

Strikes

A strike is a mutual agreement among workers (whether members of a union or not) to a temporary work stoppage to obtain—or to resist—a change in their working conditions. The term is thought to have nautical origins because sailors would stop work by striking or taking down their sails. A strike or potential strike is considered an essential element of the collective bargaining process. Many labor leaders claim that collective bargaining can never be more than a charade without the right to strike. Major strikes have been declining in frequency in recent years, as unions in both the public and private sectors have lost a large measure of economic clout and political support. Public employee strikes also have been declining for another reason as well. A great percentage of public sector strikes in the 1960s and early 1970s were over one issue: recognition of the union for purposes of collective bargaining. Because recognition strikes tend to be one-time issues and because many states have in the last three decades passed comprehensive public employee relations laws, public sector labor strife has been less than it once was.

The use of strikes is becoming somewhat outmoded. The use of economic force can be too damaging and unpredictable in today's economy, and, consequently, the strike is viewed as a last-resort means of producing an agreement. Moreover, it is sometimes argued that the fundamental character of the strike is changing due to the maturing of collective bargaining relationships. Violence is sometimes incidental to strikes nowadays, but physical force no longer plays a central role. Rather, the parties tend to view the strike as a continuation of the bargaining process. Indeed, negotiations may avidly continue during the entire length of a strike. Again, it is important to remember that both sides have an overriding interest in common—the economic vitality of the employer and the concomitant maintenance of the employees' jobs. Another general factor affecting strike behavior is what singer Bob Dylan refers to as "Union Sundown." Because the public's image of unions has changed, they are no longer considered weak underdogs struggling for justice in the workplace. In contrast, many segments of the population see them as too powerful and too greedy. Because organized labor now seeks to achieve many of its goals through political means, such as lobbying and electioneering, it cannot be oblivious to its public standing.

The Air Traffic Controllers' Strike

Strikes are often compared to warfare—never more so than when the strike results in the complete destruction of the union. This is understandably rare, but the Professional Air Traffic Controllers Organization (PATCO) was the rarest of unions. Not only was it one of the very few unions to support the Republican Party candidate, Ronald Reagan, for president in 1980, but it also was the first major union to make job stress and burnout major collective bargaining issues.

On July 29, 1981, 95 percent of PATCO's 13,000 members went on strike. PATCO had rejected the federal government's final offer. The union's position was that it wanted twice-a-year cost-of-living increases that would be one and a half times greater than inflation; a four-day, 32-hour workweek without a compensating salary cut; and retirement after 20 years at 75 percent of base salary. As one striking controller put it, "Where are they going to get 13,000 controllers and train them before the economy sinks? The reality is, we are it. They have to deal with us."

In response, the U.S. government cut back scheduled flights and reduced staff at smaller airports. Then it brought supervisors and retired controllers into service and ordered military controllers to civilian stations. Then the ghoulish wait began. It would only take one midair collision and the deaths of hundreds for the situation to radically change to the union's favor. PATCO was loudly critical of the safety of the nation's "fill-in" air traffic control system. The union's president menacingly suggested, "I hope that nothing happens!" He told the secretary of transportation, "If passengers are killed, it'll be your responsibility." Luckily, while there were some near misses, no one was hurt.

Finally, President Ronald Reagan addressed the nation on television. After reminding viewers that it is illegal for federal government employees to strike and that each controller signed an oath asserting that he or she would never strike, he proclaimed, "They are in violation of the law, and if they do not report for work within 48 hours, they have forfeited their jobs and will be terminated." Just over 1,000 controllers reported back. Most thought that the president was bluffing, but he wasn't. The union's assets were frozen by the courts, some PATCO leaders were literally hauled away to jail in chains, and the Department of Transportation started formal proceedings to decertify the union.

With its members fired, with practically no public support, and with the "fill-in" system working better every day, PATCO—the union that had broken ranks with labor to support Republican presidential candidate Reagan—called for labor solidarity. The response was lip service. All of the major labor leaders verbally supported the strike and deplored the president's efforts at "union busting," but they did nothing else. United Auto Workers President Douglas Fraser said that the strike "could do massive damage to the labor movement. That's why PATCO should have talked to the AFL-CIO council"—before the strike. Had any of the other major airline unions joined in the strike, the system would surely have been shut down. But none of these unions felt that they had any obligation to support the controllers in any way that mattered.

In late October, the Federal Labor Relations Authority formally decertified PATCO—the first time that it had ever done so to any union of government workers. In December PATCO filed for bankruptcy. In the end, more than 11,000 controllers, who stayed on strike, lost their jobs permanently.

The strike and subsequent firing of the controllers has had a chilling effect on public sector strikes for three decades. If the federal government would fire nearly all of the controllers (who must undergo one year of training), there was no doubt that other workers requiring less training would be fired just as fast. Before the PATCO strike, the leaders of the postal workers unions, facing upcoming contract talks, were making noises about how they did not know if they could "control" the membership. *Control* here is a code word for a possible illegal wildcat strike—one that breaks out without an appropriate vote. After the PATCO strike, not a word has been heard about "controlling" the postal workers. They and all the other federal unions had been tamed by the only president of the United States who was also a union leader (Reagan was president of the Screen Actors Guild during the 1950s).

A CASE STUDY | The Spectacular Rise and Modest Decline of Public Employeee Unions

In his first of many bestselling books on economics, *American Capitalism: The Concept of Countervailing Power* (1952), John Kenneth Galbraith put forth his theory that when one group gets too powerful in a pluralist free society such as the United States, another group or coalition will spring up to counter or oppose its power. This is exactly what has happened to the public sector union movement; it grew to be so successful that it inspired a counter-revolution in the treatment of unionized public employees.

Just how successful were they? A few statistics will tell the tale. In 1960 31.9 percent of private sector employees belonged to unions compared to just under 11 percent of public sector employees. Fifty years later, in 2010, reflected a radically different reality: only 6.9 percent of the private sector was unionized while 31.9 percent of the public sector was (*Wall Street Journal*, March 1, 2011). What happened to cause bv this reversal? Simply put: as traditional unionized rust-belt industries (autos, coal, rubber, steel, etc.) needed fewer workers due to automation and foreign competition, the service sector that took up the slack in employment numbers was far less hospitable to unions. Meanwhile, the public sector unions were taking full advantage of their natural monopoly and rapidly expanded their numbers, their scope of bargaining, and their political influence.

While many issues have contributed to the revolt against public employee unions, none is more prominent than pensions. It is generally true that government jobs in large jurisdictions offer significantly greater fringe benefits than most private companies. While one could hardly claim to justify aristocratic advantages on the basis of a few more holidays or sick leave, government pension plans provide an example of the extraordinary advantage that public employees enjoy at the expense of the common citizenry. For example, almost all (90 percent) full-time government employees at all jurisdictional levels are eligible for lifetime pensions. This compares to 18 percent of employees in the private sector (*U.S. News*, October 2010). As public sector unions grew in numbers and influence over the last 50 years, the gap between total remuneration (pay and benefits) has continued to widen. This disparity, increasingly noticed, has, with the help of Republicans and the Tea Party, helped to fuel this counterrevolution.

When pension plans for government employees began to emerge during the second and third decades of the twentieth century, their rationale was quite logical and simple. In the absence of such programs, there was a tendency to retain on the payroll employees who were too old to perform their normal duties. Since it is not a social tendency to reward many years of faithful service with dismissal, employees frequently remained on the payroll as a matter of gratitude. At a time when state, county, and municipal political machines almost always kept a variety of their stalwarts on the payroll with "no-show" jobs, this practice of compassionate corruption was neither unreasonable nor unparalleled.

The drawbacks of retaining decrepit employees notwithstanding, it was observed that it was both kinder to the employee and cheaper for the taxpayer to provide pensions for those grown old in the public service. What started out as a measure to provide for the old age of public servants has, several generations later and in too many cases, turned into a rip-off of the public treasury.

The public is generally aware of pensions at half-pay after 20 years for members of the armed services. Paralleling the military pension program are the

(*continued*)

A CASE STUDY | *Continued*

civilian paramilitary organizations such as police and fire departments. Again the rationale for a retirement plan providing for half-pay after 20 years of service is supplied by the inherent dangers and physical strains of such work. The dangers that police officers and firefighters face are certainly real. Nevertheless, it is the individual sanitation worker, the trash collector, who is more likely to be injured on the job. Admittedly, however, few sanitation workers, in contrast to police and firefighters, have had occasion to die in the line of duty. Heavy trashcans can literally be backbreaking, but seldom lethal.

In many jurisdictions, pension benefits are not simply computed on the basis of one's salary, but on the basis of one's total earnings during the previous year or two or three. Consequently, it is possible for an employee who worked a great deal of overtime during his 20th year on the job to retire with up to three-fourths of his base pay. Such public largess is no longer limited to military and paramilitary services. With the advent of aggressive public employee unions in the 1960s, an ever-increasing number of public servants in all categories of employment gained the privilege of retiring at half-pay after 20 years of service. But because of the method of computation, the general impression of merely half-pay benefits is often misleading.

In stark contrast to the situation in the larger jurisdictions, retirement provisions for public employees in many smaller jurisdictions are sometimes grossly inadequate. But the trends established by the larger jurisdictions are unmistakable. The United Auto Workers was delighted to have achieved a 30-year retirement program at less than half-pay in 1973, when at the same time some large municipal jurisdictions had as a reality a 20-year retirement program at half-pay or more for most, if not all, of their employees. All this had been achieved in many larger jurisdictions in just over a decade of municipal union militancy.

Such remarkable success was due in large part to the "hidden" nature of pension benefits. Since such monies tend to come out of future budgets, the incumbent executive can frequently bring himself labor peace at the price of a fiscal headache for a future incumbent of his office—not to mention taxpayer gouging. Union members have been quite willing to accept "smaller" salary increases in exchange for increased pension benefits. They could hardly have made a wiser financial investment.

A study of municipal labor relations in New York City by Raymond D. Horton of Columbia University offers a detailed account of how this unhealthy situation came about. While the lessons of New York are not wholly transferable to other jurisdictional contexts, Horton's analysis of municipal union–management relations as essentially a political struggle is a highly plausible explanation of why the leadership groups of municipal unions throughout the nation have been so remarkably successful in obtaining financial gains for their members. Simply put, the union leaders have been the better politicians. Their acceptance of a militant posture directly followed the recognition that the nontraditional forms of political behavior used by the civil rights movement had been exceedingly productive for other interest groups in the city as well as the nation. Couple this with the fact that management is really a misnomer for the web of competitive political relationships existing among the various public officials involved with the collective bargaining process, and you have the basis for the rapid advances of municipal unions.

Horton viewed municipal labor relations as "a political contest" between career civil servants and elected public officials. With both sides protecting mainly their own interests, the public has been the big loser while the unions have been the big winners. Since the 1960s the mayors of New York and other major cities have sought to depoliticize the labor relations process. By removing themselves from the actual negotiations and installing intermediary impasse machinery, they abdicated a large portion of their authority over the public purse.

An impasse is a condition that exists during labor–management negotiations when either party feels that no further progress can be made toward a settlement unless the process of negotiating changes. The most common techniques used to break the impasse are mediation and arbitration.

Mediation or conciliation is any attempt by an impartial third party to help settle disputes. A mediator has no power but that of persuasion; the mediator's suggestions are advisory and may be rejected by both parties. Mediation and conciliation tend to be used interchangeably to denote the entrance of an impartial third party into a labor dispute. However, there is a distinction. Conciliation is the less active term. It technically refers simply to efforts to bring the parties together so that they may resolve their problems themselves. Mediation, in contrast, is a more active term. It implies that an active effort will be made to help the parties reach agreement by clarifying issues, asking questions, and making specific proposals.

Arbitration is the means of settling a dispute by having an impartial third party (the arbitrator) hold a formal hearing and render a decision that may or may not be binding on both sides. The arbitrator may be a single individual or a board of three, five, or more (usually an uneven number). When boards are used, they may include, in addition to impartial members, representatives from both of the disputants. In the context of labor relations, arbitrators are selected jointly by labor and management, recommended by the Federal Mediation and Conciliation Service, by a state or local agency offering similar referrals, or by the private American Arbitration Association.

Compulsory arbitration is a negotiating process whereby the parties are required by law to arbitrate their dispute. Some state statutes concerning collective bargaining impasses in the public sector mandate that parties who have exhausted all other means of achieving a settlement must submit their dispute to an arbitrator. The intent of such requirements for compulsory arbitration is to induce the parties to reach agreement by presenting them with an alternative that is certain, even though it may be unpleasant in some respects to everyone involved.

(*continued*)

◤ A CASE STUDY | *Continued*

The most common effort to adjust public sector collective bargaining in the absence of the legalized strike has been to introduce some form of binding arbitration. But this raises a host of difficult problems. Arbitration inherently undercuts the bargaining process itself. If both sides are convinced a dispute will go to arbitration, they will tend to spend most of their time posturing rather than negotiating or compromising. Moreover, arbitration cannot resolve the concern that the sovereign—the state and not its employees—makes public policy. And arbitrators' decisions are not automatically sensible or in the public interest. Sometimes, they may even disregard a jurisdiction's ability to pay for the awards they authorize.

The nature of the arbitration of public sector labor disputes is also related to the remoteness of the "market" as a constraint on the total compensation of employees. In fact, the economic aspects of public sector labor relations tend to work best when cities are on the threshold of bankruptcy and therefore the "market" is not so remote.

Consequently, because of the nature of the arbitration process, it has not been unusual that whenever union leaders were unhappy about the wage offer they received from the mayor's representatives, they would directly or indirectly threaten a strike (even though strikes may be illegal) that would trigger the impasse machinery of "neutral" third parties who were quite willing to "split the difference." Why did these "neutrals" wind up giving away the store? Horton suggests three reasons: (1) it was not their responsibility to advocate the city's bargaining position; (2) they lacked the "muscle" of a mayor or his chief negotiator; and (3) if neutrals wished to be selected for future employment in impasse situations, they could not afford to develop pro-management reputations.

Of course, the justification for this approach was labor peace. After a series of highly disruptive and embarrassing strikes, peace was essential. This was certainly the perception in New York City. But, according to Horton, this peace was one of capitulation. The result was higher taxes for the public and strong union support for the mayors in their campaigns for re-election. Aligning himself with those who feel that New York City's municipal unions are too strong for the public good, Horton advocated a re-politicization of the negotiating process. Nor does Horton shy away from this re-politicization stance when politics turns to conflict. "For public officials [and the public] always to equate labor peace with the public interest represents a kind of public death wish that ensures only that the municipal labor relations process will work better for organized civil servants than for anyone else."

Horton, while writing in the 1970s, was a prophet. He predicted that the unions would continue to win, to gain more and more advantages for their members, until the politicians developed the political will to challenge them in the political arena. This finally happened in a big way and in many parts of the nation at the same time in 2011. There were two pressing reasons for this counterrevolution: the sheer expense of union dominance and the fact that the public sector unions had overwhelmingly aligned themselves with the Democratic Party. Consequently, when Tea-Party-supported Republican Party stalwarts gained control of both the governor's office and the state legislature in states such as Wisconsin and Ohio, they took the opportunity to both punish their political opponents and put their state's finances in better fiscal order by reducing both union political influence and their members' financial benefits. For example, Wisconsin and Ohio reduced public employee bargaining rights for most employees. Consequently, pensions and health care would no longer be bargained over. Suddenly employees who contributed little or nothing for those benefits had to make substantial contributions out of their own pockets in order to save their state's fiscal health—and as punishment for supporting Democratic candidates.

The future nature of public employee pensions is obvious and is already becoming apparent in some jurisdictions; it portends multi-tier pension benefits for public employees. Defined-benefit plans, the traditional pension, will gradually be supplanted by defined-contribution plans. Those who have been in the system for a substantial period retain their generous defined-benefit plans. Those who entered more recently may have a less generous defined-benefit plan, meaning they must work more years for full benefits. Finally, the newest hires may not have a defined-benefit plan at all but will instead have modest contributions made to a 401(K)-type plan.

Three things seem certain as we enter the brave new world of constrained public sector finances. First, as is already the case in many jurisdictions, new employees will have their pension benefits severely constrained compared to their older coworkers who got there first. And this will be done with the compliance of the unions who are naturally more interested in protecting the benefits of current employees at the expense of future ones.

Second, there will be fewer and fewer traditional pensions for new employees. A modest pension might be combined with a 401(K)-type plan. Hybrid plans like this have already been adopted by the state of Utah, Orange County, California, and Atlanta, Georgia.

And third, employees with these new-style 401(K) plans will be obligated to manage their own pension assets, for all the good and ill that this portends. After this becomes commonplace, public employee pensions will be pretty much the same as those in the private sector where traditional pensions have practically disappeared. But this will happen gradually and not without a fight. But you cannot fight arithmetic. And the arithmetic clearly suggests that the traditional defined-benefit union-negotiated pension may eventually disappear.

For Discussion: *How fair is it that older public sector employees have far more generous pension benefits than their younger colleagues? Are the generous benefits that have been traditionally available to public employee union members being curtailed more because of fiscal necessity or because they supported Democratic candidates in what are now Republican-controlled jurisdictions?* ▸

SUMMARY

The function of a personnel agency is service to line management. Typical services include recruiting, selection, training, evaluation, compensation, discipline, and termination.

Selection is the oldest function of the public personnel administration. Job relatedness is now the main consideration in developing a selection device because the legality of any test hinges on its validity, on its ability to predict job success. Those responsible for the preparation of examinations now have no choice but to develop them on the assumption that they will have to be defended in a court challenge.

The perversion of most civil service merit systems for private, administrative, and especially partisan ends is one of the worst kept, yet least written about, secrets in government. While the vast majority of civil service employees within the merit system enter, perform, and advance on the basis of their own talents and the design of the system, at the same time and within the same system there are other employees who enter the system and advance according to criteria other than those provided for by merit system regulations.

The advent of the civil service commission as a political device was not synonymous with the development of personnel administration as such. The commission impetus was decidedly negative and heavily moralistic. Its goals were to smite out "evil" as personified by the spoils system. Viewed historically and dispassionately, one could argue that considerable good in the guise of executive discretion also got washed away with the evil.

The ultimate goal of the current reinventors of public personnel administration is the expectation that government personnel officers must always remember the customer—that they shift from being reactive processors of paperwork to responsive consultants and advisers.

Public personnel departments have traditionally had the dual function of simultaneously representing management while enforcing and interpreting civil service regulations. This institutionalized degree of conflict over what role personnel should play on what occasion is reaching resolution because public sector unions reject the proposition that personnel management in the public sector has an equal responsibility to employees and to management.

Collective bargaining encompasses both the negotiating process that leads to a contract between labor and management on wages, hours, and other conditions of employment as well as the subsequent administration and interpretation of the signed contract. However, the public sector is incredibly fragmented in terms of collective bargaining. There is no national law on the subject. States and cities vary widely in their practices. Because the law differs so widely, substantial burdens are placed on national labor unions and dispute resolution personnel who work in different jurisdictions.

REVIEW QUESTIONS

1. What is the difference between a civil service system and a merit system?
2. Why do netherworld operations tend to evolve in so many aspects of public personnel administration?

3. Why is civil service reform a never-ending process of which the reinventing-personnel movement is just the latest manifestation?
4. What has the U.S. Supreme Court said about the constitutionality of patronage appointments?
5. How do labor relations practices in the public sector differ from those in the private sector?

KEY CONCEPTS

Civil service   A collective term for all nonmilitary employees of a government. Paramilitary organizations, such as police and firefighters, are always included in civil service counts in the United States. Civil service employment is not the same as merit system employment because all patronage positions (those not covered by merit systems) are included in civil service totals.

Civil service reform   Efforts to improve the status, integrity, and productivity of the civil service at all levels of government by supplanting the spoils system with the merit system; efforts to improve the management and efficiency of the public service; or the historical events, the movement, leading up to the enactment of the Pendleton Act of 1883.

Collective bargaining   Bargaining on behalf of a group of employees, as opposed to individual bargaining, in which each worker represents only himself or herself.

Competitive sourcing   The act of exposing government activities to competition with the private sector. The objective is to focus on the most effective and efficient way to accomplish the agency's mission, regardless of whether it is done by civil servants or contractors.

Impasse resolution   A condition that exists during labor–management negotiations when either party feels that no further progress can be made toward a settlement—unless the process of negotiating changes. The most common techniques used to break an impasse are mediation, fact-finding, and arbitration.

Management development   Any conscious effort on the part of an organization (such as rotational assignments or formal educational experiences) to provide a manager with the skills needed for future duties.

Merit system   A public sector concept of staffing that implies that no test of party membership is involved in the selection, promotion, or retention of government employees and that a constant effort is made to select the best-qualified individuals available for appointment and advancement.

Patronage   The power of elected and appointed officials to make partisan appointments to office or to confer contracts, honors, or other benefits on their political supporters. Patronage has always been one of the major tools by which political executives consolidate their power and attempt to control a bureaucracy.

Performance appraisal   The formal methods by which an organization documents the work performance of its employees. Performance appraisals are typically designed to change dysfunctional work behavior, communicate perceptions of work quality, assess the future potential of employees, and provide a documented record for disciplinary and separation actions.

Personnel   A collective term for all of the employees of an organization. The word is of military origin—the two basic components of a traditional army being materiel and personnel. *Personnel* is also commonly used to refer to the personnel management function, or the organizational unit responsible for administering personnel programs.

Position classification   The use of formal job descriptions to organize all jobs in a civil service merit system into classes on the basis of duties and responsibilities, for the purposes of delineating authority, establishing chains of command, and providing equitable salary scales.

Spoils system The practice of awarding government jobs to one's political supporters, as opposed to awarding them on the basis of merit.

Strike A mutual agreement among workers (whether members of a union or not) to a temporary work stoppage to obtain—or to resist—a change in their working conditions.

Unions Groups of employees who create a formal organization (the union) to represent their interests before management.

MySearchLab® EXERCISES

Apply what you learned in this chapter on MySearchLab (*www.mysearchlab.com*).

BIBLIOGRAPHY

Argyris, Chris. (1964). "T-Groups for Organizational Effectiveness," *Harvard Business Review* (March–April).

Ban, Carolyn, and Norma Riccucci, eds. (1991). *Public Personnel Management*. New York: Longman.

Barr, Stephen. (2000). "A Barrel of Plum Jobs for One Side or the Other," *Washington Post* (November 9).

Branigan, William. (2007). "Gonzalez Defends Actions on U.S. Attorney Firings," *Washington Post* (April 19).

Business Wire. (2005). "U.S. Office of Personnel Management Awards Monster Government Solutions Contract for Federal Government's Online Job Sites" (April 2002).

Fainaru, Steve. (2007). "Cutting Costs, Bending Rules and a Trail of Broken Lives," *Washington Post* (July 29).

General Accounting Office. (1995). *An Overview of the Federal Contracting Out Program* (March).

Government Accountability Office. (2004). *Competitive Sourcing: Greater Emphasis Needed on Increasing Efficiency and Accountability* (February).

Gruber, Amelia. (2004). "George Bush's Ambitious Management Reforms Agenda Is Only Beginning to Show Results," *Government Executive Magazine* (July 15, 2004).

Hays, Steven W., and Richard C. Kearney, eds. (1995). *Public Personnel Administration: Problems and Prospects*, 3rd ed. Englewood Cliffs, NJ: Prentice Hall.

Horton, Raymond D. (1972). *Municipal Labor Labor Relations in New York City*. New York: Praeger.

Ingraham, Patricia, and Carolyn Ban, eds. (1984). *Legislating Bureaucratic Change: The Civil Service Reform Act of 1978*. Albany: State University of New York Press.

Kearney, Richard. (2000). *Labor Relations in the Public Sector*, 3rd ed. New York: Marcel Dekker.

Kingsley, J. Donald. (1944). *Representative Bureaucracy: An Interpretation of the British Civil Service*. Yellow Springs, OH: Antioch Press.

Krislov, Samuel. (1967). *The Negro in Federal Employment*. Minneapolis: University of Minnesota Press.

Lacey, Marc. (2001). "Public Lives: Old Ties Give Bush Aide Cachet; Job Gives Him Power," *New York Times* (February 19).

Mosher, Frederick. (1982). *Democracy and the Public Service,* 2nd ed. New York: Oxford University Press.

Mosher, William E., and J. Donald Kingsley. (1936). *Public Personnel Administration.* New York: Harper.

Office of Management and Budget. (2006). *Report on Competitive Sourcing: Fiscal Year 2005.*

———. (2007). *Report on Competitive Sourcing: Fiscal Year 2006.*

Partlow, Joshua and Walter Pincus. (2007) "Iraq Bans Security Contractor," *The Washington Post* (September 18)

Peters, Charles. (1993). "Tilting at Windmills," *The Washington Monthly* (May).

———. (1994). "Tilting at Windmills," *The Washington Monthly* (November).

Rosenbloom, David H. (1971a). *Federal Equal Employment Opportunity.* New York: Praeger.

———. (1971b). *Federal Service and the Constitution.* Ithaca, NY: Cornell University Press.

Rosenbloom, David H., and Jay Shafritz. (1985). *Essentials of Labor Relations.* Reston, VA: Reston.

Shafritz, Jay M. (1973). *Position Classification: A Behavioral Analysis for the Public Service.* New York: Praeger.

———. (1975). *Personnel Management in Government: The Heritage of Civil Service Reform.* New York: Praeger.

Shafritz, Jay M., Norma Riccucci, David H. Rosenbloom, Katherine Naff, and Al Hyde. (2001). *Personnel Management in Government,* 5th ed. New York: Marcel Dekker.

Tompkins, Jonathan. (1995). *Human Resource Management in Government.* New York: HarperCollins.

Van Riper, Paul P. (1958). *History of the United States Civil Service.* Evanston, IL: Row, Peterson.

Wurf, Jerry. (1966). "Personnel Opinions," *Public Personnel Review* (January).

RECOMMENDED BOOKS

Bissinger, Buzz. (1997). *A Prayer for the City.* New York: Random House. An insider's account of Edward Rendell's first term as mayor of Philadelphia; includes an extensive account of how Rendell tamed the municipal unions and thus brought the city back from the brink of bankruptcy.

Condrey, Stephen E., and Robert Maranto, eds. (2001). *Radical Reform of the Civil Service.* Lanaham, MD: Lexington Books. A collection of assessments of current public-personnel-reinventing efforts.

Freedman, Anne. (1994). *Patronage: An American Tradition.* Chicago: Nelson-Hall. An engaging historical analysis of the rise and modest fall of political patronage, from the spoils system of the nineteenth century to the most recent Supreme Court decisions curtailing it.

Heclo, Hugh. (1977). *A Government of Strangers: Executive Politics in Washington.* Washington: Brookings Institution. The now-classic analysis of how political appointees and career executives cope with each other in the federal bureaucracy.

Kearney, Richard C. (2008). *Labor Relations in the Public Sector,* 4th ed. Boca Raton, FL: Taylor and Francis. The rules of the game in governmental collective bargaining, at all levels of government.

Mosher, Frederick C. (1982). *Democracy and the Public Service,* 2nd ed. New York: Oxford University Press. The best short history of the U.S. Public Service and the impact that an ever-increasing professionalism has had on it.

RELATED WEB SITES

www.afge.org
American Federation of Government Employees (AFGE)
AFGE is the largest federal employee union, representing 600,000 federal and Washington, D.C., government workers nationwide and overseas. The AFGE site has news, current issues, legal information, and ways to become involved in the organization. The site also maintains links to all of the federal departments where the union has workers.

www.afscme.org
American Federation of State, County, and Municipal Employees (AFSCME)
AFSCME is the nation's largest public employee union, with more than 1.6 million active and retired members. The site has news, blogs, videos, legal issues, and other information for those in the union.

www.astd.org
American Society for Training and Development (ASTD)
ASTD is dedicated to workplace learning and performance professionals. The site has information about its conferences, education programs, publications, and public policies. The site also contains the organization's online magazine, TD, which covers best practices, emerging technologies and trends, and a range of issues relevant to workplace learning professionals.

www.jobsfed.com
Federal Jobs Digest
A list of federal government employment opportunities. The site's search engine allows queries by type of employment, agency, and area of the country.

www.wfpma.com
World Federation of Personnel Management Associations (WFPMA)
The WFPMA represents more than 450,000 management professionals in over 70 national personnel associations around the world. The site has information about awards, news, research, publications and events.

Social Equity

KEYNOTE: Three Thousand Years of Sexual Harassment

Joseph, the Bible tells us, was sold into slavery by his older brothers for "twenty pieces of silver" (Genesis 37:28). Taken to Egypt by a slave merchant and sold to Potiphar, the captain of Pharaoh's guards, Joseph's talents served his master so well that Potiphar "made him overseer over his house."

Joseph, a natural administrator, was on the fast track, as slavery goes, until his career was derailed by an unfounded claim of sexual harassment. Potiphar's wife "cast her eyes upon Joseph." One day when they were alone in the house, "she caught him by his garment, saying lie with me." Joseph immediately fled, leaving "his garment in her hand."

Poor Joseph. He goes to work one day, and the next thing he knows he's running away. But where to? In those days there was no Equal Employment Opportunity Commission to whom Joseph could complain about workplace sexual harassment. Besides, slaves did not have the right to complain about anything anyway—least of all a workplace free of sexual intimidation. While it is bad enough to be harassed, it is worse to be framed and jailed—which is just what happened next to Joseph. Potiphar's wife claimed that Joseph had approached her and had run away when she cried out, leaving his garment behind as evidence. When Potiphar heard this false accusation, "his wrath was kindled." And Joseph was put into prison.

Fortunately, this particular story of sexual harassment has a happy ending. While in prison, Joseph's skills in long-range business forecasting came to the attention of the pharaoh, who needed a dream interpreted—something about seven thin cows eating seven fat cows. Joseph's warning of a coming famine so impressed Pharaoh that Joseph began his rise to the top of the Egyptian bureaucracy. It just goes to show that sometimes an ex-convict can be a very effective employee.

More than 3,000 years later, Joseph's problem with sexual harassment at work arrived on the docket of the U.S. Supreme Court. While too late to help Joseph, the Court ruled in 1986 on a similar case. In *Meritor Savings Bank v. Vinson*, sexual harassment that creates a hostile or abusive work environment, even without economic loss for the person being harassed, was declared illegal—because it was in violation of Title VII of the Civil Rights Act of 1964. (Title VII is that portion of the act that prohibits employment discrimination because of race, color, religion, sex, or national origin.)

This case sought to establish ways by which to judge whether or not sexual harassment exists in any given set of circumstances. Thus the Court held that Title VII is violated when the workplace is permeated with discriminatory behavior that is sufficiently severe or pervasive to create a discriminatorily hostile or abusive working environment. The standard laid down by the Court is that of an objectively hostile or abusive environment—one that a reasonable person would find hostile or abusive. Whether an environment is "hostile" or "abusive" can be determined only by looking at all the circumstances: the frequency of the discriminatory conduct, its severity, whether it is physically threatening or humiliating (or only an offensive utterance), and whether it unreasonably interferes with an employee's work performance. The effect on an employee's psychological well-being is also relevant in determining whether the environment is abusive.

But this standard was not detailed or clear enough to provide sufficient guidance to employers and the lower federal courts. So the Supreme Court had to expand on the 1986 standard in the 1993 case of *Harris v. Forklift Systems*. Teresa Harris worked as a manager at an equipment rental company for more than two years. Throughout Harris's time of employment, the male president of Forklift Systems often insulted her because of her gender and often made her the target of unwanted sexual innuendos. For example, he said to Harris on several occasions, in the presence of other employees, "You're a woman. What do you know?" and "We need a man as the rental manager."

Again in front of others, he suggested that the two of them "go to the Holiday Inn to negotiate [Harris's] raise." He even asked Harris and other female employees to get coins from his front pants pocket. When Harris complained about this conduct, the company president said he was surprised that Harris was offended, claimed he was only joking, and apologized. He also promised he would stop. Based on this assurance, Harris stayed on the job. But a few weeks later the problem began anew. Harris quit, and then she sued Forklift Systems, claiming that the president's conduct had created an abusive work environment for her because of her gender. The lower federal courts held that the situation had not created an abusive environment. The courts found that the comments would offend any reasonable woman but that they were not "so severe as to be expected to seriously affect [Harris's] psychological well-being."

The Supreme Court agreed to hear this case to resolve the conflict over just what constituted a "sexually abusive" work environment. Associate Justice Sandra Day O'Connor, in writing the majority opinion of the Court, asserted that Title VII's protections necessarily had to "come into play before the harassing conduct leads to a nervous breakdown." Victims do not have to prove "concrete psychological harm," only that the offending conduct "would seriously affect a reasonable person's psychological well-being." Thus the new standard holds that "so long as the environment would reasonably be perceived, and is perceived, as hostile or abusive, there is no need for it also to be psychologically injurious." In effect, there is no need to wait for it to lead "to a nervous breakdown." O'Connor concluded that "while psychological harm, like any other relevant factor, may be taken into account, no single factor is required" because this is not, and by its nature cannot be, "a mathematically precise test."

The story of Joseph may be the first recorded instance of on-the-job sexual harassment. More than three millennia later, the issue is still being debated within the courts. Progress has certainly been slow. But the quest for social equity at the office seems to be finally passing into a phase of resolution.

For Discussion: *How has it come about that the sex discrimination prohibition of the Civil Rights Act of 1964 has been applied to sexual harassment? What are the Supreme Court's rulings about the minimal obligations of employers regarding sexual harassment?*

WHAT IS SOCIAL EQUITY?

Social equity is fairness in the delivery of public services; it is egalitarianism in action—the principle that each citizen, regardless of economic resources or personal traits, deserves and has a right to be given equal treatment by the political system. Even though the United States has not lived up to this ideal, and has not provided equality to all its men and women throughout its history, it has nevertheless been constantly moving in that direction. Political theorist Jean-Jacques Rousseau warned in *The Social Contract* (1762), "It is precisely because the force of circumstances tends always to destroy equality that the force of legislation must always tend to maintain it." The United States has a long tradition of using legislation to mitigate the "force of circumstances" that so often inhibits equality. For example, in the early nineteenth century, free public schools made education gradually available to all classes. In 1862 the Homestead Act made it possible for any citizen to own 160 acres of public land if he or she would live on it for five years. The Civil War of 1861–1865 can be viewed alternatively as conflict over the nature of intergovernmental relations or a moral crusade to bring "equality" to those in bondage. The twentieth century witnessed an outpouring of legislation that gave new rights to workers, women, and minorities. This has gone so far that social equity, in addition to efficiency, is now a major criterion for evaluating the desirability of any public policy or program.

Government organizations have a special obligation to be fair—to pursue social equity both with their employees and the public—because they represent the citizenry. This is in distinct contrast to business organizations, which represent private interests such as stockholders. It is often asserted that corporations have a social responsibility, that they have a moral and ethical duty to contribute to society's well-being—obligations far beyond just seeking a profit in a legal manner. But others, such as economist Milton Friedman, feel that the resolution of social problems is the task of governments, not businesses, and that managers who spend money to alleviate social problems act irresponsibly.

Mandating Social Equity

There's a long tradition of government forcing private organizations to better treat their employees. Better treatment was inhibited by social Darwinism, Charles Darwin's (1809–1882) concept of biological evolution applied by others to the development of human social organization and economic policy. American social Darwinism applied Darwin's concepts of "natural selection" and "survival of the fittest" to society in general. Thus practices such as child labor, the employment of children in a manner detrimental to their health and social development, were justified. Efforts by the labor movement and social reformers to prevent the exploitation of children in the workplace date back well into the nineteenth century. As early as 1842, Connecticut and Massachusetts legislated a maximum 10-hour workday for children. In 1848, Pennsylvania established a minimum working age of 12 years for factory jobs. But it would be 20 more years before any state had inspectors to enforce child labor laws. And it would not be until the late 1930s that federal laws would outlaw child labor (mainly through the Fair Labor Standards Act of 1938). The practice was so entrenched that earlier federal attempts to outlaw child labor were construed by the Supreme Court as being unconstitutional infringements on the power of the states to regulate conditions in the workplace. So achieving social equity for children was an uphill battle that lasted more than a century because, in large measure, of the social Darwinist belief that the "fit" children would survive and that this was all part of a normal process of "natural selection."

Child labor is just one example of how government regulation has been used to further social equity. The whole thrust of the labor and women's movements that began in the nineteenth century and the post–World War II civil rights movement was to obtain legislation that would equalize the employment and social prospects of unions, women, and minority group members. The fine-tuning of those public policies is an ongoing process. The Supreme Court cases discussed in the keynote dealt with sexual harassment, a variant of sexual discrimination. While it is impossible to predict future cases, it seems certain that the Court will be ruling on the subject well into this century. The quest for social equity is never-ending. While legislation seeks to cope with gross abuses, the subtleties are left to the courts.

The New Public Administration

By the late 1960s, serious questions were being raised concerning the state of the discipline and profession of public administration. Dwight Waldo, having noted that public administration was "in a time of revolution," called a conference of younger academics in public administration, through the auspices of his position as editor-in-chief of *Public Administration Review* and with funds from the Maxwell School of Syracuse University. Held in 1968 at Syracuse University's Minnowbrook conference site, the event produced papers that were edited by Frank Marini, then managing editor of *Public Administration Review,* and published in 1971 under the title *Toward a New Public Administration: The Minnowbrook Perspective.* The goal of the meeting was to identify what was relevant about public administration and how the discipline had to change to meet the challenges of the 1970s. H. George Frederickson, now a professor at the University of Kansas, contributed a paper, "Toward a New Public Administration," which called for social equity in the performance and delivery of public services.

Frederickson's new public administration called for a proactive administrator with a burning desire for social equity to replace the traditional, impersonal, neutral, gun-for-hire bureaucrat. While this call was heeded by few, it was discussed by many. The basic problem with the new public administration's call for social equity was that it was also a call for insubordination—something that is not lightly tolerated in bureaucracies. Victor Thompson immediately attacked the new public administration movement in his aptly titled *Without Sympathy or Enthusiasm* as an effort by left-wing radicals to "steal the popular sovereignty."

Thompson need not have worried. All these "radicals" did was talk—and write. From the 1970s to the present day, and still led by Frederickson, they have produced an endless stream of conference papers and scholarly articles urging public administrators to show a greater sensitivity to the forces of change, the needs of clients, and the problem of social equity in service delivery. This has had a positive effect in that now the ethical and equitable treatment of citizens by administrators is at the forefront of concerns in public agencies. Reinforced by changing public attitudes, the reinventing-government movement, and civil rights laws, the new public administration has triumphed after a quarter century. Now it is unthinkable (as well as illegal), for example, to deny someone welfare benefits because of his or her race or a job opportunity because of his or her sex. Social equity today does not have to be so much fought for by young radicals as administrated by managers of all ages.

Victor Thompson (1912–) ∎
One of the most gifted stylists in the literature of public administration. Thompson is best known for dealing deftly with bureaucratic interactions and dysfunctions. In his most influential work, *Modern Organization,* he reminds us that "one must not forget that clients are notoriously insensitive to the needs of bureaucrats."

THE CHALLENGE OF EQUALITY

Equality is an American ideal. In 1776 the Declaration of Independence proclaimed that "all men are created equal, that they are endowed by their Creator with certain unalienable rights." These are rights derived from natural law, which all people have and which cannot be taken away or transferred. Yet the Declaration as well as the subsequent Constitution denied these rights to a large group of residents. Because the Constitution was initially oblivious to the plight of African Americans, Supreme Court Associate Justice **Thurgood Marshall** pointedly rejected the view that Americans should celebrate the Constitution as the source of all that is good in the nation. On the contrary, he said of the founders that "the government they devised was defective from the start, requiring several amendments, a civil

Thurgood Marshall (1908–1993) ∎
The civil rights lawyer who successfully argued the *Brown v. Board of Education* case before the Supreme Court and who in 1967 was appointed by President Lyndon B. Johnson to be the first African American member of that court.

war, and momentous social transformation to attain the system of constitutional government, and its respect for individual freedoms and human rights, we hold as fundamental today." Marshall's harsh rhetoric notwithstanding, all discussions of equality in the United States must begin with the issue of race.

Racism

Race can be defined as a large group of people with common characteristics presumed to be transmitted genetically. Which characteristics are properly included has been a subject of debate. They range from physical characteristics that are immediately observable, such as color of hair, skin, and eyes, to the subtler aspects of emotions and aptitudes. Some races even have genetic susceptibility to certain diseases or physical disorders. Rational people of all races are often uncomfortable talking about race. There is a depth of feeling about past injustices that is dangerous to bring to the surface in polite conversation. Yet no subject is more important in administering the public affairs of a multiracial society. The issues must be faced and discussed even if they cannot be immediately resolved.

Up to the middle of the twentieth century, race was used as a way of distinguishing among national groups. This practice is traceable to eighteenth-century distinctions among people according to language. It became a method of attempting to define a hierarchy of races, with the so-called Anglo-Saxons at the top and others arranged along supposedly developmental lines. In recent times, in American political language, race has come to designate issues or attitudes concerning citizens of African origin. Other minority groups are called *ethnics*. Originally, the term applied only to European ethnics. The term is now more likely to refer to the new ethnics, both those who have long been here and those who are more recent arrivals—for example, the Hispanics and the Vietnamese. Technically, every American except for white Anglo-Saxon Protestants is a member of an ethnic group. And now that they are in the minority, many of them have begun to claim that they are an ethnic group, too. A politician may be said to be practicing ethnic politics when he tells his Irish constituents of his support for a united Ireland, his Jewish constituents of his support for a strong state of Israel, and his Hispanic constituents of his strong support for bilingual education. Ethnic politics does not have to be substantive; sometimes it is nothing more than a "photo opportunity" of the politician eating ethnic food or attending an ethnic cultural festival or wedding.

A racist can be defined as any person or organization that either consciously or unconsciously practices racial **discrimination** against a person on the basis of race (or ethnicity) or supports the supremacy of one race over others. The most notorious of American racist groups has been the **Ku Klux Klan (KKK)**. But anyone who is insensitive to the feelings of racial minorities and uses racially demeaning language or diction out of genuine ignorance may also be considered racist. Such people might deny they are racist; however, offended minority groups might still perceive them to be so. This is especially true with what is known as stealth racism— racist acts readily apparent to African Americans but virtually invisible to whites. Well-to-do middle-class nonwhites are routinely kept under greater surveillance at shopping places, find it difficult to get taxis, are automatically presumed to be dangerous, and are given unequal service in restaurants and airports. Such lack of

Discrimination ■
Bigotry in practice; intolerance toward those who are of different races or have different religious beliefs.

Ku Klux Klan (KKK) ■
The most infamous U.S. terrorist organization; a racist white supremacist group established in the South following the Civil War. The KKK has a long history of intimidation, beatings, and murders of blacks, as well as other racial and religious minorities. Early in the twentieth century, the KKK had considerable political power; it dominated politics in a dozen states. Today, the KKK has only the slightest influence; it has traveled from the mainstream to the lunatic fringe.

respect, such affronts to honor, are difficult to deal with by legislation. The Civil Rights Act of 1964 mandated equal access to expensive hotels and restaurants. But it still hurts when an African American guest dressed in a tuxedo is mistaken for a waiter or the valet parking attendant. That's stealth racism.

What distinguishes African Americans from other ethnic Americans is not so much their color—many other groups are nonwhite—but their ancestors, who came to the United States not as the "huddled masses yearning to breathe free," as is engraved on the pedestal of the Statue of Liberty, but as slaves. And slavery has uniquely colored the African American experience to the present day.

The Bitter Heritage of Slavery

Slavery, which began in colonial times, was addressed, albeit obliquely, in various parts of the Constitution. Article I, Section 2, stated that slaves are to be counted for purposes of congressional appointments as "three-fifths" of a person. Article I, Section 9, stated that Congress could not pass any law banning the importation of slaves until 1808 (which it did). Article IV, Section 2, said that persons "held in service"—meaning runaway slaves—who escaped had to be returned. This was upheld by the *Dred Scott v. Sandford* decision of the Supreme Court.

Abraham Lincoln was, even before he became president, the most eloquent spokesman against slavery. He told the Illinois Republican State Convention on June 16, 1858, "'A house divided against itself cannot stand' [the Bible, Mark 3:25]. I believe this government cannot endure, permanently half slave and half free. I do not expect the Union to be dissolved—I do not expect the house to fall—but I do expect it will cease to be divided. It will become all one thing, or all the other." He was right.

In September 1862, President Abraham Lincoln, acting as commander in chief during a time of war, issued the Emancipation Proclamation, which became effective on January 1, 1863. The proclamation declared that all people held in slavery "are, and henceforth shall be, free; and the executive government of the United States, including the military and naval authorities thereof, will recognize and maintain the freedom." The Thirteenth Amendment was passed in 1865 to quell the controversy over the constitutionality of the Emancipation Proclamation and to settle the issue of slavery in the United States forever.

The history of slavery in the United States is still relevant today because it is the underlying basis for African American claims for special treatment. Some argue that reparations are due and point to the Civil Liberties Act of 1988. This law authorized the payment of $20,000 to all living Japanese Americans who were interned by the U.S. government during World War II. The act authorized a total of $1.25 billion in reparations payments. Of the 120,000 Japanese Americans who were interned, about 70,000 were still alive when the act was passed. But these payments to Japanese Americans went to the still-living victims. There are no direct victims of slavery still living. There is not much sympathy for reparation for slavery when most Americans are not descendants of slave owners but descendants of people who came to the United States after the Civil War—often with little more than the clothes on their backs. Still, the unfinished business of mitigating the heritage of slavery led to the second reconstruction.

Dred Scott v. Sandford **(1857)** ■ The second case in which the U.S. Supreme Court declared an act of the Congress (the Missouri Compromise) to be unconstitutional (the first was *Marbury v. Madison* in 1803). Dred Scott (1795–1858) was a slave who was taken to a free state in the North. The question before the Court was whether residence in a free state was sufficient basis for declaring Scott a free man. The Supreme Court in a 7-to-2 ruling said no. The chief justice, Roger Brook Taney, wrote in the Court's opinion, "The right of property in a slave is distinctly and expressly affirmed in the Constitution . . . ." While it helped to further entrench the Court's right to judicial review, the Court's holdings—that blacks could not become citizens and that the United States could not prohibit slavery in unsettled territories—did much to make the Civil War inevitable, especially because the decision made a legislative solution to the slavery issue virtually impossible.

From Reconstruction to Second Reconstruction

While the Thirteenth, Fourteenth, and Fifteenth Amendments attempted to settle the issues of slavery and civil rights, the issue of the former slaves remained. After Reconstruction many states enacted Jim Crow laws, which effectively made African Americans second-class citizens.

This second-class status was supported by the Supreme Court in the separate but equal doctrine. In *Plessy v. Ferguson* (1896), the Court held that segregated railroad facilities for African Americans, facilities that were considered equal in quality to those provided for whites, did not violate the equal protection clause of the Fourteenth Amendment. In a dissenting opinion Justice John Marshall Harlan wrote, "We boast of the freedom enjoyed by our people. . . . But it is difficult to reconcile that boast with a state of the law which, practically, puts the brand of servitude and degradation on a large class of our fellow citizens, our equals before the law. The thin disguise of 'equal' accommodations for passengers in the railroad coaches will not mislead anyone, or atone for the wrong this day done."

More than half a century later the Court overturned the *Plessy* decision and nullified this doctrine when it asserted that separate was "inherently unequal." In *Brown v. Board of Education of Topeka, Kansas* (1954), the Court decided that the separation of children by race and according to law in public schools "generates a feeling of inferiority as to their [the minority group's] status in the community that may affect their hearts and minds in a way unlikely ever to be undone." Consequently, it held that "separate educational facilities are inherently unequal" and therefore violate the equal protection clause of the Fourteenth Amendment. According to Chief Justice Earl Warren, "We come then to the question presented: Does segregation of children in public schools solely on the basis of race, even though the physical facilities and other 'tangible' factors may be equal, deprive the children of the minority group of equal educational opportunities? We believe that it does."

This decision, one of the most significant in the century, helped create the environment that would lead to the second reconstruction: the civil rights movement and legislation of the 1960s. The first reconstruction, immediately after the Civil War, gave African Americans their freedom from slavery. But the laws as enforced and customs as practiced did not allow for the full rights of citizens. That came in the 1960s, when public sentiment was aroused and legal action was taken to ensure equal rights for all Americans.

An Administrative Fix for Racism

The problem with the second reconstruction, with its outpouring of equal employment opportunity and civil rights legislation, was that the government formally got into the business of examining people's blood lines. Official race categories were established by the Equal Employment Opportunity Commission (EEOC), which had been created by the Civil Rights Act of 1964. The South once had miscegenation laws, declared unconstitutional in *Loving v. Virginia* (1967). Miscegenation laws meant that if one of your ancestors was African, you could not marry someone whose ancestors were all European. Now, in a reversal of fortune, if one of your ancestors is African, you are entitled, under affirmative action provisions of equal opportunity laws, to preferential treatment in employment.

Reconstruction ■
The post–Civil War period when the South was divided into military districts and the states that were formerly part of the Confederacy were brought back into the Union. The official end of Reconstruction was 1876, when the last federal troops were withdrawn.

Jim Crow ■
A name given to any law requiring the segregation of the races. All such statutes are now unconstitutional. But prior to the Civil Rights Act of 1964, many southern states had laws requiring separate drinking fountains, separate rest rooms, separate sections of theaters, and so on.

Second-class citizen ■
A person who does not have all of the civil rights of other citizens. Historically, African Americans were called, and because of segregation and discrimination often considered themselves to be, second-class citizens. But since the civil rights movement and the new laws that flowed from it, there can be no second-class citizens in the United States. Nevertheless, the phrase is still used in various contexts.

BOX 12.1 | What *Plessy* Did

What made the "separate but equal" doctrine particularly insidious was the fact that it derived not just from custom and the Jim Crow laws (laws requiring racial segregation) of the South; it was famously promulgated by the U.S. Supreme Court. In *Plessy v. Ferguson* (1896) the Court held that segregated railroad facilities for African Americans, facilities that were considered equal in quality to those provided for whites, were legal. This case didn't just happen. Homer Plessy, at the time a 30-year-old shoemaker from New Orleans, volunteered to test an 1890 Louisiana law providing for "equal but separate accommodations for the white and colored races" on railroads. So on June 7, 1892, Plessy bought a first-class ticket on the East Louisiana Railway. Plessy was so white looking (he only had one black great-grandparent) that he had to inform the train conductor that he was "a colored man." As expected, the conductor then asked him to transfer to the "colored" car. When Plessy refused, in one of American history's first sit-ins, he was duly arrested for crimes "against the peace and dignity of the state."

Four years later Plessy's case reached the Supreme Court. His lawyers urged the Court to reject the "equal but separate" law because it violated the equal protection clause of the Fourteenth Amendment. But the Court saw no such violation.

The majority opinion stated that "the object of the [Fourteenth] amendment was undoubtedly to enforce the absolute equality of the two races before the law, but in the nature of things it could not have been intended to abolish distinctions based upon color, or to enforce social, as distinguished from political, equality"

The Court felt that reasonableness was the essence of the case:

> the case reduces itself to the question whether the statute of Louisiana is a reasonable regulation. . . . Gauged by this standard, we cannot say that a law which authorizes or even requires the separation of the two races in public conveyances is unreasonable. . . .

The Court even denied the plaintiff's "assumption that the enforced separation of the two races stamps the colored race with a badge of inferiority. If this be so, it is not by reason of anything found in the act, but solely because the colored race chooses to put that construction upon it." The *Plessy* case was a disaster for civil rights. Instead of striking down a Jim Crow law in one state, it allowed the Supreme Court to formally sanction the doctrine. This made it easier for race-based legislation to be expanded and sustained. *Plessy* put the stamp of inferiority on every American of African descent. ▲

The Supreme Court has also recognized additional race categories that are protected by the federal civil rights laws. In *Shaare Tefila Congregation v. Cobb* (1987), it held that Jews could bring charges of racial discrimination against defendants who were also considered Caucasian. And in *Saint Francis College v. Al-Khazraji* (1987), it held that someone of Arabian ancestry was protected from racial discrimination under the various civil rights statutes.

In addition to employment advantages, recognized minority group members have been granted set-asides—government purchasing and contracting provisions that set aside or allocate a certain percentage of business for minority-owned or female-owned companies. The use of set-asides was upheld by the Supreme Court in *Fullilove v. Klutznick* and *Metro Broadcasting v. FCC* but restricted in *City of Richmond v. J. A. Croson* and *Adarand Constructors v. Pena*.

Fullilove v. Klutznick (1980) ■ The Supreme Court case holding that Congress has the authority to use quotas to remedy past discrimination in government public works programs.

Metro Broadcasting v. FCC (1990) ■
The Supreme Court case holding that the Federal Communications Commission could use "benign race-conscious measures" to increase minority ownership of broadcast licenses.

City of Richmond v. J. A. Croson (1989) ■
The Supreme Court case holding that a minority set-aside program designed so that 30 percent of city construction contacts went to minority-owned firms was too rigid.

EQUAL EMPLOYMENT OPPORTUNITY

Equal employment opportunity (EEO) is a concept fraught with political, cultural, and emotional overtones. Generally, it applies to a set of employment procedures and practices that effectively prevent any individual from being adversely excluded from employment opportunities on the basis of race, color, sex, religion, age, national origin, or other factors that cannot lawfully be considered in employing people. While the ideal of EEO is an employment system devoid of both intentional and unintentional discrimination, achieving this ideal may be a political impossibility because of the problem of definition. One person's equal opportunity may be another's institutional racism or institutional sexism. Because of this problem of definition, only the courts have been able to say if, when, and where EEO exists.

Nevertheless, it must always be remembered that EEO laws and programs were created to remedy very real problems of bigotry and sexism—problems that are still with us today. The word that summarizes workplace intolerance toward those who are different is *discrimination*. In employment, this is the failure to treat equals equally. Whether deliberate or unintentional, any action that has the effect of limiting employment and advancement opportunities because of an individual's sex, race, color, age, national origin, religion, physical handicap, or other irrelevant criteria, is discrimination—and illegal.

Origins of Affirmative Action

It was not until the Kennedy administration that EEO became a central aspect of public personnel administration. Between 1961 and 1965, the civil rights movement reached the pinnacle of its political importance and became a dominant national issue. Indeed, it was a sign of the times when Kennedy declared, "I have dedicated my administration to the cause of equal opportunity in employment by the government." His Executive Order 10925 of March 6, 1961, for the first time

---

BOX 12.2 | Race and Ethnic Identifications Approved by the U.S. Equal Employment Opportunity Commission

Hispanic or Latino—A person of Cuban, Mexican, Puerto Rican, South or Central American, or other Spanish culture or origin regardless of race.

White (Not Hispanic or Latino)—A person having origins in any of the original peoples of Europe, the Middle East, or North Africa.

Black or African American (Not Hispanic or Latino)—A person having origins in any of the black racial groups of Africa.

Native Hawaiian or Other Pacific Islander (Not Hispanic or Latino)—A person having origins in any of the peoples of Hawaii, Guam, Samoa, or other Pacific Islands.

Asian (Not Hispanic or Latino)—A person having origins in any of the original peoples of the Far East, Southeast Asia, or the Indian Subcontinent, including, for example, Cambodia, China, India, Japan, Korea, Malaysia, Pakistan, the Philippine Islands, Thailand, and Vietnam.

American Indian or Alaska Native (Not Hispanic or Latino)—A person having origins in any of the original peoples of North and South America (including Central America), and who maintain tribal affiliation or community attachment. ▲

required that "affirmative action" be used to implement the policy of nondiscrimination in employment by the federal government and its contractors.

Affirmative action first meant the removal of "artificial barriers" to the employment of women and minority group members. Special efforts were made to bring more members of minority groups into the federal service. These included recruitment drives at high schools and colleges heavily attended by minorities. Agencies were encouraged to provide better training opportunities for minority group members.

The Kennedy program was carried forward and expanded by the Johnson administration. The Civil Rights Act of 1964 declared that "it shall be the policy of the United States to ensure equal employment opportunities for Federal employees." It also created the Equal Employment Opportunity Commission (EEOC) to

***Adarand Constructors v. Pena* (1995)** ■
The Supreme Court case holding that set-asides could only be used when a minority group has suffered actual discrimination.

Is This the End of Affirmative Action?
President Barack Obama took his oath of office January 20, 2009. With the accession of an African American to the highest office in the land many voices said that racial discrimination is dead. After all, he received the votes of a clear majority of those who voted in the presidential election. If he could rise to such heights, then all other African Americans had similar opportunities for achievement. Not so fast, many others declare. Obama was born half black, but was raised by whites. Both of his parents earned Ph.D.s. He graduated from the best prep school in Hawaii, then from Columbia University and Harvard Law School. He had a great start in life and made the most of it. His "head start," so to speak, was so great that early in his presidential campaign black critics complained that he wasn't black enough, that he hadn't truly shared the post-slavery experience of other African Americans. It's these citizens, many argue, who still need the advantage of affirmative action to compensate for the historic discrimination they and their families suffered. Obama's election, while a landmark event, only marginally changes the facts on the ground for most of his fellow African Americans. How true is this?

Goals ■

Realistic objectives that an organization endeavors to achieve through affirmative action. Quotas, in contrast, restrict employment or development opportunities to members of particular groups by establishing a required number or proportionate representation, which managers are obligated to attain, without regard to equal employment opportunity. To be meaningful, any program of goals or quotas must be associated with a specific timetable—a schedule of when the goals or quotas are to be achieved.

EEO plan ■

An organization's written plan to remedy past discrimination against, or underutilization of, women and minorities. The plan itself usually consists of a statement of goals, timetables for achieving them, and specific program efforts.

combat discrimination in the private sphere. The coordination of all equal employment activities for federal employees was assigned to the Civil Service Commission.

The continuing rationale for government-sanctioned affirmative action programs was provided by President Lyndon Johnson in a June 4, 1965, speech at Howard University: "You do not take a person who, for years, has been hobbled by chains and liberate him, bring him up to the starting line of a race and then say, 'You are free to compete with the others' and still justly believe you have been completely fair."

The next major development in the evolution of the EEO program came in 1969, when President Nixon issued an executive order requiring agency heads to "establish and maintain an affirmative program of equal employment opportunity." It was also during the Nixon administration, when the federal courts associated affirmative action with specific **goals** and timetables for minority hiring, that the term was altered to include compensatory opportunities for hitherto disadvantaged groups.

The Equal Employment Opportunity Act of 1972 solidified the Civil Service Commission's authority in this area and placed the program on a solid statutory basis for the first time. It reaffirmed the traditional policy of nondiscrimination and empowered the commission to enforce its provisions "through appropriate remedies, including reinstatement or hiring of employees with or without back pay . . . and issuing such rules, regulations, orders, and instructions as it deems necessary and appropriate." It also made the commission responsible for the annual review and approval of agency **EEO plans** and for evaluating agency EEO activities. The act also brought state and local governments under the federal EEO umbrella for the first time. The EEOC, hitherto primarily concerned with the private sector, was given equal authority over the nonfederal public sector. In 1979, as part of the overall federal civil service reforms then taking place (see Chapter 11), the enforcement aspects of the federal EEO program were transferred to the EEOC. So after starting out with enforcement authority over just the private sector in 1964, the EEOC by 1979 had been given responsibility for enforcing equal employment opportunity at all levels of government as well.

The Case for Affirmative Action

The case for affirmative action, for special efforts to recruit and advance minorities and women in employment, has always been based on statistics. According to

TABLE 12.1

Median Weekly Earnings by Race and Gender

	Men	Women
All Races	$825	$689
White	$850	$705
Black	$673	$592
Hispanic	$586	$524
Asian	$972	$748

Source: U.S. Bureau of the Census and Bureau of Labor Statistics, *Annual Demographic Survey* (2011). http://www.bls.gov/news.release/pdf/wkyeng.pdf.

the Bureau of the Census, white college graduate males earned about $72,000 in 2006. But black and Hispanic males with the same education earned 30 percent less. Even among high school graduates, black men earned 25 percent less than whites. These economic disparities in income carry over into rates of home ownership. In 2002 the national rate for home ownership was 68 percent, but for blacks it was 48 percent (up from 42 percent in 1990).

These disparities exist because of continuing patterns of discrimination that are easily traced back to the days of slavery. The only way to overcome and get beyond the adverse impact of systemic discrimination is to implement a vigorous affirmative action program. To repeal affirmative action and force minorities to compete on the proverbial "level playing field" would only perpetuate the existing patterns of discrimination.

Affirmative action offers advantages that go beyond its immediate beneficiaries. As civil rights activist Roger Wilkins wrote, "Racist and sexist whites who are not able to accept the full humanity of other people are themselves badly damaged—morally stunted—people." They, too, are victims of racism and sexism—even if it is their own. Affirmative action programs that bring them into contact with a more diverse group of associates will help liberate them from their own ignorance. They can go from being "morally stunted" to morally elevated.

And the same that can be said of people can be said of organizations. The less damaged they are by racism and sexism, the more productive they will be. This is the effect of diversity management—directing the work of a racially and culturally heterogeneous group of employees to bring a more varied set of perspectives to organizational problems. This variety can translate into greater productivity. Concerns for diversity that started as part of EEO programs are now less a matter of social equity than organizational survival. The simple demographic fact is that whites will be a continuously decreasing part of the national workforce. For large organizations, the future can be summed up in three words: "Diversify or die!"

The Case Against Affirmative Action

The case against affirmative action can be stated very simply: It is unfair. It negates Dr. Martin Luther King's "dream that my four little children will one day live in a nation where they will not be judged by the color of their skin, but by the content of their character." Well-meaning opponents of affirmative action (as opposed to lunatic fringe racists) favor equal employment opportunity. They hold that race or sexual discrimination is wrong no matter who does it. Racial and sexual preferences in hiring women, blacks, or other ethnic minorities are not only inherently discriminatory, but they are also in violation of the Civil Rights Act of 1964, which prohibits discrimination against anybody—even whites.

Despite its best intentions, affirmative action programs have had the effect of stigmatizing minority workers as those who got their jobs not because of their intrinsic merit but because of pressure to fill a formal or informal quota. Thus such programs damage both the self-confidence and self-image of their beneficiaries while creating resentment among those denied such employment opportunities. Minorities who advocate affirmative action are essentially saying, critics charge, that they cannot compete on merit.

Adverse impact ■
When a selection process for a particular job or group of jobs results in the selection of members of any racial, ethnic, or gender group at a lower rate than members of other groups, that process is said to have adverse impact. Federal EEO enforcement agencies generally regard a selection rate for any group that is less than four-fifths, or 80 percent, of the rate for other groups as constituting evidence of adverse impact.

Systemic discrimination ■
Use of employment practices (recruiting methods, selection tests, promotion policies, etc.) that have the unintended effect of excluding or limiting the employment prospects of protected-class persons. Because of court interpretations of Title VII of the Civil Rights Act of 1964, all such systemic discrimination, despite its "innocence," must be eliminated where it cannot be shown that such action would place an unreasonable burden on the employer or that such practices cannot be replaced by other practices that would not have such an adverse effect.

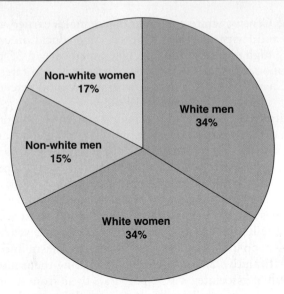

FIGURE 12.1

A numerical argument for diversity: The U.S. workforce in 2009

Source: U.S. Bureau of Labor Statistics (2010).

Finally, opponents of affirmative action argue that if compensatory benefits are to be provided, they should be based on class, not race. Why should a child from a black professional family making more than $100,000 a year be given special educational and employment opportunities when there is greater need for such opportunities in the case of a child from a poor white family with an income close to the national median? Besides, class-based preferences could gain the widespread political support that affirmative action now seems to lack.

Representative Bureaucracy

In 1944 J. Donald Kingsley, coauthor of the first full-scale text on public personnel administration, had published his historical analysis, *Representative Bureaucracy: An Interpretation of the British Civil Service.* In 1967 Samuel Krislov, a constitutional law scholar, expanded on Kingsley's concept of a governing bureaucracy made up of representative elements from the population being ruled. In *The Negro in Federal Employment,* Krislov examined the advantages of "representation in the sense of personification" and thereby gave a name to the goal for the movement for the fullest expression of civil rights in government employment—representative bureaucracy.

In a subsequent work in 1974, also entitled *Representative Bureaucracy,* Krislov explored the issues of merit systems, personnel selection, and social equity. Krislov asked more directly, how could any bureaucracy have legitimacy and public credibility if it did not represent all sectors of its society? So, thanks in large part to Krislov, the term *representative bureaucracy* grew to mean that all social groups have a right to participation in their governing institutions. In recent years, the concept has developed a normative overlay—that all social groups should occupy bureaucratic positions in direct proportion to their numbers in the general population. Today, representative bureaucracy is commonly used as a shorthand phrase for the ultimate goal of equal employment opportunity and affirmative action programs.

Reverse Discrimination

Reverse discrimination is a practice generally understood to mean discrimination against white males in conjunction with preferential treatment for women and minorities. The practice had no legal standing in civil rights laws. Indeed, Section 703(j) of Title VII of the Civil Rights Act of 1964 holds that nothing in the title shall be interpreted to permit any employer to "grant preferential treatment to any individual or group on the basis of race, color, religion, sex, or national origin." Yet affirmative action programs necessarily put some white males at a disadvantage that they would not have otherwise had. Reverse discrimination is usually most keenly perceived when affirmative action policies conflict with older policies of granting preferments on the basis of seniority, test scores, and so on.

The practice of reverse discrimination was finally given legal standing when the U.S. Supreme Court, in *Johnson v. Santa Clara County* (1987), upheld an affirmative action plan that promoted a woman ahead of an objectively more qualified man. Critics contended that this turned Title VII's requirement that there be no "preferential treatment" upside down because for the first time the Court sanctioned and gave legal standing to reverse discrimination. This was not illegal sex discrimination because Paul Johnson was not actually harmed. The Court reasoned that he "had no absolute entitlement to the road dispatcher position. Seven of the applicants were classified as qualified and eligible, and the Agency Director was authorized to promote any of the seven. Thus, the denial of the promotion unsettled no legitimate firmly rooted expectation on the part of [Johnson]." While Johnson was denied a promotion, he remained employed with the same salary and seniority, and he remained eligible for other promotions.

Race has always been a hot issue in American politics. But affirmative action policies were tolerated, if not actually supported, by most of the public until a sea change in public opinion began to occur in 1990. That was the year that Republican Senator Jesse Helms of North Carolina, running for reelection against Harvey Gantt, the black mayor of Charlotte, used a notorious television commercial in the last week of the campaign. Over a pair of white hands crumpling a job rejection letter, a voice announced, "You needed that job, and you were the best qualified, but it had to go to a minority because of a racial quota." Helms, who was well behind in the polls, then decisively won reelection.

Affirmative action is a wedge issue—it drives people apart. Since the 1980s, the Republicans have been quite astute in using the wedge. They branded the Democratic Party the champion of special privileges for minorities. This wedge deserves much of the credit for driving traditionally Democratic blue-collar voters into the political arms of the Republicans.

The raw political fact is that affirmative action has lost the support of whites. According to a 2009 *Quinnipiac University* poll, 64 percent of whites oppose it. When a vast majority of citizens are opposed to reverse discrimination (which to many is just another term for affirmative action), it is absurd to brand them all as

TABLE 12.2

Affirmative Action: A Chronology

1941   President Franklin D. Roosevelt issues Executive Order 8802, which (1) required that defense contractors not discriminate against any worker because of race, creed, or national origin, and (2) established a Committee on Fair Employment Practice to investigate and remedy violations.

1944   J. Donald Kingsley's *Representative Bureaucracy* develops the concept that all social groups have a right to participate in their governing institutions in proportion to their numbers in the population.

1948   President Harry S. Truman issues Executive Order 9981, which mandated the racial integration of the military and naval forces of the United States and called for an end to racial discrimination in all federal employment.

1961   President John F. Kennedy issues Executive Order 10925, which for the first time required that "affirmative action" be used to implement the policy of nondiscrimination in employment by the federal government and its contractors.

1964   The Civil Rights Act prohibits discrimination on the basis of race, color, religion, sex, or national origin in most private sector employment; creates the Equal Employment Opportunity Commission for enforcement.

1965   President Lyndon B. Johnson issues Executive Order 11246, which required federal government contractors to have affirmative action programs.

1969   President Richard M. Nixon's "Philadelphia Plan" imposes affirmative action quotas on federal building contractors in Philadelphia.

1971   The Supreme Court attacks restrictive credentialism when in *Griggs v. Duke Power Company* it rules that Title VII of the Civil Rights Act of 1964 "proscribes not only overt discrimination but also practices that are discriminatory in operation"; thus, if an employment practice operating to exclude minorities "cannot be shown to be related to job performance, the practice is prohibited."

1972   The Equal Employment Opportunity Act amends Title VII of the Civil Rights Act to include prohibitions on discrimination by public sector employers.

1978   The Supreme Court in *Regents of the University of California v. Bakke* rules that a white male applicant denied admission to medical school in favor of minorities with lesser objective credentials was discriminated against and had to be admitted; but at the same time the Court holds that race was a factor that could be taken into account in admissions decisions.

1979   The Supreme Court in *United Steelworkers of America v. Weber* upholds an affirmative action program giving blacks preference in selection of employees for a training program.

1980   The Supreme Court in *Fullilove v. Klutznick* (1980) holds that Congress has the authority to use quotas to remedy past discrimination in government public works programs.

1984   The Supreme Court in *Fire Fighters Local Union No. 1784 v. Stotts* rules that courts may not interfere with seniority systems to protect newly hired minority employees from layoff.

1987   The practice of reverse discrimination was finally given legal standing when the U.S. Supreme Court, in *Johnson v. Santa Clara County*, upholds an affirmative action plan that promoted a woman ahead of an objectively more qualified man.

1989   The Supreme Court in *Wards Cove Packing v. Antonio* puts the burden of proof on the plaintiff in equal employment opportunity cases.

1991   The Civil Rights Act of 1991 overturns the *Wards Cove* decision.

1995   In reaffirming his administration's support for affirmative action, President Bill Clinton asserts that "affirmative action should not go on forever."

TABLE 12.2 (Continued)	

Affirmative Action: A Chronology

1996	The state of California repeals affirmative action by ballot initiative.
1998	The state of Washington repeals affirmative action by ballot initiative.
2003	The Supreme Court in two cases involving the University of Michigan reaffirms taking race into account in admissions decisions (*Grutter v. Bollinger* and *Gratz v. Bollinger*) but disallows automatic point systems in *Gratz*.
2007	The Supreme Court rules against considering race to integrate schools in *Parents v. Seattle* and *Meredith v. Jefferson*.
2008	The state of Nebraska passes a ban on affirmative action through ballot initiative. The state of Colorado rejects the proposed ballot initiative to repeal affirmative action.
2009	The Supreme Court strikes down a New Haven, Connecticut, decision to throw out a firefighter test that promoted too few minorities in *Ricci v. DeStefano*.

racists. True, opposition to affirmative action is a credo of racism. But most who oppose it are not racists; they simply believe that the present EEO program does not further equality, that it will ultimately be found to be unconstitutional, and that while it was once needed to jump-start black Americans into the economic mainstream, it now—on the whole—does more harm than good.

Justifying Diversity

The legal rationale for affirmative action—in effect, reverse discrimination—was to provide a remedy for past practices of discrimination. But how do you justify the continuation of such remedies when the practices they were designed to remedy were increasingly long in the past? This is the question that confronted the Supreme Court in 2003 in two cases concerning the University of Michigan.

In *Grutter v. Bollinger*, the Court agreed that the University of Michigan Law School could continue to give advantages to minority applicants for admission. But the justification for such preferences was not to remedy past practices of discrimination but to further diversify for its own sake. The majority opinion written by Justice Sandra Day O'Connor held that the Constitution "does not prohibit the law school's narrowly tailored use of race in admissions decisions to further a compelling interest in obtaining the educational benefits that flow from a diverse student body." In this 5-to-4 decision, the Court asserted that "effective participation by members of all racial and ethnic groups in the civic life of our nation is essential if the dream of one nation, indivisible, is to be realized." Justice Lewis F. Powell had initially advocated the diversity rationale in the 1978 *Bakke* decision. In this 2003 case the Court endorsed Justice Powell's "view that student body diversity is a compelling state interest that can justify the use of race in university admissions."

But even in accepting that diversity is a "compelling state interest," the Court has asserted that this interest, no matter how "compelling," must be temporary because such compellance flies in the face of the Fourteenth Amendment's requirement for equal treatment. In an unusually blatant appeal to a future Supreme Court, Justice O'Connor stated, "Race-conscious admissions policies must be limited in time. This requirement reflects that racial classifications, however compelling their goals, are potentially so dangerous that they may be employed no more broadly than the interest demands. Enshrining a permanent justification for racial preferences would offend this fundamental equal protection principle." She concluded, "All governmental use of race must have a logical end point." Then she quite literally provided the end point: "We expect that 25 years from now, the use of racial preferences will no longer be necessary to further the interest approved today."

So the Court has ruled that racial preference for diversity's sake may extend another 25 years—but did not provide explicit criteria for their termination. In an unusually scathing dissenting opinion Justice Antonin Scalia asserted that the "mystical 'critical mass' justification" for racial preferences "challenges even the most gullible mind." The "critical mass" refers to the oft-asserted "fact" that significant numbers of minorities are needed in schools for everyone's betterment. The "gullible minds" seem to include the five justices that approved O'Connor's majority opinion. Scalia observed that the same academics who are among the strongest advocates of diversity tolerate "tribalism and racial segregation" on their own campuses, including "minority-only student organizations, separate minority housing opportunities, separate minority student centers, even separate minority-only graduation ceremonies."

In a parallel case involving the University of Michigan's undergraduate admissions process, *Gratz v. Bollinger*, the Court held that a point system that automatically gave black students an overwhelming advantage in admissions was unconstitutional. Race may still be taken into account but not in such a "nonindividualized, mechanical" way. This means that affirmative action/reverse discrimination admissions (and hiring) programs may continue as before—so long as no hard numbers that look, smell, or sound like quotas are attached to them. Justice O'Connor expected a "highly individualized, holistic review of each applicant's file." Race is just one factor among many. To those who are annoyed that race is a factor at all (because they believe the Constitution should be color-blind), the Court has said, in effect, "just wait 25 years."

President George W. Bush had his administration formally ask the Court to reject both of Michigan's admissions programs as barely disguised quota systems. On first hearing of the Court's support for its version of diversity, the White House (on June 22, 2003) issued a presidential statement. It praised the Court "for recognizing the value of diversity on our nation's campuses." It then said, "Like the court, I look forward to the day when America will truly be a color-blind society." You could almost hear the president frustratingly shouting between the lines: "But why do we have to wait 25 years?"

The election of Barack Obama to the White House in 2009 further stoked the argument that affirmative action was no longer necessary in the United States. After all, if an African American could be elected to the highest office in the land, it could be assumed that the times really had changed. And during Obama's first year in office, the Supreme Court sent a signal that it might be growing less supportive of affirmative action measures. In the case of *Ricci v. DeStefano* (2009), the Court struck down a New Haven, Connecticut, decision to throw out a firefighter test that promoted too few minorities. While once again avoiding answering the

Has *Brown v. Board of Education* (1954)
▶ **IN THE NEWS** | **Been Reversed?**

Just when you think things are settled for the next 25 years, Sandra Day O'Connor retires from the Supreme Court and the newly constituted Court seems to reverse her opinion on diversity. In a 5-to-4 decision, the Court rejected public school diversity plans from Seattle, Washington, and Louisville, Kentucky. The 2007 holding in *Parents Involved in Community Schools v. Seattle School District* and *Meredith v. Jefferson County Board of Education* declared that the two districts each failed to constitutionally justify "the extreme means they have chosen—discriminating among individual students based on race" in making school assignments. While these decisions do not eliminate race as a factor in assigning students to local schools, it makes it far more difficult, if not impossible, to assign them solely because of their race.

Chief Justice John Roberts's majority opinion stated that "accepting racial balancing as a compelling state interest would justify the imposition of racial proportionality throughout American society." Furthermore, "simply because the school districts

may seek a worthy goal does not mean they are free to discriminate on the basis of race to achieve it." Before *Brown v. Board of Education* (1954), "school children were told where they could and could not go to school based on the color of their skin. The school districts in these cases have not carried the heavy burden of demonstrating that we should allow this once again—even for very different reasons." Finally, he concluded that: "The way to stop discrimination on the basis of race is to stop discrimination on the basis of race."

After all, "distinctions by race are so evil, so arbitrary and invidious that a state bound to defend the equal protection of the laws must not invoke them in any public sphere." However, this last sentence was not written by the current Supreme Court but by Thurgood Marshall (later the first black justice on the Supreme Court) when he argued the *Brown* decision before the Court as the lead attorney for the National Association for the Advancement of Colored People. So has *Brown* been reversed or really affirmed in its essence? ▶

question regarding the ultimate constitutionality of affirmative action, the Court continued to narrow what it will consider fair in the realm of racial preferences.

The Ongoing Role of Race in Public Administration

If the role of racial discrimination in the United States had drifted from the everyday thoughts of most Americans by 2005, the aftermath of Hurricane Katrina reminded the nation that race continues to play a major role in government and society. As New Orleans was evacuated in the days and hours before Katrina struck, images of city residents left behind to ride out the storm in the Superdome demonstrated an obvious racial divide. Almost all of the individuals lining up outside of the mammoth sports stadium were African Americans. While the city was attempting to protect its residents in a "shelter of last resort," one could not help but wonder why those unable to get out of the city were overwhelmingly black. The absence of white faces, even in a predominantly black city, made for striking television images. In the week following Katrina's landfall, the images grew even starker, with pictures of thousands of African Americans suffering without food or water in the stifling Louisiana heat. These shocking photos reignited the national debate about the relationship between race and government policies. This

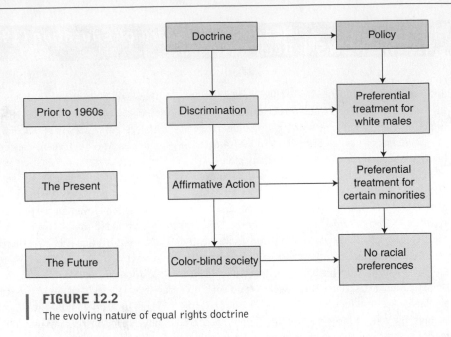

FIGURE 12.2
The evolving nature of equal rights doctrine

debate is bound to have an impact on public administrators charged with providing equal protection under the law to 300 million Americans.

NONRACIAL DISCRIMINATION

Equal employment opportunity has been most controversial when race is at issue. However, it is equally illegal to discriminate against someone for reasons of sex, age, or disability.

Sex Discrimination

Sex discrimination is any disparate or unfavorable treatment of a person in an employment situation because of his or her gender. The Civil Rights Act of 1964 (as amended by the Equal Employment Opportunity Act of 1972) makes sex discrimination illegal in most employment, except where a **bona fide occupational qualification** is involved.

Sex discrimination in employment was by no means a significant concern of the civil rights advocates of the early 1960s. Its prohibition only became part of the Civil Rights Act of 1964 because of Congressman Howard "Judge" Smith (1883–1976) of Virginia. As chairman of the House Rules Committee in 1964, Smith was one of the most powerful men in Congress—and as unlikely a hero as the women's movement will ever have. As the leader of the South's fight against civil rights, he added one small word—sex—to prohibitions against discrimination based on race, color, religion, and national origin. He felt confident this amendment would make the proposed law ridiculous and cause its defeat. Smith was an "old style" bigot: To his mind, the one thing more ridiculous than equal rights for blacks was equal rights for women.

Bona fide occupational qualification (BFOQ) ■
A good-faith exception to EEO provisions; a job requirement that would be discriminatory and illegal were it not necessary for the performance of a particular job. For example, female sex would be a BFOQ for a wet nurse.

The "sex discrimination" amendment was opposed by most of the leading liberals in Congress. They saw it as nothing but a ploy to discourage passage of the new civil rights law. The major support for adopting the amendment came from the reactionary southern establishment of the day. There was no discussion of sex discrimination by the Senate. The momentum for a new civil rights law was so great that Smith's addition not only failed to scuttle the bill, but also went largely unnoticed. The legal foundation for the modern women's movement was passed with almost no debate or media attention. Once Smith and his supporters realized the true impact of what they were doing, they sought to withdraw the amendment before the final vote but the few female members of Congress stopped this by insisting that it be done by a recorded, as opposed to a voice, vote. The male members did not want to be embarrassed by voting against women, so the amendment remained in the bill.

Although the sex discrimination prohibition was included in the new civil rights law almost in secret, word quickly got out. The new law brought into being the Equal Employment Opportunity Commission to enforce its various provisions. During the first year of the new commission's operation, more than one-third of all of the complaints it received dealt with sex discrimination in employment. Typical complaints included inadequate consideration of female applicants for promotion, "help wanted" ads for separate male- and female-labeled jobs, and higher retirement benefits for male workers. All these practices and more were made illegal by Title VII. Over the next four decades, Judge Smith's unintended gift to the nation's women became the judicial reference for countless court cases and out-of-court settlements.

Women, far more than minorities, have been the greatest beneficiaries of affirmative action. Women are now almost a quarter of the medical and legal professions (and nearly half of all medical and law students), more than 30 percent of all natural scientists and 40 percent of all college professors, and about 60 percent of all public officials. While some complain of a **glass ceiling** that many women find difficult to break through, many others are happy to note that it is only a matter of time before it falls down by itself.

Glass ceiling ■
The unseen barrier through which an organization's highest-level positions can be seen but not reached. Women and minorities often perceive that a "glass ceiling" prevents their advancement to the top.

Sexual Harassment

When the Civil Rights Act of 1964 prohibited sex discrimination in employment, it would not have occurred to anyone to say or imply that the new law had anything to do with sexual harassment. The phrase "sexual harassment" was not even in the language. Yet today, for all legal purposes, sex discrimination includes sexual harassment—the action of an individual in a position to control or influence the job, career, or grade of another person and who uses such power to gain sexual favors or punish the refusal of such favors. Sexual harassment on the job varies from inappropriate sexual innuendo to coerced sexual relations.

The courts are only gradually giving us a general idea of what behavior should not be permitted on the job. Although there was universal agreement that sexual harassment was bad, there was no agreement as to where the normal give-and-take between the sexes ended and sexual harassment began. An old maxim of the common law in such situations was that "there is no harm in asking [for sex]"! But the harm was always there. Countless women left jobs rather than submit to sexual requests. Countless others, out of sheer economic necessity, continued on in humiliation and fear.

In 1980, after the lower federal courts had decided that sexual harassment was sex discrimination in a variety of cases, the EEOC issued legally binding rules that defined and prohibited sexual harassment.

Unwelcome sexual advances, requests for sexual favors, and other verbal or physical contact of a sexual nature constitute sexual harassment when:

1. submission to such conduct is made either explicitly or implicitly a term or condition of an individual's employment;
2. submission to or rejection of such conduct by an individual is used as the basis for employment decisions affecting such individual; or
3. such conduct has the purpose or effect of unreasonably interfering with an individual's work performance or creating an intimidating, hostile, or offensive working environment.

Finally, in 1986, the Supreme Court issued its first ruling on sexual harassment. In *Meritor Savings Bank v. Vinson*, it held that "a violation of Title VII [of the Civil Rights Act of 1964] may be predicated on either of two types of sexual harassment: harassment that involves the conditioning of concrete employment benefits on sexual favors, and harassment that, while not affecting economic benefits, creates a hostile or offensive working environment." The hostile environment standard was expanded on in *Harris v. Forklift Systems*, discussed in the keynote.

In 1998, the Supreme Court offered further refinements in four sexual harassment cases. In *Oncale v. Sundowner Offshore Services*, the Court held that same-sex claims of harassment are permissible. In *Gebser v. Lago Vista Independent School District*, the Court held that school districts are not responsible if teachers harassed students when the school administrators did not know about it. In *Faragher v. Boca Raton, Florida*, the court held that an employer could be held financially liable for harassment by a supervisor. And in *Burlington Industries v. Ellerth*, the Court held that employers were liable for the threatening sexual advances of a supervisor even when the threats are not carried out and the harassed employee suffers no adverse effects.

Despite the clearly established illegality of it, sexual harassment remains a continuing problem. In 1995, the U.S. Merit Systems Protection Board released a survey, based on a questionnaire sent to 8,000 federal employees, that found that 44 percent of women and 19 percent of men said that they had been the victims of "uninvited, unwanted sexual attention." However, most of what was being complained about were the less severe forms of harassment—sexual teasing, jokes, and questionable remarks. A male referring to a female coworker as "honey" or "sweetie" or "doll" is not guilty of criminal sexual assault. But such verbal assaults, if perceived as inappropriate, do constitute sexual harassment, are inappropriate, and may be **actionable**.

Actionable ■
Provides adequate reason for a grievance or lawsuit.

Pregnancy Discrimination

A 1978 amendment to Title VII of the Civil Rights Act of 1964 holds that discrimination on the basis of pregnancy, childbirth, or related medical conditions constitutes unlawful sex discrimination. The amendment was enacted in response to the Supreme Court's ruling in *General Electric Co. v. Gilbert* (1976) that an employer's exclusion of pregnancy-related disabilities from its comprehensive disability plan did not violate Title VII.

The amendment asserts that a written or unwritten employment policy or practice that excludes from employment opportunities applicants or employees

IN THE NEWS | A New Civil Right—the Right for Women to Breastfeed Their Infants in Public

Physicians agree! Mother's milk is best. Children will be better off—less diarrhea and fewer infections—if they are nursed by their mothers rather than given a bottle of formula by a nanny. Mothers are better off by reducing their risk of breast and ovarian cancer. So what's the problem? Too many mothers seeking to feed their infants in the way nature intended have been hassled by people who find this natural process to be publicly offensive and possibly even in violation of public indecency laws.

The problem is cultural. Too many citizens associate the female breast with adult sex rather than with infant food. The same people who "know" that breastfeeding is best for infants, mothers, and society are uncomfortable when confronted with it in public.

Nevertheless, attitudes are changing and governments are in the forefront of this revolution in nursing. According to *Newsweek* (June 11, 2007), 38 states now guarantee a woman's right to breastfeed wherever she may be. And the Breastfeeding Promotion Act was introduced in Congress in 2011. This law, if enacted, would be an amendment to the Civil Rights Act of 1964. In 1964, when the act was passed, nobody would have thought that it would someday be applied to breastfeeding. Remember that it was the federal government with new laws and extensive public awareness campaigns that took the lead in changing attitudes about smoking. Is a similar change, nurtured by American governments at all levels, about to occur in regard to public breastfeeding? ◣

because of pregnancy, childbirth, or related medical conditions is a **prima facie** violation of Title VII.

While this amendment to Title VII did not require an employer to offer a specific number of weeks of maternity leave, the Family and Medical Leave Act of 1993 requires employers—in both the public and private sectors—with at least 50 workers to allow up to 12 weeks of unpaid leave (for childbirth, care of spouse or parent, new adoption of child, and so on) during a 12-month period for all employees (whether male or female) employed for at least a year.

Prima facie ■
Latin for "at first sight"; on the face of it; presumably. Said of a fact that will be considered to be true unless disproved by contrary evidence.

Age Discrimination

Ageism is discrimination against those who are considered "old." During the second presidential debate of the 1984 election, when there had been great speculation about Ronald Reagan's ability to continue to perform as president because of his age, Reagan literally turned the election around when he said, in answer to a question about his age, "I will not make age an issue in this campaign. I am not going to exploit, for political purposes, my opponent's youth and inexperience." Reagan went on to defeat the much younger Walter Mondale in a landslide.

Because not everybody has the Great Communicator's ability to turn the issue of age on its head, the Age Discrimination in Employment Act (ADEA) exists. First passed in 1967 and often amended, this law prohibits employment discrimination on the basis of age and (with certain exceptions) prohibits mandatory retirement. The law applies to all public employers, private employers of 20 or more employees, employment agencies serving covered employers, and labor unions of more than 25 members.

The ADEA prohibits help-wanted advertisements that indicate preference, limitation, specification, or discrimination based on age. For example, terms such as "girl" and "35–55" may not be used because they indicate the exclusion of qualified applicants based on age. Many states also have age discrimination laws or provisions in their fair employment practices laws. Some of these laws parallel the federal law and have no upper limit in protections against age discrimination in employment; others protect workers until they reach 60, 65, or 70 years of age. In 1983 the Supreme Court, in *Equal Employment Opportunity Commission v. Wyoming*, upheld the federal government's 1974 extension of the ADEA to cover state and local government workers.

Disabilities Discrimination

The federal government has a long history of legislative efforts to provide employment for the disabled. Disabled veterans were the first people formally given employment preference, toward the end of the Civil War. In 1919, just after World War I, employment preferences were extended to the wives of disabled veterans as well. However, it was not until the Vocational Rehabilitation Act of 1973 that federal contractors and subcontractors were required to take affirmative action to seek qualified handicapped individuals for employment. This act also provided the now accepted definition of a handicapped or disabled individual:

1. A person who has a physical or mental impairment that substantially limits one or more of such person's major life activities
2. A person who has a record of such an impairment
3. A person who is regarded as having such an impairment

Reasonable accommodation ■ Those steps needed to accommodate a handicapped employee's disability (e.g., adequate workspace for an employee confined to a wheelchair) required of an employer unless such steps would cause the employer undue hardship.

A qualified handicapped individual, according to the act and with respect to employment, is one who with reasonable accommodation can perform the essential functions of a job in question.

But it was not until the passage of the Americans with Disabilities Act (ADA) of 1990 that there was a comprehensive federal law to ban discrimination against physically and mentally handicapped individuals in employment, transportation, telecommunications, and public accommodations. All employers with more than 15 workers—not just federal contractors as before—are required to accommodate disabled employees. New buses and trains must be accessible to people in wheelchairs. Telephone companies have to provide hearing- or voice-impaired people with equipment to place and receive calls from ordinary telephones. Renovated or new hotels, stores, and restaurants must be wheelchair accessible. Existing barriers must be removed, if that is "readily achievable." Businesses that can demonstrate that these changes would be too costly or disruptive may be exempt from the law.

According to the ADA, "No covered entity shall discriminate against a qualified individual with a disability because of the disability of such individual in regard to job application procedures, the hiring, advancement, or discharge of employees, employee compensation, job training, and other terms, conditions, and privileges of employment." Among those protected by the act are individuals who are in or have successfully completed rehabilitation for drug abuse or alcoholism. However, the act states that "homosexuality and bisexuality are not impairments and as such are not disabilities under this Act." In seeking to limit the applicability of the ADA to those with traditional disabilities, the ADA also specifically excludes transvestism, pedophilia, compulsive gambling, kleptomania, and pyromania.

While the U.S. Supreme Court has not ruled that AIDS is a directly covered disability under the ADA, it has signaled the possibility that it might be. In its decision in *School Board of Nassau County v. Arline* (1987), the Court held that a public school teacher with the contagious disease of tuberculosis was "a handicapped individual" within the meaning of the Rehabilitation Act. Therefore, protection against employment discrimination was provided by the law. This case has been the basis for some lower court rulings that the Rehabilitation Act protects persons with AIDS from employment discrimination. In 1998 the Court offered its first substantial review of the ADA in *Bragdon v. Abbott*. Here it held that people with the HIV infection that leads to AIDS—people with no AIDS symptoms as yet—were protected by the ADA. While the scope of the case was limited, its tone strongly suggested that people with AIDS would also be protected.

The Equal Employment Opportunity Commission, which enforces the provisions of the ADA, requires that an employer may not ask about the existence, nature, or severity of a disability and may not conduct medical examinations until after it makes a conditional job offer to the applicant. This prohibition ensures that an applicant's disability that is not obviously apparent is not considered prior to the assessment of the applicant's non-medically related qualifications. At this pre-offer stage, employers can ask about an applicant's ability to perform specific job-related functions. After a conditional offer is made, an employer may require medical examinations and may make disability-related inquiries if it does so for all entering employees in the job category. If an examination or inquiry screens out an individual because of disability, the exclusionary criterion must be job related—and the employer must be able to demonstrate that the essential functions of the job cannot be performed with reasonable accommodation.

Sexual Orientation Discrimination

The long history of discrimination against and hostility toward homosexuals—gays and lesbians—has been subsiding considerably in recent decades. While sexual orientation is not protected by the federal civil rights laws, many federal agencies have internal regulations prohibiting discrimination on the basis of sexual orientation. In addition, 21 states and more than 140 local jurisdictions have laws or executive orders that forbid sexual orientation discrimination in employment. In addition, four states have laws prohibiting sexual orientation discrimination in public workplaces only.

The core problem of dealing with the civil rights of gays and lesbians is that the activity that defined them (sexual relations with a member of the same sex) was a crime in many states. This, however, is no longer the case. In 2003 the Supreme Court in *Lawrence v. Texas* declared unconstitutional the Texas ban on "consensual sodomy" and in effect asserted a broad constitutional right to sexual privacy. Justice Anthony M. Kennedy in the majority opinion wrote that the case concerned "two adults who, with full and mutual consent from each other, engaged in sexual practices common to a homosexual lifestyle. The petitioners are entitled to respect for their private lives. The State cannot demean their existence or control their destiny by making their private sexual conduct a crime."

In an extremely strong dissenting opinion Justice Antonin Scalia said that the ruling "effectively decrees the end of all morals legislation," and could possibly pave the way for "judicial imposition of homosexual marriage, as has recently occurred in Canada." This case overruled a 1986 decision in which the Court upheld Georgia's sodomy law (*Bowers v. Hardwick*). The 2003 decision effectively nullified sodomy laws in the 13 other states besides Texas that still had such laws. The 2003 *Lawrence* decision on homosexual rights has its origins in the 1965 case of *Griswold v. Connecticut*, which first asserted that there was a constitutional right to bedroom privacy even when the word *privacy* does not appear in the Constitution.

Of course, one of the most hotly debated matters related to employment discrimination is the official policy of the U.S. government regarding the service of gays and lesbians in the military. For most of the nation's history, the armed forces wouldn't accept homosexuals into their ranks. If a soldier was found to be gay or lesbian, he or she was discharged from the service, often in a dishonorable manner. It wasn't until 1993 that this policy changed with a key decision on the part of President Bill Clinton. Acting on one of his key campaign promises, Clinton ordered any homosexual or bisexual person serving in the military not to disclose his or her sexual orientation while serving in uniform. Clinton also ordered military superiors to refrain from asking a service member's orientation in the absence of discovering them engaged in a homosexual act. Despite some strong public reaction against the policy, Clinton stuck by "don't ask, don't tell," which his successor, George W. Bush, maintained during his eight years in office.

In 2008, Barack Obama campaigned on the promise that he would repeal the policy if elected. Obama not only indicated his belief that the policy was discriminatory in nature, but he also justified his position by pointing out the practical considerations of maintaining a ban on openly homosexual individuals in the armed services. In particular, he contended that the policy cost the government millions of dollars to replace troops kicked out of the military, and that it deprived the military of key personnel in such critical areas as linguistics.

By the time Obama arrived in the White House in 2009, there was growing pressure to repeal "don't ask, don't tell" and let gays and lesbians serve openly in the military. Once he arrived in the White House, however, Obama was slow to repeal the policy. Instead, he announced that he would need to confer more with his Chiefs of Staff before ending the rule. His administration was even put in the awkward position of defending "don't ask, don't tell" when the policy was challenged in court. It appeared that Obama didn't want to draw the same type of negative public reaction that Clinton had had to deal with during his first year in office, and thereby preserve some of his political capital to fight other fights (e.g., the economic stimulus and health care reform). Eventually, with public opinion overwhelmingly in support of ending "don't ask, don't tell," and with support from the leaders of all the branches of the U.S. military, Congress passed and President Obama signed the repeal in December of 2010. The armed forces finalized the process of ending the policy during the summer of 2011 and by the fall of that year openly gay Americans could serve their country in the military.

PUBLIC ADMINISTRATION AND SOCIAL EQUITY

All public administrators have an obvious obligation to advance social equity. However, this obligation can be legitimately and honorably interpreted in several ways. First is the obligation to administer the laws they work under in a fair manner. It is hard to believe today that this first obligation was once controversial.

Griswold v. Connecticut (1965) ■

The U.S. Supreme Court case that, in holding that the state regulation of birth control devices was an impermissible invasion of privacy, helped to establish privacy as a constitutionally protected right under the Ninth and Fourteenth Amendments. Justice William O. Douglas wrote, in the majority opinion, "The First Amendment has a penumbra where privacy is protected from governmental intrusion." He asked, "Would we allow the police to search the sacred precincts of marital bedrooms for telltale signs of the use of contraceptives? The very idea is repulsive to the notions of privacy surrounding the marriage relationship."

Before the passage of the 1960s civil rights legislation—mainly the Civil Rights Act of 1964 and the Voting Rights Act of 1965—minorities and women were routinely denied equitable treatment. For example, when the two female justices of the U.S. Supreme Court—Sandra Day O'Connor and Ruth Bader Ginsberg—graduated from law school, neither could obtain jobs with any major law firm. Today all large employers in the public and private sector are legally obligated to provide equal employment opportunity—and legally liable if they don't.

Going the Extra Mile

But it is one thing to simply avoid being in violation of the law; it is another matter altogether to actively seek to foster its spirit. Thus the second way of interpreting obligations to advance social equity is to feel bound to proactively further the cause—to seek to hire and advance a varied workforce. The attitude requires a specific approach: "It is not enough to go out and find qualified minorities. You must go out, find them, and then qualify them." This is why the U.S. armed forces have been so much more successful in their affirmative action efforts than the society as a whole. They bring minorities into their organizations as young recruits and nurture them as they grow—just the same as they have been doing with white males for 200 years.

This going the "extra mile" is the spirit of the new public administration. These are not two ends of a continuum, with passive attitudes toward social equity at one end and proactive attitudes at the other. These are different ways of looking at the administrative world and one's responsibilities within it as an individual, as a citizen, and as an administrator.

Inspiring Social Equity

Still there is one other aspect to advancing social equity that is best illustrated by a story. In 1963 George C. Wallace, then governor of Alabama, dramatically stood in the doorway of the University of Alabama to prevent the entry of black students and the desegregation of the University. It was a major media event. Wallace, backed up by the Alabama National Guard, stood waiting at his designated chalk mark on the pavement wearing his TV network microphone. As was prearranged, the deputy U.S. attorney general, Nicholas Katzenbach, backed up by 3,000 federal troops, ordered Wallace to allow a black student, Vivian Malone, to enter. After a long-winded speech about federal encroachment on states' rights, Wallace stepped aside and Katzenbach escorted Malone to the university cafeteria.

This incident is a famous aspect of the civil rights movement. Journalist Jacob Weisberg in his *In Defense of Government* adds an element to this well-known story that shows government at its best. After Malone entered the cafeteria, she got her tray of food and sat alone. Almost immediately some white female students joined her. They sought to befriend her, as they would any new student. According to Weisberg, "That's the most powerful part of the story because it is about a change that good government inspired but could not force." Then as now governments can go only so far in forcing social equity. But there is no limit to the amount of inspiration it can provide to encourage people to do the right, decent, and honorable thing. This encouragement has a name. It is called moral leadership.

A CASE STUDY | Social Equity Through Social Insurance

Middle Ages ■
The historical time period that divides the classical world of Greece and Rome from the modern period; generally from the fall of Rome to the Italian Renaissance.

Industrial revolution ■
A very general term that refers to a society's change from an agrarian to an industrial economy. The Industrial Revolution of the Western world is considered to have begun in England in the eighteenth century.

Craft unions ■
Labor organizations that restrict membership to skilled workers (such as plumbers, carpenters, electricians, etc.) as opposed to industrial unions that seek to organize all workers in an industry.

Factors of production ■
The resources used to produce goods and services. There are three traditional factors: land, labor, and capital. Recently, management (or entrepreneurship) has come to be considered a factor as well.

An anonymous Washington wit once observed that the federal government is basically just a large insurance company with a defense business on the side. While seemingly outrageous on the surface, this comment becomes more and more reasonable if its implications are closely examined. The reality is that most—far more than half—of the federal budget goes to insurance programs: Social Security, Medicare, Medicaid, welfare, and food stamps are the most obvious. But the federal government also runs insurance programs for banks (Federal Deposit Insurance Corporation), for pensions (Pension Benefit Guaranty Corporation), and for home mortgages (Department of Housing and Urban Development), among others. In terms of money, these programs represent more than 60 percent of the federal government. Defense—that business on the side—accounts for only 20 percent.

So how did the federal government evolve into the world's largest insurance business? The answer lies in the historical development of the American welfare state. The problem the welfare state was created to ameliorate was elegantly posed by Anatole France in his 1894 novel *The Red Lily*: "The law, in its majestic equality, forbids the rich as well as the poor to sleep under bridges, to beg in the streets, and to steal bread." Thus social equity in terms of political and civil rights is inadequate if not accompanied by minimal economic rights. This other side of the equity coin, often summed up in one word—*welfare*—has a long lineage.

Some biblical scholars contend that the commandment "Thou shalt not kill" contained the essence of a welfare program. After all, if a wandering desert tribe did not help those members in need (the ill, the old, the widowed and orphaned), they would surely die. Thus we can conclude that the social provision of welfare services has always been mandated from above—sometimes high above.

Economic security has often been an elusive goal. During the Middle Ages merchants and craft workers, any group with a common business intent, might form guilds or mutual aid societies. While primarily created to regulate prices and employment standards, they also offered welfare benefits to members in times of poverty or illness. Beginning in the sixteenth century, friendly societies, the forerunners of fraternal organizations, emerged. They would grow rapidly during the Industrial Revolution and would often evolve into modern craft unions. They allowed members to provide for their own welfare by paying into funds for life insurance, burial expenses, and other forms of assistance in times of need. Many of these organizations still thrive in the United States and are well known: the Free Masons, the Odd Fellows, the Benevolent and Protective Order of Elks, and the Royal Order of Moose.

The rapid industrialization of the late nineteenth century transformed the concept of the worker. They were viewed less and less as human beings and more and more as factors of production. Like any other nonhuman resource, the laborer was increasingly a specialized "cog" in the manufacturing process. Workers also felt threatened by massive immigration from Europe, which assured a ready supply of "hands" to take their place. Finally, increasing urbanization made workers almost completely dependent on their wages—the proportion of factory workers who could "retreat" to a family farm continued to dwindle.

When the problem of what to do with displaced workers and their families grew too much for traditional charity to handle, the state stepped in. The English Poor Law of 1601 was the first systematic codification of English ideas about the responsibility of the state to provide for the welfare of its citizens. It provided public funds to pay for relief. It distinguished between the "deserving" and the "undeserving" poor. Relief was local and community controlled. Almshouses and poor farms were also established. This essential structure was the tradition the English settlers brought with them when they colonized North America.

The first colonial poor laws featured local taxation to support the destitute, distinguished between the "worthy" and the "unworthy" poor, and had relief as a local responsibility. This tradition continued until well after the American Civil War. It was up to local officials to decide who was worthy of support and how that support would be provided. Relief was made as unpleasant as possible in order to "discourage" dependency. Those receiving relief could lose their personal property as well as the right to vote.

Four important demographic changes happened in America beginning in the mid-1880s that rendered the traditional systems of economic security increasingly unworkable:

1. The Industrial Revolution transformed the majority of working people from self-employed agricultural workers into wage earners working for large, impersonal organizations. In an agricultural society, personal prosperity was linked to one's labor. Anyone willing to work hard enough could usually provide at least a bare subsistence for themselves and their family. But when one's income is primarily from wages, one's economic security can be threatened by factors outside one's control—such as recessions, layoffs, failed businesses, and so on.
2. Urbanization increased along with the shift from an agricultural to an industrial society. Americans moved from farms and small rural communities to large cities; that's where the industrial jobs were. In 1890, only 28 percent of the population lived in cities. By 1930 this percentage had exactly doubled, to 56 percent.
3. This trend toward urbanization contributed to the disappearance of the extended family and the concomitant rise of the nuclear family. Today we tend to assume that "the family" consists of parents and children—the so-called nuclear family. For most of human history, we lived in "extended families" that included children, parents, grandparents, and

(continued)

Relief ■
Public assistance programs for the poor. Direct relief referred to straight welfare payments. Work relief referred to any of the numerous public works projects initiated specifically to provide jobs for the unemployed.

A CASE STUDY | *Continued*

other relatives. The advantage of the extended family was that when a family member became too old or infirm to work, the other family members assumed responsibility for the individual's support. But when the able-bodied left the farms to seek employment in the cities (or other countries), the parents or grandparents usually stayed behind.

4. Finally, thanks primarily to better health care, modern sanitation, and effective public health programs, Americans began to live significantly longer. In the three decades from 1900 to 1930, average life spans increased by 10 years. The result was a rapid growth in the number of older citizens from 3 million in 1900 to 7.8 million by 1935.

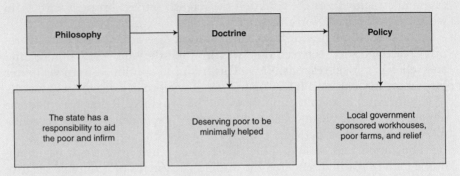

FIGURE 12.3
The Traditional Doctrine of Welfare.

The net result of this complex set of demographic and social changes was that America was older, more urban, more industrial, and had fewer of its people living on farms in extended families. The traditional strategies for the provision of economic security were becoming increasingly fragile—and with the Great Depression, they would be overwhelmed.

There were, generally speaking, three basic approaches to the Great Depression that began in 1929:

1. Do nothing because nothing needed to be done. The current problem was just another dip in the inevitable boom-and-bust economic cycle. Prosperity would eventually be just around the corner—just as it always had been. Nevertheless, the problem remained that prosperity was taking too long to turn the corner.

2. Rely on "volunteerism" or private charity. Traditional charitable good works were widespread in a nation with a large churchgoing population. But the problem was too huge for a nation that had lost half its total wealth by the end of the first three years of the Depression. Six years after the Depression began, President Franklin D. Roosevelt would say in his second inaugural address, "I see one-third of a nation ill-housed,

ill-clad, ill-nourished." The nation was simply too ill for the "pill" of charity to make it better.

3. Expand welfare programs. Even before the Depression hit, the states had been forced to deal with the problems of economic security in a wage-based, industrial economy. **Workers' compensation** programs had been established by most states. Once the Depression hit, all levels of government responded with expanded relief and public works programs. The main strategy for providing economic security to the elderly, in the face of the demographic changes just discussed, was to provide various forms of old-age "pensions." These were welfare programs, eligibility for which was based on financial need. By 1934, most states had such "pension" plans. However, these plans were so restrictive in eligibility and so minimal in payments that they were almost wholly inadequate to the task.

The essential problem with these three approaches was that the Depression just continued. While the New Deal of President Franklin D. Roosevelt fought the Depression traditionally with massive relief and public works programs, it also sought to change the debate on how to deal with economic insecurity. A long-term permanent program of social insurance, already widespread in Europe, would become the alternative to the current patchwork of ad hoc solutions.

Social insurance, as conceived by President Roosevelt, would address the permanent problem of economic security for the elderly by creating a work-related, contributory system in which workers would provide for their own future economic security through taxes paid while employed. Thus it was an alternative both to reliance on welfare and to radical changes in our capitalist system. In the context of its time, it can be seen as a conservative, yet activist, response to the challenges of the Depression. State-sponsored efforts to provide for economic security would come to be seen as the practical alternative to the siren calls of those who preached socialism.

Social insurance has been the pragmatic answer to a variety of widespread problems—from disability and death to old age or unemployment. It is

Workers' compensation ◼ Industrial accident insurance designed to provide cash benefits and medical care for a worker injured on the job and monetary payments to survivors for a worker killed on the job. This was the first form of social insurance to develop widely in the United States. Workers' compensation was first developed in Germany and Great Britain in the 1880s. By 1920, all but a handful of states had laws encouraging workers' compensation in private industry.

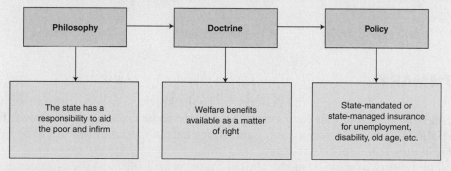

FIGURE 12.4
The Social Insurance Approach to Welfare.

(continued)

> **A CASE STUDY** | *Continued*

immediately obvious to think of death, disability, or unemployment as conditions that led to a loss of income and that can be ameliorated by a pooling of risk. It may be strange at first to think of old age or retirement in this same way. But social insurance looks at retirement much as it looks at death: A loss of income has occurred because of a cessation of work. Social insurance seeks to solve the eternal problem of economic security by pooling the assets (the insurance contributions) from a large social group and providing income to those members whose economic security is being immediately threatened.

As President Franklin D. Roosevelt signed into law the Social Security Act on August 14, 1935, he stated, "We can never insure one hundred percent of the population against one hundred percent of the hazards and vicissitudes of life, but we have tried to frame a law which will give some measure of protection to the average citizen and to his family against the loss of a job and against poverty-ridden old age."

Nevertheless, the Social Security Act did not quite achieve all the aspirations its supporters had hoped by way of providing a "comprehensive package of protection" against the "hazards and vicissitudes of life." Certain features of that package, notably disability coverage and medical benefits, would have to wait until 1954 and 1965, respectively. But it did provide a wide range of programs. In addition to the program we immediately think of as Social Security (old-age pensions), it included unemployment insurance and aid to dependent children. But this was just the beginning. The act would be amended time and again to become the foundation of the American welfare state. (For details on the current welfare program, see Chapter 4. For the current status of Social Security, see the case study in Chapter 13.)

For Discussion: *Why does social equity necessarily have two faces—civil rights and economic rights? Why has the American welfare state evolved as a pragmatic, not an ideological, solution to the pressing problem of social equity?* ▶

SUMMARY

Social equity is fairness in the delivery of public services; it is egalitarianism in action—the principle that each citizen has a right to be given equal treatment by the political system. Government organizations have a special obligation to be fair because they represent the citizenry.

The history of slavery in the United States is still relevant today because it is the underlying basis for African American claims for special treatment. Equal employment opportunity, created to mitigate the heritage of slavery, is a concept fraught with political, cultural, and emotional overtones. Generally, it applies to employment practices that prevent any individual from being adversely excluded from employment opportunities on the basis of race, color, sex, religion, age, or national origin. The problem with equal employment opportunity programs is that they put the government into the business of examining people's bloodlines.

Well-meaning opponents of affirmative action (the means by which EEO is to be achieved) favor equality. They hold that racial and sexual hiring preferences are not only inherently discriminatory, but they are also in violation of the Civil Rights Act of 1964, which prohibits discrimination against anybody. Affirmative action has become a wedge issue—an issue that drives people apart. Since the 1980s, the Republicans have been quite astute in using this wedge to brand the Democratic Party the champion of special privileges for minorities.

When the Civil Rights Act of 1964 prohibited sex discrimination in employment, nobody would have said that the new law had anything to do with sexual harassment. Yet today, for all legal purposes, sex discrimination includes sexual harassment. A 1978 amendment to the act holds that discrimination on the basis of pregnancy, childbirth, or related medical conditions also constitutes unlawful sex discrimination.

The federal government has a long history of legislative efforts to provide employment for the disabled. But it was not until the passage of the Americans with Disabilities Act in 1990 that there was a comprehensive federal law to ban discrimination against physically and mentally handicapped individuals in employment, transportation, telecommunications, and public accommodations.

REVIEW QUESTIONS

1. Why is social equity a critically important value for public organizations?
2. What is the difference between equal employment opportunity and affirmative action?
3. Why is a representative bureaucracy the inherent goal of all affirmative action programs?
4. Is reverse discrimination both legal and ethical?
5. How did the Civil Rights Act of 1964 eventually make sexual harassment illegal?

KEY CONCEPTS

Affirmative action   A term that first meant the removal of "artificial barriers" to the employment of women and minority group members; now it refers to compensatory opportunities for hitherto disadvantaged groups—specific efforts to recruit, hire, and promote qualified members of disadvantaged groups for the purpose of eliminating the present effects of past discrimination.

Child labor   Originally, the employment of children in a manner detrimental to their health and social development. Now that the law contains strong child labor prohibitions, the term refers to the employment of children below the legal age limit.

Discrimination   Bigotry in practice; intolerance toward those who have different beliefs or religions. In employment, the failure to treat equals equally. Any action that has the effect of limiting employment and advancement opportunities because of an individual's sex, race, color, age, national origin, religion, physical handicap, or other irrelevant criteria is discrimination.

Equal employment opportunity   Employment practices that prevent any individual from being adversely excluded from employment opportunities on the basis of race, color, sex, religion, age, national origin, or other factors that cannot lawfully be considered in employing people.

New public administration   An academic advocacy movement for social equity in the performance and delivery of public services; it called for a proactive administrator with a burning desire for social equity to replace the traditional impersonal and neutral gun-for-hire bureaucrat.

Racist Any person or organization that either consciously or unconsciously practices discrimination against another person on the basis of race (or ethnicity) or supports the supremacy of one race over others.

Representative bureaucracy The ultimate goal of equal employment opportunity and affirmative action programs.

Reverse discrimination Discrimination against white males in conjunction with preferential treatment for women and minorities.

Second reconstruction The civil rights movement and legislation of the 1960s. The first reconstruction, immediately after the Civil War, gave blacks their freedom from slavery. But the laws as enforced and customs as practiced did not allow for the full rights of citizens. That came in the 1960s, when public sentiment was aroused and legal action was taken to ensure equal rights for all Americans.

Sex discrimination Any disparate or unfavorable treatment of a person in an employment situation because of his or her sex.

Sexual harassment The action of an individual (either a supervisor or coworker) in a position to control or influence another's job, career, or grade who uses such power to gain sexual favors or punish the refusal of such favors. Sexual harassment on the job varies from inappropriate sexual innuendo to coerced sexual relations.

Title VII That part of the Civil Rights Act of 1964 that prohibits employment discrimination because of race, color, religion, sex, or national origin and created the Equal Employment Opportunity Commission as its enforcement vehicle.

MySearchLab® EXERCISES

Apply what you learned in this chapter on MySearchLab (*www.mysearchlab.com*).

BIBLIOGRAPHY

Armas, Genard (2003*a*). "Census Figures Show Economic Gains by Blacks," *Las Vegas Review-Journal* (April 26).

———. (2003*b*). "Earnings Potential Still Subject to Gender, Race Gaps," *Las Vegas Review-Journal* (March 21).

Bishop, Peter C., and Augustus J. Jones Jr. (1993). "Implementing the Americans with Disabilities Act of 1990," *Public Administration Review* 53 (March–April).

Boller, Harvey R., and Douglas Massengill (1992). "Public Employers' Obligation to Reasonably Accommodate the Disabled under the Rehabilitation and Americans with Disabilities Acts," *Public Personnel Management* 21 (Fall).

Cose, Ellis (1993). *The Rage of a Privileged Class.* New York: HarperCollins.

Fineman, Howard, and Tamara Lipper (2003). "Spinning Race," *Newsweek* (January 27).

Fletcher, Michael A. (2003). "Changes to Title IX Considered: Proposal Would Allow Scholarship Limits," *Washington Post* (January 24).

Frederickson, H. George (1980). *New Public Administration.* University: University of Alabama Press.

Henry, William A., III. (1994). *In Defense of Elitism.* New York: Doubleday.

Jamieson, David, and Julie O'Mara (1991). *Managing Workforce 2000: Gaining the Diversity Advantage.* San Francisco: Jossey-Bass.

Kingsley, J. Donald (1944). *Representative Bureaucracy: An Interpretation of the British Civil Service.* Yellow Springs, OH: Antioch Press.

Klein, Joe (1995). "The End of Affirmative Action," *Newsweek* (February 13).

Krislov, Samuel (1967). *The Negro in Federal Employment.* Minneapolis: University of Minnesota Press.

———. (1974). *Representative Bureaucracy.* Englewood Cliffs, NJ: Prentice Hall.

Marini, Frank, ed. (1971). *Toward a New Public Administration.* San Francisco: Chandler.

Marshall, Thurgood (1987). "An African-American's Perspective on the Constitution," *Vanderbilt Law Review* 40.

McAllister, Bill (1995). "The Problem That Won't Go Away: A New Survey Finds Complaints of Sexual Harassment Are Still Widespread in Federal Offices," *The Washington Post National Weekly Edition* (November 20–26).

Pellicciotti, Joseph M. (1991). "Exemptions and Employer Defenses under the ADEA," *Public Personnel Management* 20 (Summer).

Riccucci, Norma M. (2002). *Managing Diversity in Public Sector Workforces.* Boulder, CO: Westview.

Robinson, Robert K., et al. (1993). "Sexual Harassment in the Workplace: A Review of the Legal Rights and Responsibilities of All Parties," *Public Personnel Management* 19 (Spring).

Schlessinger, Arthur M., Jr. (1965). *A Thousand Days: John F. Kennedy in the White House.* Boston: Houghton Mifflin.

Sowell, Thomas (1984). *Civil Rights: Rhetoric or Reality.* New York: William Morrow.

Thomas, R. Roosevelt, Jr. (1990). "From Affirmative Action to Affirming Diversity," *Harvard Business Review* 68 (March–April).

Thompson, Mark (2009). "Dismay over Obama's 'Don't Ask, Don't Tell' Turnabout," *Time* (June 9).

Thompson, Victor A. (1961). *Modern Organization.* New York: Knopf.

———. (1975). *Without Sympathy or Enthusiasm.* University: University of Alabama Press.

Waldo, Dwight (1968). "Public Administration in a Time of Revolution," *Public Administration Review* 28 (July–August).

Weisberg, Jacob (1996). *In Defense of Government: The Rise and Fall of Public Trust.* New York: Scribner.

Wilkins, Roger (1995). "The Case for Affirmative Action," *The Nation* (March 27).

Williams, John (2001). "The Clint Eastwood Verdict Makes My Day," *Business Week Online* (October 6). http://www.businessweek.com.

RECOMMENDED BOOKS

Arredondo, Patricia (1996). *Successful Diversity Management Initiatives: A Blueprint for Planning and Implementation.* Thousand Oaks, CA: Sage. A how-to-do-it manual for workforce diversity program implementation; presents a prototype for measuring both qualitative and quantitative results.

Katznelson, Ira (2005). *When Affirmative Action Was White: An Untold History of Racial Inequality in Twentieth-Century America.* New York, W.W. Norton and Company. An examination of racial inequity and its relationship to government policies that are believed to benefit blacks but that have actually benefited whites.

Olson, Walter K. (1997). *The Excuse Factory: How Employment Law Is Paralyzing the American Workplace.* New York: Free Press. A review of the unintended consequences of the Americans with Disabilities Act whereby it has become difficult to fire slacking employees because of the protections the act offers for those with frivolous physical and mental "problems."

Reese, Laura A., and Karen E. Lindenberg (1998). *Implementing Sexual Harassment Policy: Challenges for the Public Sector Workforce*. Thousand Oaks, CA: Sage. A review of the problems and opportunities of creating organizational policies for forestalling and dealing with sexual harassment.

Sowell, Thomas (1990). *Preferential Policies: An International Perspective*. New York: William Morrow. An around-the-world tour of affirmative action policies and practices.

West, Cornel (1993). *Race Matters*. Boston: Beacon Press. An explanation of how the intellectual frameworks about race used by both blacks and whites impede racial progress and understanding.

RELATED WEB SITES

http://aad.english.ucsb.edu
Affirmative Action and Diversity Project
This site from the University of California at Santa Barbra presents diverse opinions regarding affirmative action topics, rather than taking a singular pro or con position. Its goal is to help lend many different voices to the debates on affirmative action.

http://jan.wvu.edu/links/adalinks.htm
Americans with Disabilities Act Document Center
Links to documents concerning themselves with the Americans with Disabilities Act.

www.usdoj.gov/crt/
Civil Rights Division of the U.S. Department of Justice (DOJ)
This DOJ division's Web site provides news and resources concerning the enforcement of the nation's civil rights laws and constitutional protections; also allows individuals to file complaints with the DOJ.

www.usccr.gov
Commission on Civil Rights (CCR)
The site offers publications on the CCR's activities and information on myriad civil right issues.

www.pay-equity.org
National Committee on Pay Equity (NCPE)
NCPE is a coalition of women's and civil rights organizations; labor unions; religious, professional, legal, and educational associations; commissions on women; state and local pay equity coalitions; and individuals working to eliminate sex and race-based wage discrimination and to achieve pay equity.

www.titleix.info
Title IX information
Title IX is a law passed in 1972 that requires gender equity for men and women in every educational program that receives federal funding. The site gives information about Title IX, tracks news stories where fights about Title IX are taking place, and encourages people to get involved in the fight to protect Title IX and ensure it is followed.

www.eeoc.gov
U.S. Equal Employment Opportunity Commission (EEOC)
The EEOC is the primary unit of the federal government that enforces the nation's employment laws. This site has news, information, and ways to file claims concerning equal employment opportunities and abuses.

Public Financial Management

KEYNOTE: A Tale of How Two States and Their Governors Weathered the Fiscal Storms of 2011

It was the best of times for Republicans. It was the worst of times for Democrats. The 2010 midterm elections not only saw the Republicans and their Tea Party allies take control of the U.S. House of Representatives by the highest margin in half a century, but they also gained control of a majority of governorships and state legislatures. The ill feelings between the parties at the national level would now find its counterpart in state government.

Meteorologists are fond of saying that conditions are prime for major storms. When barometric pressure plummets, humidity increases and winds flow from the right direction, storm clouds are likely to appear on the horizon. The confluence of these weather ingredients often occur in the American heartland during the springtime, creating tremendous tornados and thunderstorms that leave behind terrible carnage in their wake.

During the early months of 2011 a mixture of political, economic, and personal factors produced a different type of storm that threatened the fiscal health of the American states, including many in the Midwest where spring storms are part of the fabric of life. As with the tornados that devastate lives and properties where they strike, the fiscal twisters of 2011 left behind devastation in terms of government programs as well as the political reputations and careers that were caught in their path.

While there were many fiscal storms during 2011, none was more turbulent, destructive, and highly publicized than the one that blew through Wisconsin. At the center of this storm was a fairly young first-term governor who made national headlines for his role in an epic budget battle that was watched on television by much of the nation. This is the story of Wisconsin Governor Scott Walker (1967–) and his management (or mismanagement, depending upon your point of view) of the budget crisis that stood out in a season of fiscal tempests that battered the nation.

Nothing about Scott Walker predicted that he would be the catalyst of dramatic events that would engulf the usually mild political environment in that mid western state. Walker was no novice to politics. This Eagle Scout had been in elective office practically his entire adult life. He was first elected to the Wisconsin State Assembly in 1993 and served until 2002 when he was elected County Executive of Milwaukee County. After two four-year terms he ran for governor as a fiscal and social conservative, winning with 52 percent of the vote. As the election results were being finalized on the night of November 2, 2010, the final ingredient had been added to a mix that would produce one of the most contentious budgetary storms in the history of the American states.

The fiscal storm that engulfed Wisconsin in 2011 began to form long before Scott Walker came to power in January of that year. The Great Recession of 2008 and 2009 had left Wisconsin and other states short on revenue and long on budget shortfalls. The influx of federal stimulus dollars had helped to lessen the intensity of the budget pain endured in 2010, but as 2011 approached the stimulus money was gone and record shortfalls appeared imminent in "America's Dairyland."

With fiscal conditions deteriorating during the fall of 2010 the midterm election approached, with a governor's race headlining a packed ballot. Wisconsin had been seen as one of the nation's more competitive political environments for generations. Both Democrats and Republicans had success in winning statewide offices during the past quarter century and control of the legislative houses had vacillated between parties.

While both parties have done well in Wisconsin, the Democrats had a great run in the years leading up to 2010. President Obama had carried the state easily in 2008 and a Democrat had been governor for the last eight years. But the political tides had shifted in 2010 and Republicans were optimistic as November approached. The stagnant economy and a mounting budget deficit in the state left the incumbent Governor Jim Doyle wounded to the point where he was a political liability as election day neared. Public opinion polls indicated that the elections of 2010 would not be kind to Democrats.

During the election candidate Walker had pledged to not raise taxes in order to balance the state budget if elected. Instead Walker campaigned on the position that fiscal health required dramatic cuts in state spending and in the size and scope of state government. He vowed to bring fiscal discipline to Wisconsin and to find the waste and unnecessary spending that Republicans claimed was prevalent in their state capital of Madison. With the political winds at his back, Walker scored a solid victory on election day and thus guaranteed that the spring of 2011 would be a turbulent one in terms of budget matters.

It didn't take long for the fiscal storm to ignite after the fledgling Walker administration began to operate. Buoyed by public opinion favoring cutting spending and with the help of a Republican-controlled legislature, the new governor quickly established plans to address the budget shortfall. His campaign pledge to cut state government was kept by his budget proposal to the state legislature.

Walker announced in February that he wanted to eliminate 1,200 state jobs and significantly cut the benefits packages of state employees as part of his attempt to balance a budget that was facing a $3.6 billion deficit. Walker also called for deep cuts in aid to public schools and local governments while setting up increases in private school aid. While his proposals drew the ire of many in the state, it was Walker's proposal to end the right of state employees to bargain collectively that acted as the catalyst for the political firestorm that would engulf Madison for much of the spring.

Wisconsin's public employee unions, in tune with the tenor of the fiscal times, recognized that the size of the budget deficit in the state would require that they make some sacrifices in wages and benefits. In comparison with their private sector counterparts, public employees had faired well during the difficult economic environments in the years leading up to 2011. In fact, public employees in Wisconsin and beyond had had a pretty good run for decades (See Chapter 11 keynote for details.) Public opinion in the state was supportive of benefit cuts to state employees; and with Republican control of both the executive and legislative branches, nothing was more predictable than that public employees would feel substantial cuts during this budget cycle.

What was not predictable was Governor Walker's decision to not only seek concessions from state employee unions, but to attempt to strip public employees from jurisdictions throughout the state from having the right to collectively bargain with their governments on most employment matters. The Republican governor claimed that removing collective bargaining rights of state and local government employees was necessary if the state and local governments were going to get control of their long-term fiscal problems. Walker argued that as long as the public employee unions had the power to bargain over benefits and working conditions, they would be able to extract excessive benefits from the state's various governments.

To put it mildly, the unions strongly disagreed with this premise. The unionized state government workers were willing to accept benefit cuts that obligated them to pay modest portions of the costs of their medical insurance and pension plans. However, Walker's drive to take away collective bargaining pushed public employee unions into a state of outright rebellion, resulting in state workers and many of their supporters swarming Madison and peacefully occupying the Capital rotunda as a means of protesting the governor's move. National media descended upon Madison and cameras focused on the circus-like atmosphere developing in the capital. Something big was brewing in Wisconsin, and the 24-hour cable news networks wanted to capture it live. Once the circus began, it continued for weeks and became a fixture on broadcast and cable news programs.

As noted earlier, the Wisconsin public was initially behind Walker's calls for state employees to make sacrifices as part of his plan for fiscal solvency in the state. Unions were simply not that popular with the residents of the Badger State. Even in a state that was the first to allow public workers to unionize in 1959, and was famous for its role in developing a strong corps of civil servants since the progressive era of the early twentieth century, public employee unions did not have a great deal of political capital to use in the budget negotiations. That is, they didn't have much until Scott Walker made his push to take away their collective bargaining rights.

The public may have no love for the generic "public employee," but they certainly have respect for firefighters, police officers, and especially teachers, who are very much public employees. In trying to take away collective bargaining rights from unions representing these respected professions, Walker had inadvertently turned what were once considered overpaid state employees into a sympathetic group of civil servants. From the public's perspective, the unions had to give up some of their cushy benefits but they didn't have to be killed off.

As Governor Walker watched his public ratings fall, he altered his proposal by removing firefighters and police unions from the bill, claiming public safety as the reason for the shift. As Walker modified his proposal, many of the Senate Democrats took a different path—they left the state! In an attempt to prevent a quorum necessary to vote on the union proposal, Democratic legislatures bolted for hiding places across the state border in Illinois. They hid from the officers that the governor sent to bring them back. They hid from their families and friends. But somehow TV news reporters always seemed to be able to find them and record interviews about their personal plight as a recluse and their political fight with a governor they accused of being unwilling to compromise.

With many Democrats in exile and his budget proposals stagnating in the legislature, Walker scrambled to find a way out of the mess. Republicans in the legislature suddenly discovered that they could pass the collective bargaining repeal without a quorum because the bill did not involve the spending of state dollars. On March 9 the bill passed the Senate without the Democrats present, effectively ending the collective bargaining rights for state and local government workers in areas such as pensions and employee benefits. Governor Walker had achieved his goal. Wisconsin's public employee unions had been emasculated; but at what cost?

A budget deficit of the magnitude that Wisconsin was facing in 2011 required difficult decisions. No matter what path Scott Walker took he was destined to take some serious hits in terms of his standing with the public. While some political damage was inevitable for Walker, his decisions to go after the collective bargaining rights that the unions had enjoyed for decades was a classic case of overreach. The elimination of collective bargaining rights had very little impact on the short-term effort to balance the state budget. In the long term-eliminating these rights will certainly save the state some costs. But in the short term it only served to give the unions the high ground in the debate and increase opposition to his entire budget plan.

Walker may very well have been able to get the lion's share of the cuts he desired with fairly moderate impact on his standing on the state if he had not taken a hard-lined stance on collective bargaining. By preserving his public standing, Walker could have used a more incremental approach to reduce the union's clout in budgetary matters over the course of his four years in office. It wasn't as if the public employee unions were going to suddenly become popular with the public. Instead Walker's strategy resulted in a dramatic rise in the number of Wisconsinites who had very unfavorable views of him. Consequently, it now seems likely that he will have to survive a recall effort in his second year of office if he is to even to serve out his term. Simply put, it didn't have to be that way.

Walker's fellow first-term Republican governor Tom Corbett of Pennsylvania seems to have learned from the troubles of his counterpart in Wisconsin. Like Walker, Corbett (1949–) also began his term with years of experience in elected office (he was the Attorney General of Pennsylvania for the previous six years). Facing a similar deep fiscal crisis in 2011, Corbett proposed major cuts to education and welfare programs in the commonwealth. A 50 percent cut in state support for higher education was particularly upsetting to students at state-supported universities. Corbett seem somewhat insensitive to the pain of these cuts when he responded to critics by suggesting that since at least six of the campuses sit atop natural gas deposits, the colleges should start drilling for gas to make up their budget shortfalls. Remarks like these made Corbett very unpopular with the public and his poll numbers plummeted during the spring. As he struggled to get the Pennsylvania legislature to pass his budget, Corbett had to negotiate a new contract with the largest government employees' union in the state, the American Federation of State, County and Municipal Employees (AFSCME).

As the budget debate intensified in the state capital of Harrisburg, Governor Corbett could have aggressively challenged the unions, mimicking Walker's hard-line approach. Instead, Corbett opted to limit the number of fights he would face by striking a deal with AFSCME. In this deal the unions agreed to a one-year wage freeze and to pay 5 percent of their health insurance premiums instead of 3 percent. In turn they would receive a 4 percent total pay increase over the next three years. The deal was so amenable to the unions that many conservatives in the Keystone State claimed that Corbett had sold out to the unions. While drawing the ire of the right, Corbett's decision on the unions helped him to pass his budget rather easily and with substantial cuts in government spending. By August his poll numbers were rebounding and it looked like he had survived the fiscal storm that greeted him when he arrived in office.

Budgeting during a fiscal crisis will inevitably take its toll on those making the difficult decisions. There simply is no way to please everybody when cutbacks are taking place, and political fights are part of the landscape. Scott Walker made the mistake of taking on fights that would have been better left for another day, and it undercut the ability of his administration to govern. Tom Corbett avoided a fight with the unions when he had enough going on already; this allowed him to emerge from a budget crisis in fairly solid standing.

These two governors arrived in office during fiscal storms and chose not to find a hiding place to ride out the poor conditions. Both Corbett and Walker made tough choices that came with costs to their administrations. Walker just picked one fight too many and it jeopardized his future as Wisconsin's chief executive. The meteorological lesson here also applies to politics: when storms hit, it's best to limit your exposure to the elements and to emerge after the deluge in condition to get back to work.

For Discussion: *Who was the more effective governor for the long term: Walker of Wisconsin, who confronted the unions head on, or Corbett of Pennsylvania, who took a softer, more conciliatory approach? How did your state deal with the fiscal storms of 2011?*

THE IMPORTANCE OF PUBLIC FINANCIAL MANAGEMENT

The flow and management of funds is the lifeblood of our system of public administration. No policy, however farsighted, no system of administrative performance, however well crafted, can function unless it is associated with the flow of funds that will make it possible. Like other parts of the story of public administration covered so far, the system of public financial management rests on designs and reforms adopted over many years. Administrators need to understand how that system has been designed, what it is intended to do, what it is capable of doing, and especially what it is *not* capable of doing. As with the machinery of government and the system of intergovernmental relations, many aspects of the design of the American system of public financial management go back to our deepest political traditions and compacts—to the ideas of the founders at the Constitutional Convention. Others, such as the idea of the welfare state, go back only a few generations. Still others, such as the concept of "user pays," are at their height.

Six Principles

At the Boston Tea Party in 1773, America's pioneers began to lay down the design of this country's system of public financial management when they cast cargoes of tea into Boston Harbor rather than pay reasonable taxes on them to England.

> **TABLE 13.1**

The Federal Government's Fiscal Posture—FY 2011

Where the Federal Government Gets Its Revenue

Source	Percent
Individual Income Taxes	29%
Borrowing	33%
Social. Security and Social Insurance	24%
Corporate Income Taxes	8%
Excise Taxes	2%
Other Taxes (i.e., estate, gift)	4%

Where the Federal Government Spends Its Funds

Area of Expenditure	Percent
National Defense	23%
Social Security	19%
Medicare/Medicaid	21%
Other Discretionary Spending	14%
Interest on the Federal Debt	7%
Other Mandatory Spending	16%

Source: Budget of the United States, fiscal year 2011 figures. http://www.cbo.gov/ftpdocs/120xx/doc12039/HistoricalTables%5B1%5D.pdf.

When they shouted their slogan, "No taxation without representation," they were also asserting a cardinal value—a design principle—for the future system of public financial management in America. Taxation and public spending must be voted for; they must have, in effect, the stamp of democratic approval. This had not been the way most governments to that date had operated. States and potentates had levied and extracted taxes as a matter of the exercise of power. Then they kept or spent the money as they chose. America's founders made democratic consent to these things a fundamental design feature. This is why the Constitution requires that all tax legislation must originate in the House of Representatives, the legislative branch most responsive to the popular will.

At the heart of the design of the American system of public financial management are the following six principles:

1. *Democratic consent:* Taxation and spending should not be done without the explicit **consent of the governed.**
2. *Equity:* Governments should be equitable (treat people in similar circumstances similarly) in raising and spending taxes.
3. *Transparency:* What governments do in raising and spending funds should be open to public knowledge and scrutiny.

Consent of the governed ■
The notion that the institutions of government must be based on the will of the people.

4. *Probity:* There must be scrupulous honesty in dealing with public funds, of which legislators and administrators are the stewards, not the owners.
5. *Prudence:* These stewards should not take undue risks with public funds.
6. *Accountability:* Those who deal in public funds can and should be regularly called to account for their stewardship through legislative review and audit processes.

These normative principles are "shoulds," but they are all too often breached in real life. Public financial management can be abused. Democratic consent is lacking when government is conducted in secret. Concerns for equity often yield to **pork barrel** favoritism toward areas, clients, or groups. Without transparency, probity, and prudence, the inherent caution so essential to the management of public funds is thrown to the winds. Governments then may incur substantial losses through risky investments or negligence.

Balanced Budgets

A balanced **budget** is a budget in which receipts are equal to or greater than outlays. A government that has one is financially healthy. The advantages of a balanced budget, not spending more than you take in, are obvious. But there are also advantages to "unbalanced" budgets, those that require public borrowing. The "extra" spending can stimulate the economy during economic downturns and provide needed public works and public support for the less fortunate. But these considerations must be weighed against the danger that large deficits over a significant period can devalue the currency, kindle inflation, and have such a **crowding-out** effect on capital markets that an economic depression (or recession) occurs. Note that it is only the federal government that has the option of long-term deficit spending. The states all have constitutional or statutory provisions mandating balanced budgets (at least at the beginning of each year).

The Fiscal Year

Fiscal means having to do with taxation, public revenues, or public debt. The fiscal year is a 12-month accounting period without regard to a calendar year. The fiscal year for the federal government, through fiscal year 1976, began on July 1 and ended on June 30. But Congress, in part because of the invention of air conditioning, increasingly stayed in Washington through the summer. Because it usually waited until the last minute to pass the various appropriations bills, federal agencies increasingly had to depend on **continuing resolutions** for their funding. Finally, Congress realized how silly this was and simply moved the beginning of the new fiscal year to the end of the summer. Since fiscal year 1977, fiscal years for the federal government begin on October 1 and end on September 30. The fiscal year is designated by the calendar year in which it ends (e.g., fiscal year 2010 was the fiscal year ending September 30, 2010). Not all state and local governments follow the federal example. Most states begin their fiscal year on July 1, but a few use the first day of April, September, or October.

Fiscal is also used as an all-purpose adjective to refer to anything to do with government finances. Thus fiscal integrity is a characteristic of a government budget that spends no more than anticipated revenues. A balanced budget has fiscal integrity; a budget with a significant deficit does not. You will be deemed to have fiscal integrity when the person so deeming agrees with your fiscal policies. If that same person disagrees with your policies, you may be deemed so lacking in fiscal responsibility as to be considered fiscally irresponsible.

BUDGETING THEORY AND PRACTICE

Budgeting is the single most important decision-making process in public institutions. The budget itself is also a jurisdiction's most important reference document. In their increasingly voluminous formats, budgets simultaneously record policy decision outcomes, cite policy priorities as well as program objectives, and delineate a government's total service effort.

A public budget has four basic dimensions. First, it is a political instrument that allocates scarce public resources among the social and economic needs of the jurisdiction. Second, a budget is a managerial or administrative instrument: It specifies the **ways and means** of providing public programs and services; it establishes the costs of programs and the criteria by which these programs are evaluated for efficiency and effectiveness; it ensures that the programs will be reviewed or evaluated at least once during the budget year or **budget cycle**. Third, a budget is an economic instrument that can direct a jurisdiction's economic growth and development. Certainly at the national level—and to a lesser extent at the state and regional levels—government budgets are the primary instruments for redistributing income, stimulating economic growth, promoting full employment, combating inflation, and maintaining economic stability. Fourth, a budget is an accounting instrument that holds government officials responsible for the expenditure of the funds with which they have been entrusted. Budgets also hold governments accountable in the aggregate. The very concept of a budget implies that there is a ceiling, or a spending limitation, that literally (but theoretically) requires governments to live within their means.

The Taft Commission

Prior to 1900, the processes of public financial management in America lacked overall objectives. A particular need—to build a road, finance a war, or meet the costs of civil service and military pay—inspired an appropriate allocation by Congress. In the twentieth century, the growing scale and complexity of government led to calls for budgetary reform. In 1912, the **Taft Commission** recommended a national budgeting system. Writing in 1918, William F. Willoughby (1867–1960), a member of the Taft Commission, outlined developments that were leading to the creation of modern budget systems in state governments. In *The Movement Towards Budgetary Reform in the States*, Willoughby argues that budget reform would involve three major threads: (1) how budgets would advance and provide for popular control, (2) how budgets would enhance legislative and executive cooperation, and (3) how budgets would ensure administrative and management efficiency. This is rather prophetic when you consider the topics of some of our everyday headlines: taxpayers' revolts, "Proposition 13" movements, and other

Ways and means ■
The methods by which a state gains its funds, supplies, and other necessities. The English House of Commons has had a Committee on Ways and Means at least since 1644. The U.S. House of Representatives has had a Ways and Means Committee since 1795. All national tax legislation must originate in the House Ways and Means Committee.

Budget cycle ■
The timed steps of the budget process, which include preparation, approval, execution, and audit.

Taft Commission ■
The 1912 Commission on Economy and Efficiency, chaired by the president, that called for a national budgetary system. Its recommendations were incorporated into the Budget and Accounting Act of 1921.

forms of expenditure and revenue limitation laws (thread 1: popular control); continued infighting between the executive and legislative branches over budgetary control, deficits, and balanced budgets (thread 2: executive-legislative cooperation); and the effectiveness, or lack of it, in overburdened budgeting systems in maintaining managerial practices (thread 3: management effectiveness). Finally, in 1921, the Budget and Accounting Act was passed, bringing into being the Bureau of the Budget and the General Accounting Office (GAO), responsible for budgeting and auditing, respectively. (See Chapter 14 for further details on the GAO.)

At first, budgetary and compliance procedures remained simple, with budgets constructed of "line items" allocating funds to particular expenditure categories in each department—so much for salaries, furniture, paper, and so on. The process of auditing was correspondingly simple, emphasizing the examination of the extent to which expenditures had been in compliance with the purposes for which funds were allocated.

The 1930s saw the advent of increasingly larger government domestic programs and concomitant expenditures. Consequently, budgeting became of increasing importance. However, budgetary theory—that is, how to rationally allocate government resources—was woefully inadequate. The emphasis was on process and line-item budgeting, which stressed accountability and control. Performance budgeting (allocating funds for sets of activities), which stressed work measurement, much as scientific management, was increasingly advanced and used as an appropriate management-oriented budgetary process. Nevertheless, there remained little integration of the budgetary process with rational policymaking and decision making. In 1940, **V. O. Key Jr.** wrote an article bemoaning the lack of a budgetary theory. Greatly concerned about the overemphasis on mechanics, he posed what was soon acknowledged as the central question of budgeting: "On what basis shall it be decided to allocate X dollars to activity A instead of activity B?" Key went on to elaborate on what he considered the major areas of inquiry that should be researched to develop a budgeting theory. This, along with continuing pressure for even greater increases in the size of government programs, would set the stage for the major advances to come—but they would not be coming until after World War II.

The Influence of Keynes

The British economist **John Maynard Keynes** showed how government spending could be critical in managing an economy, by stimulating demand when resources were underutilized and unemployment was high. His thinking created the notion of budgetary policy as an instrument—in some respects the primary instrument—by which a nation could execute **macroeconomic** policy. All U.S. presidents since Franklin D. Roosevelt have used Keynes's theories to justify deficit spending to stimulate the economy, whether or not they admit it. Even President Richard M. Nixon admitted, "We're all Keynesians now." Keynes observed in his *General Theory* that "practical men, who believe themselves to be quite exempt from any intellectual influences, are usually the slaves of some defunct economist." He even provided the definitive economic forecast when he asserted that "in the long run we are all dead."

Aaron Wildavsky, in successive editions of *The Politics of the Budgetary Process*, highlighted the extent to which budgeting was a political and economic rather

---

V. O. Key Jr. (1908–1963) ■
The political scientist who did pioneering work in developing empirical methods to explore political and administrative behavior.

John Maynard Keynes (1883–1946) ■
The English economist who wrote the most influential book on economics of the past century, *The General Theory of Employment, Interest, and Money* (1936), which called for using a government's fiscal and monetary policies to positively influence a capitalistic economy.

Macroeconomics ■
The study of the relationships among broad economic trends such as national income, consumer savings and expenditures, capital investment, employment, money supply, prices, government expenditures, and balance of payments. Macroeconomics is especially concerned with government's role in affecting these trends.

than a mechanical process. Later, economists James M. Buchanan and Gordon Tullock of the "public choice" school presented government budgeting as a battle among beneficiaries seeking to capture funds to their own ends. Instead of a lack of budgetary theory, as in 1940, we are now abundantly served with it.

The Influence of Hayek

The Austrian-born economist Friedrich August von Hayek (1899–1992) became a British subject in 1938. But when World War II broke out and his academic peers, such as his close friend Keynes, were offered significant positions in the civil service, he was blacklisted from such work because of his Austrian background. (Austria had been incorporated into Germany; and no German—even a forsworn one—could be trusted with war work.) This had the unintentional but beneficial effect of giving him the time to write what became his most enduring and influential book. *The Road to Serfdom* (1944).

Hayek's *Road* argued that "the unforeseen but inevitable consequences of socialist planning create a state of affairs in which, if the policy is to be pursued, totalitarian forces will get the upper hand." To Hayek, state intervention in the economy in Great Britain and the United States differed only in degree, not in kind, from the fascism of Hitler and the communism of Stalin. The evil to be resisted was collectivism whether it wore a swastika or not. By asserting that allied economic policies were headed in the direction of Nazi policies, Hayek was being deliberately provocative and controversial. According to Hayek, "there is scarcely a leaf out of Hitler's [economic] book which somebody or other in England or America has not recommended us to take and use for our own purposes." Thus the "road" to serfdom was a collectivism that would ultimately lead to a Hitler-like totalitarian tyranny. Consequently, open market capitalism, a political system with minimal state planning and regulation, offered the only logical means to maintain prosperous and free societies.

Hayek's book, which can be condensed into five words—government planning leads to dictatorship—was an immediate sensation on both sides of the Atlantic. But it made Hayek decidedly unpopular in a postwar Britain that was implementing the socialist agenda of the Labour Party. So after a messy divorce that alienated him from even more friends and colleagues, Hayek moved across the pond to the University of Chicago.

In a world moving increasingly toward centralized planning, Hayek seemed more like a crank than a prophet during the next two decades. Nevertheless, his work became the foundation of the modern conservative movement. He not only inspired important disciples such as Margaret Thatcher and Ronald Reagan, but his writings have become a major part of the intellectual basis of the modern American Tea Party movement. Physically dead since 1992, he, meaning his ideas, has never been more alive.

The Objectives of Budgeting

The analysis of economists Richard and Peggy Musgrave in *Public Finance in Theory and Practice* provides a key to the understanding of the objectives of public

Aaron Wildavsky (1930–1993) ■ The author of *The Politics of the Budgetary Process* (1964; 4th ed., 1984), which reveals the tactics public managers use to get their budgets passed and explains why rational attempts to reform the budgetary process have always failed.

financial management. They postulate that government revenue raising and spending serve one of the following four objectives:

1. *Allocation:* Ensuring that an appropriate level of funding flows into sectors of the economy where it is required.
2. *Distribution:* Ensuring that the balance in public funding between regions, between classes of people in society, between public and private sectors, and between government and business reflects public policy.
3. *Stabilization:* Using public spending to stabilize the macroeconomy (or in some cases parts of it) as prescribed by Keynes.
4. *Growth:* Using the power of government spending to facilitate economic growth and wealth creation.

When we look at the budget of the national government—or of a state or local government—we can use this perspective for analysis. Is this a budget aimed at supporting growth in the economy? If so, what are its strategies—perhaps a lower tax on business and less government regulation? Is this a budget aimed at distributional objectives? Perhaps it seeks to assist cities and the long-term unemployed? Or it may be designed to stabilize the economic cycle—to stimulate demand during a slump or to moderate it in a boom. There is often disagreement over just how to achieve stated goals. Those who espouse supply-side economics believe that lowering tax rates, especially on marginal income, encourages fresh capital to flow into the economy, which in turn generates jobs, growth, and new tax revenue. Because this concept was adopted by the Reagan administration, it has been popularly called Reaganomics, even though Reagan's actual economic policies were a mélange of supply-side thinking, monetarism, old-fashioned conservatism, and even Keynesianism. While economist Arthur Laffer is generally credited with having "discovered" supply-side economics, the underlying premises of it were established more than 200 years ago by Alexander Hamilton in *The Federalist*, No. 21 (1787). Hamilton presented this argument:

> It is a signal advantage of taxes . . . that they . . . prescribe their own limit; which cannot be exceeded without defeating the end proposed—that is, an extension of the revenue. When applied to this object, the saying is as just as it is witty, that, "in political arithmetic, two and two do not always make four." If duties are too high, they lessen the consumption; the collection is eluded; and the product to the treasury is not so great as when they are confined within proper and moderate bounds.

Of course, one person's supply-side economics may be another's **voodoo economics.** Politicians are not always crystal clear in articulating what values and objectives underlie their budgetary strategies. Sometimes when these objectives have crass political motives—tax loopholes for campaign contributors—it is not polite or honorable to publicly admit them. Often, because budgets have grown so enormously complicated and detailed, those who are responsible for them literally do not fully understand the import of what they are doing—budgetarily speaking. Remember that it was David A. Stockman, Reagan's director of the Office of Management and Budget from 1981 to 1985, who, in 1981, confessed to readers of the *Atlantic Monthly* that "none of us really understands what's going on with all these numbers."

Voodoo economics ■
Presidential candidate George Bush's 1980 description of Republican primary opposition candidate Ronald Reagan's economic policy proposals. After joining Reagan as the vice-presidential nominee on the 1980 (and the 1984) ticket, Bush thought he had better not say it anymore. And he didn't. But the press never let him forget it. When in 1982 he denied ever having said it—"I didn't say it. I challenge anyone to find it"—NBC News then showed a videotape of him using the phrase (*Newsweek*, May 23, 1988). Since then, he hasn't denied saying it.

BOX 13.1 | The Budget Maximizing Bureaucrat

As in poker, bluff and overstatement are key tactical tools of departments and spending advocates during budget processes. Aware that their bids will be subject to some degree of cutback, bidders build in a protective tactic by providing for cutback in the original level of bid. This is not lying, but playing a tough game in which there are no rewards for losers. The game itself is regulated. There are rules in budget preparation as to the inflation indices that are to be used, the ways in which costs are to be estimated and programs are to be documented. But there are no limits on the ambitions of agency heads who want to maximize their agency budgets and their program's importance. In the often perverted world of government one may be only as important as the size of one's budget. The bureaucratic battle cry of "mine is bigger than yours" is heard often during the perennial budget wars. This phenomenon is universal. As Sir Humphrey Appleby in *The Complete Yes Minister* explains to a British civil service colleague, "we measure success by the size of our staff and our budget. By definition a big department is more successful than a small one." ◣

The Two Types of Budgets

There are two basic kinds of budgets. The most common, and what most people think of when the word *budget* comes to mind, is the operating budget. This is a short-term plan for managing the resources necessary to carry out a program. "Short term" can mean anything from a few weeks to a few years. Usually an operating budget is developed for each fiscal year, with changes made as necessary.

The second kind is the capital budget process that deals with planning for large expenditures for capital items. Capital expenditures should be for long-term investments (such as bridges and buildings), which yield returns for years after they are completed. Capital budgets typically cover 5- to 10-year periods and are updated yearly. Items included in capital budgets may be financed through borrowing (including tax-exempt municipal bonds), savings, grants, revenue sharing, special assessments, and so on. A capital budget provides for separating the financing of capital, or investment, expenditures from current, or operating, expenditures. The federal government has never had a capital budget in the sense of financing capital programs separately from current expenditures.

WAVES OF INNOVATION IN BUDGET MAKING

The structure and format of government budgets has been the subject of successive waves of innovation throughout the twentieth century. Why should this be so? It is simply because the ultimate statement of what a government stands for and spends is to be found in its budget. The budget is the key focal point of public administration. It places huge power in the hands of those who shape it. To the executive, the bureaucrat, and the "budgeteers," it is of incessant interest because of its timeless potency.

The Executive Budget

The first conceptual breakthrough in budgeting was really the conception that there could be a government budget at all—that is, a single document bringing

Representative government ■
A governing system in which a legislature freely chosen by the people exercises substantial power on their behalf.

Committee ■
A subdivision of a legislature that prepares legislation for action by the respective house or that makes investigations as directed by the respective house. Most standing (full) committees are divided into subcommittees, which study legislation, hold hearings, and report their recommendations to the full committee. Only the full committee can report legislation for action by the entire legislature.

Hill ■
The U.S. Congress, because it is literally situated on a hill. It is 88 feet above sea level, while the White House is 55 feet above sea level. Now there can be no doubt about which is the "higher" branch of government.

together in one place the revenue, expenditure, and financing plans of government. Until the twentieth century, budgeting in **representative governments** was decidedly a legislative, not an executive, function. Congressional or state legislative **committees** would appropriate funds for an agency without regard for the other agencies of government. Without overall coordination there was considerable confusion and ample opportunity for both incompetence and corruption. The movement toward an executive (or comprehensive) budget in the United States began in the states and was adopted by the federal government with the Budget and Accounting Act of 1921. Today all state governments except South Carolina use some variation of the executive budget.

An executive budget is both a technical process and a physical thing. First it is the process by which agency requests for appropriations are prepared and submitted to a budget bureau under the chief executive for review, alteration, and consolidation into a single budget document that can be compared to expected revenues and executive priorities before submission to the legislature. Then it becomes a tangible document, the comprehensive budget document for an executive branch of government that a jurisdiction's chief executive submits to a legislature for review, modification, and enactment. The president's budget is the executive budget for a particular fiscal year transmitted to the Congress by the president in accordance with the Budget and Accounting Act of 1921, as amended. Some elements of the budget (such as the estimates for the legislative branch and the judiciary) are required to be included without review by the Office of Management and Budget or approval by the president. After all, the president has no say in the budgets of the other branches of government. It is just convenient to include the comparatively small budgets of other branches in the overall document. The president's budget is the president's "wish list"—his suggestions to Congress. Every president's budget is "dead on arrival" the moment it is formally sent to the **Hill**, because Congress always makes extensive changes. The same considerations apply to state governors. Thus a governor's budget is an executive budget prepared by a state governor.

Not all of the national budget is open to public scrutiny, however. The "black budget" is the classified (secret) portion of the federal budget that hides sensitive military and covert projects. According to journalist Tim Weiner in *Blank Check*, "The black budget is a challenge to the open government promised by the Constitution. Today close to a quarter of every dollar in the Pentagon's budget for new weapons is cloaked in blackness. . . . Every dollar spent in secret defies the Framers' intent that the balance sheet of government should be a public document."

Line-Item Budgeting

The line-item budget was the original budget format—each item of expense had a literal line in a ledger book. It classified budgetary accounts according to narrow, detailed objects of expenditure (such as motor vehicles, clerical workers, or reams of paper) used within each particular agency of government, generally without reference to the ultimate purpose or objective served by the expenditure. It was useful as a record of expenditures and the criteria against which audits could measure compliance.

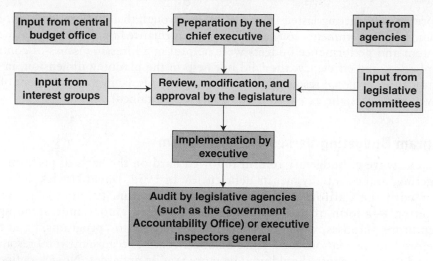

FIGURE 13.1
The executive budget process

The line-item budget is still widely used. Most local governments use it either as their basic budget format or as a supplement to more sophisticated formats. Because it offers such comprehensive details on proposed expenditures, legislators interested in fine-tuning executive budget recommendations are particularly partial to it because it allows for greater control and oversight.

While the traditional line-item budget was a great step forward, it had a major weakness. It might allow the test to be made as to whether funds had been spent on the purposes for which they had been appropriated, and that truly was (and is) an important test. But it gave no inkling as to how well these appropriations had been spent, whether they had resulted in "value for money."

Performance Budgeting

The concept of performance budgeting, first tried in New York City in the early 1900s, was the first major step beyond the line-item budget. Performance budgeting required a performance measure to be stated alongside each line item so that elementary calculations of unit cost and efficiency could be made. Line items were grouped, or categorized, in functional terms. For example, a sanitation (trash collection) department's workload could be determined on the basis of the number of houses and businesses served, which made it relatively easy to calculate how much trash is generated each week, month, or year. Using this measure, the efficiency of collection could be compared to a base period and a base cost. At this elementary level, comparisons in relative efficiency could be made from year to year, and in concept, between governments (in practice, intergovernmental comparisons required standardized measurement, which usually did not exist).

Performance budgeting, which was in its prime after being officially sanctioned by the Hoover Commission of 1949 (see Chapter 3), stressed using the budget process as a tool for work measurement and efficiency analysis. The heyday of performance budgeting lasted from the 1950s through the 1960s, and even today in some local governments you can still find performance budgets. However, while line-item and performance budgets were helpful in addressing issues of control, compliance, and efficiency, they did not help in the planning dimension, in the identification of global resource allocation to purposes, or in the assessment of effectiveness (that is, the extent to which goals were attained).

Program Budgeting Versus Incrementalism

The next wave of budgetary reform followed hard on the heels of performance budgeting, and essentially met its deficiencies. In 1954, David Novick, an economist with the California-based **RAND Corporation**, proposed "program budgeting"—a form of budgeting that would permit global understanding of expenditure purposes, which consolidated spending into "programs," and that therefore laid foundations for a focus on effectiveness, because the total resources directed to any purpose should now be more readily apparent. Novick defined a program as "the sum of the steps or interdependent activities which enter into the attainment of a specified objective."

RAND Corporation ■
A think tank created by the U.S. Air Force in 1947 and located in Santa Monica, California. The name is an acronym for research and development, and came from Project Rand, in which Douglas Aircraft agreed to provide civilian advice to the Air Force about developing new bombers. Separated from Douglas in 1948, the RAND Corporation was located in Santa Monica partly on the grounds that it was better to have a think tank of this kind away from the political pressures of Washington.

If a budget were to consist of large slabs of spending, called programs, directed toward particular objectives, the fragmentation problem common to line-item and performance budgeting would be overcome. Compliance could still be monitored, but the monitoring of efficiency and effectiveness would also be facilitated. And instead of being primarily an instrument of control and management information, the budget would become a planning document, and a document supporting the comparison of alternative expenditures at some meaningful level of aggregation. These were important conceptual breakthroughs.

The team that fashioned program budgeting at the RAND Corporation had an ambitious program, for they proposed not merely a rewrite of budget structure but a new framework for the analysis of policy and the review of accomplishment. They proposed not just program budgeting but planning-programming budgeting. This was a linked system with elements of forward planning, which they termed "the analytical comparison of alternatives," the allocation of resources in the framework of a multiyear cycle, and budgeting related to broad program groups rather than individual items. The "package" was named PPBS; it was intended "to create a new environment of choice." The document was now no longer about "Where are we?" but about "Where do we want to go?" It seemed that the theorists were at last making a contribution that had the potential to reshape government budgeting, planning, and resource allocation in a fundamental way.

Budgeting during the 1960s was dominated by PPBS—the planning, programming, budgeting system. First installed in the Defense Department during the Kennedy administration, it seemed to represent the height of rationality for the budget process. According to Schick, the stages of budget reform went from the development of budgetary theory, with its concerns for accountability and control, which were the hallmark of the line-item budget, to performance budgeting, with its emphasis on managerial efficiency, to PPBS, which stressed objectives, planning, and program effectiveness.

In 1965 Lyndon Johnson mandated the use of PPBS for all federal agencies. The application of PPBS, which required among other things that agencies detail program objectives and indicators for evaluation, make five-year expenditure forecasts, and generate numerous special cost-benefit analyses and zero-based reviews of program activities, marked perhaps the zenith of the management systems approach to public administration. Implemented hastily, with insufficient time for understanding, training, and development, the across-the-board implementation of PPBS failed quickly, leaving a platform for cynics and incrementalists to lambaste national initiatives and planning indiscriminately for many years.

PPBS was never without its critics. In 1964, Aaron M. Wildavsky published *The Politics of the Budgetary Process*, his immensely well-received critique of how budgeting was, in reality, an incremental process sharply influenced by political considerations. Incremental budgeting is a method of budget review that focuses on the increments of increase or decrease in the budget of existing programs. Incremental budgeting, which is often called traditional budgeting, is a counter-school of thought to more rational, systems-oriented approaches, such as PPBS or zero-based budgeting. But this old approach nicely takes into account the inherently political nature of the budget process and so will continue to be favored by legislative appropriations committees, if not by budget theorists. As Wildavsky wrote, "The largest determining factor of the size and content of this year's budget is last year's budget." And this is still overwhelmingly true, despite the reinventing-government movement and the devolution revolution of the 1990s.

In 1969 Wildavsky wrote a devastating critique of PPBS. Aside from stating flatly that he thought PPBS was unworkable, Wildavsky demonstrated how the planning and analytical functions of PPBS were contradictory to the essential nature of budgeting.

What was once mandatory for all federal agencies and widely adopted by state and local jurisdictions, by the end of the decade was officially "un"-adopted by the federal government and was widely considered to be unusable in its original format. Nevertheless, the influence of PPBS as a major budgeting process remains. Where it is still in use, however, it tends to exist in a hybrid instead of a pure form.

Wildavsky, who would later form and be the first dean of the University of California at Berkeley's Graduate School of Public Policy, was greatly influenced by Charles Lindblom, under whom he studied while a doctoral student at Yale. Incremental approaches to budgeting, or what would later be called "traditional budgeting," was the counter-school of thought to the management systems emphasis. The principal contention of the incrementalists (such as Wildavsky and Lindblom) was that budgets are inherently political and that studying budgeting and budgets is useful because it explains how and what choices (political compromises) have been made. Wildavsky even rebutted V. O. Key's classic question, "On what basis shall it be decided to allocate X dollars to activity A instead of activity B?," as unanswerable and irrelevant. What mattered was that the process of budgeting should facilitate decision making and assist in obtaining consensus about policy goals and program objectives.

Zero-Based Budgeting

In 1952 Verne B. Lewis continued the quest for the development of a theory of budgeting that Key had sought a dozen years earlier. In his "Toward a Theory of Budgeting," Lewis presented a theory of alternative budgeting. His analysis

Verne B. Lewis (1913–2001) ■ A federal budget officer. After retiring from the U.S. Department of Agriculture, he taught public administration at the University of Washington.

marked an important link to the PPBS systems of the 1960s and, especially, to the zero-based budgeting systems of the 1970s.

Lewis advocated budget submissions prepared in a manner that would facilitate comparison and demonstrate a range of choices for service and funding levels and, at the same time, have the final choice to provide realistic contracts—that is, specific, realistic expectations for the individual program managers. The implied rationale for this process almost seems to be a restating of Key's classic budgeting equation: For X level of funding, Y level of service can be provided; for $X + 1$ funding, $Y + Z$ services, and so on.

Alternative budgeting, Lewis's preferred solution, was a means to overcome traditional budgetary review techniques that focus on item-by-item control rather than on scaling levels of program services and goals to varying levels of funding. Lewis, a realist, saw clearly the influence of other factors such as "pride and prejudice, provincialism, and politics" in budgetary decisions. His hope was for the advent of budgeting systems that could overcome these noneconomic and nonrational factors.

The next stage of budget reform after PPBS, zero-based budgeting (ZBB), would fully incorporate Lewis's concept of alternative budgeting. Management consultant Peter A. Phyrr first developed it for Texas Instruments and then for the state of Georgia while Jimmy Carter was governor. In 1976, presidential candidate Carter made the installation of zero-based budgeting a campaign promise, and in 1977, as president, he ordered its adoption by the federal government. The initial reaction to ZBB paralleled the reaction to PPBS in the 1960s, only the downfall of ZBB was even more rapid.

Zero-based budgeting is a budgeting process that is, first and foremost, a rejection of the incremental decision-making model of budgeting. It demands a rejustification of the entire budget submission (from ground zero), whereas incremental budgeting essentially respects the outcomes of previous budgetary decisions (collectively referred to as the budget base) and focuses examination on the margin of change from year to year. So, under ZBB, an agency would have to rank each of its programs according to importance and face the possibility of the least important ones being discontinued.

In large part, ZBB failed because the conditions that had prevailed for most of the previous budgeting systems reforms had changed. In an era of acute resource scarcity, ZBB had little utility because there was little real chance that funding could be provided for any program growth. Critics assaulted ZBB as a fraud; some called it a nonsystem of budgeting. ZBB's fate in the federal government was tied to the Carter presidency. After the inauguration of a new president (Reagan) in 1981, it was quietly rescinded. Still, numerous state and local governments use ZBB techniques or some adaptation of ZBB. Now that the hype has subsided, ZBB remains an important part of public budgeting.

CONTEMPORARY BUDGET REFORM

It is useful to consider three important contemporary budget questions because they remain unanswered and are likely to be so far into the future. Should an integrated national budget and financial statement be created? Can multiyear budgetary cycles be effectively controlled through shorter-term political processes? And, finally, can a budget process with a greater policy focus be created?

Integrated Budgets

The concept of an integrated national budget and financial statement is an important one. No corporation would expect its shareholders to be content with less than an integrated **balance sheet** and operating statement. Yet the rule in government has too often been that the balance sheet is missing and the **operating statement** incomplete. The completion of the operating statement, after all, was the reason why the budget concept itself was originally created: to present a single document integrating at one view what was to be raised and spent. In 1967, the President's Commission on Budget Concepts reaffirmed the need for just such a unified budget, and one was adopted in 1969.

A unified budget is one in which receipts and outlays from federal funds and trust funds (such as Social Security) are consolidated. When these two fund groups are consolidated to display budget totals, transactions from one fund group to another (interfund transactions) are deducted to avoid double counting. The fiscal activities of **off-budget federal agencies** are not included in the unified budget. And this is precisely the problem. Because billions and billions of dollars of "off-budget" spending exists outside the unified budget, the budget is not all that "unified" after all. Some expenditures of this type were created to avoid political scrutiny of the costs of new programs, some represent the "black" expenditures of the intelligence community, and some are represented by the budgets of public enterprises whose financial affairs can be excluded from the unified budget if that will help the administration (as it usually does) to understate the total size of government spending. The goal of transparency in public financial administration is a strong argument for reform in this area, with the ultimate goal being an annual consolidated financial statement—both balance sheet and operating statements—which is unified, inclusive, and prepared on independently validated standards as to accounting, estimating, and valuation. Only then can we claim to have a mature budgetary document in line with community expectations and private sector norms.

Multiyear Budgets

A second long-standing but essentially unresolved issue in budgeting concerns the need of some program areas for multiyear funding—for financing that extends over a number of years. Just as business demands certainty from government as to the rules of the game, so does effective public administration in many areas, from major infrastructure investment to strategic research. Effectively, the federal government uses a multiyear budget for a wide variety of programs, such as transfer payments to the states based on statutory formulas, **entitlement programs,** multiyear appropriations for construction projects, and, of course, long-term borrowing authority. Yet, our legislators might argue, if they do not have the opportunity annually to apportion public funds, how can they take an integrated view and place funds where today's priorities lie?

A strong case can be made for a biennial or triennial budget cycle. The advantages of such a horizon would include a better matching of known funding with the needs of longer-term projects and allocations; an ability for government and business alike to plan with certainty over several years; and the containment

Balance sheet ■
A summary of the financial worth of an individual or organization broken down by assets (what is owned) and liabilities (what is owed). It is called a balance sheet because total assets balance with, or are equal to, total liabilities plus net worth.

Operating statement ■
The detailed financial information that supplements a balance sheet.

Off-budget federal agencies ■
Agencies, federally owned in whole or in part, whose transactions have been excluded from the budget totals under provisions of law (e.g., the Federal Financing Bank). The fiscal activities of these agencies are presented in an appendix to the federal budget.

Entitlement program ■
Any government program that pays benefits to individuals, organizations, or other governments that meet eligibility requirements set by law. Social Security is the largest federal entitlement program for individuals. Others include farm price supports, Medicare, Medicaid, unemployment insurance, and food stamps.

of the necessary political wrangling over budget making so that the crescendo of horse trading would occur less frequently. This would thus allow politicians, lobbyists, and bureaucrats more time to do other things—to consider longer-term policies, to engage in in-depth scrutiny of the implementation of programs, and perhaps to concentrate on cooperative rather than adversarial aspects of their responsibilities.

FINANCING PUBLIC EXPENDITURE

There are three basic elements to public financial management: (1) taxing, (2) spending, and (3) saving. Yes, unlike the federal government, many state and local jurisdictions do not spend all their funds each year. Contingency and "rainy day" accounts are common at the subnational levels. Still, taxing and spending are the essential elements of public finance. And it is a pointless chicken-egg argument as to which comes first. But they eventually have to be reconciled—sort of. Spending must always equal taxing plus borrowing. Because tax revenues tend to be **elastic**, one can only estimate yearly revenues. A booming economy will bring in a surfeit of taxes; a sluggish economy will bring in less revenue than before. This is why budget makers so often paint a rosy scenario—an all-too-optimistic estimate of economic growth and interest-rate levels made by budgeteers so that the estimated deficit will seem less than realistic estimates would suggest. But beware the rosy scenario! If you are a budget maker, it will strain your credibility. If you are a consumer of budgets, it will set you up for a fall. Whether scenarios are rosy, neutral, or harsh, the fact remains that budget making involves the task of matching revenues and expenditures so that government can function in the coming year.

Governments have eight principal means of financing their spending requirements. This is something of an advance from biblical times, when revenue from tax collectors and forced seizure of property were the main available strategies. Today, governments must choose from the following:

1. Imposing a **direct tax**
2. Imposing an **indirect tax**
3. Collecting revenue by imposing user charges for government customers
4. Obtaining grants from another level of government or an aid agency
5. Making profits from the activities of public enterprises
6. Borrowing from the public through bonds, or from private lenders through loans
7. Using innovative finance techniques, **public-private partnerships**, franchises, or the licensing of private sector providers
8. Using earnings from savings or investments, if any

Each of these methods of raising government revenue involves complex issues of policy, such as incidence (on what group the tax will fall), effectiveness (whether the tax will succeed in yielding the revenue it should), equity (whether it is fair), and administrative ease and cost. If these financing options are still insufficient, governments may turn to privatization, cost cutting, or the termination of programs to reduce the scope of what must be financed.

Elastic ■
The up-and-down nature of tax revenues; they increase or decrease depending on overall economic conditions.

Direct tax ■
A tax (e.g., an income tax) paid to a government directly by a taxpayer. Article I, Section 9, of the U.S. Constitution holds that "no capitation, or other direct tax shall be laid, unless in proportion to the census or enumeration herein before directed to be taken." This inhibited the enactment of the federal income tax until the Sixteenth Amendment of 1913 changed the Constitution to allow for direct taxation.

Indirect tax ■
A tax (e.g., a sales tax) paid to a third party, who in turn pays it to a government.

Public-private partnerships ■
Joint efforts on the part of local governments and the business community to plan for, generate public support for, and pay for major social programs or construction projects that will be mutually beneficial.

Taxation

General taxation (or a general property tax in the context of local government) is the most traditional means of financing public services. A tax is a compulsory contribution exacted by a government for public purposes. This does not include

> **TABLE 13.2**

Landmarks in Federal Budget Practices

1921	The Budget and Accounting Act establishes a Bureau of the Budget in the Department of the Treasury and the General Accounting Office as an audit agency of Congress.
1939	The Reorganization Act transfers the Bureau of the Budget from the Treasury to the White House.
1950	The Budgeting and Accounting Procedures Act mandates the performance budgeting concepts called for by the Hoover Commission.
1961	The Department of Defense installs a planning programming budgeting system (PPBS).
1965	A PPBS is made mandatory for all federal agencies by the Johnson administration.
1970	The Bureau of the Budget is given more responsibility for managerial oversight and renamed the Office of Management and Budget.
1971	PPBS is formally abandoned in the federal government by the Nixon administration.
1974	The Congressional Budget and Impoundment Control Act revises the congressional budget process and timetable and creates the Congressional Budget Office.
1977	Zero-based budgeting is required of all federal agencies by the Carter administration.
1981	Zero-based budgeting requirements are rescinded by the Reagan administration. David Stockman, director of the Office of Management and Budget, tells the *Atlantic Monthly* that "none of us really understands what's going on with all these numbers."
1985	The Gramm-Rudman-Hollings Act is signed into law; it seeks to balance the federal budget by mandating across-the-board cuts over a period of years.
1986	The Supreme Court, in *Bowsher v. Synar*, invalidates certain provisions of the Gramm-Rudman-Hollings Act.
1990	The Budget Enforcement Act amends the Gramm-Rudman-Hollings Act to require that new spending be balanced by new taxes or spending reductions.

(Continued)

▶ **TABLE 13.2 (Continued)**

Landmarks in Federal Budget Practices

	The Credit Reform Act (in response to the savings and loan scandal) tightens requirements on federal lending and loan guarantees.
	The Chief Financial Officers Act requires federal agencies to create a chief financial officer position to oversee agency finances.
1993	The Government Performance Results Act requires agencies to justify their budget requests on the basis of the results or outcomes to be achieved.
1997	Agencies are required to submit strategic plans, including mission statements and performance goals.
1998	A Government-Wide Performance Plan is first presented with the federal budget.
2000	Agencies must now advise Congress as to how well they met the performance objectives and goals set out in their strategic plans.
2004	The OMB no longer makes budget projections beyond 5 years, ending the practice of 10-year projections that had been in place since 1971.
2009	The White House ends the practice of putting war costs in supplemental budgets and instead counts spending for the Iraq War in the overall budget.
2011	The House of Representatives passes a Balanced Budget Amendment to the Constitution but the Senate does not.

employee and employer assessments for retirement and social insurance purposes, which are classified as insurance trust revenue.

Taxes are generally perceived by a public to be legitimate if they are levied by that public's elected representatives. Indeed, one of the causes of, and principal rallying cries for, the American Revolution was that there should be "no taxation without representation" because "taxation without representation is tyranny." Consequently, practically all taxes at all levels of government are now enacted by popularly elected legislatures.

People have been making poignant remarks about taxes since ancient times. For example, the first-century Roman historian Suetonius reported on a complaint presented to the Emperor Vespasian about taxes on the public toilets (in effect, user fees) in Rome. The emperor took a coin that came from this tax, stuck it in the complainer's nose and asked, "Does it smell?" Hardly even waiting for the answer of "no," he continued: "Yet it comes from urine." Since then, nothing has been in such bad odor that it could escape taxation. Sometimes tax reform is not as much reform as the addition of new kinds of taxes. New things to tax come about by the inventiveness of fiscal experts or by new technology. A vivid example is presented by James Kendall in his biography of Michael Faraday, one of the pioneers in the development of electricity. When Faraday was first explaining his invention to the British chancellor of the exchequer, he was interrupted with "the impatient inquiry: 'But, after all, what use is it?' Like a flash of lightning came the response: 'Why, sir, there is every probability that you will soon be able to tax it!'" Whether urine or electricity, it is all part of the cosmic, all-encompassing governmental revenue stream.

Taxes are one of the most volatile of political issues. Walter Mondale, in accepting the Democratic Party's presidential nomination in 1984, said, "Taxes will go up. And anyone who says they won't is not telling the truth." He lost by a landslide. George Bush in accepting the Republican Party's presidential nomination in 1988 said, "Read my lips. No new taxes!" He won by a landslide. So there is a lesson in this. Bush's lips, however, did not speak the truth. He raised taxes, and this was very much held against him when he futilely sought reelection in 1992.

There are major differences between the federal and state-local revenue systems. The federal system has experienced a trend toward less diversity; more than two-thirds of its general revenue is provided by the federal income tax and the several insurance trust funds (such as Social Security). State and local revenue systems, in contrast, depend on a greater variety of revenue sources (such as property taxes, income taxes, sales taxes, user charges, lotteries, and federal grants). While local governments still rely primarily on the property tax, their states—with a few exceptions—rely largely on the state personal income tax. In addition, state sales and business taxes provide a significant source of income. This mélange of taxing authorities creates great disparities in the state-local tax burden. A resident of New York may pay hundreds or thousands of dollars in state income taxes, while a resident of Texas—which has no state income tax—pays none. Virginians have to pay more than double the sales taxes paid by Vermonters. There are even greater variations in property taxes. A house in one jurisdiction may be assessed at three times the amount of an identical house in another.

The Ability-to-Pay Principle

Historically the art of taxation has been defined as "so plucking the goose as to obtain the largest amount of feathers with the least possible amount of hissing." While this definition is usually attributed to **Jean-Baptiste Colbert**, efforts to reduce the "hiss" have continued unabated. Two of the classic means of doing this are using the "ability-to-pay" principle or "hiding" the taxes.

The ability-to-pay is the principle of taxation that holds that the tax burden should be distributed according to a person's wealth. It is based on the assumption that as a person's income increases, the person (whether an individual or a corporation) can and should contribute a larger percentage of income to support government activities. The progressive income tax is based on the ability-to-pay principle.

Jean-Baptiste Colbert (1619–1683) ■ King Louis XIV's controller general of finance.

The personal income tax is based on ability-to-pay, in that the tax rate is applied against income. But income is more than just money; it is any asset that increases one's net worth, and yet income taxes are not necessarily a straight tax on all of one's income in a given year. Remember all those millionaires that the press annually discovers who do not pay any tax on their income? They are able to do this because it is not their total incomes that are subject to taxation but their adjusted gross incomes. All taxpayers have the right to exclude certain kinds of incomes from their gross incomes for tax purposes. For example, interest from state and local bonds is exempt from federal taxation. Thus a millionaire whose sole income came from investments in such bonds would pay no federal income tax. (To ensure that such citizens pay at least something, there is now an "alternative minimum tax"—but emphasis is on the "minimum.") The taxpayer may also subtract deductions and exemptions from taxable income. Then the taxpayer can deduct a host of expenses, as long as they are allowed by the tax laws: medical care, state and local taxes (if a federal return), home mortgage interest, and charitable contributions. A taxpayer can itemize deductions or take a minimum standard deduction, which is a precalculated weighted average. Progressive tax rates are then applied to the taxable income to determine how much tax is due.

All states except Alaska, Florida, Nevada, South Dakota, Texas, Washington, and Wyoming have personal income taxes, as do many cities. Thus residents of Baltimore, Cleveland, Detroit, New York, and Philadelphia, for example, must pay personal income taxes to three different governments: federal, state, and local. With so many taxes at so many levels of government, it is no wonder that **tax avoidance** has become a national pastime rivaling even baseball. The very wealthy J. Pierpont Morgan (1836–1913) provided the intellectual foundation of tax avoidance when he said, "No citizen has a moral obligation to assist in maintaining the government. If Congress insists on making stupid mistakes and passing foolish tax laws, millionaires should not be condemned if they take advantage of them." The Tax Reform Act of 1986, designed to make tax avoidance more difficult by closing many **tax loopholes**, was with good reason informally, cynically, and accurately referred to as the "Tax Accountant's Full Employment Act."

The Flat Tax

An income tax that is flat has no brackets; it charges the same rate to each taxpayer. The concept has been put forward in a variety of proposals for reform of the federal income tax. This has long been advocated by prominent Republicans in the Congress such as Jack Kemp of New York in the 1980s and Richard Armey of Texas in the 1990s. It even became a major issue in the 1996 presidential race when millionaire publisher Steve Forbes based his campaign for the Republican presidential nomination on it.

The flat tax is attractive in large measure because it is so simple and seemingly fair. Everybody just pays the same percentage of their income. Tax returns could be completed on a postcard. Nevertheless, Democratic Party members tend to oppose it because it grossly violates the ability-to-pay principle. A flat tax is inherently regressive in that the poor pay proportionately more than the rich. When the idea became a major issue in the 1996 Republican primary elections,

Tax avoidance ■
Planning one's personal finances to take advantage of all legal tax breaks, such as deductions and tax shelters.

Tax loophole ■
An inconsistency in the tax laws, intentional or unintentional, that allows the avoidance of some taxes. An intentional tax loophole is tax expenditure. A tax expenditure for one person is a often viewed as a loophole by another. Tax loopholes are perfectly legal; but they have an unsavory reputation as the handiwork of special interest lobbyists.

ALTERNATIVE Theories | Progressive versus Flat Tax

Progressive Tax	Flat Tax
Tax rate rises with income	Tax rate unaffected by income
Multiple tax brackets	Single tax bracket for all
Complicated rules	Simple rules
Appears unfair	Appears fair
Favored by politicians	Favored by the wealthy
Opposed by political right	Opposed by the political left
Greater government revenue	Lower government revenue ◤

Note that ever since Adam Smith argued in *The Wealth of Nations* (1776) that the progressive income tax based on the ability-to-pay is the best tax policy, the wealthy have been counterarguing that the rich should pay at the same rate as the poor. What do you think is the best tax policy: a progressive tax or a flat (meaning regressive) tax?

the accounting firm of Price Waterhouse did an analysis reported in *U.S. News & World Report*. It found that a couple with two children and an income of $60,000 would pay 2 percent more if there was a 21 percent flat tax instead of the current system. However, if that same family earned $300,000, they would have an effective tax cut of 31 percent.

Many forces in the economy are natural enemies of a true flat tax. Charitable and religious organizations do not want to lose the deductions that encourage contributions to them. The housing industry is concerned that the loss of the home mortgage interest deduction would depress housing prices. Corporations worry that the elimination of tax deductions for new equipment purchases would hurt profits. And public financial analysts express concern that a flat tax at the oft-mentioned rate of 17 percent could not raise enough revenue to run the government.

User Charges

User charges are specific fees that users or consumers of a government service pay to receive that service. For example, a homeowner's water bill, if based on usage, would be a user charge. Other examples include toll roads and bridges and charges to use public swimming pools. If a sports team plays on a publicly owned field that has been fenced in, gate takings should be the basic source of finance for that operation. Public transportation is a little different. There, some of the costs need to be recovered from riders. But because the existence of public transportation saves government the need to build new freeways, and because the limitation on the resulting number of commuter automobiles lessens air pollution, public transportation also offers obvious advantages. Accordingly, it is customary and proper for publicly owned transportation systems to be financed partly from user charges and partly from taxation. Freeways, because gasoline taxes are used to pay for them, are financed in this manner. Freeways provide some obvious public

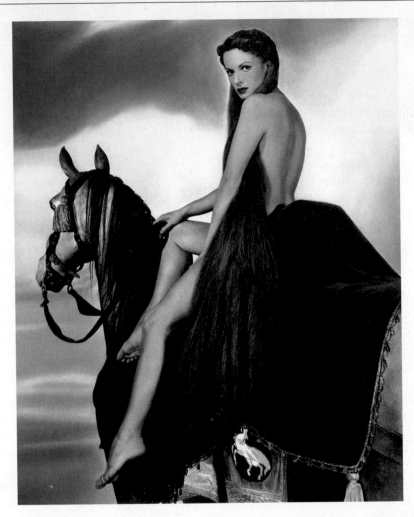

Maureen O'Hara, bare but for her hair, in the title role in the 1955 film *Lady Godiva*, acts out the most famous tax revolt in history. In 1057, so the legend goes, the vassals of Lord Leofric in Coventry, England, complained about their tax burden to his wife, Lady Godiva. Nice lady that she was, she then pleaded with her husband to lower the levy. Nasty fellow that he was, he agreed, but only if she would ride naked through the streets of the town. He didn't think she would do it. But she did. Then he kept his word, reduced the taxes, and thereby established public nudity as an effective tax reduction technique. Godiva chocolates, first made in Belgium in 1926, were introduced to the United States in 1966 with a massive advertising campaign featuring Lady Godiva's tax-revolting ride. Market research had determined that drawings of a naked woman on a horse combined with the subliminal advocacy of lower taxes would sell expensive chocolates to the Americans. After all, the only people who could afford them were already in a high tax bracket!

goods, such as mobility for the car-owning public and a capability for business to truck its products around. But on the other hand, particular freeways do benefit selectively the commuters that are able to access them. These commuters, some argue, should incur a user charge—that is, they should pay a toll—but this is not always politically possible.

While user charges are voluntary in theory, in practice they are often unavoidable. Few citizens consider municipal water and sewer connections among life's little options. Being essential, the charges are in actuality taxes that dare not use their name. Many user charges are more easily avoided. For example, if you do not attend a state university, you do not have to pay their fees—except for your portion of the overall subsidy such institutions receive through general taxation. If you do not hunt or fish, you need not buy a state license to do so. And if you do not build an extension to your house, you need not pay for a local building permit.

User charges are often treated as earmarked tax revenue in that the funds they produce may only be used for legislatively determined purposes. Thus charges for hunting and fishing licenses are often earmarked for wildlife conservation programs.

Earmarked tax ■
A tax whose revenues must, by law, be spent for specific purposes. For example, a state gasoline tax may be earmarked for highway construction.

Grants

Grants represent an important category of revenue for state and local governments in the United States, as well as in other federal systems such as Australia and Germany. As we have seen in Chapter 4, there are hundreds of federal grant programs, particularly reaching into the areas of health, welfare, and infrastructure (programs involving transportation, water, and sewerage). There are, as well, block grants designed to bolster the financial position of poorer states and regions. The block grants may be automatic, based on population. But when grants are a function of population size, counting people becomes a matter of counting money. Local jurisdictions, especially the big cities, often complain that they are shortchanged in grant money because of a census undercount—the contention that people are missed by the census because they move, are illiterate, or are fearful of filling out government forms, or for other reasons. Because the count is critical for congressional districting and for the funding level of many intergovernmental grant programs, jurisdictions are apt to make an issue of what they consider to be an undercount.

THE PROBLEM OF DEBT AND BUDGETARY MANIPULATION

Nowhere can the urgency of developing adequate standards of public financial management and reporting be seen more clearly than in the management of debt. The ability to incur debt is in many respects a hallmark of governments. They usually exist, in part, to undertake projects whose benefits will go on for many generations. This is why Alexander Hamilton wrote in an April 30, 1781, letter to Robert Morris that "a national debt, if it is not excessive, will be to us a national blessing." Of course, there have always been those who disagree with Hamilton's famous sentiment. Andrew Jackson, while a candidate for president, wrote to L. H. Colman on April 26, 1824, "I am one of those who do not believe that a national debt is a national blessing. . . . It is calculated to raise around the administration a moneyed aristocracy dangerous to the liberties of the country." This essential argument continues today among contemporary politicians.

Debt is a way of matching costs with those who benefit from the borrowing, of seeing that future generations pay their share of the costs of roads or buildings we put in place now, of ensuring "intergenerational equity." In the United States, tens of thousands of governments can issue bonds and incur debt. These range from the federal government to the tiniest local governments.

The national debt is the total outstanding debt of a central government. The national debt is often confused with the nation's budget deficit in a given year. The debt is, in effect, the total of all the yearly deficits (borrowing) that have not been repaid, plus accumulated interest. It is President Herbert Hoover who is usually credited with first saying: "Blessed are the young for they shall inherit the national debt."

Deficit financing is a situation in which a government's excess of outlays over receipts for a given period is financed primarily by borrowing from the public. Deficit financing, and especially the general acceptance of it by economic theorists, is largely a phenomenon of the last hundred years. Depending on the economist you listen to, a large deficit is either considered a major drag on the economy or a significant stimulus.

Abuse of Public Debt

Borrowing is a tool that has a clear purpose in public administration. It is a tool that in the right circumstances public administrators should use with confidence. It is also a tool notoriously open to abuse. There are six main categories of such abuse:

1. Borrowing to finance operating (or "recurrent") expenditure
2. Borrowing beyond the level of repayments the community can meet
3. Borrowing under poorly structured contracts that leave the borrower no protection against large interest-rate hikes by the lender
4. Borrowing to finance projects that give no return (like public monuments) or are highly speculative (like building facilities to host sporting events, the tenure of which cannot be guaranteed)
5. Borrowing where government lacks the administrative capacity to manage or implement projects without major losses
6. Borrowing where there is widespread corruption and where a high proportion of the funds borrowed will be creamed off in payments to corrupt politicians and administrators, rather than applied to the purpose for which the funds were ostensibly borrowed

These risks are compounded by the fact that politicians often view borrowing as politically preferable to imposing higher taxes. Borrowing is virtually invisible to the electorate. If the projects produced by it are impressive, politicians see a painless way of "buying" votes—especially when the proverbial chickens do not come home to roost until a subsequent administration.

Overcoming these problems is not straightforward. There is not a high level of understanding and debate of these issues in the community. It is genuinely hard to assess the masses of confusing data that project boosters disseminate. Democratic oversight through legislative committees is of varying effectiveness. And audit scrutiny is often too late.

Municipal Bonds

A bond is a certificate of indebtedness issued by a borrower to a lender that constitutes a legal obligation to repay the principal of the loan plus accrued interest. Municipal bonds are the debt instruments of subnational governments. This causes some confusion because they appear to refer only to bonds issued by a local government. Yet bonds issued by states, territories, or possessions of the United States, or by any municipality, political subdivision (including cities, counties, school districts, and special districts for fire prevention, water, sewer, irrigation, and other purposes), or public agency or instrumentality (such as an authority or commission) are subsumed under the rubric "municipal bonds." While the interest on municipal bonds is exempt from federal taxes, state and local exemptions may vary. Tax-exempt bonds allow jurisdictions to borrow money at lower than commercial market interest rates. The buyers of the bonds find them attractive because their high marginal tax rates make a tax-free investment more advantageous than a taxable one paying even higher interest.

The Rating Agencies

The problem of abuse of public debt is critically important for citizens, administrators, and honest politicians. But it is also very important to lending institutions. After all, borrowing is a two-sided activity: There can be no borrowing without some institution agreeing to lend. International financial markets are composed of many thousands of lenders. Their capability of assessing the merits of a project a government wishes to fund by borrowing will vary greatly. Large lenders financing big governments might have an acute idea as to the merits of projects and the creditworthiness of borrowers, but the thousands of smaller governments and smaller lenders may well see each other "through a glass darkly"—that is, very imperfectly indeed.

The New York ratings agencies, Standard and Poor's and Moody's, exist to fill this gap, which they do by rating or assessing the creditworthiness of borrowers (public or private) and assigning them a credit rating—just like those that have long been assigned to individuals and businesses. However, at the scale of borrowing a government undertakes, the difference between a triple A rating and a rating of merely double A might amount to millions of dollars in loan repayments. Bond rating systems differ, but the highest or most **gilt edge** are triple A; the lowest rating of **investment grade** bonds is triple B. Bonds rated below double B are generally considered speculative or junk. The ratings agencies have independent teams of analysts permanently assigned the task of reassessing ratings, and governments are keen to persuade the agencies of the safety and security offered by their prudent financial management approaches.

The role these agencies have come to play in the financial management of governments is crucial. On the one hand, they are a clearinghouse for information and confidence. No doubt their activities facilitate lending that might not otherwise occur. On the other hand, they are not value free. By upgrading the ratings of the bonds of governments whose actions accord with their ideology, they impose a value scale on policy decisions throughout the world. It is a value scale that rewards balanced budgets and reductions in government expenditure. It gives a tilt

Gilt edge ■
A popular term for a stock, bond, or other security with the highest rating (for safety of investment) or for a negotiable instrument with similar safety.

Investment grade ■
Refers to securities that fall into the top four categories, AAA to BBB or Aaa to Baa, for Standard and Poor's and Moody's ratings, respectively. Some institutions are required by law to buy only investment-grade issues.

IN THE NEWS | What Rating Would the Rating Agency Get?

In August of 2011 Standard and Poor's (S & P), the bond rating agency, made the decision to downgrade the credit rating of U.S. government securities from the highest possible level of safety, AAA, to AA+. The downgrade of U.S. Treasury securities was the first in the history of the nation and set off a dramatic sell-off on Wall Street, with stock values plummeting by over 1,000 points. Representatives of Standard and Poor's stated that their decision to downgrade the safety of U.S. securities was based largely on the federal government's inability to work toward getting control over the ballooning national debt. In essence, S & P was warning that the government's ever-mounting debt and dysfunctional government had made it a less safe bet to be able to pay back the interest and principal on the bonds and Treasury notes that investors purchased from the U.S. Treasury.

While S & P found the federal government to be a more risky investment option than it was in the past, many people had concerns about just how reliable the rating agency itself is. Looking at its recent track record with some of the biggest fiscal failures in Europe, it seems that Standard and Poor's may be performing as badly as the fiscal situations it rates. Consider the record: In 2006 S & P rated Ireland with its highest debt rating of AAA, the same rating that the United States had until August of 2011. Ireland's economy had been flourishing for years and the "Celtic Tiger" appeared to many to be in a sound fiscal situation. However, the fiscal condition of Ireland was actually much more fragile than portrayed. By 2008 Ireland's fiscal situation had deteriorated to the point where the European Union was exploring how it could provide loans to bail the country out of its financial mess. It wasn't until after the fact that S & P caught up with reality; it finally downgraded Ireland's debt rating in March of 2009.

In 2006 Iceland was given a AA+ rating by S&P, the second highest rating available, and the same rating that the United States held after its 2011 downgrade. The fairly strong grade given to Iceland proved to be highly suspect when the small island nation teetered near bankruptcy in 2008 and its national currency crashed.

Even Greece, which has become the poster child for fiscal messes, received a solid A rating from S & P as late as 2009. By 2011 the likelihood of Greece actually defaulting on its bonds was quite high, and its debt worries were putting a drain on the European Union economy as a whole.

In the end, S & P's decision to downgrade the financial rating of the United States may prove to be warranted. Clearly the mounting federal debt and the inability of the divided government to effectively come up with a plan to curb that debt raise questions about the long-term fiscal safety of U.S. securities. But as Nate Silver of the *New York Times* wrote on August 8, 2011, "it may be worthwhile to adopt a contrarian investing strategy that specifically bets against S & P's ratings." Given S&P's big misses in recent years Silver may be on to something. ◣

to "the level playing field." And of course, these agencies work in secret and are not subject to any form of democratic accountability. When Standard and Poor's in 1995 rated Detroit triple B, Baltimore A, and Minneapolis triple A, it made judgments that will affect the overall quality of life in those cities for years to come. Minneapolis, because it has the best possible rating, will save millions. It will have more money to spend on police and parks than cities such as Detroit and Baltimore, which will have to spend those "extra" millions on interest.

Debt and Economic Recovery

Demand for goods and services is the driving force behind economic vitality. In the U.S. economy, most demand is derived from private sources such as businesses and individuals. However, when a recession occurs that causes demand from private sources to lessen, this in turn causes businesses to cut back on their operations, including employees. Generally, demand eventually increases as the prices for goods and services reach the point where it's attractive for investors and consumers to re-enter the markets. However, when businesses and individuals either lack the financial resources or are too afraid to spend their capital, it can lead an economy from an ordinary economic downturn into a deep recession or even a depression. Such was the case in the Great Depression of the 1930s, and such was the concern with the recession of 2008 and 2009. The collapse of the nation's housing market and banking industries in the fall of 2008 had many economists concerned that the economy was on the brink of falling off the cliff and dropping into the first depression in almost 70 years.

This concern led Congress to pass the American Recovery and Reinvestment Act of 2009, which was designed to pump badly needed capital into the struggling U.S. economy. The act, commonly referred to as the "Federal Stimulus," included tax cuts, expansion of unemployment benefits, and increased spending in the education, health care, infrastructure, and energy sectors. In all, the legislation came at a price tag of $787 billion, raising hopes that the law would help lead the nation out of recession, but also generating significant concern that the price tag of the stimulus would increase the size of the federal budget deficits and national debt. The nonpartisan Congressional Budget Office (CBO) estimated that enacting the bill would increase federal budget deficits by $185 billion over the remaining months of fiscal year 2009, by $399 billion in 2010, and by $134 billion in 2011. This heavy debt would only contribute to the federal government's already mammoth debt, which stood at nearly $12 trillion in late 2009. Proponents of the stimulus package argued that this added debt was worth it because the money pumped into the economy prevented the nation from a complete failure of the economic system. Opponents argued that the economy would emerge from recession without the influx of government cash, and that the added debt would cripple economic growth in the next decade. Both sides had a point.

At the national level, government debt can be a very dangerous thing. If the federal government borrows to the point where investors question its ability to pay back those debts, it becomes difficult for the government to continue finding investors who want to buy the federal bonds and notes that allow the national government to pay off its debt. When Standard and Poor's downgraded the debt rating of the United States in August of 2011, this fear became more justified than ever before. High debt also brings with it the risk of higher inflation because the value of the dollar is likely to decrease as the economic stability of the government that issues those dollars becomes more suspect. While these risks are real, so is the risk of letting a highly damaged economy slip closer to the precipice of recession. As the U.S. economy crawled along in 2010 and 2011, many argued that the focus on controlling debt was holding back the ability of government to push a more robust economic recovery. Let the debate go on.

Bonds, Debt, and Emergency Recovery

The terrorist attacks of September 11, 2001, and the major destruction from Hurricane Katrina in 2005 had a major impact on the area of municipal bonds

IN THE NEWS | Something Else to Fear

There are many things that elicit fear among people. Snakes, spiders, terrorists, and earthquakes are just a few of the things that can cause people to lose sleep at night. While the list of frightening things is extensive, the term "debt ceiling" never appeared on anybody's list of phobias until the summer of 2011, when debt ceiling joined the top tier of frightening terms.

For even the most hardened scholar of fiscal policy, the term *debt ceiling* rarely drew any attention and certainly no fear or anxiety. In the United States the amount of money that the federal government can owe investors who buy securities such as Treasury notes and bonds is limited by the Congress. Over the years as the nation has not collected enough taxes to pay for spending, the Treasury has had to sell more and more government-backed securities in order for the government to pay its bills.

Before 1917, Congress had to authorize every issuing of debt by the Treasury by an individual vote. As this process became more cumbersome and time consuming, during World War I, Congress opted to institute a debt ceiling that allowed the Treasury to incur debt up to the established amount. This process of periodically raising the debt limit became a common and largely unnoticed feature of fiscal policy. So during the past half century the debt ceiling was raised 74 times, with each president from John F. Kennedy to George W. Bush signing these increases without controversy or ceremony.

This all changed in 2010 when Tea Party candidates for Congress began to pledge that they would oppose raising the debt limit unless the federal government made significant reductions in expenditures. They argued that the high levels of government spending under the Obama administration, including the large stimulus legislation, had exacerbated an already serious debt problem. But they felt that a vote on the debt ceiling could be used as tactic to achieve fiscal balance. When dozens of those Tea Party candidates were elected to Congress, the stage was set for an unprecedented showdown on this previously innocuous budgetary process.

Throughout the first half of 2011, the debt ceiling debate cast a long shadow on proceedings in the nation's capitol, with the broader American public slowly becoming aware that a term most had never heard of threatened the very stability of the national and world economies. As the world's largest single source of investment, the U.S. Treasury has an enormous impact on global financial conditions.

If the debt ceiling was not raised, the possibility existed that the United States would not have enough funds to pay its creditors (i.e., anyone holding bonds or Treasury bills) the interest and principal it owed them became realistic. Simply put, without the ability to borrow more money, the United States couldn't pay all of its bills. The ramifications of that possibility were quite terrifying to the little old lady expecting her Social Security check as well as to the government of China, which holds billions in U.S. Treasury notes.

As the August 1, 2011, deadline approached, the prospects of the government defaulting on its debt played havoc with the financial markets; public concern with the debt ceiling also magnified. Eventually, a compromise was struck between Democrats and Republicans in Congress and President Obama that provided for the debt ceiling to be increased until 2013, with a process to reduce the federal debt established in the interim. Notably, most Tea-Party-affiliated members of Congress voted against the deal, along with the most liberal members among the Democratic caucus.

While the aftermath of the debt ceiling crisis of 2011 left confidence in government badly shaken and the world financial markets battered, it appears that fear about the debt ceiling may become a normal part of everyday life in the United States. The battles from the summer of 2011 appear destined to be repeated in 2013 and beyond as the nation wrestles with its debt problem. Thus the debt ceiling, along with spiders, snakes, earthquakes, and ghosts, will continue to keep some Americans up at night for years to come. ◣

and finances. Both 9/11 and Katrina left local and state governments with substantial financial difficulties that usually discourage investors from investing in municipal bonds for governments and authorities. After the disasters in New York and Louisiana, municipal governments needed massive amounts of money to rebuild destroyed infrastructure at the same time that tax revenues dried up because of crippled local economies. Not surprisingly, Standard and Poor's warned investors of possible downgrades of New York City and New Orleans municipal bonds in the wake of their catastrophes.

To help New York recover after 9/11, Congress, New York State, and local governments created a special financing mechanism that reassured private investors that it would be safe to invest in bonds from the city and Port Authority. In fact, a whole new category of municipal bonds, called Liberty Bonds, has been used to pay for the redevelopment of lower Manhattan after the destruction wrought by the terrorist strike. These bonds are part of a broader economic stimulus law signed by President Bush in March 2002 that let New York City real estate developers obtain lower borrowing rates by selling bonds in the municipal bond market. Despite some controversy over how the revenue is being used, the Liberty Bond provision has been essential to the rebirth of the area around "Ground Zero."

Liberty Bond ■
Refers to tax-exempt private activity bonds used to finance capital projects in New York City after the terrorist attacks of September 11, 2001.

While this new bond helped New York City recover from 9/11, New Orleans's efforts to rebuild after Katrina may take much longer. The widespread nature of the destruction in New Orleans caused a significant loss in the city's tax base—most notably from property taxes. According to the Congressional Budget Office (CBO), in 2006 the City of New Orleans had about $800 million of outstanding bonds, with the water and sewer authority holding another $198 million and the convention center obligated to about $500 million more. It has been extremely difficult for New Orleans to meet these bond obligations without significant revenue coming in during the city's recovery period. For example, the Convention Center Authority pays its bond debt through taxes on hotels and restaurants. With the city's tourism trade in shambles for a number of years after Katrina, the Convention Center Authority had a hard time meeting its obligations to bondholders. All major ratings firms issued warnings on debt issued by New Orleans and its special purpose districts but did not downgrade any bonds. The lack of downgrades was caused by the belief that both the state and federal government would step in and keep the city and its authorities from defaulting on their financial obligations. These beliefs turned out to be well founded, as the federal government guaranteed nearly $1 billion to support New Orleans and other local government debt service.

In the post-Katrina era the federal government also went back to the 9/11 recovery playbook and developed special purpose bonds to help the Gulf Coast recovery. As part of the rebuilding effort, the federal government introduced a special class of private activity bonds called Gulf Opportunity Zone Bonds. As with Liberty Bonds, states or municipalities are permitted to issue bonds, with the proceeds used to pay for acquisition, construction, and renovation of non-residential real property. The Gulf Opportunity Zone legislation authorized just under $8 billion in tax-exempt bonds for the Katrina-ravaged areas, with the hope that the same type of rebirth stimulated in lower Manhattan will occur along the Gulf of Mexico Coast.

IN THE NEWS | Cutback Management: Looking under the Sofa Cushions for Change

If you're like most college students, you have periods when money gets tight. During those lean times you may find yourself looking under the sofa or under your car seats to find some extra cash to see you through until your next paycheck. While governments may operate on a much larger operating budget than you do, the mammoth Washington bureaucracy engages in its own version of looking under the cushions when dollars are hard to come by. Such was the case during the economic downturn of 2008 and 2009, when the federal government was faced with record budget deficits. During President Obama's first cabinet meeting in April of 2009, the new chief executive challenged his department head to identify at least $100 million in collective cuts to their administrative budgets, separate from those identified in Fiscal Year (FY) 2010 budget. While $100 million is quite a bit of money to the average person, it amounts to little more than loose change to a federal government whose budget is more than $3.5 trillion. Nevertheless, the federal agencies had to dig the money up from somewhere if they were to meet the specified goals of the president, and thus came up with an array of measures to locate cost savings.

Some of the savings identified by the federal departments and agencies were strikingly simple. For example, the Department of Justice announced that it would start using double-sided photocopying to save paper and ink expenses, with corresponding savings of more than half a million dollars per year. At the U.S. Forest Service, the decision to no longer repaint new white vehicles in nice shades of forest green helped the service trim thousands of dollars from its annual budget. The Secretary of the Department of Homeland Security decided that the security of the nations would not be damaged

if her agency e-mailed documents rather than printing them out, leading to a savings of more than $300,000 per fiscal year.

Even the mighty armed forces located a few areas that could save Uncle Sam some coin. The Air Force high brass decided that instead of buying specially formulated jet fuel for its aircraft, it would use standard commercial-grade fuel mixed with a military-grade additive. This choice had no impact on aircraft performance but trimmed about $50 million dollars from the Defense Department budget. Not to be out done by the "fly boys" over at the U.S. Air Force, the U.S. Army identified cost savings by packing more soldiers onto R&R (rest and relaxation) flights, and the U.S. Navy saved by deleting unused e-mail accounts.

In the end, the federal agencies met President Obama's challenge and came back with $102 million in savings. This sum amounted to only 0.006 percent of the projected deficit for FY 2010 and didn't come close to solving the federal government's budget crisis. Nevertheless, the fact that more than $100 million dollars could be identified through the government equivalent of looking under the sofa cushions demonstrates that there are vast inefficiencies in the federal bureaucracy. As the FY 2010 budget savings were located, the Office of Management and Budget (OMB) signaled that the exercise in frugality was a prelude to more aggressive belt-tightening in future budget cycles. It remains to be seen how much more change can be found. ◣

DATA FROM: Jonathan Wesiman, "In a Savings Shocker, the Government Discovers That Paper Has Two Sides," *Wall Street Journal* (July 29, 2009); The Office of Management and Budget "Meeting the $100 Million Savings Challenge" (July 27, 2009), http:// www.whitehouse.gov/omb/blog/09/07/27/Meetingthe100MillionSavingsChallenge.

Stealth Budgeting: Hiding the True Costs of the Iraq War

War is hell—and it's damn expensive. While much of the nation's anger toward the war in Iraq has been justifiably focused on the thousands of dead and wounded American soldiers, the large financial cost of the war has been somewhat lost on the public. This fairly low profile for the major fiscal impact of the war can be partially attributed to the way the costs of the war are calculated.

Before the war in Iraq was initiated, Bush administration economists estimated the cost of the war to total somewhere between $100 and 200 billion. Interestingly, the director of the Office of Management and Budget (OMB) argued that those estimates were too high and that the war would end up costing about $60 billion. In the end, even the $200 billion figure would prove to be laughably low.

Even though the uncertainties of a war always preclude exact estimates of financial impacts, it has become clear that the war will cost somewhere between 5 and 10 times the estimates put out by the Bush administration in 2003. Let's start with the best estimates from government itself. In 2006 the Congressional Budget Office (CBO) estimated the cost of the war to come in around $500 billion. While much higher than the 2003 White House estimates, the CBO projection was widely panned for hiding many of the real costs of the war. Among the harshest critics of both the OMB and CBO estimates was former Clinton economic adviser and Nobel Laureate Joseph Stiglitz. In particular, Stiglitz and his colleague Linda Blimes of Harvard University argue that the government cost projections for the war exclude many of the true financial costs of the conflict.

First, Stiglitz and Blimes argue that the Bush administration's projections did not include many of the real budgetary costs of the war, and point to a number of ways in which costs have been hidden. For example, the cost estimates from the chief executive did not include the lifetime disability and health care costs associated with caring for more than 16,000 wounded veterans. With about 20 percent of the wounded vets returning with severe brain trauma, the long-term costs for

IN THE NEWS | The Gift That Stops Giving

The gift card has become a favorite in contemporary American life. You may have received one of these cards from your aunt for your high school graduation, or maybe your grandparents gave you one for Christmas last year. If you haven't used the card yet, you'd better hurry up, because your state government might beat you to it. Most states are strapped for cash, and in attempt to find revenue anywhere they can, they're increasing efforts to claim "abandoned property" as their own. Abandoned property can be anything from a dormant bank account to a car left at a public parking garage. If the government gives notice to the public to come and get its property and there's no response, the government can claim that property as its own. This goes for those ubiquitous gift cards that Americans have become so fond of. Every year, about

$7 billion worth of gift cards go unredeemed. When this happens, the value of the cards usually reverts to the retailers that issued them. However, cash-starved state governments have had a different idea. They now covet these unused cards as a revenue source. For example, the state of New York, with its $7 billion fiscal year 2009 budget deficit, was able to pocket about $10 million in unredeemed gift cards. Retailers have protested the collection acts of states such as New York, but states continue to hunt down the unused cards. After all, if citizens have forgotten they had the cards, the less likely they'll be to complain about the government taking the unused portions. ◣

DATA FROM: Erica Alini, "Governments Grab Unused Gift Cards," Wall Street Journal (June 30, 2009).

care will be extremely high. Many of these wounded warriors will need constant care in skilled nursing facilities for the remainder of their lives, with the public paying the substantial costs.

Stiglitz and Blimes also note that the administration did not include the increasing costs of recruiting and retaining soldiers to serve in the nation's armed services during a time of war. To get young Americans to join the military during an unpopular and very dangerous war, the Pentagon has had to turn to increased recruiting tools. Among these strategies to attract young warriors have been larger financial incentives such as enlistment bonuses and educational benefits. Even more importantly, to retain trained and experienced soldiers in the military, the Bush administration employed enhanced re-enlistment bonuses and improved benefit packages that also cost a great deal of money.

Beyond the undervaluing of recruiting and health care costs, the impact of the war on the overall federal budget has often been overlooked. In particular, because much of the war is being paid for through borrowing, the costs of interest on this debt should be included in the overall price tag of the conflict. However, none of the official government estimates include these "indirect" costs of the war. Similarly, the official cost estimates for the Iraq War ignore more complex economic measures such as the lost earnings of military personnel and the lost opportunity to use war funds in other areas such as transportation, education, and the environment.

In the end, it should come as no surprise that the Bush administration wanted to show the public the lowest possible price tag for the war. With the public confidence in the war at very low levels, any reminder of the high financial costs of the conflict only exacerbated the negatively charged attitudes of the American public. And while President Bush may have been criticized for not reading a lot of books on history, he was well aware that when the public turns on a war they can turn on the leader running the war.

President Lyndon Johnson also knew this, and tried his best to hide the costs of the Vietnam War from the American public. As the cost of Vietnam mounted during the 1960s, Johnson became desperate to limit the damage the war was having on his administration. While he couldn't hide the nightly body counts from the war, he did his best to hide the war's price tag. To do this he utilized an accounting maneuver that involved the mammoth Social Security Trust Fund. For years Americans had been paying into the Social Security Trust, but not many had started to take out benefits, thus leaving an apparent surplus of revenue. While in reality this trust fund was not actually a surplus (see the case study at the end of this chapter), the large sum of cash turned out to be a useful political tool for LBJ. In his fiscal year 1969 budget, Johnson added the Trust Fund revenue to the government's regular budget to turn an otherwise war-created budget deficit into an apparent budget surplus.

For Johnson, the accounting voodoo was not enough to offset the public outrage about the overall impact of the war in Vietnam, and he did not seek his party's renomination for president. While President Bush did win reelection in 2004, both his ability to lead and his legacy have been undermined by the Iraq War. Ultimately, accounting tricks and economic calculations can only go so far before the real numbers catch up with you.

ECONOMIC POLICY

Isolationism, an option in foreign policy, is most decidedly not a possibility with a government's financial policies. Contemporary financial policies cannot stand alone. They are inherently part of the nation's overall economic policies.

Economic policy, the process by which a nation manages its trade, business, and finances, generally consists of three dimensions: (1) fiscal policy, (2) monetary policy, and (3) those other facets of public policy with economic implications, such as energy policy, farm policy, and labor union policy. The interaction of these dimensions of economic policy is crucial, because none operates in a vacuum. While monetary policy basically exercises control over the quantity and cost (interest rates) of money and credit in the economy, fiscal policy deals with the sizes of budgets, deficits, and taxes. Other policy areas, such as housing policy (also dependent on interest rates) and programs dependent on deficit spending, involve aspects of both monetary and fiscal policy, and vice versa. However, their interrelationship does not exist with regard to implementation. Monetary policy, while receiving major inputs from the president and other executive agencies, is the responsibility of the Federal Reserve Board, an independent agency. Fiscal policy, while receiving similar inputs from the Federal Reserve Board, is primarily the responsibility of the president and Congress. The degree of equality and subsequent share of responsibility varies within a stable range. While a president may wish to spend this or that amount, only Congress has the constitutional ability to levy taxes (although tax laws, like any others, must be signed or vetoed by the president). Also limiting a president's discretion over economic policy is the fact that so much of it is controlled by prior decisions to fund, for example, welfare, entitlement, and pension programs, which are not easily changed.

Monetary Policy

Monetary policy consists of a government's formal efforts to manage the money in its economy in order to realize specific economic goals. Three basic kinds of monetary policy decisions can be made: (1) decisions about the amount of money in circulation; (2) decisions about the level of interest rates; and (3) decisions about the functioning of credit markets and the banking system.

Controlling the amount of money is, of course, the key variable. In 1913, the United States passed into law the Federal Reserve Act, which created a strong central bank: the Federal Reserve. Like most central banks, the Federal Reserve System is empowered to control the amount of money in circulation by either creating or canceling dollars. The implementation of money control is achieved through the process of putting up for sale or buying government securities, usually termed open-market operations, which means that the Federal Reserve competes with other bidders in the purchasing or selling of securities. The difference is that when the Federal Reserve buys securities, it pays in the form of new currency in circulation. If it sells some of its securities, it decreases money available, because in effect it absorbs currency held by others. This does not mean, however, that the money stock fluctuates greatly. It steadily increases. It is in the margin of the increase that money supply has its impact. Through the use of the two other tools, the Federal Reserve can attempt to affect investments and loans. First, it

Money supply ■
The amount of money in the economy.

can change its discount rate—the interest rate it charges other banks for loans of money that these banks can use to make loans. Second, it can change the reserve requirement—the amount of money a bank must have on hand in comparison with the amount of money it may have out on loan.

Fiscal Policy

Fiscal policy consists of the manipulation of government finances by raising or lowering taxes or levels of spending to promote economic stability and growth. Stability and growth must be combined, because stability without growth is stagnation. The use of fiscal policy for economic objectives is a decidedly recent phenomenon. For the greater part of the 200-plus-year history of the United States, fiscal policy was not a factor. The national budgetary policy was premised on expenditures equaling revenues (a balanced budget). In fact, with the exception of war years, budgeting before the 1900s was primarily an exercise in deciding how to get rid of excess revenues, generated primarily by tariffs. This is not to say that modern fiscal policies would not have saved the nation considerable distress from assorted recessions and depressions, but the nineteenth century held that the economy followed a natural order. The first major tampering with the natural order of things came in 1913, with the advent of the federal income tax and the establishment of the Federal Reserve System. The Great Depression of the 1930s, along with the initiation of Social Security and unemployment compensation programs, provided the first recognition of the need for a national economic policy. However, legitimization of the goal of a national economic policy came with the passage of the Full Employment Act of 1946. The act not only created a Council of Economic Advisers for the president, but it also prescribed objectives for economic prosperity and charged the president with ensuring their achievement.

Basically, fiscal policy offers discretionary and built-in courses of action. Discretionary fiscal policy, which involves changing policy, has two major facets: the level of receipts and the level of expenditures. The major fiscal policy actions of recent years are replete with tax cuts and temporary reductions. Given the time lags involved in legislating tax changes, it is easy to see why presidents have preferred to wage fiscal policy battles in terms of government spending. The second dimension involves built-in fiscal stabilizers—that is, preset or automatic policy. These are the transfer payments, the progressive tax rates, and the changing federal budget deficits and surpluses that move automatically to counter economic downturns or to control excessive periods of demand and business activity. For example, as people are laid off from work in a recessionary period, payments for unemployment compensation mount automatically. This increases the federal budget deficit, which in turn stimulates the economy and moves to offset the economic downswing. If the economy heats up, both regular and overtime wages increase, fueling demand for goods and services and creating inflation. As personal income increases, however, more and more people move into higher tax brackets. Thus the tax structure functions as an automatic stabilizer by absorbing more personal income and restraining demand for goods and services.

Tariff ■
A tax imposed on imported products. A duty is distinguished from a tariff solely by the fact that the duty is the actual tax imposed or collected, while the tariff, technically speaking, is the schedule of duties. However, in practice the words are often used interchangeably.

Transfer payments ■
Payments by a government made to individuals who provide no goods or services in return. All of the social welfare programs at all levels of government that provide subsistence income support are transfer payment programs. They are often referred to as *entitlement programs* because one becomes entitled to transfer payments if one meets criteria established by the authorizing legislation.

Progressive tax ■
Any tax that has people of greater wealth paying a larger percentage in tax than people of lesser means. Income taxes are often progressive.

A CASE STUDY | Social Security Reform from Clinton to Obama

Social Security is the popular name for the Old Age, Survivors, and Disability Insurance (OASDI) system established by the Social Security Act of 1935. At first, Social Security covered only retired private sector employees. In 1939, the law was changed to cover survivors when the worker died and to cover certain dependents when the worker retired. In the 1950s, coverage was extended to include most self-employed persons, most state and local employees, household and farm employees, members of the armed forces, and members of the clergy. Today, almost all jobs are covered by Social Security.

Disability insurance was added in 1954 to give workers protection against loss of earnings due to total disability. The Social Security program was expanded again in 1965 with the enactment of **Medicare**, which assured hospital and medical insurance protection to people 65 years of age and over. Since 1973, Medicare coverage has been available to people under 65 who have been entitled to disability checks for two or more consecutive years and to people with permanent kidney failure who need dialysis treatment or kidney transplants. Amendments enacted in 1972 provided an automatic cost-of-living adjustment (COLA).

The biggest problem with Social Security is demographics. In 1950 the ratio of taxpaying workers to pensioners was 120 to 1. In the year 2030 it will be two to one. This is why Social Security payroll taxes have risen from 1 percent in 1940 to 7.65 percent in 2002. (Of the 7.65 percent, 6.2 percent is for traditional Social Security pensions; the remainder goes to fund Medicare.) And that percentage is for both employees and employers—so it is double if you are self-employed.

Brookings Institution analyst Paul C. Light contends that if you want to understand American politics, you must first study Social Security. "Those who care about budget deficits must know something about the single largest program on the domestic ledger; those who care about electoral politics must know something about the central concern of older voters; those who care about trust in government must know something about the lack of confidence in Social Security among young and old Americans alike." Nevertheless, even with all its problems and deficiencies, Social Security remains "the most important program for helping elderly women and minorities."

The critical importance of Social Security as an antipoverty program can be summarized with a few statistics. According to the Social Security Administration, in 2007 almost 90 percent of all citizens over age 65 received benefits. For 23 percent of them, Social Security was their only income. For 35 percent, it represented 90 percent or more of their income. And for 64 percent of them, it represented 50 percent or more of their income. And that Social Security income in December 2007 averaged $1,218 a month

(continued)

Medicare ■
The national health insurance program for the elderly and the disabled authorized by a 1965 amendment to the Social Security Act. The two parts of Medicare—hospital insurance and medical insurance—help protect people 65 years of age and older from the high costs of health care. Also eligible for Medicare are disabled people under 65 who have been entitled to Social Security disability benefits for 24 or more consecutive months (including adults who are receiving benefits because they have been disabled since childhood).

Cost-of-living adjustment (COLA) ■
An increase in compensation in response to increasing inflation. Some labor union contracts and some entitlement programs (such as Social Security) provide for automatic COLAs if inflation reaches predetermined levels.

▶ **A CASE STUDY** | *Continued*

for men and $935 a month for women. Nearly 50 million citizens currently rely on monthly Social Security payments. And they tend to be experienced voters.

Social Security is not a static program. Discussions to expand and contract it have been going on since its inception. For its first four decades it kept expanding with additional classes of workers being covered and new benefits added. The high watermark of this expansion occurred in 1972 when benefits started being automatically adjusted for inflation. But by the 1980s it had become obvious that something had to be done if the system was to retain its long-term viability. So in 1981 President Ronald Reagan appointed the bipartisan National Commission on Social Security Reform (known as the Greenspan Commission for its chair, Alan Greenspan). The commission's recommendations, which were signed into law in 1983, sought to make the system fiscally solvent by raising Social Security taxes from 5.4 percent to its present rate of 6.2 percent, taxing the benefits themselves to recover a portion of benefits paid out to higher-income recipients, and gradually raising the age at which one could receive full benefits from 65 to 67.

In 2001 President George W. Bush, motivated as much by ideological zeal as actuarial necessity, appointed the President's Commission to Strengthen Social Security—a bipartisan 16-member group "to study and report recommendations to preserve Social Security for seniors while building wealth for younger Americans." Then Governor Bush had campaigned for president in 2000, pledging to take Social Security to its "logical conclusion" by allowing Americans to use part of their Social Security contribution to create "Personal Retirement Accounts." These accounts—unlike the current Social Security program, which provides benefits only for recipients, their spouses, and dependent minor children—would facilitate wealth creation. Similar in concept to individual retirement accounts and 401(k) accounts, the accumulated assets could be inherited as they would be personally owned and not subject to the vagaries of politics.

President Bush followed up on his campaign promise by formally introducing a proposal in 2005 that called for reform of Social Security that included elements of privatization. In this excerpt from his 2005 State of the Union speech, Bush makes his case for the creation of voluntary personal retirement accounts:

> As we fix Social Security, we also have the responsibility to make the system a better deal for younger workers. And the best way to reach that goal is through voluntary personal retirement accounts. Here is how the idea works. Right now, a set portion of the money you earn is taken out of your paycheck to pay for the Social Security benefits of today's retirees. If you're a younger worker, I believe you should be able to set aside part of that money in your own retirement account so you can build a nest egg for your own future.
>
> Here's why the personal accounts are a better deal. Your money will grow, over time, at a greater rate than anything the current system can

deliver—and your account will provide money for retirement over and above the check you'll receive from Social Security. In addition, you'll be able to pass along the money that accumulates in your personal account, if you wish, to your children and/or grandchildren. And best of all, the money in the account is yours, and the government can never take it away.

While there was considerable national debate on the merits of such accounts and how they might be gradually implemented, the commission issued its report at a most unfortunate time: at the end of 2001 when the United States was deep in a recession and the stock market's decline was so severe that it was being compared to that of the Great Depression. This more than anything else took the wind out of the sails of this proposal. Consequently, the whole matter of reform and the creation of personal accounts to be invested in the stock market was quietly dropped from the national agenda.

ALTERNATIVE Theories | Traditional Social Security Pensions versus Private Pension Accounts

Traditional Social Security	Private Pension Accounts
Guaranteed by government	Not guaranteed by government
Payments set by law	Payments set by the market
Benefits die with the pensioner	Accumulated wealth inheritable
Low but steady rate of return	Variable rate of return ◣

Note that the debate over personal retirement accounts is seldom framed as an either/or decision. Since it is recognized by most analysts that a minimal government pension be available to those unable or unwilling to provide for themselves, the question usually asked is how much (what percentage) of current Social Security contributions should be diverted to personal accounts? What percentage would you recommend and why?

Since being introduced, Bush's plan for Social Security reform met with great resistance in Congress. The only certainty is that reform efforts will continue. The current system is simply not sustainable.

Obviously something must be done. But it is hard to muster the political will to deal with a problem that is still decades away. Both Presidents Bill Clinton and George W. Bush sought to reform the system. But Clinton, who once thought that Social Security reform would be part of his legacy to the nation, instead spent his second term lying about his Oval Office sexual escapades and fighting impeachment. Then his successor's reform efforts were sidetracked by a recession and the war on terrorism.

President Obama did not quickly champion Social Security reform on taking office in 2009. Perhaps he was too busy dealing with other major problems, such as two wars, a collapsing economy, health care reform, and climate change. Or maybe he learned from the failures of both Clinton and Bush and decided to move more cautiously on the matter. Early in his

(continued)

administration he offered more modest ideas for how the system could be preserved. In particular, the 44th president focused his attention on creating more revenue for the system through increased payroll taxes for people making more than $250,000 a year and by bolstering pension plans for individuals to ensure that more Americans will have supplements to Social Security benefits when they retire.

While President Obama moved cautiously on the issue of Social Security reform, the Chairman of the House Budget Committee, Paul Ryan, introduced a much bolder plan. In January of 2011 the Republican congressman from Wisconsin released a plan that called for a partial privatization of Social Security and a shift in Medicare that would provide recipients with vouchers to get medical insurance in lieu of the current insurance provided by government itself. The "Ryan Plan" received a less-than-welcoming response from the public, and even Republican members of Congress and GOP presidential hopefuls were distancing themselves from the proposal as the elections of 2012 neared.

Only two facts remain: (1) reform must come, and (2) the sooner it comes, the less painful it will be. One prevalent suggestion is to gradually raise the retirement age to 70 but exempt those baby boomers who are about to retire. If no one feels any immediate pain, this fix for the system becomes more politically palatable.

For Discussion: *Why will it be politically so difficult to achieve a consensus on reforming the Social Security program? Why is it that the baby-boom generation is in effect forcing political leaders to reform the system sooner rather than later? Why has President Bush's proposal to partially privatize Social Security failed to attract support?* ▶

SUMMARY

Budgeting is the single most important decision-making process in public institutions. The budget itself is also a jurisdiction's most important reference document. In their increasingly voluminous formats, budgets simultaneously record policy decision outcomes, cite policy priorities as well as program objectives, and delineate a government's total service effort.

There are two basic kinds of budgets. The most common is the operating budget: a short-term plan for managing the resources necessary to carry out a program. Usually an operating budget is developed for each fiscal year. The second kind is the capital budget; it deals with planning for large expenditures such as bridges and buildings. Capital budgets typically cover 5- to 10-year periods.

An executive budget is both a technical process and a physical thing. First, it is the process by which agency requests for appropriations are prepared and submitted to a central budget office for review, alteration, and consolidation. Then, it becomes a tangible thing, the comprehensive budget document for an executive branch of government that a jurisdiction's chief executive submits to a legislature for review, modification, and enactment.

General taxation (or a general property tax in the context of local government) is the most traditional means of financing public services. There are major differences between the federal and state-local revenue systems. The federal system has experienced a trend toward less diversity; more than two-thirds of its general revenue is provided by the federal income tax and the several insurance trust funds (such as Social Security). State and local revenue systems, in contrast, depend on a greater variety of revenue sources (such as property taxes, income taxes, sales taxes, user charges, lotteries, and federal grants). While local governments still rely primarily on the property tax, their states—with a few exceptions—rely largely on the state personal income tax.

Deficit financing is a situation in which a government's excess of outlays over receipts for a given period is financed primarily by borrowing from the public. Politicians often view borrowing as politically preferable to imposing higher taxes. Borrowing is virtually invisible to the electorate. If the projects produced by it are impressive, politicians see a painless way of "buying" votes—especially when the proverbial chickens do not come home to roost until a subsequent administration.

Economic policy, the process by which a nation manages its trade, business, and finances, generally consists of three dimensions: (1) fiscal policy, (2) monetary policy, and (3) those other facets of public policy with economic implications, such as energy policy, farm policy, and labor union policy. While monetary policy basically exercises control over the quantity and cost (interest rates) of money and credit in the economy, fiscal policy deals with the sizes of budgets, deficits, and taxes.

REVIEW QUESTIONS

1. Why is government budgeting—meaning the allocation of public resources—an inherently political process?
2. What are the goals and tactics of a budget-maximizing bureaucrat?
3. What is the difference between an operating budget and a capital budget?
4. Why has the executive budgeting process evolved to be the most common means by which public budgets are developed and approved?
5. How is the ability-to-pay principle incorporated into all progressive taxing systems?

KEY CONCEPTS

Budget process   The total system a jurisdiction uses to make decisions on government spending needs and how to pay for them. The main difference between federal and state-local budget processes is that the state and local jurisdictions must have balanced budgets each year.

Budget surplus   The amount by which a government's budget receipts exceed its budget outlays for any given period.

Capital budgeting   A budget process that deals with planning for large expenditures for capital items such as bridges and buildings.

Deficit financing   A situation in which a government's excess of outlays over receipts for a given period is financed primarily by borrowing from the public.

Executive budget   The budget document for an executive branch of government that a jurisdiction's chief executive submits to a legislature for review, modification, and enactment.

Incremental budgeting   A method of budget review that focuses on the increments of increase or decrease in the budget of existing programs. Incremental budgeting, which is often called traditional budgeting, is a counter-school of thought to more rational, systems-oriented approaches, such as zero-based budgeting.

Line-item budget   The classification of budgetary accounts according to narrow, detailed objects of expenditure (such as motor vehicles, clerical workers, or reams of paper) used within each particular agency of government, generally without reference to the ultimate purpose or objective served by the expenditure.

National debt   The total outstanding debt of a central government.

Progressive tax   Any tax that has people of greater wealth paying a larger percentage in tax than people of lesser means. Income taxes are often progressive.

Regressive tax   Any tax that has people with lower incomes paying a higher overall percentage of their income in tax than people of greater income. Sales taxes are examples of regressive taxes.

Tax   A compulsory contribution exacted by a government for public purposes.

Unified budget   The present form of the budget of the federal government, in which receipts and outlays from federal funds and trust funds (such as Social Security) are consolidated.

Zero-based budgeting   A budgeting process that is a rejection of the incremental decision-making model of budgeting. It demands a rejustification of the entire budget submission (from ground zero), whereas incremental budgeting essentially respects the outcomes of previous budgetary decisions (collectively referred to as the budget base) and focuses examination on the margin of change from year to year.

MySearchLab® EXERCISES

Apply what you learned in this chapter on MySearchLab (*www.mysearchlab.com*).

BIBLIOGRAPHY

Anderson, Martin (1988). *Revolution*. New York: Harcourt Brace Jovanovich.

Basler, Roy P., ed. (1953). *The Collected Works of Abraham Lincoln*, vol. 2. New Brunswick, NJ: Rutgers University Press.

Blais, Andre, and Stephane Dion, eds. (1991). *The Budget-Maximizing Bureaucrat*. Pittsburgh: University of Pittsburgh Press.

Boettke, Peter J. (1992). "Friedrich A. Hayek (1899–1992)," *The Freeman* (August).

Buchanan, James, and Gordon Tullock (1962). *The Calculus of Consent*. Ann Arbor: University of Michigan Press.

Caiden, Naomi (1983). "Guidelines to Federal Budget Reform," *Public Budgeting and Finance* 3 (Winter).

Cassidy, John (2000). "The Price Prophet," *The New Yorker* (February 7).

DiCamillio, Mark, and Mervin Field (2009). "Big Decline in Governor's and Legislature's Job Ratings. Corresponding Drop in Voters' Belief That State Is Heading in the Right Direction," *The Field Poll*, Release 2272. http://field.com/fieldpollonline/subscribers/Rls2272.pdf.

Dror, Yehezkel (1964). "Muddling Through—'Science' or Inertia," *Public Administration Review* 24, No. 3 (September).

Frederickson, H. George (1995). "Misdiagnosing the Orange County Scandal," *Governing* (April).

Galbraith, John Kenneth (1981). *A Life in Our Times*. Boston: Houghton Mifflin.

Gingrich, Newt (1995). *To Renew America*. New York: HarperCollins.

Gore, Al (1993). Report of the National Performance Review, *From Red Tape to Results: Creating a Government That Works Better and Costs Less*. Washington: U.S. Government Printing Office.

Grieder, William (1981). "The Education of David Stockman," *The Atlantic Monthly* (December).

Hayek, Friedrich A. (1944). *The Road to Serfdom*. Chicago: University of Chicago Press.

———. (1960). *The Constitution of Liberty*. Chicago: University of Chicago Press.

Herszzehorn, David (2009). "Deal Reached in Congress on $789 Billion Stimulus Plan," *New York Times* (February 11).

Hunt, Michael (1997). *Lyndon Johnson's War: America's Cold War Crusade in Vietnam, 1945–1968*. New York: Hill and Wang.

Hyde, Albert C., ed. (1992). *Government Budgeting: Theory, Process, Politics*. Monterey, CA: Brooks-Cole.

Kendall, James (1955). *Michael Faraday*. London: Farber and Farber.

Key, V. O., Jr. (1940). "The Lack of a Budgetary Theory," *American Political Science Review* (December).

Lewis, Verne (1952). "Toward a Theory of Budgeting," *Public Administration Review* (Winter).

Light, Paul C. (1985). *Artful Work: The Politics of Social Security Reform*. New York: Random House.

———. (1994). *Still Artful Work: The Continuing Politics of Social Security Reform*, 2nd ed. New York: McGraw-Hill.

Lynch, Thomas D. (1995). *Public Budgeting in America*, 4th ed. Englewood Cliffs, NJ: Prentice Hall.

Lynn, Jonathan, and Antony Jay (1984). *The Complete Yes Minister*. New York: Harper and Row.

Miranda, Rowan (1994). "Privatization and the Budget Maximizing Bureaucrat," *Public Productivity and Management Review* (Summer).

Montgomery, Lori, and Paul Kane (2011). "White House, Congressional Leaders Reach Debt Limit Deal," *Washington Post* (July 31).

Musgrave, Richard R., and Peggy B. Musgrave (1984). *Public Finance in Theory and Practice*, 4th ed. New York: McGraw-Hill.

Mysak, Joe (1995). "Winking at Debt," *New York Times* (June 23).

Novick, David (1968). "The Origin and History of Programming Budgeting," *California Management Review* 11 (Fall).

Owen, Jeffery G. (2003). "The Stadium Game: Cities versus Teams," *Journal of Sports Economics* (August).

Phyrr, Peter A. (1977). "The Zero-Base Approach to Government Budgeting," *Public Administration Review* 37 (January–February).

Quinn, K., P. Bursik, C. Borick, and L. Raethz (2003). "Do New Digs Mean More Wins? The Relationship between a New Venue and a Professional Sports Team's Competitive Success," *Journal of Sports Economics* (August).

Regan, Tom (2006). "Iraq War Costs Could Top $2 Trillion," *Christian Science Monitor* (January 10).

Samuelson, Robert. J. (2009). "California's Reckoning—and Ours," *Newsweek* (August 3).

Schick, Allen (1966). "The Road to PPB: The Stages of Budget Reform," *Public Administration Review* 26 (December).

———. (1973). "A Death in the Bureaucracy: The Demise of Federal PPB," *Public Administration Review* 33 (March–April).

———. (1977). "Budget Gap," *Public Administration Review* (September–October).

———. (1978). "The Road from ZBB," *Public Administration Review* 38 (March–April).

———. (1983). "Incremental Budgeting in a Decremental Age," *Policy Sciences* (September).

Shenk, J. W. (1995). "Hidden Kingdom: Disney's Political Blueprint," *American Prospect* (Spring).

Silver, Nate. (2011). "Why S&P's Ratings Are Substandard and Porous," http://fivethirtyeight.blogs.nytimes.com/page/2//

Steinhauer, Jennifer (2009). "Coffers Empty, California Pays with I.O.U.'s," *The New York Times* (July 2).

Strop, Leigh (2003). "Report: Social Security Deficit to Boom," *Washington Times* (July 29).

Suetonius (1931). *The Lives of the Twelve Caesars*. New York: Modern Library.

Stiglitz, Joseph, and Linda Blimes (2006). *The Economic Costs of the War in Iraq: An Appraisal Three Years after the Beginning of the Conflict*. Harvard University Faculty Working Paper Series. http://ksgnotes1.harvard.edu/Research/wpaper.nsf/rwp/RWP06-002/$File/rwp_06_002_Bilmes_SSRN.pdf.

Weiner, Tim (1990). *Blank Check: The Pentagon's Black Budget*. New York: Warner Books.

Wildavsky, Aaron (1969). "Rescuing Policy Analysis from PPBS," *Public Administration Review* 29 (March–April).

———. (1984). *The Politics of the Budgetary Process*, 4th ed. Boston: Little, Brown.

Willoughby, William F. (1918). *The Movement towards Budgetary Reform in the States*. New York: D. Appleton and Company for the Institute of Government Research.

Woo, Stu, and Ryan Knutson (2009). "California Budget Deal Closes $26 Billion Gap," *Wall Street Journal* (July 21).

RECOMMENDED BOOKS

Blais, Andre, and Stephanie Dion, eds. (1991). *The Budget-Maximizing Bureaucrat: Appraisals and Evidence*. Pittsburgh: University of Pittsburgh Press. Everything you need to know about bureaucratic empire builders and how to help them or thwart them.

Bland, Robert L., and Irene S. Rubin (1997). *Budgeting: A Guide for Local Governments*. Washington: International City/County Management Association. A succinct survey of the theory, obstacles, and practicalities of budgeting at the local level; offers many examples of how budgets are assembled and what municipal budget manuals need to contain.

Gosling, James J. (2009). *Budgetary Politics in American Governments*. New York: Routledge. A comprehensive survey of budgetary practices at all levels of government.

Mikesell, John L. (2010). *Fiscal Administration: Analysis and Applications for the Public Sector*, 8th ed. Boston, MA: Wadsworth. The standard text on managing governmental funds.

Wildavsky, Aaron (1992). *The New Politics of the Budgetary Process*, 2nd ed. New York: HarperCollins. The last update of Wildavsky's *Politics of the Budgetary Process* (initially published in 1964); one of the most influential books in the history of public administration.

RELATED WEB SITES

www.cbo.gov
Congressional Budget Office (CBO)
The CBO plays a major role in calculating the budgetary and fiscal projections that inform the decisions made by Congress. The CBO Web site includes economic forecasts, deficit and debt estimates, and projections for the solvency of entitlements programs such as Social Security and Medicare.

www.federalreserve.gov
Federal Reserve System
The major organ of monetary policy in the United States maintains a Web site that gives access to Federal Reserve meeting minutes and policy decisions, and provides explanation on how the reserve works and how the money is being used.

www.gfoa.org
Government Finance Officers Association (GFOA)
The purpose of GFOA Web site is to promote the professional management of governments by identifying and developing financial policies and best practices and promoting their use through education, training, facilitation of member networking, and leadership.

www.nasbo.org
National Association of State Budget Officers (NASBO)
NASBO serves as the professional organization for all state budget officers. The site allows access to reports and analysis on state budgets and provides budget officials with overviews of best practices for the management of public financial resources.

www.publicdebt.treas.gov
U.S. Bureau of Public Debt
This bureau, a branch of the U.S. Treasury, borrows the money needed to operate the federal government. The site contains valuable information about the selling of Treasury bills, notes, and bonds.

Program Audit and Evaluation

KEYNOTE: Captain Bligh's Program Evaluation of the Mutiny on the *Bounty*

For more than two centuries the ultimate South Seas adventure story has been the tale of the *Bounty* and its mutiny. But this is no tall tale; there really was a mutiny on the *Bounty* in 1789. William Bligh, the captain, and Fletcher Christian, the mutinous officer, were real people. A trio of Hollywood's greatest character actors (Charles Laughton in 1935, Trevor Howard in 1962, and Anthony Hopkins in 1983) have played Bligh—first as a sadist, then as an overbearing bureaucrat, and finally as a frustrated corporate climber. They were paired with Fletcher Christians who were among the greatest romantic leads of their day (Clark Gable, Marlon Brando, and Mel Gibson). The dramatic tension between these two estranged friends is the core of the film, of the mutiny, and of the legend.

Bligh was chosen to be the ship's captain because he was a young officer with Captain **James Cook** when Cook visited Tahiti in 1777. Cook, before he was killed by the local residents of Hawaii, wrote that the breadfruit plant would be excellent food for the slaves of the British-owned West Indian plantations. This is why the

**James Cook
(1728–1779)** ■
The explorer who first sailed English ships to Australia, New Zealand, Antarctica, and many Pacific islands. While visiting Hawaii he was killed—literally hacked to pieces—by locals who wished to discourage tourism.

Jamaican slave owners lobbied the navy for the voyage. Bligh was one of the very few naval officers in England who had actually been to Tahiti and knew the people there. Besides, Bligh's wife had an uncle who was one of the plantation owners who successfully lobbied the government for the voyage. The uncle then continued his lobbying efforts on Bligh's behalf. While his political sponsor brought Bligh's name to the forefront of consideration, there is no doubt that Bligh was as fully qualified for the command as any officer in England. The *Bounty* command was considered such a choice assignment, one that could really make one's reputation, that Bligh, then a merchant ship captain, accepted the job for a vastly reduced salary (from 500 down to 50 pounds a year) and at the rank of lieutenant. So while Bligh was the captain of the *Bounty*, he was only a lieutenant in the Royal Navy. Bligh then chose Christian because he wanted his friend from two earlier voyages to the West Indies along for the ride. Good company can be scarce on the high seas unless you plan for it!

The *Bounty*'s mutiny was in reality a pathetic little affair as mutinies go. While passions ran high, the decks did not run red with blood. The crew totaled 44, but only 12 of them actually were mutineers. Aside from Bligh's bruised ego, nobody was really hurt. No blood was shed, and no shots were fired. After much shouting, the mutineers put Bligh and 18 other men in a 23-foot lifeboat, fully expecting all of them to perish. But Bligh, in one of history's most remarkable feats of seamanship, sailed that tiny, overloaded craft 3,618 miles to the Dutch colony of Timor, in present-day Indonesia. There he found passage home to England. Had Bligh and his lifeboat colleagues died, there would have been no mutiny in that the world would never have known of it. The *Bounty* would have just been presumed lost at sea—a common enough occurrence in those days.

The mutiny became a cause célèbre because Bligh's account of it, his program evaluation, *The Mutiny on Board H.M.S. Bounty*, was published soon after he returned to England in 1790. It was an instant best seller, what with its tales of the exotic South Seas with casual sex, betrayal, and a desperate voyage of survival. Adding to the sensationalism was the simple fact that this kind of thing had never happened before in the Royal Navy. Mutiny was a word used for insubordination, for resisting or complaining about orders. But to take over—to steal—one of His Majesty's ships was unthinkable for two reasons. First, under the **articles of war**, mutiny was punishable by death. Second, there was quite literally no place in the entire world where one could hide from the enormous Royal Navy. Thus Christian and company could only have committed such an act because they were deranged by the allures of Tahiti. Bligh's account, being first, supported the derangement theory and forever defined the terms of the mutiny. He wrote, "The mutineers had flattered themselves with the hopes of a more happy life among the Otaheiteans [Tahitians] than they could possibly enjoy in England." Bligh's analysis for the underlying causes have been quibbled with and expanded on but never subsequently refuted:

> The women at Otaheite [Tahiti] are handsome, mild and cheerful in their manners and conversation, possessed of great sensibility, and have sufficient delicacy to make them admired and beloved. The chiefs were so much attached to our people, that they rather encouraged their stay among them. . . . Under these, and many other attendant circumstances, equally desirable, it is now perhaps not so

Articles of war ■
The traditional laws governing the behavior of military and naval personnel. The United States used articles of war from 1775 to 1950, when they were superseded by the Uniform Code of Military Justice.

much to be wondered at, though scarcely possible to have been foreseen, that a set of sailors, most of them void of connections, should be led away; especially when, in addition to such powerful inducements, they imagined it in their power to fix themselves in the midst of plenty, on one of the finest islands in the world, where they need not labour, and where the allurements of dissipation are beyond anything that can be conceived.

Bligh knew that there would be a clash of cultures when his normally sexually repressed and especially sex-starved crew met the sexually liberated Tahitians. But after a few weeks at most, they would all be back at sea. The problem was that the *Bounty* stayed in Tahiti for almost six months—mainly because Bligh wanted to make sure that the breadfruit shoots had rooted properly so that they would survive the anticipated seven-month voyage to Jamaica. This delay gave the men time to establish extremely strong relationships with the local women. In his analysis, the "allurements of dissipation" that Bligh only hints at are the prime causes of the mutiny. Bligh saw nothing else amiss. As he wrote, "Had their mutiny been occasioned by any grievances, either real or imaginary, I must have discovered symptoms of their discontent, which would have put me on my guard." Modern audiences of the films about the mutiny often think the crew revolted because of Bligh's harsh discipline and frequent whippings. But this is looking at eighteenth-century management practices with twentieth-century eyes. Lash for lash, Bligh was actually far less harsh than other captains of his era. Statistical analysis of the number and severity of floggings shows that Bligh used corporal punishment sparingly. According to historian Sven Wahlroos, "It was not his physical cruelty but, rather, his humiliating tongue—in an era when a man's honor was more important than his life—that contributed heavily to the most famous mutiny of all time." A very strong case can be made that Bligh, far from being too harsh, was too lenient. He allowed the crew almost total freedom to cavort among the Tahitians both on shore and on ship. This is what made it impossible to reassert traditional discipline on the return voyage. But the imagery of the floggings and the pleasure the actors playing Bligh gave to his countenance during the floggings has made his name a byword for a seagoing **martinet**.

Bligh was an astute organizational climber. He was not about to let those who would lead a life of dissipation ruin his naval career. Knowing that any officer who loses a ship by mutiny would be **court-martialed**, he craftily started making his case, writing his program evaluation while still in the lifeboat. Any court-martial is essentially an evaluation of whether an officer has conducted himself appropriately. Bligh had. But he also knew he had to defend himself before three courts:

1. The formal court-martial, which he had every reason to believe would be a formality that would (and did) exonerate him
2. The informal court of naval opinion, which would determine whether he would ever be given another command
3. The court of public opinion

He won all three at first. He was acquitted by the court-martial; the navy kept promoting him (eventually to admiral) and giving him progressively more responsible assignments; and the public initially considered him to be a great hero. But

Martinet ■
A strict disciplinarian. The word comes from an inspector general in the army of France's Louis XIV, Jean Martinet, who was so despised for his spit-and-polish discipline that he was "accidentally" killed by his own soldiers while leading an assault in 1672.

Court-martial ■
A military court that tries members of the armed forces for violations of military law.

A contemporary portrait of William Bligh (1754–1817), captain of the *Bounty*. Because the *Bounty's* saga has lent itself so well to novels and movies, readers (and viewers) often forget that this story is a case study in public policy and, particularly, program evaluation. True, the *Bounty* was a Royal Navy ship, but she was built as a merchant ship, was commanded by an officer (Bligh) with years of experience in merchant ships, and was on a merchant ship's mission. Today, private corporations have the National Aeronautics and Space Administration put satellites in space for them. In the eighteenth century it was the Royal Navy that was on the cutting edge of technological and navigational skills, so it was quite reasonable that its members would undertake such a "scientific" mission. The Navy was only being responsive to the request of influential planters in Jamaica. These West Indian businessmen just wanted a cheap source of fuel for their slaves. Believing that Tahiti, an island in the South Pacific, had a nourishing plant—breadfruit—that could thrive in their climate, they used all their considerable influence to get the Navy to do the job for them. Just like today's corporate executives, they lobbied their government to take on their breadfruit research and development costs. Governments, then and now, are happy to accede to such requests in the hope that a relatively small investment would engender substantial economic development and concomitant taxes. The absolute immorality of doing something designed to make slavery a more economically viable institution never occurred to the English colonists, the Royal Navy, or the crew of the *Bounty*. While the *Bounty* was not a slave ship, it nevertheless was on a slaver's mission. This mission gave the *Bounty* its name. Originally a merchant ship named *Bethia*, it was rechristened to reflect the king's "bounty" to his West Indian subjects—and their subject slaves.

two years later, during the court-martial of the few mutineers who were captured, new information surfaced that branded him a villain.

Without ever using the phrase, Bligh was a practitioner of the "defensive program evaluation." His assessment of the mutiny prevailed at first because there were no contemporary contradictory evaluations. British Prime Minister Winston Churchill once bragged during World War II that history would look kindly on his actions because he, as a professional writer, intended to write it. Bligh was no Churchill, to be sure, but they both knew the advantages of writing the history in which you participated—before the other guy does.

However, Bligh was not completely forthcoming in his analysis. He only told of one of the reasons for the mutiny. According to naval historian Richard Hough, there were two other major contributing factors: Fletcher Christian's tender sensibilities and the fact that Bligh was overwhelmingly detested by everyone on board. Bligh seems to have been unusually obnoxious and bad tempered. He was the worst kind of **Theory X** manager, giving so many orders that they often contradicted each other. When the resulting foul-ups occurred, he tended to blame anyone but himself—and his blame was expressed by language so constantly obscene and insulting that it shocked—yes, shocked—sailors who were, as sailors, thoroughly experienced with obscene and insulting language. By constantly impugning the honor and integrity of every sailor and officer on board, he created a situation such that, when push came to shove, not one officer would take his side. A mutiny must be led by officers for the simple reason that only they knew how to navigate. There would be no point in taking over a ship if you couldn't go anywhere with it. This is why the focus of the analysis of the mutineers' motivation has been on Christian. The lower-deck men encouraged and supported him because they knew he had grievances, and they wanted to return to Tahiti. Indeed, Christian, as a gentleman, would have felt obligated to challenge Bligh to a duel because of his verbal abuses had they been on land.

Bligh was absolutely correct about there being nothing amiss for him to discover. The mutiny was less a plot than a spontaneous outburst. Christian was in despair over his relationship with Bligh. He was effectively suicidal and preparing to jump ship in a makeshift raft when a fellow crew member, noticing his preparations, said the men were "ready for anything." Thus the mutiny began spontaneously because Bligh's treatment of Christian had pushed him over the proverbial edge.

What happened on the *Bounty* in 1789 was no different from what seems to happen a few times each year in the U.S. Postal Service—an overbearing supervisor psychologically pushes a mentally delicate clerk too far. So the clerk comes to work one day with a gun and kills the supervisor, a few bystanders, and maybe himself. True, the mutiny was aggravated by the allures of Tahiti, but its underlying cause was less a matter of sadistic perversion than bad management. The single most significant management blunder was the absence of the squad of marines almost always assigned to naval ships. Marines in all major navies originated not as soldiers to be landed on hostile shores, but as jailers for the sailors. Unfortunately the *Bounty* was a small ship, less than 90 feet long by 24 feet wide. With a crew of 44 there was simply no room. Many other naval ships visited Tahiti and other friendly Polynesian islands before and after the *Bounty*. They did not suffer mutinies, but they had marines.

Theory X ■
The traditional managerial assumptions that people dislike work and therefore must be coerced or threatened to put forth adequate efforts.

And there was one other contemporary element to the *Bounty* mutiny. One of the most respected accounts of the mutiny, Richard Hough's *Captain Bligh and Mr. Christian*, suggests that its underlying cause was sexual harassment. This suggestion is a mixture of fact and speculation. It was fact that the traditions of the Royal Navy included "rum, sodomy and the lash." We know that the *Bounty* made ample use of rum and the lash. Because sodomy was a capital offense, it was never lightly discussed. According to Greg Dening, shipmates on Bligh's two earlier voyages with Christian "remarked on Bligh's infatuation with the active, charming young man [Christian] who had begged—for the experience of it—to join his crew even at no pay, so long as Bligh permitted him 'to mess with the gentlemen.'" It was a fact that Bligh showed extreme favoritism toward Christian—a favoritism that stopped as the return voyage began. The speculation is that the 26-year-old Christian was not the macho romantic portrayed by Hollywood but that he had a homosexual relationship with Bligh before Tahiti, which he was reluctant to resume after his Tahitian interlude. And all accounts of the *Bounty*'s odyssey, including Bligh's, agree that Bligh was the only member of the ship's company who didn't have a sexual liaison with any of the Tahitian women. Hough concludes that Bligh's pressure on Christian to resume their previous, not unprecedented, relationship led to the angst that forced Christian over the mental edge. If so, he would not have been the last worker driven crazy by a sexually harassing boss.

A court-martial declared that Lieutenant Bligh was personally blameless for the mutiny. He was then promoted to captain and given another ship—this time with marines. He returned to Tahiti for a second cargo of breadfruit plants, which were successfully delivered to Jamaica in 1793. The irony of all this was that even after a successful second voyage, it did not do any good. The West Indian slaves did not like breadfruit and would not eat it. The whole program was a total failure except for the blockbuster movies, the more than 2,500 books published on the adventure, and the still-thriving Tahitian tourist industry.

Popular imagery aside, Captain Bligh's adventures conveniently provide modern public managers with five valuable lessons about the politics of program evaluation:

1. *Be first.* Bligh arrived back in England just as promptly as he could. His account of the mutiny, mostly written on his voyage home, was practically ready for the printer. The first evaluation of a major program defines the parameters and sets the tone for the others that inevitably follow. Bligh's assertion that it was lust—and not lashes—that motivated the mutineers has never been completely refuted. Even though many subsequent analyses have shown Bligh's leadership style to be a major contributing factor, his **spin** on events is still spinning.
2. *Have friendly evaluators.* Your best friend at evaluation time is your own pen—or computer. Imagine a continuum with yourself at one end and your worst enemy at the other—and everybody else aligned according to their affection for you. It is far better to have an evaluation written by someone leaning toward you on that continuum. Is arranging for an evaluation to be biased in your favor cheating or simply effective **public relations**? Hey, we're not talking objective social science here; we are talking management survival. The methodologies naturally differ.

Spin ■
Efforts by an administration or an individual political actor to manipulate the media to contain, deflect, and minimize an unraveling scandal or other embarrassing or politically damaging revelation. The purpose is to keep the situation from spinning out of control.

Public relations ■
The management of the public's perception of a political figure or an agency. Cunning politicos throughout the ages have instinctively practiced effective public relations.

3. *Disseminate your evaluation.* Just as the old adage says that there is no such thing as bad publicity, there is no such thing as too much dissemination of an evaluation. It creates notoriety and fame. In the entertainment business it means that whatever you did, good or bad, someone will hire you or offer you a book contract. There is no way of assaying how much good Bligh's widely disseminated account of the mutiny did him, but this much is for sure. Honor after honor and high office after high office came to him. So it probably did a great deal of good. Besides, it proved he could write. To the extent that real life—and especially public policy and its administration—is an essay contest, he won. Fletcher Christian lost. His name has become a synonym for a disloyal officer in large part because he never told his side of the story. Had he returned to England and challenged Bligh to a duel of evaluations, he might have been hanged for it—but Bligh's honor would have been at least sullied.

4. *Don't tell all.* Bligh knew more about events leading to the mutiny than he put in his report. He knew he stayed in Tahiti longer than necessary. He knew that he had allowed shipboard discipline to become so lax that the decks were filthy and some of the sails had been allowed to rot from neglect. He knew much more about Christian's motivations and mental state than he admitted. His report did not lie about these things. It was just self-servingly less comprehensive than it could have been. Bligh, no more paranoid than many a manager today, knew he did not have to say bad things about himself because so many of his enemies would be happy to do that for him. And they did. The mutineers and alleged mutineers who were captured in Tahiti and returned in chains for court-martial gave a devastating indictment of Bligh's management style. Only thereafter did Bligh become in the public mind what we still think of as "a Captain Bligh."

5. *Impeach the integrity or methodology of critics—or simply ignore them.* Bligh's court-martial was **pro forma**. However, while Bligh was off on his second two-year breadfruit-to-Jamaica expedition, the 10 members of *Bounty*'s crew who were arrested in Tahiti were court-martialed in England. (Christian and the other mutineers fled with the *Bounty* to Pitcairn's Island, where they remained for the rest of their lives.) The crew's account of events on the *Bounty* fleshed out Bligh's earlier evaluation to such an extent that Bligh lost his stature as a national hero. Edward Christian (Fletcher's brother) wrote a stinging rebuttal to Bligh's assessment in *A Short Reply to Captain Bligh's Answer* (1795). Bligh then published a pamphlet attacking his accuser's methodology and facts. Edward Christian then published a rejoinder pamphlet attacking Bligh's attack on him. The attacks by supporters of either side continue to this day.

Pro forma ■
A Latin phrase meaning "as a matter of form" or "a mere formality." The phrase applies to requirements or agreements that are presumed to have no real effect on behavior.

If you think that the mutiny and the debate it has fostered are ancient history, consider that its essence reoccurs every day in the United States. The nation is a ship in which we all sail. Indeed, the "ship of state" is a nautical metaphor that has been used since ancient times. All citizens are obligated on the voyage of their lives to obey the shipboard laws. Many people, especially young men the same ages as the *Bounty* crew, "mutiny" by violating the law of the land. They steal. They kill.

They rape. The same people who would defend Christian and company offer a similar defense for these new-style mutineers—they lived in an oppressive environment and were treated too harshly by those who were "in charge." Those who would defend Bligh, who feel that there can be no excuse for mutiny, today assert that there can be no excuse for breaking the law.

To the extent that we as a society refuse to excuse crime and demand longer prison sentences under increasingly harsh conditions, we are all "Captain Blighs." The debate over the mutiny is really a debate over the legitimacy of mutiny itself. Christian supporters will find ways to rationalize crime, will seek to understand the motivation of the criminals, and will demand more ameliorative programs, such as increased public housing. Bligh supporters see no excuse for crime of any kind anywhere. To those who demand such things as more public housing as a preventive measure, they say that the nation has been on a public housing building boom since the 1980s—only these "public houses" are called jails.

For Discussion: *Was Bligh's published account of the mutiny and the events that followed a good example of the assertion made in Chapter 1 that public administration is an essay contest? Are Bligh's five lessons about the politics of program evaluation still valid today?*

WHAT IS AN AUDIT?

Bligh knew that on his return to England he would be subject to an audit, a word derived from the Latin word *auditus*, meaning "a hearing." *Auditorium* retains this original meaning. Bligh's audit, because he was a naval officer, took the form of a court-martial. But even if there had been no mutiny, Bligh's conduct would have been audited—reviewed by his administrative supervisors. Today, *audit* is used to refer to any independent examination, any objective assessment of something. In public administration, *audit* refers to either of two common activities:

1. The official examination of a financial report submitted by an individual or organization to determine whether it accurately represents expenditures, deductions, or other allowances determined by laws and regulations; or
2. The final phase of the government budgetary process, which reviews the operations of an agency, especially its financial transactions, to determine whether the agency has spent its money in accordance with the law, in the most efficient manner, and with desired results.

In all cases an audit connotes comparison with some standard. Bligh knew that his behavior would be measured against that of other naval officers. Administrators expect that their performance will be compared to that of other administrators with comparable responsibilities. And financial statements are audited to determine when they are in accord with generally accepted accounting standards. The essence of auditing is measuring something against a good example in order to make a critical, evaluative judgment.

Virtually all modern organizations, from a local tennis club to the U.S. government, have auditors whose basic task is to certify that the financial accounts of the organization are correct. Auditing has become a major branch of the accounting profession, with complex professional standards and procedures for admission, practice, and reporting. Large accounting firms such as Price Waterhouse are widely known throughout the developed world. In themselves they are multinational organizations of substantial size and complexity. The audit certifications of such firms are attached to the formal financial reports of all major corporations. This independent examination of the financial accounts of organizations is a process designed to establish that they comply both with the law and with national accounting standards. These pictures of an organization's financial position are essential requirements for confident decision making by senior managers, by boards of directors, and by stockholders.

Multiple Applications

Audit continues to evolve. Many new applications of the term now exist besides its traditional use for financial reports. Thus it is possible to have a management audit—an independent examination of an organization's management posture (policies, practices, and performance of management within an organization)—or a performance or efficiency audit. An audit undertaken within a single organization may seek to combine elements of the financial audit, the efficiency audit, and the management audit. To such global intentions the term *comprehensive audit* is often applied.

The concept of independent audit has not been limited to financial and managerial issues. Many other kinds of independent assessments are also called audits. For example, an environmental audit may seek to examine compliance with environmental laws and sound environmental practices. An energy audit may seek to independently assess how an organization uses or wastes energy. Water or telecommunications audits may do the same to help an individual or organization reduce its utility bills. And a social audit may assess social issues within an organizational context. Audit processes have in common a focus on the present and the immediate past. When the social or environmental effects of a future proposal such as a new airport or highway are examined, they are usually referred to as a social impact, or environmental impact, statement. Logically we cannot audit something that has not yet happened, although it is often possible to analyze or predict future impacts.

Independent examinations—audits—of an organization's finances or performance can be conducted internally or externally, by an organization's own staff, or by outsiders from a public (meaning private sector) accounting firm. In government the outsiders could be an independent audit arm of government such as a comptroller general's office. Large organizations are normally subject to both internal and external auditors. An internal audit group, independent of line management and with a reporting line sufficiently high in the organization, may seek to provide management with objective advice quickly so that problems can be identified and rectified before they grow worse. The external auditor not only comes from outside, but often reports outside as well—to elected representatives, stockholders, or whomever it is that holds ultimate responsibility for an organization's destiny. Often, an efficient internal audit unit can simplify and prepare the ground to make the work of external auditors quicker and more focused. Nevertheless, neither internal nor external auditors alone are likely to be adequate for a large and complex organization—especially in the public sector where accountability is critically important.

A History of Auditing

Government auditing goes back to ancient times. There are records of a Chinese audit function in the eleventh century B.C.E. and in Athens in the fourth century B.C.E. Modern audits in government, though, really developed in the nineteenth century when the growth of public sector activities became so complex that an independent and objective assessment of financial management became essential. With huge sums of money moving around global empires in the nineteenth century, the opportunities for corruption were effectively limitless. In this context it made financial sense to create strong government audit units with clear links to the top of government. Great Britain created its Office of Comptroller-General in 1857. It had independent links to a Parliamentary Committee of Public Accounts and strong legislative backing to enforce access to accounts and the disclosure of information. The U.S. General Accounting Office was established in 1921. Headed by the comptroller general of the United States, it is an agency of, and reports directly to, Congress. However, there were many other examples of government audit in the United States earlier than this. The progressive reform movement early in the twentieth century fought, often quite successfully, for state and local governments to have an appointed civil service commission to curtail patronage abuses, as well as an elected controller/comptroller whose job it was to inhibit financial abuses.

The establishment of prestigious and relatively independent national audit organizations like the Comptroller and Auditor-General in Great Britain and the General Accounting Office in the United States helps the audit function to stand above corruption and apart from the political administration of the day. Often the prestige and renown of the individual in charge of an audit office can be important in personifying the integrity and credibility of the office—particularly when (as is inevitable) some of its findings turn out to be unpalatable to the ruling administration.

The Government Accountability Office

Today, most people assume that it is the president who is responsible for the performance and accountability of the federal bureaucracy. That was certainly not the case in the nineteenth century, when it was assumed that Congress had the overwhelming responsibility for the national administration. But when Theodore Roosevelt became president in 1901, he led a two-decade-long cry that the president be given greater authority. Finally, after a variety of high-level commissions endorsed the notion that the president be given significant administrative responsibility, Congress passed the Budget and Accounting Act of 1921. The first half of the act (the "budget") gave in to the reform advocates by creating a Bureau of the Budget in the Department of the Treasury. This new bureau was authorized to prepare an executive budget and was given additional staff to conduct continuing studies of efficiency. So, long before the Bureau of the Budget was renamed the Office of Management and Budget in 1970, it had a significant management role.

Congress, however, was institutionally suspicious of presidential power. So the second half of the act (the "accounting") created the General Accounting Office (GAO) as a congressional support agency to audit federal government expenditures and to assist Congress with its legislative oversight responsibilities. Because these two agencies have become so central to the administrative well-being of the federal government, Herbert Emmerich in *Federal Organization and Administrative Management* has called their creation "probably the greatest landmark of our administrative history except for the Constitution itself."

The GAO, which officially became the Government Accountability Office in 2004, is directed by the comptroller general of the United States, who is appointed by the president with the advice and consent of the Senate for a term of 15 years. While the GAO originally confined itself to auditing financial records to see that funds were properly spent, during the 1960s it redefined its mission to include overall program evaluation. Its responsibilities include conducting financial as well as performance audits of all federal government agencies. Indeed, it was always intended that it be so. The 1921 act specifically authorizes the comptroller general to "make recommendations looking to greater economy or efficiency in public expenditures." And "all departments and establishments" are required by the act to turn over "any books, documents, papers or records" that the comptroller general "or any of his assistants or employees" requests. Long before President Ronald Reagan popularized the phrase "trust but verify" in regard to nuclear weapons treaties with the Russians, Congress was taking this attitude with the president. Think of the GAO as the "Office of Verification" for Congress. In a typical year the GAO completes around 1,000 major reports for the members of Congress.

Often the information provided by the Government Accountability Office is delivered to Congress in written reports that include specific recommendations. According to the GAO's own estimates, the agency made 2,700 recommendations to improve government operations between 2000 and 2004, with 83 percent of those suggestions being implemented. However, there are numerous occasions every year where GAO staff provide testimony to congressional committees (217 times in 2004) or provide formal briefings to members of Congress. The issues covered may concern conventional financial management, but often the scope of reports and briefings goes to matters of vital policy import of which Congress might otherwise not have been aware. For example, in fiscal year 2004 the GAO reported to Congress on Social Security reform, Defense Department procurement, the use of private contractors in Iraq, military peacekeeping operations, the No Child Left Behind Act, the Defense of Marriage Act, the renewable energy policy, tax policy, computer policy, flu vaccinations, managing human resources, the United Nations Oil for Food program, and lapses in security at federal agencies. The scope of these topics illustrates how far removed a modern national audit agency is from the kind of green eyeshade, quill pen audit that existed in the past. These are truly adventures in public policy where the auditor is not so much a "private" as "public" detective and the client not a rich widow but Uncle Sam himself.

Despite the wide scope of policy and performance investigations that the GAO undertakes, financial management remains a central concern. On the revenue side, the GAO identifies many cases where government agencies are not pulling in the money owed. The GAO found out, for example, in one of its studies that the Internal Revenue Service is less likely to catch high-income people who do not file tax returns than lower-income people, and that Medicare contractors were not bothering to recover monies owed by other insurers. On the expenditure side, each year brings new examples of waste identified by GAO—for example, how Stanford University had overcharged the Office of Naval Research or how inadequate controls over Department of Defense subcontractors cost the federal government millions of dollars each year. Overall the, GAO measured its financial savings to the government at $35.4 billion in 2003, or a $78 return on each dollar in its budget.

The GAO, with its $464 million budget and a staff consisting of 3,200 accountants, lawyers, engineers, and other employees, is the largest government auditing agency in the United States. The GAO is vast both in size and reputation. Its national visibility and reputation for institutional integrity has made it a model for other levels of government. Every major subnational government has its auditors. They range from the elected auditor general of a state government to the local accounting firm retained by a small school board. Indeed, the state-level auditor is effectively part of a plural executive, the *de facto* arrangement of most state governments, because most governors share executive authority with other independently elected officers, such as a secretary of state, treasurer, attorney general—or an auditor.

BOX 14.1 | What's in a Name?

In 2004, the 83-year-old General Accounting Office officially changed its name to the Government Accountability Office. While still going by the acronym GAO, this organization's name change could be considered an act of "truth in labeling." While accounting has always been an important role for the GAO, this function is just one aspect of the office's broad mission. According to its Comptroller General David Walker, only 15 percent of the GAO's workload deals with the area of accounting. In reality, the GAO has been much more involved with the evaluation and analysis of government programs than with keeping the government's books. An examination of the agency's personnel helps to demonstrate the multifaceted nature of the contemporary GAO. You'll still find CPAs among the GAO's staff, but you're more likely to find economists, policy analysts, and lawyers inhabiting the agency's offices. The GAO's staff does conduct audits to make sure tax dollars are being spent appropriately, but more often its employees are engaged in projects that attempt to measure the efficiency and effectiveness of programs. For example, the GAO has been highly engaged in the evaluation of the Social Security system and other federal entitlement programs. In addition, the agency has been deeply involved in examinations of the logistics and resource allocation of the U.S. military in Iraq. In this capacity it has evaluated the effectiveness of such endeavors from the security of its position within the legislative branch of government. Thus the GAO of today is much more than a group of grizzled bean counters with accounting ledgers. Instead, it's the government entity that is responsible for making sure the country gets the most bang for its tax buck. ◣

Source: Adapted from the GAO Web site, http://www.gao.gov/about/rollcall07192004.pdf.

TYPES OF AUDIT

The GAO in its *Standards for Audit of Governmental Organizations, Programs, Activities, and Functions* maintains that a comprehensive audit program should include the following three types of audit:

1. *Financial and compliance:* Determines (a) whether the financial statements of an audited entity present fairly the financial position and the results of financial operations in accordance with generally accepted accounting principles and (b) whether the entity has complied with laws and regulations that may have a material effect on the financial statements.
2. *Economy and efficiency:* Determines (a) whether the entity is managing and utilizing its resources (such as personnel, property, space) economically and efficiently, (b) the causes of inefficiencies or uneconomical practices, and (c) whether the entity has complied with laws and regulations concerning matters of economy and efficiency.
3. *Program results:* Determines (a) whether the desired results or benefits established by the legislature or other authorizing body are being achieved and (b) whether the agency has considered alternatives that might yield desired results at a lower cost.

Compliance Audit

The oldest and most traditional form of auditing activity is known as a *compliance audit*. Here the auditor is looking for the extent to which, in the financial management of an organization, financial inputs have been managed in compliance with the law and accepted standards and conventions for the treatment of accounting information. In the past, a traditional compliance audit was embodied by the annual visit of the auditor to remote parts of the organization, where the auditor would check each entry in financial journals and ledgers, making sure that arithmetic and balances were correct and that no mistakes had been made. At the end of this process, the auditor would certify that the financial records were correct.

The value of this traditional form of audit is clear. Officials dealing with funds could not simply dispose of them as they wished, keeping no records or records that could not be understood. The advent of traditional auditing meant that every public official had to (1) expect and prepare for a regular visit by the auditor, (2) keep accounts in a manner officially prescribed (often by regulations), and (3) make those records available for the auditor's scrutiny. In some jurisdictions the audit might be accompanied by an inventory of stores and equipment—hence, the at times derisive references to compliance audits as involving the counting of paper clips. In fact, the compliance audit was and remains a powerful primary tool for preventing many types of corruption.

But compliance audits often go beyond financial reviews. Voluntary compliance is the basis of a civil society. No government has the resources to force all of its citizens to comply with all of the criminal and civil laws. Consequently, all governments are more dependent on compliance than they would ever like to admit.

IN THE NEWS | Auditing Iraq

When a major financial scandal led to the demise of the Enron Corporation in 2002, the corporate world was quite shaken. What auditors had exposed was an elaborate scam in which company officials had concealed debts and exaggerated profits by manipulating Enron's accounting practices. While the illegal practices were taking place for quite some time, it took government examiners years to sort through the complex financial arrangements of the seventh largest company in the United States. But if exposing Enron seems like a massive undertaking for government auditors and accountants, just imagine the difficulty of auditing the financial aspects of the war in Iraq.

For starters, no one was shooting at the individuals auditing Enron executives. But in Iraq the process of auditing financial transactions requires accountants to carry spreadsheets as well as wear Kevlar body armor. By its very nature, war is chaotic and efforts to find financial irregularities are extremely complicated. This difficulty is magnified by some of the irregular financial transactions that necessarily take place in the theater of war. For example, consider the difficulty in following the audit trail of enormous amounts of cash.

During a period between May 2003 and June 2004, nearly $12 billion in cash, mainly in $100 bills, was sent from the United States to Iraq. Once in Iraq the cash was distributed to U.S. Army officers at the rank of major or above. These officers were to use the "Benjamins" to help with reconstruction projects throughout Iraq. The catch, or lack thereof, was that there were really no standards distribution or accounting practices in place to track where the money went. This action led Democratic Congressman Henry Waxman to tell National Public Radio that "It's hard even now to imagine $12 billion in hundred-dollar bills, wrapped into bricklike bundles, then put on huge pallets and brought over by troop carrier airplanes to be dispersed in a war zone." The situation left government examiners overwhelmed.

With no shortage of fraud and corruption taking place in Iraq, it might be expected that the Pentagon would quickly ramp up its auditing efforts regarding the war. But Defense Department leaders seem to have done just the opposite. After sending auditors to Iraq after the start of the war in 2003, the Defense Department's inspector general suddenly withdrew the auditors in 2004. The "retreat" of the army auditors was justified as appropriate because there were other government agencies like the Government Accountability Office (GAO) looking at the financial dealings in Iraq. However, critics lambasted the "auditor reduction" as a way for the Defense Department to avoid uncovering many of the glaring cases of fraud, corruption, and waste plaguing American military actions in a country with no tradition of good government honestly administered.

Despite the withdrawal of Defense Department auditors in 2004, GAO and the special inspector for Iraq Reconstruction have been able to discover more than a few egregious cases of financial wrongdoing in Iraq. For example, the GAO found that the military lost track of nearly 190,000 AK-47 assault rifles and pistols intended for use by Iraqi security forces. More troubling is the fact that these missing weapons had most likely landed in the hands of insurgents to be used against Americans. It was also found that military contractors such as Halliburton have commonly overbilled the federal government for services and supplies: these civilian employees used funds for extravagant purposes such as staying in five-star hotels in Kuwait. Such financial accounting measures helped prompt the GAO Comptroller General David Walker to scold the Defense Department for its "atrocious financial management" and inability to provide adequate oversight of more than $1 billion a week spent on the war. According to Walker: "If the Department of Defense were a business, they'd be out of business." But is it fair to use peacetime accounting standards in a war zone? ▶

Internal Revenue Service (IRS) ■ The federal agency, established in 1862 within the Treasury Department, responsible for administering and enforcing the internal revenue laws, except those relating to alcohol, tobacco, firearms, and explosives (which are the responsibility of the Bureau of Alcohol, Tobacco, Firearms and Explosives). The IRS mission is to encourage and achieve the highest possible degree of voluntary compliance with the tax laws and regulations.

The best single example of massive voluntary compliance is the U.S. federal income tax system, which is essentially administered by self-assessment and voluntary payment. The much-dreaded audit by the federal government's tax-collecting agency, the **Internal Revenue Service**, is an assessment not just of whether a citizen has paid taxes due, but also of whether the taxes were calculated in the appropriate manner. Compliance auditing is also undertaken by funding agencies to judge whether a grantee is acting (i.e., spending its grant funds) in accordance with the granter's policies or preset guidelines. For example, the aptly named Office of Federal Contract Compliance Programs within the Department of Labor works to ensure that (1) there is no employment discrimination by government contractors because of race, religion, color, sex, or national origin; and (2) there is affirmative action to employ veterans and handicapped workers.

But compliance auditing is inherently limited. Conceptually it is part of a control system that focuses on the "inputs" or resources used in administration, not the "outputs" or results. An organization might well be able to comply with the letter of the laws concerning accounting for public monies and yet seem to achieve nothing. By the 1960s government auditors at all levels became increasingly discontented with performing such a confined role, of effectively "fiddling while Rome burned," by concentrating only on financial transactions rather than looking at the overall performance of the organization.

Performance Audit

The possibility of auditors extending their scope from assessing compliance with law and regulations to the wider role of assessing efficiency and effectiveness began to be discussed late in the 1960s. By 1972, the General Accounting Office was formally advocating adopting such a wider role. The GAO's enabling legislation had from the beginning given it the legal basis for this expansion of its mission. Efficiency and effectiveness audits are the two steps in the performance audit chain, but in practice they may be telescoped into a single performance or comprehensive audit of the organization. An efficiency audit compares the activities of an organization with the objectives that have been assigned to it. In a sense, an efficiency audit still entails a compliance notion—though it is now the extent to which the organization has complied with and realized its objectives that is being examined. Such an extension of the auditor's role is compatible with an instrumental view of administration, since it is implementation of the objectives set by political leaders that is being reviewed. They and their constituents want to know how responsive the organization has been to their will and how effective they have been in playing the instruments of state.

When the scope of audit is extended beyond the efficiency of an organization to its effectiveness, attention now turns from the extent to which politically set objectives have been achieved to the broader question of whether the objectives themselves were right in the first place. This further extension of scope has been controversial, since it places the auditor firmly in the role of policy evaluator. Is this an appropriate role for an auditor? Does it invite political controversy of a kind that might reflect on the independence of the audit function? If auditors criticize political leaders or suggest that government policies are inappropriate, the audit entity itself could lose the capacity to review programs in a way that will be perceived as not only objective, but also above the normal political fray. Effectiveness or performance auditing in government is thus an inherently political activity that must be dressed in apolitical clothes. It must be free of methodological bias as a matter of science at the same time that it is perceived to be free of political bias as a matter of strategy.

Internal Audit

So far we've focused on the audit of governmental programs and activities by external auditors, such as the Government Accountability Office. However, line managers are often reluctant to wait until an external examination finds problems in their organizations. It is therefore common to find internal audit groups within larger governmental organizations. Such groups need to have a reporting line high in the organization (such as to the chief executive officer or to an audit committee at the highest level). They need adequate clear authority and support as well as resources and the right to enter all parts of an organization. Internal audit functions vary in the tasks they pursue and the way tasks are assigned to them. Sometimes (especially if the organization is a major cash handler), they may need to have a significant compliance audit role. In other circumstances they can virtually serve as independent troubleshooters, providing early warning to top management of emerging problems. While any such internal audit unit must have an **audit program** showing what it intends to focus on, CEOs sometimes give substantial latitude to internal auditors to roam freely around the organization and to add items to their audit program without top-management approval. In this sense they function as **inspectors general**.

Internal auditors are always in danger of losing their independence to line management. To ensure that the degree of independence needed for effectiveness is maintained, three key principles must be observed:

1. Location outside line management
2. A high reporting line for audit results
3. Reasonable latitude in selecting assignments

There is a significant role in the public sector for private accounting firms serving as auditors. Large public corporations, especially those operating under corporations law, normally employ accounting firms in some or all of their audit functions. The Government Accountability Office itself, quite appropriately, has been audited by a private accounting firm (Price Waterhouse). There can be many occasions when such firms with their wide networks and expertise can play an invaluable role in public audit.

However, those who imagine that the whole of government audit can or should be placed in the hands of private accounting firms are in the minority. While public administration remains a large, complex, and specialized field, with its own framework of accountability leading back to democratically elected representatives, there will remain a need for specialist internal and external audit capacities, such as the Government Accountability Office, within government.

Audit program ■
The detailed steps and procedures to be followed in conducting the audit and preparing the report. A written audit program should be prepared for each audit, and it should include such information as the purpose and scope, background information needed to understand the audit objectives and the entity's mission, definitions of unique terms, objectives, and reporting procedures.

Inspector general ■
The job title (of military origin) for the administrative head of an inspection or investigative unit of a larger agency.

PROGRAM EVALUATION

A program evaluation is the systematic examination of any activity or group of activities undertaken by government to make a determination about their effects, both short and long range. Program evaluation is distinguished from management evaluation (also called organization evaluation) because the latter is limited to a program's internal administrative procedures. While program evaluations use management and organizational data, the main thrust is necessarily on overall program objectives and impact.

Policy Analysis Is Not Program Evaluation

The terms *policy analysis* and *program evaluation* are often used interchangeably, but they mean different things. A policy analysis is a set of techniques that seeks to answer the question of what the probable effects of a policy will be before they actually occur. A policy analysis undertaken on a program that is already under way is more properly called a program evaluation. Nevertheless, the term is used by many to refer to both before- and after-the-fact analyses of public policies. All policy analysis involves the application of systematic research techniques (drawn largely from the social sciences and based on measurements of program effectiveness, quality, cost, and impact) to the formulation, execution, and evaluation of public policy to create a more rational or optimal administrative system. A formal program evaluation effort normally implies that a relationship of "arm's length" independence has been established between the program and those evaluating it. In-house evaluations, however well conducted, are likely to be suspected of special pleading on behalf of the agency concerned.

Of course, program evaluations have always been done by executives, legislators, and their captains. (Remember Bligh!) But as old government programs expanded and new programs were initiated in the 1960s, program evaluations came out of the shadows. By the beginning of the 1970s, it was generally conceded that many of the Great Society programs initiated during the Johnson administration

---

ALTERNATIVE Theories | Neutral Policy Analysis versus Partisan Policy Analysis

Neutral Analyses Are:	Partisan Analyses Are:
honest	biased
apolitical	political
disinterested	interested
methodologically sound	methodologically suspect
focused on facts	focused on advocacy

Note that all of these characteristics are tendencies, not absolutes. Thus a partisan policy analysis could be methodologically sound. However, political partisans are not well known for the soundness of their research methodologies. What kind of analyst would you prefer to be: neutral or partisan? Which would be more fun?

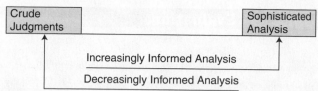

To the extent that we make judgments on governmental policies
from affirmative action to zoning ordinances we all do policy analysis.
A judgement on a policy issue requires an analysis, however superficial.
Policy analysis can be viewed as a continuum from crude judgments
made in a snap ("The governor is an idiot and all his policies are stupid!")
to the most sophisticated analysis using complicated methodologies
("I have just administered an I.Q. test to the governor and he really
is an idiot."). Policy analysis is like sex. Everybody does it, but
there is a relatively small group that does it professionally.

FIGURE 14.1

The policy analysis continuum

were not working nearly as well as had been originally hoped. As these and other social programs came under increasing criticism, the field of program evaluation gained increasing prominence.

Aaron Wildavsky, in his 1972 *Public Administration Review* article "The Self-Evaluating Organization," provided an insightful discussion about the difficulties of evaluating public programs in a dynamic political environment. Wildavsky wrote that the "ideal organization would be self-evaluating. It would continuously monitor its own activities so as to determine whether it was meeting its goals or even whether these goals should continue to prevail. When evaluation suggested that a change in goals or programs to achieve them was desirable, these proposals would be taken seriously by top decision makers. They would institute the necessary changes."

But the problem with evaluation, according to Wildavsky, was that no matter how compelling the case for change, change was precisely what evaluation emphasized most and organizations abhorred most. Most public managers, he argued, are hard-pressed to cope with day-to-day operational demands, so they strive for stability—not constant reorder and reformulation. The costs of change had to be borne, too, and evaluation seldom considered this. Finally, since the most politically feasible organizational strategies would be ones that minimized disruption, managers would tend to resist or ignore evaluation.

Legislative Program Evaluation

The General Accounting Office (now known as the Government Accountability Office), under the leadership of **Elmer Staats**, also helped elevate the general quality and value of program evaluation by setting evaluation standards and working actively to professionalize program evaluation as part of the **expanded scope of auditing**. Many state governments would initiate legislative evaluation commissions based on the GAO idea. Some state legislatures—most notably Hawaii,

Elmer Staats (1914–2011) ■
The comptroller general of the United States from 1966 to 1981.

Expanded scope of auditing ■
Evaluating the results and effectiveness of a government activity in addition to delving into the traditional financial compliance concerns of auditing.

IN THE NEWS | The Politics of Evaluation

Wildavsky's arguments notwithstanding, evaluation would not be denied. In 1967, Edward Suchman of Columbia University published the first major work on evaluation theory, *Evaluation Research*. Suchman's work argued that evaluation was essentially a field of study; that evaluative research and practice can and must be studied in a general context outside of evaluation applications in the various fields of specialization; and that evaluation was generic. *Generic?* Yes. But in whatever context it surfaced, it was also intensely political. Evaluation researcher Carol H. Weiss discovered these four "less legitimate"—meaning wholly political in the worst sense of the word—reasons for evaluation:

1. *Postponement:* The decision makers may be looking for ways to delay a decision. Instead of resorting to the usual ploy of appointing a committee and waiting for its report, they can commission an evaluation study, which takes even longer.

2. *Ducking responsibility:* Sometimes one faction in the program organization is espousing one course of action and another faction is opposing it. The administrators look to evaluation to get them off the hook by producing dispassionate evidence that will make the decision for them. There are cases in which administrators know what the decision will be even before they call in the evaluators, but they want to cloak it in the legitimate trappings of research.

3. *Public relations:* Occasionally, evaluation is seen as a way of self-glorification. Administrators

believe that they have a highly successful program and look for a way to make it visible. A good study will fill the bill. Copies of the report, favorable of course, can be sent to boards of trustees, members of legislative committees, executives of philanthropic foundations who give large sums to successful programs, and other influential people. . . . The program administrators' motives are not, of course, necessarily crooked or selfish. Often, there is a need to justify the program to the people who pay the bills, and they are seeking support for a concept and a project in which they believe. Generating support for existing programs is a common motive for embarking on evaluation.

4. *Fulfilling grant requirements:* Increasingly, the decision to evaluate stems from sources outside the program. Many federal grants for demonstration projects and innovative programs are tagged with an evaluation requirement—for example, all projects for disadvantaged pupils funded under Title I of the Elementary and Secondary Education Act are required to be evaluated. . . . To the operators of a project, the demands of starting up and running the new program take priority. Plagued as they often are by immediate problems of staffing, budgets, logistics, community relations, and all the other trials of pioneers, they tend to neglect the evaluation. They see it mainly as a ritual designed to placate the funding bodies, without any real usefulness to them. ◣

Wisconsin, and Michigan—have organized separate program evaluation staffs similar to the GAO. Another method used by state legislatures is that of the legislative commission. New York's Legislative Commission on Expenditure Review pioneered this concept, whereby a separate program evaluation staff, under an executive director, reports to the joint leadership of the legislature. New Jersey, Illinois, and Virginia now use variations of this theme. A third format exists whereby the evaluation function is located in a discrete committee that is linked to the several appropriations committees. Connecticut and North Carolina offer examples of this.

In 1976, Colorado, after a major lobbying effort by **Common Cause**, would become the first state to enact a sunset law—the requirement that government agencies and programs have termination dates. Many other jurisdictions subsequently enacted them as well. They require formal evaluations and subsequent affirmative legislation if the agency or program is to continue. Although the purpose of a finite life span of, say, five years is to force evaluation and to toughen legislative oversight, the effect is to subject programs to automatic termination unless the clock is reset. Despite its widespread popularity, such time-bomb evaluation is not without risks. There are limits to the abilities of any legislature's staff to do the kind of thorough evaluation required to make sunset meaningful. And, of course, the political reality is that the evaluation might become a tool of bipartisan infighting. Requiring organizations to submit evaluation data for review and to justify their programs may amount to little more than burying the legislature in an avalanche of insignificant paper—something at which agencies have a demonstrated prowess. Furthermore, some agencies, such as police, prisons, and mental health institutions, will be rightly skeptical of the chances of their programs being shut down. Nevertheless, by the mid-1970s evaluation was—and remains—a vital and integral part of public administration.

Common Cause ■
A Washington, D.C.-based public interest lobby founded in 1970 and devoted to making public officials more accountable to citizens and to improving government performance.

Types of Evaluation

There are many types of program evaluation and many perspectives from which it can be undertaken. For example, an *ex ante facto* evaluation, such as an environmental effects statement, might seek to assess the impacts and outcomes of a program before that program is implemented: Should the outcomes or impacts identified prove problematic, such a study may lead to a program being aborted, or at least significantly modified. A process evaluation may examine aspects of a program's operations while they are in place, and its results may be absorbed directly into the organization's management processes. An *ex post facto* evaluation, postmortem, or debriefing looks at a program or operation after it has been completed, and it has particular relevance when the nature of an activity is iterative, like dealing with a forest fire emergency, or a serious heat wave such as the one in Chicago in 1995 that claimed hundreds of lives. Such studies seek to establish the changes to policy, infrastructure, or operations that would allow a similar circumstance to have more positive results when it next occurred.

Perspectives in program evaluation also vary according to the discipline or paradigm from which they are conducted. Managers will usually think in terms of managerial paradigms and look at the nature and appropriateness of objectives, and the efficiency and effectiveness with which objectives were pursued. Lawyers may stress issues such as authority, compliance, equity, process, and culpability in examining an issue. A political analysis may look at issues of representation and accountability. Clearly, the purpose of undertaking the evaluation needs to determine the kind of evaluation to be adopted and the skills required in the evaluation team. Other decisions will include the type of supporting data and research to be used (and the provision of a budget to fund it); the extent to which there will be public hearings or consultations as part of the evaluative process; and whether there are hidden agendas to continue, terminate, or transform the program.

The zealous evaluator has one cardinal principle: Everything is evaluatable. There are no exceptions. However, many a public manager, while agreeing that most programs can be evaluated, will also argue that there are plenty of exceptions. In actuality, it is more a question of degree. Some programs have a high degree of "goal ambiguity"—a quality that can greatly inhibit evaluation. The public sector, because it tends to provide services rather than produce products, has always had more difficulty in defining its output—in measuring its goals. Further complicating matters is the fact that the different functions of government invariably involve different types of evaluation measurement. In evaluating highways we can focus on accidents, injuries, and fatality rates, which seemingly represent hard data; but the "data" quickly become soft once we move to such functions as parks, mental health, services for the elderly, education, and training programs for the unemployed.

Evaluation Standards

Generally speaking, evaluations refer to three standards against which a program can be evaluated: (1) compliance, (2) efficiency, and (3) effectiveness/relevance. These standards indicate the fundamental questions that must be asked of any program.

The first category of questions, compliance, essentially asks an auditing question: Are government business transactions being conducted in accordance with law? This can be broken down into more specific questions:

1. Were all financial transactions involving the acquisition and expenditure of resources consistent with legislative and administrative authorization/ regulation?
2. Are financial records and statements rendered in accord with prescribed accounting standards?
3. Are they accurate and free from fraud?

Most evaluations for ensuring compliance on a regular basis are performed by various audit and control units.

Questions of efficiency can be asked: Are government agencies getting optimum productivity out of the resources that they expend? More specific questions can be asked:

1. Is responsibility for specific tasks clearly delegated?
2. Are employees adequately qualified to perform their tasks?
3. Is the waste of resources being avoided?

Efficiency evaluation can also be readily used for comparative analysis: pitting various units, regions, or similar organizations against each other to ascertain who is more efficient and, conversely, who is less so. But sometimes this kind of competition can prove counterproductive. For example, Jay Shafritz, Albert Hyde, and David Rosenbloom tell the story in *Personnel Management in Government* of a GAO audit of the U.S. Postal Service. After a new **postmaster general** sought to foster competition among post offices by generating a list of top offices in productivity, the Postal Service's productivity and mail volume appeared

Postmaster general ■
The chief executive officer of the U.S. Postal Service appointed by its nine-member board of governors.

No Child Will Be Left Behind—If Teachers Cheat

The pressure for productivity improvement in the public sector has been nowhere more intense than in local school districts. With funding incomes increasingly dependent upon student performance on standardized tests, teachers in some of the largest school districts have used a time-honored improvement technique—cheating. Not by the students but by their teachers. The methods vary: encourage potentially low-scoring students to stay home on the day of the test, seat test-challenged students next to high achievers to encourage the copying of correct answers, or for guaranteed results, simply have the teachers take the completed tests home and change the answers to improve tests scores. In March 2011 a series of articles in *USA TODAY* revealed 1,610 cases of test-score tampering in six states and Washington, D.C., during 2009 and 2010. But this is the tip of an iceberg. If large numbers of teachers were having "eraser parties" in Atlanta, Georgia, over many years, it seems reasonable to assume that teachers in other school districts also had access to erasers. The single fact remains that if success, financial rewards, and promotions are to be determined by statistics, there will always be those who will manipulate those statistics to their advantage.

to increase nationwide. After starting at the bottom of the list, the Washington, D.C., post office reported consistently increasing mail volumes and productivity until it ranked at or near the top. The Postal Inspection Service estimated that the total amount of mail handled was inflated more than 60 percent. Sometimes the totals were overstated by as much as 110 percent. According to the GAO, these estimates were "supported by hours of videotape records showing individuals reweighing the same mail over and over to inflate volumes and by sworn statements from supervisors and employees admitting record falsification." The GAO concluded that "the most common reasons given by employees for participating in the fabrication were the pressure from higher management to achieve production levels that were unrealistic and a belief that their careers would suffer if these productivity levels were not met." Now "pressure for increased productivity" can be added to the list of all-purpose excuses such as "the devil made me do it" and "the dog ate my homework."

But it has been the third category of questions, those concerning effectiveness, that seem to now dominate the program evaluation environment. Questions of effectiveness ask, "Is the expenditure of government resources for a specific purpose contributing sufficiently to the achievement of that purpose?" This general question then can in turn be subdivided:

1. Are the various purposes involved in a program compatible?
2. How much of a reduction has there been in the problem?
3. Could the commitment of additional resources to the program have brought about significantly greater advances toward the objectives?
4. What would have happened if the program had not existed?

Despite the close relationship between the effectiveness and efficiency aspects of a program's operations, they can have an inverse relationship to one another. Thus it is possible to have a program that is relatively inefficient but nonetheless effective (it squanders resources but nevertheless gets the job done) or one that is relatively efficient but ineffective (it may use its resources optimally but nevertheless has little impact on the problem it was designed to ameliorate).

Management Control: Evaluation in a Microcosm

Control is that aspect of management concerned with the comparison of actual versus planned performance, as well as the development and implementation of procedures to correct substandard performance. Control, which is inherent to all levels of management, is a feedback process that ideally should report only unexpected situations. Some management control systems regularly report critical indicators of performance so that management will have advance notice of potential problems.

As we have seen, audits and evaluations provide important perspectives through which managers and elected officials may make evaluative judgments about the efficiency and performance of programs and organizations. However, it is not the only such perspective. On a day-to-day basis, within the organization, the manager must receive continual feedback, make judgments, and exercise corrective and directive control. Herbert Kaufman, in *Administrative Feedback: Monitoring Subordinates' Behavior*, notes that not all feedback is welcome. When organizations are rife with corruption, as is all too often the case with public administration, leaders "may resort to the strategy of discouraging feedback about administrative behavior because they privately approve of the behavior they know they should, according to law and morality, prevent." Such leaders want to be managers, but most specifically do not want to appear to be "in control" in case "a pattern of offenses by subordinates is disclosed." They want to be able to make "a credible claim that they, too, were victimized" by their organization's ne'er-do-wells. This is the tactic of the police chief (played by Claude Rains) in the 1941 movie *Casablanca* who was "shocked, shocked!" that gambling had been going on (as he pocketed his winnings) in Humphrey Bogart's nightclub.

Management control exists to ensure that managers are made aware on a day-to-day basis of developments within their program or organization so judgments and corrective actions can be taken. The process can be described as "evaluation in a microcosm." As with formal, external evaluation, the manager is likely to have strategic objectives in mind and to be forming progressive but increasingly formed judgments about the extent and rate at which objectives are being achieved. If they are not being achieved, or being achieved too slowly or in the wrong way, the manager will often "exert control" by stepping in and providing program managers with direction. The nature of this direction will reflect management style and the gravity of the position. It may range from a facilitative discussion of available options to a stormy injunction to "shape up or ship out."

Often the audit process focuses on assessing the adequacy of management control systems as a whole. Effective control seeks to ensure that all members of an organization are working together toward organizational objectives. It should provide an early warning system if strategic assumptions are wrong or if the environment has changed. An effective management control system will deploy many of the tools of longer-term evaluation; that is, it will involve references back to goals and objectives, the selective use of performance standards and performance measures to see whether and how well objectives are being achieved. It will also use informal networks and the **grapevine**, which helps to provide timely information and knowledgeable hunches as to what is happening "in the trenches." A framework of control that is well conceived, uses timely information, and is flexible can help the program or organization to avoid disaster. On the other hand, if the system of management control is heavy-handed, based on poor or incomplete information, and excessively rigid, it can frighten out innovation and fail to perform its key task of short-term evaluation and correction. This is what happened with the space shuttle *Challenger* disaster (see Chapter 2).

Grapevine ■
The informal means by which organizational members give or receive messages. The word is derived from the practice of stringing early telegraph wires from tree to tree in a vine-like fashion.

Evaluation and the Democratic Process

One of the distinguishing features of public administration in democratic societies is the extent to which government is conducted in a "fishbowl." The electorate and elected members of legislatures expect to be able to see clearly how governmental programs and organizations are functioning in "real time" so that policy adjustments and changes in direction can be made—and so that debate can occur about the practicalities of program implementation as well as about the theoretical niceties of policy.

Executive branch internal evaluations—essentially "self"-evaluations—are normally incorporated into the management process. More and more budget offices are undertaking this role. Agencies need to be sure that they are accomplishing their objectives, that they are making progress. Of course, this "thirst" for evaluation may be induced from various motives. The noblest is the good management practice of assessing progress so that problem areas can be identified and remedial action taken. Equally necessary, though considerably less noble, are program evaluations undertaken for political considerations. A common gambit here is the "defensive program evaluation," whereby possibly controversial programs are evaluated to create, in effect, "good" report cards to show legislative committees or at least to provide some counterarguments against evaluations by others that might produce less-favorable results. This is what Captain Bligh instinctively knew he had to do. As a program evaluator, he was far ahead of his time!

The processes of audit and evaluation in government, and indeed many aspects of the exercise of day-to-day management control within public organizations, are no longer conducted in the expectation of secrecy. Rather, the expectation is that decisions and actions are likely to be publicly audited, evaluated, debated, and discussed. Many state and local governments have sunshine laws that exist to this end. The federal government's Sunshine Act of 1977 requires all independent regulatory commissions to give advance notice of the date, time, place, and agenda of their meetings. Closed meetings are allowed if circumstances warrant, but citizens have the right to take agencies to federal court if they feel that closed meetings were not justified. On the whole, this is a healthy development likely to weigh against corruption and incompetence, which fester best in dark places.

A CASE STUDY | Jeremy Bentham, the Philosopher of Policy Analysis and Program Evaluation

The ancient Greek philosophers and the political analysts that they inspired over the next two millennia were concerned with grand theories of the state and governance, of war and peace, and of power and politics. But with the rise of cities, with the advent of a merchant or middle class, and with the new problems and opportunities brought about by the Industrial Revolution, things had to change. Governments had to get increasingly involved with the minutiae of public policy and its administration. Someone had to start thinking about the relatively small issues, less about war and peace and more about how best to collect taxes, build sewers, and design prisons. This is where Jeremy Bentham (1748–1832) comes in. He was a one-man think tank for a great many of the petty details of governance. In consequence he is considered one of the founders of the practice—indeed, the science—of policy analysis.

Bentham was often referred to as a child prodigy because he was reading English by age three, Latin by four, and French by six. At 12 he was sent off to Queen's College, Oxford, graduated in 1763, and immediately undertook the formal study of law. The family hoped he would join his father in the family legal business. But, on hearing the lectures of the leading legal scholars of the day, he became disillusioned and disappointed with English law—but not discouraged. While called to the bar in 1769, instead of practicing law, he decided to devote his life to reforming it. By "it" he meant both the established doctrines of the law as well as the laws themselves. While the life of a reformer seldom pays well, he worried not—especially after his father died and left him independently wealthy. Even today the life of the mind is ever so eased by a healthy inheritance.

Bentham is best known as the British philosopher who held that self-interest was the prime motivator and that a government should strive to do the greatest good for the greatest number. He wanted institutions to justify themselves on the practical grounds of the level of useful welfare achieved. He was thereby the prophet of the movement called Utilitarianism, which held that an action is right if and only if its performance will be more productive of pleasure than pain, more productive of happiness than unhappiness—than of available alternatives. In his best-known book *Introduction to the Principles of Morals and Legislation* (1780), Bentham wrote that "nature has placed mankind under the governance of two sovereign masters, pain and pleasure. It is for them alone to point out what we ought to do, as well as to determine what we shall do."

By using the principle of utility to explain all human motivation, Bentham felt he had found the key to a science of human welfare. The overall welfare of a society would be measured by how well off were each of its members. Thus governments, through their policies, should strive to achieve the "greatest happiness for the greatest number." This was not an attitude that endeared him to the British aristocracy who, as a class, were determined

Bar ■
The once real but now imaginary partition across a court; lawyers stood at this bar to argue their cases. Thus to be "called to *the* bar" meant that you were thought to be enough of a lawyer to plead a case in court.

to keep themselves happy at the direct expense of the lower social classes. But the French were so pleased with Bentham's egalitarian musings that in 1792 he was made an honorary citizen of the fledgling French Republic. Those French revolutionaries regarded him as one of their own.

By holding that governments were created because of man's desire for happiness and not by divine intervention, Bentham antagonized both the monarch and the church—which denounced utilitarianism as "godless philosophy." His beliefs, writings, and actions made Bentham the major intellectual force behind social reform in nineteenth-century England. What actions? Bentham, a truly gentle man, was an intellectual agitator. He bought a house in Westminster near the British Houses of Parliament. He named his house "Hermitage" and there, unmarried, he devoted his life to writing and reform. On virtually every day of his life he wrote about 15 pages of proposals for and commentary on legislation. He was conveniently located to frequently entertain—rather, educate—members of both Houses of Parliament. Not only was he a one-man think tank, he was also a one-man lobbying organization. Ultimately, he succeeded in that his ideas, premised on their utility, contributed to all the major social and legal reforms in nineteenth-century Britain.

The difference between Bentham and other would-be reformers was that Bentham sought to develop techniques to deal with policy questions—techniques that others could use to apply to yet unknown problems. In effect, Bentham's patrimony is so great because he was the first methodologist in policy analysis. He showed the way to find a way.

Bentham admittedly did not originate the principle of utility, which can be traced back to the ancient Greeks. He first read of it in Joseph Priestley's 1768 *Essay on the First Principles of Government*. However, he was the first to rigorously and mathematically apply the principle to current and proposed public policies. Bentham was the first to empirically examine public policy problems, to use the investigation of social facts as a justification for reforming the law on a matter. A hundred years later this would be called a Brandeis brief, a legal argument that takes into account not only the law, but also the technical data from social or scientific research that have economic and sociological implications for the law as well as society. This kind of legal argument was pioneered by Louis D. Brandeis (1856–1941), who later served on the U.S. Supreme Court (1916–1939). It was a Brandeis brief, for example, that helped win the 1954 *Brown v. Board of Education* case, when, with testimony from psychologists about the effects of segregation on black children, the lawyers for Brown proved that separate education facilities were inherently unequal. "Bentham brief" would be the more intellectually honest phrase.

Bentham demanded that all laws and policies answer the question "Who benefits?" And if the proposal didn't meet his test of the "greatest happiness for the greatest number," then it was not deserving of enactment. Above all, Bentham urged practical, pragmatic solutions to the problems of crime, education, welfare, and public health, among others. He felt that he had a genius for

(*continued*)

> ▶ **A CASE STUDY** | *Continued*

legislation, for recommending new policies that should be enacted into law—which is exactly what he spent his life doing. And he demanded that legislators be guided not by their party but by his principle of utility. To do otherwise is to be dishonorably immoral. That is why his most influential work is called *An Introduction to the Principles of Morals and Legislation*. After all, the whole point of legislation is to do the moral, the ethical, thing. Isn't it?

For Discussion: *Is Bentham's criterion for a successful program as one offering the "greatest happiness for the greatest number" still valid as the underlying basis for a program evaluation? Is Bentham's principle of utility still visible in current social legislation and public administration practices?* ▶

SUMMARY

Organizations have auditors whose basic task is to certify that financial accounts are correct. New applications of auditing have evolved beyond this traditional meaning. Thus it is possible to have a management audit, a performance audit, or an efficiency audit. An audit undertaken within a single organization may seek to combine multiple auditing elements. Such efforts are called comprehensive audits.

A comprehensive audit program typically includes three types of audit: (1) financial and compliance, which determines whether the funds were properly spent and whether the law was complied with; (2) economy and efficiency, which determines whether resources have been used economically and efficiently; and (3) program results, which determine whether desired results have been achieved. The establishment of relatively independent audit organizations has helped the audit function to stand above corruption and apart from the political administration of the day.

Policy analysis and program evaluation are often confused and are often used interchangeably, but they are not the same. A policy analysis is a set of techniques that seeks to answer the question of what the probable effects of a policy will be before they actually occur. A policy analysis undertaken on a program that is already in effect is more properly called a program evaluation. Evaluations refer to the standards against which a program can be evaluated: compliance, efficiency, and effectiveness/relevance. These standards indicate the fundamental questions that must be asked of any program.

REVIEW QUESTIONS

1. Why is an audit so often considered to be the final phase of a budgetary process?
2. What is the mission of the U.S. Government Accountability Office?
3. What is the difference between a formal compliance audit and a performance audit?
4. What organizations undertake governmental program evaluations, and why do they do it?
5. Are program evaluations more likely to be undertaken for political or for managerial reasons, or both?

KEY CONCEPTS

Audit   An independent examination, an objective assessment of something; typically the financial reports of an individual or organization to determine whether they accurately represent expenditures and are in compliance with accounting standards and laws.

Compliance audit   The traditional form of auditing where the auditor is looking for the extent to which an organization's funds have been managed in compliance with the law and that accepted standards and conventions for the treatment of accounting information have been used.

Evaluation research   An attempt to assess specific policy options by conducting experiments, assessing their outcomes, and recommending whether the new concept should be broadly applied.

Government Accountability Office (GAO)   A support agency of the U.S. Congress created by the Budget and Accounting Act of 1921 to audit federal government expenditures and to assist Congress with its legislative oversight responsibilities. Originally named the General Accounting Office.

Internal audit   The function of audit groups within a larger organization. They vary in the tasks they are assigned. Sometimes they have a compliance audit role. In other instances they serve as independent troubleshooters, providing early warning to top management of emerging problems.

Management control   That aspect of management concerned with the comparison of actual versus planned performance as well as the development and implementation of procedures to correct substandard performance.

Performance audit   An audit that compares the activities of an organization with the objectives that have been assigned to it.

Program evaluation   The systematic examination of any activity undertaken by government to make a determination about its effects, both short term and long range.

MySearchLab® EXERCISES

Apply what you learned in this chapter on MySearchLab (*www.mysearchlab.com*).

BIBLIOGRAPHY

Bagby, Meredith (1994). *The First Annual Report of the United States of America*. New York: HarperCollins.

Ball, Ian M. (1973). *Pitcairn: Children of Mutiny*. Boston: Little, Brown.

Bligh, William. (1961). *The Mutiny on Board H.M.S.* Bounty. New York: New American Library.

Bowring, John, ed. (1962). *The Works of Jeremy Bentham*, 11 vols. New York: Russell and Russell.

Brown, Judith R. (1984). "Legislative Program Evaluation: Defining a Legislative Service and a Profession," *Public Administration Review* (May–June).

Brown, Richard E., and Ralph Craft (1980). "Auditing and Public Administration: The Unrealized Partnership," *Public Administration Review* (May–June).

Chelimsky, Eleanor, ed. (1984). *Program Evaluation: Patterns and Directions*. Washington: American Society for Public Administration.

Comptroller General of the United States (1981). *Standards for Audit of Governmental Organizations, Programs, Activities and Functions*. Washington: General Accounting Office.

Dening, Greg (1992). *Mr. Bligh's Bad Language: Passion, Power and Theatre on the Bounty.* Cambridge, England: Cambridge University Press.

Emmerich, Herbert (1971). *Federal Organization and Administrative Management.* University of Alabama Press.

Hodge, G. (1993). *Minding Everybody's Business: Performance Management in Public Sector Agencies.* Melbourne, Australia: Montech Pty.

Hough, Richard (1973). *Captain Bligh and Mr. Christian.* New York: E. P. Dutton.

Hyde, Albert C., and Jay M. Shafritz, eds. (1979). *Program Evaluation in the Public Sector.* New York: Praeger.

Kaufman, Herbert (1973). *Administrative Feedback: Monitoring Subordinates' Behavior.* Washington: Brookings Institution.

Kearns, Kevin P. (1996). *Managing for Accountability.* San Francisco: Jossey-Bass.

Kelly, Paul Joseph (1990). *Utilitarianism and Distributive Justice: Jeremy Bentham and the Civil Law.* New York: Oxford University Press.

Konigsberg, Eric (1993). "Waste Watchers," *The New Republic* (April 5).

Morrison, Philip, and Emily Morrison, eds. (1961). *Charles Babbage and His Calculating Engines.* New York: Dover.

Normanton, E. L. (1966). *The Accountability and Audit of Governments.* Manchester, England: University of Manchester.

Postema, Gerald J. (1986). *Bentham and the Common Law Tradition.* New York: Oxford University Press.

Rivlin, Alice (1971). *Systematic Thinking for Social Action.* Washington: Brookings Institution.

Shafritz, Jay M., Albert C. Hyde, and David H. Rosenbloom (1986). *Personnel Management in Government*, 3rd ed. New York: Marcel Dekker.

Suchman, Edward (1967). *Evaluation Research.* New York: Russell Sage Foundation.

Wahlroos, Sven (1989). *Mutiny and Romance in the South Seas: A Companion to the Bounty Adventure.* Topsfield, MA: Salem House.

Webber, Carolyn, and Aaron Wildavsky (1986). *A History of Taxation and Expenditure in the Western World.* New York: Simon and Schuster.

Weiss, Carol H. (1972). *Evaluation Research.* Englewood Cliffs, NJ: Prentice Hall.

Wildavsky, Aaron (1972). "The Self-Evaluating Organization," *Public Administration Review* 32, No. 5 (September–October).

RECOMMENDED BOOKS

McDavid, James C., and Laura R. L. Hawthorn (2006). *Program Evaluation and Performance Measurement: An Introduction to Practice.* California: Sage Publications. A thorough overview of the methods and tools used in the evaluation of government programs.

Normanton, E. Leslie (1966). *The Accountability and Audit of Governments: A Comparative Study.* Manchester, England: University of Manchester Press. The classic study of how governments have conducted audits throughout history and throughout the world.

Sylvia, Ronald, Kathleen Sylvia, and Elizabeth Gunn (2004). *Program Planning and Evaluation for the Public Manager*, 3rd ed. Prospect Heights, IL: Waveland Press. A systems approach to monitoring and reviewing internal processes, as well as conceptualizing outcome evaluations.

Weiss, Carol H. (1997). *Evaluation: Methods for Studying Programs and Policies.* Englewood Cliffs, NJ: Prentice Hall. A primer on evaluation that deals with both the politics of why it is undertaken as well as the techniques of how to do it.

Wholey, Joseph S., Harry P. Hatry, and Kathryn E. Newcomer, eds. (2004). *Handbook of Practical Program Evaluation,* 2nd ed. San Francisco: Jossey-Bass. A comprehensive reference, offering all the how-to "nuts and bolts."

RELATED WEB SITES

www.agacgfm.org/homepage.aspx
Association of Government Accountants (AGA)
The site has news and information for government accountability professionals.

www.governmentauditors.org
Association of Local Government Auditors (ALGA)
The ALGA provides resources to individuals who perform financial audits of counties, cities, and towns. The association's Web site has information about recent audits as well as job postings.

www.bsa.ca.gov
California State Auditor (CSA)
California's State Auditor is responsible for assuring that state expenditures are done legally. The CSA Web site includes reports and recommendations on how California can most effectively manage its financial resources.

www.dcaa.mil
Defense Contract Auditing Agency (DCAA)
The DCAA plays a pivotal role in ensuring that defense spending is being done in an efficient and legal manner. The site includes online publications about the techniques used to audit various aspects of military programs.

www.gao.gov
U.S. Government Accountability Office (GAO)
The GAO examines the effectiveness and efficiency of federal programs and spending. This site has reports, laws, policies, and news pertaining to the U.S. government and federal accountability.

GLOSSARY

Accountability   The extent to which one must answer to higher authority—legal or organizational—for one's actions in society at large or within one's particular organizational position.

Administration   The management and direction of the affairs of governments and institutions; a collective term for all policymaking officials of a government; the execution and implementation of public policy.

Administrative doctrine   The rules, procedures, and ways of doing things that reflect the basic values of an organization.

Affirmative action   A term that first meant the removal of "artificial barriers" to the employment of women and minority group members; now it refers to compensatory opportunities for hitherto disadvantaged groups—specific efforts to recruit, hire, and promote qualified members of disadvantaged groups for the purpose of eliminating the present effects of past discrimination.

Agenda setting   The process by which ideas or issues bubble up through the various political channels to wind up for consideration by a political institution such as a legislature or court.

Assets   All money, property, and money-related rights (such as money owed to one) owned by a person or an organization. Capital assets or fixed assets are those things that cannot be turned into cash easily (such as buildings); current assets or liquid assets are those things that can be turned into cash easily (such as cash or goods for sale); and frozen assets are those things that are tied up (for instance, because of a lawsuit).

Audit   An independent examination, an objective assessment of something; typically the financial reports of an individual or organization to determine whether they accurately represent expenditures and are in compliance with accounting standards and laws.

Big lie   An untruth so great or so audacious that it is bound to have an effect on public opinion.

Block grant   A grant distributed in accordance with a statutory formula for use in a variety of activities within a broad functional area, largely at the recipient's discretion.

Bribery   The giving or offering of anything of value with intent to unlawfully influence an official in the discharge of duties; a public official's receiving or asking for anything of value with the intent to be unlawfully influenced.

Brownlow Committee   A committee appointed by President Franklin D. Roosevelt in 1936 for the purpose of diagnosing the staffing needs of the president and making appropriate recommendations for the reorganization of the executive branch.

Budget   A financial plan serving as a pattern for and control over future operations—hence, any estimate of future costs or any systematic plan for the utilization of the workforce, material, or other resources.

Budget cycle   The timed steps of the budget process, which includes preparation, approval, execution, and audit.

Budget process   The total system a jurisdiction uses to make decisions on government spending needs and how to pay for them. The main difference between federal, state, and local budget processes is that the state and local jurisdictions must have balanced budgets each year.

Budget surplus   The amount by which a government's budget receipts exceed its budget outlays for any given period.

Bureau movement   The efforts of progressive reformers early in the twentieth century to apply scientific methods to municipal problems. Their efforts led to the creation of research bureaus, which in turn created the academic field of public administration.

Bureaucracy   The totality of government officers; all of a government's employees; a general invective to refer to any inefficient organization encumbered by red tape or a specific set of structural arrangements.

Bureaucrat bashing   Either justified criticism or inappropriate condemnation of public employees.

Bureaucratic dysfunctions   The pathological elements of bureaucratic structures that often make them inefficient in operation; the pressures on workers to conform that cause them to adhere to rules as an end rather than a means.

Bureaucratic impersonality   The dehumanizing consequences of formal organizational structures eliminating personal and emotional consideration from organizational life so that the individual bureaucrat functions only as a cog in an ever-moving machine.

Cabinet   The heads of the executive departments of a jurisdiction who report to and advise its chief executive; examples include the president's cabinet, the governor's cabinet, and the mayor's cabinet.

Cabinet government   The British system, whereby the cabinet as a whole, rather than only the prime minister who heads it, is considered the executive, and the cabinet is collectively responsible to the Parliament for its performance. In addition, the cabinet ministers are typically drawn from among the majority party's members in Parliament, whereas in the United States the cabinet secretaries are only from the executive branch.

Capital budgeting   A budget process that deals with planning for large expenditures for capital items such as bridges and buildings.

Casework   The services performed by legislators and their staffs at the request of and on behalf of constituents.

Categorical grant   A grant that can be used only for specific, narrowly defined activities—for example, to construct an interstate highway.

Charisma   Leadership based on the compelling personality of the leader rather than upon formal position. The word *charisma* is derived from the Greek word for "divine grace." The concept was first developed by Max Weber, who distinguished charismatic authority from both the traditional authority of a monarch and the legal authority given to someone by law.

Chief of staff   The military title for the officer who supervises the work of the other officers on a commander's staff; civilian supervisor of an overall management team who reports directly to the chief executive officer.

Child labor   Originally, the employment of children in a manner detrimental to their health and social development. Now that the law contains strong child labor prohibitions, the term refers to the employment of children below the legal age limit.

Civil service   A collective term for all nonmilitary employees of a government. Paramilitary organizations, such as police and firefighters, are always included in civil service counts in the United States. Civil service employment is not the same as merit system employment, because all patronage positions (those not covered by merit systems) are included in civil service totals.

Civil service reform   Efforts to improve the status, integrity, and productivity of the civil service at all levels of government by supplanting the spoils system with the merit system; efforts to improve the management and efficiency of the public service; or the historical events, the movement, leading up to the enactment of the Pendleton Act of 1883.

Classical theory   The original theory about organizations that closely resemble military structures.

Code of ethics   A statement of professional standards of conduct to which the practitioners of a profession say they subscribe. Codes of ethics are usually not legally binding, so they may not be taken too seriously as constraints on behavior.

Collective bargaining   Bargaining on behalf of a group of employees, as opposed to individual bargaining, in which each worker represents only himself or herself.

Common law   The totality of judge-made laws that initially developed in England and continued to evolve in the United States. Whenever this kind of law—which is based on custom, culture, habit, and previous judicial decisions—proved inadequate, it was supplanted by statutory laws made by legislatures. But the common law tradition, based upon precedent, is still the foundation of the American legal system, even though much of what was originally common law has been converted into statutes over the years.

Compliance audit   The traditional form of auditing, in which the auditor is looking for the extent to which, in the financial management of an organization, funds have been managed in compliance with the law, and to which accepted standards and conventions for the treatment of accounting information have been used.

Congressional oversight   The total means by which the U.S. Congress monitors the activities of executive branch agencies to determine if the laws are being faithfully executed.

Constitutional architecture   The administrative arrangements created by a government's constitution—from the separation of powers to the requirement that specific departments be created or services performed.

Contingency theory   An approach to leadership asserting that leadership styles will vary in their effects in different situations. The situation (not traits or styles themselves) determines whether a leadership style or a particular leader will be effective.

Corruption   The unauthorized use of public office for private gain. The most common forms of corruption are bribery, extortion, and the misuse of inside information.

Council of government (COG)   An organization of cooperating local governments seeking a regional approach to planning, development, transportation, environment, and other issues.

Deficit financing   A situation in which a government's excess of outlays over receipts for a given period is financed primarily by borrowing from the public.

Devolution   The transfer of power from a central to a local authority.

Dillon's rule   The criteria developed by state courts to determine the nature and extent of powers granted to local governments.

Dirty hands dilemma   A graphic phrase for the tendency of public officials to commit an act generally considered to be a wrong to further the common good. This is a dilemma in the sense that doing bad seems to lead to something good.

Discrimination   Bigotry in practice; intolerance toward those who have different beliefs or religions. In employment, the failure to treat equals equally. Any action that has the effect of limiting employment and advancement opportunities because of an individual's sex, race, color, age, national origin, religion, physical handicap, or other irrelevant criteria, is discrimination.

E-commerce   Selling and buying over the Internet, whether wholesale or retail.

E-government   Conducting any aspect of government business operations over the Internet—from providing information by government to paying bills to government.

Empowerment   Giving a person or organization the formal authority to do something.

Equal employment opportunity   Employment practices that prevent any individual from being adversely excluded from employment opportunities on the basis of race, color, sex, religion, age, national origin, or other factors that cannot lawfully be considered in employing people.

Evaluation research   An attempt to assess specific policy options by conducting experiments, assessing their outcomes, and recommending whether the new concept should be broadly applied.

Executive branch   In a government with separation of powers, the part responsible for applying or administering the law. Thus a president, governor, or mayor and their respective supporting bureaucracies are the executive branches of their respective jurisdictions. But not all of the federal bureaucracy is part of the executive branch. Some agencies, such as the General Accounting Office, are directly responsible to Congress. Others, such as the Federal Trade Commission (and other regulatory agencies), have been held by the Supreme Court not to be part of the executive branch.

Executive budget   The budget document for an executive branch of government that a jurisdiction's chief executive submits to a legislature for review, modification, and enactment.

Executive Office of the President (EOP)   The umbrella office consisting of the top presidential staff agencies that provide the president with help and advice in carrying out his major responsibilities. The EOP was created by President Franklin D. Roosevelt under the authority of the Reorganization Act of 1939. Since then, presidents have used executive orders, reorganization plans, and legislative initiatives to reorganize, expand, or contract the EOP.

Federalism   A system of governance in which a national, overarching government shares power with subnational or state governments.

Federalism, cooperative   The notion that the national, state, and local governments are cooperating, interacting agents, jointly working to solve common problems, rather than conflicting, sometimes hostile competitors, pursuing similar or possibly conflicting ends.

Federalism, dual   The nineteenth-century concept, now no longer operational, that the functions and responsibilities of the federal and state governments were theoretically distinguished and functionally separate from each other.

Federalism, marble-cake   The concept that the cooperative relations among the varying levels of government result in an intermingling of activities; in contrast to the more traditional view of layer-cake federalism, which holds that the three levels of government are totally or almost totally separate.

Federalism, New   The Republican efforts begun during the Nixon administration to decentralize governmental functions by returning power and responsibility to the states. This trend was continued in the 1980s by the Reagan administration and culminated in the 1990s movement toward devolution.

Federalism, picket-fence   The concept that bureaucratic specialists at the various levels of government (along with clientele groups) exercise considerable power over the nature of intergovernmental programs.

Financial report   A written statement—also called an accountant's certificate, accountant's opinion, or audit report—prepared by an independent accountant or auditor after an audit.

Fiscal federalism   The financial relations between and among units of government in a federal system. The theory of fiscal federalism, or multi-unit government finance, is one part of the branch of applied economics known as public finance.

General staff   A group of officers in a military's headquarters that assists their commanders in planning, coordinating, and supervising operations.

Government Accountability Office (GAO)   A support agency of the U.S. Congress created by the Budget and Accounting Act of 1921 to audit federal government expenditures and to assist Congress with its legislative oversight responsibilities.

Grace Commission   An attempt made by the Reagan administration to have business leaders study and reform the federal government; much was studied, little was reformed.

Grant   An intergovernmental transfer of funds (or other assets). Since the New Deal, state and local governments have become increasingly dependent upon federal grants for an almost infinite variety of programs.

Group cohesion   The shared beliefs, values, and assumptions of a group that allow it to function as a team.

Group dynamics   The subfield of organization behavior concerned with the nature of groups, how they develop, and how they interrelate with individuals and other groups.

Hawthorne experiments   The late 1920s and early 1930s management studies undertaken at the Hawthorne Works of the Western Electric Company near Chicago. Conducted by Elton Mayo and his associates from the Harvard Business School, the studies became the most famous management experiments ever reported.

Higher law   The notion that no matter what the laws of a state are, there remains a higher law, to which a person has an even greater obligation. A higher law is often appealed to by those who wish to attack an existing law or practice that courts or legislators are unlikely or unwilling to change.

Honor   The internalized moral compass by which individuals ascertain correct behavior in public and private life; the perception by others of one's reputation for integrity.

Hoover Commissions   The post–World War II efforts to reorganize the federal government.

Implementation   Putting a government program into effect; the total process of translating a legal mandate, whether an executive order or an enacted statute, into appropriate program directives and structures that provide services or create goods.

Incremental budgeting   A method of budget review that focuses on the increments of increase or decrease in the budget of existing programs. Incremental budgeting, which is often called traditional budgeting, is a counter school of thought to more rational, systems-oriented approaches, such as zero-based budgeting.

Incremental decision making model   A view of the public policymaking process that assumes that small decisions made at the margins of problems are the usual reality of change.

Integrity   The core of honor. Those who have integrity live up to their stated principles, values, and, most important, their word. A person whose word is his or her bond gives the full faith and credit of his or her whole being to keeping commitments.

Intergovernmental relations   The complex network of interrelationships among governments; the political, fiscal, programmatic, and administrative processes by which higher units of government share revenues and other resources with lower units of government, generally accompanied by special conditions that the lower units must satisfy as prerequisites to receiving the assistance.

Internal audit   The function of audit groups within a larger organization. They vary in the tasks they are assigned. Sometimes they have a compliance audit role. In other instances they serve as independent troubleshooters, providing early warning to top management of emerging problems.

Leadership   The exercise of authority, whether formal or informal, in directing and coordinating the work of others.

Learning organization Peter Senge's term for organizations in which new patterns of thinking are nurtured and where people are continually learning together to improve both the organization and their personal lives.

Line-item budget The classification of budgetary accounts according to narrow, detailed objects of expenditure (such as motor vehicles, clerical workers, or reams of paper) used within each particular agency of government, generally without reference to the ultimate purpose or objective served by the expenditure.

Management A word that refers both to the people responsible for running an organization and to the running process itself; the use of numerous resources (such as employees and machines) to accomplish an organizational goal.

Management control That aspect of management concerned with the comparison of actual versus planned performance as well as the development and implementation of procedures to correct substandard performance.

Management development Any conscious effort on the part of an organization, such as rotational assignments or formal educational experiences, to provide a manager with the skills needed for future duties.

Managerial revolution James Burham's concept that as control of large businesses moved from the original owners to professional managers, society's new governing class would be not the traditional possessors of wealth—but those who have the professional expertise to manage, to lead, large organizations.

Managerialism An entrepreneurial approach to public management that emphasizes management rights and a reinvigorated scientific management.

Mandating One level of government requiring another to offer—and/or pay for—a program as a matter of law or as a prerequisite to partial or full funding for either the program in question or other programs.

Merit system A public sector concept of staffing that implies that no test of party membership is involved in the selection, promotion, or retention of government employees and that a constant effort is made to select the best-qualified individuals available for appointment and advancement.

Micromanagement A pejorative term for supervising too closely. Any manager may be guilty of micromanagement for refusing to allow subordinates to have any real authority or responsibility, thereby ensuring

that subordinates can neither function as, nor grow into, effective managers. Also used to refer to interference by legislators with the minutiae of administration for the benefit of their constituents.

Moral leadership Leading people in specific directions of action and thought based on morals and decency.

Motivation An amalgam of all of the factors in one's working environment that foster or inhibit productive efforts.

National debt The total outstanding debt of a central government.

Needs hierarchy Abraham H. Maslow's five sets of goals or basic needs arranged in a hierarchy of prepotency: physiological needs (food, water, shelter, etc.), safety needs, love or affiliation needs, esteem needs, and the final need for self-actualization.

Neoclassical theory Theoretical perspectives that revise, expand, and/or are critical of classical organization theory.

New public administration An academic advocacy movement for social equity in the performance and delivery of public services; it called for a proactive administrator with a burning desire for social equity to replace the traditional impersonal and neutral gun-for-hire bureaucrat.

New public management A disparate group of structural reforms and informal management initiatives that reflects the doctrine of managerialism in the public sector.

Nonprofit organization An organization created and operated for public or societal purposes (such as alleviation of poverty) rather than private benefit purposes (such as return on shareholders' investments).

Objective A short-term goal; something that must be achieved on the way to a larger overall achievement.

Organization A group of people who jointly work to achieve at least one common goal.

Organization development An approach or strategy for increasing organizational effectiveness. As a process it has no value biases, but it is usually associated with the idea that effectiveness is found by integrating the individual's desire for growth with organizational goals.

Organization theory A set of propositions that seeks to explain or predict how groups and individuals behave in differing organizational arrangements.

Organizational culture The culture that exists within an organization; a parallel but smaller version of a societal culture.

Paradigm An intellectual model for a situation or condition.

Patronage The power of elected and appointed officials to make partisan appointments to office or to confer contracts, honors, or other benefits on their political supporters. Patronage has always been one of the major tools by which political executives consolidate their power and attempt to control a bureaucracy.

Performance appraisal The formal methods by which an organization documents the work performance of its employees. Performance appraisals are typically designed to change dysfunctional work behavior, communicate perceptions of work quality, assess the future potential of employees, and provide a documented record for disciplinary and separation actions.

Performance audit An audit that compares the activities of an organization with the objectives that have been assigned to it.

Performance management The systematic integration of an organization's efforts to achieve its objectives.

Personnel A collective term for all of the employees of an organization. The word is of military origin— the two basic components of a traditional army being materiel and personnel. Personnel is also commonly used to refer to the personnel management function or the organizational unit responsible for administering personnel programs.

Planning horizon The time frame during which the objectives of a strategic plan are to be achieved.

Pluralism A theory of government that attempts to reaffirm the democratic character of society by asserting that open, multiple, competing, and responsive groups preserve traditional democratic values in a mass industrial state. Pluralism assumes that power will shift from group to group as elements in the mass public transfer their allegiance in response to their perceptions of their individual interests.

Political culture That part of the overall societal culture that determines a community's attitudes toward the quality, style, and vigor of its political processes and government operations.

POSDCORB The mnemonic device invented by Luther Gulick in 1937 to call attention to the various functional elements of the work of a chief executive.

Position classification The use of formal job descriptions to organize all jobs in a civil service merit system into classes on the basis of duties and responsibilities, for the purposes of delineating authority, establishing chains of command, and providing equitable salary scales.

Postbureaucratic organization Constantly changing temporary organizational systems; task forces composed of groups of relative strangers with diverse skills created in response to a special problem, as opposed to continuing need.

Postmodernism The belief that constant change is a new fact of life for large organizations that are living on the edge, on the boundary, between order and chaos.

Principles of management Fundamental truths or working hypotheses that serve as guidelines to management thinking and action.

Privatization The process of returning to the private sector property or functions previously owned or performed by government.

Productivity A measured relationship between the quantity (and quality) of results produced and the quantity of resources required for production. Productivity is, in essence, a measure of the work efficiency of an individual, a work unit, or a whole organization.

Professional A member of an occupation requiring specialized knowledge that can be gained only after intensive preparation. Professional occupations tend to possess three features: a body of academic and practical knowledge that is applied to the service of society, a standard of success theoretically measured by serving the needs of society rather than seeking purely personal gain, and a system of control over the professional practice.

Program evaluation The systematic examination of any activity undertaken by government to make a determination about its effects, both short term and long range.

Progressive tax Any tax that has people of greater wealth paying a larger percentage in tax than people of lesser means. Income taxes are often progressive.

Public administration Whatever governments do, for good or ill. It is public administration's political context that makes it public—that distinguishes it from private or business administration.

Public interest The universal label that political actors wrap around the policies and programs that they advocate.

Public policy Decision making by government. Governments are constantly concerned about what they should or should not do. And whatever they do or do not do is public policy.

Public program All those activities designed to implement a public policy; often this calls for the creation of organizations, public agencies, and bureaus.

Racist Any person or organization that either consciously or unconsciously practices discrimination against another person on the basis of race (or ethnicity) or supports the supremacy of one race over others.

Rational decision-making model A view of the public policymaking process that assumes complete information and a systematic, logical, and comprehensive approach to change.

Red tape The ribbon that was once used to bind government documents; the term now stands as the symbol of excessive official formality and overattention to prescribed routines.

Reengineering The fundamental rethinking and redesign of organizational processes to achieve significant improvements in critical measures of performance, such as costs or quality of services.

Regressive tax Any tax that has people with lower incomes paying a higher overall percentage of their income in tax than people of greater income. Sales taxes are examples of regressive taxes.

Regulation The totality of government controls on the social and economic activities of its citizens; the rulemaking process of those administrative agencies charged with the official interpretation of laws.

Regulatory commission An independent agency created by a government to regulate some aspect of economic life.

Reinventing government The latest manifestation of the progressive tradition of continuously improving government—this time with an emphasis on privatization.

Representative bureaucracy The ultimate goal of equal employment opportunity and affirmative action programs.

Republic A form of government in which sovereignty resides in the people who elect agents to represent them in political decision making.

Reverse discrimination Discrimination against white males in conjunction with preferential treatment for women and minorities.

Rule of law A governing system in which the highest authority is a body of law that applies equally to all (as opposed to the traditional "rule of men," in which the personal whims of those in power can decide any issue).

Scientific management A systematic approach to managing that seeks the "one best way" of accomplishing any given task by discovering the fastest, most efficient, and least fatiguing production methods.

Second reconstruction The civil rights movement and legislation of the 1960s. The first reconstruction, immediately after the Civil War, gave blacks their freedom from slavery. But the laws as enforced and customs as practiced did not allow for the full rights of citizens. That came in the 1960s, when public sentiment was aroused and legal action was taken to ensure equal rights for all Americans.

Self-directed work team A work group that will accept responsibility for its processes and products—as well as for the behavior of other group members.

Separation of powers The allocation of powers among the three branches of government so that they are a check upon each other. This separation, in theory, makes a tyrannical concentration of power impossible.

Sex discrimination Any disparate or unfavorable treatment of a person in an employment situation because of his or her sex.

Sexual harassment The action of an individual in a position to control or influence another's job, career, or grade who uses such power to gain sexual favors or punish the refusal of such favors. Sexual harassment on the job varies from inappropriate sexual innuendo to coerced sexual relations.

Spoils system The practice of awarding government jobs to one's political supporters, as opposed to awarding them on the basis of merit.

Staff principle That a unit of a larger organization should have primary responsibility to think and plan, to ponder over innovations and plan for their implementation.

Stakeholder Any individual or group that might be affected by the outcome of something. All decisions have their stakeholders. The responsible public decision maker seeks to obtain the maximum possible stakeholder satisfaction.

Standards of conduct A compendium of ethical norms promulgated by an organization to guide the behavior of its members. Many government agencies have formal codes (or standards) of conduct for their employees.

Strategic management A philosophy of management that links strategic planning with day-to-day decision making. Strategic management seeks a fit between an organization's external and internal environments.

Strategic plan The formal document that presents the ways and means by which a strategic goal will be achieved.

Strategic planning   The set of processes used by an organization to assess the strategic situation and develop strategy for the future.

Strategy   The overall conduct of a major enterprise to achieve long-term goals; the pattern to be found in a series of organizational decisions.

Strike   A mutual agreement among workers (whether members of a union or not) to a temporary work stoppage to obtain—or resist—a change in their working conditions.

SWOT analysis   A review of an organization's strengths, weaknesses, opportunities, and threats. This technique is widely used to examine the viability of strategic plans.

Systems theory   A view of an organization as a complex set of dynamically intertwined and interconnected elements, including its inputs, processes, outputs, feedback loops, and the environment in which it operates and with which it continuously interacts.

Tactics   The short-term immediate decisions that, in their totality, lead to the achievement of strategic goals.

Tax   A compulsory contribution exacted by a government for public purposes.

Technocracy   A contraction of "technical" and "bureaucracy," which refers to the high-tech organizational environments of the postmodern world.

Theory X   The assumptions that the average human being has an inherent dislike of work; that most people must be threatened to get them to put forth adequate effort; and that people prefer to be directed and to avoid responsibility.

Theory Y   The assumptions that work is as natural as play, that workers can exercise self-direction and self-control, and that imagination, ingenuity, and creativity are widespread.

Think tank   A colloquial term for an organization, or organizational segment, whose sole function is research, usually in the policy and behavioral sciences.

Title VII   That part of the Civil Rights Act of 1964 that prohibits employment discrimination because of race, color, religion, sex, or national origin and that created the Equal Employment Opportunity Commission as its enforcement vehicle.

Total quality management (TQM)   A phrase for quality control in its most expanded sense of a total and continuing concern for quality in the production of goods and services.

Trait theory   An approach to leadership that assumes leaders possess traits that make them fundamentally different from followers. Advocates of trait theory believe that some people have unique leadership characteristics and qualities that enable them to assume responsibilities not everyone can execute. Therefore they are "born" leaders.

Transformational leadership   Leadership that strives to change organizational culture and directions. It reflects the ability of a leader to develop a values-based vision for the organization, to convert the vision into reality, and to maintain it over time.

Unified budget   The present form of the budget of the federal government, in which receipts and outlays from federal funds and trust funds (such as Social Security) are consolidated.

Unions   Groups of employees who create a formal organization (the union) to represent their interests before management.

Vision   A view of an organization's future. The purpose of strategic management is to make such a vision a reality.

Vision statement   The identification of objectives to be achieved in the future.

Watergate   The scandal that led to the resignation of President Richard M. Nixon. Watergate itself is a hotel-office-apartment complex in Washington, D.C. When individuals associated with the Committee to Reelect the President were caught breaking into the Democratic National Committee Headquarters (then located in the Watergate complex) in 1972, the resulting cover-up and national trauma was condensed into one word: Watergate. The suffix "-gate" has grown to refer to any political crime or instance of bureaucratic corruption that undermines confidence in governing institutions.

Whistle-blower   An individual who believes the public interest overrides the interests of his or her organization and publicly blows the whistle on— meaning exposes—corrupt, illegal, fraudulent, or harmful activity.

Zero-based budgeting   A budgeting process that is a rejection of the incremental decision making model of budgeting. It demands a rejustification of the entire budget submission (from ground zero), whereas incremental budgeting essentially respects the outcomes of previous budgetary decisions (collectively referred to as the budget base) and focuses examination on the margin of change from year to year.

APPENDIX

Additional Sources

Chapter 1 "snow buttons" *U. S. News and World Report*, January 17, 1994

Chapter 2 "Just what is it . . ." Speech of January 29, 1916

"Remember, democracy . . ." Letter to John Taylor, April 15, 1814

". . . that my oath . . ." Letter to A. G. Hodges, April 4, 1864

Chapter 3 ". . . are supervisors in California, judges in . . ." *Governing*, May 1989

Chapter 4 "What the judges say . . ." Hughes speech, May 3, 1907

"States are not colonies . . ." *Economist*, November 26, 1984

"On bended knee . . ." Ibid.

"We do not want to be in the importing . . ." *Washington Post National Weekly*, September 18–24, 1995

Chapter 5 "The nation's honor . . ." Speech in Cleveland, January 29, 1916

". . . about a man who drives into Moscow . . ." *New York Times*, May 3, 1995

"Most of the material should not have been secret . . ." *Christian Science Monitor*, July 18, 1973

"When I order abandon ship . . ." *Time*, August 19, 1991

"Stand up, you man-eating . . ." *American Heritage*, October 1977

". . . have a duty to refrain . . ." *Times* (London), April 15, 1993

". . . that people shouldn't require . . ." *U.S. News and World Report*, January 19, 1981

"McNamara went to the World Bank . . ." *New York Times*, April 15, 1995

"He kept his mouth shut . . ." *Newsweek*, April 24, 1995

"I think it's about 25 years . . ." *New York Times*, April 15, 1995

Chapter 6 "I found Rome . . ." Michael Grant, *The Founders of the Ancient World* (1991)

"No rule of war . . ." *Military Maxims* (1827)

"With 2,000 years . . ." Norman F. Dixon, *On the Psychology of Military Incompetence* (1976)

"There is nothing so practical . . ." Alfred J. Marrow, *The Practical Theorist: The Life and Work of Kurt Lewis* (1969)

Chapter 7 ". . . the giant power wielded . . ." H. Balzac, *Bureaucracy* (1901)

Chapter 8 ". . . if Congress . . . passed a law . . ." C. G. Dawes, *The First Year of the Budget of the United States* (1923)

". . . every revolution evaporates . . ." Kafka, quoted in *Newsweek*, October 14, 1968

". . . clocks look bureaucratic . . ." *Newsweek*, October 31, 1994

"All at once, five postal . . ." *New York Times*, June 6, 1993

Chapter 9 ". . . the public be damned." Remark to reporter on October 8, 1882

Chapter 10 "Federal Centers for Disease Control . . ." *New York Times*, July 10, 1995

"The Presidency is not merely an . . ." *New York Times*, September 11, 1932

"This brand is cynically . . ." *Washington Post National Weekly*, February 5–11, 1990

". . . each year the military spends . . ." *U. S. News and World Report*, May 24, 1993

Chapter 12 "Effective January 1, 1997, the University . . ." *New York Times*, July 22, 1995

". . . the nation's first governor . . ." *Pittsburgh Post Gazette*, June 2, 1995

Chapter 13 "What the hell . . ." *New York Times*, December 18, 1994

"No citizen has a moral obligation . . ." *New York Times*, April 16, 1995

INDEX

Page numbers in bold indicate illustrations or photos.
Page numbers followed by a "t" indicate material in tables.